MASS MEDIA AND VIOLENCE

VOL. XI

A Report to the
National Commission on
the Causes and Prevention of
Violence

by
David L. Lange
Robert K. Baker
Sandra J. Ball

November 1969

Library of Congress Catalog Card Number: 72-604084

For sale by the Superintendent of Documents, U.S. Government Printing Office
Washington, D.C. 20402 - Price $2.50

PREFACE

When a government commission undertakes to evaluate any aspect of media performance, it is properly a delicate inquiry in a society which prizes free expression. There is no room for polemics when media performance is called into question, for the ultimate issue may become whether free expression is feasible. There was, however, no point during our investigation when the resolution of this issue was in serious doubt.

We are not sufficiently arrogant to essay an answer to all of the questions subsumed under the title of these two volumes. Particularly in the news area, there are few answers and many questions of judgment. While we have attempted to provide the kind of information and analysis relevant to these judgments, we can suggest neither that our list of considerations is complete nor that any rigid formula will be satisfactory for all occasions. In the context of our concern with the media and violence, however, while continuing to believe fully in the concept of free expression, it is clear that the media—including their educational and professional organizations—have shown an apalling lack of concern about the effects of particular media practices and little interest in research to determine how, under any reasonable standard, they might do better.

From the outset many people asserted, sometimes quite vituperatively, that it was not only improper but unconstitutional for a governmental body even to study the media. We reject this position. Government, as any other group in our society, is as entitled to speak out on all issues and this includes commenting on media performance. If the government's statements are to rise above the level of diatribes or platitudes, they must be based on research and reasoned deliberation of the issues. This is what we have attempted to accomplish. This Commission has no sanctions to impose, and we do not believe that studies of this kind have any chilling effect upon the exercise of First Amendment rights. Indeed, uninformed comment by government officials is more likely to chill, if only because the irrational tends to be frightening.

A new era in communications is very near. Technological developments, presently being adopted, make possible twenty broadband channels to each home. If competing forms of communication do not develop simultaneously, plenary control over access to such a system by one or two, even three corporations is unacceptable in a society which values free expression. If the ultimate in concentration of media control ever arrives, there is no reason to believe that government control would not be better. At least the government is apt to be more responsive than a self-perpetuating corporate management with such tremendous power. Today we are moving in that direction and one thing seems clear: the policies of the First Amendment can no longer be secured simply by keeping the government out.

Part I of the Task Force Report begins with a summary of the philosophical and historical antecedents which underlie our First Amendment tradition. It then proceeds to discuss the development, structure, and functions of the contemporary media. This overview of the media is essential not only to an understanding of what the media are today, but also to an intelligent formulation of what they might be tomorrow.

Part II of the report, addressed to the news media, does not focus on the pathology of American journalism. There are, to be sure, a number of well-documented cases of news suppression, and the occasional rudeness, pomposity, and simplemindedness of some newsmen is well known. There is little those outside the professional and news organizations can do to improve manners, and there is no point in admonishing against what even the least principled members of the profession recognize is wrong.

We have tried to address problems which we regard as inherent in what are relatively broadly accepted practices and values of American journalism. But, just as the general quality of American journalism cannot be assessed by examining only *The New York Times, The Louisville Courier Journal, The Bend Oregon Bulletin,* or the network news department, our report will not be equally applicable to all news organizations.

Our analysis is not value-free. Although there is a place in American journalism for advocacy, the major news media view themselves as a source of unbiased information. It is this news function on which we focus our concern. We strongly endorse the view that the journalist reporting hard news is obligated not to take sides on the many issues which confront and sometimes divide our society. The continued viability of the First Amendment depends mostly on a credible presentation of the kind of information which will enable our citizens to discharge their democratic responsibilities and to provide the news in a format likely to produce the minimum amount of audience distortion during assimilation. This is the journalist's most important obligation. Similarly, news values and practices which consistently distort information in a direction likely to exacerbate intergroup tensions—which the tendency to equate news with emotional impact clearly does—are a liability to a society which should be committed to the orderly resolution of their differences.

In a speech to the Overseas Press Club, William Wirtz observed that criticism of the press by anyone even remotely associated with government is a notably unrewarding occupation. In part this is no doubt due to the belief of some journalists that, as Mr. Wirtz went on to describe, "an essential balance against the power of government to corrupt absolutely is the power of the press to be critical beyond criticism." Throughout this report we have offered our views on the many issues which confront American newsmen and suggested the ways in which journalists' values and practices should be changed. As our comments are not equally applicable to all news organizations, our solutions will not be equally persuasive to all newsmen, publishers, and broadcasters. As we will repeat in the conclusion of the News Section of this report, we can only recommend their implementation where they are found both applicable and persuasive. The government can no more legislate good journalism than it can legislate good manners. More important than the adoption of specific suggestions is that each news organization make an independent determination of the efficacy of its own policies and practices. There will never be agreement among the many news organizations or other institutions, including the government. Yet, such diversity is what the First Amendment is all about, and that is the great strength of American journalism.

Public concern for violence in entertainment television programming has been with us since at least 1954. This is the focus of Part III of our Report.

From 1954 to the present day, the networks and the National Association of Broadcasters—the trade association representing a majority of local commercial stations—have answered public concern with three principal arguments:

First, they have asserted that there is no conclusive evidence that violence on television causes viewers to behave violently. Even a nodding acquaintance with the research literature on the causes of violent behavior teaches that violent behavior is usually the result of interacting social forces of which television program content may be one. It is unlikely that anyone can show, except in the unusual cases, that television or any other single factor is anything more than a contributing cause among the nexus of forces which act on the human personality. Surely there are other factors which contribute to violent behavior, some of them undoubtedly more important than television. Others, such as weak parental influence or bad schools, may increase the potential of television to do harm. Just as important is the implicit suggestion in the industry response that before any action is taken to reduce the amount or kind of violence to which our children are exposed, the harmful relationship must be conclusively demonstrated. Again, any familiarity with research on human behavior teaches that such propositions are rarely, if ever, capable of proof of the kind we have come to expect in determining the guilt of an accused felon. The decision must rest, as do other business decisions made by the industry and decisions in other areas of social policy, on the basis of the weight of the evidence and the potential risk of harm.

The second principal response has been that the industry will sponsor the research to determine the relationship between viewing violence and violent behavior. It is sufficient to note that although such promises were made first in 1954 and continued through 1964, by October 1967 the amount of research sponsored by the industry on this issue was so small as to be insignificant and that which was supported by the industry was, from the outset, clearly undertaken as a defensive move. By the time of our first set of hearings, the industry had shifted to the position that the reason they had undertaken no research is that it was not a researchable problem. Yet, within a matter of weeks after the second set of hearings in December, the networks had met and agreed to promote new research, and NBC had authorized the expenditure of $500,000 over the next five years.

The third major response of the industry over the years has been that they are going to reduce the amount of violence on television. Such promises were made in hearings before the Senate Subcommittee on Juvenile Delinquency in 1954, 1961, and 1963. Some studies in the files of the subcommittee indicate that the quantity of violent programs increased as much as 300 percent between 1954 and 1961. In 1961, the networks told the subcommittee that it takes eighteen months to two years to effect program changes capable of reducing violence. Two years later another set of hearings discovered that, with the exception of CBS, there had been no statistically significant reduction in the amount of violence.

After the tragic assassinations in the spring of 1968, there was much publicity in the trade and regular press about how the networks were reducing violence on television. Content analysis contracted by the Media Task Force indicate there was no such reduction by October 1968.

As before Senator Dodd's subcommittee on Juvenile Delinquency, in testifying before the Commission, the industry again asked for more time. We hope they will put it to better use than they have in the past.

Acknowledgments

The Media Task Force Report is the product of a group effort. While it is impossible to identify separately individual contributions, it is both necessary and desirable to identify major areas of responsibility, major contributors, and those to whom we are most heavily indebted for both their time and patience.

The most difficult task was faced by our consultants who were asked to set aside the many pressing demands on their time to prepare under impossible deadlines papers on which to base this report. Without their generous cooperation no report would have been feasible.

Our requests for information and access to personnel placed the greatest burden on the three commercial television networks. Each cooperated fully and promptly in assisting us to secure the information and material we needed. Special thanks is owed to Elmer Lower of ABC News and Richard Wald of NBC News for informally discussing news practices with us early in the formulation of this study. Similarly, special thanks is owed to the lawyers for the respective networks, Robert Evans and Ralph Goldberg at CBS, Corydon Dunham at NBC and Mark Roth at ABC, for handling our requests for information and tapes of entertainment programming promptly and efficiently. Aid was also received from Jack Valenti and Edward Cooper of the Motion Picture Association of America and from Douglas Anello of the National Association of Broadcasters.

In December of 1968 we invited about 50 journalists and six or seven representatives with minority perspectives to Washington for a three-day conference and we appreciate their insights to the news profession and how it works.

With regard to the news section of our report, three individuals must be singled out for extraordinary contributions: Ben H. Bagdikian of the Rand Corporation, Norman Isaacs of the *Louisville Courier-Journal*, and William L. Rivers of the Stanford School of Communication. Where their contribution is taken from a published source it is footnoted, but our borrowing from their unpublished work and oral comments is quite extensive in several chapters. Moreover, they frequently provided important leads to other source materials.

It is somewhat easier to assign final responsibility for analysis and conclusions within the Media Task Force staff. David Lange wrote the first two chapters of "Violence and the News Media" on the basis of papers submitted by consultants.

The remainder of the report, "Violence and the News Media", was written by Robert K. Baker. Significant portions of this section drew heavily on staff papers prepared by F. Clifton Berry, Jr., Steffen W. Graae, and David Lange. In addition, Linda J. Schacht made several essential research contributions to the formulation of the news section.

The section on "Television Entertainment and Violence" was under the direction of Sandra J. Ball. Assisting her on research were Carolyn McClelland, Linda J. Schacht, and Deborah Cutler.

As one might expect, the weaknesses and fallacies of the report must be credited to the Co-Director responsible for the relevant section—Robert K. Baker for "Violence and the News Media" and Sandra J. Ball for "Television Entertainment and Violence."

RKB

Bangkok, Thailand
20 November, 1969

I would like particularly to thank the social scientists who participated directly and indirectly in Part III. Their ideas, and counsel contained in papers submitted to the Media Task Force or in conversation were invaluable. In this respect, I am particularly indebted to Dr. Arline H. Sakuma.

S.J.B.

CONTENTS

APPENDICES

Witnesses

October 16, 17, 1969

Bradley Greenberg, Department of Communication, Michigan State University.

Joseph T. Klapper, Director, Office of Social Research, Columbia Broadcasting Systems, Inc.

Leonard Berkowitz, Department of Psychology, University of Wisconsin at Madison.

Percy Tannenbaum, Annenberg School of Communication, University of Pennsylvania.

George Gerbner, Dean of the Annenberg School of Communication, University of Pennsylvania.

Otto N. Larsen, Department of Sociology, University of Washington at Seattle.

Alfred R. Schneider, Vice President and Assistant to the Executive Vice President, American Broadcasting Company.

Robert D. Kasmire, Vice President, National Broadcasting Company.

Leo Bogart, Executive Vice President and General Manager of the Bureau of Advertising of the American Newspaper Publishers Association.

December 18, 19, and 20, 1969

Robert MacNeil, British Broadcasting Company.

Ben. · H. Bagdikian, Journalist and Press Critic, currently at the Rand Corporation.

Norman E. Isaacs, Executive Editor of the *Louisville Courier-Journal* and the *Louisville Times.*

John F. Dille, Jr., President of the Communicana Group.

Jack Valenti, President, Motion Picture Association of America.

The Honorable Rosel Hyde, Chairman of the Federal Communications Commission.

Dr. Lawrence Kubie, Psychiatrist.

The Honorable Nicholas Johnson, Federal Communications Commission.

James Casey, Assistant U.S. Attorney, Northern District of Illinois.

Thomas A. Foran, United States Attorney for the Northern District of Illinois.

Leonard H. Goldenson, President, American Broadcasting Companies, Inc.

Elmer W. Lower, President of ABC News.

Frank Stanton, President, Columbia Broadcasting System, Inc.

Richard S. Salant, President of CBS News.

Julian Goodman, President of National Broadcasting Company, Inc.

Reuven Frank, President of NBC News.

Chapter 1

THE PRINTED MEDIUM

The mass media in the United States are a blend of journalism and showmanship, information and entertainment, and professional altruism and marketplace opportunism. These are obviously qualities which, if not entirely antithetical, at least cannot be relied upon to coexist in perfect harmony. When they clash, the discord is important, for, if one thing is clear about the American media, it is that they touch our lives in ways far too intimate and complex to ignore.

Traditionally, of course, the media, and more particularly the news media, have given us our perceptions of the world around us. It is one of our richer, if less solidly grounded, beliefs that the media provide a "marketplace" in which one man's ideas and opinions can be compared with or joined to those of another. We expect the media to take an active role in the processes of government through criticism, through interpretation, even through the advocacy of action, and we encourage all these functions by according to the press as an institution essentially the same freedom of speech that we enjoy as individuals.

Beyond all this, however, we have become a nation of the entertained, and it is the media, for the most part, who provide our entertainment. Indeed, our appetites for entertainment, far more than our quest for knowledge, have brought the media from the economic position represented by the individual printer of two centuries ago to the status of a major business industry. In the process, the media themselves have changed in ways that invite attention.

The media today pervade our culture to a degree unmatched by any other social institution. From the tens of thousands of available titles, theoretically, an adult can choose from among some 1,750 daily newspapers; 578 Sunday papers; more than 8,000 weekly newspapers; more than 22,000 periodicals, including nearly 150 magazines of "general editorial" content; or from among tens of thousands of new books put out by the nation's more than 1,700 publishing houses.[1] Listeners with radios can choose from among more than 4,200 AM and 2,200 FM radio stations, and those with phonographs can select from the 35,000 phonograph records, including 10,000 new releases the market provides annually. For those who prefer to watch, there are some 840 television stations and more than 13,700 motion picture theatres and

Some media are available to nearly everyone, and nearly everyone makes some use of them. Most (95 percent) American homes include at least one TV set; nearly all (99 percent) own at least one radio. In a typical weekday, 82 percent of adults watch television; the average time invested is more than two hours. Two-thirds of America's adults listen to the radio, on the average more than an hour a day. More than nine out of every ten adults read a magazine sometime during the month and approximately three-fourths of the adult population read one or more newspapers on a typical weekday. Although movie-going is less universal, a third of the adult population sees at least one film in a typical month.

If these figures indicate that the media do indeed play an important role in the lives of American adults, it is no less true that the nation's children are heavily exposed to media influences—for better or worse. In particular, young people spend even more time with television than do their elders. Substantial evidence indicates that children from low-income families—children in the ghettos, for example—spend even more time watching television than do their counterparts in more priviledged classes. One study found that while middle class teenagers watch television on Sunday for an average of four hours; black teenagers, however, devoted six hours to their sets.[2] For most of these children, as for most Americans generally, television provides more than entertainment: it also provides Americans with the single most important and credible source of news about the world around them.[3]

Statistics as to media use vary, to be sure, and we have included here a composite of figures cited in several sources. Nonetheless, from any standpoint, the media clearly play an important, and perhaps critical, role in daily American living. The media, and television in particular, have gradually assumed more and more of the role formerly occupied by schools, churches, and family groups in providing a nation with its values, its goals, and its standards of conduct.

It becomes a matter of no small importance, then, to inquire into the content and effects of the media with regard to violence. It is equally important to know what forces shape the media. On the one hand, the media are a multi-billion dollar business, which makes them susceptible to the competitive pressures that influence all major business enterprises. With the exception of motion pictures and books, the media are sustained by advertising revenues. In the typical case, therefore, the pressures of competition become an urgent, literal, life-or-death need to attract audiences sufficiently large to earn the advertising revenues necessary to sustain them. Where advertisements do not provide the source of income, direct sales to consumers do, and the urgent need for mass acceptability remains much the same. These pressures do not insure that the public interest will always be served.

In the past these pressures have led to the familiar excesses of newspaper circulation wars in which sex, violence, and sensationalism have been served up in generous portions by publishers hungry for audiences. Today, they contribute to the selection of television programming aimed for the most part at the broadest possible audiences. Because media entertainment more than media information can attract audiences, these pressures also explain the growing influence of entertainment values—the "show-business ethic," as it has been called—upon the whole spectrum of media content.

In short, any study of the relationship between violence and the media must take into account the conflicting nature of the media as institutions.

We must, on the one hand, appreciate the heritage of free expression that has come to us in large part because of the struggle of the press against censorship and regulation. No clearer evidence can sustain the high value Americans place upon a free press than the fact that the press is the only private institution specifically protected by the Constitution. All media today directly descend from the American press and they have naturally come to share in the hard-won freedom of the press.

Yet, as we have said, the media today comprise institutions far different from the press of two centuries ago. The forms have changed. Circulation has increased beyond anything then dreamed of. Competitive pressures have increased and in response the media have learned from sheer necessity the art of manipulating vast audiences for economic gain. In the process of this growth and change, the ability of any single man to gain access to the "marketplace of ideas" has become all but extinct.

Clearly, then, the media merit study by anyone who would know more about the structure of American society. But when violence becomes the issue, the study is obligatory. For much of what we know of violence in all its forms we understand as observers and students of the mass media, not as participants.

A. History of the American Press*

> The way to get at the nature of an institution, as of anything else that is alive, is to see how it has grown.

—A. G. Keller

1. England

When, in 1476, William Caxton established his printing press at Westminster and began to publish books and pamphlets, he brought to England a craft already well established on the Continent. 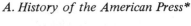 The impact was enormous. Knowledge of the world beyond the experience of the individual was no longer limited by the occasional tales of travelling minstrels or messengers from afar. Knowledge was no longer the exclusive province of the few who could afford the one or two hand-lettered manuscripts that one artisan could produce in an entire year. In unprecedented numbers, people could now question, doubt, criticize, explore, suggest, persuade, and teach. In short, development of the press brought the power to manipulate the environment and affect people's thoughts well beyond the range of the human voice. By 1620, Francis Bacon could regard its "force, effects and consequences," on a par with gunpowder and the compass for having "changed the appearance and state of the world."[4] In retrospect, his claim

---

*Much of the material in this portion of this report is from a paper, "Historical Development of the Media in American Life," prepared for the Task Force by Dr. Jay W. Jensen, head of the department of journalism, and Dr. Theodore Peterson, dean, College of Communications, University of Illinois at Champaign-Urbana.

was no hyperbole. Printing in fact did play an impressive part in shaping intellectual life and in the diffusion of culture, in the development of the nation-state and the rise of capitalism, and in transforming the nature of religion and politics.

From the ranks of anonymous artisans and minstrels, printing elevated men of letters to personages famous in their own lifetimes and sometimes long after their deaths. By standardizing language, printing fostered the development of national literatures. Although it did not immediately revolutionize scientific thought, printing led ultimately to the dissemination of scientific ideas and to the formation of a scientific community. The press provided the means for spreading scientific thought across national borders.

Equally significant was printing's contribution to growth in the spirit of rationality. As Herbert Muller has observed, "In thought generally it both fortified and supplemented the classifical tradition of rationalism by more empirical sense, or concern with fact. Accordingly, it had much to do with the revolutionary developments to come, notably the rise of science and of democracy."[5]

Printing undoubtedly did contribute to the rise of democracy. Early empires, although essentially loose confederations, extended over vast expanses of territory. Printing aided centralization of political allegiances by spreading common beliefs, common values, and common goals over wide geographic areas.

In religion, too, printing served both as a force for maintaining the established order and as a force for change. But change dominated. Printing broke the Church's monopoly over knowledge. Although he berated printers for their money-mindedness, Martin Luther called printing "God's highest act of Grace."

Established institutions became threatened. Andrew Fletcher, the Scot patriot, recognized the importance of controlling communication when he noted in 1704, "I believe that if a man were permitted the right to write all the ballads he need not care who should make the laws of a nation." The phenomenon was also recognized by established authorities on the Continent and in England. They responded with attempts to control the source of the threat. Although all had some effect, none could either silence or control the press completely. The tension between the government and the press has been as old as the press itself.

The struggle for press freedom in England became a part of the larger struggle of the people to achieve a responsive constitutional government. Since that slow movement of power—from crown to nobility to people—had profound implications for the extent and kinds of repression, one needs a grasp of its broad outlines to understand the development of freedom of the press in England.

When the infant printing industry started to develop, the Tudors—Henry VII, Henry VIII, Edward, Mary, Elizabeth I—sat on the throne. Though generally popular for bringing stability after the sanguinary civil wars of feudal times, the Tudors, both powerful and arbitrary, governed efficiently in an era of national expansion, consolidation, and the revival of classical learning, an era when challenge to the wealth and power of the Catholic Church was inevitable.

As printing developed, the King, rather than put it under the jurisdiction of courts or Parliament, assumed control as an inherent royal prerogative. He had unlimited authority to regulate and to control. So long as printing remained a mere adjunct of letters, however, neither King nor Parliament showed much interest in interfering with it. But as the number of books increased, and particularly as their authors engaged in religious and political controversy, the Tudors concentrated control of the press in the hands of the King and his council. This system of controls established by the tight-ruling Tudors set the pattern for succeeding periods.

One of the earliest control devices was the grant of patents of monopoly to printers. In exchange for good behavior, printers were given permits to publish selected categories of books, such as school books, religious books, law books, histories, and plays. The system was so effective it flourished for two centuries, reaching its culmination in the monopolistic Stationers Company, an exclusive organization of privileged printers chartered by the Crown to admit and expel members to the printing trades, to penalize offending printers, and to regulate the press in the interest of the Crown.

From patents, the Tudors moved to a second type of control—licensing. Although licensing took various forms, its essential purpose remained the same: to require the printer to submit manuscripts for official review and approval prior to publication.

The most comprehensive regulation of the Tudor period evolved from Elizabeth's Star Chamber decree. Promulgated in 1586, it remained in effect until 1637. The decree limited the number of printers, apprentices, and presses, gave the Stationers Company power of search and seizure, and required the licensing of all books. Law books were licensed by the justices, and all others by the Archbishop of Canterbury or the Bishop of London. Administration and enforcement became the responsibility of the Stationers Company and of ecclesiastical officials.

The early Stuarts made the courts and Parliament the instruments for controlling discussion. The gradually eroding power of the monarch made an efficient new means for controlling thought and discussion necessary. In this setting, the law of seditious libel developed to deal more effectively with ideas that challenged the existing order. The old law of treason, which had been adequate to put down armed rebellion, was too cumbersome to invoke against controversial pamphleteers. The Star Chamber provided precedent for subsequent prosecutions of seditious libel by laying down four propositions in 1606: (1) Libel against an ordinary person was a criminal offense; (2) libel against a deceased person was an offense; (3) the prosecution could be either in court or before the Star Chamber; and (4) truth was no defense. By implication, a fifth soon emerged: It was as criminal to publish libelous or seditious material as to create it.

During the Puritan Revolution and the Cromwellian interregnum, the press was, at times, almost entirely free, and at times under restrictions nearly as stringent as those of Elizabeth's reign. The powerful Stationers Company was undermined, and the Star Chamber's enforcement powers were abolished.

With the Restoration in 1660, the Stuarts shared power to control the press with Parliament. Charles II, late in his reign, ended the Crown's long alliance with the Stationers Company. Under William of Orange, after the

Bloodless Revolution, restrictions on the press reached a low point. Licensing became too cumbersome and ineffective a method under a two-party system of Parliamentary government and it was allowed to lapse. Only seditious libel and a ban on reporting the activities of Parliament remained.

Although government control of the press had not disappeared by the 18th century, new techniques seemed necessary. The propertied middle class recognized the crude, direct methods of the Tudors as anachronistic, and those means of control gradually vanished. In their place emerged the more subtle but no less effective control by taxation, by subsidy, and by prosecution under due process.

Usually, taxation and subsidy worked in tandem. Taxes aimed at eliminating marginal publications and undermining the financial health of the survivors in order to make them susceptible to subsidy. Meanwhile, however, political leaders, political parties, and the government itself secretly paid writers and editors to give them editorial support.

By the American Revolution, England had come a long way. It was, in the judgment of H.J.Muller, the freest country in Europe, with the most vigorous press, the most open debate and the most influential public opinion.[6]

2. Early America

During this same period, the American press had begun to grow. Its nature and practices heavily influenced by its English and continental forebears, the early colonial press repeated the struggle of the British press for independence. As in England, the press was viewed as a threat to both church and state; the authorities responded with licensing, direct censorship, sedition laws, legislative privilege, and patronage. As in England, the efforts met with only partial success, for powerful newspapers started to grow in the principal American cities.

After the mid-17th century, the demand for information in the growing Colonies exceeded the supply provided by gossip in the coffeehouse, letters from abroad, and packets of English newspapers delivered by accommodating sea captains. The growth of periodicals, however, was retarded by the firm control exercised by church authorities, colonial governors and their councils, because these authorities, like their English counterparts, regarded a controlled press as useful and a free press as dangerous.

Philadelphia was two years old in 1685 when William Bradford set up his printing shop there. His first publication, an almanac, was censored in advance and he was warned not to print without a license. In 1690. Bradford has trouble again. This time the authorities seized his press and subjected him to trial, the first in the Colonies with freedom of the press at issue. He was jailed for seditious libel. That same year, Benjamin Harris published the first newspaper in America, *Publick Occurrences*. It did not survive the first day. The first issue carried an account of the French and Indian wars that could be construed as critical of colonial policy; therefore, the governor and council of Massachusetts invoked their licensing power to shop further publication.

Licensing survived in the Colonies at least through 1722, when Andrew Bradford, son of William, was brought before the authorities for offensive publications. The younger Bradford, after making abject apologies, was ordered not "to publish anything relating to or concerning the Affairs of this Government, or the Government of any other of his Majesty's Colonies" without prior permission.[7]

A more sophisticated remedy for controlling the press soon found official favor and eventually displaced licensing as the preferred control. The law of seditious libel was accepted in the Colonies, even by libertarians, until the end of the 18th century.

The 18th century libertarians believed that the press would be free if there were no prior censorship, if the defendant could plead truth as a defense to a charge of seditious libel, and if juries rather than judges would resolve the issue of whether the material was libelous. Such powers for the jury secured in England by Fox's Libel Act of 1792, took longer to gain acceptance in America.

Courts served as the forum for some seditious libel prosecutions. Truth as a defense emerged as the principal issue. John Peter Zenger was charged with sedition for publishing articles criticizing New York's Governor Cosby in 1735. The jury accepted his defense of truth and concluded the material was not seditious. He was acquitted. The verdict, as popular as Governor Cosby was unpopular, however, had no practical effect in New York or elsewhere in the Colonies. Over 60 years later, a Jeffersonian chief justice of New York still contended that truth served as no defense to a charge of seditious libel. Although the Zenger case is sometimes taken as a milestone in the march to freedom of the press, it was little more than an incident that received an inordinate amount of publicity.

The courts may have been a threat and a deterrent to colonial publishers, but, as in England in the 18th century, the legislature zealously and effectively restricted the press. The popularly elected colonial assemblies, which needed no jury to indict or to convict, used their power to punish "breaches of parliamentary privilege" to try individuals for spoken or written words that had angered their members. Turning to the House of Commons for precedent, the assemblies punished as seditious almost any utterance that they thought questioned their authority, conduct, or reputation.

Despite these controls, the press managed a slow growth in the 18th century. In the first quarter, five newspapers began in Colonial seaports which were centers of commercial, cultural, and political activity. By midcentury, the Colonies had more than a dozen papers. More important than their number, though, they had changed from weak, inconsequential organs with circulations of a few hundred into significant propaganda voices with circulations as high as 3,000. As the conflict between Tories and Patriots deepened, the papers grew rapidly in number and in circulation. Publishing, even without political subsidy, became a profitable business. The publisher, with his access to an important tool for molding public opinion, became a significant public figure, and the press started to play an important role in the process of social change.

3. Philosophical Antecedents

The constructive role of the press in the growth of this nation would not have been possible without a strong philosophy of free expression. But that philosophy developed even more slowly than the press. Most colonists simply did not comprehend the utility of a doctrine that allowed freedom to express views and opinions different from their own and they accepted with little opposition the early controls that the government imposed on the press.

Most of the early English libertarians offered only limited or self-serving defenses of free expression. John Milton's *Areopagitica*, written in 1644, is often quoted as a classic defense of press freedom. In fact, however, Milton regarded freedom of the press as no more than the abolition of licensing, and he proposed to deny freedom to anyone who questioned the fundamental political and religious order. The freedom he wanted was for those of his own persuasion or with "neighboring differences."

Other libertarians—John Locke and Roger Williams, for example—conceived freedom of the press as the abolition of prior censorship and of licensing. The Levellers, who in the 1640's were at the forefront of the libertarian movement in England, shared this limited view; many of them would return to prosecution for sedition, according to historian Leonard W. Levy, and even John Lilburne on occasion favored the enforcement of the licensing procedure so long as he was exempt.

Although well reasoned and comprehensive statements about free expression seemed rare, Americans could read one early in the 18th century in *Cato's Letters*, which went through a half-dozen editions in book form between 1733 and 1755, and were widely and extensively printed in the colonial papers. "Cato," the pseudonym of Whig journalists Thomas Gordon and John Trenchard, wrote three-quarters of a century after Milton and the Levellers, and had a broader concept of free expression. He contended that the government should conduct itself in the interests of the people; that the people had the responsibility of making sure that the public business was transacted in their interest; and that only a free press could subject the government to public scrutiny. He conceded the necessary of some laws to curb seditious utterances, provided they were reasonable and rarely imposed. But, he believed, truth should be a defense against seditious libel. In short, Cato was that rare creature, a libertarian who would tolerate opinions that offended him.[8] For the most part, however, from Cato's time until the end of the 18th century, there was no genuinely original philosophical writing about free expression in the Colonies.

When the American tradition of a free press did begin to emerge, it came from the bitter interaction of contending interests, each working for its self-interest; first in the controversy over the adoption of a Bill of Rights, later in the furor over the Alien and Sedition Acts of 1798. As it turned out, the tradition went far beyond the conventional thinking of the 18th century, and it had respectable philosophical arguments to sustain it.

Persuasive evidence supports the view that the framers of the Constitution were not quite the practicing libertarians that conventional history has sometimes painted them. Delegates to the Constitutional Convention of 1787 met with the press excluded, and not one of them protested the rule of secrecy. Some 55 years ago, Charles Beard, in *An Economic Interpretation of the Constitution*,[9] wrote that the Constitution owed far less to abstract concern about rights than to the self-interest of the men who drafted it. More recently, Professor Levy, in his *Legacy of Suppression*, has cogently

developed the thesis that the generation that adopted the Constitution, the
Bill of Rights, and the various state constitutions, did not believe in a broad
scope for freedom of expression, especially in political matters. The Bill of
Rights, he concluded, was more the chance product of expediency than the
happy product of principle.[10]

The Bill of Rights resulted from the contest between the Federalists, who
favored a strong national government, and the Antifederalists, who preferred
a league of more or less independent states. One view held that, since the
national government had only enumerated powers, it had no authority to
regulate the press. The Anti-federalists, however, regarded the Bill of Rights
as essential in order to protect the state's interests. It would prevent the
central government from imposing any restrictions on speech and the press,
and it would reserve the power to regulate the press to the states.[11]

In 1798, war with France was imminent. The Federalists in power passed
the Alien and Sedition Acts to deport troublesome aliens and curb seditious
utterances. One of the four measures provided punishments of up to two
years in prison and a fine of $2,000 for writing, printing, or uttering any
"false, scandalous and malicious" statement against the government of
Congress "with intent to defame . . . or to bring them . . . into contempt or
disrepute." The act embodied the principles for which libertarians had
fought: criminal intent had to be demonstrated, truth was a defense, and the
jury decided whether the words were libelous.[12]

When the act was used to intimidate printers and publishers, when juries
were quick to convict, the Republicans saw it as a Federalist attempt to
create a one-party press and one-party government. Their attack on the
sedition laws broke with the conventional doctrines of free expression.

There were many contributors to the attack, but one of the most eloquent
and philosophical was Tunis Wortman, a New York lawyer. Calm, persuasive,
free from polemics, Wortman urged that governments exist to protect the
liberties of their citizens, that the citizen has the right to dissolve the
government, and that free expression is indispensable to the preservation of
the citizen's rights. He rejected criminal libel as incompatible with a
democratic society, and asked, in effect, "Of what use is liberty of doing that
for which I am punishable afterwards?"[13]

Most commonly associated with the classical libertarian view, however, are
John Milton, Thomas Jefferson, and John Stuart Mill. They argued
eloquently, and their reputations have overshadowed others who wrote with
no less brilliance or intellectual vigor. Separately, none of the three expressed
a comprehensive philosophy; but together, their writings embody a set of
unified principles.

Although Milton is invariably cited as an early champion of free
expression, he in fact scarcely qualifies as a libertarian by modern standards.
His conception of freedom of the press was narrow: it was an end to
licensing, and no more. Once an offensive work was published, the
government could punish, and for Milton the categories of offensive works
were many. Milton's main contribution to the classical tradition was his idea
of the self-righting process in which truth emerges from the unfettered
competition of ideas in the marketplace. Coming before the widespread
acceptance of the natural rights doctrine, he also provided a religious base for

free expression. He saw freedom of expression as God's will; man could not be virtuous without it.[14]

Jefferson, on the other hand, regarded free expression as one of man's inalienable natural rights; a child of the Enlightenment, he accepted its optimistic assumptions. He saw man as essentially good unless corrupted by ignorance or bad institutions, and he put strong faith in man's rationality and perfectability. Like Locke, Jefferson believed that men entered into governments of their own volition to protect their natural rights and that, therefore, the best government had only a light hand on its citizens. But to be capable of self-government, the individual citizen had to be educated and well-informed. Although individuals might be mistaken in their application of reason, the majority would invariably reach sound decisions. Thus social change would result from unrestricted discussion.

The press, Jefferson believed, had an important part to play in making government function effectively. Besides promoting the grand search for ultimate truth, it could perform such utilitarian tasks as enlightening the citizenry, expediting the political process, and safeguarding personal liberties. To Jefferson, the press remained the best means of "enlightening the mind of man, and improving him as a rational, moral and social being." It was the channel for providing the citizen with the facts and opinions needed for self-government, and the watchdog to sound a warning when individual rights were threatened.[15]

While Jefferson's defense of free expression was only partially posited on its political utility, John Stuart Mill rested his entire case on individual and social utility, rejecting any claim to free expression as a natural right. For Mill, the good society was one in which an individual was free to think and act as he chose. He feared most a tyranny of the majority. In his view, each individual must accord to others the same wide latitutde of freedom he claimed for himself.

Mill's defense of free expression centered on four propositions: first, as opinion is silenced, truth may be silenced as well; second, even a wrong opinion may contain an element of truth necessary to discovery of the whole truth; third, even if the commonly accepted opinion is the whole truth, people will hold it not as rational belief but as a prejudice if they have not had to defend it; fourth, the commonly held opinion loses its vitality and its effect on character and conduct if it is not contested.[16]

With Mill, Americans arrived at a multi-faceted libertarian philosophy of freedom of expression and freedom of the press. It rested on a concept of negative liberty—freedom from any external restraint. Under this libertarian view, the press should be free to publish without prior restraint and without affirmative responsibility. Men needed this wide latitude of freedom in their quest for truth, to bring about social change through the peaceable means of discussion, conversion, and consensus, and to check the excesses of government.

The people need not fear the vast freedom granted the press, according to classical libertarian theory, for free expression carried built-in safeguards. Most men, as moral beings, would use their freedom responsibly. For every man who abused his freedom, there were many others to expose or correct him. And the greatest safeguard of all was the preeminent good sense of the majority, which would arrive at sound judgment if the channels of communication were left unrestricted. In short, the press would function as a vast marketplace of ideas.

The tradition did condone libel laws, which provided recourse in the courts for defamation. It did condone obscenity laws, although what constituted obscenity was a perennial matter of dispute. And it did condone mild sedition laws. But even with those limitations, the theory offered unprecedented freedom to speak and to write.

4. The Philosophy as Law*

The legal structure of free speech and press has grown as slowly as the philosophy of free expression. England's well-known scholar of jurisprudence, William Blackstone, supposed that freedom of the press meant simply no prior censorship. But Blackstone and other legal scholars who followed him found no fault with the idea of imposing sanctions for "abuse" of that freedom. As we have seen, even some philosophers were willing to accept this concept. Early state court decisions in the United States, as well as many later state constitutions, reflected the principle that the press was "free"—but responsible for abuses of the freedom.

The adoption of the first amendment itself did little to affect these early interpretations of the legal content of free speech and press. The first amendment was resolved as a compromise during the hectic negotiations between Federalists and Antifederalists. The language of the amendment reflects this compromise in its vagueness:

> Congress shall make no law respecting the establishment of religion, or prohibiting free exercise thereof; or abridging the freedom of speech, or press; or the right of the people peaceably to assemble, and to petition government for a redress of grievances.

Attempts to construe the language literally in order to resolve specific controversies almost certainly result in failure. Nowhere does the amendment define either free speech or freedom of the press. This understanding does not ignore whatever sense of direction or policy the language suggests, one cannot read the amendment without taking into account the "gloss" which the circumstances of its enactment provided, and the subsequent judicial interpretations in the context of specific controversies.

To a surprising degree, the gloss is recent; much of it, immediate. Not until 1919, in *Schenck* v. *United States*,[17] did the U.S. Supreme Court begin seriously to define the legal boundaries of freedom of expression in the United States. Even more starting is the fact that more than half of the cases which legal scholars might agree deserve particular study have been decided within the past fifteen years. In short, despite the age of the first amendment, the precise content of freedom of speech and press under the amendment has only recently begun to be defined.

The emerging definitions are not entirely clear. But the obscenity cases

---

*Much of the discussion in this section is based upon a paper prepared for the Media Task Force by Professor Harry Kalven of the University of Chicago Law School. The conclusions suggested here are the responsibility of the Task Force, however, and do not necessarily represent Professor Kalven's conclusions.

make it relatively clear that ideas and speech may not be suppressed merely because they are heretical or contrary to the prevailing moral climate. It also seems clear that the doctrine of seditious libel, once the great instrument for controlling freedom of expression in England and the Colonies, can find no room in contemporary American life. Finally, it seems clear that freedom of speech and press means more than freedom from prior censorship. Indeed, prior censorship itself may not always be forbidden; instead, the relevant question asks the extent to which expression, including speech and press, is protected at all stages of publication.

Some aspects of speech and press yield to regulation; for example, the right to regulate matters which do not affect what is said, but rather when, where, and how it is said. The regulatory powers of the Federal Communications Commission provide an excellent example, both because they illustrate an important, practical application of this principle and because they illustrate the difficulties inherent in deciding when regulation of speech "traffic" becomes unacceptable regulation of speech content. The FCC, on the one hand, must observe the first amendment's prohibition against Congressional abridgement of freedom of the press and, more specifically, the prohibition against censorship imposed by section 326 of the Communications Act of 1934. At the same time, the act requires broadcasters to employ their franchise in the "public interest, convenience and necessity." Rather clearly, whether broadcasters serve the public interest depends at least partly upon what is said.

When does permissible regulation become impermissible abridgement? That has occupied most of the attention of courts that have considered the limits of the first amendment. A number of tests have been suggested for determining the validity of efforts to control the content of publications; but no single, integrated theory of first amendment freedoms has been stated in any case.

The theory that has enjoyed perhaps the longest run in the courts—and the widest popular understanding—is the so-called "clear and present danger" test. It stems from an opinion written by Mr. Justice Holmes in the U.S. Supreme Court's 1919 decision in *Schenck* v. *United States*. Schenck widely disseminated literature condemning World War I and its supposed Wall Street sponsors, and he urged draftees to resist induction. He and his comrades were charged with having violated the Espionage Act. The Supreme Court affirmed their conviction and sentence. Holmes wrote:

> We admit that in many places and in ordinary times the defendants in saying all that was said in the circular would have been within their constitutional rights. But the character of every act depends upon the circumstances in which it is done . . . The most stringent protection of free speech should not protect a man in falsely shouting fire in a theater, and causing a panic. It does not even protect a man from an injunction against uttering words that may have all the effect of force . . . The question in every case is whether the words used are used in such circumstances and are of such a nature as to create a clear and present danger that they will bring about the substantive evils Congress has a right to prevent. It is a question of proximity and degree.[18]

The clear and present danger test amounts to a rule that the content of speech will not be subject to government regulation unless what one says or writes may contribute immediately and proximately to the occurrence of some activity which itself is subject to government regulation. The test, obviously, does not lend itself to certainty. Instead, it requires an individual assessment of a questioned utterance in the context of a given situation.

Whether the clear and present danger test remains a valid prescription for determining the amenability of content to regulation is itself uncertain. In cases before the Supreme Court dealing with the Smith Act, which aimed at Communists in the early years of the last decade, a majority of the justices appeared to find the Holmes formula unmanageably vague. In particular, it seemed inadequate to measure publications that, although involving substantial issues conceivably affected in some important way by the utterance in question, do not present a clear cause-and-effect relationship. Similarly, the Holmes formula, it would seem, has little evident applicability to the regulation of violence as it appears in media content.

Yet in our concern with violence and the media, two highly significant lessons do appear in the first amendment cases. First, the courts will probably not draw any substantial distinction between news or information and entertainment content in the media. The point may appear somewhat surprising at first, because entertainment, as we know it popularly in the media, is commonly believed not to result in substantial contributions to truth or knowledge. Yet important ideas can clothe themselves in fiction or other forms of entertainment as surely as in the evening newscast or editorial page. Because we cannot readily draw a line between the worthwhile and unworthwhile, a rule that generally accords to all communications, the protection of the first amendment, without an effort to distinguish between entertainment and nonentertainment content, would undoubtedly be desirable.

The second lesson, however, teaches that, although neither entertainment nor news may be regulated generally, possibly one or the other or both may be subject to minimal restraints that may have a direct or indirect bearing upon violence in the society. To the extent that the advocacy of violence may be regulated in individuals under the clear and present danger or some other test, the media will necessarily feel the restraint, if only indirectly. Beyond that, an analogy between violence and obscenity can conceivably provide a rationale for regulating violence in the media.

In the most general terms, obscenity now yields to regulation when the questionable matter appeals primarily to the reader's prurient interest, patently offends, has utterly no redeeming social value, or it is disseminated with the cynical attitude of the panderer. It is fashionable to speak of these elements as defining "hard-core" obscenity or pornography. There is also evidence in recent cases indicating that the Supreme Court may be willing to permit a somewhat more stringent regulation in the dissemination of material to minors.

Conceivably, as Professor Kalven suggests, an area of "hard core violence" might be established within which the first amendment might permit regulation of media content. He is quick to point out, however, that the analogy between violence and obscenity strains belief, and the obscenity cases themselves have been less than satisfactory. In particular, the concept of obscenity carries with it our traditional acceptance of prurience as a topic subject to regulation. From the stocks to public whippings to *The Scarlet Letter*, we know about sex and dark urges, and we readily understand efforts to regulate here, whether or not we agree with them. Not so with violence. Much of our culture accepts violence as a normal occurrence without real definition or without much thought about the forms of violence; to try to separate unacceptable violence from the acceptable would require initially an exploration into concepts hitherto largely ignored, and likely to be of little use.

The U.S. Supreme Court has considered the regulation of violence only once—in 1948, in *Winters* v. *New York*.[19] In that case, a statute purporting to regulate printed matter "devoted to the publication and principally made up of criminal news, police reports, or accounts of criminal deeds, or pictures or stories of deeds of bloodshed, lust or crime" was overturned by six members of the Court—after three arguments. The majority opinion rested upon the vagueness of the statute; it did not reach the underlying issues. Yet the writer of the opinion tried at some pains to avoid suggesting that no such statute could succeed. At the beginning of his opinion, Justice Reed wrote:

> We recognize the importance of the exercise of a state's police power to minimize all incentives to crime, particularly in the field of sanguinary or salacious publications with their stimulation of juvenile delinquency.[20]

And again at the conclusion he stated:

> To say that a state may not punish by such a vague statute carries no implication that it may not punish circulation of objectionable printed matter, assuming that it is not protected by the principles of the First Amendment, by the use of apt words to describe the prohibited publications.[21]

Since 1947, when it decided *Winters*, the Court has considered numerous obscenity cases but no other case directly involving violence as a principal issue. And so the amenability of violence in media content to regulation remains a matter for speculation. Within this area for speculation a few general predictions may be advanced.

First, it seems clear, any effort to control the appearance of violence in media content should be supported by clear evidence of its effects upon the audience. If, indeed, a balance can be struck against first amendment protection and in favor of regulation, the need for that balance will almost certainly help determine the success or failure of the proposal to regulate. Second, the proposal itself will demand clear, specific, and precise draftsmanship, both in the subject matter of the regulation, as well as in the end to be realized. The *Winters* case makes it clear that nothing less can suffice. Third, greater regulation on behalf of children than adults can probably the sustained under the first amendment.

These are, as we have said, speculations. They are not blueprints for action. Indeed, as our conclusions and recommendations will point out, what we have learned to date about the relationship between the media and violence makes the case for legislative "solutions" less than clear. There is virtually no evidence to support any legislative action regulating the content of violence in news reporting, with the possible exception of information likely to aid rioters during periods of civil disorder. And on this latter point, the drafting difficulties are apt to be so great as to make constitutional regulation impossible.

The speculations here do suggest the outlines of some possible ways in which the philosophy of free expression, hard won after three centuries of conflict and not yet fully defined after two centuries of protection under the first amendment, might be reconciled at some future date with this country's concern for the effects of the constant barrage of violence in the entertainment media. This is particularly true with regard to regulation aimed at limiting access by children without parental consent.

5. The Historical Role of the Press*

The emergence of the press as an institution essentially free from government interference or regulation—yet possessed of powerful means for influencing the society in which it functions—has resulted inevitably in an important role for the press in the process of social change within this country. We have explored the struggle of the press to gain its freedom. We turn now to an examination of the ways in which the press has contributed to the development of a nation while gaining its own independence. To understand the role the press might take in the resolution of today's divisive issues, we must know what role it has played in past crises.

The press has never been a monolith. At no point in its history could we say that all the elements of the American press promoted this change or anchored that stability. When one newspaper has advocated an action, many others have opposed it. Trends and centers of gravity exist, but no concerted action. The press has distinctively changed even as it has served as an instrument of change.

The attitudes of the American press of the Revolutionary period are significant. To oppose the tax controls imposed by the Stamp Act, some editors suspended publication, which aroused citizens who had come to depend upon them. Others published without the stamp, or without a title or masthead to identify them as newspapers. Several issued wild satires—among them, skull and crossbone decorations—on the Stamp Act itself.

Of course, not all the editors and pamphleteers of the Revolutionary period wanted war, or even separation from England. But as the Colonies moved closer to war with England, the "radical" editors, who had been quite the weakest group, gathered numbers and strength. When the Revolutionary War began, many Whigs who had argued for the middle course were drawn into the ranks of the radicals.

---

*The material in this section and the next is from a paper prepared for the Task Force by Prof. William L. Rivers of the department of communications, Stanford University, Stanford, Calif.

Revolutionary newspapers went to 40 thousand homes and were widely distributed among friends and neighbors. In all, considering the level of literacy and the makeshift communications facilities, Revolutionary sentiment was widely dispersed by the press of the period. It became an effective lesson in the power of the press, a lesson not lost on others who understood the use of power. So convinced was General Washington of its value, he issued a plea to patriot women asking them to save all available material for conversion into paper for printing.

The relationship between the press and the government, however, has not always been warm, as the initial efforts by authorities to control the press have made clear. From the first, officials have had to adapt to the anomaly of an information system that is *of,* but not *in,* the government, which produced a natural struggle between the press and government. The "strong Presidents," revered by many historians and political scientists— Washington, Jefferson, Jackson, Lincoln, Theodore Roosevelt, Wilson, and Franklin Roosevelt—understood and used the press most adroitly. Much of the history of American government pivots on the use of the press as an instrument of political power. Our founding fathers, eminently practical, knew how to use the press. The stern figure of George Washington becomes less austere when viewed through the prism of his worried statement to Alexander Hamilton regarding the farewell address:

> The doubt that occurs at first view is the length of it for a News Paper publication . . . . All the columns of a large Gazette would scarcely, I conceive, contain the present draught.[22]

Nowhere did this pragmatism find clearer expression than in the establishment of the "party press" newspapers and journals that served as the official organs of polemics and politics. Both Jefferson and Washington had revealed their usefulness while Jefferson served in Washington's cabinet. Alexander Hamilton, Washington's chief lieutenant, established *The Gazette of the United States* to trumpet the cause of Washington's Federalists. Eager to develop an editorial voice for anti-Federalism, Jefferson enlisted Philip Freneau, a talented poet-journalist who had become famous as "The Poet of the Revolution" to act as paid "translator" in Jefferson's office—and also to publish a party newspaper.

Freneau moved to Philadelphia and established *The National Gazette*, which soon became the loudest anti-Federalist voice. It also became President Washington's strongest critic. The President protested the attacks as "outrages on common decency," and he questioned Jefferson closely regarding Freneau's reason for coming to Philadelphia. He had simply lost his translating clerk, Jefferson replied, and had hired Freneau to replace him. "I cannot recollect," Jefferson told Washington, "whether it was at the same time, or afterwards, that I was told he had a thought of setting up a newspaper . . . ."[23]

When Jefferson was elected President, he found that none of the Washington and New York newspapers had sent reporters to chronicle the move of the Capital from Philadelphia to Washington. He persuaded a young printer named Samuel Harrison Smith to set up shop on the mudflats of the

Potomac, luring him with printing-contract patronage. Smith's *National Intelligencer* was the preeminent newspaper for more than a decade, and served Jefferson well.[24]

When Andrew Jackson became President, he established *The Washington Globe*. Its editor, Amos Kendall, was so significant a member of the famed "Kitchen Cabinet" that a Congressman of the time declared, "He was the President's thinking machine, his writing machine—aye, and his lying machine." Jackson was not content, however, to have a single organ grinding his tune. At one point, fifty-seven journalists were reported to have been on the government payroll.[25]

The party press began to wane after Jackson, but the period continued to be far from tranquil. American newspapers, which had always aimed at the highly literate, now began to direct their appeal to the masses. Other editors had tried to establish "penny papers," but none succeeded until Benjamin H. Day brought out his *New York Sun* in 1833. Before the *Sun,* editors had been charging six to ten dollars a year in advance for subscriptions—more than many a skilled worker could earn in a week. Day's *Sun* was not only inexpensive, it emphasized local news and, at least initially, gave special play to human interest, crime, and violence. The *Sun* soon had a circulation of 8,000.

The *Sun* and the other penny papers were certainly sensational, and they are often remembered chiefly for that quality. But perhaps they deserve a better memory. Beyond sensationalism, they achieved what more sober journals had largely failed to do: they appealed to the common man and helped to make him literate. More important, they made him believe that he, too, had a voice in the leading affairs of his time, for they mixed in with the sensationalism readable reports on domestic and foreign government.

During this same period of Jacksonian Democracy, the abolitionists began the fierce agitation that marked three decades. Though not the first time that the press had embarked upon crusade and counter-crusade, it set the stage for the press to assume the on-going roles of accuser and champion which they could still fill today.

The party press had all but died in 1860, when the Government Printing Office was established, thus cutting off many of the lucrative printing contracts that Washington papers had enjoyed. The party press declined, too, because of the growth of Washington bureaus of the strong New York newspapers. A President or a Congressional leader could benefit only moderately from establishing a party organ when alert reporters for James Gorden Bennet's *New York Herald* or Horace Greeley's *New York Tribune* were covering Washington more ably than any Washington newspaper. By this time, the Associated Press started to distribute dispassionate reports to a variety of papers, ushering in the period of "objective reporting." Thus began an era of independence that shaped a concept of self that the press has never relinquished.

From the end of the Civil War to the end of the 19th century, power was atomized in the world of the American press. Editors discovered that their influence did not depend on party affiliation. Instead of seeking support from party leaders, they sought to build their own centers of strength among readers.

It resulted in a series of experiments somewhat like the "penny press" era of the early 19th century. The difference was that America itself was changing radically during the latter part of the century. Arthur M. Schlesinger's *Rise of the City, 1878-1898,* analyzes the exploding urbanization of the period. During the decade from 1880 to 1890, more than five million immigrants came to the United States, and nearly four million in the next decade.[26]

The press changed to meet the new conditions of American life. The number of newspapers increased from 850 in 1880 to 1,967 in 1900. More important, whereas ten percent of all adults subscribed in 1880, twenty-six percent did in 1900. This change came about, not only because of increased educational opportunities and because of revolution in printing technology, but especially because of the promotion of a new journalism of the common man. Led by Joseph Pulitzer and pushed too far by William Randolph Hearst (whose contests with Pulitzer brought on yellow journalism), metropolitan newspapers invited the immigrants into the American community with splashy crusades and stunts. Himself an immigrant, Pulitzer set forth his essential aims in a signed statement in the first issue of his *New York World:*

> There is room in this great and growing city for a journal that is not only cheap but bright, not only bright but large, not only large but truly Democratic—dedicated to the cause of the people rather than that of the purse potentates—devoted more to the news of the New than the Old World—that will expose all fraud and sham, fight all public evils and abuses—that will serve and battle for the people with earnest sincerity.[27]

Pulitzer allowed Hearst to push him too far into sensationalism, and Hearst carried journalism into outrageous fiction. Other editors similarly exceeded rational bounds. That they were also deeply involved in affairs of great moment is generally agreed upon by historians of the period. A few argue, for example, that Hearst promoted the Spanish-American War with relentless propaganda. He sent a famous illustrator, Frederic Remington to Cuba. Remington cabled: "Everything is quiet. There is no trouble here. There will be no war. Wish to return." Hearst responded: "Please remain. You furnish the pictures and I'll furnish the war."[28]

6. Sensationalism

To the early American journalist, "news" was primarily something on which to base editorial opinion. He felt no obligation to inform the public about matters which did not support his view. As Robert Park has suggested: "He refused to take the responsibility of letting his readers learn about things that he knew ought not to have happened."[29] Some straight, factual reporting appeared, but it was primarily limited to noncontroversial subjects. Horace Greeley best described the range when he advised a friend about to start a country paper:

> [The] subject of deepest interest to a human being is himself; next to that, he is most concerned about his neighbors. . . . Do not let a new

church be organized, or a new member be added to one already existing, a farm be sold, a new house be raised, a mill be set in motion, a store be opened, nor anything of interest to a dozen families occur, without having the fact duly though briefly chronicled in your columns.[30]

A combination of circumstances led to the reporting of facts, unta.nted by opinion, as news: The breakdown of the relationship between the press and political parties; the development of large Washington staffs by the New York papers; the growth of urban populations and the consequent inability of the press to build circulation by covering each barn raising; the development of advertising support; the invention of the steam press; the growth of the Associated Press and its need to serve editors of all political hues; and the attempts to expand circulation by appealing to the semiliterate, with emphasis on sex and violence, preferably in combination.

When the first penny press was established by Benjamin Day on Sept. 3, 1833, he recognized that, if he was to expand circulation, he would have to appeal to the semiliterate, non-newspaper reader. And this meant emphasis upon emotion for its own sake—sensationalism.

Mr. Day put very little emphasis on editorial opinion; his focus was on local happenings and violence. Six months after the *New York Sun* was founded, it reached a circulation of 8,000, nearly twice that of its nearest rival. Once the *Sun's* new readers had the habit of reading newspapers, the *Sun* began to offer more significant information. Simultaneously, the recently franchised laboring class showed more interest in the operations of government.

Day's format was similar to that of other penny papers founded during the 1830's. James Gordon Bennett's *New York Morning Herald* concentrated on crime news. During the 1830's, a total of 35 penny papers were founded in New York. None survived except the *Sun* and the *Herald*. Nevertheless, in other cities penny papers succeeded with similar formats and news policies—a great deal of local news, human interest stories, and substantial doses of entertainment.

During the 1850's, however, the trend was away from this kind of sensationalism. The *New York Tribune*, founded in 1841 by Horace Greeley, typified this trend. The *Tribune* sold for a penny, but rather than make unabashed appeals to emotionalism, the *Tribune* reported facts and serious discussions of the issues of the day. It could rival its competitors when it came to sensational crime stories, but this was not its main appeal. The *Tribune* was read by all classes—farmers, the workingman, educators, and politicians. Greeley had raised the press of the masses from the vulgar level of sensationalism to a force for stimulating thought. More important, the *Tribune* was a financial success.

Greeley's assistant, Charles Dana, eventually took over the *New York Sun*. By this time, even the *Sun* and *Herald* were offering more substantial material. The increasing literacy and interest of their readers required it.

As late as 1889, even in the large cities, a good deal of emphasis was still placed on brief accounts of events of interest primarily to the individuals involved. It was also about this time that Charles Dana discovered that, by making literature out of the news, circulation could be greatly enhanced. But the appeal was limited. Manton Marble, editor of the *New York World* before its takeover by Joseph Pulitzer, said there were not 18,000 people in New York to whom a well-conducted newspaper could appeal.

As in 1833, this left a large, semi-literate group ripe to be tapped. This time it was Joseph Pulitzer and William Randolph Hearst who employed sensationalism to expand circulation by appealing to large masses of theretofore non-newspaper readers.

In the past, the function of disseminating information had been overshadowed by efforts to entertain; but the yellow journalism that now began in the 1890's went well beyond any reasonable standard. Edwin Emery has described it thusly:

> It seized upon the techniques of writing, illustrating, and printing which were the prize of the new journalism and turned them to perverted uses. It made the high drama of life a cheap melodrama, and it twisted the facts of each day into whatever form seemed best suited to produce sales for the hallowing news boy. Worst of all, instead of giving its readers effective leadership, it offered a palliative of sin, sex, and violence. The process was begun by Joseph Pulitzer in the mid-1880's, but when the young William Randolph Hearst entered the New York market he was able to put Pulitzer to shame when it came to appealing to the emotions of the public.[31]

Typical of these practices were the headlines carried in the *New York Journal* in the fall of 1896, a period during which its circulation jumped by 125,000 in a single month:

> "Real American Monsters and Dragons"—over a story of the discovery of fossil remains by an archeological expedition. "A Marvelous New Way of Giving Medicine: Wonderful Results From Merely Holding Tubes of Drugs Near Entranced Patients"—a headline which horrified medical researchers. "Henry James New Novel of Immorality and Crime; The Surprising Plunge of the Great Novelist in the Field of Sensational Fiction"—the journals way of announcing the publication of *The Other House*. Other headlines included: "The Mysterious Murder of Bessie Little," "One Mad Blow Kills Child," "What Made Him a Burglar? A Story of Real Life in New York by Edgar Saltus," "Startling Confession of a Wholesale Murderer Who Begs to be Hanged."[32]

In the election of 1900, Hearst opposed McKinley's campaign for the Presidency. And the opposition did not cease after McKinley and Theodore Roosevelt won the election. In April 1901, in an editorial in the *New York Journal*, he declared "if bad institutions and bad men can be got rid of only by killing, then the killing must be done." Two months before that, a quatrain had appeared in the *Journal* which read:

The bullet that pierced Goeble's breast,
Cannot be found in all the West.

Good reason, it is speeding here
To stretch McKinley on his bier.[33]

Goelbe, the governor of Kentucky, had recently been shot. In September 1901, President McKinley was assassinated by an anarchist. Shortly thereafter, Hearst's *Journal* changed its name to the *American*.

The last round of sensationalism began with birth of the *Illustrated Daily News* on June 26, 1919. In the next 6 years, together with two other tabloids, it would build a combined circulation of a million and a half readers who were attracted to the tabloid-style format and the extensive use of photography. Again the target of the sensational newspapers was the theretofore non-reading public. The circulation balance of the existing dailies was not unduly affected. The *Illustrated Daily News'* initial circulation of 200,000 the first month dropped to 26,000 the second month. At this point, it was discovered that its appeal was not among the readers of the *New York Times*, but among the immigrant and poorly educated American-born population. Its publishers made sure that it was placed on news stands where only foreign language newspapers were sold. Pictures sold the paper.[34]

The second of the three newspapers was William Randolph Hearst's tabloid, the *Daily Mirror*. The third was the *Daily Graphic*. The *Mirror* originally challenged the *News* on relatively straight, journalistic standards, but the *Graphic* was as lurid and sensational as possible. The *Graphic* made a practice of writing first person stories, signed by persons in the news, which were in turn headlined, "I Know Who Killed My Brother," "He beat Me—I Love Him," or "For 36 Hours I Lived Another Woman's Love Life."[35]

For those who think that today's press at times goes to excess, consider the following paragraphs from Edwin Emery's *The Press in America*:

Climax year of the war of the tabloids was 1926. First the Broadway producer, Earl Carroll, gave a party at which a nude dancing girl sat in a bathtub full of champagne. Before the furor had died down, the tabloids discovered a wealthy real estate man, Edward Browning, and his 15-year-old shopgirl bride. This was "hot" romance indeed and the pair became Daddy and Peaches to all of America. The *Graphic* portrayed them frolicking on a bed with Daddy saying "Woof! Woof! I'm a Goof!" Gauvreau decided to thrill his shopgirl audience with the details of Peaches' intimate diary, but at that point the law stepped in.

Next into the spotlight stepped wealthy socialite Kip Rhinelander, who charged in court that his bride of a few months had Negro blood, a fact he had not known at the time of the marriage. The sensational-hungry reporters balked at the climax of the trial when the judge ousted them before the attractive Mrs. Rhinelander was partially disrobed to prove a point for the defense. But Gauvreau hastily posed a bare-backed chorus girl among some of his reporters, pasted likenesses of court participants in place of the reporters' faces, and hit the street with a sell-out edition. The *Graphic* said in small type that its sensational picture was a "composograph" but most of its readers assumed that it was the real thing.

Meanwhile the desperate editors of the *Mirror* had dug up a four-year-old murder story in New Jersey. In 1922 a New Brunswick,

New Jersey, minister named Edward Hall and his choirsinger sweetheart, Eleanor Mills, were found dead, apparently suicides. The *Mirror* succeeded in having the minister's widow brought to trial and for months the New Jersey town became one of the most important filing points for press associations and big newspapers in America. One witness became "the pig woman" to the 200 reporters at the trial. Unfortunately for the *Mirror*, Mrs. Hall was acquitted and sued the paper for libel.

While the Hall-Mills story was running, Gertrude Ederle swam the English Channel to become America's heroine for a day. In late August of 1926 former President Charles Eliot of Harvard, and "the Sheik" of motion pictures, Rudolph Valentino died. The *Daily News* gave Valentino six pages of space and Eliot one paragraph, thereby setting off more irate complaints from serious-minded folk. But "Valentino Dies With Smile as Lips Touch Priest's Crucifix" and "Rudy Leaped from Rags to World Hero" were tabloid copy, and the death of an educator was not. In most of the press, too, Valentino rated the most attention.

A second sensational murder trial was drummed up in the spring of 1926. A corset salesman named Judd Gray and his sweetheart, Mrs. Ruth Snyder, had collaborated in disposing of the unwanted Mr. Snyder. When it came time for Mrs. Snyder's execution in the electric chair at Sing Sing the *Graphic* blared to its readers:

"Don't fail to read tomorrow's *Graphic*. An installment that thrills and stuns! A story that fairly pierces the heart and reveals Ruth Snyder's last thoughts on earth; that pulses the blood as it discloses her final letters. Think of it! A woman's final thoughts just before she is clutched in the deadly snare that sears and burns and FRIES AND KILLS! Her very last words! Exclusively in tomorrow's *Graphic*."

It was the photography-minded *News* which had the last word, however. The *Graphic* might have its "confession" but the *News* proposed to take its readers inside the execution chamber. Pictures were forbidden, but a photographer, Tom Howard, strapped a tiny camera to his ankle and took his picture just after the current was turned. The *News* put the gruesome shot on its front page, sold 250,000 extra copies, and then had to run off 750,000 additional pages later.[36]

Sensationalism began a general decline in 1926. After 1930, the *Mirror* was never profitable. The *Graphic* went out of business in 1932. The newspapers of the 1930's devoted more space to politics and economics and foreign affairs; yet they maintained their yen for crime, violence, and sex. In the late 1930's and early 1940's interpretive reporting, which began during World War I, became more widely accepted. It provided perspective and background for news of important human activities that were far from sensational. The "why" received some recognition as, now more than ever before, people needed to understand the events, due in part to the complex social legislation introduced during the Roosevelt administration.

REFERENCES

1. The figures cited in this paragraph and the next are based upon statistics appearing prepared for the Task Force by Dr. Leo Bogart, excutive vice president of the Bureau of Advertising, American Newspaper Publishers Association, and Prof. Jack Lyle of the Department of Journalism, University of California at Los Angles. Both Dr. Bogart's paper, "How the Mass Media Work in America," and Professor Lyle's paper, "Contemporary Functions of the Media," appear in the Appendix.
2. Testimony of Dr. Bradley Greenberg Before the NCCPV, Oct. 16, 1968.
3. *Ibid.*
4. Francis Bacon, *Novum Organum,* Aphorism 129.
5. Herbert J. Muller, *Freedom in the Western World* (New York: Harper & Row, 1963), p. 192.
6. *Ibid.,* p. 313.
7. Levy, *Freedom of Speech and Press in Early American History* (Harper & Row, Inc., Torchbook ed. 1963). p. 50.
8. *Ibid.,* pp. 119-120.
9. Charles A. Beard, *An Economic Interpretation of the Constitution* (New York: Macmillan Co., 1913). p.
10. Leonard W. Levy, Legacy of Suppression, (Cambridge, Belknap Press, 1960).
11. Levy, *op. cit., Footnote 5, pp. 274-275.*
12. Frank Luther Mitt. *American Journalism, 1690-1960* (New York: The Macmillan Co., 3d ed., 1962), p. 148.
13. Levy, *op. cit.,* Footnote 5, pp. 283-289.
14. John Milton, *Areopagitica* (New York Crofts; Classics, 1967). See also Peterson, Jenson, and Rivers, *Mass Media and Modern Society,* (New York: Holt, Rinehart & Winston, 1965), pp. 89-91, and Siebert, Peterson, and Schramm, *Four theories of the Press* (Urbana: University of Illinois Press, 1956), pp. 46-47.
15. *Thomas Jefferson, Life & Selected Writings,* ed. by A. Koch & W. Peden (New York: The Modern Library, 1944). See also Peterson et al., *Mass Media,* pp. 95-97; and Siebert et al., *Four Theories,* pp. 45-46.
16. John Stuart Mill, *On Liberty (New York: Crofts Classics, 1947. See also Peterson et al., Mass Media,* pp. 98-98; and Siebert et al., *Four Theories,* pp. 45-46.
17. 249 U.S. 47.
18. 249 U.S. at 52 (1919).
19. 333 U.S. 507.
20. *Ibid.,* p. 510.
21. *Ibid.,* p. 520.
22. James E. Pollard, *The Presidents and the Press* (New York: The Macmillan Co., 1947), p. 23.
23. *Ibid.,* p. 12.
24. Douglass Cater, *The Fourth Branch of Government* (Boston: Houghton-Mifflin, 1959), p. 76.
25. *Ibid.,* p.77.
26. Arthur M. Schlesinger, *The Rise of the City, 1878-1898 (New York: The Macmillan Co., 1933).*
27. *New York World,* May 11, 1883.
28. Mott, *op. cit.,* p. 529.
29. Robert E. Park, "The Natural History of the Newspaper," in *Mass Communications,* Wilbur Schramm, Ed. (Urbana: University of Illinois Press, 1964), p. 12.
30. *Ibid.,* p. 18.
31. Edwin Emery, *The Press and America: Aninter pretative History of Journalism* (New York: Prentice-Hall, 2d ed., 1965), pp. 514-516.
32. *Ibid.,* pp. 424-524.
33. *Ibid.,*
34. *Ibid.,*
35. *Ibid.,* pp. 627-628.
36. *Ibid., p.*

Chapter 2

FROM MEDIUM TO MEDIA

By the end of the 19th century, both the nation and the press had changed drastically from the 18th century environment that had contributed and shaped their values. A colony of Englishmen was becoming a nation of immigrants. The press stood at the threshold of revolutionary new technology that would change the medium of the printed, the spoken, and the seen. And in the meantime, a new status for the press loomed on the economic horizon.

A. Newspapers

Lincoln Steffens took a long look at newspaper journalism across the United States in 1897 and shared his findings with the readers of *Scribner's* magazine. Talking shop the previous spring, the executive heads of twoscore great newspapers had spoken of their properties as factories, he reported, and had likened the management of their editorial departments to that of department stores. "Journalism today is a business," he wrote, somewhat in awe at his discovery.

Indeed, with the beginning of the new century, journalism had become a very big business. The personal journals of colonial days and the party organs of the first half of the 19th century had fallen far behind. Education, industrialization, mass production of newspapers—all had combined with shrewd editorial judgment to turn the craft of journalism into a business. Pulitzer's *World,* which he had bought for $346,000 in 1883, was deemed to be worth $10 million little more than a decade later, and it employed 1,300 people.[1] Many other newspapers, especially those that promoted themselves as "people's champions," similarly grew large. Circulations in the hundreds of thousands became common.

B. Magazines

As the 20th century began, magazines, too, started to become giants. Although Andrew Bradford had published the first American magazine in 1741 (a few days before Benjamin Franklin had founded the second), for more than a century the magazines suffered from small circulation, from too little advertising, and from limited editorial vision. Not until the 1890's were

S. S. McClure, Frank Munsey, and Cyrus H. K. Curtis able to bring magazine content into harmony with the tastes and interests of the great middle class. Munsey put *Munsey's Magazine* on sale at ten cents in 1893, and Curtis began to sell his *Saturday Evening Post* at five cents a short time later. Both began to teach other magazine publishers what they had learned from newspapers: By appealing to the masses, they could sell their publications at less than cost, draw huge lists of readers, and lure advertising dollars. Shortly after the turn of the century, the *Ladies Home Journal* became the first magazine to reach a circulation of one million. Edward W. Bok, the editor, built circulation by giving women readers practical advice on running a home and on rearing a family, by trying to elevate their standards in art and architecture, and by crusading against public drinking cups and patent medicines.

This was the period, too, when the muckrakers—Lincoln Steffens, Ida Tarbell, Ray Stannard Baker, and the others—were exerting a stunning impact on government with their exposes.

Newspapers and magazines have not been static in the decades since the 1890's and early 1900's, but many of the ingredients that went into the success of the newspapers and magazines of that period are staples today.

C. Movies

Even as newspapers and magazines were sprinkling their columns with entertaining items, a medium that was almost entirely entertainment was beginning in the cities—the nickelodeon, forerunner of the giant film industry. It was born at a time when the democratic movement was fullblown and urbanization had brought the multitudes to the cities. Motion pictures had wide audience appeal from the start. Originally little more than peepshows in the penny arcades of the 1890's, the early movies offered vaudeville bits, slapstick routines, and jerky scenes of boxing matches.[2]

The movies went from the penny arcades to vaudeville shows, then traveling carnivals and amusement parks. The first movie with a solid story line, Edwin S. Porter's *The Great Train Robbery*, was a distinct success in a Pittsburgh theater that featured only movies. Within a year, five thousand other small theaters were built. Most of these nickclodeons were in the largest cities, especially those with high concentrations of foreign born. Film was a form of entertainment that even recent arrivals could afford and enjoy. Admission was usually five cents.

In these early days, movies had not become respectable enough for the upper classes. The movies had trouble developing at first when so many who sponsored film making believed that long features would only bore audiences. D.W. Griffith was impatient to make full-length movies, but his backers would allow him to go no further than two reels (about twenty minutes' playing time). Then Adolph Zukor, an independent operator, imported a four-reel French Play, *Queen Elizabeth,* starring Sarah Bernhardt in the title role. It played before a fashionable audience in New York in 1912, and Zukor became convinced that audiences could enjoy a full evening's entertainment at the movies. He began to produce long films. Griffith then broke away from his cautious backers to film *The Birth of a Nation,* which opened at the Liberty Theater in New York in March 1915, with an admission charge of two dollars. But a step from this success came the burgeoning of film-making companies, especially when theaters moved from laboring-class districts into middle-class neighborhoods. First, novelty brought new audiences, then the big production converted them to move going. Paul Rotha, a film producer and critic, has written:

> During this period, therefore, from about 1912 until 1920, the very marvelling of the general public, watching every new film with mouth agape, was sufficient for the studios to become established on a practical basis capable of mass production.[3]

By the time that novelty had gone, the studios had built the "star" system, and names like Charlie Chaplin, Mary Pickford, Douglas Fairbanks, Francis X. Bushman, and Beverly Bayne attracted movie-goers across the nation.

As the industry grew, the costs of production went up as well. The star system, which did so much to attract audiences, made the stars valuable properties. Their high salaries and the necessity for established studios rocketed the costs of moviemaking. The motion picture became institutionalized. Studios chose locations other than the rooftops and city streets that had served the early shoestring operations. Artificial lighting replaced the sun. Scripts replaced the improvisations of directors and cameramen. Equipment became refined—and therefore more expensive. Producers needed more and more money to complete feature films. And to bring the greatest return on their money, moviemakers tried to turn out a product that would attract the widest possible public. Like newspapers—but in a much shorter time span—movies became big business.

D. Radio

The business of radio began as inauspiciously as had the motion picture industry. Broadcasting had been a free-for-all in its earliest days. No effective regulation prevailed: government power was limited to a 1912 act concerned only with radio telegraphy. Eventually government regulation came at the request of the industry itself, and as protection for an instrument of communication that pioneer broadcasters thought would be useful primarily in the dissemination of culture. Many thought that owners of receiving sets would have to support radio by paying an annual license fee. They only profit would come from the sale of sets and other radio equipment. David Sarnoff of the Radio Corporation of America argued at the time that radio deserved an endowment "similar to that enjoyed by libraries, museums, and educational institutions." He believed, Gleason Archer wrote in *Big Business and Radio,* that "philanthropists would eventually come to the rescue of a hard-pressed industry."[4]

Almost all the pioneers rejected the notion that advertising would support radio. Herbert Hoover, who was then Secretary of Commerce, declared at the First Annual Radio Conference in Washington: "It is inconceivable that so great a possibility for service . . . be drowned in advertising matters." Even *Printer's Ink*, the advertising trade weekly, stated in 1922 that radio advertising would be offensive: "The family circle is not a public place, and advertising has no business intruding there unless it is invited." *Radio Broadcasting* magazine complained about advertising that had begun to invade radio:

> Concerts are seasoned here and there with a dash of advertising paprika. You can't miss it; every little classic number has a slogan all its own, if it is only the mention of the name—and the shrill address, and the phone number—of the music house which arranged the program. More of this sort of thing may be expected. And once the avalanche gets a good start, nothing short of an Act of Congress oɾ a repetition of Noah's excitement will suffice to stop it.[5]

The rise of radio as a major disseminator of news and entertainment had begun with the broadcasting of the 1920 presidential election by KDKA. It took on major impetus when sponsored programs were broadcast experimentally on WEAF in 1922. Three million radio sets were available to listeners by the time of the 1924 presidential election. By then, 556 broadcasting stations were on the air, and the Radio Corp. of America was growing rapidly.

Throughout the early years, despite the growth of advertising, radio sets and equipment sales formed by far the most lucrative aspect of broadcasting. Then the Radio Corp. of America formed a broadcasting subsidiary, the National Broadcasting Co., in 1925. The following year, another network began, first as the Judson Radio Program Corp., then as United Independent Broadcasters. It finally began its broadcasting operations in 1927 and changed its name to the Columbia Broadcasting System. With 19 stations in its Red and Blue Networks in 1926, NBC had 48 by the end of 1927; CBS had 16 in 1927 and 28 in the following year. Thus, little more than three decades after Guglielmo Marconi had succeeded in transmitting a message by wireless across his father's Bolognese estate, the vast structure of broadcasting was taking shape. In 1934, powerful independent stations that had been seeking advertising together formed the Mutual Broadcasting System.

Meanwhile, Congress had finally recognized the confusion over the use and allocation of wavelengths and had passed the Radio Act of 1927. That act was followed by the Communications Act of 1934, which created the Federal Communications Commission to regulate broadcasting in "the public interest, convenience, and necessity." Congress gave the FCC the power to license broadcasting stations, to assign wavelengths, and to suspend or revoke the licenses of stations not serving the public interest.

By 1934, radio had firmly established itself as an advertising medium. The star system became readily adaptable to the increasingly popular entertainment programs and broadcasting executives quickly exploited it.

E. Television

In a sense, television has no history. Radio provided for television a station structure, a network structure, an advertising support structure, even a time structure that divided programs into 15-minute, half-hour, and hour segments. Given these facts, the novelty and visual impact of the new medium, and the growing leisure time, television became established without having to struggle. Television took over the motion picture-radio star system; and specialization, which had grown slowly in the newspaper world and only a little faster in movies and radio, was almost instantaneous in television. Even government control was ready made in the FCC.

In essence, then, television provided for itself only the technical competence that allowed telecasting. It became a primitive reality in the 1920's and so near refinement by 1938 that David Sarnoff announced that home television "is now technically feasible." World War II interrupted television development; but by January, 1948, the nation had 102,000 television sets—two-thirds of them in New York. By April, the number of sets had more than doubled. Ten years later, four out of five American homes had television sets. As television operations demanded more and more of the national networks' time, attention, and money, national radio began to wither. Soon, national broadcasting, except for brief news reports and scattershot programs, became telecasting, and radio stations began to find their reason for being in local broadcasting. Television had won the day.

F. The Media in Contemporary American Life

In the final sections of this background inquiry, we will consider the content of the media so that we may better understand the role that violence occupies and the role of the media operators, in particular, the journalist or communications professional.

1. Media Content: A Brief Overview

The American mass media provide something for nearly everyone at one time or another. But the usual appeal is to the broadest possible audience. The result, for the most part, is a fairly predictable blend of information and entertainment, distinguished chiefly by its efforts neither to demand nor offend.

Typically, the broadcast media prefer entertainment while the print media favor news and information. Newspapers, on the other hand, devote from as little as six percent to as much as twenty-five percent of their news and editorial space to "popular amusements." The rest of their content appears to be slightly more serious.[6] Obviously, however, television can offer serious programs containing hard information, while newspapers often afford light entertainment.

Television network entertainment programming tends to run in cycles, and TV news programs emphasize the photogenic. Radio stations, once the source of numerous dramatic programs long since eclipsed by television, now tend to offer music, news, and sports and, more recently, "open-mike" programs—with an occasional leftover transcription of "Boston Blackie." Newspapers, too, provide a familiar format with "hard" news of the world, national, and local events blended with lighter, brighter features, sports, and business coverage—and, of course, the ubiquitous comics. More recently, a so-called "underground press" has begun to flourish in larger cities across the country. Previously a protest organ, it now shows increasing signs of falling into the "establishment" patterns which its editorials and, for that matter, its news items, rail against; and underground news syndicates provide features in much the way AP and UPI do. Magazines, books, and motion pictures provide perhaps the greatest variety of content; among these media, there is almost literally something for everyone.

No reasonably literate American today is apt to be unaware of these general outlines of media content. But for those who wish to go beyond the level of common knowledge to a seriously sophisticated understanding of media content, the way is not easy. Many studies have been conducted to determine the content of relatively isolated examples of the media or to determine the content within a specific area of concern. Some advertising and marketing enterprises perform continuing analyses for specific purposes—generally to assist media buyers in selecting vehicles for advertising purposes. These and similarly limited sources provide some useful data, but the data are limited by the scope of the researcher's interest and absence of general availability.

Americans use their media in a variety of ways and for enormous amounts of time. As we have seen, 95 percent of American homes have at least one TV set, and during a typical weekday, 82 percent of adults watch television for an average of more than two hours. Those in lower-income homes watch more TV than those with a higher income. Bogart reports, for example, that the "average" person in a home with less than $5,000 income occupies himself with television for 2 hours 27 minutes daily; viewers in homes over $10,000 income watch television about 1 hour 45 minutes.[7]

2. The Media and the Professionals

As Bogart and others have suggested,[8] the media owners and operators offer one of the most direct means of resolving the problems posed by violence in media content.

The media require the diverse talents of many types of men. At the top of the media structure, the owners and managers of the major media businesses, the newspaper publishers, broadcast station operators, and network presidents or vice presidents, for example, are often little distinguishable from their counterparts in other business organizations. Yet they are the men who establish the basic policies of their enterprises, and typically represent most of the good as well as bad in American business. Motivated by the prospect of profit, at least as much as by the opportunities for public service, they have brought the media into the poorest American home as well as the richest. But they have largely produced media designed more to sell products than to enlighten or to inform.

The media owners and managers may establish basic policy, including policy as to content, but others must translate policy into action. Throughout the middle levels of the media, the media "gatekeepers" perform these functions. The gatekeepers' role is most critical, for they ultimately decide what is published or broadcast. Newspaper editors and broadcasting news directors decide what events to cover, what stories and photos or newsreel footage to run, how to report the selected stories, and where to place the story in the context of the day's or week's events. In much the same way, producers, program directors and feature editors determine the media's entertainment content.

To fulfill these functions, the media need a diversity of talent and a talent for diversity. Few major business enterprises tolerate as wide a range of colorful personalities as the metropolitan daily newspaper, for example. Yet the gatekeepers tend almost inevitably to reflect the values of the American middle class, from which most of them have come and which sustains their professional status. Numerous studies of the gatekeepers demonstrate that much of what we read or see or hear in the media reflects the gatekeepers' own background. Thus, the media tend to offer all Americans—black or white, rich or poor—the kind of fare that a white, middle-class background finds acceptable. Although much that is worthwhile exists in the middle-class background, those who do not share this background must often see an inviting but unattainable life, with consequent frustration and alienation.

The professional status of the media operators, although often asserted and generally acknowledged, remains dubious. For many, the question of professional status is relatively unimportant. Television entertainment program producers, it would seem, probably spend little time wondering about the matter; their business, as they see it, is essentially show business. But the journalist's claim to professionalism is a different proposition; traditionally, they have regarded themselves as professionals and they jealously guard their privileges, though not always their obligations.

Despite their incalculable influence upon the lives of most Americans, and despite the claims of the press to professional status, the gatekeepers and other journalists subject themselves to few, if any, professional standards that are not self-imposed and self-enforced. Journalists are not licensed, of course; the history of the press's struggle with censors suggests that licensing would unacceptable, even without the first amendment. Although a number of professional associations and societies have promulgated codes of ethics, the codes are usually vague and general and are rarely, if ever, enforced against violators. Compliance is voluntary. For the same reasons that prevent licensing, no state board is empowered to bar journalists from practice on grounds of failure to adhere to even the barest minimum professional standards.

In a profession without readily enforceable codes of ethics and without standards for admission to practice or for disbarment, the professional education of its practitioners is of more than ordinary importance. Yet the would-be journalist or other media operators must meet no minimum educational level. Whether the press today realizes the professional importance of journalism education and continuing education programs for practicing journalists remains to be seen. What is clear, however, is this: The press must base its claim to professionalism upon something firmer than outworn tradition and blind reliance on the first amendment. The journalism and communications schools can do much to provide that support.

Meanwhile, however, the media and the gatekeepers are subject to little in the way of organized, continuing evaluation and criticism. Although professional organizations sponsor some exercises in self-examination, those efforts tend to produce few substantial changes. Rare is the case, for example, in which a journalist is subjected to punishment or to other sanction for transgressions. Are there no transgressors, or does one who sews his own hair shirt make sure that it fits loosely?

When a threat of criticism from outside the media appears, media operators can be counted on, in the main, to meet the threat with portentous warnings against the undoing of our free press, coupled with promises of increased attention to self-regulation.

No one would deny that the first amendment should not be subverted. Ironically, however, the media themselves may ultimately bring about their undoing—and, in the process, the undoing of much that makes sense in the philosophy of free expression.

Increasingly, the people have been asking, directly and through their government, if the media have not abused their freedom. If the media continue to put off a serious answer to that question—if they block even the means to find an answer—possibly those critics who believe that they know the answer without need for further inquiry and who are prepared to take drastic "corrective" action may prevail. To avoid that possibility, the media themselves may be required to take equally drastic steps to restore their right to the people's confidence.

The challenge is, in a real sense then, to the professionalism of the media; the job is for the professionals. Their success or failure in meeting the challenge looms as an important test as to how long freedom of expression remains feasible in our society.

REFERENCES

1. Edwin Emery, *The Press and America:An Interpretative History of Journalism* (New York: Prentice-Hall, 2d. ed., 1965), p. 98.
2. Theodore Peterson, Jay W. Jensen, and William Rivers, *The Mass Media and Modern society* (New York: Holt, Rinchart & Winston, 1965), p. 49.
3. *Ibid.,* pp. 50-51.
4. *Ibid.,* p. 27.
5. *Ibid.,* p. 55.
6. Lyle, Appendix II B
7. Bogart, Appendix II A
8. *Ibid.*

Chapter 3

FUNCTIONS AND CREDIBILITY

> Those who make peaceful revolution impossible
> will make violent revolution inevitable.
> —John F. Kennedy

> All social progress is laid
> to discontent.
> —Abraham Lincoln

Conflict is part of the crucible of change. It may yield progress or repression. But conflict is not a state of social equilibrium. Whether conflict is resolved by violence or cooperation will depend in part upon the actors' perceptions of the world about them. Providing an accurate perception of that world is the media's most important responsibility. Conflict may be resolved by force, but, in every conflict, there is a point short of the use of force that would be to the mutual advantage of the participants and society. Violence takes its toll on the victor, the vanquished, and the nation.

Conflict cannot be resolved rationally unless each participant has an accurate perception of the intentions and goals of others. Mutual trust must exist. Confidence must exist in the desire of each person to reach a nonviolent and mutually satisfactory accommodation of divergent interests. And a rough equivalency must exist in the conflicting groups' perceptions of reality. The media cannot make the unwilling seek mutual accommodation, but they can make an extremist of the moderate. Regardless of their performance, the media will never be able to assure the non-violent resolution of conflict, but they can assure the violent resolution of conflict.

In our increasingly complex and urban society, interdependence has increased greatly and the need for cooperation between various groups has grown in direct proportion. The rate of change has grown geometrically and the requirement for information about this changing environment has expanded in a similar progression. At the same time, the individual's capacity to acquire knowledge through personal experience has increased only marginally, if at all. Similarly, his ability to communicate with others informally has increased only slightly, and is totally inadequate. Rational and non-violent readjustment to a changing society requires accurate information about our shifting environment.

The news media are the central institutions in the process of intergroup communication in this country. While face-to-face communication has an

33

important role in intergroup communication and may serve a mediating role in the process of persuasion, to the extent that the news media are regarded as credible, they are the primary source of information.

Never before have the American news media been so defensive while being so successful. Today, more information is disseminated faster and more accurately than ever before. The standards of reporting and the sense of responsibility have improved measurably since the beginning of this century. But the changes in American society have been more than measurable; they have been radical. The issues, more numerous and complex, require greater sophistication and time to report adequately. The need for more and different kinds of information has mushroomed. The broadening of the political base and the growth of direct citizen participation in politics and institutional decisionmaking require not so much a larger flow of words as a more sophisticated treatment of information.

An apparent unwillingness by the journalism profession to analyze its utility in a rapidly evolving democratic society has resulted in a sometimes blind adherence to values developed in the latter half of the 19th century. Old practices have been abandoned only when the most contorted rationalizations have been unable to provide any support. Energy has been wasted on mischievous attempts to justify practices of the past and to explain why they are serviceable for the present. Little attention has been given to what will be needed in the next two decades.

When the layman inquires about today's practices, he is frequently told that "news is what I say it is and journalism is best left to journalists." This kind of arrogance does not lead to understanding between the public and the news media. If the media cannot communicate their own problems to the American people, there is little hope that they can function as a medium of communication among the several groups in society.

Have the media failed to achieve perfection or to perform the impossible? Walter Lippman has written:

> As social truth is organized today, the press is not constituted to furnish from one edition to the next the amount of knowledge which the democratic theory of public opinion demands . . . . When we expect it to supply such a body of truth, we employ a misleading standard of judgment. We misunderstand the limited nature of news, the illimitable complexity of society; we over-estimate our own endurance, public spirit, and all-round competence. We suppose an appetite for uninteresting truths which is not discovered by any honest analysis of our own tastes . . . Unconsciously the theory sets up the single reader as theoretically incompetent, and puts upon the press the burden of accomplishing whatever representative government, industrial organization, and diplomacy have failed to accomplish. Acting upon everybody for thirty minutes in twenty-four hours, the press is asked to create a mystical force called "public opinion" that will take up the slack in public institutions.[1]

To suggest that the media cannot compensate for the defects of other institutions is quite different from urging that all is well.

The journalists do not have principal roles in making the news and have only limited power to determine what will be read, watched, or believed. But they do have the power to determine the relative availability, and non-availability, of millions of daily transactions, their mode of presentation, and the context in which they will be cast. While this view suggests that the responsibility for disaffection with the media should not be placed entirely on the profession and their employers, it also suggests that they stand in the best position to do something about it.

The inadequacy of traditional journalistic values is clearest in the case of television. It has not yet defined its role in the news communication system. A desire to be first with the news, linked with the logistical problems of providing pictures and action, plus an inherited show-business ethic, have imposed serious limitations on the medium. The heavy reliance of a majority of Americans for their news on a medium that is unwilling or unequipped to provide no more information than the front page of a newspaper has resulted in additional stress. The limited number of channels, television's relatively greater impact, and a preoccupation with pictures substantially increase the burdens of the medium. Finally, the requirement that television serve a truly mass audience and that it be licensed and subject to regulation by a Congressional agency has made it both more timid and more responsible than other media.

Although the development and growth of radio and television news have generated some thought among the print media about their changing role, reorientation has been painful and slow.

As a result of changes in technology, financial and political organization, the educational level of the public and its shifting information needs, the forces of dislocation continue to operate on the news media. Technological developments could, within the next two decades, radically reconstitute the media.

The news media have vigorously urged the government to recognize the people's right to know. Harold Cross, a newspaper attorney, has summed up the argument:

> Public business is the public's business. The people have a right to know. Freedom of information is their just heritage. Without that the citizens of a democracy have but changed their Kings.[2]

Lately, a similar argument has been used to meet a perceived threat of government intervention. Said Walter Cronkite:

> When we fight for freedom of the press, we're not fighting for our rights to do something, we're fighting for the people's right to know. That's what freedom of the press is. It's not license to the press. It's freedom of the people to know. How do they think they're going to know? By putting television news or newspapers or any other news source under government control?[3]

The press vigorously asserts its right to the access to government information and defends the first amendment on the ground that the people have a right to know. Rightly so. But if the people have a right to know, somebody has the obligation to inform them: an obligation to provide the accurate information necessary to rational decision-making and a rational response to a changing environment. That obligation devolves upon the news media.

A. Functions of the News Media

Again Walter Lippman has said it best:

> If the country is to be governed with the consent of the governed, then the government must arrive at opinions about what their governors want them to consent to. How do they do this? They do it by hearing the radio and reading in the newspapers what the corps of correspondents tell them is going on in Washington and in the country at large and in the world. Here we perform an essential service . . . we do what every sovereign citizen is supposed to do, but has not the time or the interest to do for himself. This is our job. It is no mean calling, and we have a right to be proud of it and to be glad that it is our work.[4]

The purpose of communicating news should be to reduce uncertainty and to increase the probability that the audience will respond to conflict and change in a rational manner.

Harold D. Lasswell suggested the media have three functions:

> "(1) *Surveillance* of the environment, disclosing threats and opportunities affecting the value position of the community and the component parts within it; (2) *correlation* of the components of society in making a response to the environment; and (3) *transmission* of the social inheritance."[5]

These are primary functions of the news media today.

Surveillance of the environment describes the collection and distribution of information about events both inside and outside a particular society. Roughly, it corresponds to what is popularly called "news." *Correlation* of the components of society to respond to the environment includes news analysis, news interpretation and editorials, and prescriptions for collective response to changing events in the environment. *Transmission* of culture includes messages designed to communicate the attitudes, norms, and values of the past and the information which is an integral part of these traditions. This third category is the educational function of the media.

In 1947, the Commission for a Free and Responsible Press set forth five goals for the press so it could discharge its obligation to provide the information the public has the right to know:

1. A truthful, comprehensive, and intelligent account of the day's events in a context which gives them meaning.
2. A forum for the exchange of comment and criticism.
3. A means of projecting the opinions and attitudes of the groups in the society to one another.
4. A method of presenting and clarifying the goals and values of society.
5. Full access to the day's intelligence. [6]

Although most of these suggestions drew on recommendations or ideas generated by editors and publishers, the media greeted the Commission's report with hostility and it received a rather general denunciation in columns and editorials and at professional meetings.

Perhaps most important to the non-violent resolution of social conflict are two much more specific objectives: 1) The news media should accurately communicate information between various conflicting groups within society and the circumstances surrounding the conflict; and 2) they must make the "marketplace of ideas," a fundamental rationale for the first amendment, a reality.

The news media cannot perform their important functions unless they have the public's confidence. Any decline in the credibility of formal channels of communication will invariably result in the development of informal channels of communication. Under conditions of mild stress, such channels may serve moderately well to provide accurate intelligence on the surrounding environment, but it is impossible for such informal channels to serve the needs of the people in a democratic society as effectively as a free and responsible news media. Moreover, during periods of great stress, complete reliance on informal channels of communication can result, and has resulted, in a completed breakdown of social norms, and has produced irrational responses. The credibility of the media is a function of the perceptions of its audience, not "truthfulness" in some abstract, Olympian sense. The basic issue of media credibility today is whether the media are presenting a biased or distorted picture of the world through selective reporting, rather than a concern for fabrication of facts. Nevertheless, if the audience does not believe that the media are providing all relevant facts, it will rely on informal channels of communication and its own imagination to supply the perceived omissions, creating a substantial potential for distortion.

It therefore matters little whether the news media have favored one particular point of view over another. What does matter is the effect of media practices and values on the public's perception of the media's credibility, on the public's perception of reality, and the manner in which these practices and values might be changed to facilitate more effective communication of the information the public has a right to know. In some instances, an allegation of bias will be the result of deviation from some abstract concept of "truth;" as frequently, however, it will be the result of the media's failure to tell its audience what it would like to hear.

B. Credibility of the News Media

A crisis in confidence exists today between the American people and their news media. The magnitude of the problem is open to debate; its existence is not. Concern ranges from a high-level official at the *New York Times*, who believes that readers see the editorial policy of the *Times* controlling the content of news, to a western newspaper editor, committed to improving race relations, who believes his paper's standing and credibility in the white community have declined as a result of his commitment. It extends from the network news commentators, who hypothesize the public chose not to believe the scenes of disorder broadcast during the 1968 Democratic National

Convention in Chicago, to the general manager of a midwestern metropolitan television station who has run over one hundred five-minute spots dealing with race relations and speculates that his station has alienated a significant part of its white audience.

The concern is not totally unfounded. In a recent issue of the *International Press Institute Bulletin* it was reported:

> In the United States, where journalists have long enjoyed a special position compared with colleagues elsewhere, a disquieting development has been noted. . . . Newspapers, it appeared in surveys, were no longer trusted by their readers, who felt that they lie, manufacture news and sensationalize what they do report . . . . For the press of America and elsewhere, its own communication problem of reestablishing the trust of the readers may prove harder to solve than the technical and economic problems which beset it.[7]

There is evidence that the news media have been developing a credibility problem, at least since the early 1960's. One study of a medium-sized California city found that respondents discounted, on the average, a third of what they read in the newspapers and a fifth of what they saw on television.[8] A 1963 study—two years before the Watts riots—showed that, among Los Angeles Negroes, only 32 percent felt the metropolitan dailies would give a black candidate coverage equal to that given a white opponent; only 25 percent felt Negro churches and organizations had a chance equal to that of white organizations of getting publicity in the daily press; and 54 percent felt the daily press was not fair in treatment of race relations issues.[9]

Yet there is little hard evidence of any widespread public belief that the facts provided by the media are false. The primary objection seems to be that the news media either omit important facts or slant the presentation of the facts they do report. In Chicago, for example, the evidence suggests that the objection was to the media's failure to provide adequate coverage of the provocations by the demonstrators toward the police, and some objection to network personnel who were perceived as critical of the police.[10]

For example, a survey in a large midwestern city conducted while the events of Chicago were still fresh in the public conscience found that among viewers interested in civil disorders: "Foremost, viewers desire more 'honest' coverage." Approximately 49 percent of the Negroes and 41 percent of the whites believed that television stations are hiding the "truth" in their coverage of rioting;

> they desire that the coverage of rioting be more candid and the "truth" be told. In terms of specifics, one-half (52 percent) of the whites and one-third (36 percent) of Negroes request more "balanced" or "fair" news coverage. . . . In addition, some viewers maintain that stations are unfair in their coverage of riot situations because they focus solely on the sensational rather than balance it with the mundane. Thus, both Negroes and whites believe that stations should de-emphasize the sensational aspects of riot coverage or, in some cases, eliminate it entirely.[11]

C. The Importance of Being Credible

When the public does not believe the information they receive from the news media or think the media are omitting important facts, there will be increased reliance on less formal sources for information. Ordinarily, this means they ask their friends and neighbors, or worse, they supply the information from their own imaginations. The consequences of such a breakdown of formal channels of communication can be very serious.

Shortly after the bombing of Pearl Harbor, for example, the credibility of the media was seriously questioned by a large number of Americans, because, in part, they did not trust the source of much of the pertinent information—the Roosevelt administration—and because, in part, of the adoption of wartime censorship.

In their pioneer study of rumor, Allport and Postman analyzed more than 1,000 rumors from all parts of the country during World War II. Of these, almost 67 percent were categorized as "hostility (wedge-driving) rumors." These included such "news" as the Jews were evading the draft in massive numbers, American minority groups were impairing the war effort, and Negro servicemen were saving ice picks in preparation for revolt against the white community after their return home. Another 25 percent of the rumors were classified as "fear (bogy) rumors," e.g., the government is not telling the truth about the destruction of our fleet at Pearl Harbor or, in another instance, a collier was accidentally sunk near Cape Cod Canal and New Englanders believed that an American ship filled with Army nurses had been torpedoed, killing thousands of nurses.[12]

Similarly, almost any after-action report on the recent civil disorders will confirm that rumors run rampant during periods of great stress and almost invariably involve gross exaggerations. The direction of the exaggeration depends upon the community in which the rumors circulate. In the black community, for instance, rumors prevail about extreme police brutality or about camps like the concentration camps in Germany during World War II. In the white community, it is not uncommon to hear that Negroes are arming themselves to invade the white section of town.

The direction of distortion of information received through informal communication is almost invariably toward the group's preconceptions. In one series of experiments reported by Allport and Postman, they first showed one of twenty subjects a picture of people in a subway car. One person in the group was black and the rest were white. There appeared to be some dispute among them. A white man held a razor in his hand. The subject of the experiment viewed the picture and was asked to describe it to the next person; the second, to repeat the description to the third, and so on. In over half the experiments using white subjects, the final version had the Negro (instead of the white man) brandishing the razor. Among the possible explanations for this distortion, all were related to the subject's preconceptions about blacks:

Whether this ominous distortion reflects hatred and fear of Negroes we cannot definitely say. In some cases, these deeper emotions may be the assimilative factor at work. And yet the distortion may occur even in subjects who have no anti-Negro bias. It is an unthinking cultural stereotype that the Negro is hot tempered and addicted to the use of razors as weapons. The rumor, though mischievous, may reflect chiefly an assimilation of the story to verbal-clichés and conventional expectation.[13]

A review of the literature on rumor indicates that at least two conditions are prerequisite to their circulation: an event that generates anxiety—an event about which people feel some need to know—and a state of ambiguity concerning the facts surrounding than event.[14] The extreme case for these two conditions is a major event, such as the assassination of prominent public figure, and non-coverage by any of the news media. These conditions can also exist where the event is reported and anxiety aroused but the message is characterized by a high degree of uncertainty. Such uncertainty can result either from the omission of significant facts or the lack of credibility of the communicating medium. Under these circumstances, the message recipient has considerable latitude to supply the missing information from his own imagination or adopt the speculations of others he receives through informal channels of communication. Such informal communications are popularly referred to. as rumor.

At the very least, rumors tend to reinforce present positions, and in most cases the recipient will move further toward one of the attitudinal extremes than if he had received the kind of full and fair account of significant facts a skilled journalist can provide.

In an era that demands the subjugation of our emotional attitudes about race, either a decline in credibility of the media or the failure of the media to meet the demand for information on issues of race relations will solidify rather than dissolve prejudice. The same is true in varying degrees on other issues, depending upon the strength of audience predispositions.

A full and credible presentation of the news also serves the interests of the news organization. The eventual impact of increasing polarization will reduce the media's ability to hold a mass audience. Through the process of selective exposure, people will tend to listen to those voices that agree with their special point of view.[15] Where the society is highly polarized, it will become increasingly difficult for the media to communicate effectively except by tailoring their presentation to the predisposition of particular audiences. What will develop is a series of media, each appealing to a small section on the continuum with strongly held and relatively homogeneous views. Under such circumstances, intergroup communication substantially decreases.

D. Credibility and Audience Bias

Accusations that the news media are biased are frequently the result of strong political, attitudinal, or behavioral convictions. Many of the same charges of bias, for example, are raised against the media from both extremes of the political spectrum. The charges made by the conservatives at the 1964 Republican convention, for instance, remind many observers of those made by liberal Democrats throughout the years.[16]

A 1960 study showed a much greater perception of political bias in the *Dallas News* among Catholic priests than among Baptist ministers. More significant, it found that, among *all* clergy, the perception of political bias increased if the individual thought the paper unfair to his religious group. [17] If the reader gives the newspaper low marks for accuracy or fairness on one subject, he is likely to apply it to others. [18]

Further, experimental studies on attitude change also suggest this situation is general. Hovland and Sherif reported that respondents tended to distort the location of other points of view as a function of their own position on the continuum. Thus, those at either extreme tend to shift the midpoint toward themselves, thereby exaggerating the extremity of other positions as well as putting the objective neutral position "on the other side."[19] A member of the John Birch society, for example, may perceive former Chief Justice Earl Warren as a Communist, while students on the far left may regard Hubert Humphrey as an arch-conservative at best and a Fascist at worst. Clearly, strongly committed persons at eithe end of the spectrum will regard a newspaper that follows an objective and neutral course as biased and lacking in credibility.

The news media are inevitably bound by this paradox. Traditionally, they have attempted to extricate themselves by distinguishing between "news" and "editorial comment." More recently, a third category, "news analysis," has been added. Newsmen are increasingly recognizing that some degree of interpretation inheres in the very act of reporting, regardless of the medium. At a minimum, interpretation results from individual differences in physical perception and social and cultural background.

The news media will not be able to meet the communications needs of the country in the coming decades until they acknowledge—at least to themselves—that the old distinction between "news" and "editorial comment" is inadequate.

REFERENCES

1. Quoted by Robert E. Park, "The Natural History of the Newspaper," in *Mass Communications,* Wilbur Schramm, Ed), (Urbana: University of Illinois Press, 1960), p. 13.
2. Harold Cross, *The People's Right to Know* (New York: Columbia University Press, 1956), p. xiii.
3. Walter Cronkite, *"The Whole World is Watching,"* Public Broadcast Laboratory, Broadcast Dec. 22, 1968, script p. 56.
4. Walter Lippmann, "The Job of the Washington Correspondent," *Atlantic,* January, 1960, p. 49.
5. Harold D. Lasswell, "The Structure and Function of Communication in Society," in Schramm, *op. cit.,* footnote 1, p. 130.
6. Robert M. Hutchins, Chairman, *A Free and Responsible Press,* Commission on Freedom of the Press (Chicago: University of Chicago Press, 1947), pp. 20-21.
7. *International Press Institute Bulletin,* January 1969, p. 4. See also Norman Isaacs, "The New Credibility Gap—Readers vs. The Press," *American Society of Newspaper Editors Bulletin,* February 1969, p. 1.
8. Jack Lyle, *The News in Megalopolis* (San Francisco: Chandler, 1967), pp. 39-42.
9. *Ibid.,* p. 171.
10. Thomas Whiteside, "Corridor of Mirrors: The Television Editorial Process, Chicago," *Columbia Journalism Review* (Winter 1968/69), p. 35-54.
    Commenting on his involvement in the events in Chicago, Walter Cronkite said, "I am ashamed of having become emotionally involved, if we are talking about on-air involvement, when our own man was beat up before our eyes on the floor of the convention. I became indignant, said there were a bunch of thugs out there I

think on the floor. I shouldn't have. I think that's wrong." Broadcast Dec. 22, 1968, 8:30 p.m. edt, by the Public Broadcast Laboratory, script p. 43.

11. The Survey was commissioned by WFBM-TV at the direction of Eldon Campbell shortly after the assassination of Senator Kennedy and was performed by Frank N. Magid Associates. We appreciate the generosity and cooperation of Messrs. Campbell and Magid in making it available to us and discussing it with us. Unfortunately it was not completed in time for us to make more extensive use of it. pp. 130-131.

12. Gordon Allport and Leo Postman, *The Psychology of Rumor,* (New York: Holt, Rinehart & Winston, 1947).

13. Gordon Allport and Leo Postman, "The Basic Psychology of Rumor," in *The Process and Effects of Mass Communication* (Wilbur Schramm, Ed.) (Urbana: University of Illinois Press, 1955), p. 153.

14. Tamotsu Shibutani, *Improvised News: A Sociological Study of Rumor* (Bobbs-Merrill 1966).

15. Lazarsfeld, Berelson, Gaudet, *The People's Choice,* New York: Columbia University Press, (1948); Cartwright, "Some Principles of Mass Persuasion: Selected Findings of Research on the Sale of United States War Bonds," *Human Relations,* II (1949), pp. 253-67; Starr & Hughes, "Report on an Educational Campaign: The Cincinnati Plan for the United Nations," *American Journal of Sociology* (1950), pp. 389-400; Cannel & MacDonald, "The Impact of Health News on Attitudes and Behavior," *Journalism Quarterly* (1956), pp. 315-23.

16. Lyle, *op. cit.,* footnote 8, p. 171.

17. *Ibid.,* pp. 44-45.

18. James E. Brinton, et al. *The Newspaper and Its Public,* (Stanford University, Institute for Communications Research, undated).

19. Carl Hovland and Muzafer Sherif, *Social Judgment* (New Haven: Yale University Press, 1961).

Chapter 4

INTERGROUP COMMUNICATION

You can't write a terribly exciting story
about a boring football game. What . . . that
again has nothing to do with ideology; it's
simply that the newspapers—this one
included—hold up a mirror to the world.
If what they see is a boring picture, I'm afraid
that what the readers get is a boring story
quite often.

Clifton Daniel, Former Managing Editor,
New York Times

So long as the news media rely on the mirror of society theory of journalism as their main defense, their critics will have a monopoly on both facts and logic. Fortunately, some journalists have rejected the mirror theory. Bill Moyers, publisher of *Newsday*, has said:

> For a long time, there's been a myth about journalism, a myth shared by people who read us and view us, and a myth shared by those of us who are in the profession. That myth has been that newspapers are sort of, simply, mirrors of the world, as someone has said, that we simply reflect what is happening . . . . I think part of the cure for this exaggerated myth is simply if journalism admits that objectivity's a myth; we will diffuse the great expectations people have which we can never fulfill, and that is that we can look down from Olympus and tell people, "what is true."

Once the fetish for objectivity is set aside, journalists should begin to examine their craft in terms of the information requirements of a democratic society. Even if objectivity is a myth, fair and balanced surveillance are goals worth pursuing.

Accuracy, balance, and fairness are important in the resolution of conflict for several related reasons. Most important is that individual and collective responses to a changing environment, regardless of how carefully thought out, will be irrational if based on misinformation. All irrational responses do not necessarily fail, but success with them is purely coincidental. Failure not only breeds frustration, it also generates mistrust among groups. To the extent that the synthetic world of news does not square with the experience of large numbers of citizens, the credibility of the news media will be impaired. As a result, increased reliance on informal channels of communication will prevail. Finally, unbalanced surveillance will produce disparity in the perception of important underlying facts among the several groups in conflict in our society. Disagreements more easily resolve when the views of the underlying facts are approximately the same. Nowhere is the importance of the mass media in intergroup communication more apparent than between blacks and whites.

A. Communication Between Blacks and Whites: A Case Study

> We believe that the greatest single need
> in America today is for communication
> between blacks and whites.
> —NBC News, "Summer 1967:
> What We Learned."

A communication gap stretches wide between the black and white communities. Insulated from each other geographically, socially, and politically, they have primarily the mass media as a medium of intergroup communication. The news media did not request this job, but when the need for communication became critical, they were the one institution in society equipped to do the most about it.

By the middle 1960's, the gap had not been bridged. For example, a 1967 survey by the Louis Harris organization on the causes of Negro rioting is shown in table 1.

Table 1.—The understanding gap: Causes of Negro rioting

Cause	Whites' Belief (percent)	Negroes' Belief (percent)
Outside agitation	45	10
Police brutality	8	49
Joblessness	34	67
Inadequate housing	39	68
Inadequate education	46	61

Forty-five percent of whites, but only 10 percent of Negroes, consider "outside agitation" a major cause of riots. What do the whites know that Negroes don't? How can two groups of people, living in the same country, in the same cities, have such different pictures of reality? Do the Negroes, conversely, know something that the white community does not?

If blacks and whites cannot agree even on the basic facts underlying the racial crisis in this country, there is little likelihood that we will be able to make any significant progress toward a joint resolution of the American dilemma, and any resolution unilaterally imposed will most probably be violent.

The Louis Harris poll makes clear the great disparity between the black and white man's view of the racial crisis. Take the issue of police brutality, for example. A bureau chief of one of the national news magazines had been assigned to Chicago several years prior to the convention disorders. While there, he had heard complaints from ghetto residents about police brutality; his practice, typically, was to dismiss them as imagined slights or, at worst, verbal abuse. He never paid much attention. Later he returned to Chicago for the Democratic national convention. After his experiences this time and those of the reporters under him, he was solidly convinced that there was such a thing as police brutality in Chicago. One thing seems clear: the failure of the press to report on police brutality is one factor that contributes to the notion by whites that it is not a major factor in Negro discontent. The failure to report in this case was mainly the product of ignorance and indifference.

The Kerner Report emphasized that this country is rapidly moving toward two societies. Just as important is the fact that America has always been two societies, one black and one white, separate and unequal. The pervasiveness of segregation, both North and South, has resulted in very little candid two-way communication between blacks and whites. Until the early 1960's, the personal experience of most whites with Negroes was largely in the Negroes' rendering of menial services to the white community. The remainder of any communication was through the media.

The CBS documentary, "Black History: Lost, Stolen or Strayed," [1] has brilliantly documented the manner in which blacks were portrayed in motion pictures and radio. An analysis of 100 motion pictures involving Negro characters, made during the 1940's, found that in 75 cases the portrayal was a disparaging stereotype. In only 12 cases was the Negro favorably presented as an individual human being.[2] Large-circulation magazines were indifferent toward the Negro. While there were exceptions among the journals of opinion and magazines with a cause, "During the 1930's both *Collier's* and the *Saturday Evening Post* ran a number of fiction pieces about the Negro, all of them in a quaint dialect that today seems almost incomprehensible. Roark Bradford wrote of the Widow Duck and Uncle Charlie and life at Little Bee Bend Plantation, and Octavus Roy Cohen chronicled the misadventures of his most endurable character, Florian Slappey. But their characters were stereotypes, and the life of the Negro wasn't really like that, even then."[3] Until the late fifties, most news coverage of blacks was limited to Negroes involved in crime, sports, or entertainment.

Until recently, what most white Americans knew about blacks was that some of them were pretty good athletes, they had lots of rhythm, a lot of them were criminals—possibly by instinct—and they could be very good entertainers. Many Americans, to be sure, had either met or heard of people like Ralph Bunche, but the mere fact that such Negroes were regarded as exceptions, of course, proves the rule. Southern whites, some quite sincerely, were convinced that their Negroes were happy; and the only way trouble could come would be through outside agitation.

Omitting the black press, no medium of communication was reporting the Negro struggle for equality. Were this owing solely to ignorance, perhaps it could be ignored. The great paradox however, is that when Gunner Myrdal was writing his now-classic "American Dilemma" 25 years ago, one of his most important sources of information about the state of race relations was

Southern newspaper reporters—they knew the story but could not write it.[4] This fact can only be attributed to the parochial attitudes, ignorance, and, in some cases, venality of Southern publishers.

Typically, publishers both North and South have been allies of the black man only when he was in conflict with elements outside the publishers' own community. The strong editorial views exchanged between Northern and Southern newspapers prior to the Civil War, for example, is well known.

1. Nineteenth Century Coverage of Blacks

The Northern papers criticized the South for not reporting slave insurrections, thus allowing many of their readers to continue in their illusion that the Negro was content with slavery. The Northern papers played up the Carolina slave revolts of the 1800's with sensational stories of destruction and havoc, but North Carolina papers practically ignored them. Although the Northern papers probably overplayed the extent of the revolts, they had at least acknowledged their existence.[5]

On Jan. 31, 1831, William Lloyd Garrison brought out the first issue of the *Liberator,* a four-page paper entirely devoted to the abolition of slavery. Garrison had total dedication:

> He who oppugns the public liberty overthrows his own . . . There is no safety where there is no strength; no strength without union; no union without justice; no justice where faith and truth are wanting. The right to be free is a truth planted in the hearts of men . . .[6]

Garrison was the prototype of the combatant editor. Although there were other abolitionists, he was so vehement and self-righteous that he made as many enemies in the North as he made in the South. It was a prosperous time, and many Northerners who had no stake in slavery wanted to preserve their comfort by compromising the differences between North and South. Garrison wrote:

> These are your men of "caution" and "prudence" and "judiciousness." Sir, I have learned to hate those words. Whenever we attempt to imitate the Great Exemplar, and press the truth of God in all its plainness upon the conscience, why, we are imprudent; because, forsooth, a great excitement will ensue. Sir, slavery will not be overthrown without excitement—a most tremendous excitement.[7]

Garrison was opposed not only by many of the leading newspapers of the day, but also by Postmaster General Amos Kendall, who argued that each issue of the *Liberator* circulated in a Southern state was a threat to the public peace, and therefore allowed southern committees to remove the *Liberator* from the mails. Even the state of Massachusetts conspired against the *Liberator,* which was published in Boston; officials tried to forbid its export.

Not until 1850 did American opinion—shaped in part by the pressure of world opinion—begin to square with the views of the abolitionist. By then, many abolitionists had suffered physically at the hands of mobs. One, Elijah Lovejoy, had been killed by a mob in Alton, Ill. Such action helped to make abolitionists of the greatest editors. By 1854, Horace Greeley of the *New York Tribune* was publishing editorial attacks on slavery that were so vehement that his critics accused him of brutality. Samual Bowles of the *Springfield Republican,* William Cullen Bryant of the *New York Evening Post,* Joseph Medill of the *Chicago Tribune*—all thundered against slavery.

Greeley's *New York Tribune* responded to the Emancipation Proclamation with the headline "GOD BLESS ABRAHAM LINCOLN." But the Natchez, Mississippi, *Courier* editorialized "A monkey with his tail off is a monkey still." In 1865, the Jackson, Mississippi *Daily News* urged, "We must keep the ex-slave in a position of inferiority. We must pass such laws as will make him feel his inferiority." The *Chicago Tribune* answered; "We tell the white men of Mississippi that the men of the North will convert the State of Mississippi into a frog pond before they will allow any such laws to disgrace one foot of soil in which the bones of our soldiers sleep and over which the flag of freedom waves."[8]

After Reconstruction, Jim Crow began to sweep the South. In 1898, the Charleston, S. C., *News and Courier,* satirized:

> As we have got on fairly well for a third of a century, we can probably get on as well hereafter without [Jim Crow] .... If there must be Jim Crow cars on the street railways .... And if there are to be Jim Crow cars, moreover there should be Jim Crow waiting saloons at all stations, and Jim Crow eating houses. There should be Jim Crow sections of the jury box and a separate Jim Crow dock and witness stand in every court—and a Jim Crow Bible for colored witnesses to kiss.[9]

But satire became reality: 8 years later the same paper was urging that "only mass deportation could solve as grave a problem as the presence of Negroes."[10]

During the 19th century, discrimination was not limited to the Southern press. Over a hundred years ago, Willie A. Hodges, a Negro, sought to have his opinions published in Benjamin Day's *New York Sun.* Hodges was told that the *Sun* did not shine for black men. This provided the impetus for the birth of the *Rams Horn* in January 1847, one of the earliest of approximately 3,000 Negro newspapers that have been published in this country, and that have kept alive the hopes and strengthened the discontent of the Black community.[11]

2. The Twentieth Century: The First Fifty Years

Until the mid-fifties, the Northern press almost completely ignored blacks and black protest, but not without notable exceptions: The Sweet trial in Detroit in 1926; the successful campaign to bar Judge John J. Parker's confirmation to the U. S. Supreme Court; the Scottsboro trials in the early 1930's. Yet, in 1944,Gunnar Myrdal concluded:

> "No feasible widening of the reporting of Negro activities in the white press will substitute for the Negro press. What happens to Negroes will continue to have relatively low 'news value' to white people, and even the most well-meaning editor will have to stop far short of what Negroes demand if he wants to satisfy his white public ... Whether or not this forecast of an increasing circulation for Negro papers comes true, the Negro press is of tremendous importance."[12]

Another exception, at least for a time, was the Montgomery, Ala., *Advertiser.* When the Klan was run out of Alabama during the 1920's, it was in part the result of the efforts of the *Advertiser's* publisher, Grover Hall. Hall had castigated and ridiculed the nightriders and met their threats by wearing his pistol to the office. He mobilized community opinion against the Klan by emphasizing the threat of such organizations to lawful government.

Although during the Scottsboro trials Hall did characterize the nine defendants as "beasts" and "apes," after the court testimony in the third trial proved that the boys had been framed, he changed his editorial position, went to a Negro meeting, and then publicly apologized for his earlier remarks.[13]

When the Supreme Court decided *Brown* v. *Board of Education* in 1954, Hall's son had assumed control of the paper. Shortly after the desegregation decision, the younger Hall took an editorial position opposing the White Citizen's Council—describing them as "manicured Ku Klux Klansmen." That was until an address by Senator James O. Eastland drew a crowd of 15,000 active or potential Citizen's Council members to a meeting in Montgomery. Then the *Advertiser* did an about face. Even small meetings of the Council began to be front-page news. The White Citizen's Council frequently dominated the "letters to the editor" column. When Martin Luther King, Jr., addressed 12,000 people in the Cathedral of St. John the Divine, in New York, the story was given three paragraphs and placed at the bottom of one of five stories appearing in that issue on the White Citizen's Council.[14]

Asked about this shift in policy by Ted Poston, a reporter for the *New York Post,* Hall responded:

> "Well, what the hell would Jimmy Wechsler [editor of the *New York Post*] have done in a small community like this when most of the important people in town had joined the White Citizens Council and when it had mustered a fifteen-thousand membership."[15]

At least two other Southern newspapers have made a serious effort toward balance in reporting race relations over the years: The Greenville, Miss., *Delta Democrat,* under the direction of Hodding Carter III, and prior to that under his father; and the *Atlanta Constitution,* whose policies were largely the result of the influence of its publisher, the late Ralph McGill, and its former managing editor, Eugene Patterson, now in the same position at *The Washington Post.* Whether the *Constitution* will continue its traditionally balanced approach after the departure of these two fine journalists remains to be seen.

The Southern press was not the only medium subject to outside pressures. During both World Wars, evidence abounded of official concern about the exposure of Negroes in the press and reports of the mistreatment of Negro troops. Threats of clamping special censorship on the *Crisis,* the *Messenger,* the Chicago *Defender* were made by Attorney General Mitchell Palmer during World War I. In some Mississippi cities, whole shipments of the *Defender* were confiscated or destroyed.[16]

Yet ignoring black Americans was not totally the result of antiblack attitudes by media personnel. Poor people do not make news, black or white. The American press has traditionally been aristocratic, not democratic, and an important factor in determining newsworthiness of any story is prominence. American society simply did not produce many prominent Negroes or black institutions. The American press discriminated against the poor, both black and white.[17]

Nevertheless, the performance of the Southern press up through the earlier fifties won no medals from integrationists, North or South. Southern newspapers and Southern radio and TV stations carried very little news about Negroes and gave scant or little attention to news involving racial issues. Negroes were not referred to as "Mr." or "Mrs." There was, in fact, no effective communication between the white and Negro communities on any level in the mass media.[18]

Hodding Carter has summarized the performance of the Southern press:

> The obvious errors, the obvious omissions, the obvious commissions by the Southern press are monumental. In the past it has been said that the church is the most segregated aspect of contemporary American life. I could say that for years the Southern press was as segregated as the church ever dreamed of being.[19]

3. Progress in Black Coverage: The 1950s

The first consistent progress toward balance in the coverage of race relations began a short time after the Supreme Court's 1954 decision to strike down the doctrine of "separate but equal." That decision gave the Negro struggle for equality legitimacy within the white community, and its potential impact was enormous; but it did not assure broad-based coverage by the white media.

On Dec. 1, 1955, Mrs. Rosa Parks, formerly an officer of the local NAACP, boarded a bus on Cleveland Avenue, in Montgomery, Alabama. A short time later, a white man boarded the bus and the driver ordered Mrs. Parks to get up and give the white man her seat. Mrs. Parks said, "No." She was arrested. The news spread quickly through the Negro community. Within 24 hours, there was a mass gathering. It was decided that the following Monday, Negroes—75 percent of Montgomery's bus riders—would walk to work. The clergymen would spread the word from their pulpits on Sunday morning. A young Baptist minister, Dr. Martin Luther King, Jr., accepted responsibility for circulating printed notices to Montgomery's 50,000 Negro residents.[20]

The bus boycotts, the freedom rides, the sit-ins, the parades, and the picketing that followed this incident caught the attention of Northern newsmen. These events were unusual, they represented conflict, they had a potentially wide impact, there was action, and the response of the official and nonofficial white South sometimes provided violence. In short, these reactions fitted almost any reporter's definition of "news." Most important, they provided material uniquely suited to the new medium, television.

If only the leaders such as Dr. King had simply called a press conference, briefed the reporters present, and instructed them to go out and report on the deplorable state of race relations in America! If they had, of course, very few if any, of the white media would have written the story; in many instances, they could not because they did not know how. Even if they had, few people in the white community would have read it. And if whites had read it, few would have perceived the urgency of the situation. Some still don't. The

Negro community not only had to get the attention of the white media, they also had to get the attention of the white audience.

The campaign of sit-ins, parades, and picketing at least provided some news coverage of black problems. White Americans, for the first time, were learning that blacks existed as humans, not chattels, and were unhappy about something. Whites also learned that the Negro proposed to do something about his discontent.

Northern audiences responded and, although blind to their own more subtle forms of discrimination, they sympathized with the plight of the Southern Negro. The manifestations of racism in the South were infinitely less subtle than those in the North. Separate public facilities, separate schools, separate restaurants, the sometimes blatant police brutality which surfaced for the television cameras during non-violent demonstrations—all were practices that Northern audiences found easy to deplore. The television media, presented with action, brought the human aspect of the story to the American home with unprecedented impact and directness.

The national television networks also brought the message to the South. Little wonder, therefore, that many white southerners became irritated and upset. For the first time in their lives, they saw Southern Negroes asserting their rights on national television. Initially, many refused to believe it. They wondered where the networks found these unbelievable Negroes. Threaten men's cherished illusions, and frequently they become angry and respond with disbelief—sometimes with violence.

The Southern news media were not quick to change old habits. In 1961, the American Broadcasting Co. released a documentary titled "Walk in My Shoes," The story suggested that white people take a long hard look at what it meant to be black. Only one of the five ABC affiliates in the state of Florida carried the program.[21]

During the riots in Birmingham, Alabama, in 1963, the *Birmingham News* devoted most of its prime space to the bloody riots in Cyprus. The disorders in Birmingham were given only a brief space at the bottom of page four to make passing mention—without many details, of course—of the local rioting then going on between Birmingham's Negroes and Bull Connor, with his police dogs and fire hoses."[22]

When Medgar Evers was murdered, the Jackson, Mississippi, *Clarion Ledger* discovered that the accused killer had been taken as a very young child to California for a brief period. Most of the rest of his life had been spent in the Mississippi Delta. The newspaper headline said "CALIFORNIAN ARRESTED IN EVERS CASE."[23]

Unbalanced coverage in the South was not always the result of unfettered choice. In many instances, it was to avoid the consequences of perceived economic threats and of community opinion. William B. Monroe, Jr. former chief of NBC News in Washington, D.C., tells of his experience when he was chief editorial writer for the *New Orleans Item.* The newspaper had been liberal enough to support Adlai Stevenson; but when it received a letter to the editor on a racial subject from a Negro man, it did not print it. The Negro had been an electrician in the Navy during World War II; when he returned to New Orleans, the white electricians union would not admit him. The letter "was couched in entirely reasonable language, but its viewpoint was that of resentment against discrimination. The newspaper did not publish the man's letter because the opposition newspaper was already using the *Item's* relative liberalism as a sales tool with advertisers, and the publisher felt that the *Item* could not afford a too pro-Negro image."[24] The problem had been made particularly acute for Southern newspapers because the target of many civil rights demonstrations became what could ordinarily be relied upon as one of the more liberal allies of the press by Southern standards—the business community. Outside of voting, one of the chief problems was segregated business facilities. In Greenville, Miss., the *Delta Democrat* covered the boycott of a local shop and give it extensive publicity. The next day, the owner met his friends from the newspaper in the coffee shop as they did every day, and screamed "Why are you doing this to me?"

Northern reporters who covered the civil rights movement in the South were frequently harassed. Richard Valeriani was clubbed on the back of the head at the courthouse in Marion, Alabama, while working for NBC. The Haleyville *Alabamian* editorialized that Mr. Valeriani was a "propagandist" and a "carpetbagger" and suggested that much of the racial demonstrating was the result of collusion between Negroes and television photographers. Under these circumstances, the newspaper felt, it was too much to expect southerners to be friendly and hospitable. The editorial was reprinted with approval in Jackson, Mississippi.[25]

Karl Fleming, *Newsweek's* Los Angeles Bureau chief, relates a similar experience in which he and Claude Sitton, now National Affairs Editor for the *New York Times,* were involved shortly after the slaying of three young civil rights workers in Mississippi. They had gone to the courthouse to question the sheriff and his deputy. When they left, they were approached by some of the local residents, "who proceeded to tell us in no uncertain terms that if we didn't get the hell out of town, they were going to kill us. Their Negroes were really happy; they ate a lot of watermelon and picked cotton and everything was fine until we damn Yankee newspapermen came around to stir up trouble."[26] That night some men came to their motel accompanied by a half-gallon of corn whiskey and two, double-barreled, 10-gauge shotguns. Sitton and Fleming were convinced to spend the night in another town.[27]

Many Southern reporters, however, sympathized with Northern brethren. Ted Poston, a black reporter for the *New York Post,* has observed:

> Nowhere else have I met a more knowledgeable, decent, and frustrated group of newspapermen than those with whom I worked down South. I can say truthfully that I owe my life to several of these men. Without their warnings and assistance, I could have been lynched on any of three occasions when I was chased out of town by mobs—the last one led by three sheriff's deputies.[28]

Today, the number of Southern publishers and broadcasters who consciously engage in distortion of the news is diminishing, but a hard core will always not allow their readers and viewers "to know what ought not to have happened." Yet the problem of unconscious distortion, of viewing the news from a perspective that makes unbalanced surveillance inevitable, is substantial and will continue:

... A North Carolina publisher ... complained to United Press International: "As a new subscriber to U.P.I., I am beginning to realize why newspapers are so loaded with nothing but racial news centered around such people as Martin Luther King. In trying to get some items worthy of reading last night, I found long and constant harangues coming over the wire about this questionable person during his visit with an even more questionable organization in North Carolina." Checking up, a U.P.I. executive discovered that only one story on Martin Luther King had been dispatched that night, that it reported that King was entering a retreat of the Southern Christian Leadership Council, and that the story was only 150 words long.[29]

B. Communication Between Blacks and Whites

In October 1963, Turner Catledge of the *New York Times* noted the disparity in coverage between North and South:

> We've had open season on the south here now for some time, and it seems to me that, especially when you read the editorial pages in the North some people are too much concerned about what's going on somewhere else and too little concerned about what's going on right at their own door ... There seems to be a disposition, especially on our editorial pages, to demand that the southerners accept some sort of an emotional change in this matter, which they're not going to do. Integration is coming to the south. It's coming very slowly, but it's not wanted. Is it wanted any more in Minnesota or in New York? I think this is the question our readers are entitled to have us explore.[30]

The expansion of coverage of the black community by the Northern press, conceived in crisis, remains crisis-oriented. Almost all publishers and broadcast owners, most editors, and the majority of reporters do not know their black communities well enough to perform the function of surveillance on any basis other than traditional news values and practices. These, unfortunately, are not adequate.

1. The Need for a Black Perspective

When a story breaks in the black community, the white news media are sufficiently competent at reporting how many people were hurt, how much property was damaged, the number of police used, who said what. Most are not, however, very competent at doing the kind of analysis necessary to place the event in context and give it significance.

Until recently, and the exceptions remain few, the news organizations have not regularly covered the black community. Few news "beats" existed in the ghetto.[31] The reporters did not know its aspirations. Today, enough reporters, both North and South, are capable, qualified, and willing to learn the skills necessary to provide adequate coverage. Too few publishers and broadcast owners, however, are willing to let them do it.

The essential requirement for any individual or organization to function as a medium of communication between two groups as diverse as blacks and whites is an understanding of both communities. The reporter must see problems from the perspective of both groups and he must be able to speak in terms that both will understand. The only way the white media can hope to understand the black community is by becoming involved in the black community. This involvement includes hiring blacks in professional positions. Most of the intergroup communication in this country has been from the white community to the black community; very little has been in the other direction. The white community cannot listen unless someone carries the message, a message based on understanding the black man.

Unfortunately, the evidence suggests, not many editors care to acquire the basic knowledge necessary to survey the black community adequately. Approximately 500 newspaper editors were present in 1965 when Floyd McKissick, then director of CORE, offered to have each editor's local CORE chapter take the editor on a personal insider's tour of the ghetto in their city. Six months later, Norman Isaacs of the *Louisville Courier-Journal* asked Mr. McKissick how many had accepted the offer. "Two" he answered; the *Louisville Courier-Journal* and the *Oakland Tribune.*

Had these editors gone into the ghettos, they might have begun to learn the answers to some of the questions put by Benjamin Holman, formerly with the Justice Department's Community Relations Service and now with NBC news:

> Have you ever wondered what it's like to be seven years old, and black, in a slum school? Have you ever tried to find out how a young, unskilled Negro husband tries to provide for his family? Have you ever thought about the aspirations of a Negro teenager? Do you know what soul food is? What do you know about the myriad of block clubs and organizations in the ghetto community? What really goes on in ghetto pool rooms? Do attitudes of Negro youngsters about sex differ from those of whites? What is the meaning of the ritual of those store- front churches? What does a young Negro father tell his son about being Black in America? Why are there seemingly so many taverns in Negro neighborhoods? What are the latest in-group jokes in the ghetto? There is a fascinating world of humor, pathos, aspirations, frustrations, toil, heartbreak, violence, and joy right under your nose.

The news organization that does not know the answers to these questions cannot possibly do a balanced job of surveillance.

It is not the editor or publisher who writes the story, some may argue, and accordingly it does not really matter whether he knows the black community. He does, however, set the standards and policies that determine the allocation of reporting resources, the amount of time or space alloted, the style in which material shall be prepared, the policies toward coverage of the black community, and the system of rewards and punishments. During the 1930's and 1940's. even white reporters in the South could have done a better job of covering the Negro community.

If the publisher, broadcaster, or editor refuses to know his community beyond what he can learn at the country club or his wife can relate from her bridge club, then he must rely on reporters who are willing to accept the responsibility; and in turn, must relinquish some of the control he has traditionally exercised. To trust the reporter's discretion was done long ago in some news organizations for foreign correspondents and more recently for the Washington correspondents. The news executive who neither learns nor delegates his authority, infringes the people's right to know. He denies them important information. He contributes to simplistic, inaccurate, and stereotyped illusions of the reality of the black community and, worse, he impairs his credibility and allows a condition to persist that promotes rumors.

2. There Can Be Progress

Progress is being made by those who seek to know their community and are concerned. In Connecticut, for example, several of the media have begun to establish lists of black leaders in each community, in order to learn the organizational structure of the community, to know who has influence, how many followers they have, and what their goals are. From this approach comes an appreciation of the spectrum of views in the black community.

Just as important, again in Connecticut, some of the news organizations are not only finding out who the leaders and organizations are, but they are also establishing personal communication with them. One television station assigns reporters to cover these organizations on a regular basis. Such a policy can involve something as simple as calling the organization every week or two and inquiring what they are doing, what plans they have, what programs they are thinking about adopting, or what shifts in policy have occurred, and in discussing current events. To make sure that the reporters are doing their job and to assist management, the news director of the station can require the reporters to file weekly reports on the coverage of their "beats."

White media operators make much of the fact that they cannot find out who speaks for the black community. No one speaks for it, no more than anyone speaks for the white community. George Wallace, John Lindsay, Ronald Reagan, Edward Kennedy, James Eastland, John Gardner, Richard Nixon, or Ralph Nader: none speaks for the white community; each speaks for his own constituency, and that constituency may shift depending on the issue. So it is with the black community. A range of organizations and leaders has varying influence and shifting constituencies. Only by meeting with the black leaders and the black organizations can the media begin to get an accurate notion of how important each is to the black community, how many followers or adherents they have, what views they have on a variety of problems, and how they would react to fast-breaking news stories. Armed with this kind of knowledge, the white media can begin to put fast-breaking stories involving blacks in perspective. To achieve balance, they will not have to go to the nearest street corner and ask whomever happens along for the view of the black community. Nor will they have to rely on traditional news standards which usually dictate a selection of the most vocal spokesman. They will know who are the leaders.

There is another advantage to knowing the black community. People both within and without the media have pointed out that some news media, usually classified as liberal, are overly timid about criticizing black leaders or about taking an editorial position opposed to a program of a black organization. As one observer put it: "If a white man came in and proposed that the Government do so and so, the news organization would say it was ridiculous. But let a black man propose it and they take it seriously."

It is not necessary to embrace the doctrines of Stokely Carmichael, Malcolm X, or other advocates of black power to conclude that they were never able to get their views across to the vast majority of white people. It is sufficient to simply read some of their books [34] or speeches.

On an issue such as black power, the major responsibility for distortion rests with the media. The issue, relatively new, was one in which the media can be most effective. With Malcolm X or the Nation of Islam, the public had little or no actual experience, a condition where media influence is greatest. And, because whites were barred from Muslim meetings, no white could learn information that might contradict what the media reported. Here is an example in which approximately the same conditions existed:

> Tiring of his routine on Saturdays during the football season, a New York sports writer began writing fictitious stories about the spectacular exploits of Sammy Chang, a whirlwind halfback for Plainfield New Jersey Tech. There is no Plainfield Tech. Chang does not exist. But the writer had presented the fictitious facts so vividly that in the balloting for the Little All America team, Chang received the greatest number of votes.[35]

Most of the distortion is not the result of any conscious effort on the part of the media to give black power a bad name. The major causes, rather, are the media's indifference toward and lack of perspective on the black community, the resultant relatively greater dominance of the media's traditional high value on conflict, and the inadequacy of objective formula reporting.

Life magazine, for example, has editorially committed itself to integration, and it has great sympathy for the Negro cause. In a study of all integration crisis photographs that appeared in Life during 1962 and 1963,[36] however, more than half of those photographs show violence rather than passive resistance; in addition, more than ten percent of these photographs portrayed Black Muslims. *Ebony,* roughly the black press equivalent of *Life*, during the same period, showed violence in only twenty percent of its photographs and only one percent were of Black Muslims.

Similarly, what has the press done to distinguish between rejecting black inferiority and a philosophy of white hate? If the Negro is to reject the notion that white is right, that straight hair, thin lips, and light skin are inherently more beautiful than knappy hair, wide lips, and black skin, he is being taught to admire whites less. This, however, is something quite different from teaching that whites are to be hated. Similarly, it is impossible to explain to the black man the reason he has been cast in a subordinate position for three hundred years, without recounting the offenses of the white community against him. Finally, there are a good many blacks who believe that today's institutions do not meet the needs of the nation or of the black community. These institutions were built and are operated by whites. It does not follow, however, that to advocate radical changes in these white institutions necessarily betrays a racist position. Many white students today advocate the same. The Crime Commission recommended radical changes in the institutions that administer criminal justice. The Kerner Commission recommended radical changes in white institutions. Many prominent white politicians have advocated radical change in white institutions. No one has suggested these men are racists, however, even though they attack white institutions.

3. The Black Community and the White Press

Much of the antipathy of militant blacks toward the white news media centers on the unwillingness of the press to explore the nature of black power in depth. In reporting on the advocates of black pride or black power, the news organizations have shown a greater willingness to accept the radical statements and simply to repeat them than to explore their significance and to place them in proper perspective. Karl Fleming, Los Angeles Bureau Chief for *Newsweek,* has said:

> The advocates of Black Power and the treatment they have received by the press are undoubtedly one of the factors behind this situation. Perhaps no better example can be put forth than the way we've treated Stokely Carmichael. Let me make it clear that this is no polemical defense of Carmichael; I know him and I know how erratic he can be at times. He is sort of a hysterical Barry Goldwater, but the difference is that the press was almost uniformly defensive of Goldwater. They would go to interminable lengths to give him a second chance, going back and saying Well, did you really mean this, Senator, or would you like to clarify this? Exactly the reverse is true of Carmichael. The press has uniformly, and I think deliberately, set out to distort what this guy was trying to say about Black Power.[37]

The press functions not only to survey, but also to criticize, and responsible criticism has understanding as its prerequisite. If the media do not first make the effort to understand the black community, they cannot intelligently criticize it. If they do not criticize, they are abdicating another of their obligations to the people. But criticism without understanding becomes a hit-or-miss proposition and leads to black animosity toward the media and a consequent drying up of news sources. Yet, much of the sting from critical editorials lessens if the subject of the editorial believes he has had at least a fair opportunity to be understood.

Similarly, the media cannot do an adequate in-depth report without understanding. Consider the following account of the Nation of Islam's first major encounter with the news media. In the spring of 1959, Louis Lomax asked Malcolm X whether the Nation of Islam, of which he was then one of the leaders, would cooperate in being filmed as a television documentary program for the Mike Wallace show, known for featuring controversial subjects. Late that year the program was broadcast.

The documentary began with a recording of a play presented by the Black Muslims. Titled, *The Trial,* it depicts the white man being tried by the rest of the world for crimes against blacks. The prosecutor's summation characterizes the nature of the charges:

> I charge the white man with being the greatest liar on earth. I charge the white man with being the greatest drunkard on earth. I charge the white man with being the greatest swine-eater on earth. Yet the Bible forbids it. I charge the white man with being the greatest gambler on earth. I charge the white man, ladies and gentlemen of the jury, with

being the greatest murderer on earth. I charge the white man with being the greatest peacebreaker on earth. I charge the white man with being the greatest adulterer on earth. I charge the white man with being the greatest deceiver on earth. I charge the white man with being the greatest trouble-maker on earth. So therefore, ladies and gentlemen of the jury, I ask you, bring back a verdict of guilty as charged.

The jury brought in a verdict of guilty and the applause of the audience was so thunderous it drowned out the judge's voice as he sentenced the white man to death.[32]

Commenting on this broadcast in his autobiography, Malcolm X said:

"The Hate That Hate Produced"—the title—was edited tightly into a kaleidoscope of "shocker" images . . . Mr. Muhammad, me, and others speaking . . . strong-looking, set-faced black men, our Fruit of Islam . . . white-scarved, white-gowned Muslim sisters of all ages . . . Muslims in our restaurants, and other businesses . . . Muslims and other black people entering and leaving our mosques . . .

Every phrase was edited to increase the shock mood. As the producers intended, I think people sat just about limp when the program went off.

In a way, the public reaction was like what happened back in the 1930's when Orson Welles frightened America with a radio program describing, as though it was actually happening, an invasion by "men from Mars."

No one jumped from any windows, but in New York City there was an instant avalanche of public reaction. It's my personal opinion that the "Hate . . . Hate . . ." title was primarily responsible for the reaction. Hundreds of thousand of New Yorkers, black and white were exclaiming "Did you hear it? Did you see it? Preaching hate of white people!"[33]

Contrast the treatment of Carmichael with Douglass Cater's observation on the coverage of Congress:

Members of the press often apply a deliberate censorship. One neophyte reporter who unwittingly quoted in print a rash remark revealing bigotry on the part of a leading Congressman told me he was afterward chastised by several of his press colleagues for his indiscretion.[38]

Under such circumstances, alienation of many black militants should surprise no one. More and more, as a result, newsmen are being barred from the meetings of black organizations and blacks are refusing to be news sources. During the first week of the news program, Martin Agronsky's "Washington," WTOP-TV sought a filmed interview with students at Howard Law School who had recently been involved in a protest movement. The students refused to take part in filmed interviews because the station would have an opportunity to edit their remarks. They agreed, however, to appear at the studio that evening for a live broadcast and did. Other Negro organizations have permitted only black newsmen to be present at meetings, presumably because they then have an even chance of having the proceedings fairly reported.

Nevertheless, some of the blacks' objections to the media are imagined slights. In view of the history of past transgressions and the lack of understanding on the part of many blacks about how the media work, any mistreatment is apt to be regarded as evidence of discrimination.

But the impact of the imagined slights can be reduced if the media initiate, and the black community responds to, a closer association between the reporters and their black news sources. Many organizations, both political and private, exploit the news media to achieve their particular ends. More white organizations than black know how to prepare and distribute a press release, know whom to contact if they have a story they want told, know how to present a story to the news organization, know what deadlines must be met, and know the terms on which they can deal with the news media. Because of the heritage of segregation and the past practice of the white press to ignore blacks, however, this kind of public relations capability has not developed in the black community to the same extent that it has in the white community. Yet the media rely on such efforts by non-media organizations. Black coverage deserves the same advantages.

At least two things can be done. First, there must be a conscious recognition of this condition by the media. To achieve balanced surveillance, they must compensate for this lack of public relations know-how among black organizations in their own community by inviting representatives of the organizations to attend seminars designed to instruct them in the methods of obtaining publicity: Whom do you call when you have something you think is newsworthy? How do you present if? How far in advance must the particular media organization be notified? What kinds of things make news?

At the same seminar, the media should advise the Negroes candidly about the problems of the news organization. The media should: (1) explain why only a small part of the information or material gathered can be printed or broadcast each day; (2) invite them to inquire about reports which they believe treated them unfairly and be prepared to offer explanations; (3) indicate that they cannot promise everything reported about the Negroes will be good, but that they will make a sincere effort to be fair; (4) instruct them in the methods by which they can provide information to the media without fear of being quoted, e.g., background briefings, off-the-record statements, not for direct-attribution statements. In short, the media should instruct Negroes in the methods of using the media to that extent necessary to place them on an equal footing with other organizations and news sources in the community.

Such an approach would help establish an integrated perspective on society. Integrated employment in news organizations would also help.

4. Integrated Newsrooms

Most city rooms and broadcast studios a decade ago were almost totally white, and it has caused apprehension on the part of the Negro community. In the mid-1950's, it was very difficult to find a black face in the American press corps. Progress did not begin until the approach of the sixties, although the motive was more a desire for integration by progressive editors than a desire to develop pipelines into the Negro community. Blacks were hired as reporters, not as black reporters.[39]

By 1964, not much progress had been achieved. The American Newspaper Guild could name only 45 Negroes working as reporters, copyreaders, or deskmen on metropolitan daily newspapers in the United States. At best, not more than 100 Negroes had such jobs, yet the U. S. Bureau of Census estimated 50,000 jobs of the kind described.[40]

In 1967, the Kerner Commission found that fewer than five percent of the news editorial employees in the United States were Negroes. Fewer than one percent of the editors and supervisors were Negroes, and most of those worked for Negro-owned organizations. A poll in 1968, sponsored by Columbia University and B'nai B'rith, found that Negroes—who represent over 11 percent of the nation's population—constitute 4.2 percent of all news media editorial employees. The highest percentage of Negro employees were reported by magazines—an average of 5.1 percent, and the lowest by radio and television stations and network respondents—2.7 percent.

C. Sumner Stone, the first Negro television news commentator, began in 1965 with a daily news-analysis program. Today, according to a *Newsweek* survey: "The 5 to 7 p.m. time slot hardly looks like an NAACP convention, but nearly every metropolitan area outside the South is kept informed by at least one Negro newsman."[41]

The major networks declined to give their statistics to the Columbia study group; but their replies to the Violence Commission showed their employment of Negroes to be considerably higher than this 2.7 percent figure for industry, generally.[42] The employment by the three commercial networks is:

	Professional Negroes (percent)	Nonprofessional non-white (percent 3.9)
ABC	3.9	10.2
CBS	4.5	15.7
NBC	4.0	8.6

Many of the non-white professionals have been hired during the last year. For example, of the 29 professional Negroes employed by NBC in both their network radio and TV news operations, seventeen have been hired within the last year, 25 within the last two years—only four have been with the network for more than two years.

In addition, the networks have made an effort to improve the number of their representatives from minority groups. NBC has a news-writing program in which twelve nonwhites have been enrolled, and has made a commitment to train a total of 21 minority group members at a total cost of $127,551 annually. ABC's professional and technical trainee programs for Negroes began on July 1, 1968, with four Negroes enrolled by September 1968. The unions primarily involved in television work—AFTRA, SAG, Writer's Guild, and Director's Guild—have stated their complete willingness to cooperate. CBS initiated its first training program last year.

Several individual stations surveyed by the Mass Media Task Force of the Violence Commission have either started special training programs for

Negroes or have emphasized Negro recruitment for regular employment or management training programs. These efforts include WLWT's (Cincinnati) training program for "hard-core" unemployed, KFMB's (San Diego) on-the-job training program for minority group members, and its junior year internship for a student from Hampton Institute in Virginia.

A number of stations have cooperated with local schools and universities by offering use of staff and equipment for Radio-TV courses. WSAV-TV (Savannah) took the initiative in requesting the state Department of Education to establish Radio-TV vocational training programs and offered to donate $100,000 in equipment to encourage the program. Two stations, KAKE-TV (both Wichita), cooperate in an explorer scout TV training program in which young men produce, sell time, and air six variety programs. Twenty-nine Negro employees work at WRC-TV and radio, an NBC owned and operated station in Washington, D.C., and contrary to the findings of the survey reported in the *Columbia Journalism Review,* a number of stations employ seven to twenty Negroes—with a number of these in editorial positions.

However, stations in two cities with high concentrations of minorities—Mexican-Americans in San Diego and Negroes in Savannah—showed practically no representation from these groups among their station personnel. In Savannah, WTOC-TV employed one Negro, WSAV-TV four. In San Diego, the record was a little better; two stations, KOGO-TV and KEBS-TV, employed one Mexican-American each; KFMB-TV had two, and KCST-TV kept no records. By contrast, television and radio stations in Washington, D.C. reported high employment of minority group members, including Spanish-Americans and Orientals.

The Columbia University survey of the news media showed that newspapers reporting in their nationwide survey had an average of 4.7 percent Negro editorial employees. *The Washington Post,* one of the Commission's survey papers, listed the largest proportion of Negro employees among newspapers: 388 Negroes, including 50 editorial employees, out of a total of 1850 employees—20.9 percent. At the other end of the spectrum, the *Evening Tribune* of San Diego and the *Cincinnati Enquirer* each reported only one professional Negro on its staff.

One constant theme expressed by the journalists is that the media do not need journalists on welfare to cover poverty, segregationists to cover the Klan, policemen to cover the police beat, or black journalists to cover black news. Some news organizations, such as the ABC network, have integrated crews and refuse to cover an event if being black is a prerequisite for admission. What these journalists suggest is that the media need educated, sophisticated, imaginative, and aware journalists to cover the whole of society.

But this does not mean that there is no need to make a special effort to recruit Negroes and members of other minority groups. It should be done because it is right, and also because it is beneficial to the news organization, which will then be better able to achieve perspective on their community if they are in daily contact with peers who are black. In the process of associating on the job with members of the black community, news staffs will become more sensitive to minority issues and take one more step toward balanced reporting. Like many Americans traveling to Southeast Asia who cannot distinguish between Vietnamese, Thais, Chinese, and Cambodians, many white American newsmen cannot distinguish between the various shades of militancy and philosophy of the blacks. Only by prolonged association can they begin to achieve the necessary skill and insight.

Moreover, the very presence of black reporters in a news organization helps allay the antipathy of some blacks toward the media. This aversion is approaching serious proportions. Recently Karl Fleming observed:

> Personally, I feel a kind of despair because I see the day coming when it may become impossible for the white press and for me as an agent thereof to cover this story. The last time around was bad enough. But I think this hostility has reached the point where in some places and certainly in some organizations, it has become absolutely impossible for a white reporter to even get in and find out what's going on.[43]

Greater use may have to be made of black reporters to cover some black stories than their numbers would dictate. But it is an undesirable practice. The sooner the news media succeed in gaining the perspective required to cover the ghetto the way they do the rest of the community, and the sooner they establish the same close relationship with their black news sources as they have with white institutions, the sooner the reporter's color will not matter. The media cannot complain about restrictions on white reporters until they have developed reporters capable of covering the black community as well as they do the white community.

Reporting black news should not be the only assignment of the black reporter, however. Equally important is to have him cover events in which whites or mixed groups are involved. If the black reporter's perspective is limited only to those experiences gained in the black community, the reporting he produces is just as likely to be distorted as that of the white reporter ignorant of the black community.

In one respect black reporters are probably clearly more qualified to serve as a conduit for intergroup communication than their white counterparts. The essential requirement of the reporter who is to serve this function is familiarity with both communities. Blacks are more knowledgeable about the white community than whites are about the black community.

5. What Facts Are Significant?

Beyond integrating their news staffs and their perspective on the community, news organizations can do much individually or collectively to expand their awareness of the communication needs of the community they serve. The first step would be to study the communication gap between the various groups in the community. Useful lessons can be drawn from a study, such as recently commissioned by WFBM-TV in Indianapolis, Indiana.[44] Taking a representative sample of 400 Negro and 400 white households, the survey explored a wide range of subjects and issues: the social and economic characteristics of the black and white communities, black militancy; the relative concern with the quality of municipal services, neighborhood conditions, housing, employment, education, police relations; attitudes toward civil rights and civil unrest; and finally, the role of television in the community. Not surprisingly, white and black perceptions of the same issues differed widely in several instances.

In another example noted earlier, the Louis Harris survey found that 49 percent of Negroes and only eight percent of whites thought police brutality was a significant factor in Negro rioting. The two groups obviously have somewhat different perceptions of the problem—probably because, until relatively recently, the white press largely ignored instances of police brutality. This suggests why, on the one hand, the white community does not see police brutality as significant, and why, on the other hand—because many of the targets of police brutality have been Negroes and the vehicle for communicating such "news" within the black community has been word of mouth—the black community will tend to exaggerate the extent and ferocity of police brutality. The solution to this disparity in perception is for the media to cover, regularly and systematically, incidents that may involve police misconduct in the black community. This approach will increase the awareness of the white community, and, as the media become credible with the black community, it will provide through formal channels of communication a more accurate portrayal of the extent of the problem, and thus displace rumors as the main source of information.

Consider also the following example of what can be done with a straight news story reported by Martin Hayden, editor-in-chief of the *Detroit News:*

> . . . [A] few years ago, a police sergeant in the traffic division was murdered by a Negro at one of the exit ramps of the Edsel Ford Expressway. This occurred during one of those summer periods of tension, and thoughtful community leaders were severely troubled by the possibility of racial explosion. Two exacerbating factors were at work on the community. On the one hand, there was a conviction among too many whites that a largely "criminal" Negro population was carrying its war against the police to the point where all Negroes condoned Negro lawlessness and where no Negro would cooperate with police efforts to catch a Negro ciminal. At the opposite pole, there was the too general opinion among Negroes that brutality was the rule of the Detroit Police Department, that any Negro in police hands was lucky to emerge alive and whole. The tragic death of the police sergeant was to disprove both points.
>
> The officer had chased a reckless driver up the ramp from the expressway. As he was being questioned, the driver suddenly lunged at the officer, pulled his service revolver from its holster, knocked the policeman down with one shot, shot him several more times as he lay on the ground, and then fled.
>
> Officers answering radio calls in the largely Negro neighborhood found an abundance of Negro witnesses, who described the killer and gave the license number of his car. Within an hour, officers were at the killer's house. At the door, they were met by the killer's wife, whose initial question was, "Is the policeman dead?" The police found the dead officer's service revolver under the killer's bed.

Here was a "cop killer" caught immediately after the event by the dead officer's friends and colleagues. In another era, he might have been taken away in a morgue wagon, his peremptory execution masked by a claim that he resisted arrest. But it didn't happen. He was delivered to the station unmarked, and at no time thereafter was there any defense claim that he was mistreated.

All these details were reported in the following morning's newspaper. The key facts—that Negro witnesses brought about the quick arrest and that all the civil rights of the accused were protected by the arresting officers—stood as editorial contradiction of the preachments of racial extremists, both white and black.[45]

The *Detroit News* has also tried to deal with Negro concern over police brutality by reporting the number of cases in which police officers have killed people: Three in 1962; four in 1963; six in 1964; and, at that time, eight in 1965—six of the men killed were white and two were Negroes.[46] Addressing themselves to the concern of the white community and their frequent indictment of Negroes as criminals and fear that the streets are unsafe, the *Detroit News* emphasized other statistics:

> ... that most crimes are nonracial—that is, Negroes commit crimes against Negroes, and whites against whites—and that an even greater percentage of killings result from family quarrels or arguments, usually drunken, between people who know each other. We point out that such crimes are beyond preventive action by the police and could not be averted if there were an officer on permanent station in every block.[47]

Another major concern of many middle-class whites is that the integration of their neighborhood will have a depressing effect on home property values; this concern intensifies when a black attempts to move into a white neighborhood. At least three newspapers around the country have assigned reporters to do an in-depth investigation of the effect of integration on property values. Juanita Green of the *Miami Herald* went to the county records to find out what had happened to the price level of homes in newly integrated neighborhoods. She found that they had either remained stable or risen.[48] Such reporting won't make the bigot welcome a newly arrived black neighbor, but the elimination of such myths should make it easier for some and force others to confront their own consciences.

> For newspapers and broadcasting, as for other segments of society, it was clear that, however the racial crisis would be handled, it would not be unbiased. In fact, because the mass media catch the society in a magnified and concentrated form, the editor who bemuses himself with the notion he is unbiased can only contribute to the confusion. If we have learned nothing else in the last ten years, certainly we have seen that the man who says, "I treat everybody alike, regardless of race, creed, or color, on a first-come, first-serve basis," is either a fool or a knave. The *differences* between people—and what we do about them—are what this racial crisis is all about.[49]

Reporting which values and those facts which dispel illusions contrasts radically with the "we are-mirrors-of-society" theory of journalism. It is a conscious selection of the information that enables the people to function more knowledgeably and more rationally in discharging their obligations as citizens in a democracy.

REFERENCES

1. "Of Black America: CBS News Special" Broadcast Tuesday, July 2, 1968, 10-11 p.m., e.d.t.
2. Gordon Allport, *The Nature of Prejudice.* (Cambridge, Mass: Wesley Pub. Co., 1954)
3. Theodore Peterson, "Magazine Content: The Nude in 'Jubilee' and Other Pleasures," Speech at School of Journalism, University of Minnesota, Minneapolis, April 16, 1968, p. 4.
4. Ralph McGill, *The Black American and the Press,* Jack Lyle, ed. (Los Angeles: Ward Ritchie Press: 1968), p. 29.
5. George P. Hunt, Managing Editor of *Life,* "The Racial Crisis and the News Media: An Overview," in *Race and The News Media* Paul L. Fisher and Ralph Lowenstein, ed., (New York: Anti-Defamation League of B'nai B'rith, 1067), p. 12.
6. Wendell Philips Garrison and Francis Jackson Garrison, *William Lloyd Garrison: The Story of His Life Told by His Children,* Vol. 1 (New York: The Century Co., 1885), p. 200.
7. Vernon L. Parrington, "The Romantic Revolution in America," *Main Currents in American Thought,* II (New York: Harcourt, Brace & Co. 1927), p. 356.
8. George P. Hunt, *op. cit.* footnote 5, p. 13.
9. *Ibid,* pp. 13-14.
10. *Ibid,* p. 14.
11. Armistead S. Pride, in Lyle *op.cit.* footnote 4 pp.3–4.
12. Henry Lee Moon, "Beyond Objectivity: The Fighting Press," in Fisher and Lowenstein, *op. cit.* footnote 5 pp.137.
13. Ted Poston, "The American Negro and Newspaper Myths," *Ibid.* p. 65.
14. *Ibid.* pp. 64-65.
15. *Ibid.* p. 66.
16. Moon, *op. cit.* footnote 12, pp. 135-36.
17. Lyle, *op. cit.* footnote 4, p. xii-xiv.
18. William B. Monroe, Jr. "Television: The Chosen Instrument of the Revolution," in Lyle, *op. cit.* footnote 5, p. 85.
19. Hodding Carter, in Lyle, *op. cit.* footnote 4, p. 38.
20. Louis E. Lomax, *The Negro Revolt* (New York: Signet, 1963), pp. 92-93.
21. Joseph L. Brechner, "Were Broadcasters Color Blind," in Lyle, *op. cit.* footnote 5, p. 99.
22. Poston, *op. cit.,* footnote 13, p. 66.
23. Carter, *op. cit.* footnote 19, p. 49.
24. Monroe, *op. cit.* footnote 18, p. 84.
25. *Ibid.* p. 86.
26. Karl Fleming, in Lyle, *op. cit.* footnote 4, p. 30.
27. *Ibid.*
28. Poston, *op. cit.* footnote 13, pp. 66-67.
29. William Rivers and Wilbur Schramm, *Responsibility in Mass Communication,* rev. ed. (New York: Harper and Row), p. 185.
30. Quoted by Hunt, *op. cit.* footnote 5, p. 15.
31. New York city ghetto News science project. 32.
32. Lomax, *op. cit.* footnote 20, pp. 181-182.
33. *The Autobiography of Malcolm X* (New York: The Grove Press, 1964) pp. 236-238.
34. *Ibid;* Stokely Carmichael and Charles V. Hamilton, *Black Power: The Politics of Liberation in America* (New York: Vintage Books 1967).
35. Rivers and Schramm, *op. cit.* footnote 29, p. 149.

36. Leslie Sargent, Wiley Carr, and Elizabeth McDonald, "Significant Coverage of Integration by Minority Group Magazines," *Journal of Human Relations,* Vol. 14, No. 4 (Fourth Quarter, 1965).

37. Fleming *op. cit.* footnote 4, p. 31.

38. Douglass Cater, *The Fourth Branch of Government* (New York: Vintage Books, 1959) p. 55. The passages which follow indicate that the self-censorship may cover a range of subjects: "Senators have been seen to stagger drunkenly onto the Senate floor and deliver unintelligible harangues without creating a ripple in the press. Considering the great glare of publicity that beats down on Congress, the unillumined corners are the more curious.

   This protectionism even covers some of the collective activities of Congress. Year in and year out minor frauds on the public understanding are committed without being duly noted by the press. Each year, for example, the House Appropriation Committee or one of its subcommittees virtuously makes deep cuts in appropriations bills for funds already contractually obligated. Each year this action is duly rewarded by newspaper accounts that the Committee has 'slashed' the budget by such and such an amount. And later each year the Committee quietly restores the cut in its 'supplemental' appropriations. Yet, one reporter told me, though tempted he wouldn't dare lead his story with the fact that 'the congressmen have made this cut with the full expectation, as in former years, of restoring it later in the Session when the public isn't looking.' pp. 55-56.

39. Martin S. Hayden, Editor in Chief, The Detroit News, "A View From Detroit," *The Media and the Cities* (Charles N. Daly, Ed.) (Chicago: Chicago University Press, 1968), p. 64.

40. Fisher and Lowenstein, *op. cit.,* footnote 5, p. 8.

41. Quoted by Woody Klein, "The New Revolution: A Postscript," in Fisher and Lowenstein, *op. cit.* footnote 5, p. 158.

42. Additional data are provided in Appendix II-G

43. Fleming in Lyle, *op. cit.,* footnote 4.

44. Preliminary survey report sponsored by WFBM-TV Indianapolis, and performed by Frank Magid and Associates.

45. Hayden, *op. cit.* footnote 39, pp. 28-29. 46.

46. *Ibid.* p. 31. 47.

47. *Ibid.*

48. See testimony of Norman Isaacs at NCCPV hearings, Dec. 18, 1968, transcript, p. 184.

49. Lawrence S. Fanning, "The Media: Observer or Participant?" in Fisher and Lowenstein, *op. cit.* footnote 5, pp. 107-108.

Chapter 5

THE MARKETPLACE MYTH:
ACCESS TO THE MASS MEDIA

To give the news impartially, without
fear or favor, regardless of any party,
sect or interest involved.

—Credo of *New York Times*,
August 19, 1896

The First Amendment presupposes that right
conclusions are more likely to be gathered
out of a multitude of tongues than through
any kind of authoritative selection. To
many this is, and always will be, folly; but
we have staked upon it our all.

—Judge Learned Hand,
United States v. *Associated Press*,
52 F. Supp. 362 (S.D. N.Y.) (1943)

It is the purpose of the First Amendment to
preserve an uninhibited marketplace of ideas
in which truth will ultimately prevail,
rather than to countenance monopolization
of that market, whether it be by the Government
itself or a private licensee.

—Mr. Justice White,
Red Lion Broadcasting Co. Inc.,
v. *Federal Communications
Commission, 89S. Ct. 1794
(1969).*

Unbalanced and inaccurate surveillance of minority groups is not
solely the product of the nation's segregationist heritage. Negroes,
Mexican-Americans, Japanese, Chinese-Americans, and Indians have more
difficulty securing media access than white Americans; yet another barrier
exists, this one more from an ideological than from a racist heritage. The

outstanding characteristics of ideas that have difficulty gaining access are that they are new, that their proponents lack prominence by traditional media standards, and that they threaten the values of the social group to which the broadcaster or publisher belongs. In the last fifteen years, substantial progress has been made toward providing more coverage of the activities—demonstrations and protests—of minority groups and marginal progress in coverage of their ideas. What is needed, however, is more attention to minority views and less attention to the physical dramatization of conflicting ideas.

Much of the American first amendment tradition and philosophy is founded, as we have seen, on the 18th century libertarian's assumption of how the press would function in the search for truth and reason. A press unfettered by government, the libertarian believed, would create a marketplace of ideas similar to the classical economist's marketplace for goods and services. This kind of marketplace, the theory ran, would produce truth in much the same way Adam Smith's classical economics market assured the optimum allocation of goods and services. So long as men were reasonable, and a majority honest, the speculations and abuses of the few would be more than offset by the majority. Truth, justice, and a rational world would inevitably emerge.

Like Adam Smith's marketplace for products, however, certain conditions must be met before the marketplace of ideas can function according to theory. In Smith's marketplace, there had to be a sufficient number of sellers and purchasers that none could affect price; as a corollary, Smith's theory abhors monopolies or conspiracies in restraint of trade. Similarly, one of the underlying assumptions of a smoothly functioning marketplace of ideas is the equal opportunity to take ideas to the public. No control should prevail over access to the marketplace. The government has dealt with monopolization of goods and services through the antitrust laws. There is some evidence the courts are moving toward a theory of the first amendment that will allow the government to act to prevent monopolization in the distribution of ideas. Whether the government acts and how much it does will depend largely on how serious the problem becomes.

In 1790, The United States had a total of eight daily newspapers and 83 weeklies. When the Constitution was adopted, 97 percent of the population lived in places so small that they were not even called towns. Of the remaining three percent, most lived in towns whose populations were under 25,000—most only a few thousand. Under these conditions, the individual could make his opinions known by giving a speech on Sunday outside the local church or by getting a printer to put up a broadside and by posting it in taverns and in other public gathering spots around town. With relative ease he could have an impact.

Today, unless the individual has access to formal channels of communication, it is almost impossible for him to have an impact. His ability to communicate widely is extremely limited. As a minimum, an effective marketplace requires access on approximately equal terms by all those with messages. Long ago, perhaps, a newspaper might have been started with relatively little capital by one whose views were strong enough to demand that they be aired. Even today, it is probably possible to blanket a city the size of Washington, D.C., with a four-page broadside for about $1,500.

Sometimes, television, radio, and newspaper advertising space can be purchased to carry a non-commercial message. These are communication outlets, but obviously they are not available to all; for many, they would be less than adequate.

Access to the American public for the message bearer is limited by both mechanical and human constraints. Present mechanical limitations of the media make it impossible for more than a fraction of the potential communications to be carried to society at large. Existing newspapers, magazines, radio and television stations, and other media in this country could not possibly simultaneously accommodate the individual views of the 125 million Americans over the age of eighteen. Obviously, there is neither sufficient space nor time.

Mechanical limitations lead to human limitations. Because the media cannot carry all of the messages, someone must select and reject. The process of selection thus becomes a limitation of critical importance, and the media owners and gatekeepers are the first barriers to media access.

Under the traditional view of the first amendment, the role of the gatekeeper and the right of the owner to choose, are plenary. It makes no difference whether the choice is representative or honest, or whether it meets the public's requirements for information.

The nation's broadcasters, publishers, and editors decide who shall have the opportunity to be heard—an understandable and pragmatically necessary process. But, with the present structure of the communication business, it results in a marketplace far different from the 18th century concept of a marketplace for ideas. The ultimate barrier to communication is, of course, the audience. The significance of that barrier depends in part on how media operators choose to present the news. That the media print or broadcast a message does not guarantee that the audience will pay attention or will retain the message. Yet here, too, the media have some control.

A. Access: The News Media Audience

Although the audience is at the end of the communication process, its role as a barrier to new ideas is more conveniently discussed first because audience characteristics that impede communication are also operative, in varying degrees, on newsmen.

There has always been a tendency among journalists to regard the bulk of their audience as not very bright.[3] This makes it relatively easy to excuse themselves of all responsibility when the message is garbled. In theory, the journalist is a professional and the audience is his client. In fact, most newsmen know very little about their audience except that it includes their editors and publishers, their friends and neighbors, and their peers. Moreover, few seem to have any serious desire to learn much about their larger audience. If they devoted more attention to the needs of their real clients, the public, it would become clear that to an important degree journalists must share responsibility when messages don't get through.

Audiences tend to expose themselves to media messages that support their predispositions. A study by Wilbur Schramm and Richard Carter, for example, found that Republicans are approximately twice as likely as

Democrats to watch a Republican-sponsored telecast. While those opposed to a particular view have a tendency to avoid such material, the great bulk of what passes for "news" in the modern media is not labeled pro-Republican, pro-Democrat, nor is it attached to any other ideology. The opportunity for selection is far less in the case of news. Moreover, in such media as radio and television, which are linear and fugitive, the opportunity for selective exposure on hard news programs is practically nil. If a viewer watches the news—and two-thirds of Americans regard television as their most important news source—it is difficult for him to avoid a particular segment; his choice is limited to turning the set off. Regular viewers of news programs can be expected, therefore, to receive exposure to almost everything that is broadcast. The decision whether or not to watch a particular documentary program is more likely to be made on the basis of the issue, than on the point of view presented. Again, the opportunity for selective exposure is very low.

In contrast to television hard news programs, a newspaper story is regarded as highly successful if it is read by 30 percent of the audience. Newspaper stories presented without any predictable slant, however, cannot be sorted on the basis of the reader's predispositions. Selection, like the documentary, will be subject oriented. On the editorial page, when the reader is familiar with the publisher's position on various issues, selective exposure will be operative.

The second characteristic that may distort the media's message is selective perception. Some people go to incredible lengths to assimilate information in a manner that supports their personal prejudices.[6] A group of subjects shown a subway poster portraying a Caucasian, a Negro, and an Oriental, and labeled, "It Takes All Kinds of People to Make a City Run," will tend to interpret the poster to fit their attitudes on racial equality. Those believing in equality tend to see the poster as a strong appeal for racial tolerance; those not supporting equality more frequently interpreted the poster as suggesting a city needs Negro garbage men, maids, and Chinese laundries. To prejudiced subjects, it is obvious that by performing these functions, members of these minority groups could be good citizens.

It does not follow, of course, that it is pointless to report facts that do not support public preconceptions. That, in any given instance, part of the audience may misinterpret the message only suggests that the media cannot change attitudes instantly. A member of the National Mobilization Committee has stated: that the amazing aspect of the audience response to television coverage of the Chicago disorders at the Democratic convention was not that 70 percent of the American people were sympathetic toward the police; rather it was that 20 percent thought the police were wrong. Changing attitudes to conform with changes in reality is a slower process that some believe, but the news media must continue to report reality, regardless of how comfortably it fits audience illusions or desires. Every idea begins as a minority point of view.

Like selective exposure and perception, selective retention is also governed by audience predispositions.[7] In one instance, shortly after President Kennedy was elected, two groups of college students were asked to read an article favorable to the President-elect. The pro-Kennedy students learned the material sooner than the anti-Kennedy students.

A third characteristic of audience communication behavior suggesting limitations on the ability of the media to change opinions was well documented for the first time during an investigation of voting behavior in the 1940 election.[8] Many voters who had changed their positions indicated the change was primarily influenced by other people, not the mass media. An attempt was made to identify such people and they were labeled "opinion leaders."[9] Additional studies, involving drug buying by doctors [10] and adaption of new agricultural techniques,[11] have been made on the interplay between media, opinion leaders, and their followers. Many of these studies also found that opinion leaders paid far more attention to the mass media than did their followers. People who are not influenced directly by the media are influenced by those who are. A second consideration, which indicates that this phenomenon is not as limiting a factor as some seem to believe,[12] is that in most of the studies, relatively immediate action was sought on the issue involved. Under such circumstances, the role of opinion leaders will be substantially greater.[13] This finding is consistent with Shibutani's conclusion that rumors are more carefully scrutinized when immediate action is required.[14] The implication is that, where no immediate action is required, as in the vast majority of news reports, the cause-and-effect relationship is more likely to be direct and, concomitantly, the mediating role of opinion leaders is less.[15] It also suggests that laboratory experiments that require immediate action—e.g., answering questions—would tend to have an inherent bias toward findings that the influence of the media is less than it would be in a more natural setting.

Another relevant fact is that there are not merely two classes of people—those who support a particular point of view and those who oppose it. Ordinarily, on any issue, opinion ranges from strong supporters to strong opponents, and somewhere in the middle are those who have not made up their minds. Evidence also exists that the processes of selective exposure, perception, and retention do not operate on "new" issues.[16] Thus, the media have more effect on whether to deploy ABM's than on the desirability of prohibition legislation.

Similarly, media messages are more likely to influence audience opinions on such issues as student disorders where people have few preconceptions than they are on such issues as national elections, where audiences already may have developed strong opinions. To be sure, audiences may have some general predispositions about young people, about how an educational institution should be run, and about the role of faculty, administration, and students in the decisionmaking process. But on a new issue, these broader attitudes may conflict. For example, a person could believe that university faculties and administrators are eggheads in an ivory tower who do not prepare young people to function in the outside world, and the same person could simultaneously believe that law, order, and property are sacred values. If, on the one hand, the information presented in the media emphasizes the students' desire for courses more closely related to their needs after graduation—e.g., at Howard Law School recently, students thought that more emphasis should be put on poverty law than international law—then the reader or viewer might very well sympathize with the students. If, however, the emphasis is placed upon conflict, violence, and destruction of property, an individual holding these conflicting views might oppose the students because, even when there is some small mention in the news account of the inadequacy of the curriculum, he would be opposed to violence. Among audience members who rank order and obedience to the law high in their system of values, media emphasis on the disruptive and unlawful aspects of dissent impedes the communication of minority views. In addition, at least one study suggests that messages that produce a high level of anxiety—as messages with a high quantum of violence are apt to do—tend to communicate less effectively.[17] Messages that disturb the audience and offer no solution may be ignored altogether.[18]

Neither the studies referred to in this chapter, nor, indeed, all the audience studies available are likely to provide complete answers to the question of how the journalist can overcome audience bias and get his message through the way he intended it. Most of these studies are unrelated to this issue. They were attempts to study voting behavior, or the effectiveness of propaganda, or training films, etc. There is, however, remarkably little evidence that practicing journalists are even interested in what information is available. At the least, schools of communication and journalism, as the repository of intellectual talent, could contribute by exploring the problem more fully and preparing a generation of journalists who regard distorting audience characteristics as a barrier to the effective communication that can be lowered through the reasoned application of research findings.

B. Access: The Newsman's Perspective

> The ability to present news objectively and to interpret it realistically is not a native instinct in the human species; it is a product of culture which comes with the knowledge of the past and acute awareness of how deceptive is our normal observation and how wishful our thinking.
>
> —Walter Lippmann

The audience is neither the first nor the most important barrier to access. The newsman's perspective is relevant in at least two respects. First, to the extent that it is responsible for not reporting or biased reporting of the events that frequently give rise to dissent, it creates the need for access. Second, it is an obstacle to the presentation of views by those who are unhappy with the status quo, and when dissidents do secure media coverage, it is only a partial cure because the technique for gaining access (demonstrations and other forms of protest) is frequently emphasized at the expense of the ideas for which access is sought.

Consider the following accounts of the same event:

STUDENT PICKETS
MARCH IN CAPITAL

Washington (AP)—Students picketing for peace marched four abreast in spring-like weather to Arlington National Cemetery Saturday, demonstrating their hopes for disarmament and an end to nuclear testing.

STUDENT MARCH ON CAPITAL
TINGED BY BEARDED BEATNICKS

By Robert E. Baskin, Washington Bureau of the *News.* Washington—Left-wing student peace marchers—with a definite beatnik tinge—marched through the streets of the capital Saturday on a pilgrimage to the Tomb of the Unknown Soldier in Arlington National Cemetery.

The first story was written by the Associated Press, the second by Robert E. Baskin, Washington bureau chief of the *Dallas News.*[19] In each case, it appears the reporters were simply holding up Clifton Daniel's mirror.

Selective exposure, perception, and retention not only affect the audience; they also affect the newsman. Like their audience, journalists bring their own set of preconceptions to their craft, preconceptions produced by their environment, their position in the community, their business relationships, and the requirement that they earn a profit. The biases are both conscious and unconscious. In both cases, however, the remedies are the same: acknowledge the problem exists and, through a combination of conscious effort, changed perspective, and new institutional arrangements, work toward the elimination of systematic distortion.

A gatekeeper is any person who is so situated in the news gathering and disseminating process that he has control over the content and form of the news. Although the term has been applied to news sources, in this chapter it is used exclusively to refer to media personnel.

One of the earliest gatekeeper studies was performed by David Manning White and reported in 1950.[20] It was the examination of the editor of a newspaper with about 30,000 circulation in a midwestern community of about 100,000 population, whose job was to select material from the wire services for the front page. During the week analyzed, Mr. Gates (a pseudonymn) used approximately 10 percent of the 12,400 column inches received from the three wire services.

The 56 phrases he used in justifying rejection of material divided into two main categories: the story was unworthy of being reported (423 rejections), and the selection from many reports of the same event (910 rejections).

One rejected story had the notation, "he's too red." Another was marked, "Never use this"; it dealt with Townsend Plan, which Mr. Gates felt was of doubtful desirability. Another story was marked, "don't care for suicides."

One story on the trial of Cardinal Mindzenty was rejected with the notation "propaganda," it dealt with this statement by Samuel Cardinal Striech:

> It is very unfortunate that our news agencies are not giving their sources of information in their day by day reports on the trial of Cardinal Mindzenty. It should be made clear that restrictions have been made on a few American correspondents who have been present at the trial.[20a]

Mr. Gates, of course, had no way of knowing whether the story was true or false, but apparently resented the obvious implications of the quote, and decided his readers should not have the opportunity to exercise their independent judgment. The story was also rejected when received from the other two wire services.

These were isolated instances, but they do indicate this particular editor had some definite opinions on what news was fit to print based on something other than a neutral standard. In sum, approximately 16 pieces were rejected as "propaganda," the remainder were apparently rejected for reasons unrelated to content. Gates was found to be conservative both in his politics and his style. He consistently avoided sensationalism and insinuations. Professor White summarized:

> It is a well-known fact in individual psychology that people tend to perceive as true only those happenings which fit into their own beliefs concerning what is likely to happen. It begins to appear (if Mr. Gates is a fair representative of his class) that in his position as "gatekeeper" the newspaper editor sees to it (even though he may never be consciously aware of it) that the community shall hear as a fact only those events which the newsman, as a representative of his culture, believes to be true.[20b]

Louis Donohew approached the effect of publisher's opinions on news content from a different direction.[21] He attempted to measure publishers' attitudes, their perceptions of community opinion, and objective data on community conditions, on the content of the newspaper. He chose to examine Medicare, a subject of some salience in 1962, when it was debated before the Congress. He examined the issue during January, May, June, and July of 1962 in all the afternoon newspapers that subscribed to Associated Press in the State of Kentucky.

Beginning with the hypothesis that publishers would follow the journalist's credo that the publishers' opinions should be on the editorial page but not in the news columns,[22] Donohew examined the ratio of favorable to unfavorable paragraphs on Medicare carried by each paper, the total number of paragraphs on the issue, and the display of the Medicare stories both on page one and in other sections of the newspaper. If the hypothesis that the publishers' attitudes, perceptions of community opinion, or the actual economic conditions within the community had no effect upon the play of the story, then there would only be random correlations between the coverage and these three factors. At least two of these factors, it was found, were strongly correlated to the treatment of the story at a level well beyond coincidence.

The greatest single factor operating in the process of news selection was the publishers' attitudes toward Medicare. The publishers' perceptions of community opinion, e.g., how the community would have voted on the issue, were not significantly related to the coverage. In those communities that would apparently be in the greatest need of Medicare, the publishers seemed to be opposed to it. Newspapers that were more favorable to Medicare in most instances had publishers who favored Medicare and they usually supported it editorially. Generally, these were the papers with relatively greater circulation. They tended to serve urban communities with larger white collar populations, with fewer people receiving old age assistance, and with fewer people in the $3,000 or less income bracket, but with more doctors per thousand population. The contrary was found in papers that were less favorable to Medicare. Little or no relationship existed between coverage by the papers and the percentage of readers over the age of 65, the percentage of the vote given John F. Kennedy, the level of unemployment, or the level of education.

Systematic exclusion was approached from a third direction by Professor Warren Breed.[23] He compared the content of newspapers with community studies, by examining a book of cartoons rejected by popular publications and by interviewing newsmen.

The subject matter from the community studies was selected on the basis of Professor Breed's opinion of material that might be suppressed. Typically, Professor Breed's study shows that the media have a tendency not to report such items as: elite individuals or groups, usually business, gaining advantage in a privileged manner; negative aspects of religion, such as lack of piety or respect, by parishioners, discontent shown by the clergy, or "human weakness" in church relationships; doctors acting in a selfish, rather than a professional, fashion; national or community pride or integrity in question; shortcomings in mothers, judges, or other institutions which middle-class white society regards highly.

The power and class of favored individuals do not provide a complete explanation, however, because mothers, overseas GI's, members of churches, and unknown soldiers are not normally regarded as elite groups. The dominant cultural patterns and values also provide protection from media exposure. Values such as capitalism, the home, religion, health, justice, the nation, and the community, also receive favored treatment. Similarly, the media's reluctance to discuss social class or social inequality, as the antithesis of the American creed, indicates another bias favoring established values.

News may also be given play more or less depending upon its position in the newspaper. The front page is the prime time of daily newspapers. During the 1952 presidential campaign, Richard M. Nixon was charged with accepting $18,235 from some 76 California supporters. A study by Arthur Rowse indicates that many Republican papers placed the story on the back burner:

> Any review of the way thirteen evening papers displayed the Nixon story makes it clear that editors were in no hurry to get the news into the paper. They were even less enthusiastic about getting it onto the front page. Of the thirteen evening papers studied, only four put the story on the front page at the first opportunity on Thursday afternoon ... The four papers using the report on the front page included only one pro-Eisenhower paper, the *Chicago Daily News,* which spotted the newsworthiness of Peter Edson's column and played it up with a three-column headline on the first page ... Three other evening papers used the story the first day but buried it inside the paper. ... Five evening papers apparently did not use the Nixon story

in their editions of record until the next day ... One paper, the New York *Journal American,* could not find room on the front page for the story until Sunday, the fourth day the news was available.

Of the eighteen morning papers studied—all pro-Eisenhower on their editorial pages—only eight allowed the Nixon affair on the front page of their Friday editions of record. Of the remaining ten morning papers, seven used the story somewhere in their editions of record on Friday. But three omitted it entirely from the issues studied.[24]

Relations with the business community and the process of self-examination indicate a somewhat more conscious form of distortion. Ben Bagdikian has described it thus:

[Newspapers] are part of a Geneva Convention of Newspaper Warfare which provides that whatever else the parties may do, they shall not escalate their competition to the point where they shall first, expose each other's errors and omissions; second, write about the other's front office problems even if these affect the public welfare; and third, never disturb the business establishment.[25]

In 1966, the Bell-McClure syndicate offered serialization of Ralph Nader's book, *Unsafe at Any Speed,* to over 700 newspapers. None of them accepted.[26]

The *Jackson Clarion-Ledger* and *News* jointly owned newspapers in Jackson, Mississippi, were brought before the U.S. District Court on charges alleging violation of the federal laws barring overtime pay. A permanent injunction was issued barring continuation of the offending practices. Reporters from the Jackson papers were ordered to stay away from the court and they did. Not a single word appeared in any of the Jackson papers.[27]

Reporters Hank Messick and Jim Savage, of the *Boston Herald,* were told to stop inquiries concerning complicated stock transactions in Universal Marion Corporation in which Joseph Linsey had an interest. Mr. Linsey, a well-known Boston businessman and philanthropist, was president of a company that owned stock in the Herald-Traveler Corporation. Mr. Messick was subsequently dismissed and Mr. Savage quit after his request for "permission" from the *Herald* to interview Mr. Linsey was ignored.[28]

Frequently, distortion is the product of sloth and indifference. Provided the opportunity to get something for nothing, many newspapers take it. One editorial from the *Industrial News Review* in Portland, Oregon, was published in 59 newspapers. Distributed during the reign of Latin Dictator Trujillo, it began: "Today the Dominican Republic is a bulwark of strength against communism and has been widely cited as one of the cleanest, healthiest, happiest countries on the globe. The guiding spirit of this transformation has been Generalissimo Trujillo." The *Miami Herald* editorialized, "Somehow dahlias, daisies, pine trees, and 65° weather are not the picture that most people visualize when they think of the Dominican Republic, but yet this is what ..." And two weeks later in the *Hartford Courant,* "somehow dahlias, daisies, pine trees and 65° weather," etc. This editorial was supplied free of charge and was published in 59 newspapers with apparent disregard of whether it was based on truth or the Dominican Government's public relations program.[29]

Consider also the following coincidence: [30]

> Secretary of Interior Udall has become a symbol of the Kennedy Administration—arrogance coupled with overriding, zealous activity to run roughshod over private interests and spread Government control. He is a prime example of the danger of bestowing too much power on Government agencies . . . .
> —July 17, 1963, Republican
> Congressional Committee

> Secretary of Interior Stewart L. Udall has become the symbol of the New Frontier Administration—arrogance coupled with overriding, zealous activity to run roughshod over private interests and speed Government control of our lives and properties. He is a prime example of the danger of handling too much power . . . .
> —July 22, 1963, Item in
> *Delaware State News.*

William Allen White, former editor of the Kansas *Emporia Gazette,* expressed the problem this way:

> If he is a smart go-getting-up-and-coming publisher in a town of 100,000 to 1,000,000 people, the publisher associates on terms of equality with the bankers, the merchant princes, the manufacturers and the investment brokers. His friends unconsciously color his opinion. If he lives with them on any kind of social terms in the City club, he must more or less merge his views into the common views of the other capitalists. The publisher is not bought like a chattel. Indeed, he is often able to buy those who are suspected of buying him. But he takes the color of his social environment.
>
> He is pretty generally against organized labor. He is too often found opposing the government control of public utilities. He instinctively fears any regulation of the stock exchange. The right to strike seems to the rich publisher and his Chamber of Commerce friends to be sheer anarchy. It is inevitable that the managing editor and the editorial writers who want to hold their jobs take their professional views and get their professional slant from their boss, the man who signs the payroll check.
>
> So it often happens, alas too often, that a newspaper publisher, reflecting this unconscious class arrogance of the consciously rich, thinks he is printing news when he is doctoring it innocently enough. He thinks he is purveying the truth when much that he offers seems poison to hundreds of thousands of his readers who don't move in his social and economic stratosphere . . .
>
> The worst of it is that, bad as he is, the crookedest, rich, property minded publisher is vastly better than he would be if he was operating under a government-controlled press. For on seven sides out of ten,

the most prejudiced, unscrupulous publisher is fair and his columns in those areas are reasonably dependable. [31]

While this may overstate the case, if it is intended to apply to all publishers, it is still certainly true of too many today.

To the extent there is a trend, it appears that the direct influence of publishers in altering reporters' stories is declining. In the 1930's, Leo Rosten provided a questionnaire to be filled out anonymously by Washington correspondents. Among the statements on the questionnaire was "My orders are to be objective, but I *know* how my paper wants stories played." To this, more than 60 percent of the correspondents answered, "yes," indicating they felt some pressure to slant their dispatches in a manner consistent with their publisher's leanings. Another statement said "In my experience I have had stories played down, cut or killed for policy reasons." To this, slightly more than 55 percent wrote, "yes."

When the same questions were asked in the early 1960's, less than ten percent replied "yes, my orders are to be objective, but I *know* how my boss wants stories played," and only slightly over seven percent replied that stories had been killed, or played down for policy reasons. [32] Similarly, for hard network news programs and national newsmagazines, the evidence suggests that outside influence by advertisers or non-news network executives is practically nil.

While these findings on Washington correspondents may provide some comfort, the absence of pervasive publisher influence on Washington correspondents does not necessarily mean their brethren in other parts of the country fare as well. The Washington correspondents are, as a group, amongst the most able professionals in journalism. Their distance from the home office makes control more difficult, and their generally high level of competence gives them somewhat more independence than reporters of lesser recognized talent.

C. Access: News Media Structure and Competitive Practices

By the mid-20th century, the structure of the news media as we know it today was largely formed and is the structure with which we must begin our concern. The news media are represented by a multitude of individual examples, but with very few exceptions the major news media share common characteristics imposed by their common economic and business orientation.

Two characteristics stand out. First, many news media are sensitive to their need for large audiences to a degree individual members of their audience may find difficult to comprehend. Second, the media tend toward concentration of ownership, influence, and control, as do other major businesses.

1. The News Business

Much of the news media's close to neurotic response to criticism is owing to what Ben Bagdikian has described as the "built-in schizophrenia" of American journalism. The news media "have to be godless, profit-making corporations and, at the same time, be selfless community institutions devoted to the unbiased education of the public." This inner conflict of American journalism cannot be ignored.

The news media with the largest audiences—radio, television, newspapers, magazines—depend upon advertising revenues. The sums involved are large. Radio and television advertisers paid more than $3.2 billion in 1967 to present their products to the American public.[33] Newspaper publishers received more than $5 billion from their advertisers, and magazine publishers' advertising income equaled $1.3 billion. The media's advertising revenues have consistently represented 3.5 percent of consumer expenditures in the United States.[34]

Although the sums paid for advertising are high, the number of businesses that contributes these sums is relatively small. In 1967, 100 advertisers contributed 30 percent of all money spent on national advertising and 80 percent of the expenditure for national TV advertising. More than a fourth of TV advertising dollars was spent by the ten largest advertisers. This concentration in media spending by advertisers is matched by concentration in advertising-agency billings: 30 percent of total 1967 agency billings, and 46 percent of TV billings were placed by only ten agencies.[35]

No one denies that the media are generally very profitable, although exactly how profitable is a source of some dispute. Most consistently decline to disclose their finances. Federal Communications Commission data indicate that 1967 earnings before taxes for radio were approximately $80.8 million on revenues of $907.3 million.[36] Television earned pre-tax profits of $414.6 million on revenues of $2.3 billion.[37] Profits on television station operations average approximately 30 percent of gross revenues and about 16 percent for the three national networks.[38] The networks and their fifteen owned and operated stations earned $55.8 million on revenues of $953.3 million in 1967, down from earnings of $78.7 million on revenues of $903.9 million in 1966.[39] Earnings for fifteen network owned and operated stations were 39.6 percent of revenues.

Pre-tax earnings in 1967 of the TV networks and their fifteen owned and operated stations were $160.1 million on assets of $147.3 million, almost 109 percent return on book value of assets.[40]

The newspaper business, simply in terms of physical production of papers, is larger than most of the manufacturing industries in the nation's economy. The economic value of its production is greater than that of the drug industry or the meat products industry, and roughly equivalent to that of the petroleum refining industry.[41] Since World War II, the newspaper industry has grown substantially. The number of employees increased from less than 250,000 in 1946 to more than 350,000 in 1966, a rate of growth far greater than that of all manufacturing industries. Daily newspaper circulation now stands at more than 61.5 million compared to less than 51 million in 1946. Newspaper advertising revenues have increased about 400 percent since 1946. Although between 1950 and 1966 newspapers' share of total advertising has declined from 66.3 to 49.1 percent because of the growth of television, they continue to be the single largest advertising medium. This preeminent position of the newspapers in advertising is largely owing to their 61 percent share of the expenditures by local advertisers for local media.

Other indications of the growth of the newspaper industry since World

War II include an increase in the average number of pages in daily newspapers from 22 to 53, the increase in newsprint consumption from 3.5 to 9 million tons per year, and the increase in annual capital expenditures from $80 million to over $169 million.

Like television, the print media rank among the more profitable businesses in the United States. The print media, overall, earn about 18 percent on gross revenues.[42] Estimates for the average earnings of medium-sized and larger daily newspapers range up to 30 percent.

In these circumstances, it is not surprising that the media are frequently accused of paying too much attention to their advertisers and too little attention to the public who, if journalists are professionals, should be regarded as their clients.

Criticism of direct advertising pressures upon publishers is one of the most durable. It is personified in the snivelling publisher who kills the story of a department store owner's divorce under threat of losing the store's substantial advertising revenues. Evidence to prove that assertion is, however, in very short supply. Newsmen asked about it replied that a news operation is most vulnerable to advertising pressure when it is economically weak and, correspondingly, it is most able to resist pressure when it is strong. In a one-newspaper town, advertisers may be more subject to newspaper pressures than vice versa. In at least one instance, a daily newspaper published a list of companies whose news releases should not be printed because they do not advertise in the paper.[43] This, of course, is as objectionable as exercise of influence in the other direction.

On television news programs, direct influence by advertisers is essentially nonexistent. The case is somewhat different for documentaries. Here it appears primarily in terms of the choice of subjects for documentaries.

> Documentaries, however, are the most crucial part of the television journalism, because they provide the mass audience with the only kind of programming about vital issues in depth. There is abundant evidence that despite protestations about plenty of hard-hitting documentaries, the networks consistently shy away from subjects which will be unpopular, either by failing to attract large ratings and thus sponsor interest, or by alienating some section of the community.[44]

There are also exceptions among newspapers. On the afternoon of March 29, 1968, word was received at the copy desks of both afternoon Chicago papers that under no circumstances was the word "Carson's" to appear in the banner headline of the next edition. That was the afternoon of a large fire in a store owned by Carson Pirie Scott & Co. The explanation by the *Chicago Journalism Review:*

> Carson's is a big advertiser, and somebody in their advertising department might not like seeing the name of his institution in the bad company of other words like "fire," "ablaze," or "holocaust." Of course, maybe nobody cared particularly either, since it was a fact, and not even the advertising department could do anything about that. Newspapers, however, weren't about to take a chance on the latter.[45]

The report goes on to suggest that much of the coverage featuring clothes and fashion, travel, and business news is designed to keep advertisers happy—good news on these subjects deserves to be printed. "In contrast, Operation Breadbasket's boycott of A & P Food Stores was pointedly ignored by the downtown dailies—until young blacks tore through a North Side A & P."[46]

A similar motivation has been ascribed to the *Boston Globe* and the *Boston Traveler* decisions to print misleading weather information during the Easter shopping period.[47]

More important than the influence of particular advertisers is the effect of policies adopted to maximize profits. With high fixed costs, there is pressure to maintain the maximum possible audience.

For the print and electronic media, the cost of production has little correlation to circulation. If a newspaper or news magazine goes to the expense of gathering the news and selling and preparing the advertising messages to support it, the incremental cost of extra press runs is relatively low. The equipment is already there, and newsprint and ink costs for a medium-sized newspaper typically are about 26 to 28 percent of total expenses. For larger newspapers it is considerably lower. The pressure is greater for television. It costs television no more to produce a program whether 30 or 30 million people watch. Yet, the single most important measure of revenues will be the projected cost per thousand television households delivered. If enough viewers are delivered for the network to break even, additional viewers produce additional revenues at no additional cost. It is for this reason that the pressures on the news media to attract and maintain audience may seem quite out of proportion to small shifts in ratings or circulation. Although network news officials insist that a few points change in the ratings are not important to them, an examination of the emphasis placed on news program ratings in the trade press and institutional advertisements in magazines like *Broadcasting* strongly suggests otherwise.[48]

The accusation has frequently been made that the news media cater to the lowest common denominator in public taste. Very few critics—none so far as we know—have undertaken to explain how news executives determine what appeals to the lowest common denominator. It is simply one of those clichés that have gained acceptance among those who think the media should meet their particular standards. Certainly, if "lowest common denominator" means that the media appeal solely to the uneducated, they are wrong. Were this so, the majority of educated Americans would turn to smaller circulation media—as many of those at the top of the educated spectrum have done.

More likely, the effect is for the media to present material of the broadest possible appeal, necessarily aiming at middle America. It is also true that the same high premium is placed on not offending any significant segment of the audience.[49] It is this requirement that makes it more difficult for new ideas to gain access and limits reporting on those conditions which give rise to much of today's dissent.

The need not to offend is greatest for national news media and those with large circulation in metropolitan areas. To limit audience alienation, large circulation media prefer to report ideas or factual stories that are either inoffensive or on which there is relatively broad agreement or wide acceptance. When they must report controversial ideas or offensive facts, they prefer to speak through the person of a recognized figure—a government official, prominent businessman, or recognized expert. Although exceptions are made for news commentators, like Eric Sevareid, who have sufficient national stature to entitle them to broadcast such opinions, in the main television rarely covers new ideas until they are talked about by people of recognized importance.

Although preference is given to action to attract large audience, the networks seek to avoid offending. Both practices are apparent from the following description of Vietnam coverage by Robert MacNeil:

> At CBS, Vietnam hands used the expression, "shooting bloody" to describe the filming they had to do to get on the air. It was not that they were ordered to shoot only war scenes, but when they shot a political story or the progress of the pacification program as well as war scenes, it would be the action film which the program producers selected. Night after night for two years, American families have seen badly wounded Americans, sacks of dead Americans being loaded for shipment home, sprawled heaps of small, dead Vietnamese bodies. There are those who believe that this portrayal of horror has sickened Americans and turned many against the war, which has seemed increasingly pointless. Yet the horror has been heavily edited, and that may also have had a political impact . . . . . The grisly truth has been shown in the screening rooms of the network news departments. There would be close-up footage, with sound, of a young soldier, whose leg has been shot away a moment before, screaming obscenities at the medics, pleading with them in desperation to stop his agony.[50]

Avoidance of the controversial is not the result of a directive or other overt expression of policy. As with other newsroom taboos, journalists soon learn what is and what is not acceptable through newsroom gossip and observation. When particular kinds of items are consistently rejected, no one has to tell them they are wasting their time turning in more.[51]

2. News Media Concentration

The second aspect of the news business that inhibits a marketplace of ideas is concentration of control, cross-ownership within the same market, and the relative homogeneity of perspective among news media owners.

At the close of 1968, there were 671 commercial and 169 educational television stations.[52] Of the commercial stations, all but a handful were affiliated with or owned by one of the three commercial networks. Each of the three national networks owns five VHF stations in major markets and together are affiliated with 542 stations—CBS, 192; NBC, 200; and ABC, 150.[53] One hundred and forty of the non-commercial stations are affiliated with the National Educational Television network.

Many of the nation's commercial radio outlets are tied together by network ownership or affiliation. CBS owns and operates seven AM—FM stations and is affiliated with 244 other stations and, in addition, operates the

CBS Pacific network with 21 affiliates. ABC also owns six AM–FM stations and, operating four separate networks, has some 900 affiliates. Of the remaining approximately 4,700 commercial radio stations serving the country, 696 are affiliated with one of the 44 smaller networks.[54]

Those commercial TV and radio stations that are network affiliates receive network news programs and, in addition, as of 1966, Associated Press serviced 2,600 domestic radio and 324 television stations; the UPI service went to 3,078 broadcasters, 320 radio-TV stations.[55]

The prominence of chain ownership in both radio and television has increased steadily. In 1939, 39 chains owned 109 AM radio stations or 14.3 percent of all AM radio. In 1967, 373 chains owned 1,297 AM stations or 31.4 percent of the total. The pattern is similar in television. In 1956, 81 chains owned 203 TV stations or 45.8 percent. In 1967, chain ownership had grown until 147 chains owned 459 stations or 73.6 percent.[56] Although the number of commercial television outlets between 1956 and 1967 increased from 443 to 623, the number of station owners remained constant, 321.

Newspapers have no exact counterpart to the three broadcasting networks, but the major wire services and news and feature syndicates perform much the same function. The older of the two major wire services—Associated Press—provides news and features to more than 1,200 member daily and weekly newspapers. United Press International serves nearly as many newspaper subscribers.

[O]nly 16.4 percent of the dailies receive a service other than AP or UPI. And most of these are large dailies which also receive both AP and UPI. The *New York Times* Service has one hundred subscribers, the *Chicago Daily News* more than seventy. None of the other approximately forty-five supplemental news agencies serve as many as sixty dailies. The only foreign news service received by more than one or two newspapers is Reuters, with forty-one subscribers.

Obviously, large segments of the population rely on AP or UPI for their picture of the world. Their newspapers and their broadcasting stations subscribe to no alternate source of non-local news.[57]

Beyond these common sources of news and feature content, there is a tendency toward ownership of the nation's newspapers by fewer and fewer publishers. In 1910, over 600 cities had competing daily newspapers; by 1965, there were only 43 cities with fully competitive dailies.[58] In 97 percent of daily newspaper markets, only one owner is represented.[59] The 50 largest dailies capture 39 percent of total daily circulation.[60] In 1910, only 62 of the more than 2,600 daily newspapers were owned by 13 chains.[61] Today, more than half (59 percent) of the total daily newspaper circulation belongs to 871 dailies owned by 157 chains, and one group alone accounts for 6 percent of the total.[62] One witness before the Senate Antitrust and Monopoly Subcommittee in 1968 projected that at the present rate of expansion all the daily newspapers would be chain owned within twenty years and all Sunday papers within thirteen years.[63] Nearly two-fifths of the chain-owned papers are owned by twenty chains, and more than one-fourth are owned by twelve chains. Nineteen of the 25 largest newspapers in the country are chain owned.

The trend toward one-newspaper cities has made the problem of cross-ownership of media within the same market more acute. In the fall of 1968, there were 55 cities in which there was ownership or control of a television station by a monopoly newspaper, plus six more cities in which the newspapers were operating under a joint publishing agreement and one or both of the papers owned a television station. In 23 of the 55 cities, the monopoly newspaper controlled the *only* television station in the city. In 78 cities, the only daily newspaper owned or controlled the only AM radio station. Overall newspaper ownership of radio and TV stations did not significantly increase during the 1960's, and most of the TV-newspaper combinations resulted from acquisitions that occurred some years ago. In view of the increasing number of single-daily cities, however, any additional newspaper acquisitions of television or AM radio facilities should be closely examined.

3. Acquisition of Suburban Newspapers

One of the most important competitive developments in the newspaper field has been the rise of the suburban, or "community." daily. This growth is a countertrend operating against the increasing number of single-newspaper cities. Between 1945 and 1962, for example, the weekday circulation of suburban dailies in the 10 largest metropolitan areas rose from 2.8 million to 5 million, an increase of 80 percent, while the circulation of metropolitan dailies rose only 2 percent, from 16.2 million to 16.5 million.[64] Just as suburban merchants are taking business from the downtown merchants, suburban newspapers are effectively competing for circulation growth that might otherwise go the downtown papers by default.

The city dailies are responding, of course. Many have adopted zoned or regional editions, in which separate sections are added to the downtown papers that are distributed in particular suburban areas. These separate sections carry local news and advertising sold to local merchants at a rate substantially less than that for advertising appearing in the paper's total circulation sections. Zoned editions are evidently the most effective competitive weapon available to the downtown daily facing major suburban competition—short of acquisition of the suburban competitor.

As the suburban papers grow and thrive, metropolitan papers will increasingly be tempted to meet this new competition by the easiest means—acquisition. By acquiring its suburban competitors, a downtown paper can take advantage of suburban growth without the expense and trouble of zoned editions and without improving its own product to provide comprehensive, in-depth, area-wide news coverage. It can promote the "two newspapers on every doorstep" concept without sacrificing advertising revenues and with each of the commonly owned papers freed from the urgency of sharpening its performance, and it can institute combined advertising rates that will effectively forestall the entry of new competition. Should the trend to downtown-suburban mergers continue to develop, another source of new voices in the community would be cut off.

Within the last two years, the Justice Department has won two cases which suggest that such a trend can be prevented under the antitrust laws. One case involved the acquisition of the *San Bernardino Sun-Telegram* by the downtown *Los Angeles Times*. The acquisition took place in 1964, involved the purchase by the largest daily newspaper in Southern California, or, to put it another way, the acquisition by the only remaining Los Angeles morning daily of the largest morning daily newspaper within 75 miles of Los Angeles. The District Court found that the acquisition violated the Clayton Act, and has ordered divestiture of the *Sun* in order to restore it as an independent competitive force. The decision is on appeal by the defendant, but if affirmed, it will be an important roadblock against the trend toward concentration of the newspaper market in Southern California. The decision will also provide a valuable precedent applicable to other situations where a trend toward acquisition of suburban competitors may be developing.

4. Syndicated Features

Another problem area closely related to the competitive struggle between metropolitan dailies and the emerging suburban competitors is "syndicated features." Major newspaper syndicates acquire copyrighted materials, such as columns, comics, and crosswords, and they engage in the business of licensing newspapers to publish these features. Over the years a practice has developed whereby unduly broad exclusive territorial rights to the features have been sold to the metropolitan papers.[65] The effect of this practice has been, of course, to deprive many non-metropolitan newspapers of the opportunity to purchase and publish many popular features. Sometimes the area of exclusivity extends out for more than a hundred miles around the city in which the large daily publishes, and thus includes wide areas in which the metropolitan daily is not even a significant competitive force. Sometimes newspapers will even buy features they do not publish, simply to keep them out of the hands of their competitors. Numerous complaints have been received by the Department of Justice, which has had negotiations with some of the major syndicates to determine if the problem can be alleviated through a consent settlement.

On Sept. 14, 1966, the Department of Justice secured a consent decree from the *World-Journal-Tribune*. The defendant agreed to waive exclusive right to publication in the New York city area of nineteen features formerly appearing in the three merged papers, The *Herald Tribune, World-Telegram & Sun,* and *Journal-American.*[66]

Like distributors of syndicated features, both Associated Press and United Press International have a long history of business practices which substantially increase barriers to entry by newcomers and discriminate against smaller news organizations.[67]

5. Joint Publishing Agreements

In approximately two dozen cities there have emerged—some quite recently—arrangements under which newspaper publishers combine their production facilities and commercial functions but retain separate ownership and separate control of news and editorial departments. Most such arrangements have the following characteristics: Establishment of a third corporation to manage and operate the business functions of both newspapers (sometimes one newspaper acts as the managing partner); composing, stereotyping, and printing the newspapers of both parties in a single plant; consolidation of advertising and circulation departments; allocation of the morning field to one newspaper and the evening field to the other (this often includes the shutting down of one or more newspapers); allocation of the Sunday field to one newspaper or the other; pooling of profits by the parties to the agreement; and the establishment of either forced or optional combination advertising rates. Sometimes the parties technically reserve to themselves the right to fix their advertising rates independently, but this reservation is a mere formality when profit pooling is involved.

Profit pooling is the most offensive feature of these joint arrangements because it necessarily removes much of the incentive for either party to the agreement to try to increase its circulation at the expense of the other. Marked increases in advertising rates have been observed shortly after some of these arrangements were put into effect. Nor can continuation of commercial competition between the papers be expected when the advertising and circulation departments are not kept separate in fact as well as in form. Arrangements whereby competing newspapers simply pool manufacturing and distributing functions is not necessarily undesirable or illegal. An arrangement of this kind can make possible savings in plant, equipment, and labor costs; insistence on inefficiency is not one of the objectives of current antitrust laws. But profit pooling and price fixing are designed to improve profits, not by eliminating inefficiency, but by eliminating all commercial competition between the papers, and to that extent are probably unlawful under current antitrust decisions.

It was on this basis that the Department of Justice challenged the legality of a joint publishing agreement between the *Arizona Daily Star* and the *Tucson Daily Citizen* as a *per se* violation of Section 1 of the Sherman Act. The agreement, in effect since 1940, provided for profit pooling, agreement on advertising rates, and allocation of markets. Also involved in that case was a challenge to the 1966 acquisition of the *Star* by the *Citizen* on the grounds that it violated Section 7 of the Clayton Act. At the time suit was brought these two papers were the only daily newspapers published in Tucson, Arizona. The district judge in that proceeding has already indicated that he regards certain aspects of the operating agreement unlawful, although no final decree has been entered (July 4, 1969).

Related is a bill now in the hearing phase before the Senate Antitrust and Monopoly Subcommittee. Originally introduced as the "failing newspaper act" it has been relabeled the "newspaper preservation act." Hearings were suspended at the end of June 1969, pending the disposition of the Tucson newspaper litigation. The objective of the bill would exempt from the antitrust laws mergers and joint newspaper operating agreements involving one or more "failing newspapers"—which are defined to include any paper that "appears unlikely to remain or become a financially sound publication." This is a radical extension of the traditional antitrust exemption provided for failing companies. In addition to unduly relaxing the failing company defense already available to merging companies, the bill would legalize the profit-pooling and price-fixing features of joint publishing agreements. The bill has been strongly opposed by many suburban dailies on the ground that such an exemption would place them at a severe competitive disadvantage.

While there is a definite trend toward concentration of the control of news sources, recently there is a good deal of evidence that the government has taken an active interest in stopping this trend and possibly reversing it. Until recently, in the whole history of the antitrust laws the Justice Department has filed only about a dozen cases in the newspaper field.[68] In part this was no doubt owing to the recognition that there may not always be an exact correlation between maintaining advertising competition and promoting the social values inherent in a multiplicity of voices. In recent years there has been some refinement of antitrust doctrine and a sharpening of the tools of analysis that have provided new confidence. In 1967, the Department challenged the attempted acquisition of the American Broadcasting Co. by International Telephone and Telegraph Corp. (ITT). Among the grounds urged for disallowing the merger were that ITT was a potential entrant into broadcasting and CATV, and that ITT was an important source of the technology and engineering skills needed to multiply channels for mass communication. More recently the department took a position before the FCC opposing cross-ownership.

On Jan. 30, 1963, the Federal Communications Commission made clear it was opposed to combined broadcasting-newspaper advertising rates—a practice that makes entry of new media and survival of old media more difficult. On June 21, 1965, the Commission adopted a proposed rule making an interim policy that would have prevented chain ownership of more than three (two VHF) television stations in any of the top 50 markets, but the Commission has already made exception to this guideline on at least four occasions. This year the Commission launched a broad investigation of broadcast ownership that will include cross-ownership, chain ownership, and ownership by diversified corporations.

While we would not oppose government efforts at de-concentration, as a practical matter the administrative and political problems that would have to be overcome make substantial progress unlikely. With the exception of ownership of television stations by newspapers in the same market, the limited government resources available would be better directed toward preventing additional concentration, eliminating competitive practices, and planning for the future development, particularly of CATV, along lines most conductive to providing a marketplace for ideas.

D. Access: Coverage of Protest

The increased frequency of boycotts, sit-ins, picketing, parades, and large-group protest meetings has generated public and governmental concern over the news media's—and particularly television's—coverage of these events. In the late 1950's and early sixties, many southerners believed that if the media would not cover these events, they would not happen. Today many in the North share that view. Some Americans thought such events were one continuous dramatic production staged for and sometimes by the television networks. Criticism has ranged from claims that the media distort the events they report to bald assertions that they incite riots simply by their presence.

At one time, a demonstration, a boycott, a sit-in, or any other form of confrontation, even when non-violent, almost guaranteed coverage by the news media. Today, the greater number of non-violent demonstrations have reduced their efficacy as a technique for access, but still appeal to traditional news values and provide the action desired by television.

Apparent to any observer of the American scene for the past fifteen years is that this technique for gaining access is used by those who have not been admitted through traditional channels. General Motors, the President of the United States, or the Chamber of Commerce do not need a parade or physical confrontation to attract media attention. Dissenters have the problem of attracting not only media attention, but also public attention. The non-violent demonstration is a press conference for those who cannot otherwise command the attention of the media and its public. Although demonstrations would probably occur infrequently if the media did not cover them, press conferences would also occur less frequently if the media did not cover them. Those who object to nonviolent demonstrations may object to the format of the press conference, just as often they disagree with the message.

The criticism that "media coverage of conflict causes conflict" proceeds from an inaccurate assumption: that media coverage is both a necessary and sufficient condition for conflict. It is neither. The causes lie elsewhere, in social conditions and tensions.

One of the earliest accusations that television was the cause of violent eruptions in the process of social change is that of former New Orleans Mayor deLesseps Morrison. Integration of New Orleans schools was less than peaceful. At first he attempted to place the responsibility on Leander Perez, political boss of an adjoining parish. When that met with little success he labeled television the primary villain. Blaming television was an afterthought; the real cause of violence was his own neutrality toward the Supreme Court's desegregation order, the unlawful posture of the governor, the Louisiana state legislature's policy of massive resistance and refusal to support the local school board, and the neutrality of civic leaders.[69] Where government and civic leaders are willing to cooperate in securing orderly social change, it seems clear that the press can be of assistance without seriously damaging its traditional standards of journalism.[70]

The immediate effect of non-coverage of protest would probably be less protest; for those who subscribe to the ostrich theory of journalism, this may be the short-term answer. But protest is an attempt to communicate, to tell the public that the social machine is in trouble.

America continually readjusts its intergroup relations in the pursuit of certain fundamental democratic values. Readjustment, however, can generate severe tension. As de Tocqueville has said:

> Only a consummate statecraft can enable a king to save this throne when after a long spell of oppressive rule he sets to improving the lot of his subjects. Patiently endured so long as it seemed beyond redress, a grievance comes to appear intolerable once the possibility of improving it crosses men's minds. For the mere fact that certain abuses have been

remedied draws attention to the others and they now appear more galling; people may suffer less but their sensibility is exacerbated.

The alternative to continuous readjustment is massive repression, which would produce a society neither dynamic nor democratic. Without media attention, the tensions of change could not be identified, much less alleviated.

Media performance is subject to criticism on at least two grounds. As suggested earlier, to the extent the media have not focused on the conditions underlying much of today's protest they have reduced the likelihood that these problems would be met before growing to such serious proportions. Even here, however, the failure of the media performance cannot be regarded as the only cause. Some of these conditions were covered but were largely ignored. The second criticism is that the news media slight the causes of protest at the expense of reporting the manifestations of discontent, physical confrontation.

If there were systematic balanced surveillance of the community, the need for demonstrations as vehicles for communication would not be so great. If the news media did not place such a high value on conflict and action, the character of protest might be quite different. If the public and its government had attended to the problems which beset them today, our society would not be in such a state of upheaval.

1. Influence of Media Presence

One commentator has said, "Nothing, but nothing, ever happens the same way it was after you put a TV or movie camera on it! The fundamental problem is that TV reporters are so conspicuous that, without intending to, they can't help but influence their own coverage."[71] To the extent his presence is obtrusive, no reasonable and honest newsman can deny that his presence has an effect on the event he is covering. Another has observed,

> "A newspaper reporter equipped with pencil and pad subtly influences the event he is covering; a still photographer with his cameras dangling about his neck may change it more. And a television camera crew, with their lights and large equipment, can transform the event into an entirely different scene. So much so, in fact, that it is questionable if TV is capable of reporting the news objectively."[72]

Reporting the news objectively, in this sense, means reporting it as it would have happened if the newsman were not present. There is little doubt that his presence has an effect on the behavior of protestors. Consider the following description of television coverage of a picket line:

> By now it was something after 8 p.m. and the television crews needed something to show on the 10 o'clock news ...
>
> Up came the three-man television crew: a camera man with a hand-held camera, a sound man and light man. Very discreet in the dark.
>
> "May as well get it."
>
> You could sense the disappointment in his voice, because pictorially it wasn't much of a demonstration.
>
> The light-man held up his 30-volt frezzi and laid a four-foot beam of

light across one section of the picket line. Instantly the marchers' heads snapped up, their eyes flashed. They threw up their arms in the clenched Communist fist. Some made a V with their fingers, and they held up their banners for the cameras . . .[73]

Obviously, it was not the same event once the cameras were on.

As on other decisions regarding coverage, it is important to apply neutral journalistic principles in deciding whether to cover an event. What many critics of protest coverage do not acknowledge is that others stage events for the benefit of the press. Yet, was the distortion any greater than the "unreal" hearing which followed the circulation of this memorandum to a congressional committee:

1. Decide what you want the newspapers to hit hardest and then shape each hearing so that the main point becomes the vortex of the testimony. Once that vortex is reached, *adjourn* . . . .

4. Do not permit distractions to occur, such as extraneous fusses with would-be witnesses, which might provide news that would bury the testimony which you want featured.

5. Do not space hearing more than 24 or 48 hours apart when on a controversial subject. This gives the opposition too much opportunity to make all kinds of counter-charges and replies by issuing statements to the newspapers.

6. Don't ever be afraid to recess a hearing even for five minutes, so that you can keep the proceedings completely in control so far as creating news is concerned.

7. And this is most important: don't let the hearings or the evidence ever descend to the plane of a personal fight between the Committee Chairman and the head of the agency being investigated. The high plane of a duly authorized Committee of the House of Representatives *examining* the operations of an Agency of the Executive Branch for constructive purposes should be maintained at all costs.[74]

The congressional hearing undoubtedly would have been a different event if it would have been held at all, were it not for the anticipated presence of the media. Nor is the staging of congressional hearings new. The above memorandum was circulated in 1943 by the counsel of a House committee investigating the Federal Communications Commission.

Publicity is frequently the end product and not the sideline of the committee's work. In some of the more notable probes, the final committee conclusions have been a matter of scant importance. After two particularly sensational ones of recent years—the MacArthur dismissal inquiry and the Army-McCarthy hearings—the chairman sought to dispense with the formality of a report altogether, each making vague assertions that the public had "the facts" and could form its own judgments. The responsibility to come up with remedial legislation is often forgotten in the shuffle.[75]

Committee hearings are not the only activities of government officials that are staged or doctored. It is only necessary to recall one of the more recent episodes in which Senator Edward Kennedy's Subcommittee on Indian Education set off on a tour of Alaska, only to have some Republican members bolt the excursion on the charge that the trip was "a stage-managed scenario" to boost Kennedy's presidential prospects. There was apparently no objection that the tour was frankly designed to generate publicity to improve the educational and anti-poverty programs for Eskimos and Indians.[76] Similarly, President Johnson's interview with White House correspondents was edited under the supervision of administration aides. "CBS and ABC both protested to White House officials but were told that the remarks the President was concerned about were matters of security. When pressed, they admitted they meant the President considered them politically sensitive."[77] Only CBS advised viewers that the interview had been edited under White House supervision. Estimates of total federal expenditures on public relations and public information run as high as $400 million annually.[78]

The argument persists that demonstrators holding up clenched fists differ from Congressional hearings contrived to focus on a particular point or other public information activities of the government. The demonstrators know what they are doing; they consciously conduct themselves before the camera. If they hold up clenched fists they want to communicate this message to the public. Most of them, however, have some additional message. Although demonstration and confrontation are vehicles for access, something else rides in the vehicles. The media go to a demonstration, make the demonstration the story, but they ignore the message. In doing so they are performing about as well as if they had reported that the President held a press conference, but forgot to tell the public what the President said.

2. Media Incitement to Violence

With respect to the possibility that the presence of the media may incite demonstrators to real violence, rather than threats of violence or hostile gestures, the solution does not lie in prohibiting coverage. If the conduct promoted by the media's presence is socially undesirable and not constitutionally protected, a law can prohibit such conduct. Where conduct is unlawful, arrest the demonstrator. But denying all demonstrators access simply because some of them may engage in unlawful activity prescribes too broad a remedy for an otherwise narrow problem, and clearly would be unconstitutional. Most demonstrators do not engage in unlawful violence simply to get on camera; less extreme conduct usually suffices. Denying coverage to all demonstrators attempts to discourage indirectly that which cannot be prohibited directly: infringing dissident's first amendment rights. However unwise the hostile message from the disaffected may be, the conditions under the first amendment that justify the limitation of speech, including symbolic speech, are few. That the message is unwise is not one of them.

Protestors usually have little to gain in the way of access to the media by engaging in unlawful or violent behavior. Indeed, the more violent their behavior, the more likely the media will focus on that to the exclusion of the views for which access is sought. Moreover, the revulsion of most Americans to violence means that regardless of the soundness of their view, when the message comes across mixed with lawless behavior audience acceptance is substantially reduced. The dignified 1963 March on Washington, D.C., was a much more effective vehicle for communicating views than the performance of the New York Yippie contingent at the 1968 Democratic National Convention.

Nevertheless, protestors do engage in unlawful or violent behavior for several reasons:

1. Sometimes the grievances of demonstrators include police brutality. To bring the excesses of the police into public view, they may seek to provoke them when television cameras were present.

2. The demonstrators may wish to illustrate the depth of their conviction in the rightness of their cause by risking jail sentences or other punitive action.

3. The demonstrators regard the law they are violating as unconstitutional and seek a court test.

4. Frequently, there is a large group that supports the goals of the demonstrators, but is not willing to engage in the extreme tactics they adopt. Under such circumstances, the more radical members seek to generate a confrontation with the police for the purpose of surfacing the "venality" of the "establishment" and thereby convince those on the fringe that any means necessary should be adopted to secure shared objectives.

5. The demonstrators may seek to generate such a massive official overresponse as to force a breakdown in the administration of criminal justice and thereby illustrate how corrupt is the entire system.

As a case in point, the report of the Violence Commission's Chicago Task Force, *Rights in Conflict,* abundantly reveals many complex motivations for unlawful or violent behavior.

The provocation may be mild or severe, lawful or unlawful. The response of the authorities to the 1963 march in Selma, for example, was an overresponse by the police, for they were provoked by demonstrators who wished only to peaceably exercise their first amendment rights. Television coverage, because of its revelation of this truth, undoubtedly contributed to the passage of the 1964 Civil Rights Bill.

The overresponse of the police in Chicago during the Democratic National Convention discloses a reaction to severe verbal provocation, threats of extreme violence, and, in some instances, physical assault and other conduct by demonstrators. Yet the police responded with more force than was necessary to enforce the law. Many newsmen were surprised, therefore, that the majority of the public sympathized with the police.

So long as the media continue to cover demonstrations, some demonstrators will continue to provoke the police. To this extent, coverage may contribute to the level of violence. But the incentive is the same whether the television cameras are present or not. The objective is overreaction by police, and publicity will be achieved through the print media and informal channels if television is not present.

Media coverage, then, does provide some incentive to violence; but it also provides a disincentive.

First, as suggested earlier, nobody, including demonstrators, wants to have his unlawful acts recorded on camera. Secondly, the presence of the media also tends to have a restraining influence on the use of violence by the authorities. During the late fifties and early sixties, Justice Department lawyers encouraged media coverage of civil rights demonstrations in the belief that it restrained the police.[79] Former Attorney General Nicholas Katzenbach has acknowledged the constructive role of television coverage:

> The bitter segregationists' view of [the civil rights movement] is that the demonstrators are following the cameras, not vice versa. To them, it is the Northern press and the television networks which seem to be the motive force in the civil rights movement. This idea apparently motivated many of the toughs during the 1961 freedom rides in Selma and elsewhere. Almost their first moves were against the cameras.
>
> Yet news coverage has been a powerful deterrent to racial violence in the South. For every assault on newsmen, many more incidents have been defused by their presence. Reporters and cameras, particularly the network-television cameras, which symbolize the national focus on Southern violence, have had a tempering as well as instructional effect.[80]

In Chicago, many officers removed their badges to avoid identification and frequently smashed cameras to destroy evidence of their misconduct. They did not want the public to know what had happened.

Media coverage thus reduces the immediate violence that results from overresponse by the police. But police violence has a fallout effect that may promote more extreme confrontations or even induce a shift to covert tactics, because they are less risky than public confrontations. When non-violent demonstrations become impractical because of personal risk, the disaffected can do nothing or they can resort to more extreme tactics. While many will certainly be deterred by massive applications of police force, others may very well decide to go underground.

3. Coverage of Demonstrations

Another source of tension between the news media and the police during demonstrations was highlighted by the Walker Report: "The police are never enthusiastic about the presence of newsmen in large—crowd situations . . . ."[81] Conflict between the police, who want to maintain or restore order, and reporters, who wish to provide full coverage of a volatile event, does arise as it did in Chicago. Mayor Daley and the Chicago police accused the media of interfering with the maintenance of order. Newsmen, in turn, complained of excessive restrictions on their coverage. That there is some truth to both complaints makes the problem no easier to resolve.

It does suggest that, where a demonstration is anticipated, the press and the police should discuss their competing interests in advance. TV should certainly arrange to avoid blinding officers with kleig lights and flashbulbs. It does not follow, however, that such conduct by some members of the press justifies indiscriminate retaliation by police. The police should also keep in mind that, as in Chicago, not everyone with a camera or strobe unit represents the press. Many protest organizations have their own cameramen and some persons were impersonating television network newsmen in

Chicago. Nothing, it is clear now, pleased some demonstrators more than indiscriminate police violence toward the news media.

If a member of the press refuses to obey a lawful police order to cease interfering with or to stop obstructing police efforts at crowd control, he is properly subject to arrest. Under no circumstances, however, can police justify the confiscation of film, notes, or audio tapes. Nor is there any excuse for the destruction of equipment, or the use of force against a reporter unless he is resisting arrest. This problem has confronted reporters for a long time. If the present Federal Civil Rights Act proves inadequate, consideration ought to be given to enacting the necessary amendments. Police violence of the kind in Chicago clearly generates a threat to the gathering of news for transmission in interstate commerce, and it impairs the most fundamental of an American's civil rights—his first amendment right to know.

Unless the police intend to engage in improper conduct, it is also in their best interest to have reporters present. Consider the following incident:

> In Chicago some time ago, the Negro comedian Dick Gregory complained, a few days after he had been arrested in a demonstration, that the police were brutal in making the arrest. WMAQ in Chicago carried Gregory's statement and then, without comment, reran the film showing Gregory being arrested. The film did not bear out Gregory's accusation of brutal treatment, and the Chicago police were grateful that the station was able to show exactly what had happened.[82]

Large demonstrations normally require a permit by demonstrators and pre-planning by both demonstrators and police. The press, if it decides to cover the event, ought to pre-plan and consult with both the demonstrators and the police. Under such circumstances, if all parties conduct themselves reasonably, the problem lessens in accommodating the desire of the demonstrators for coverage, the obligation of the police to maintain public safety, and the right of the press to provide adequate coverage. The police and the demonstrators can help enormously by negotiating a permit agreement far enough in advance to permit planning by the media. Authorities occasionally delay issue of a permit as long as possible on the theory that it will discourage people from participating, but this is reprehensible and, if chaos results, the authorities must accept responsibility for the consequences.

Generally, the presence of the media improves the behavior of those present. Most demonstrations involve important political and social issues. Each side seeks adherents. However attractive violence may be to the few, it has little appeal to the vast majority of Americans. In Chicago, the various groups of demonstrators attempted to give dissidents a choice. They tried to warn protestors when a particular line of activity might lead to arrest or violence, and they tried to instruct those who did not wish to participate to avoid these activities. This policy shows that some dissident groups recognize that, if demonstrations are to be successful tomorrow, they cannot lead inevitably to bloody confrontation today; otherwise, the protestors cannot attract people to their movement, people who, while strongly supporting the objectives, either fear or have no appetite for violence. They need such broad support for their success.

The news media can take additional steps to offset whatever incentive they may provide for violence, first by balanced coverage of the confrontation. At least four elements require balanced treatment:

1. The purpose of the demonstration. What is the nature of the grievance? Why are the demonstrators there?

2. The events leading up to the demonstration. Have other remedies been sought, such as administrative relief or negotiations, either on the grievances or on the right to demonstrate? If so, what has been the response of the objects (city officials, university officials, etc.) of the demonstration?

3. The demonstration. How many people were present? How did they conduct themselves? Do not focus only on the most extreme conduct or dress.

4. What provocations, if any, were directed toward the police? Why were the demonstrators trying to provoke the police? Did the police use more force than was necessary to maintain order? Were there any extenuating circumstances, such as physical exhaustion or security for a presidential candidate?

The first element is important because particular grievances frequently cause demonstrations. As suggested earlier, failure to cover the grievance compares to announcing that there has been a presidential press conference but neglecting to relay what the President said. Moreover, if the demonstration forms part of the strategy of confrontation—designed basically to provoke police—then the public has a right to know about it. Similarly, if the purpose is to get arrested and to convey to the public the depth of a dissident conviction, the public should know that. Also, knowledge of the purpose of demonstrations will aid the news organization in deciding whether to cover the event at all and, if so, the amount of resources to allocate to the coverage. It will help them avoid groups whose only purpose is to get on camera.

Information on the second element tells the public whether the group involved has been reasonable in attempting to resolve its grievances. If it has not, the public will undoubtedly have little sympathy for them. If it has, the public will probably conclude that its action was justified and place responsibility for the consequences of the demonstration with those who could meet the grievances. Such coverage will provide an incentive to the aggrieved to pursue less drastic remedies, as well as give similar incentive to responsible officials to take reasonable steps to remedy the grievances.

The third element provides the public with a representative portrayal of the kind of people involved, the number who felt sufficiently strong about the grievances to appear, and the dignity with which they conducted themselves. If all the coverage of demonstrators focuses only on the most extreme behavior, no incentive remains for dignified and orderly conduct.

The fourth element determines the justification for the official response and which party to the confrontation ought to be held responsible for any violence that resulted. Such coverage provides incentives to demonstrators to avoid extreme provocations and to the police to avoid the use of excessive force.

The issue of provocation presents a special problem. Many provocations are obscenities, not appropriate for either broadcast or for print media. Some people have suggested that the media have an obligation to disseminate the language of provocation anyway. Among those who once subscribed to this theory, at least in reporting on the Walker Report, was Norman Isaacs of the *Louisville Courier—Journal.* But the response from his readers was so overwhelmingly negative that he decided not to do it again. The problem remains, however, and the solution is to describe in abstract terms the nature and severity of the provocations.

Television has acute problems in providing balanced coverage of this kind for at least three reasons. First, television communicates in two modes, audio and visual. Certain kinds of visual portrayals can have an impact out of proportion to the accompanying verbal statements. Where pictures become available of some elements, and are especially dramatic, extra effort is needed to balance them with commentary. Under some circumstances, it may be impossible to present certain picture sequences and retain balance; then, perhaps, the sequence ought to be eliminated or softened. Second, certain segments of the audience are less receptive to verbal than visual messages. Eric Sevareid is worth a thousand pictures only for those who understand him. When commentary is accompanied by very dramatic film clips, it is especially difficult to provide balance.

The second characteristic that makes balanced television reporting difficult applies to almost any kind of story. With only 30 minutes to cover all the news, network television can provide little more than a headline service. There is a similar bias in this direction because of television's visual presentation. As Walter Scott, NBC board chairman has said: "Because television is a visual medium, it may scant the background and significance of events to focus on the outward appearance—the comings and goings of statesmen instead of the issue that confronts them."[83] The network news departments and those of many local stations do as well as they can in the time available. The necessity of expanding the evening network news broadcasts from 30 minutes to an hour is plain. The format of that hour should be altered from the present formula to a mixture of hard news and news magazine presentations—a cross between "Walter Cronkite" and "60 Minutes" on CBS, "Huntley—Brinkley" and "First Tuesday" on NBC, in the style of "Martin Agronsky's Washington" on WTOP—TV in Washington, D.C.

The third reason television coverage tends to be less well balanced than other media is that the entertainment ethic is somewhat stronger in television and, accordingly, action scenes tend to dominate.

We do not suggest the abandonment of action sequences. In some instances, film, by far the most effective means of communicating the forceful, human aspects of a story, is a good attention getter. But once television has the audience's attention, it should also provide the audience with valuable information.

* * * *

The media can reduce confrontations and demonstrations by giving more balanced coverage to the community, by opening traditional access channels to those with new, different, and minority views. Such changes in media performance will not eliminate protest altogether because other reasons exist. In many universities, for example, the dissenting students have control of the one medium of mass communication in their community, the school newspaper, which usually favors the dissidents both in the quality and quantity of its coverage. If one seeks to lay the whole explanation for confrontation on inadequate media access, he must somehow find a plausible explanation for the university phenomenon.

Where media attention is a positive incentive to demonstrate, it is also a remedial phenomenon that compensates for imbalanced surveillance. The solution, then, is not to ignore demonstrations, but to correct the conditions which, if they did not give them birth, were at least the midwife. Once done, to the extent demonstrations are an access problem they will diminish. Similarly, the standard for determining whether an event will be covered should place more emphasis on the nature of the grievance, the number of people affected, the severity of the grievance, and less emphasis should be placed on the willingness of the aggrieved to engage in violence and the likelihood that they will.

REFERENCES

1. Walter Gieber, "Attributes of a Reporter's Role" (San Francisco State College: unpublished mimeo), p. 27.
2. Wilbur Schramm, ed., *Mass Communications,* (Urbana: University of Illinois Press, 1954), p. 195.
3. John Hohenberg, *The News Media; A Journalist Looks at His Profession* (Holt, Rinehart & Winston, 1968), pp. 294–297.
4. Paul F. Lazarfield, Bernard Berelson, and Hazel Gaudet. *The People's Choice* (New York: Columbia University Press, 1948); Shirley A. Star and Helen McGill Hughes, "Report of an Educational Campaign: The Cincinnati Plan for the United Nations," *American Journal of Sociology* (1950) pp. 389–400; Charles F. Cannell and James C. MacDonald. "The Impact of Health News on Attitudes and Behavior," *Journalism Quarterly* (1956), pp. 315–323; Dorwin Cartwright, "Some Principles of Mass Persuasion: Selected Findings of Research on the Sale of United States War Bonds," *Human Relations* (1949), pp. 253–267.
5. Wilbur Schramm and Richard F. Carter, "Effectiveness of a Political Telethon," *Public Opinion Quarterly* (1959), pp. 121–126.
6. Daniel M. Wilner, *"Attitude as a Determinant of Perception in the Mass Media of Communication:* Reaction to the Motion Picture,'Home of the Brave,' " (University of California, Los Angeles Library unpublished PhD dissertation, 1951); Gordon Allport and Leo J. Postman "The Basic Psychology of Rumor," *Transactions of the New York Academy of Sciences,* Series II (1945), pp. 61-81; Eunice Cooper and Marie Jahoda "The Evasion of Propaganda," *Journal of Psychology* (1947). p. 1525; Patricia L. Kendall and Katherine M. Wolf, *The Personification of Prejudice as a Device in Educational Propaganda* (New York: Bureau of Applied Social Research,

Columbia University, 1946); Herbert H. Hyman, and Paul B. Sheatsley, "Some Reasons Why Information Campaigns Fail," *Public Opinion Quarterly* (1947), pp. 412–423; Patricia L. Kendall and Katherine M. Wolf. "The Analysis of Deviant Cases in Communications Research," in *Communications Research,* Paul F. Lazarsfeld and Frank N. Stanton, eds., (New York: Harper & Bros., 1949).

7. Herbert H. Hyman and Paul B. Sheatsley, "Some Reasons Why Information Campaigns Fail," *Public Opinion Quarterly* (1947), pp. 412–423; Claire Simmerman and Raymond A. Bauer. "The Effect of an Audience Upon What is Remembered," *Public Opinion Quarterly* (1956), pp. 238–248; Virginia Seeleman, "The Influence of Attitude upon the Remembering of Pictorial Material,"*Archives of Psychology,* No. 258 (1941); Jerome M. Levine and Gardner Murphy, "The Learning and Forgetting of Controversial Material," *Journal of Abnormal and Social Psychology* (1943), pp. 507–517.

8. Lazarfeld, *et al., op. cit.* footnote 4.

9. Melvin L. DeFleur and Otto N. Larsen, *The Flow of Information* (New York: Harper & Bros., 1958); Elihu Katz, "The Two-step Flow of Communication: An Up–to–Date Report on an Hypothesis," *Public Opinion Quarterly* (1957), pp. 61–78; Robert K. Merton, "Patterns of Influence: A Study of Interpersonal Influence and Communications Behavior in a Local Community," in *Communications Research 1948–49,* Paul F. Lazerfeld and Frank Stanton, eds., (New York: Harper & Bros., 1949); Elihu Katz, and Paul Lazarfeld, *Personal Influence: The Part Played by People in the Flow of Mass Communications* (Glencoe, Illinois: The Free Press, 1955).

10. James Coleman, Herbert Menzel, and Elihu Katz, "Social Processes in Physicians' Adoption of a New Drug," *Journal of Chronic Diseases* (1958), pp. 1–19.

11. James H. Copp, Maurice L. Sill, and Emory J. Brown, "The Function of Information Sources in the Farm Practice Adoption Process," *Rural Sociology* (1958), pp. 146–157; Bryce Ryan and Neal Gross, "The Diffusion of Hybrid Seed Corn in Two Iowa Communities," *Rural Sociology* (1943), pp. 15–24; North Central and Rural Sociological Subcommittee, *Social Factors in the Adoption of Farm Practices* (Ames, Iowa: Iowa State College, 1959); Paul C. Marsh and Lee Coleman, "Group Influences and Agricultural Innovations: Some Tentative Findings and Hypotheses," *American Journal of Sociology (1956), pp. 61;* George M. Beal, Joe M. Bohlen, and Everett M. Rogers, "Validity of the Concept of Stages in the Adoption Process," *Rural Sociology* (1957), pp. 166–168.

12. Joseph Klapper, *The Effects of Mass Communication* (New York: The Free Press, 1960), p. 252.

13. Ithiel deSola Poole, "The Mass Media and Their Interpersonal Social Functions in the Process of Modernization," in *Communication and Political Development* (Lucien Pye, Ed.) (Princeton University Press, 1963) Chapter 14; Tamotsu Shibutani, *Improvised News* (Bobbs, Merrill 1966).

14. Shibutani, *op. cit.,* footnote 13.

15. *Ibid.*

16. A. D. Annis and N. C. Meier, "The Induction of Opinion through Suggestions by Means of Planted Content," *Journal of Social Psychology* (1934), pp. 65-81; Martin F. Herz, "Some Psychological Lessons from Leaflet Propaganda in World War II," *Public Opinion Quarterly,* pp. 471-486; Arnold M. Rose, "The Use of Propaganda to Reduce Prejudice," *International Journal of Opinion and Attitude Research* (1948), pp. 220-229; Carl I. Hovland, "Effects of the Mass Media and Communication," in *Handbook of Social Psychology* Sindzey Gardner, ed. (Cambridge, Mass,: Addison-Wesley Publishing Co., 1954), pp. 1062-1103; Irving J. Janis and Seymour Feshbach. "Effects of Fear–Arousing Communications," *Journal of Abnormal and Social Psychology* (1953), pp. 78-92; Carl Hovland and Wallace Mandell, "Is There a Law of Primacy in Persuasion?" *American Psychologist* (1952), p. 538.

17. Irving, L., Janis and Seymour Feshbach, "Effects of Fear Arousing Communication," *Journal of Abnormal and Social Psychology* 1953), pp. 78-92.

18. Roy Popkin, *The Environmental Services Administration* (New York: Frederick A. Praeger, 1967), p. 186.

19. William L. Rivers, *The Opinion Makers* (Boston: Beacon Press, 1965), p. 180.

20. *Journalism Quarterly* (1950), pp. 383-390.
    For other studies dealing with various aspects of gatekeeper performance, see: Walter Gieber, "Across the Desk," *Journalism Quarterly* (Fall 1956), pp. 423-32; Walter Gieber and Walter Johnson, "The City Hall Beat," *Journalism Quarterly* (1961), pp. 289-97; Walter Gieber, "Private versus Public Role of the Newsman," paper presented to Association for Education in Journalism, 1963; Walter Gieber, "The City Desk: A Model of News Decisions," a paper presented to the Association for Education in Journalism, 1964; Walter Gieber, "Role Playing Among Reporters," paper presented to Association for Education 1965. Walter Gieber, "A City Editor Selects the News," paper presented to American Sociological Association, 1961; Ithiel de Sola Poole and Irwin Shulman, "Newsmen's Fantasies, Audiences and News Writing," *Public Opinion Quarterly* (1959), pp. 145-58; Leo Rosten, *The Washington Correspondents,* (New York: Harcourt, Brace, 1937); Robert P. Judd, "The Newspaper Reporter in a Suburban City," *Journalism Quarterly* (1961), pp. 35-42; Dan D. Nimmo, *Newsgathering in Washington,* (New York: Atherton Press, 1964); Roy E. Carter, "Newspaper Gatekeepers and the Sources of News," *Public Opinion Quarterly* (1958), pp. 133-44; Jack M. McLeod and Searle E. Hawley, Jr., "Professionalization Among Newsmen," *Journalism Quarterly* (1964), pp. 529-37; Alex S. Edelstein and J. Blaine Schulz, "The Weekly Newspaper's Leadership Role as Seen by Community Leaders," *Journalism Quarterly* (1963), pp. 565-74; Merrill A. Samuelson, "A Standardized Test to Measure Job Satisfaction in the Newsroom," *Journalism Quarterly* (1962), pp. 286-91; Douglass Cater, *The Fourth Branch of Government* (Boston: Houghton Mifflin, 1959); William L. Rivers, *The Opinion Makers* (Boston: Beacon, 1965); Walter Gieber, *Gatekeepers of News of Civil Rights and Liberties* (Berkeley: Department of Journalism, University of California).
20a.*Ibid.*
20b.*Ibid.*
21. Lewis Donohew, "Newspaper Gatekeepers and Forces in the News Channel," *Public Opinion Quarterly* (1967), pp. 61-68.
22. Canon 5, The Canons of Journalism, American Society of Newspaper Editors, Appendix II-D.
23. Warren Breed, "Mass Communications and Socio-cultural Integration," *Social Forces* (1958), pp. 109-116.
24. Arthur E. Rowse, *Slanted News* (Boston: Beacon Press, 1957), p. 124.
25. Ben H. Bagdikian, quoted in *Failing Newspaper Act,* Hearings before the Subcommittee on Antitrust and Monopoly of the Committee on Judiciary, U.S. Senate, July 12-26, 1967, part I, p. 311.
26. *Ibid.*, p. 395.
27. "Ethics and the Press: Conflicts of Interest, Pressures Still Distort Some Papers Converage," *The Wall Street Journal* July 25, 1967; reprinted in *Failing Newspaper Act, op. cit.,* footnote 25, p. 440.
28. *Ibid.*, p. 439.
29. William L. Rivers, *Failing Newspaper Hearings, op. cit.,* footnote 25, p. 397.
30. William L. Rivers, *The Opinion Makers, op. cit.,* footnote 19, p. 197.
31. William Allen White, "Publishers Menace Their Own Freedom," quoted in George L. Bird, *et at., The Press and Society* (New York: Prentice-Hall, Inc., 1951), pp. 74-75.
32. William Rivers, *op. cit.,* footnote 19, pp. 175-178.
33. "AM-FM Broadcast Financial Data, 1967" FCC Public Notice 27306, Feb. 7, 1969-B.
34. Some of the factual material in this section is drawn from Dr. Bogart's paper for the Task Force (reprinted as Appendix II-A). The conclusions are those of the Task Force and do not necessarily reflect Dr. Bogart's views.
35. *Ibid.*
36. FCC Public Notice, *op. cit.,* footnote 33.
37. "TV Broadcast Financial Data," FCC Public Notice 26097, Dec. 31, 1967.
38. Bogart, *op. cit.,* footnote 34.
39. "TV Broadcast Financial Data, 1966," FCC Public Notice 5317, Aug. 25, 1967.
40. *Ibid.* The 1967 earnings may be atypical; earnings in 1966 were $186.8 million on

assets of $126 million, a 148% return on book value of assets.

41. John G. Udell, *The Growth of the American Daily Newspaper; An Economic Analysis* (Madison: Bureau of Business Research and Service, School of Commerce, University of Wisconsin, 1965).
42. Bogart, *op. cit.*, footnote 34.
43. Brian McNamara, *Failing Newspaper Hearings, op. cit.*, footnote 27, p. 419.
44. Testimony of Robert MacNail before the NCCPV, Dec. 18, 1968, transcript, p. 21. Howard K. Smith had such an experience on a "News and Comment" program on the political obituary of Richard Nixon. The show included a 2-minute interview with Alger Hiss. "/T/ here was a prompt rush for the door by several sponsors of *other* ABC programs, apparently on the theory that breaking a contract is better business than staying in the vicinity of adult reportage. At the end of the season, Smith's own sponsor deserted him. But the starkest display of apologetic journalism came from two of the ABC stations that refused to broadcast the program, then blacked out references to it in the next day's news reports."
45. "Giving Readers the Business," *Chicago Journalism Review*, October 1968, p. 3.
46. *Ibid.*
47. William L. Rivers, *Failing Newspaper Hearings, op. cit.*, footnote 29, pp. 394-395.
48. See also, "The Whole World is Watching," Public Broadcast Laboratory Broadcast, Dec. 22, 1968, at 8:30 p.m., script p. 18.
49. There is some research on this point, most of it quite old: See, discussion and sources cited in Klapper, *op. cit.*, footnote 12, pp. 38-43. One or two additional studies will be published in the next year.
50. Robert NacNeil, "The News on TV and How It Is Unmade," *Harpers*, May 1968, p. 75.
51. Testimony of Robert MacNeil, NCCPV Hearings, Dec. 18, 1968, transcript p. 21.
52. *1969 Broadcasting Yearbook*, p. 11.
53. *Ibid.* pp. E8-E15.
54. *Ibid.* pp. E8-E-18.
55. Bryce Rucker, *The First Freedom* (Southern Illinois University Press, 1968, p. 67.
56. *Ibid.* pp. 189-194.
57. *Ibid.* p. 68.
58. Bogart, *op. cit.*, footnote 3.
59. *Ibid.*
60. *Ibid.*
61. Rucker, *op. cit.*, footnote 55, p. 20.
62. Bogart, *op. cit.*, footnote 34; Rucker, *op. cit.*, footnote 25, p. 282.
63. Rucker, *Failing Newspaper Hearings, op. cit.*, footnote 25, p. 281.
64. Kenneth R. Byerly, "Newspaper Battle in Suburbia: Goliath vs. David," *Media/Scope* (August 1964), pp. 58-66.
65. Loyal B. Phillips, former president and publisher of late *Evening Independent* of St. Petersburg, Fla., testified: "In many cases the dominant newspaper holds exclusive contracts on the best editorial columns, women's features, comics, etc . . . In some instances the metropolitan dailies control publishing rights on syndicated features for smaller nearby cities, thus preventing publication in small city newspapers. Sometimes the dominant newspapers tie up syndicated features without using them." Testimony before the Antitrust Subcommittee of the Committee on the Judiciary Hearings on Concentration of Ownership in News Media, Mar. 14, 1963. The Transcript is in the office of Chairman Emanual Celler. "The *Philadelphia Evening Bulletin* pays $250 a week for Drew Pearson on the condition that Pearson will not be sold to any other paper in Pennsylvania, in Delaware, and in part of New Jersey." William Rivers, *Failing Newspaper Hearings, op. cit.*, footnote 25, p. 395. For a discussion of the role of synicated features in the economics of newspaper publishing see Rucker, *op. cit.*, footnote 55, pp. 60-79.
66. *United States V. World-Journal-Tribune, Inc.*, Civ. 66-2967 (S.D.N.Y.).
67. The most recent recap of this history is in Rucker, *op. cit.*, footnote 55, pp. 60-79.
68. *United States V. Chattanooga News-Free Press Co*, Crim. 7978 (E.D. Tenn: 1940) *United States V. Lorain Journal Company*, Civ. 26823 (N.D. Ohio: 1949) aff'd 342 U.S. 143 (1951); *United States V. The Namsfield Journal company*, Civ. 28235

(N.D. Ohio: 1951); *United States V. The Kansas City Star Co.* (Crim. 18444): 240 F. 2d 643 (8th civ. 1957) *cert.* denied 354 U.S. 923 (19); *United States V. The Kansas City Star Co.,* (Civ 7989; *United States V. Witchita Eagle Publishing Co., Inc.,* Civ. W 1876 (D. Kansas): (1959); *United States V. Times Picayune Publishing Company,* Civ. 1797 (E.D. La.: 1950) rev'd 345 U.S. 594 (19); *United States V. Harte-Hanks Newspapers, Inc.* Crim 15393 (N.D. Tex). See 170F. Supp. 227 (N.D. Tex., 1959); *United States V. The Lima News,* Civ. 64-178 (W.D. Ohio: 1964); *United States V. Lindsay-Schaub Newspapers, Inc.* Civ. 6748D (E.D. Ill.: 1967).

69. See Robert L. Crain, "Desegregation in New Orleans," Part III on *The Politics of School Desegration* (Garden City, N.Y.: Doubleday, 1969), pp. 235-322.

70. William R. Carmack, "Media Role in Aiding Social Change," *American Journal of Ortho-psychiatry,* (1959), p. 539; Stewart E. Perry, "The Conflict for the News Editor in Desegregation Disturbances: A Case Study in an American Social Process," *Psychiatry* (1963), pp. 352-367. In each of these cases there was a commitment by the community elite to avoid violence. Over a two-year period prior to integration in New Orleans, WDSU-TV repeatedly stated editorially that Southern cities that accepted integration peacefully had better future prospects and that "beating up freedom riders and calling on the empty legal doctrine of inter-position [which the Louisiana legislature did] were not the tactics of sane or reasonable people." William B. Monroe, Jr., "Television: The Chosen Instrument of the Revolution," *Race and the News Media* Paul L. Fisher & Ralph Lowenstein ed., (Anti-Defamation League of B'nai B'rith, 1967), pp. 85-86.

71. Richard Salant, quoted in George N. Gordon and Irving A. Falk, *TV Covers the Action,* (New York: Julian Messner, 1968), p. 166.

72. Sophy Burnham, "Telling It Like It Isn't," *New York Times Magazine,* Sept. 16, 1968, p. 13.

73. *Ibid.* p.14.

74. Douglass Cater, *The Fourth Branch of Government* (New York: Vintage Books, 1959), pp. 58-59.

75. *Ibid.* pp. 59-60.

76. *Time,* Apr. 18, 1969, pp. 22-23.

77. Robert NacNeil, *The People Machine* (New York: Harper & Row, 1968, pp. 315-316.

78. William L. Rivers and Wilbur Schramm, *Responsibility in Mass Communication* (New York: Harper & Row, 1969), p. 97.

79. Lawrence Fanning, *Race and the News Media,* p. 110.

80. Quoted by Monroe, Jr.*op. cit.,* footnote 70, p. 88.

81. Daniel Walker, *Rights in Conflict, A Report to the National Commission on the Causes and Prevention of Violence* (New York: Bantam, 1968), p. 303-304.

82. Monroe, jr. *op. cit.,* footnote 70, pp. 91-92.

83. Quoted by MacNeil, *op. cit.,* footnote 50, p. 75.

Chapter 6
COVERAGE OF CIVIL DISORDERS

In contrast to demonstrations, coverage of civil disorders raises slightly more difficult and serious issues. Some police officials believe that coverage of civil disorders in other cities encourages violence in their jurisdictions and, once a disturbance has begun, local coverage contributes to the size of the crowd and escalation of violence. In the spring of 1968, the executive director of the International Association of Police Chiefs, Quinn Tamm, stated, "If destructive and fatal riots occur in American cities this year, a major share of the blame must fall upon the shoulders of sensational 'journalists' and overnight pundits of the press who are assiduously stoking the fires of unrest."

Some evidence supports this view. Morris Janowitz has written that it is " . . . impossible to rule out the contention that detailed coverage of riots had an effect on potential rioters" and on the public at large. In addition to the instance where the presence of the camera has led rioters or police to play to the television audience and thereby exacerbate tensions and aggressive behavior, the more important feature is the impact of rioting on the wider audience:

> Again we are dealing with a process of social learning, especially for potential participants. Rioting is based on contagion, the process by which the mood and attitudes of those who are actually caught up in the riot are disseminated to a larger audience on the basis of direct contact. Television images serve to spread the contagion pattern throughout urban areas and the nation. Large audiences see the details of riots, the manner in which people participate in them, and especially the ferment associated with looting and obtaining commodities which was so much at the heart of riot behavior. Television presents detailed information about the tactics of participation and the gratifications that were derived . . . The media disseminate symbols of identification used by the rioters and their rationalizations. The mass media serve to reenforce and spread a feeling of consciousness among those who participate or sympathize with extremist actions, regardless of the

actions' origins. In particular, television offers them a mass audience far beyond their most optimistic aspirations.[1]

Prior to the disorder in Watts in 1965, the American news media had little recent experience in covering the civil disorders which have plagued the nation since. Media personnel made errors of judgment, as did others involved in these civil disorders. The judiciary, for example, was not equipped to handle the large number of arrests and arraignments required in Watts in 1965, Detroit in 1967, or Washington, D.C., and Chicago in 1968. Detention facilities were inadequate. The police were trained to act as individuals or groups of two and three. This training was clearly inadequate to deal with the massive disturbance which required a well disciplined force acting in unison in groups of 20 or more. The National Guard's performance in Detroit made it clear that special training and rules of conduct were necessary if they were to function efficiently and not contribute to racial tension. It was not until after the Kerner Commission recommended special training for Guard troops and the Attorney General and the International Association of Police Chiefs sponsored a conference at Airlie House in December 1967 for law enforcement officials from major cities that substantial progress began. Although the slow response of other organizations directly charged with maintaining the peace in our cities does not justify the errors of media performance, it does suggest that the media have a good deal of company. Moreover, it contains another important lesson: because an organization makes mistakes in the course of a civil disorder—whether it be the police or the news media—it does not necessarily follow that their role should be abolished. The mistakes should not be repeated and the salutary activities should be continued.

The most important function the news media serve during periods of civil disorder is communication of accurate information. Almost invariably, if a modicum of journalistic responsibility is exercised, the information relayed by the news media will be more conservative than the rumors that would circulate in its absence. When suggesting non-coverage, most critics overlook the possibility that the information that will dominate is more likely to escalate violence than media coverage.

The media, however, cannot cover events in any manner they please, nor is their past performance flawless. The decision to bar media coverage is a dangerous one, and the substitution of governmental news sources is undesirable. Although the latter alternative might provide information that most white adults believe, in many communities the majority of young blacks and important segments of the young white population would not.

Only four media practices—perhaps more accurately malpractices—make the desirability of coverage a close question. The first is media dissemination of rumors. The second is live coverage that informs potential looters and arsonists of the deployment of police or otherwise aids them in evading apprehension. Third is coverage that is apt to draw people to the scenes of a disorder when police seek to disperse the crowd. Last is the coverage of violent or other events likely to have a high emotional impact on the viewer without providing perspective—a practice defended by the television newsman on the ground that pictures do not lie. Some news organizations engaged in all four of these practices in the coverage of the 1965 Watts disorder.

A. Watts

John McCone, chairman of the commission which investigated the Watts disorder, concluded that any investigation of the news media coverage would be counter-productive; he believed that even if news coverage did contribute to the disturbance, the Commission had more to lose by criticizing than it could possibly gain through making suggestions that might persuade the media to modify their practices.[2] The McCone Commission's observation on the media were limited to three very mild paragraphs. The one specific comment was on coverage of a meeting of community leaders called to determine what might be done to quell the rioting started the night before. The television media were present. The meeting became a public forum where complaints from members of the Watts community were aired. Among the complaints were charges of police harassment, use of poverty funds to pay high salaries to city bureaucrats, and that Mayor Yorty, elected in 1960 with strong support from the black community, had ignored their problems.

The mother of the man whose arrest had sparked the disorders was present. She had also been arrested. Addressing the group, she said, "I am the woman who was arrested last night . . . But I'm not here to talk about that. I'm here to ask you, please, to help me and to help others in this community to calm the situation down so that we will not have a riot tonight." Voices in the audience endorsed her plea.

At that point, a young man about 16 years old seized the microphone: "It's like this, the way the policemens treat you round here, I'm going to tell you something. It ain't going to be lovely tonight whether you like it or not!" Those present showed their disapproval with whistles and jeers. He continued:

> I was down on Avalon last night, and we the Negro people have got completely fed up! They not going to fight down here no more. You know where they going to fight? They're after the Whiteys! They going to congregate. They don't care! They going out to Inglewood, Playa del Rey, and everywhere else the white man supposed to stay. They going to do the white man in tonight. And I'm going to you you . . . "

There was no question that the meeting was newsworthy. It is even possible that the young man's statement was newsworthy. It is doubtful, however, that the people who broadcast it had any notion of whether this young man had a following, whether there was any truth to what he said, or whether he was representing only himself and trying to steal a little air time.

One of the moderates at the meeting who saw the telecast responded: "Man, how come you come here stooging us like that? The white man ain't interested in nothing. Look to me like he want us to riot!" Another said: "Sure, baby! If that's the way they want to read it, that's the way we'll write the book!"[3]

Television told it the way it wasn't. This kind of coverage invites overresponse by the white community. It generates resentment in the black community. The Los Angeles performance should set to rest forever the myth that the camera cannot lie. What was reported was true, but the message received was probably 99 percent false. The news media must show more concern for the accuracy of the message *received*. It is not enough that the message *sent* is literally true. Showing the most dramatic aspect of the unusual can distort the message as much as false statements. By focusing only on the statement of the boy, a small slice of a significant event, the media misled and angered parts of their audience.

The second objection to the coverage of the Watts disorder, even more serious, was the indiscriminate dissemination of rumor. The most valuable function the media can serve in periods of high stress is to provide accurate information. When the media disseminate every available rumor, however, a good case can be made for eliminating coverage. Consider the following descriptions of media reporting on Watts:

> Chief Parker's office resembled the locker room of a team that has just won the world series. A television crew with live cameras was parked there permanently. Up to 20 reporters, filling the air with smoke and babble, were in constant attendance, moving out only to file stories and meet deadlines. Every report, every rumor that came in was immediately relayed raw and without qualification . . .
>
> Television and radio faithfully transmitted each of these reports without evaluation, and the listener, who was in no position to make any judgment, and who never learned that the ominous snipers downtown were a couple of drunks or that the location of the men seen loading shotguns was that of the Hollywood police station, assumed the worst and made it a banner weekend for gunshop owners, with sales up more than 250 per cent.
>
> Chief Parker told the press he continued to believe the rioting was unorganized, but that "I will say that other elements moved into it." The *Los Angeles Times* "interpreted" this as "Parker Hints Muslims Took Part in Rioting."[4]

This kind of reporting leaves the media with almost no useful function to serve during periods of civil crisis.

The third lesson from Watts teaches that live coverage can provide information to would-be looters and arsonists about the deployment of police and troops, and thereby assist them in evading apprehension. During the Watts disorders, live television coverage came via helicopter. While such coverage may have provided fast and accurate information to the public and to the police about the scale of the disorders, it also may have had a harmful effect.[5] At the Poughkeepsie Conference, sponsored by the Kerner Commission, representatives from the television industry agreed that live television coverage of Watts also inflamed the issue. Network news executives, as a result, expressed doubts that television would ever again present live coverage of a civil disorder.[6]

B. The 1967 Disturbances

In his charge to the Kerner Commission, President Johnson expressly requested they investigate "What effect do the mass media have on riots?"

The Commission reached three conclusions:

> First, that despite instances of sensationalism, inaccuracies, and

distortions, newspapers, radio, and television, on the whole, made a real effort to give a balanced, factual account of the 1967 disorders.

Second, that despite this effort, the portrayal of the violence that occurred last summer failed to reflect accurately its scale and character. The overall effect was, we believe, an exaggeration of both mood and event.

Third, and ultimately most important, we believe that the media have thus far failed to report adequately on the causes and consequences of civil disorders and the underlying problems of race relations.[7]

Many media representatives interpreted the report as having vindicated their performance. If measured against the more extreme allegations made against the media prior to the report's release, such may be the case, but it cannot be concluded from the report and the studies on which it was based that all the media learned their lessons in Watts.

The Commission found that the main causes of the imbalance that did occur were:

[A] significant imbalance between what actually happened in our cities and what the newspaper, radio, and television coverage of the riots told us happened . . . We found that the disorders, as serious as they were, were less destructive, less widespread, and less of a black-white confrontation than most people believed . . .

[D] espite the overall statistical picture, there were instances of gross flaws in presenting news of the 1967 riots. Some newspapers printed scare headlines unsupported by the mild stories that followed. All media reported rumors that had no basis in fact. Some newsmen staged riot events for the cameras . . .

[T] he press obtained much factual information about the scale of the disorders—property damage, personal injury, and deaths—from local officials, who often were inexperienced in dealing with civil disorders and not always able to sort out fact from rumor in the confusion . . .

[T] he coverage of the disorders—particularly on television—tended to define the events as black-white confrontations. In fact, almost all of the deaths, injuries, and property damage occurred in the all-Negro neighborhoods, and thus the disorders were not "race riots" as the term

[T] he main failure of the media last summer was that the totality of its coverage was not as representative as it should have been to be accurate. We believe that to live up to their own professed standards, the media simply must exercise a higher degree of care and a greater level of sophistication than they have shown in this area—higher, perhaps, than the level ordinarily acceptable with other stories.[8]

The Kerner Commission's finding that television coverage of the disorders was generally calm is predicated on the assumption that the number of sequences is the relevant standard of measurement. Of the 955 sequences from local and national television analyzed, 27.4 percent were classified as emotional, 51.7 percent were found to be calm. These findings supported the conclusion that coverage was relatively calm. Yet the quantity of emotional versus calm material tells very little about the effect of the material broadcast on viewers. At the Democratic National Convention, CBS news devoted a total of 38 hours and 3 minutes to coverage of the convention, but only 32 minutes and 20 seconds, or 1.4 percent, were devoted to film or tape coverage of the demonstrations. On the NBC network, out of a total of 19 hours and 37 minutes of its overall convention coverage, approximately 13 minutes and 49 seconds were devoted to film or tape coverage of disorders involving demonstrations and police.[8] If all convention activities that might have been stimulated by the disorders were included in the CBS count, e.g., the speech by Senator Ribicoff, the total amount of time devoted to disorders, both calm and emotional, figures at less than 4 percent. But in view of the letters and phone calls received by the networks and the FCC, this material had a tremendous impact.

The research of Benjamin D. Singer on persons arrested during the 1967 Detroit riots also suggests that the emotional sequences tend to dominate. When asked, "What were most people doing in these riots [seen on television]," 46 percent remembered property being destroyed or looted, 28 percent perceived whites committing aggression against Negroes, 14 percent reported that they had seen fighting in a general sense, and 9 percent reported Negroes fighting against law enforcement officials and soldiers.[10]

As Martin S. Hayden, editor and chief of the *Detroit News,* has observed:

> Even though the Commission's own content analysis indicates that emotional, violent scenes were a minor proportion of the entire coverage, it remains obvious that one picture of angry blacks smashing stores, or policemen blazing away at a building, has an impact greater by far than a dozen portrayals of civic leaders urging calm or expressing concern, and another dozen dispassionate discussions of the underlying causes.[11]

A second conclusion, that the coverage was generally factual and balanced, is also suspect. To have reached the conclusion that coverage was factual and balanced, it would have been necessary to examine not only the content of the television materials broadcast, but also to have observers on the scene of the disorder to record what they saw. This was the approach taken in assessing the accuracy of the coverage of a MacArthur Day parade back in 1952.[12] Although not perfect, in the absence of having such observers, the observations of ghetto residents are the next best standard for comparison. They concluded overwhelmingly a consistent exaggeration and unrepresentative coverage.

Interviews with 567 Negroes in seven cities indicated that consistently they felt that local and national news media greatly exaggerated the rioting in the cities. Those interviewed thought that the news media focused on: (1) the amount of damage done by rioters; (2) how rampant damage was; (3) the amount of looting done; (4) how many persons were arrested; (5) the presence of guns or other weapons used by rioters. They also indicated that other crucial and widespread incidents were either never reported or, if reported, not adequately. Negroes interviewed said that sensationalism, the result of quoting uninformed sources rather than seeking out reliable sources of information, was geared to widen misunderstanding between Negroes and whites.

Ghetto residents felt that the news media placed no emphasis on the amount of police brutality or the number of deaths inflicted by police, state troopers and federal troops; on the attempts at riot control by members of the Negro community or outsiders and that such attempts were discouraged by the authorities. The local news media, Negroes contended, sympathized with and were in complete accord with city officials and police action in controlling the rioting.

Persons interviewed in ghetto areas suggested that network coverage "overplayed" and exaggerated, but that local newscasts had more balance and accuracy. Field researchers reported a high degree of hostility toward television among ghetto residents—particularly Negro teenagers—based on what they felt was a pronounced discrepancy between what they saw happening in the riots and what they saw on television.

The Kerner Commission study concluded that newspaper coverage, like television coverage, was generally calm, factual, and restrained, not emotional or inflammatory. Of the total of 3,045 riot-related articles, 502 (16.5 percent) focused primarily on legislation that should be sought and planning that should be done to prevent or control future riots. Approximately 45.8 percent focused upon the action of the disorders: defiance and mob action; police brutality; fire bombing, arson; Negro attack against enforcement agents; sniping; looting, vandalism; harm to property or persons; general disorder; and enforcement, containment or control. The newspaper analyst got less of an impression than the television analyst of the riots as a confrontation between whites and Negroes.

Newspapers tended to characterize the disorder as national, rather than local phenomena, especially when the rioting was in the newspaper's hometown—a view that squares with the Chamber of Commerce perspective of local newspapers to downplay difficulties in their community and focus upon problems of other communities. In addition, by portraying the disorders as national rather than local phenomena, the implication persisted that no special fault lay with local residents.

During the actual disorders, the newspapers in each city studied tended to emphasize the news of racial problems elsewhere. At least 40 percent of all stories originated from other than local sources. Newspapers gave almost as much headline coverage to riots in other cities as they did to the riot in their own cities. In part, this may be the result of exaggerated wire-service stories.

Martin Hayden, has suggested

> "an almost mathematical relationship between the level of exaggeration and the distance of news transmission. Detroiters following their newspapers and local TV and radio stations had no illusions: the situation was bad. Anyone trying to follow the story from California got a different mixture of fact and fiction suggesting the whole city was 'gone.' Take my word for it; Detroit is still there."[13]

Much of the responsibility, he says, can be traced to the wire service:

> The problem began with press association transmission .... On the second day of the riot UPI reported:

> Detroit—National Guard tanks rumbled through blazing, riot-torn Negro neighborhoods where gunfire left dead and wounded in the streets and entire blocks of buildings ablaze.

Our managing editor called to complain that nobody could find UPI's tanks. The press association responded with proof: a photograph of tanks in a school yard—where they stayed parked for another day while media in other cities still had them "rumbling" through Detroit's streets.

On the Friday of the riot week the trouble essentially was over. The *Detroit News* front page featured a think piece on snipers and who they might have been. Our page one picture was of two national guardsmen watching a shapely girl sashaying down the street. But UPI that morning reported:

Jumpy police and national guardsmen, using tanks and machine guns, waged war early today with savage snipers, the hard-core remnants of a riot which wracked Detroit with the worst racial violence in modern U.S. History.

A third example came over UPI wires on July 28:

Chicago—More than 200 people have been killed in the Detroit rioting but the news media have intentionally withheld the story from the public, according to Negro entertainer and civil rights activist Dick Gregory.

Ten paragraphs said Gregory had "proof" of the charge. The UPI staff in Detroit knew it was hokum. But we still are trying to live the story down. There remain people convinced that somebody achieved the remarkable and disposed of hundreds of bodies.[14]

Reports like these clarify why some newspaper editors felt that the disorders in other cities were more newsworthy.

As in Watts, the Kerner Commission learned that the media did pass on rumors:

In Detroit, a radio station broadcast a rumor, based on a telephone tip, that Negroes planned to invade suburbia one night later; if plans existed, they never materialized.

In Cincinnati, several outlets ran a story about white youths arrested for possessing a bazooka; only a few reports mentioned that the weapon was inoperable.

In Tampa, a newspaper repeatedly indulged in speculation about impending trouble. When the state attorney ruled the fatal shooting of a Negro youth justifiable homicide, the paper's news columns reported: "There were fears today that the ruling would stir new race problems for Tampa tonight." The day before, the paper quoted one "top lawman" as telling reporters "he now fears that Negro residents in the Central Avenue project and in the West Tampa trouble spots feel they are in competition and trying to see which can cause the most unrest—which area can become the center of attraction."

A West Coast newspaper put out an edition headlined: "Rioting Erupts in Washington, D.C. Negroes Hurl Bottles, Rocks at Police Near White House." The story did not support the headline. It reported what was actually the fact: that a number of teenage Negroes broke store windows and threw bottles and stones at police and firemen near downtown Washington, a mile or more from the White House. On the other hand, the same paper did not report unfounded local rumors of sniping when other news media did.[15]

Not without some justification, therefore, have some law enforcement officials doubted the efficacy of media coverage. Yet these examples are considerably weaker than those of rumors disseminated by the media during Watts.

C. 1968

This Commission did not conduct any factual investigation of the disorders that followed the assassination of Dr. Martin Luther King, Jr. Quite early, the Media Task Force considered contracting a content analysis similar to that sponsored by the Kerner Commission. After discussing the matter with research organizations, and after evaluating the utility of a content analysis without having had observers on the scene, the Task Force concluded that the possible results could not justify the expenditure.

The various fact-finding Task Forces—in Chicago, Miami, Cleveland, and San Franciso—were requested to evaluate the role of the media, but time limitations made comprehensive evaluation almost impossible. With regard to Chicago, it might have been feasible to have undertaken such a study using the substantial outtakes from both NBC and CBS as a gauge. CBS however, refused to entertain any inquiry into its "news judgment," and NBC, while not flatly refusing, expressed strong reservations.

From the Chicago, Miami, Cleveland, and San Francisco reports, from interviews with representatives of the news media, and from other sources, both public and private, we have concluded, not surprisingly, that some news organizations have made substantial progress toward responsible coverage of disorders while others, unfortunately, have made little or none.

The mayor of the District of Columbia, Walter Washington, said, toward the end of the April 1968 disorders:

> I must say at this point never in my public life have I seen a more responsive press and a more responsive media. I should say for the citizens of this city that I am appreciative for the press, radio and TV that have reported, and reported accurately, and reported well and fast, so that you could keep abreast and be assured of the condition as it advanced and progressed.

But a study conducted by the Lemberg Center at Brandeis University also indicates that coverage of urban violence needs improvement. The analysis of press reactions to 25 alleged sniping incidents in 24 cities during July and August of 1968 illustrates the effects of the newsman's pursuit of conflict upon news judgment.

The Lemberg Center study concluded that the disorders of July 23-26, 1968, in Cleveland, involving pitched gun battles between black nationalists and police, shaped press interpretations of subsequent sniping incidents in other cities. The *Cleveland Press* and the *New York Times* both characterized the Cleveland disorder as an organized plot against the police. Subsequent reports of sniping in other cities supported the view that a new phase in the course of racial conflict had begun, and this view became widespread. On August 3, 1968 the *New York Times* said in an editorial:

> ... The pattern in 1967 has not proven to be the pattern of 1968. Instead of violence almost haphazardly exploding, it has sometimes been deliberately planned. And while the 1967 disorders served to rip away false facades of racial progress and expose rusting junkyards of broken promises, the 1968 disorders also reveal a festering militancy that prompts some to resort to open warfare.[16]

Again, on Sept. 13, 1968, *Time* took note of an "ominous trend" in the country:

> Violence as a form of Negro protest appears to be changing from the spontaneous combustion of a mob to the premeditated shoot-outs of the farout few. Many battles have started with well planned sniping at police.[17]

The Brandeis study of these 25 incidents does not support this view. In 20 of the 25 disorders, there was no evidence of planning. Seventeen were traced to unplanned incidents, frequently related to police action. Of the other five incidents, only in Cleveland was there any significant evidence of planning, and even that is in doubt.[18]

Analysis of newspaper clippings and interviews with police officials from each of the 24 cities led to the following conclusions:

> 1. The overwhelming number of disorders surveyed failed to display conclusive evidence of a new type of racial violence based on conspiracy and guerilla tactics.
> 2. Initial versus later reports of sniping showed many discrepancies concerning the amount of sniping. These discrepancies included a downward revision of early sniping figures, particularly where the following items were concerned: the number of snipers involved, the number of shots fired, and the number of policemen involved as targets.
> 3. The press—at both the local and national level—was inclined toward imprecise, distorted, inaccurate reporting. In some instances, the press revealed a tendency to needlessly sensationalize the news.
>
> These findings lead to the conclusion that sniping reports have generally been exaggerated and that recent suggestions of a new 'trend' of racial violence based upon the events of last summer are highly questionable.

The Lemberg criticism of both the local and national press—the wire services, individual newspapers, and the national news magazines—sharpens to a few salient observations: early press reports were inaccurate and distorted; too little attention was given to the immediate causes of the disturbances; and, in the aftermath, few attempts (with the notable exception of the *New York Times* on the Cleveland disorders) were made to verify previous statements or to assess the tensions and grievances rooted in the community. Failing on all these fronts, the national press, in particular, was overzealous in its reports of a "trend" based on limited and unconfirmed evidence.

D. Reporting Civil Disorders

The Kerner Commission made several recommendations to improve media performance during civil disorders. The Media Task Force endorses each of them.

Much of what should be done requires only good judgment and planning. Local media should contact their law enforcement agencies, and receive briefings at least twice a year on the prospects for violent disorders and whenever a planned event has a potential for violence. At such a briefing, they should be advised of the plans the police have made for dealing with emergencies and their reasons for the planned response. When violence erupts, the police should be prepared to establish channels of communication with the news media to assure the rapid and efficient flow of information.

The need for such a system was apparent in Detroit:

> At a time of rioting, rumors are rampant and tend to grow as exhaustion sets in. Tensions rise and incidents tend to be exaggerated by overreaction. These rumors can have serious effects.
>
> Authoritative sources of information must be identified quickly, developed on a priority basis and maintained, with full reliance placed on them. Regular news conferences must be held by senior civilian and military officials; if they are not, the press will follow the sensational reports and fan the rumors. Members of the press, as feasible, should be permitted to accompany senior officials on tours of the riot areas, and to share in their evaluations in order to provide the facts to the public quickly and authoritatively. Regular formal contact with the press should be augmented by frequent background briefings for community leaders because rumors flourish at all levels.[19]

Conflict will naturally arise between the objectives of the news media and the objectives of the police. The newsmen want to report as fully as possible; the police want to prevent escalation of the disorder and to restore the peace. Yet the police and press have common interests. Full, fast, and accurate reporting can make a contribution to restoring order. On balance, the effects of coverage of civil disorders are positive; but the news organizations can take steps to reduce even further the negative effects of their reporting, and in important measure, their success depends upon the full cooperation of local officials.

Prior liaison by the media should not be limited to the police. If the news organization has followed the Task Force suggestions made earlier to establish communication with Negro and with other dissident organizations in the community, they will also tap these news sources. But development of these sources must be made prior to the disturbance; without them, there can be no balanced coverage.

Advance contact with rumor centers is also important. During the April

1968 disorders, Washington, D.C., Chicago, and several other cities established rumor centers, which consisted of a battery of telephones manned by persons provided with the latest information. Through regular reports from such a rumor center, the media can be in a much better position to determine the most frequent rumors and thereby be better able to perform their important function of destroying rumors.

Collectively, and within their own organizations, the news media can accomplish much before the disorder starts. Indeed, how much they do may determine whether it starts at all or, if it does, how much it grows.

The most controversial and difficult issue for radio and television centers on the delay of news. Where the news event is of a kind likely to symbolize past injustices to any significant group in the community, there is a danger that such an event may trigger a large-scale disorder.[20] Moreover, once a crowd has begun to gather at the scene of such an event, immediate broadcast of the event and its precise location is likely to draw additional persons to the area and add to crowd-control problems of the police, thereby contributing to the likelihood of a violent outbreak and its severity if it does occur. Consider the following example from this Commission's Miami Task Force report:

> [During the early minutes of the riot in Miami], as at all times before and after, the activities of the news media were unrestricted in the area of the disturbances. They used their own discretion in determining where to go and what to do. The fact that the disturbances were taking place was aired promptly on two radio stations serving primarily black community. One newscaster made a telephone call to one of the stations from the scene, and his report came "live" on the air in the midst of a popular rock-n-roll show. This medium, perhaps more than any other was responsible for quickly spreading the word and attracting more people to the scene with concomitant problems.[21]

No two events are exactly the same. The solution necessarily rests in the competence and good judgment of newsmen and media executives, but recent experience does suggest some of the considerations to be weighed in deciding how soon to report inflammatory incidents and how to report them without contributing to already overburdened police officials and, in some cases, to alleviate tension.

Once it is decided that the incident is potentially inflammatory or may attract a crowd to the scene, most of the newsmen with whom we have discussed the problem suggest a delay of a least 30 minutes to confirm the story, make sure the facts are clear, and to avoid exaggeration. Under particular circumstances it may require a delay of an hour or longer. Media transmittal of unconfirmed reports, emotional or unbalanced accounts, and visual portrayals of violence without perspective can do at least as much damage as news delay. Where community-wide guidelines are in effect, it is best to designate one journalist representative to determine the length of the embargo. Such centralization eliminates the competitive pressures that tend to undermine this policy. A complete embargo beyond one hour, and preferably beyond 30 minutes, probably cannot be justified.[22]

There are at least three reasons for this: (1) failure to make any report will result in the spread of unchallenged rumors; (2) additional delay will impair the credibility of the media, perhaps not for that particular incident but for future incidents; (3) persons who might otherwise travel through the area must be advised to avoid it.

News of the 1943 Detroit race riot was censored because of the war. Yet, Negroes in rural Mississippi, 700 miles away, received news of the event one day later from Pullman car porters on the Illinois Central Railroad.[23]

In June 1967, a Negro male was found dead in his cell at the Onondaga County Public Safety Building in Syracuse, N.Y. Word spread throughout the city that he had been shot. Onondaga County Sheriff Patrick Corbitt initiated a tour of the cell area and presented a statement to five Negro clergymen concerning the incident. The spokesman for the Negro ministers as well as the county coroner appeared on television. They reported that the cause of death was definitely not external injury. Some local officials believed that these immediate steps to broadcast the findings reduced the possibility of trouble.

In Washington, D.C., the shooting of a woman near 14th and U Streets by a white police officer resulted in a minor disturbance. All the ingredients for a disorder were present. Rumors had already started to the effect that a child and two women, one of them pregnant, had been shot and killed by a white policeman. One department spokesman, present at the scene, stated that it took about 1.2 seconds for the rumor to run from 14th and U Streets to 14th and Columbia Road and back, a distance of several blocks. This same officer reported that on-the-spot coverage of the incident by black journalists resulted in the quick dissemination of accurate information which calmed residents in the area. Three important factors worked together: restraint, a credible medium, and police/media cooperation.

If any doubt persists that news of an incident will travel throughout the community regardless of whether it is reported, recall that the Kerner Commission survey found that during the Detroit riot, where the news embargo extended well beyond an hour, 74 percent of the ghetto residents interviewed learned of the disorder through word of mouth. As a general rule, communications through such channels will be a gross exaggeration of any injustice that may have occurred, or even a complete fabrication. In Watts, for example, the arrest of an intoxicated driver drew a crowd. A woman wearing a barber's smock was also arrested for assaulting an officer. But, the totally false rumor was soon circulating that she was pregnant and had been roughly abused by the police.

The city of Chicago has a city-wide code which provides that news of a disturbance shall not be broadcast until the police have it under control. The difficulty with such a rule is that it may be hours, perhaps even days, before the police achieve such control. In the meantime, the public needs to know what is happening. In Detroit, for example, the first person killed, a woman, was shot while driving through the riot area. If she had listened to the radio or had watched TV at mid-morning of that day, she did not have a chance to learn of the riot because Detroit stations kept it off the air for hours at the request of Negro leadeers.

The dilemma of meeting the public's need to know and rumor suppression without contributing to the size of the crowd can be resolved by restrained reporting until the police have the situation under control or until the information is no longer likely to contribute to the disorder. The most important piece of information to withhold is the *precise* location of the disturbance. At the same time, the media can advise people to avoid the *general* area. If the police have planned adequately, they should be able to advise the media of routes to avoid and to suggest alternative routes for people who normally use the affected streets.

In cases where some delay is necessary, it is absolutely essential that the media take more than usual steps to report fully at a later date.

Many journalists believe that the basic requirements for good reporting—intelligence, judgment, lack of bias, responsibility, restraint, and balance—provide adequate standards for meeting any challenge. Certainly no set of government or industry guidelines can adequately replace these long-standing fundamentals of good journalism. Others in the news media believe, however, that coverage of disorders requires elaboration of these principles in the form of specific rules. We concur. During periods of stress, general principles are not self-executing. The guidelines adopted by many news organizations acknowledge that the problems of covering violence in an unstable, often racially troubled, social environment make more specific rules of behavior necessary.

In reporting both incidents that may grow to disorders and the disorders themselves, the media can make additional preparations within their own organizations. They can issue instructions to their staff along the lines of the guidelines discussed in Appendix II-C.

Some TV stations, for example, have already made the decision not to cover riots with live mobile television units. Rather than send conspicuous shoulder-braced sound cameras to a riot, they can plan to send the much smaller, hand-held silent cameras, plus a man with a tape recorder to pick up random sound. Similarly, they can use black and white instead of color film, which requires more light; in this way, they can reduce the need for crowd-attracting lights and apparatus. They should plan, in advance, the deployment of manpower within the news organization, what the process for assimilation shall be, and who shall exercise responsibility at each stage.

A neighborhood fight should not be called a riot. A disturbance should not be designated racial without confirmation. Accuracy should have priority over speed. The story, particularly its violent aspects, should be kept in perspective. Known visible facts should be reported in a calm, matter-of-fact manner. Lights should not be used if they heighten tension. If it becomes apparent that the media's presence attracts a crowd or causes extremists to act for the cameras, the lens should be capped and the crew withdrawn. No information, including police contingency plans that might aid rioters in evading apprehension by the police should be disseminated; reporting without specific details or delayed reporting can usually avoid this problem.

During the course of the coverage of disorders, news decisions will have to be made. In the local newsroom of a radio or television station, different men may be putting bulletins on the air, assigning TV cameramen, reviewing and editing film and scripts, and producing, in coordination with the newscasters, television and radio news programs: all these people should check their major decisions with the news director.

If, for example, the police radio carries a report of a National Guardsman being shot, it is tempting to put this on the air, because it has the surface authenticity of a police report. Many of these reports are based on rumors and are simply requests for confirmation by a police officer. The story is skimpy; no details substantiate it. During the tension of a riot, the police can act hastily and carelessly. Moreover, the day is past when everything the police say should be broadcast as "truth." The report must be confirmed.

This event supposedly happened in Cleveland: There was a police report that a National Guardsman was shot. The wire services picked it up and several radio stations put it on the air. But at least one news director decided to keep it off the air until one of his men could go to the scene and check it. It turned out that a Guardsman had simply fallen off a jeep and lain in the streets a few seconds after his fall. Nobody had been shot.

In the case of a disturbance in Washington, D.C., a report came in from a newsman on the scene that a mob was smashing windows one mile from the White House. The editor canceled out the reference to the White House as irrelevant and alarmist. The general location of the disturbance was reported, but not the exact corner. Specific instructions for avoiding the area were given to motorists.

For another possible case, a film clip comes in showing several young people looting a clothing store. A policeman is standing by, watching. Does it go on the air? Yes, if the event can be put in perspective. During the April 1968 disorders in Washington, such scenes appeared on the air. Many people objected to the showing of the clip. These scenes, they thought, gave potential looters the impression that the police did nothing. Others objected to the laxity of the police. One responsible news director has suggested that it is sufficient to point out that there was only *one* policeman present, and he would leave it to the audience to infer that the officer was not being cowardly or cynical, but was just using good judgment.

Is this adequate? A number of studies suggest that simply displaying the facts frequently results in a lost message.[24] The reporter should expressly state the reasons, or the probable reasons why the police are doing nothing. For example, where the looters outnumber the policemen, they probably cannot be apprehended without the application of deadly force; this could endanger the lives of the officers and would contribute to the tension in the community. The large-scale application of deadly force to prevent crimes against property, particularly against teenaged looters, as many of them were in Washington, D.C., may escalate the response of the extremists in the black community.

Another film clip comes in showing policemen swinging their batons at rioters. Does it go on the air? Again yes, but only if it can be put in perspective. News media face no more difficult task than to decide when a scene of violence should be broadcast and how it should be cast. At least one news director suggests that it is sufficient to broadcast such material as long as the newscaster does not make "purple" statements such as, "he swung viciously," or they "cracked skulls." He says, "let the film tell the story."

The film cannot tell the story. It represents a very small slice of the disorder. It does not tell why the police were cracking skulls; whether they were attacked by the mob; whether the mob had been ordered to disperse and refused to do so; whether they were trying to rescue an officer or another threatened person; or whether they had just lost their senses and, for no apparent reason, decided to beat up some people. Just showing the film clip openly invites every viewer to supply his own reason why, and it will be the viewer's preconceptions about rioters or police that will determine what story he receives—not the film. Just showing the film may be the easy way out of a difficult decision for the reporter, but just showing the film is not enough.

The reporting of riots often takes on the color of the policeman's viewpoint because the reporter usually goes into the riot area with the police and he normally sticks by them. If he is being shot at by the same sniper who is shooting at the police, the reporter identifies and sympathizes with the police. But he is not the police department's public relations office. If he witnesses police misconduct, he should report it. When the police perform well under extreme provocation, long hours, and accompanying tension, he should report that too.

The reporter can offset this tendency to tell the story from the official viewpoint by being especially alert to evidence of black assistance in crowd control and in cooling the situation. The Kerner Commission found the media somewhat remiss in reporting the good work done by ghetto residents.

* * *

With a few exceptions such as the Washington Post, the Media Task Force's five-city survey turned up little evidence of newspaper guidelines for the coverage of violent events.[25] Also, the failure of 50 percent of the radio stations to respond to the Task Force's questionnaire suggests limited adoption of guidelines, except at the national level.

All news organizations should give serious consideration to codifying guidelines parallel to those already promulgated by the major networks, by the Washington Post, and by other news organizations. Although no set of guidelines will cover all eventualities, the more specific they are, and the more they are discussed within the news organization, the greater the probability that the reporter or correspondent under stress will adhere to them.

Most of the initiative for developing guidelines should come from individual news organizations. Journalism is a diverse, loosely knit, pluralistic institution, and should remain so. Few critical journals and no strong professional organizations prescribe rules of conduct or levy sanctions. Little leadership comes from the schools of journalism. Professional organizations, such as Sigma Delta Chi and the American Society of Newspaper Editors, have considered riot coverage and related issues, but have not exercised strong leadership.

Electronic journalism, fortunately, does. The National Association of Broadcasters (NAB) and the Radio-Television News Directors Association (RTNDA) have both promulgated codes of ethics and standards for news broadcasting and, together with network news policies, have provided touchstones for news reporting. Standards for reporting violence for the networks and the NAB and RTNDA are similar in focus—to avoid inflammatory or morbid or sensational reporting—with the networks being the most specific.

Over the last year or so, seminars and discussion groups have discussed riot coverage and surveillance of the ghetto; these have undoubtedly heightened the awareness of participants to special needs and problems. Such activities should continue and should be initiated by national, state and local professional organizations, and by schools of journalism.

The potential for leadership in the RTNDA is underscored by the activities of its northern California chapter. After discussing the sensitive role of the broadcaster in civil disorders, the chapter designated a committee to recommend suggested guidelines. In setting out these policy guides, the RTNDA committee observed that the majority of news directors in the region felt that such a set of guidelines was necessary in this one area of coverage because, among other reasons,

"an instance of widespread civil disobedience, particularly one involving racial strife, is entirely unique from any other kind of story in that its coverage could affect the direction of its development and intensity, its duration and outcome and therefore demands exception treatment . . . "

This particular set of guidelines was endorsed by the chapter membership and submitted to station managements and law enforcement officials. Judging from the returns from the Task Force's inquiry into San Diego, the circulation of the guidelines in Northern California influenced the adoption of similar guidelines by many radio and television stations in that State. The entire RTNDA and the American Society of Newspaper Editors would do well to consider undertaking similar action nationwide.

REFERENCES

1. Cited in Hugh Davis Graham and Ted Robert Gurr, the *History of Violence in America,* Report submitted to the National Commission on the Causes and Prevention of Violence, (New York: Bantam Books, 1969). p. 440.
2. Williams L. Rivers and Wilbur Schramm, *Responsibility in Mass Communication* (New York: Harper and Row, 1969), p. 175.
3. Robert Conot, *Rivers of Blood, Years of Darkness* (New York: Bantam Books, 1967), pp. 154-155.
4. *Ibid.* p. 151.
5. William B. Monroe, Jr., "Television: The Chosen Instrument of the Revolution," in *Race and the News Media,* Paul L. Fisher and Ralph L. Lowenstein, eds. (New York: Anti-Defamation League of B'nai B'rith, 1967), p. 92.
6. *Report of The National Advisory Commission on Civil Disorders,* (Washington, D.C.: U.S. Govt. Print. Off., March 1968), pp. 205-206.
7. *Ibid.*, p. 201.
8. *Ibid.,* pp. 202-203.
9. Letter written at the direction of the Federal Communications Commission by Ben F. Waple, Secretary, to ABC, CGS, and NBC, Feb. 28, 1969, p. 2. footnote 1.
10. Benjamin D. Singer, "Journalism and the Kerner Report: The Report's Critique of Television," *Columbia Journalism Review,* Fall 1968, p. 57. ("I don't know" responses were eliminated in computing these figures.)
11. Martin S. Hayden, "A View From Detroit," in *The Media and the Cities,* Charles U. Daly, ed. (Chicago: University of Chicago Press), p. 60.
12. Kurt Lang and Gladys Engel Lang, *Politics & Television* (Chicago: Quadrangle Books, 1968), pp. 36-78.
13. Hayden, *op. cit.,* footnote 11, p. 58.
14. *Ibid.* p. 57-59.
15. Kerner Commission, *op. cit.,* footnote 6, p. 202.
16. *Sniping Incidents: A New Pattern of Violence?* (Waltham, Mass.: Lemberg Center for the Study of Violence, Brandeis University, February, 1969).
17. *Ibid.*
18. Louis H. Masotti and Jerome R. Corsi, *Shoot Out in Cleveland;* A Staff Report to the NCCPV, (Washington, D.C.: U.S. Govt. Print. Off., May 1969), *Passim.*
19. Final Report of Cyrus R. Vance, Special Assistant to the Secretary of Defense Concerning the Detroit Riots, July 23 through August 2, 1967 (August 1967).

20. Louis B. Schwartz and Stephen R. Goldstein, "Demonstrations, Picketing, Riots," *Police Guidance Manuals: A Philadelphia Model* (Philadelphia: University of Pennsylvania, 1968), pp. 24-28; FBI, *op. cit.,* footnote 1, p. 17.
21. *Miami Report,* The Report of the Study Team on Civil Disturbances in Miami, Florida during the week of August 5, 1968, (Washington, D.C.: U.S. Govt. Print. Off., 1969), p. 11.
22. A "brief voluntary moratorium" on reporting the news was one of the two characteristics common to the community wide broadcast codes that the Justice Department's Community Relations Service evaluated for the Kerner Commission in 1967. The specific period of delay, the CRS pointed out, was seldom more than 30 minutes—sufficiently long to assure accuracy and balance.
23. Ben H. Bagdikian, "Editorial Responsibility in Times of Urban Disorder," *The Media and the Cities,* Charles U. Daly, ed. (Chicago: University of Chicago Press, 1968), p. 17.
24. Wallace Mandell and Carl I. Hoveland, "Is There a Law of Primacy in Persuasion?" *American Psychologist* (1952), p. 538; Elihu Katz and Paul F. Lazarsfeld, *Personal Influence: The Part Played by People in the Flow of Mass Communications* (New York: The Free Press, 1955).
25. See Appendix II-C.

Chapter 7

JOURNALISM EDUCATION*

The only place where one can learn
to be a journalist is in
a great newspaper

— Frederic Hudson, *New
York Herald*, Circa 1870.

Young men writing in the great newspapers
were as a rule profoundly ignorant
of the simplest history or philosophy.

— Andrew Dickson White,
president, Cornell
University, 1868.

In the half-century following the Civil War, journalism education moved, haltingly, onto the American college campus. Its establishment as a college-level program was accompanied by a debate as to whether there should be collegiate preparation for the practice of journalism. From the vantage point of 1969, the resolution of the debate was never really in doubt.

During this same period America was transforming its system of higher education into a mass producer of the specialists required by a developing industrial nation. The professions, and would-be professions, were being legitimized by higher education, and it was not possible to ignore journalism.

There were those who regarded professional training as unnecessary. Journalists like Frederic Hudson of the *New York Herald* argued in the 1870's that a training school of journalism could not be made "very serviceable." He asked: "Who are to be the teachers? The only place one can learn to be a good journalist is in a great newspaper office . . . College training is good in its way, but something more is needed for journalism."[1] Many of today's journalists agree.

Sentiments such as Hudson's did not prevent the incorporation of journalism instruction into the universities. But the accompanying debate probably tended to obscure a more significant issue: the relationship of two important American institutions, the university and the press.

---

* This chapter is based almost entirely on a paper prepared for the Media Task Force by Professor I. W. Cole of the Medill School of Journalism at Northwestern University.

Because this issue was not resolved, journalism education, like Alexander Pope's Man, has existed on an "isthmus of a middle state." At one extreme, journalism education has been expected to function as a service to the press-as-business by recruiting employees and providing them with basic training—that is, functioning as a sort of campus extention of the personnel departments of the mass media. At the other extreme, journalism education has been expected to improve the press-as-a-social instrument—that is, serve the society by changing the press.

An educator of the period, Andrew Dickson White, was concerned with improving the press as a social instrument. Inaugurated as president of Cornell in 1868, he proposed to establish "departments for the instruction especially of those who intend entering public life through the newspaper or the forum." He believed that young men serving the great newspapers were, "as a rule profoundly ignorant of the simplest history or philosophy."[2]

Generally, the issue was resolved in favor of the universities serving the press as business. To a large extent, this still is the pervading influence, considerably refined, in present-day journalism programs. As a result, the journalism program is likely to reflect the needs of the press as perceived by the press; it makes journalism education a circular process, in which current newsroom practices are observed and emulated in the classroom.

In fairness to both the university and the press it should be noted that the issues are not as black and white as this summary would make them appear. More thoughtful leaders in both campus and newsrooms have sought diligently to resolve the ambivalence and ambiguity which has hampered both education for journalism and the practice of journalism. There are universities which, perhaps subliminally, view their journalism programs as being a form of public relations with the state press. There are many others that perceive a more significant fuction. Conversely there are employers of journalism graduates who regard journalism education as simply an extension of the firm's personnel department. But there are many others who are impatient with journalism schools for producing too many young men and women well drilled in yesterday's practices rather than prepared to devise tomorrow's solutions.

All professional and specialized programs in higher education have faced similar problems in this respect. In his examination of journalism and liberal education, Paul L. Dressel states:

> ... it should be observed that much of the early education in this country in all professional callings was narrowly technical. Most curricula in that day and indeed up to very recent times emphasized handbook information artd rule-of-thumb procedures while neglecting basic theory and generalized knowledge useful in the infinitely varied circumstances of everyday practice ....
>
> The most advanced views today assume that if it is to be fully effective in preparing graduates for the complicated demands of contemporary life, professional education must have not a single goal but rather three comprehensive objectives. First, because of its very nature, it must obviously inculcate the corpus of knowledge, the complement of skills, and the traits of personality and character which constitute the distinctive features of a particular craft ....

A second purpose, and one of rising importance, is concerned with the general education which all those who attend an institution of higher education must have if they are to understand, and to live competently in, an increasingly complex democratic society . . . .

Furthermore, an educational institution can hardly absolve itself of a third responsibility—that of assisting the student in gaining self-understanding, a moral grounding, and a consistent view of the world.[3]

The limitations of a system of journalism education oriented to serving the press as business are serious and the advantages few. To the extent that those newsroom practices that appear to be the most sound are selected for emulation, this approach can lead to evolutionary changes in the press, and this indeed has been an important function of journalism education. Yet the disadvantages far outweigh this very tenuous contribution.

Journalist Eugene Methvin, for example, writing in *The New Leader*, reports that some members of his profession are concerned that modern journalism may be caught in the "tradition trap." He writes:

Science Writer Blair Justice surveyed popular college journalism textbooks and found that the definition of newsworthiness has progressed little beyond the precepts developed intuitively by city editors in the days of the Hearst-Pulitzer street circulation wars. The canons of "reader psychology" generally taught place unvarying emphasis on the theme that "conflict and violence are news." They have been in an agrarian America just emerging from a century of isolation, but are they in the century of the two world wars and Fourth of July weekend highway massacres?

To test the impact of this training, Justice sent questionnaires to journalism students at six universities before and after their first journalism courses, and to journeymen editors and reporters. He submitted 20 headlines, 10 suggesting nonconflict or even harmony. Respondents were asked to rank the headlines in two ways: (1) where they would place the stories as daily newspaper editors; (2) how much personal interest they had in the news involved.

The results were startling: After exposure to journalism textbook "reader psychology," the student significantly upgraded the play they would give conflict and violence. The practicing journalists showed a similar bias. All showed a great gap between personal and news judgment, playing up stories, in which they had little interest, burying others they found personally appealing.[4]

Perhaps more serious than the passing of outmoded traditions is the failure to perform the critical role of continuous review of the efficacy of present practices and to instill in journalists a tradition of self-criticism. Schools of journalism have, from time to time, been encouraged to institutionalize a continuing critique of the press. There is little evidence of much response. Jay W. Jensen, chairman of the department of journalism of Illinois, has outlined the role:

Existing knowledge of the mass media—their character, behavior and effects—should be constantly subjected to scrutiny and criticism. Indeed, even the methods by which such knowledge is attained should be continuously criticized. This is commonplace in other units of the university.

Likewise, the values (legal, moral and cultural) underpinning the mass media—their policy, content and objectives; the rationale of their existence, the milieu of norms, imperatives and sanctions in which they operate—should be continuously examined and appraised.

Finally, the institution's arrangements which comprise the order of mass communications—their effectiveness, utility, propriety, and so on—also should be the object of continuous criticism.

For the school of journalism to do otherwise would be to abandon its proper role as a unit of the university, and therefore to abandon its responsibilities to its students, to society, and to its profession. The primary reason for its existence, as for higher education in general, is not to be found in the cultural heritage it transmits to students. This function is also performed by other agencies in society. The ultimate justification for the journalism school, as for the university, lies rather in its critical function, in its continuous critique of knowledge, values and institutions.

The school of journalism imparts knowledge, but it should impart that knowledge critically. If it fails in this respect, it has no reason for existence, except perhaps that of relieving industry of the burden of apprenticeship training. It is not enough that, in preparing students for careers, the school of journalism promotes critical consideration of those principles and techniques necessary to technical arrangements underlying and impinging upon those careers. For only thus may students be expected to pass from college into their period of technical apprenticeship with their critical faculties already honed and practiced in connecting fact with theory, values with action, ideals with reality, and the demands of life with its possibilities.[5]

The need to develop a tradition of criticism within journalism schools is more important than for other disciplines. Government review and criticism is feared undesirable, and, because of the first amendment, the threat of government action as a device for making private institutions responsive is nonexistent. Finally, the press, the critical agency for most other institutions in our society, has shown great timidity toward self-criticism.

A. The Curricula

Today there are 55 institutions offering accredited programs in journalism. Almost an equal number of other institutions offer programs with similar objectives, most of which have not sought accreditation.

In earlier days, journalism programs were for those who wished to be newspaper men. As radio and then television became part of the mass communications system, the journalism curricula in many universities were changed to reflect the emergence of the new media. Sometimes, but not always, the name of the unit offering the instruction changed from "journalism" to "communications."

The place of the journalism unit within the university hierarchy varies considerably from institution to institution. Thus, at one state university there is a department of journalism headed by a chairman, while at another there is a college of communications headed by a dean. The differences are more than semantic, however, and in the two examples cited there are substantial differences in the scope of the divisions and the responsibilities of their administrators.

In general, the typical journalism program concentrates on students who are candidates for a 4-year bachelor's degree. Three of the accredited schools depart from this pattern. Columbia University's School of Journalism offers a 1-year graduate program; Northwestern bases its curriculum on a 5-year program leading to a terminal professional Master's degree. The University of Michigan has recently eliminated professional instruction for undergraduate students, offering instead a 2-year program leading to a Master's degree.

In the typical four-year journalism program, about three-fourths of the course work offered for the bachelor's degree is taken in departments other than journalism. Usually, but not always, the bulk of the student's non-journalism program is drawn from social science and humanities departments.

The one-fourth of the total course work in subjects offered through the school of journalism is divided roughly into two parts: part of the journalism subject matter is devoted to journalism techniques, and the other part to courses emphasizing the social role of journalism. Even this sort of classification is crude; a course in reporting would fall into the journalism techniques category, yet can include excellent instruction, for example, in government and politics through reading and reporting assignments given to students.

The journalism schools themselves have contributed to some confusion by suggesting an unrealistic dichotomy between specialized courses in journalism and those courses offered by the traditional liberal arts departments. The schools point to their restrictions which prevent the student from taking excessive numbers of the journalism course offerings, and to the requirement that he take a substantial number of nonjournalism courses, as examples of the "liberal" nature of the typical journalism curriculum. Up to a point this is true, but to the extent that it has encouraged the belief that journalism courses are narrowly vocational, and nonjournalism courses are more nearly broad and general, the case has been overstated. As the late Virgil M. Hancher, while president of the State University of Iowa, noted in a 1953 address:

We forget that it is possible to become liberally educated by the teaching and study of professional or specialized subjects in a liberal manner . . .

While in general I would support the proposition that there are some things which every liberally educated man should know, I fear that we have been led into error sometimes by believing that the study of certain subject matter inevitably results in a liberal education. It is nearer the truth to say that there is no subject matter, worthy of a place in the curriculum of a modern Land-Grant college or state university, which cannot be taught either as a professional specialty or as a liberal subject.[6]

From this dichotomy between "journalism" and "non-journalism" segments of the journalism curriculum has arisen a division of labor. The journalism school concerns itself either primarily or solely with the journalism course offerings from which one-quarter of the student's undergraduate program is chosen. Typically, the journalism faculty resists encroachment by other faculties on this part of the curriculum. Conversely, the journalism school frequently plays little or no role in the formulation of courses to be offered elsewhere in the institution, courses from which journalism students choose three-fourths of their undergraduate programs. To a great extent, such a situation is an understandable by-product of the administrative structure of universities. Dressel comments, however, that the division of labor need not be as absolute as he observed it to be:

> . . . there is no real attempt, such as could rather readily be made with the small group of journalism students at any particular stage, to inventory their general background in the liberal arts courses and to build on this in the development of some of the journalism courses. Professional [journalism] faculty members . . . seem to know very little about what is being done in the liberal arts courses and make very little attempt to relate their courses to these.[7]

Since 1960, when Dressel's comment was published, there has been evidence of increasing efforts on the part of individual journalism schools to bring about better integration between the Journalism and non-journalism segments of the student's curriculum. Despite this, what Dressel describes as "the tendency to see journalism courses as discrete courses,"[8] and to see journalism as discrete from liberal arts remains very much a feature of journalism education.

What effect does the dichotomy between journalism and non-journalism courses have?

First, the ability of the journalism school to incorporate into its curriculum courses pertinent to contemporary social problems is in large part dependent on the course offerings of other departments of the institution—actions over which the typical journalism school has little or no influence. If, through the actions of other departments, such courses are available, at least two other factors determine whether these courses are incorporated. The journalism faculty may, through student advising or through curriculum requirements, encourage or discourage enrollment in such courses by journalism majors. The faculties of the departments offering such courses through prerequisites established for enrollment in the courses, make it possible or impossible for journalism students to include the courses in their program of study.

Second, in that one-fourth of the journalism student's program is offered by the journalism school, considerable freedom to reflect the changing social environment is possible. The instructor in a course in public affairs reporting, for example, may assign his student to report on problems of race, government, education, and similar subjects germane to the changing milieu. In many journalism schools such changes in emphasis would be possible without formal changes in course offerings. The principal limiting factor in most instances would be the imagination and competency of the instructor. An additional limiting factor, though probably a less important one, would be the physical location of the university of which a particular journalism school is a part, with urban locations offering more close-at-hand resources for student reports than rural locations.

Without detailed study of the academic transcripts of recent journalism graduates, it is not possible to determine the extent to which journalism schools are making use of courses offered by other departments which center on contemporary social problems. Traditionally, journalism school curricula, insofar as the non-journalism segment is concerned, are highly permissive. It seems fair to assume that if such courses are offered in institutions with journalism curricula, the journalism schools are erecting no barriers for journalism students. Further, most journalism schools have long encouraged students to take course work in the social sciences, and it is in the social sciences that many courses dealing with current social problems are found.

A 1967 study by Ray E. Hiebert, head of the University of Maryland Department of Journalism, found that a number of journalism schools that did not offer specific courses in urban affairs require their students to enroll in such courses in other departments. Surveying 130 institutions and receiving 83 responses, Hiebert found:

> A distressingly large number of schools [one-fourth of those responding] indicated that they had no courses in urban affairs reporting, required their students to take no courses in other departments that touched on the subject, and had no plans for developing a program in this area. Many of these schools are situated in rural settings, which may be the reason for their aloof position.
>
> While new programs are being developed and there are hopes and plans in the works, the survey has shown that perhaps not enough is being done—especially in view of the great magnitude of the urban problems today.[9]

The obvious question is why the journalism school response has been less than adequate.

James W. Carey, in a thoughtful paper circulated informally in the summer of 1968, suggests that in part this inadequacy is owing to the dichotomy between journalism and non-journalism courses. This practice is attacked by Carey:

> One might counter that what I am recommending starts to take the journalism curriculum into the domains of history and the social sciences. That is precisely what I am recommending. With the increasing professionalization of the social sciences—that is, in the training of professional sociologists in Sociology I—they becomes less and less relevant in organization and content to the needs of the journalist..
> This means, in part, encouraging the offering of certain kinds of courses, stepping in to create and staff courses where they are otherwise

unavailable, filling interstices in the curriculum by the redefinition of the objectives of journalism courses. . . .[10]

While not proceeding as far, nor necessarily in the manner advocated by Carey, a number of journalism schools are seeking to fill gaps in the journalism curriculum through the introduction of new or modified courses.

Columbia University's Graduate School of Journalism has brought to its students lecturers from other departments of the university. The Columbia journalism faculty has for many years used New York City as a laboratory for its reporting instruction, and more recently has placed increased emphasis on urban study and research undertaken by each student during his final weeks in the school's program.

Northwestern University's Medill School of Journalism also has, over the years, capitalized on its urban setting to use Chicago and suburbs as laboratories for student reporting assignments. In its master's degree program, in addition to traditional journalism courses, the school offers seminars on urban problems, the U.S. legal system, urban education, science and technology, politics and government, and the urban economy. These substantive seminars are taught by Medill faculty members with appropriate qualifications, and by members of other departments, such as education, business, and political science.

In 1965 Medill added a Washington, D.C., program, in recognition of the growing intercourse between the federal government and urban centers. Under this program, 15 graduate students each quarter study and report from Washington, under the direction of resident Medill faculty members. Recipients of the news stories produced are newspapers in smaller cities, which receive articles on actions in Washington which have local impact.

Other schools of journalism have taken steps in the direction of placing more emphasis on current social problems, or are in the process of so doing. For example, the University of Texas has introduced a new course, politics and the press, primarily for journalism students. In addition, in a public affairs reporting course a $20,000 grant helps to finance journalism student studies of problems of politics, transportation, taxation, and the like, while some advanced journalism students also undertake summer internships in governmental offices. The School of Communications cosponsors, on educational television, weekly programs for Americans of Mexican descent, and programs dealing with low-income areas of Austin and the residents of those areas. University of Illinois journalism students undertook the preparation of detailed reports on problems of state government in Illinois, and made the finished product available to Illinois newspapers for publication. At the University of Nebraska, a course in in-depth reporting of significant issues has been a feature of the journalism curriculum for a number of years, with substantial attention in the course going to problems and possibilities of community growth.

In all the institutions from which the above examples have been drawn, and in many others not mentioned, there are expressions of intent to undertake additional activities aimed at providing journalism majors with greater exposure to the major forces at work in society. Most of the journalism administrators interviewed in an informal telephone survey by I. W. Cole were inclined to be self-critical, and critical of journalism education in general, for moving too slowly in this respect. But on balance, the sum of the activities in the schools sampled showed evidence of progress toward deeper exposure of at least some students to important social change.

More progress is needed. James W. Carey, in the paper discussed above, asserts that a new journalism is emerging in the United States, offering opportunities for what he describes as a "golden age" of journalism education: The opportunity now exists, perhaps for the first time, to make journalism schools significant, vital, and prestigious elements within universities; and, more importantly, for such schools to become important contributors to the political and social life of the country. This opportunity has been created in part, he believes, by the emergence of students with:

> ...both the ability and the muscle to move from the campus into positions normally reserved for mature writers. More students seem to think that journalism really counts; that journalism is where the action is; that in journalism one cannot only describe the circulatory system of this fibrillating society but also create the intellectual perceptions upon which we will come to terms with the modern world... They do not avoid journalism schools, as is too frequently assumed, because [the schools] are too professional, but because they are not professional enough. [Such students] do not avoid journalism schools because such schools teach 'techniques' but because such schools teach the wrong kind of techniques and needlessly divorce the techniques of that presentation from the substance of what is presented.[11]

B. Continuing Education Programs

In August 1968, John L. Hulteng of the University of Oregon School of Journalism inventoried the continuing education programs offered during the 1967-68 academic year by all journalism schools and departments listed in *Editor & Publisher Yearbook*. Of the 82 institutions that responded, 47 reported no programs. From the remaining 35 respondents, Hulteng compiled a list of 64 continuing education programs for journalists.[12]

Some of the programs listed had been offered for the first time during the 1967-68 academic year; others had been in operation for as many as 17 years. Such programs, particularly in state universities, are a natural outgrowth of the concept of service to the institution's constituencies.

Hulteng's survey was directed to those higher institutions with some sort of identifiable journalism program. It is in these institutions that most continuing education programs are found. Some continuing education programs for journalists, however, are conducted by institutions without journalism schools. The most prestigious such program in the nation is Harvard University's Nieman Fellowships, which since its founding in 1937, has offered carefully selected journalists an opportunity to become students-at-large in the university.

The continuing education programs in journalism are, understandably, a mixed lot. Some are concerned with the most basic skills and techniques of highly specialized journalistic tasks; others with broad and sweeping social issues. Some last for a single day; others, including the Harvard program, for an academic year. Many seek to advance the public relations of institutions offering the programs, but probably most of these are not offered primarily for public relations purposes.

The programs cannot be regarded as a substitute for in-residence collegiate training, but at their best they offer the most effective means of helping the practicing journalist adapt to changing demands, provided, that is, that the profession is willing to participate.

When the Nieman grant was offered to Harvard University, President James Bryant Conant asked 10 publishers if the underlying assumptions of the program—a broad educational experience for working newsmen—were valid; all 10 said no.

> "The publishers doubted the value of a pure academic experience, compared to shorter training in specific techniques . . . In the course of a re-examination of the program in 1964 President Nathan Pusey of Harvard asked 300 publishers if they thought the program should be continued; they all said yes."[13]

Just as an increasing number of the operators of the media have become more involved in, and more sophisticated concerning, journalism degree programs, they are increasingly interested in university programs that offer mid-career educational opportunities for their staff members. And while many of the service programs offered by journalism schools draw solely on the journalism faculty for instruction, an increasing number embrace the resources of the whole university. In an address to the annual convention of the American Society of Newspaper Editors in 1959, I. W. Cole urged the editors to think of the journalism school "not as an entity in itself, but as a door to a large and complex educational institution with tremendous resources . . . we at the Medill School of Journalism offered recently a short course in crime analysis and reporting. We would have experienced great difficulty in this undertaking had it not been possible for us to mount this program in cooperation with our School of Law."[14]

While the interest in continuing education programs for journalists is present, it remains to be determined how firm the "market" for such programs will be. Herbert Brucker, past president of the American Society of Newspsper Editors who is director of the Professional Journalism Fellowships, Stanford University, poses the question this way:

> The pattern has already been set by [the American Press Insitute] at Columbia. This, also mid-career education, differs from the others in two ways. In the first place, it is devoted exclusively to journalism itself. In the second place, it is short and therefore relatively cheap. Enlightened publishers support API by contributing to its overhead, and generally they pay their share of the running expenses for each staff man they send to a seminar. They are willing to do so because they have learned through experience that in return they get back a better city editor, or circulation manager, or political reporter or whatever the man or the woman may be.
>
> The question now is whether owners and publishers see that their survival depends on more than just vocational journalistic proficiency. In a real sense it depends also on an understanding of the contemporary

world, on the part of their editiorial staffs, that is as deep and as broad as possible.

So there you have it: will newspaper owners, publishers and editors support the new mid-career, re-education programs with endowment funds and current-expense funds?[15]

What Brucker refers to as the new programs are ones which were either created or received substantial impetus from foundation funds,with the Ford Foundation in the role of the most substantial contributor:

1. Medill School of Journalism: $1,092,000 for 3-month seminars for midcareer newspaper men as well as shorter sessions which also include editors, publishers, and broadcasting executives.

2. Harvard: Expansion of the Nieman program with a $1.2 million grant.

3. Columbia University Graduate School of Journalism: $1.6 million for further development of the graduate school.

4. American Political Science Association program that brings selected members of the press and young political scientists to Washington for a year of work on staffs of members of Congress—$750,000.

5. Southern Regional Education Board: $700,000 for a variety of study and seminar programs for newsmen from the South in six regional universities.

6. Stanford University: $975,000 for a Nieman-like program for experienced journalists.

7. Six Major Urban Reporting Projects: $6.3 million since 1965.[16]

The Southern Regional Education Board program has since been given a new status which promises to obtain for it continuing support from the Southern Newspaper Publishers Association. It is also interesting to note the variety of subject matter and the variety of institutions that have been a part of the SREB program. Much of the emphasis in the SREB program has been on seminars of 3 to 5 days' duration, for groups of no more than 25 journalists, with subject matter ranging from urban problems to international affairs. In addition, a limited number of individual fellowships for one or two semesters of study at Duke, Emory, Vanderbilt, the University of North Carolina, the University of Texas, or the University of Virginia have been offered.

While the Ford Foundation journalism grant program has provided the most massive approach to encouraging mid-career education for journalists, the Russell Sage Foundation has also made significant contributions. With a Sage grant, the School of Journalism of the University of Wisconsin, for example, offers opportunities for newsmen from newspapers and television to attend a 2-semester program in the social sciences.

Faced with internal and external pressures to continually upgrade staff and undertake more complex reporting tasks, some questions have been raised as to the ability of the mass media as businesses to support the mass media as social institutions. The lead article in the January issue of the American Society of Newspaper Editors *Bulletin* proposes grants to permit individual newspapers to do more "serious probing into community, social, political, racial and economic problems."[17] This would seem to further underscore a fundamental question concerning the future of the nondegree programs for newsmen: once the input of funds, particularly funds on the order of those granted by the Ford Foundation, are gone, how many mid-career programs for journalists will be able to survive?

* * *

It is insufficient for the journalist merely to learn the presently applied technical skills necessary to his craft and receive exposure to non-journalism courses dealing with contemporary problems. The skills of today will not be good enough tomorrow. And, although many of today's problems will be with us for a long time, there will be new ones.

The journalism student, as other student professionals, must acquire those skills and perspective that will enable him continually to adapt his professional values and practices to the changing needs of the society he is trained to serve. Within the journalism school the degree candidate should have an opportunity to learn communication theory, what is known about the effectiveness of different forms of presenting the message, and a sufficient acquaintance with the methods of research to allow him to stay abreast of developments long after he has left the university. His courses in other departments must also be adapted to meet his special needs. A course in sociology for sociologists, for example, is not what the future journalist requires. He needs general instruction in the principles of sociology, a broad background in the discipline, but most important, a sufficient understanding of what sociologists can and cannot provide after he has left the university. He needs to learn how to adapt their work to the needs of journalism. It is the same with other departments.

Journalism educators on many campuses faced or still face questions concerning their academic legitimacy. While acceptance both on the campus and in the newsroom has been sufficient for the journalism schools to feel far more secure than they would have two decades ago, the memory of less happy times seems to linger.

Perhaps these factors contribute to the willingness of journalism educators to plead guilty to a variety of offenses, real and imaginary, or to be excessively aggressive in defending journalism schools against valid criticisms.

It would be difficult to maintain that journalism schools as a whole have shown great imagination or agility in reacting rapidly in a time of great social change. The fact that the same can be said of many other parts of the society hardly constitutes an excuse. At the same time, society's period of troubles has already proven for some journalism schools a time of opportunity. At the University of Iowa, a new journalism curriculum, reported to be experimental and innovative, is in the making. At a number of schools, including the University of Texas, Columbia, and the University of Michigan, efforts to bring more Negro journalists into the white mass media are in the planning or execution stages. A recent Ford Foundation grant to the American University, affiliated with the Washington Journalism Center, also has as its objective a special program to bring more minority group members into journalism. Much more, however, needs to be done.

In the history of journalism education, the 1960's may prove to be significant as the decade during which closer and more effective working relationships between the press and the university were developed. The mid-career education programs for journalists are likely to have an effect not only on the students, but also on the teachers, and, typically, these new programs involve teachers from all parts of the campus. If newsmen are discovering that academicians have answers to some social questions, it is not too much to hope that some of the academicians will discover from newsmen that the faculty members have not always been addressing themselves to the right questions.

How rapidly the partnership between press and university will grow is more difficult to predict. The journalism schools which seek to develop new techniques will be competing for development funds during a period when higher institutions face growing fiscal problems. The print and broadcast media seeking to upgrade and develop their news staff will increasingly find themselves in competition with other employers seeking essentially the same talented manpower.

Increased financial support for journalism education from the mass media undoubtedly will be required on a substantial scale, but it would be unrealistic to believe that this single source of outside support will be sufficient. Those which recognize that their existence within higher education must be based on service to the society, not simply on service to the press will do well. Those segments of the press that will be capable of benefiting from the activities of such schools will be those which recognize the validity of that position. When that stage has been reached, it may be that the support for improving communications within the society will be increasingly shared by the society at large.

REFERENCES

1. Charles F. Wingate, *Views and Interviews on Journalism* (New York: F. B. Patterson, 1875), pp. 195-196, as quoted in Albert A. Sutton, *Education for Journalism* (Evanston, Illinois: Northwestern University Press, 1945) p. 9.
2. John S. Brubacher and Willis Rudy, *Higher Education in Transition* (New York: Harper & Bros., 1958), p. 160.
3. Paul L. Dressel, *Liberal Education and Journalism* (New York: Teachers College, Columbia Universtiy Press, 1960), pp.6-7.
4. *The New Leader,* Jan. 15, 1968, p. 7.
5. Jay W. Jensen, "A Method and a Perspective for Criticism of the Mass Media," *Journalism Quarterly* (Spring 1960), pp. 261-262.
6. Virgil M. Hancher, "Liberal Education in Professional Curricula," *Proceedings of the Sixty-Seventh Annual Convention of the American Association of Land-Grant Colleges and State Universities,* Columbus, Ohio, Nov. 10-12, 1953 (Washington, D.C.: The Association, 1953), pp. 45-51 as quoted in Dressel, *op. cit.* footnote 3, p. 16.
7. Dressel, *op. cit.* footnote 3, p. 97.
8. *Ibid*, p. 98.
9. Ray E. Hiebert, "National Survey Shows Inadequate Effort by Schools to Prepare Their Students for Covering Urban Affairs," *Journalism Educator* (Summer 1968), p. 15.
10. "Comments of James W. Carey Following a Visit to the Iowa School of Journalism," p. 33.
11. *Ibid*, p. 5.
12. John L. Hulteng, "An Inventory of Continuing Education Programs Offered by Schools and Departments of Journalism," (Hulteng submitted the Inventory in August 1968, on behalf of the Association for Education in Journalism Committee on Professional Freedom and Responsibility, of which he was chairman.)

13. *The Newsman's Scope*, p. 13 (Published in September 1958, this brochure is one of a series of booklets on activities supported by the Ford Foundation.)
14. I. W. Cole, address to 1959 Convention, American Society of Newspaper Editors, Washington, D.C., as published in the Convention Proceedings.
15. Herbert Brucker, "Mid-Career Reeducation Programs" *The Bulletin* of the American Society of Newspaper Editors, (September 1968), pp. 12-13.
16. *The Newsman's Scope, op. cit.* footnote 13, pp. 3-6.
17. Bob Holmes, "Foundation Grants to Cover the News?," *The Bulletin* of the American Society of Newspaper Editors (January 1969), pp. 1-3, 11.

Chapter 8

MEDIA PRACTICES AND VALUES

Relevant to each of the foregoing subjects—intergroup communication, access to the media, and coverage of civil disorders—are the practices and values of the news media that pervade all reporting. The mechanics of assembling a newspaper or television program affect both the content and mode of presentation. The newsman's concept of news introduces a factor into his normal process of selective exposure, perception, and retention which does not afflict the nonjournalist. And the inverted pyramid style of reporting news, favored by many newspapers and the wire services, impairs the fidelity of the message and the likelihood that the viewer's perception of the event will be accurate.

News gathering and dissemination are essentially bureaucratic and contribute to news distortion. A news account is handled by a succession of gatekeepers who have an opportunity to evaluate, to change, to interpret, and to garble the message.

The structure of news organizations is hierarchical. When the values of superiors conflict with those of subordinates, the superior's values will prevail. In some news organizations the dominant values and policies are those of the publisher or owner; in others, such as newspapers in the Newhouse chain, considerable latitude prevails for editors within the simple command—make money.

The first stage in the gathering of news is the allocation of resources. Assignments are made on the basis of wire-service roundups, telephone tips, press releases, announcements of press conferences and hearings, by monitoring police and fire department wireless communications, and from hunch. In fact, if a reporter is not assigned to cover an event, for most Americans it does not exist.

When an event is powerful or exciting, i.e., has high "news" value, the newsman is pressed for time and the probability of some distortion approaches certainty. Take, for example, a fast-breaking news story moved by one of the wire services. The Associated Press and United Press International both try to break the story first, hoping thereby to increase the likelihood that subscribers to both services will use their story.

The reporter at the scene may be able to report a hundred separate facts about the event, but his first transmission is a 1-paragraph flash. Which facts does he choose? The first transmission on the wire is followed by a number of paragraphs on unrelated news stories until the wire service has assimilated enough information to sent additional paragraphs. This sequence is repeated until the story loses its "news" value or until all available facts and angles are exhausted.

The radio or television newscaster, taking the first bulletin off the wire, must decide whether to read the bulletin paragraph over the air. If he does, the listener forms his initial perception of the event on the basis of that bulletin. If the bulletin is inaccurate or misleading, and the listener doesn't hear a later, corrected broadcast, or if the radio station does not broadcast explanatory material later, he is left with an inaccurate recollection of the event. Garbling may subsequently be corrected by the listener if he sees a full television news broadcast, a complete newspaper story, or a magazine article that records the event fully and accurately and places it in perspective. Which version of the story he accepts, however, may depend upon the extent to which it fits his preconceptions, rather than the fact that it was broadcast later and, accordingly, should be more accurate. The incorrect facts, as first heard, may stick in his mind.

The same wire story, fed to a newspaper, is picked off the wire by an editor. Having more copy from the wire services and his reporters than he could possibly print, he too must decide whether the item will be included and if so, how much. His next decision is whether it will run on the front page or on the inside pages of the newspaper. Again, with a fast-breaking story, it may begin as a bulletin in an early edition and, accompanied by supplemental stories, grow into a larger front page story in a later edition. The editor must piece together the subsequent parts of the story which come over the wire intermittently.

In every case, a headline is written, compressing the essence of the story into even fewer words. If the bulletin is inaccurate, or, if the copywriter on the rim of the paper's copy desk garbles the meaning in the headline, an additional source of distortion creeps in.

Even if all information were passed by the gatekeepers with perfect fidelity, the limitations of time and space would still affect the audience's perception of its environment. A newsroom is inundated with a flood of competing information. Every news organization must select from the flood those driblets that will be allowed to surface for public view. A metropolitan newsroom, for instance, may have a half-dozen teletype machines, two newsphoto receivers, radio receivers on police and fire frequencies, dozens of press releases, hundreds of telephone tips from which to choose in a single day, and to these, add the product of the paper's own news staff. Then galvanize the organization with an impending deadline. Compress the output into a finite amount of space—column inches for a newspaper or minutes and seconds for a television news program—and the result is a package of information, selected, synthesized, honed in the greatest of haste on the basis of decisions automatically made. Clearly to produce an accurate portrayal of the environment, or to provide knowledge in a form that has more than perfunctory significance, are most difficult tasks for newsmen.

An example from the wartime experiences of a long-time wire service newsman illustrates the point. He went to London early in 1943, at a time when the wire services, AP and UP, transmitted a daily roundup of strikes at war plants around the United States. Americans, he said, understood that the wire services did a daily roundup, but the practice caused the English to misunderstand the state of America's labor relations. London newspapers played about six paragraphs total of U.S. domestic news on their front pages, and five of those six paragraphs were devoted to the AP or UP roundup of strikes at war plants. The impression of the British audience was one of widespread labor unrest in the United States. A similar result ensues from wire service roundups of civil disorder or campus protest.

In any event, the disjointed nature of news, resulting from the mechanics of the news system, may prevent an audience from ever knowing the significance of events. Tonight's 2-minute television news story about a riot in a distant city may not be followed tomorrow by a 10-minute story on the underlying causes, simply because the news director will have other stories with higher "news" values to show his audience. The disjointed riot story rides off into the limbo of the audience's memory, to reappear only when stimulated by another disjointed but related story. Yet the impression it first made colors, perhaps irrevocably, the audience's future opinion.

Each of these decisions involves what journalists call "news judgment." While a great many studies have been done on the selective processes of audiences, remarkably few have been done on the selective processes of journalists. Part of the reason for this anomaly is that many media members believe it is nobody's business but their own.

Nevertheless, it is possible to extrapolate from audience studies and apply them to journalists. While this can provide some insights into news judgment, important differences distinguish professional journalists from their audiences. One of the most significant is that a journalist is a trained listener, observer, reader, and writer. He has developed skills that aid him in selecting from a multitude of facts, opinions, and events, and in finding those items he calls "news." He is trained to present his findings in a clear, concise, and orderly manner. All journalists, it does not follow, are sagacious, able, extraordinarily perceptive unbiased, and excellent writers—many of them are not; but such is their goal and they devote much time and energy to developing these skills.

Another significant difference is that, in addition to the preconceptions each individual carries around with him, the journalist is looking at events in a peculiar way. He is trying to determine whether an event is "news" and which facts about the event make it "news." In other words, he is actively seeking something called "news," and his preoccupation with certain kinds of events and facts is apt to have a distorting effect that does not work on the non-journalist observer. What, indeed, is news?

A. The Newsman's Concept of News

News, in the most literal sense, is what you read in newspapers and news magazines, what you see and hear on television, and hear on the radio. While the definition is accurate, it is not very useful.

Several years ago, a political scientist decided that, in order to understand the operations of the federal government, it would be necessary to learn about political journalism. The nation's capital has as perceptive, articulate, and brilliant a collection of American journalists as can be found anywhere; yet, none of them was able to define news. And the few who offered succinct definitions did not agree.[1] News has been defined as the unusual, the significant; it is change, anything that interests the audience, drama, conflict, violence; it is "what I say it is."[2] The ambiguity among journalists about news is understandable. The occasions on which they must exercise their news judgment do not allow for reflection and the journalism schools have made few efforts to examine the normative question, what ought to be news.

Generally, what most contemporary newsmen mean by news is an event that happened within the last 24 hours and will attract reader interest. An event quite old, recently discovered, can be news if it can be related to a current issue of high saliency. This was demonstrated in the fall of 1968, during the hearings on the circumstances and possible deception surrounding the 1964 Gulf of Tonkin Resolution. Similarly, "trend" stories may or may not qualify as news. As James Reston has suggested, if the story of a developing trend is published before anyone notices it, it is a hard news story; if it is published after it has become a topic of discussion, it is soft. The criteria for determining reader interest are conflict or violence, firstness, novelty, human interest, impact, saliency, and, for some, proximity.

Conflict and violence—as well as sex—gained prominence in American journalism as devices for expanding readership among non-newspaper readers. These are the lessons taught by the periods of sensationalism in the 1830's, the 1890's, and the late 1920's. History also teaches that, once people begin to read newspapers, they begin to become interested in more substantial fare. Certainly the level of sensationalism practiced in the past is little in evidence today, yet the tradition— subtle and much refined—persists.[3]

This tradition sometimes provides reporters with exciting hallucinations. In 1967, Ted Poston of the *New York Post* said there had hardly been a single year since he left the South that the New York dailies, his included, had not provided at least one season of Negro scare stories "that aroused such intra-community tensions that bloodshed could well have resulted. One paper may pick up a legitimate and dramatic story of racial conflict, and then the season is on. A competitor will seek a 'new angle' on the story, only to be topped by a third or fourth rival, and pretty soon the whole city will seem to be fighting the Civil War all over again."[4] He cited some examples:

> . . . Months before the rioting of July, 1964, broke out in Harlem and in Brooklyn's Bedford-Stuyvesant section, the annual scare season had been opened—and from a rather unexpected source. The staid *New York Times* . . . It proclaimed that it had uncovered the existence of a sinister Harlem organization composed of Negro teen-agers and pre-teen-agers who had pledged to maim or murder every white person found in Harlem. Then it cited four recent isolated and unsolved slayings of white persons during apparent holdup attempts and credited them all to the new organization—the Blood Brothers.
> Every responsible social, civic, youth, and antidelinquency agency in harlem not only denounced but disproved the preposterous story. But the *Times* continued to pursue it, with its competitors panting in its path—and with the Blood Brothers' membership growing from 30 to 400 and then dropping to 90 in successive editions.

In Queens, a white student who wanted to quit college read of the Blood Brothers and got a big idea. He slashed himself with razor blades and told the police that he had been assaulted by two Negroes who called him "white man" (obviously Blood Brothers). The story got a big play in all the local dailies and made a big hit with every body except the police. They called the student in for questioning, and he broke down and confessed to the hoax.

All the papers seemed willing to drop the story except the New York *Journal-American*. In "news" stories that really should have run in the editorial column, the *Journal-American* intimated that the only "hoax" in the case was the youth's confession. Didn't everyone know the Blood Brothers were around?

The *Times* buried the Blood Brothers as abruptly as it had created them, but the scare returned in the form of stories about a group of youthful assassins called the Five Percenters, said to believe that 95 percent of all Negroes are either cattle of Uncle Toms and that only the remaining 5 percent are courageous enough to try to kill all white people and Negro policemen.

This new group was publicized editorially by the New York *Herald Tribune* . . . The *Times* denounced the Five Percenter scare, compared it with the Blood Brother myth, which it said was quite properly protested by Negro leaders. The *Times* didn't seem to recall where the blood Brothers were born.[5]

David Brinkley has said, ". . . placidity is not news. News is the unusual and the unexpected. If an airplane departs on time, arrives on time, it isn't news. If it crashes, regrettably, it is. I don't—I don't understand that complaint at all. Never have."[6]

News is the unusual, the extraordinary; it is something that doesn't happen every day. The media have no need to report each airliner that arrives safely; it is not a matter of general public interest. The objection, however, is not that the media focus upon the unusual; rather it is that they focus on the unusual aspects of the unusual, and this narrower focus means the most dramatic or violent aspect of the unusual. Recall, for example, the coverage of the meeting at Watts, devoted to discussing grievances and what could be done to calm a tense racial situation. The media focused on the extremist statements of one 16-year-old boy.[7] This was not a representative portrayal of a legitimate news event.

The unrepresentative portrayal of the unusual has been called "highlighting." The problem is generic and consists of giving the highlights of an event rather than the event itself. Moreover, there is a kind of highlight spiral. The assignment editor assigns the reporter to cover the most exciting or unusual events. The reporter, who wants to get his story in the paper or on the air and knows that space and time are short and that he is in competition with other reporters, then reports the most exciting or unusual aspects of that event. His product then goes to an editor who may cut it to include only the most exciting of the exciting. Finally, there is the executive editor (or producer in TV) who may kill the piece if it lacks the "news values" of competing products, or will institute a re-edit to cut out the less exciting parts.

This brief summary exaggerates the nature of the spiral to some extent. Some activities, like the public acts of the President, are covered whether they are exciting or not; on some days competitive pressures are weaker than others; and editors must consider the morale of their reporters and cannot always cut as ruthlessly as they would sometimes like to do. The difficulty of portraying the unusual in a representative fashion is particularly exacerbated for television because of the fee system. The correspondent may receive $25 to $150 for each time he appears on television, in addition to his base salary. This provides an incentive not only to make the most of whatever assignment he receives, but once he has secured sufficiently dramatic footage to get on to the next one and not waste time doing the kind of digging necessary to provide perspective.[8]

Attracting audiences requires conflict and drama. Conflict, to be sure, is important and should be reported, because change in our society frequently emerges from conflict. Some news organizations have, however, a capacity for manufacturing drama where none exists or to overdramatize the dramatic. In addition, the press has a tendency to focus on the conflict rather than the change that may or does emerge from it. Here is a description of some news coverage of the San Francisco Conference called to draft the United Nations Charter:

> ... This gathering necessarily followed a course governed by protocol; it involved proposal and counter proposal, preparation of texts, amendments and revisions, and eventual agreement by compromise.
>
> On many days during the weeks the Conference was in session there was nothing to report. But the reporters had to sent in their stories. Somehow there had to be news. The result on the lower levels was a series of personal items modeled after the Hollywood fan magazine and on the higher levels a distorted account of what took place. Because drama and tension were demanded by the editorial desks back home, drama and tension were manufactured at San Francisco. Hence calm was turned into the calm-before-the-storm. Silence became the silence-of-impending-conflict. The passage of time became a portentous period of delay. So completely was the task of manufacturing suspense performed that, when, after some weeks an acceptable charter was signed, the effect on newspaper readers was one of incredulous surprise.[9]

In a similar vein, Lawrence Laurent, television critic for *The Washington Post*, observed President Nixon's third television[10] news conference dealing with foreign affairs:

> The lack of conflict [in the press conference] that TV commentators often equate with "news" left reporters on all networks with little to say. The result was that the TV reporters were frequently reduced to the role of a radio announcer, describing endlessly those things that any interested viewer could see for himself.[11]

Several months later the *New York Times* observed:

Editorialists, columnists and others who for months have had little better to do than write about the serenity of the White House and the cool competence of its principal occupant have suddenly come alive with dark hints that the Administration is suffering as *Newsweek* asserted last week, "a leadership crisis of disturbing proportions."[12]

Frequently, too, the media will distort events in the direction of audience expectations, often formed from predictions the media itself makes. A study by Kurt and Gladys Lang found that television coverage of Douglas MacArthur's homecoming parade in Chicago was characterized prior to its occurrence as one of the most exceptional events in history. TV portrayed the support of the crowd as unanimous and stronger than it was and avoided direct comment on the political issues involved.

The study was conducted with monitors that described what they saw on television and compared these descriptions with those of 31 observers on the scene. Here are the descriptions of the same event, first, as reported by the network monitors:

> The scene at 2:50 P.M. at State and Jackson was described by the announcer as the "most enthusiastic crowd EVER in our city . . . . You can feel the tenseness in the air . . . you can hear the crowd roar." The crowd was described by the commentator as pushing out into the street with the police trying to keep it in order, while the camera was still focusing on MacArthur and his party. The final picture was of a bobbing mass of heads as the camera took in the entire view of State Street northward. To the monitor, this mass of people appeared to be pushing and going nowhere. And then, with the remark, "The whole city appears to be marching down State Street behind General MacArhtur," holding the picture just long enough for the impression to sink in, the picture was suddenly blacked out.

Here is the report of a second monitor:

> . . . the last buildup on TV covering the "crowd" (cut off as it was abruptly at 3:00 P.M.) gave me the impression that the crowd was pressing and straining so hard that it was going to be hard to control. I first thought, "I'm glad I'm not in that," and "I hope nobody gets crushed."

Here is the description of the same events by an observer on the scene:

> [As MacArthur passed] everybody strained but few could get a really good glimpse of him. A few seconds after he had passed most people merely turned around to shrug and to address their neighbors with such phrases: "That's all." "That was it." "Gee, he looks just like he does in the movies." "What'll we do now." Mostly teen-agers and others with no specific plans flocked into the street after MacArthur but very soon got tired of following as there was no place to go and nothing to do. Some cars were caught in the crowd, a matter which, to the crowd, seemed amusing.[13]

The role of conflict as a news value and the manner in which it leads to exaggeration from passage through numerous gatekeepers was illustrated by an experience of President Kennedy. During a 2-hour background briefing for 35 correspondents, President Kennedy stated:

> Well, I think we are more aware, probably, that we are going to incur at intervals people's displeasures. This is sort of a revolving cycle. At least I think the U.S. ought to be more aware of it, and I think too often in the past we have defined our leadership as an attempt to be rather well regarded in these countries [the Atlantic Alliance]. The fact is, you can't possibly carry out any policy without causing major frictions . . . . So I think what we have to do is be ready to accept a good deal more expressions of newspaper and governmental opposition to the United States in order to get something done than we perhaps have been willing to do in the past. I don't expect that the United States will be more loved, but I would hope that we could get more done.[14]

This was an important statement. The United States was likely to be less concerned with criticism from friendly governments. The President intended to move toward a firmer leadership role in the Atlantic Alliance. An Associated Press reporter strengthened the statement:

> President Kennedy intends to follow up his Cuban success by exerting stronger leadership over the West's Cold War policies—even at the risk of offending sensitive allies.

Correspondents not present could use either the AP story or the milder UPI report. The French and German news agencies used the AP story. The *Times* of London, known for its characteristic understatement, was about to use the UPI report when a correspondent for the BBC provided a copy of the AP story. The story in *The Times* was headlined, "TOUGH LEADERSHIP RESOLUTION BY PRESIDENT KENNEDY." A typical sentence in the story ran, "The President has made known that he will pace the foreign stage like a young lion . . ." The Paris-based, French newspaper, *Le Monde*, used the following headline:

PRESIDENT KENNEDY HAS DECIDED TO DIRECT THE WESTERN ALLIANCE WITHOUT WORRYING ABOUT OBJECTIONS OF THE ALLIES.

As the news was passed, the President's statement became stronger and the conflict greater.

Focusing on conflict is not always the cause of distortion, sometimes it is merely a preoccupation with the unusual or slighting of the ordinary. Some leaders of the anti-war movement believe that the media have placed too much emphasis on the unusual aspects of the movement and not enough on its substance. The parades of the anti-war movement are unusual; the significance of the growing discontent of Americans from all backgrounds with the war in Vietnam is unquestioned. But a great many different kinds of

Americans oppose the war; opposition ranges from the responsible to the fanatical. Some who oppose the war may properly be described as hippies or anarchists. They wear colorful clothes, use extreme language, and reject many accepted social and moral standards. The complaint has been made widely, in some instances legitimately, that during a parade or demonstration television tends to focus on the most "unusual" participants. If this is all that is shown, and it is simultaneously reported that there were 50,000 people participating in the parade, the viewer is likely to assume that all present were of the type portrayed on television, which does not square with reality. Many viewers may be misled about the nature of war protest. In fact, there are a great many people in this country who are, in every other aspect, within the "mainstream" of American thought but oppose the war and, nevertheless, participate in these demonstrations.

Consider another reported example: during the civil disorders at San Francisco State College, shortly after Dr. Hayakawa took over as acting-president, the entire nation saw pictures of him atop a sound truck ripping out wires. The car was surrounded, apparently by hostile students. The television newscast gave the impression that the entire university was in turmoil. If the viewer read the *Los Angeles Times* account the next day, he learned that the event on television represented only one episode that lasted eight or ten minutes. The rest of the day, Dr. Hawakaya was in his office receiving groups of students seeking to restore order on campus. The same day, 16,000 students attended class and did not participate in the disturbance. A few words by the television commentator would have provided the perspective necessary to communicate a representative portrayal of what had happened at San Francisco State College that day. Those words were missing.

B. Objective Versus Interpretive Reporting

Many of these complaints against today's journalism can be traced to the traditional belief that news is vaguely understood as the unfolding, event-oriented story, and the objective reporter's job is to tell the facts as he observed them about who did what, when, where, how, and why. Arguably, there is nothing wrong with that formula except that, regrettably, the "why"—if it is there at all—is last and often lost on the composing room floor.

Formula ordering of facts does not help much either. News reports are usually written in what is termed the "inverted pyramid" style. The formula takes its name from the rule that all the essential drama and facts must be compressed into the first one or two sentences of the story. Additional facts are arranged in descending order of importance.

There are several reasons for this formula. Once the writer is accustomed to it, facts fit rapidly into place. According to the folklore, readers may not read the entire story unless their attention is attracted immediately. Headlines are usually written by copy editors seated at the rim of the copy desk; their time is limited and they expect to write the headlines on the basis of the first two paragraphs. Perhaps the most important reason is that the article can be cut radically—by dropping paragraphs from the end of the story—on short notice as composing room needs may dictate.

Although the reasons for the style are easily understood, it does not encourage reflective writing. It reinforces the tendency to present drama at the expense of balance and to emphasize objectively verifiable facts—who said what, how many were injured, and how much property was destroyed—at the expense of why the event took place, its significance, and what should be done.

Formula writing also multiplies the opportunity for distortion. Consider the following example, nominated by the *Columbia Journalism Review* as the best lead from the 1968 Democratic Convention. The UPI dispatch reported:

> Chicago— Police and National Guardsmen battled thousands of antiwar protestors with clubs, rifle butts and tear gas in the heart of this convention city tonight. Hubert Humphrey was among those gassed.

The "gassing" of the Vice President was described in greater detail in the fourth and fifth paragraphs:

> Humphrey, awaiting his expected nomination at the International Amphitheater five miles away, had left his windows open on his 25th floor suite in the Hilton and taken a shower to freshen up.
> An upward draft wafted the tear gas into the suite and when Humphrey emerged he began coughing and sneezing.[15]

If the subsequent paragraphs had been cut in the composing room, the story would have been factually correct, but grossly inaccurate in the impression it left.

The inverted pyramid is, of course, not the only possible style. The chronological account has its place in news columns as well as in suspended interest stories. These take longer to fashion, but they generally heighten the dramatic qualities of the story without undue emphasis on conflict. They are more comprehensible than news presented in the standard format.

The suspended interest format (1) does not lend itself to indiscriminate shortening through elimination of later paragraphs; (2) requires the headline reader to read the entire story; and (3) requires more time to write. It is still limited by the recital of more or less objectively verifiable facts. And little by way of background or interpretation of the significance of the event is involved.

To a great extent these rigid standards for news reporting were adopted to stop editorializing in the news columns characteristic of an earlier era. In addition, the wire services, which served clients with a broad range of political views, could avoid offending any significant segment by reporting only observable facts and avoiding any attempt to provide perspective. The inadequacy of this approach became apparent in a limited way shortly after the beginning of World War I. The American people had little understanding of the events in Europe. No doubt this was in part due to the absence of prior comprehensive coverage of Europe. The growth of interpretive reporting continued during the twenties, but was limited to foreign correspondents. With the New Deal, it became apparent that traditional formula reporting on the new complex social legislation would leave the reader totally confused. Interpretive reporting was extended by larger newspapers to coverage of the nation's politics.

In 1938, Sidney Kobre, a veteran Baltimore reporter, wrote in the *Journalism Quarterly*:

> What are the next steps in American journalism if the newspapers are to be made an effective, up-to-date social institution? Certain lines of development can be pursued.
>
> The materials with which the newspaper deals are fundamentally of a psychological, economic and sociological character. It is an oversimplification to handle this material as if it were ordinary routine stuff. All aspects of human life are being methodically investigated, instead of being viewed in the usual "common-sense" traditional manner. The human body is a complicated and intricate nervous and physical system. When it breaks down only trained men can rehabilitate it. The stuff of which news is made is just as highly complicated because it relates to human behavior. Only specialized reporters with eyes sharpened in the social sciences can handle and interpret the facts intelligibly.
>
> The expert has been quietly emerging up to now from university halls and entering every field affecting industry and politics. Why not journalism?[16]

Although there is a growing agreement on the efficacy of interpretive reporting, there is substantial disagreement on what it means. Some suggest that interpretation is nothing more than backgrounding, providing the antecedent facts to place the day's events in perspective. Others refer to it as "in-depth" reporting. Edwin Canham, Editor of the *Christian Science Monitor*, has said "Background, surrounding circumstances, prior events, motivation—all are part of the real and basic news. This kind of interpretation is the best kind of reporting." Jeffrey Pond of the *New York Times* has made the case in favor in interpretive reporting:

> For example, a person has been tabbed as the mayor's choice for a job. I think you have to interpret the facts in this situation. It is not enough to say he is simply the mayor's choice. That does not tell anyone anything. He could be the mayor's choice because he will be an easy man to handle; he could be the man the mayor honestly regards as most competent for the job; the selection could be a political payoff; it could be a step to another job; it could be a way to get him out of the way for someone else. The reporter who simply says "X" is being considered is really betraying the reader's confidence; the average reader is not intimate enough with the situation. The reporter has got to tell that average reader what really is happening and why.[17]

The critics of interpretive reporting claim that it opens the door to slanted news. In response to such criticism, Lester Markel of the *New York Times* has written:

> There are, as I see it, three approaches to dealing with the news; first, the basic facts; second, the interpretation of these facts; third, the comment on them. Thus:

What Mr. Khrushchev says about Mr. Kennedy is spot news.

Why Mr. Khrushchev says these things is interpretation.

Whether Mr. Khrushchev should have said these things and what we should do about him is opinion.

It is crucial that the difference between interpretation and opinion be fully recognized. Interpretation is an *objective* appraisal, based on background, knowledge of a situation, and analysis of primary and related facts. Editorial opinion, on the other hand, is a *subjective* judgment; it is a definite taking of sides; it is likely to be exhortation . . . [18]

The test is whether, after reading the story, you know where the reporter stands.[19]

Knowledge and background of the situation are absolutely essential to effective interpretive reporting. While interpretive reporting is still largely limited to foreign affairs and politics in Washington, D. C., it is being used increasingly to report other domestic news. The need for interpretive reporting of the civil rights movement, life in the ghetto, black power, and the student revolt should be clear.

In the *Columbia Journalism Review*, Eric Blanchard has described the reporting of the Poor People's Campaign in Washington as "so pedestrian, so police-blotter superficial that the *New Yorker* envisioned newsmen asking Martin Luther King, Jr., which mountain he had visited and which night it was that he had first started having his dream."[20]

Blanchard continues with a disturbing description of the coverage of the May 29 march on the Supreme Court:

That day perhaps more than at any other time during the campaign the poor acted as the bloc they wanted to be. Negroes, with their catalog of economic needs, marched in support of Indians. The Indians were seeking "justice" from the Court, which two days before had ruled, in their eyes, against Indians by asserting that the State of Washington had a right to regulate net fishing (not just by Indians, as a matter of fact, but by everyone). Despite a 114-year-old treaty, the Indians are running a distant third to canners and sportsmen in taking fish from the waters of Puget Sound and its tributaries. Interested less in legal niceties than in food, the Indians decided on a direct-action approach to the Supreme Court. Several windows in the building were smashed; a distressed young woman hauled down the American flag.

But almost unanimously newspapers chose to emphasize the disorder almost to the exclusion of background on the Indians' problems . . . the fairest account of the day that I saw was in the *Baltimore Sun*, which subordinated the windows and the flag to the bottom of the front-page matter, while the fishing rights were cited twice on page one.

The net impact of newspaper treatment of the demonstration was almost totally negative (presumably reinforcing the attitudes of those who believe that the poor are criminals and eroding the positions of others who aren't sure yet). Reporters were careful to write only that "windows were broken," but their circumspection was spoiled by "active" headlines. The papers got a good bag from that day. The problem was they were loaded for rabbits, and that's what they got.[21]

* * *

Commercial media must attract the attention of the audience if they are to maintain the necessary financial support and to communicate with the public. Moreover, using reader interest as one criterion for determining what is news is both socially desirable as well as economically necessary. If the media do not report those matters that interest the reader they will turn to other sources for the desired information.

The difficulty with too many news organizations is that they have a tendency to do nothing more than attract the audience's attention; once they have the public's attention, they should go on to tell them something. A recent example of failure to go beyond attracting public attention is the report on page one of the *Washington Star* about an ex-convict and his wife who wanted to see their children, kidnapped a Texas Highway Patrolman, led them on a 90-mile-an-hour chase across East Texas, only to have the husband shot on entering the house where he was told he could spend 10 or 15 minutes with his children.[22] There was no explanation of why it was necessary to kidnap the officer, and there was no indication of why he could not see his children. All that was reported were the facts of the kidnapping, the chase, and the manner in which Texas authorities handled the chase and eventually killed the man. The next day the *Washington Post* ran a 7- by 5-inch picture on the front page with a similar story inside.[23] Perhaps the public has simply been trained to regard such items as "news." Yet, one can hardly suggest that it had any apparent significance, particularly page one significance.

Contrast this with the coverage by several newspapers of a senseless murder by a frustrated and deranged inventor who killed a secretary at the American Physical Society in New York. The basic facts were reported, but the *New York Times* went beyond the action. The killer had been a former mental patient and they discussed the state and federal veterans release system for mental patients. The *New York World-Telegram and Sun* listed eleven other cases involving crime by mental patients who had been released from institutions; editorialized on the inadequate release standards for mental patients from veterans hospitals; reported that the Mattewan Hospital, where the killer had been confined, had only four psychiatrists for 1,700 patients; and carried a story by the UP science editor who said that the public's indifference was to blame for such tragedies.[24]

Critics have suggested that the news media should put more emphasis on "good news." The profession has categorically rejected this suggestion. They have an obligation, they insist, to report events which involve conflict, the threat of violence, or actual violence.

Reporting on the real conditions of life undoubtedly contributes to the level of anxiety in this country. From data on radio and news listening among New Yorkers, Mendelsohn developed the point that today's citizen lives in a state of anxiety created by real conditions. This, he reported, leads to "an almost desperate sense of urgency regarding 'the news.'" In its extreme form, such anxiety can cause some persons to reject their responsibilities as members of a democratic society and avoid the information of media content altogether.[25]

In a 1962 study in Los Angeles, a correlation was found between not reading newspapers, not watching television news, and not listening to radio news. Some people almost totally ignore the news.[26] Professor Lyle often encounters respondents in field surveys who say they consciously avoid the news "because it upsets me."

The media have properly rejected the suggestion that they report "good" news simply because it is good. It apparently has not occurred to very many newsmen, however, that events should not go unreported simply because they involve a non-violent resolution of conflict. One function of the media is to aid in coordinating society's response to change. They can fulfill this function in part by telling the public how conflicts are resolved nonviolently and by giving such resolutions the same prominence they give the violent manifestations of conflict.

For the overwhelming majority of Americans, information about important social issues must come from the mass media. Giving only the objective observable facts leaves too much to the reader's preconceptions. The action must be set in context, the public must be given a representative view of events and an explanation of their significance.

The news should provide a sensitive instrument reading on vital, but remote, parts of our social machinery that the citizen cannot personally see or hear, like a human early warning system. The news system must examine itself to see if it is reporting things that really mean much anymore; or whether it selects "news" because it seemed interesting or profitable or easy in the past. It should do this because the social machinery can be destroyed by archaic, obsolete, or false readings. The task is easy for the formula reporter or editor or technician, who receives a set of traditional news values for what is news. For those newsmen who are serious about relaying what something means to men's lives, however, the job is very hard. It requires knowledge of society at a level of education and sophistication previously unknown to the general run of the news trade.

REFERENCES

1. William L. Rivers, *The Mass Media* (New York: Harper & Row, 1964) p. 74.

2. Others have also struggled with the question "What is news?": See Robert E. Park, "News as a Form of Knowledge," *Society* (Glencoe: The Free Press, 1955), pp. 71-78; Helen M. Hughes, *News and the Human Interest Story* (Chicago: University of Chicago Press, 1940) pp. xii ff.; Curtis D. MacDougall, *Interpretative Reporting* (New York: MacMillan, 1957), p. 52; Walter Gieber, "News is What Newspapermen Make it" in *People, Society, and Mass Communications* Lewis A. Dexter and David M. White eds. (New York: Free Press, 1964), pp. 173-180.

   The head of NBC news, Reuven Frank, prefers to rely on tradition and the newsman's intelligence: "There are no objective criteria by which to judge what news is. There is only an accumulated body of tradition and personal intelligence of a man who, in full possession of that tradition, makes it operative. It's news because we covered it. We covered it because we thought it would be news. If it turns out to be what we expected, it's news. If it isn't what we expect—it's not news." Reuven Frank, "TV Journalism: A Dialogue," in *The Progress In Television* A. William Blum and Roger Manveu eds. (New York: Focac Press, 1967), p. 117. Reprinted from *Television Quarterly,* Fall, 1962.

3. See Part I, Chapter 1, section on Sensationalism.
4. Ted Poston, "The American Negro and Newspaper Myths," in *Race and the News Media* Paul L. Fisher & Ralph L. Lowenstein, eds. (New York: Anti-Defamation League of B'nai B'rith, 1967), p. 67.
5. *Ibid.,* pp. 68-69.
6. "The Whole World is Watching," Broadcast by the Public Broadcast Laboratory, Dec. 22, 1968, script p. 12.
7. See Part II, Chapter 6, section on the Watts disorders.
8. "With some recent exceptions, network newsmen make their money from fees paid on top of a basic salary. Reporters contributing to television news shows receive fees ranging from $25 to $150 for each item used on a program containing commercials. A man may spend three or four days quietly digging for facts to support a story, only to find himself receiving a fee of $50 if his story is used—or nothing if the story does not pan out. His colleague, meanwhile, may use the same amount of time rushing to snatch an interview here and put together a few superficial facts there, may place ten separate pieces on the air, and may as a result pocket $500. Obviously the system discourages methodical pursuit of information. The object is to get each story on the air and move on to something else." Robert McNeil, "The News on TV and How It Is UnMade," *Harper's,* Oct. 1968, p. 74.
9. Commission on Freedom of the Press, *A Free and Responsible Press,* Robert Hutchins, Chairman (Chicago: University of Ill. Press), pp. 56-57.
10. Broadcast live on the three networks at 9 p.m. est, Mar. 4, 1969.
11. Lawrence Laurent, "Two Looks at Nixon's TV Report," *The Washington Post,* March 1969.
12. Robert E. Sample, Jr., "Nixon's Leadership: The Focus is Still Far From Clear," *New York Times,* July 13, 1969, p. E–1.
13. Kurt Lang & Gladys Engel Lang, *Politics & Television* (Chicago: Quadrangle Books), pp. 49-50.
14. William L. Rivers, *The Opinionmakers,* (Boston: Beacon Press, 1965), p. 51 ff.
15. *Columbia Journalism Review,* Fall 1968, p. 9.
16. Sidney Kobre, "The Social Sciences and the Newspaper," *Journalism Quarterly* (1938), p. 288.
17. Quoted in William L. Rivers, *The Mass Media, op. cit.* footnote 172, pp. 180-181.
18. *Ibid.,* p. 181.
19. For a well-articulated discussion and defense of interpretative reporting see "H.R. Jolliffe, A Semantic Slant on 'Objectivity' vs. 'Interpretation,'" *Journalism Quarterly,* pp. 189-193.
20. Eric Blanchard, "The Poor People and the 'White Press'" *Columbia Journalism Review* (November 1968), p. 61.
21. *Ibid.*
22. *Washington Star,* May 1, 1969, p. 1.
23. *The Washington Post,* May 3, 1969, pp. 1, A–12.
24. Sidney Kobre and Juanita Parkes, "The Newspapers Cover a Murder Case," *Journalism Quarterly* (1954), pp. 311-318.
25. Harold Mendelsohn, "Socio-Psychological Perspectives on the Mass Media and Public Anxiety," *Journalism Quarterly* (1963), p. 511.
26. Lyle Wilcox, Eds., "A Community Daily in a Changing Metropolitan Press Environment" (Los Angeles: UCLA Department of Journalism), p. 27.

Chapter 9
CONCLUSIONS AND RECOMMENDATIONS

Few American institutions are as free from responsible and systematic analysis as the American press. The press, which performs the role of reporter and critic for other institutions, has been reluctant to undertake self-analysis. Yet the products of equally few American institutions are as readily visible as that of the press. It should come as no surprise, therefore, to hear the press accused when the society fails to meet individual expectations. Frequently the accusations are ill-considered, in part because of the absence of reliable information.

Many accusations have been hurled against the news media for their real and imagined contribution to violence. "The press reports violence because violence sells the press," critics assert. "The press encourages violence because the violent seek the publicity the press provides." These are typical accusations and perhaps the most common charges that the news media fail to do enough—or do too much—about violence in our society.

The news media can play a significant role in lessening the potential for violence by functioning as a faithful conduit for intergroup communication, providing a true marketplace of ideas, providing full access to the day's intelligence, and reducing the incentive to confrontation that sometimes erupts in violence. That is a subtle and uncertain mission.

The traditional relationship between violence and the press is a matter of journalism history. Violence has had a prominent role in the press, and, at least since the time of Benjamin Day and the "penny press," violence has had some economic importance as well. Long ago, publishers learned that they could expand their readership among heretofore non-newspaper readers by openly marshalling the most exaggerated and detailed reports of violence and sex. Today there are very few new markets and the rate of literacy is high.

It is undoubtedly true that some groups have learned to use violence and the press to exploit their goals. They have learned that the media generally can be counted on to give violent behavior a prominent role in the day's news. The result is that when they seek publicity for their grievances, conflict and possibly violence may be one of the techniques used in the fairly certain knowledge that the press will make sure "the whole world is watching."

Although there is truth in this charge, it is probably a good deal less than seems to be popularly believed. First, violence is not necessary to gain media attention. In the case of television particularly, any kind of physical action or dramatization of conflict will usually suffice. Second, groups who engage in violence are apt to have their message lost because of the media tendency to focus on the violence to the exclusion of the message. Third, the use of violence, as is frequently the case in university confrontations, is a political instrument used to provoke the police and thereby radicalize large numbers of students who are sympathetic to new left goals, but ordinarily reject new left tactics.

Today, the press is less dependent upon violent content—upon titillation in general—than it may ever have been. The hard fact is that violence is not primarily what the news media have to offer today. For those who suppose that it is, that may be because it is what they have come to expect—or choose—to see and read.

Beyond that, it is the function of the news media, as the Commission on a Free and Responsible Press has put it, to provide "full access to the day's intelligence." Unless we propose to emulate the ostrich, we must expect—indeed, the public has a right to demand—that the press will report the day's intelligence including that which is violent. As with other events, when there is violence, the public has a right to know it.

We make these points forcefully because we wish to set to one side the querulous contentions of those who see in the press the source of most that is evil and who argue particularly that the press ought to "accentuate the positive and eliminate the negative." That may be a good formula for songwriting in troubled times; as a prescription for news content it is fatuous.

Yet, the media have contributed to the widespread use of confrontation as an instrument of social change by their failure to report adequately the conditions underlying current protest, by the proposals for solution of pressing social problems, and by their action-oriented coverage of conflict.

The contention that the news media are subject to manipulation by the demonstrators is only partly accurate. It has happened and will again. It is significant, we repeat, not only as an incentive to violence but, perhaps more important, for what it suggests about weaknesses of the news media which touch upon the areas that concern us. More often than not, those who object to coverage of this kind would object equally to the cure, admission of the disaffected through traditional channels.

The press does provide a marketplace for ideas, but it is not of the sort commonly supposed. The increased level of violence in the country today is partially owing to the sluggish response of our institutions to social change; but the press shares in this sluggishness, and an important part of its inadequacy is the inability of new and different voices to gain routine and peaceful access to the centralized news media.

Professor Jerome Barron has proposed one solution in the *Harvard Law Review*.[1] He urges that the first amendment requires a nondiscriminatory right of access to the media for socially important ideas with legislative, judicial, and administrative remedies. It is romantic to think in the 1960's, writes Barron, that it is possible to guarantee a free marketplace of ideas simply by keeping the government away from the press. We agree. But can the courts and legislatures do a better job? We doubt it, for it is equally romantic to think that if the courts and legislatures were granted the power to force publicity for certain ideas, they would act to protect the weak and unorthodox.

One problem in ending mass discrimination in the South, from the 17th century to the present, for example, has been the exclusion of the black communities—and the poor whites for that matter—from routine access to the mass media. Anything from them that upset the racial or economic *status quo* was censored or viciously attacked. And the judicial and legislative officials in the region were frequently more vindictive than the news media. When some newspapers and broadcasters broke this conspiracy of silence, they were harassed by law enforcement and legislative agencies. To illustrate, Gene Wirgess, Hazel Brannon Smith, P. D. East and others expressed nonconforming thoughts and suffered from the response of local courts and state governments.

On the national level, the evidence is equally discouraging. What the most powerful committees of Congress regard as the proper range of political and social ideas indicates what would happen if they were able to legislate information into the news system. Moreover, to the extent members of Congress believe that certain ideas have not received sufficient public attention in the media, they control one of the surest means of access for those ideas, congressional hearings. High government officials who seek to increase the range of debate need only speak.

The Federal Communications Commission has statutory power to force broadcasters to study the needs of their communities, to produce programming to meet these needs; further, it has the power to force a balanced treatment of issues and a fair treatment of individuals. A study of the FCC's use of this power, however, does not provide much hope. The natural history of all regulatory agencies serves as a model for power of government over ideas. Agencies like the FCC, specifically created to protect the public interest against private interest, were given powerful weapons to do it. In almost every case, within a few years they had either handed these weapons over to private interest or allowed them to atrophy through lack of use. They became, not guardians of the public interest, as the FCC should be, but service agencies for the industries involved. At the FCC this is no doubt in part owing to inadequate congressional appropriations.[2]

Judicial and legislative officials have a vested interest in the news. Senator Fannin's address to the Senate objecting to the use of funds appropriated for the Office of Economic Opportunity to support community-action newsletters is a recent example. Among the messages he objected to were these on the strike at San Francisco State College:

> The only reason the strike was called was as a last resort to bring out into the open [the student's] grievances and the present injustices and irrelevancies on the campus of a school which belongs to this community . . . . The basic truth of the strike is the freedom of self-determination of students in their education versus the present misuse of the schools by irrelevant and outside political forces such as the office of the Governor, State superintendent of schools, trustees and such boards of directors who are totally alien to the needs and desires of black and third world students. The activities and grievances of the students deserve the sympathy of the local community.

He raised objections to other items in the newsletters. One item urged that there was little difference between being in jail and life in the ghetto, and closed with the suggestion that the reader join in the fight for "identity, equality, not civil rights but human rights." Another item predicted that civil war was "almost inevitable" unless white Americans face the fact that they have a responsibility to see that "all children have some guarantees—decent economic income, housing, education, and health insurance—that exist for their own children."

Government officials or media operators are not inherently wicked. It is something much worse. Each is convinced that he possesses the truth. In the case of government officials and present broadcasters and publishers, it is probably very nearly the same truth.

Mass media openings today are in short supply, no matter who the message bearer, and these openings are made to collect huge audiences. On this basis, it costs too much to broadcast minority views, or at least, unrich minority views. A mass press also demands that the person who gets such an opening must not only appeal to an undifferentiated mass audience, but also avoid seriously offending any significant segment of that audience. If minority views were aired regularly on prime time, it would cease to be prime time. It may be quicker and more practical to get judicial, legislative or public policy action to increase the number of public channels rather than to force entry on existing channels. This process is already happening in a small way: CATV has continued to grow, the Office of Economic Opportunity has in the past supported community newsletters, and there are over 100 underground newspapers with more than a million circulation and an underground wire service.

On the broader level, no technical reason exists to prevent each community from having 20 television and several hundred voice or data channels, which would leave plenty of time and space for minority views at extremely small cost. In addition, such a communications system could be used to revitalize local politics, culture, and community interaction. In the city of Los Angeles, for example, if a group wants a public discussion of problems relating to the Santa Monica School Board, they must broadcast over a radio transmitter that covers 4,000 square miles. Similarly, it is technically feasible to construct a cable system that would allow a congressman to reach only those homes in the district from which he is to be elected. The cost of campaigning via television could be considerably reduced.

Finally, the Federal Communications Commission can make an important contribution to upgrading the performance of broadcast media without becoming involved in news content.

Section 309(a) of the Communications Act requires that they make a determination whether the licensee has operated in the public interest. While there are many objections by broadcasters today to any suggestion that the FCC become involved in determining program mix, it is clear that such objections would have been quite surprising to the Congressmen who first passed the statute and the broadcasting industry which on initial passage not only agreed, but volunteered that public service programming was one of their most important activities. In Congressional testimony which led to passage, the National Association of Broadcasters said, in part:

It is the manifest duty of the licensing authority in passing upon applications for licenses or the renewal thereof, to determine whether or not the applicant is rendering or can render adequate public service. Such service necessarily includes broadcasting of a considerable proportion of programs devoted to education, religion, labor, agricultural, and similar activities concerned with human betterment.

Broadcasting magazine editorialized in 1934:

[The Commission] cannot censor programs. But it can consider the merit of programs in passing upon applications of stations for renewal of their licenses, just as it did in deleting the stations operated by Brinkley, Baker and Shuler.[3]

Much later the Supreme Court made it relatively clear that simply meeting the technical requirements for broadcast is not sufficient:

[A]n important element of public interest and convenience affecting the issue of a license is the ability of the licensee to render the best practicable service to the community reached by his broadcast . . . . The Commission's licensing function cannot be discouraged, therefore, merely by finding that there are no technological objections to the granting of a license.[4]

The public interest standard is inchoate and requires, as all such standards do, the articulation of content by the agency charged with its enforcement. From time to time, the FCC has made some efforts to develop programing standards.[5] Yet, the recent failure of a Commission majority to endorse the development of guidelines indicates they do not accept the public interest standard as a part of their Congressional mandate.[6]

Any institutional arrangement for mass media is bound to have its defects, and many of the critics of commercial broadcasting seem to overlook the fact that any alternative will have different, perhaps more serious, defects. One important way in which the government can act positively to broaden the range of ideas in the marketplace is by providing adequate support to the present best alternative to commercial news service, the Public Broadcast Corporation.

Another proposal is to provide support for some continuing and systematic analysis of press performance. Although the news media may be sluggish, they are not immovable. If, 30 years ago, anyone had announced that most daily editors should think twice before using anything a police official said about a crime, he would have been hooted down as a radical against a free press; yet that is exactly what is beginning to happen in newsrooms today.[7] If anyone had told most network executives ten years ago that he run on prime time a TV series on the problems of people who live with cockroaches, he would have dismissed the idea as crazy. The lack of outside analysis and interaction with the public has left the whole system to drift with forces that are not clearly seen from within.

New journalistic forms are needed. After events are reported, something more is required—opinions, analysis, solutions. These opinions do not always come from the proverbial pillars of the community; frequently they will come from new voices which, at the present, have a very hard time getting into the media unless they appeal to traditional news values by creating conflict or violence. When, in the past, there were many different newspapers in one place, it might have been left to each one to give its personal analysis and it was assumed this would cover the field. But, today, we do not have this kind of multiple voice anymore. It should become habitual editorial policy to display fairly and clearly the opinions, analyses, and solutions offered by a wide variety of people, expert and non-expert, covering the spectrum, regardless of the proprietor's personal position.

Too many news organizations fear social ideas and social action. As a result, they stimulate, dissatisfy and arouse anxiety only to fall silent or limit themselves to irrelevant clichés when thoughtful solutions are required. Alternative solutions to our most urgent social problems, based on the work of our most imaginative social thinkers, and written with the clarity that only a good journalist can produce, ought to be standard practice.

America can look forward to change—the only certainty. This will require not only information about events, violent and non-violent, but ideas about what to do about these events. It is a new kind of journalism. It may start, as in the past, with the fair or objective description of physical happenings, but now it must go beyond to a fair portrayal of alternative solutions. The last generation of reporters concentrated on reporting objective physical happenings—telling the reader what he saw with his own eyes and heard with his own ears. The next generation must concentrate on describing what somebody else thinks.

A. Action by Government

Although the government's role in the communication of news is properly restricted, it is becoming increasingly evident that the policies of the first amendment cannot fully be realized simply by keeping the government out. Specifically we recommend:

A. The Corporation for Public Broadcasting be provided with a budget for news and public affairs programming comparable to that of the television networks. The three networks spent about $150 million for such programs last year. We believe that approximately $40 to $50 million should be provided to the CPB for news and public affairs. The corporation should focus on providing those services which commercial broadcasting cannot or will not perform.

This will require great restraint on the part of the government. We believe such restraint can be partially assured by requiring that all communications between government officials and the corporation relating to news content be a matter of public record, and that all hearings be open to the public.

B. The Justice Department and the Federal Communications Commission should scrutinize carefully all mergers, license applications, and license transfers which would result in greater concentration of media ownership. While generally we do not believe that it is feasible to significantly deconcentrate the industry, we do believe that, except in cases of above average performance, license renewals by television stations affiliated with a newspaper in the same community should be granted only on the condition that the station or newspaper is sold within the next 3 years. The traditional failing company exception would, of course, also apply.

C. Perhaps most important is that the government must stay abreast of new technological developments in the communications industry and be prepared to assure that further concentration of control does not occur. This is particularly important with respect to CATV. Control of access to the 20 or more channels of such a system by a single corporation is unacceptable. If CATV is to be made a common carrier, conditions for access provide one of the most difficult policy problems confronting the government. In addition, the technical specifications—e.g., whether there will be an opportunity for selection through information retrieval—and the allocation of the channels for various purposes are of crucial importance. Toward this end we would endorse the recommendation of the Telecommunications Task Force for the establishment of an executive level department for Communications planning with authority to appear in regulatory proceedings involving these issues.[8]

D. There is a good deal of confusion, particularly among practicing broadcast journalists, about what the fairness doctrine requires. We believe that the most the fairness doctrine should require is that the licensee give a representative portrayal of the arguments of various sides of an issue. If the arguments for a particular result are overwhelming, the broadcaster ought not be forced to pretend it is a close question so long as he provides a representative portrayal of opposing views. The belief that balance, regardless of the merits, is required seems to have had a dampening effect on willingness of many broadcast news organizations to treat controversial subjects. We recommend the FCC clarify this ambiguity and resolve it along the lines indicated.

E. Each year the Federal Communications Commission must pass on approximately 2,500 broadcast license renewal applications. With this kind of case load, in addition to its other many chores, it is impossible for the Commission to give individual consideration to each application. Yet the Commission is obliged to determine that each renewal will serve the "public interest, convenience and necessity." If the Commission is to effectively discharge its mandate, it must develop at least broad guidelines for such determinations in order that its staff can bring to the Commission's attention those cases that raise serious questions.

Although we do not endorse any specific set of standards we do believe that the recent dissenting opinion of Commissioners Cox and Johnson articulate the proper direction of such guidelines.[9] They include:

(1) The percentage and number of hours of news programing; (2) The percentage and number of hours of public affairs programing; (3)

Percentage of network news programs cleared; (4) Local and regional news as a percentage of total news programing; (5) Amount of locally originated prime time programing; and (6) Number of news employees.

Although these standards are relatively objective measures, it is clear that they would not be the sole guide of whether or not to renew the license. They do provide guides for determining which license renewal applications ought to be brought to the attention of the full Commission.

In addition to the kind of criteria articulated in the above dissenting opinion we would recommend the exploration of an additional standard.

The percentage or amount of time devoted to news and public affairs is only one measure of public service. Equally important as the time devoted is the quality of programing. Although we cannot accept involvement of the FCC in making judgments whether a news and public affairs programing is good or bad, it does seem appropriate for the Commission to examine the expenditures on this kind of programing. The correlation between cost and quality is hardly precise, but it is an appropriate index for consideration so long as its infirmities are recognized. Finally, it is clear that expenditures on news and public affairs programing ought not be evaluated in the abstract. The adequacy of such expenditures should be judged against the profitability of the station as a percentage of depreciated capital investment, or, in the case of stations which have been transferred since commencing operations, depreciated value of the purchase price. With regard to stations subsequently subject to sale, no readjustment of the depreciated value of assets would be allowed except the capitalized cost of securing the transfer.

This report has focused very little on the pathology of American journalism. There are, to be sure, a number of well-documented cases of news suppression and the rudeness and pomposity of some newsmen is well known. There is little those outside the profession or news organizations can do to improve manners and there is little point in admonishing against what even the least principled members of the profession recognize is wrong.

Recent governmental concern with "staged" events does require, however, that we briefly address this problem. Characteristic of the kind of response generated by the television coverage of the disorders at the Chicago convention is H.R. 9566, now pending in the House of Representatives Committee on Interstate and Foreign Commerce. If enacted, the bill would make it unlawful "for any person, with intent to deceive the listening or viewing public, to broadcast a news program which has been falsified in whole or in part." The penalty is a fine of not more than $10,000 or imprisonment for not more than 1 year, or both.

No one, of course, can endorse the broadcast of a news program that has been falsified with intent to deceive the listening or viewing public. Yet there are great dangers in such legislation to the kind of journalism we seek to promote.

Perhaps the most serious adverse effect would be to make even smaller the marketplace of ideas and reduce coverage of important social problems. Prosecution under this bill will require a jury verdict on the factual questions of whether the news was "falsified" and also whether it was done with "intent to deceive." Passing over the problem of determining whether a news event has been falsified, it is quite clear that the question of intent will be resolved by circumstantial evidence. The most important aspect of this circumstantial evidence will be how much of a falsification was involved. As our earlier discussion of audience distortion concludes, whether the jury regards the portrayal as false and if so, whether there was intent to deceive will turn in large measure on their political convictions. An important determinant of the guilt of the defendant in each case then will turn on the political views of the jury. Such a law is intolerable in a society that values free speech.

Moreover, aside from its dubious constitutionality, we believe that such legislation is unnecessary. There is almost no evidence at the present time to suggest that the conduct this bill seeks to proscribe occurs with anything but the rarest frequency. The events which gave rise to this legislation, the incidents of staging reported in *Rights in Conflict*,[10] would hardly qualify. First, there is insufficient evidence to identify the parties involved and establish that they participated in a staged event to support a criminal conviction. Second, the Media Task Force staff viewed all of the material broadcast on the three networks and none portrayed any events even remotely resembling the events described in the *Rights in Conflict*. Third, the Task Force staff viewed the out-takes (film not broadcast) and there was no evidence that they were filmed by any network crew. Fourth, the Federal Communications Commission has made it clear that it will investigate charges of staging and falsifying news broadcast where there is any extrinsic evidence to support the charge.

There is no demonstrated need for such legislation, its effect on broadcast news practices would clearly be negative, and to the extent a problem does exist, the FCC is capable of handling it under present law.

B. Action by the News Media

This report has explored the role of the media in the resolution of social conflict. We offer our recommendations for the consideration of those who have traditionally been accorded responsibility for acting in the areas upon which recommendations touch. They should be given no special significance or weight beyond whatever persuasive force they may have. Specifically, the fact that the report was funded by the government entitles our recommendations to no special weight. It is against this setting that our suggestions are made:

F. Journalists should reexamine the degree to which existing news judgments incorporate obsolete standards, including a tendency to report violence because it is sensational, rather than because it is significant. Moreover, in reporting conflict, the press should develop a special sensitivity to the danger of overstating the degree of conflict.

G. Beyond reexamining existing standards for reporting violence, newsmen should reconsider the contemporary utility of well-established news-gathering practices. Perhaps most important is that interpretive news stories—which can be written with time for calm reflection and balanced judgment—be allocated more resources and be given greater prominence. For newspapers, this means running such stories regularly on page 1. For network television, this requires expansion of the existing time slot for the evening news to 1 hour and changing to a mixed hard news/news magazine format. A similar change in format is desirable for local news. If necessary, this should be done at the expense of documentaries.

H. We strongly recommend that the news media examine carefully the problems posed when equivalent access to the media is denied. In this connection, we particularly recommend:

(1) That the media hire and train increased numbers of newsmen from minority groups.

(2) That the media provide the kind of regular surveillance of minority group activities which it applies to other segments of the community.

(3) That the media provide information to local groups about preparing press releases and, more generally securing access to the media through traditional channels short of demonstration, confrontation and violence.

(4) The use of ghetto "stringers."

(5) Inclusion of members of minority groups in day-to-day news, such as births, deaths, weddings, business promotions, opening of new businesses, and social functions.

(6) More background and in-depth stories on social issues and particularly those stories dealing with facets of the American scene with which the majority of the audience have little actual experience.

I. There is a need for greater interaction between the news media and the community and for responsible criticism of media performance. There are a number of ways in which this can be brought about:

(1) News organizations should establish and publicize the existence of grievance machinery or internal appeal boards to hear the complaints of persons who feel that their viewpoint has been unfairly excluded from the press or that the press coverage of an event in which they were involved is inaccurate. Such a program has worked well at the *Louisville Courier-Journal.*

(2) News organizations should encourage local press councils to provide a continuing exchange of views between the news media personnel and representative members of the community.

(3) Journalism schools should ingrain in their students a tradition of continuous reexamination and self-criticism through, *inter alia*, the establishment of journalism reviews and programs designed to prepare the student to apply new findings in communications theory to the practical problems of communicating the news.

(4) The establishment in other major metropolitan areas of publications like the *Chicago Journalism Review* which provide a

forum for public debate on news media performance.

(5) News organizations should freely criticize other news organizations and report on their performance the same as they would any other institution in our society.

J. Journalists should continue their efforts to upgrade their profession at a personal or individual level. We endorse the mid-career training programs offered at some universities and urge that more media owners and operators, particularly television, make time and funds available to their newsmen to take advantage of these programs.

K. We recommend that every news medium establish a code or other form of guideline to be followed in the coverage of riots or other events involving group violence. Although we do not propose to recommend specific guidelines, we suggest that at least some effort be made to establish advance contacts with the police and with various dissident groups in the community before violence erupts. We also recommend the establishment of rumor-clearance centers and close liaison between these centers and the press. In the case of reporting incidents likely to spark group violence, we recommend a minimum delay of 30 minutes in broadcasting the news, perhaps longer delays in giving the precise location of potentially explosive crowds, and very careful and restrained reporting until the police have the situation under control.

L. We recommend that news organizations resist those critics who would have them deny coverage to protest. The news media can reduce substantially whatever incentive they provide for violence by providing balanced treatment of at least four aspects of demonstrations:

(1) The purpose of the demonstration. What is the nature of the grievance? Why are the demonstrators there?

(2) The events leading up to the demonstration. Have other remedies been sought; if so, what has been the response of those addressed?

(3) The demonstration. How many people were present? How did they conduct themselves? Do not focus only on the most extreme conduct or dress.

(4) The provocations, if any, and the official response. Why were the demonstrators trying to provoke the police? Did the police use more force than necessary to maintain order? Were there any extenuating circumstances, such as physical exhaustion or personal security of political candidates?

The standard for determining whether an event will be covered should place more emphasis on the nature of the grievance, the number of people affected, the severity of the grievance and less emphasis on the willingness of the aggrieved to engage in violence or the likelihood that they will.

Several times in this report it has been suggested that the news media ought to report that which is significant—items that mean something to men's lives. We have offered no concise definition of "significant" nor rigid guidelines to determine what is and what is not significant. We agree with one journalist who responded to such a suggestion that not many newsmen he knew made an effort to report the insignificant. There is, however, a middle ground and that is where many—perhaps a majority—of newsmen stand today.

For too long, the press has been victim to what journalist Eugene Methvin has described as a "tradition trap." News is what newsmen say it is, we are told, but for too many newsmen the news is really what an earlier generation of editors and newsmen have said it was—a generation whose values were formulated on the basis of many conditions that no longer exist.

In a speech to the Overseas Press Club, Willard Wirtz observed that criticism of the press by anyone even remotely associated with government is a notably unrewarding occupation. In part, this is no doubt owing to what he went on to describe as the belief of some journalists that "an essential balance against the power of government to corrupt absolutely is the power of the press to be critical beyond criticism."[11] We cannot agree. Throughout this report we have offered our views on what is and what is not significant and the ways in which journalists' values and practices should be changed. Obviously, our comments are not equally applicable to all news organizations nor will our solutions be persuasive to all newsmen. We can only recommend their implementation where they are found both applicable and persuasive. The government can no more legislate good journalism than it can legislate good manners. More important than the adoption of specific suggestions is that each news organization make an independent determination of what is significant. There will never be agreement among the many news organizations or other institutions, including the government. Yet, such diversity is what the first amendment is all about and is the strength of American journalism.

REFERENCES

1. Jerome A. Barron, "Access to the Press—A New First Amendment Right," *Harvard Law Review* (June 1967), p. 1641.
2. This and other ideas in this chapter are taken from a speech before *mmmmmmmmmm*, Dec. 13, 1968, by Ben Bagdikian.
3. *Broadcasting*, Jan. 15, 1934. "The cases cited were those of John R. Brinkley (renewal denied, 1930), who used his station KFKB' Milford, Kansas, to promote goat-gland rejuvenation operations; Dr. Norman Baker (renewal denied, 1931), who used his KTNT, Muscatine, Iowa, to promote a cancer 'cure' and assail the medical profession; and Rev. Robert P. Shuler (renewal denied, 1931), who used his KGEF, Los Angeles, for attacks on religious and other groups. In each case the commission action was based on program content." Eric Barnouw, *The Golden Web* (New York: Oxford University Press, 1968), p. 29, footnote 4.
4. *National Broadcasting Company, Inc.* v. *United States,* 319 U.S. 190, 216 (1943).
5. See Public Service Responsibility of Broadcast Licensees, Report by the Federal Communications Commission, Mar. 7, 1946; Programming Policy, 20 Pike and Fisher Radio Regulations 1901 (1960); Ascertainment of Community Needs by Broadcast Applicants, FCC Public Notice, 19880, Aug. 22, 1968

6. See Renewal of Standard Broadcast and Television Licenses, 11 F.C.C. 2d 809 (1968); License Renewals, 10 Pike and Fisher Radio Reg. 2d 944 (1967); Renewal of Standard Broadcast Station Licenses, 7 F.C.C. 2d 122 (1967); N.Y.–N.J. Licenses Renewed, F.C.C. Public Notice, May 29, 1969.
7. Bagdikian speech, *op. cit.* Footnote 2.
8. *Final Report,* President's Task Force on Communications Policy, (Washington, D.C., mimeo: Dec. 7, 1968).
9. N.Y.–N.J. Licenses Renewed, FCC Public Notice, May 29, 1969, dissenting opinion.
10. Daniel Walker, *Rights in Conflict,* A Staff Report to the National Commission on the Causes and Prevention of Violence (New York: Bantam Books, 1968).
11. Remarks of Willard W. Wirtz, Secretary of Labor, before the Overseas Press Club of America, New York, Feb. 27, 1967.

Appendix II-A

HOW THE MASS MEDIA
WORK IN AMERICA

By Leo Bogart*

A. The Mass Media Experience

An advanced industrial society in the contemporary world is inconceivable without a well coordinated system of mass communication. Our society's complexity and specialization of function require a constant flow of information to integrate all of its components. Our bureaucratic and corporate institutions are too vast and the personnel who constitute them are too widely scattered for information to be conveyed by direct personal contact as it was in previous periods of human history. In the past two decades there has been a vast increase in the per capita utilization of mass media as well as in the range of media choices available.

The term "media" includes a wide variety of sources of information and experience. These sources differ greatly in character, organization, and social function. It is very difficult to find any common denominator by which the various media forms can be compared, except in terms of economic statistics.

No previous society has enjoyed (or suffered) so large and varied an output of mass communications as the contemporary United States. In this country today there are 1,749 daily newspapers, 573 Sunday newspapers, 8,012 weekly newspapers, 652 magazines, 2,316 business and trade publications, and innumerable school, labor union, and other special publications reflecting highly localized or transitory interests. There are 832 television stations, including 167 educational stations, and 6,480 radio stations (4,226 AM and 2,254 FM), including 355 educational or public-service stations. Seventeen hundred and sixty-seven publishing houses produce 203,470,000 textbooks and 88,400,000 trade books a year (59 percent of the latter are in hard covers and 41 percent in paperbacks; 11 percent are fiction and 89 percent are nonfiction). There are 10,034 motion picture theaters and 3,685 drive-ins that exhibit both the 178 feature films produced by Hollywood each year,

---

* Executive Vice President and General Manager of the Bureau of Advertising of the American Newspaper Publisher's Association.

and films from abroad. This does not include the total communications resources used by advertisers, who invest $6 billion in outdoor and public vehicle posters, direct-mail pieces, and miscellaneous forms of display and sales promotion.

This bewildering array of communications channels conveys to the public a continuously increasing flood of messages which steadily encroach on both our leisure and working hours. The news media make substantial use of the same national news-gathering organizations: the Associated Press serves 1,238 newspapers and 3,045 television and radio stations; United Press International serves 1,175 newspapers and 3,209 television and radio stations. Syndication and feature services diffuse identical material to numerous publications and stations. The duplication of content in different media is further augmented by the widespread public relations practice of mailing press releases and unsolicited publicity feature material directly to editors. Because of the economics of broadcasting and televising, fewer channels of information can be diffused simultaneously than in print, with the corollary result that the choices for the listener or viewer are also fewer. Television in the United States is dominated by three national networks during the evening hours when there is the greatest amount of viewers. The news services of the three networks produce most of the broadcast news that reaches the public. In a word, although a wide variety of media channels is available, media exposure tends to be concentrated in a narrow part of the spectrum of the available choices. The circulation of the twenty largest consumer magazines accounts for 41 percent of the total magazine circulation. Even in local media such as daily newspapers, the 50 largest-circulation papers account for 39 percent of the total daily circulation. The three dominant television networks attract 92 percent of the television audience during the peak viewing hours between 7:30 and 11:00 p.m.

All the mass media today are within reach of all but a fraction of the American people. Ninety-five percent of American homes have at least one television set (28 percent have two or more), and 99 percent have a radio (the household average is 4.6 sets). Ninety-five percent of the American people read a newspaper during the course of a week, and nine out of ten read at least one magazine a month. The movies attract 13 percent during an average week, and one person in three sees at least one film a month. On any given weekday, 82 percent of the adults watch television for an average of 2 hours and 17 minutes (the time spent viewing is higher for women, especially housewives, who average 2 hours and 33 minutes, than for men, who average 1 hour and 49 minutes)[1]; 66 percent listen to the radio an average of 1.3 hours; 78 percent read a newspaper (and nearly half of these read both a morning and an evening paper); and 37 percent read at least one magazine. This variety of media contacts means that people are not dependent upon any one medium as a source of information, recreation, or opinion. They get their information from different media in different dimensions, and those who are more interested in the news are precisely those who demand it from several sources each day.

Children grow up with television, but their interest shifts to radio listening during adolescence, because at that period they are attracted to both popular and offbeat music. The reading of newspapers and magazines increases when they enter adulthood, with its greater complexity of life roles and greater demands for information. Forty-three percent of adolescents between the ages of sixteen and twenty go to the movies at least once a week. This percentage drops to 17 percent among people in their twenties and 5 percent among those fifty and over. The oler part of the population, which includes a large percentage of retired and widowed persons, spends considerably more time watching television than do younger people.

An individual's utilization of mass media reflects his social class and geographical location as well as the particular period in his life. The reliance on printed material increases among people with higher education and income, while they tend to watch television less. On an average weekday newspapers are read by 89 percent of adults who have an income of $10,000 or more, and magazines by 52 percent; the percentages are 64 and 27 percent respectively among adults with under $5,000 income. The latter average 2 hours and 27 minutes a day watching television, while among the former daily viewing is only 1 hour and 45 minutes. Residents of large metropolitan areas have access to more media choices, made possible by the larger economic base of those markets. As a result of the greater accessibility of daily newspapers, specialized magazines, motion picture theaters, and bookstores, as well as of the somewhat higher educational and income levels which prevail in metropolitan areas, their residents have a considerably greater per capita exposure to printed media of all kinds and to motion pictures, than do residents of rural areas, although the amount of broadcast exposure is not substantially different.

The way in which mass-media exposure patterns differ for different types of people merely reflects the multiplicity of functions which media serve. It reveals information both about the world at large and about an individual's immediate community or specialized occupational and avocational interests. The media also are used to provide entertainment at widely varying levels of emotional involvement. These levels range from the casual scanning of a comic strip to the passionate absorption in a novel, from the housewife's use of a television soap opera as a background for her ironing to the teenage girl's emotional involvement in a romantic motion picture. Furthermore, media support and reinforce each other. Media content also reinforces direct personal experience. Media may enrich and create new life interests. But people may also turn to the media to relive or review experiences in which they have personally participated.

Media differ in the degree to which they are characterized by either parochialism or universality. Fundamentally, most media have a certain community basis. The community may be geographic, as in the case of the local daily newspaper or broadcasting station, or it may be a community of occupational or avocational interest, as in the case of a television network football broadcast or a magazine appealing to the special interests of homemakers or science buffs.

Yet the circulation of a newspaper or magazine and the number of viewers or listeners of a broadcast offer no sure criterion of meaningful communication, or of influence or impact. (Nor are they necessarily an index of how successful the medium is as a business venture; publications of identical circulation often vary widely in the amount of advertising they carry and in their profitability to their owners.) As a measure, circulation or audience size may have no relationship at all to the intensity of the communications experience which takes place as the result of exposure. Nor does intensity in any sense relate to the amount of time which people spend with different media, because the rate and volume of information flow is quite different in broadcast timebound media than it is in print, which readers may absorb at their own pace. The amount of time which an individual spends in reading reflects not only the quantity of material he examines and the intensity of his perusal, but also his reading ability, which is a function of education and social class. Better educated people read more, absorb more of what they read, and read faster.

Communication, then, is a selective process that operates at a number of levels. We choose the programs and periodicals that interest us. We remember those messages that interest or concern us most, among all those we see and hear and read. But there is also selection in the earliest stages of sensory perception. For example, when we open a newspaper page, our eyes' focus is attracted to the items which have the greatest meaning for us as readers. The nature of communication in print is inherently far more selective than it can be in a broadcast medium, which flows in time. Communication through print is at the user's speed and to his specifications, whereas in broadcasting the communicator controls the pace of transmission.

The mass media (except for the movies) have historically tended to represent increasingly individual experiences for their audiences. When once only a few people knew how to read, they read to others. With the present phenomenon of an almost universal literacy, reading has now become entirely a private matter, except in the case of parents reading to young children. With the development of the transistor, radio—once the family entertainment center—has become portable, personal, and intimate. This is now also becoming true of television as sets become smaller and mobile and as more families acquire more than one set. There remains a difference, however, between the visible, tactile, permanent record of printed communication and the intangible, evanescent nature of broadcast messages. Print is conducive to generalization and abstraction; broadcasting is directed to the immediate and specific.

People utilize the media for many reasons: they may seek inspiration, or amusement, or instruction, or a sense of participation in the great events of the time. But above all else the media experience is a pastime, an activity that people engage in at certain times of the day when they have nothing of overriding importance to do, and when they simply want to relax from chores or evade boredom. On the average, people will watch television the same number of hours a day, whether there is one channel to look at or two or three or more. Changes in programming or in the number of program choices available do not strongly affect the total time spent in viewing. Ratings are therefore not merely a measure of a program's own attractions, but of its competition in the same time period.

When the broadcaster seeks to build an audience at the expense of his competitors, his considerations are based on the particular time period, not on a need to divert people to television from other activities. At any time of day, in any given season, the demand for television entertainment is relatively inelastic. The habitual work, play, sleep, meal, and school pattern of Americans has the result that there is a certain proportion of the population before the television set at certain hours of the day. This may be as many as half of the adults at certain peak periods or only a few percent in the dull hours of the midmorning or the early afternoon. But that proportion is fairly insensitive to changes of programming content. It takes a national disaster or a political event of surpassing importance to attract more than the usual minority of housewives to the television at 11 o'clock in the morning. And no matter what the attractions of programming may be during the peak viewing hours of the evening, there will always be a certain proportion of people who will want to sleep, or who hold evening jobs, or who prefer to entertain visitors, listen to music, read, go to the movies, make love, or otherwise occupy themselves.

The viewer follows the path of least effort; he tends to watch those programs that make the fewest intellectual demands upon him, that provide easy and relaxed entertainment. Within this formula the viewer seeks a variety of content to avoid boredom.Thus, every network program department seeks to provide a balance of different program types in the course of an evening, including some of above average intellectual appeal or esthetic merit. Programs of quality may well be overrepresented in their share of broadcast time, relative to their actual appeal to the public. The latter will normally prefer entertainment to information. What is informative for one person may be merely entertaining for another, and vice versa. Nor is the boundary between information and entertainment a matter of what is timely. The fundamental difference is that information exists largely outside of time. For there is also an aesthetic element involved in acquiring information; but information often is regarded mainly as an end in itself rather than as a tool for the pleasure of learning. Entertainment and culture for most people, are pastimes which must be savored within the time dimension.

Readers and audience approach each medium with a distinctive set of expectations. Ideas or symbols which fit into the familiar mental landscape are not taken literally, but are accepted as conventional expressions of mass communications rhetoric, underserving of special attention or commentary. Hyperbole and exaggeration in advertising and campaign oratory, pontification in editorials and byline columns, excessive intimacy of tone, and insincere cordiality or humor on the part of broadcasting personalities—all of these are automatically discounted by the seasoned listener or reader as true reflections of reality. For this reason, criticism of media content must take into account not only what it conveys on the surface, but how it is interpreted by the mass audience. Even the small child who is thrilled with the mayhem of Wild West battle scenes is aware that the cowboys and Indians are really actors—"only pretending."

B. The Economics of Media

Media, like other social institutions, cannot exist without an economic base, and accordingly are big business in the United States. Daily newspapers are a $7-billion-a-year industry, of which about $5 billion is from advertisers' investments and $2 billion is the direct revenue from the public. Television is supported by $3 billion a year which is paid by advertisers for time and production. Radio yearly draws $1 billion. Magazines are a $2.5 billion industry, with $1.3 billion accounted for by advertising. Book publishing grosses $2.4 billion and motion picture theaters $1.8 billion each year. The profitability of each of the major media reflects not only its competitive position, but the degree to which its costs are fixed by a large investment in existing equipment and a commitment to an existing set of labor practices. Profits in the book publishing industry are 11 percent before taxes; in the motion picture industry they are only 4 percent. But books and movies are the only two important media that are not dependent upon advertiser support. The vast expansion of American media audiences and readers in the postwar period has its close parallels in the growth of advertising.

Advertising expenditures have represented a fairly constant percentage (around 3.5 percent) of all U.S. consumer expenditures. The growth of advertising from a $3 billion industry just after World War II to an $18 billion industry has been a reflection partly of inflation, but mostly of the very real expansion in the economy. Television has shared in this expansion and has been an important stimulus to it. The industry's profits have always reflected the state of the economy. In 1951 its earnings before taxes were $42 million. By 1966 they had risen to nearly half a billion dollars. The ratio of earnings to revenue is about 30 percent for all independent stations and 40 percent for the original 106 stations whose franchises were granted before the 1948 "freeze" on channel allocations. Profits are approximately 16 percent for the networks, whose earnings come primarily from their wholly-owned and operated stations rather than from their network operations, which return only a modest profit. The profit level for non-network stations may be compared with an average before-tax earnings ratio of about 13.5 percent for all U.S. industries in 1964–65, and with a profit level of about 18 percent in the publishing industry (which includes not only newspapers and magazines but book publishing and other allied printing trades.)

Compared with printed media, broadcasting has been highly profitable because of the comparatively low capital investment in facilities and the comparatively small payroll required to handle substantial volumes of programming time and advertising revenues. The factor which multiplies the value of the station owner's investment is his control over that freest of all commodities, the public airwaves, which he is franchised to use by the Federal Communications Commission.

Because media are big business they are difficult to acquire and expensive to start. Time, Inc. invested many millions of dollars in *Sports Illustrated* before it started to show a profit four years after its founding. Roy Thomson paid $75 million in 1967 for the Brush-Moore chain of small Ohio dailies, with an aggregate circulation of 363,000. S.I. Newhouse paid $54.2 million in the same year to acquire the *Cleveland Plain Dealer,* with a circulation of 388,000, in a fiercely competitive market. The price of a television station in a city like Lexington, Ky. is $2,500,000, as may be seen in the case of WKYT-TV, which was bought nine years earlier for $65,000 plus approximately $150,000 obligations by the co-owners. The economic structures of broadcasting and printed media differ greatly, because they entail different types of investment and labor costs. Newspapers are huge manufacturing enterprises. The 357,000 employees of newspapers in the United States put them ninth in rank among all manufacturing industries. Television and radio stations operate with far fewer personnel. There are 122,500 persons employed in all of television and radio broadcasting.

Talent and capital are unevenly distributed. Given this fact, it is not surprising that certain enterprises succeed and others fail within any field of endeavor. Concentration of ownership in the media has been brought about by the same competitive market forces whose influence has been felt in other industries which benefit from economies of scale.

Government regulations have always limited such concentration in broadcasting. Only one company (S. I. Newhouse) owns the maximum permissible number of seven television stations, eight companies own the maximum of five VHF stations, and 134 others own two or more television stations, UHF or VHF. However, even a few stations in major markets can reach an impressive proportion of the American public. (The five CBS-owned stations have only 7 percent of the total U.S. television audience during prime-time hours on weekday evenings, but the CBS network has a 37 percent share of all the viewing households.)

The Reader's Digest, Time, Inc., Cowles Publications, Curtis Publishing Co., McCall Corp., and the Fawcett, Hearst, and MacFadden publications represent 30 percent of all consumer magazine circulation. The largest magazine publisher—*Reader's Digest*—has 6 percent of all consumer magazine circulation.

Of the chains of two or more newspapers in different cities, 157 account for half of all daily newspapers and for 59 percent of their circulation. The largest single newspaper group (the Tribune Company-owned newspapers) has 6 percent of the total daily circulation. The total number of daily newspapers in the United States is approximately the same as it was twenty years ago. Although a number of economically marginal big-city newspapers have failed or merged during this period, about the same number of new dailies have started in suburban areas and in new communities. In fact, the number of cities that can boast of a daily paper is greater than ever (1,500, compared with about 1,400 in 1930 and about 1,200 in 1910.

Although in 97 percent of the nation's daily newspaper markets there is now but a single ownership, 33 percent of the total newspaper circulation represents papers published in cities where there is a competitive press.[2] This is not the only criterion by which to judge the degree to which readers have access to more than a single source of press opinion. Newspapers published in different cities often compete vigorously for the same readers and for the same advertising accounts. Metropolitan daily newspapers circulate in communities that have their own daily or weekly papers. Similarly, radio and television stations located in different cities compete for the audience in in-between areas, and for advertising revenues. Seventy magazines today publish regional or local editions. *Look* publishes 75 such editions with every issue.

The tendency toward the creation of corporate conglomerates has affected media no less than other fields of business. It has been stimulated not only by the tax laws and by accounting practices that make mergers financially advantageous, but also by a keen awareness of the impending marriage of electronics and the graphic arts. This is manifested in the acquisition of book publishing concerns by RCA (parent company of NBC) and CBS, in joint ventures such as General Learning (formed by General Electric and Time, Inc.), as well as in the further diversification of existing multi-media corporations such as Metro-Media and Downes Communications. Strong corporate links have also been forged between Hollywood and the television industry.

In 82 of the 1,506 newspaper markets a television station is owned wholly or partially by a newspaper in that city.[3] And in 216, or 14 percent of those markets, a radio station is owned by the local paper. But in only 25 of these cases is there no other competitive television voice originating in that same city, and in 35 no competitive radio voice. Because the increasing number of media vehicles has resulted in more choices for the public, all media—broadcast and print—complete more aggressively for consumer attention and for the advertiser's favor.

C. Operating the Media

The influence of the mass media in matters of taste, values, and politics represents the cumulative effect of many individual minor decisions made by media operators in response to specific situations. These decisions may be based on considerations that appear to be highly idiosyncratic at the time they are made, and which yet contribute to a total pattern whenever they resemble similar decisions made by others. Media executives help to set public standards and values; they also make judgments about what is appropriate to put before a general mass audience in depicting aspects of life which might come to the attention of only a small minority in the real world.

The major mass media have an influence in their subject matter on both public affairs (as sources of information) and the world of the arts (as entertainment). There has never been a clear distinction between journalism and politics or between popular culture and intellectual culture. From the beginning the media have attracted persons who wished to interpret the course of history to the masses of people and thereby to influence it. There have also been those who sought to convey an esthetic experience to a wider audience than could be reached in the theater, the concert hall, or the art gallery. Authors have generally sought to reach as many readers as they could, and when mass media were confined to the printed word they had no hesitation about writing for daily deadlines or, like Dickens, writing major novels in serial form.

Only in the 20th century, with the advent of the new media, do we find a broad gap between the respectability of intellectual culture and the questionable status of talented individuals who devote their skills to popular culture. The growing demands for output under severe time pressure, and the fierce competition for audiences, may have encouraged sensationalism and lowered standards of performance. As media enterprises became big business, the objectives and interests of the business office commonly came to be viewed as antagonistic to those of the people responsible for creating the product. The intellectual community viewed with increasing suspicion and hostility the activities and influence of "press lords," "movie moguls," and "Madison Avenue." The triumph of the business office was most evident in the entertainment media. Hollywood, with its star system and its "stables" of highly paid writers rewriting each others' scripts, brought to the media the idea of talent as "property," a concept that was adopted early in broadcasting.

The information media, particularly newspapers and magazines, have historically brought to their owners and managers many satisfactions beyond that of a steady income. Newspaper ownership has traditionally been linked to the expression of a community's identity and to a political point of view. The power to shape public opinion often gave newspaper owners and publishers a direct influence on political events, and this control over powerful media was often used to promote selfish and partisan interests. During the 19th century, American newspapers were often the strong voices of political parties. Among the joys of publishing at the turn of the century was the satisfaction of shaping history. Such magazine giants as Henry Luce and DeWitt Wallace were in the same tradition, and their financial success cannot be separated from their passion to articulate their beliefs in the publications they controlled. In many established media there was, and still is, a tradition of enlightened and responsible family ownership, buttressed by an established fortune. At its best, this freedom from financial concern has made possible an unbiased integrity and a dedication to the public interest.

Because newspaper publishers are apt to be established businessmen and pillars of their communities, they are often of conservative opinion. Labor and production problems are far graver for them than for operators of television and radio stations. The publisher is an employer involved in negotiations with unions in a great variety of crafts (many of them are hampered by archaic work practices). . He, as manufacturer, must manage ponderous and expensive equipment. He must supervise the handling of large quantities of paper, metal, and ink, and the logistics of distributing a bulky product through the tangled traffic of his metropolitan area.

As a businessman, the newspaper publisher is under continuous pressure, because his primary clients are close at hand in the same community. These are the local retail advertisers with whom he not only deals in business, but also with whom he often associates socially. By contrast, the television station manager derives a substantial part of his revenue from the networks and from his representatives in New York, Chicago, or Detroit, who deal not with the advertiser directly, but with his advertising agency. The television station manager is therefore less inclined than the publisher to share the attitudes and prejudices of his clients. He is part of an industry that regards itself as being a part of urban sophistication and power, and he may feel comparatively unrestrained by the parochial concerns of his own community. As a comparatively new industry, broadcasting attracts new men who may lack the newspaper owner's deep involvement in the preservation of established institutions.

In the mass media, the possession of unusual technical skills, such as the skills of writing, editing, and program production, or the skills of salesmanship or financial administration, can elevate an individual to the managerial level where policy is made. What distinguishes the mass media from other fields in which successful specialists are promoted, is that in the media, management power has a political aspect. There is probably no other field of endeavor in which people can be raised so readily to a position of tremendous political influence on the basis of what may be essentially irrelevant qualifications. Because media deal in ideas as well as in profits, the distinction between ownership and control is not exactly comparable to that between stockholders and managers in an industrial corporation. The distinction is really between those who establish the limits within which others may act and those who define policy; between those who play a watchdog role and those who are involved actively in the decision-making process.

There are few large-scale manufacturing businesses today in which an entrepreneurial dictator, in 19th-century fashion, surveys everything that goes on within his realm, counting the paper clips, and checking every overtime statement and expense account sheet. Similarly, there are few media tycoons who seek to exercise rigid control over every aspect of their operations. Big enterprises require delegation of authority. In mass communications these enterprises are responsible for a very substantial proportion of the public's media exposure, and for a large share of the influence that media wield in politics. They receive a large share of the advertising revenues, and a large amount of the criticism of program content that is often brought against the media. The absolute size of a communications enterprise can hardly be taken as an inverse index of its spirit or merit, especially when giants battle each other. In large media organizations, decisions on content are decentralized, fractionated, and made bureaucratic. In an anonymous corporate bureaucracy operated strictly as a profitable business, media (particularly magazines and newspapers) always risk losing their ethical integrity and sense of civic responsibility.

Every publication and broadcasting network has an editorial or programming formula by which the balance of its content is generally determined and which governs its essential audience appeal. The formula weighs different ingredients in the medium's potential content according to whether or not they appeal to the kinds of readers or viewers whom the management of the medium regards as its primary audience. The policymaking process by which this formula is arrived at is much more diffuse and drawn out than the focused and deliberative process that precedes the expression of a particular political viewpoint in editorials or program production.

The quantity of material produced for publication or broadcasting is far greater than the capacity of the media to disseminate it on any one day. What the public can read, see, or hear reflects the critical editorial judgment of those who act as wardens or overseers. These media "gatekeepers" are the people who control the flow of output through the media. Some, in the news media, are in the position of having to make their decisions rapidly, with inadequate time to reflect or study alternative possibilities, but usually with a shrewd awareness of the management's philosophy or bias. Others, in the entertainment media, make their judgments in a more considered and serious way, because their product involves longer intervals between deadlines and consequently less pressure.

A distinction may be made between policy decisions and action decisions. The former set long-term guidelines regarding media content and emphasis. The latter are made within an immediate framework, but these decisions also often become precedents for the setting of future policy, as well as implementing existing policy. The actions taken are the work of many hands. The reporter who covers a story, for example, is not responsible for its final position in the paper, or for its headline, or even for the actual words of his account, which are rewritten and edited. Smaller papers have smaller news staffs to write original copy, and they generally accept and run more boiler-plate material than larger papers do. The proportion of wire-service copy, relative to total editorial content, is also substantially greater in smaller papers. The telegraph editor on the local paper decides what stories to run, and the managing editor and the makeup man decide how those stories are to be played from the standpoint of length and emphasis. But before these specific decisions are made, earlier decisions have already been made by the wire-service editor on the state wire, by the rewrite man at the national wire service, and by the editors who direct and control the flow of output from the field. On a different scale, similar types of decisions are made on the output of broadcast news. Small radio stations, for example, are apt to use the wire-service bulletin copy as received, without editing or interpretation.

Many elements of media content, especially news items, are the product of a series of accidental or random events rather than of deliberate planning. Recently, a speaker at a public meeting in a New York suburb used a racial epithet in the course of a heated exchange that was irrelevant to the main business proceedings. Had no reporter been present, a handful among the several dozen people in the room might have been sufficiently exercised to pass the word along to a small circle of their interested and concerned friends. But as it happened there was a reporter present from a metropolitan daily, as a result of a very marginal editorial decision. Because he and his editors chose to consider the epithet as newsworthy and to quote it in a newspaper article, the incident suddenly was brought to the attention of over a million readers. The reporting of an event in a major medium is understood by most people to be a matter of general concern and interest, so that the unfortunate remark produced vigorous counterattacks. A controversy had been created out of what may or may not have been a "true" news event. All of this may have been completely out of scale with the fast judgments made by the reporter who covered the story and by the editor who decided to carry it with a certain degree of emphasis. News thus becomes what media choose or chance to print or to air. (The bombing of a Harlem police station on November 13, 1968, rated a front-page headline in the *Daily News* and a lead story in radio news reports, but it was "cooled" and buried deep in the inside of the *New York Times*.)

The ability of television to transform the events it transmits has become a matter of increasing concern, both to broadcasters and to society. When rioters perform for the cameras and shout, "The whole world is watching," it is apparent that the medium evokes the message and does not merely transmit it. But though the revolutionary effect of television on politics is both self-evident and novel, the newsman has never been merely a passive observer of events. He is also an actor who has the power to alter the course that events take. (Edward R. Murrow initiated the downfall of Senator Joseph McCarthy in much the same way as Emile Zola became a figure in the Dreyfus case and not merely a reporter of it.)

American mass media are staffed by writers and other creative people who include a higher-than-average proportion of political liberals, mavericks, and iconoclasts. Yet as institutions the media generally seek to maximize audience size by following known and existing tastes. There is, therefore, often an inherent tendency for them to be bland and conservative, not merely by blunting criticism of established ideas, but also by avoiding sharp innovations in style or subject matter. The mass media operator in a commercial culture understandably seeks to avoid giving offense, either to advertisers or to any significant sector of the consuming public. Left to their own devices, editors or broadcasters might produce a product that would genuinely reflect their own talents, that would express their ideals and their conceptions of their mission. They could probably trust their own instincts fairly far without fear of the consequences on audience size; for in all the major media there is a large measure of audience and advertiser inertia that cushions the shock of any shift in content or policy. Public habits, once acquired, may be taken into account by making changes in content gradual and by ensuring that the most cherished values of the society are not transgressed.

The professional pride of the media practitioner is the main safeguard against the exercise of irrational or antisocial controls on the part of media ownership. The professional looks to his peers for approval and guidance rather than to his bosses, and his peers are not necessarily the people with whom he works. They may be geographically dispersed. But he is at all times (even without their physical presence) aware of their judgment, their standards, and the need for their critical acceptance. Among any of the commercially supported mass media, it is possible to find examples of outstanding devotion to the public interest as well as many instances of total cynicism, and even some of utter corruption. If any generalization could be made about the attitudes that characterize mass media operators, it might be this: All are aware, at least to some degree, of the need to balance the profitmaking business objectives required for short-run success against the public tolerance or favor that will assure survival in the long run. Most of them are aware of the unusual traditions that link media to the political system and to the culture and of the special moral imperatives that these links impose upon those who control the flow of information and taste.

The public has only slow and subtle ways of reacting to an abuse of its interest: It may turn its attention to other competing media; rarely, it may find its leadership in the voices of advertisers or through the channels of government. Even the remote possibility of such reprisals imposes a restraint upon the media operator who regards his product as no more than another commodity to be sold at the best price the market can bear. And to such negative considerations are often added far more positive ones: Idealism, craftsmanship, and a sense of continuity with the spirited voices of the past.

D. The Influence of Advertisers

The advertiser's role in the commercial mass media is primarily to set limits on content rather than to order or shape content directly. Although it is easy enough to find individual instances of impropriety and venality, these do not appear to be broadly characteristic of the relationship between media operators and their advertisers. The kinds of pressure which an advertiser is apt to exercise are usually at a petty level. He may seek free publicity or ask for a personal favor such as getting an item onto the society page or squelching a minor accident report. More often than not, such requests are diplomatically evaded. It is rare indeed for an advertiser to attempt to influence the basic policy or editorial judgments of a reputable publication or the overall programming philosophy of a major broadcaster. Some media may voluntarily introduce editorial matter or programming in a deliberate effort to win "tie-in" advertising, but the real effect of advertisers upon the public's media fare operates in much more subtle ways. Advertisers may shape the media by giving their custom to some and withholding it from others. They do so on the basis of assumptions about how their expenditures work to best effect. Since media operators consider their output as "products" for which advertisers are customers, these products are designed with the advertisers' assumptions more or less in mind. To the extent that corporate marketing managements and the managements of large advertising agencies share a common belief that persuasive communication is essentially a matter of how much pressure is brought to bear, most advertising dollars are spent in a quest for the big audience, and the big audience continues to be the primary concern of mass media operators.

One hundred major advertisers invested 30 percent of all national advertising dollars in 1967 and 80 percent of all national television dollars. The top ten television advertisers represented 27 percent of the total. Ten advertising agencies placed 30 percent of all agency billings that year, and nearly half (46 percent) of all television billings. This concentration may merely reflect the overall structure of American industry and the large contribution made to the gross national product by a comparative handful of major corporations.

Only a comparatively small number of people actively participate in making the decisions that determine the programming philosophy of U.S. commercial broadcasting. Decisions on broadcast advertising investments are tailored to each advertising objective, yet cumulatively they are a powerful force. The prevailing philosophy of programming undoubtedly has a tremendous influence on the beliefs, outlook, and personal values of the American people, who devote a significant number of hours each week to television, and for whom television creates heroes, notions of what constitutes the good life or the interesting life, and a picture of the world at large.

In the broadcasting and advertising industries, each new program ratings report is awaited with eager apprehension and studied with great care. The dependence on ratings reflects the extreme difficulty and great cost of measuring what advertising does in terms of the one criterion which is universally accepted as being of prime importance: its effects on sales of the product. Since sales effects are difficult to measure accurately under competitive market conditions, the assumption is often made tacitly that sales response is bound to be more or less in proportion to the amount of exposure to the advertiser's message, and that the more messages distributed to the more people the more sales will be generated.[4]

In selecting individual publications or broadcast positions for a media schedule, a buyer of advertising customarily considers not only the communications attributes of each possible vehicle and the size of the audience he can reach for a given expenditure, but also how the characteristics of that audience relate to his advertising objectives. In recent years there has been a movement by advertisers away from the so-called "boxcar" statistics to a more sophisticated analysis of audience traits, with the objective of aligning the characteristics of viewers or readers to the consumption profiles for particular products and brands. For example, a media vehicle with a large proportion of young men in its audience might be suitable for a new type of shaving cream or hair-grooming product; or a medium that attracts young housewives would be appropriate for advertising baby foods, etc.

Publications and programs that appeal to restricted interests or tastes are generally distinguished by a sharply defined focus of subject matter or by unusual strength of opinion or character. If they articulate ideas that are felt intensely or that embody a group's sense of cohesion or a community's identity, the influence of such minority media (and their attractiveness to advertisers) may be quite out of proportion to their audience size. In practice, magazines afford the advertiser the greatest opportunity to reach highly specialized audiences, whereas newspapers generally blanket their communities at all social levels.

In television the segmentation of the market is clear enough in the distinctions between daytime broadcasting with its primarily feminine appeal, late-afternoon television with its large proportion of child viewers, and late evening, which draws the highest percentage of men. In these instances programming formulas simply follow the characteristic timetables of people's daily life routines. However, by far the largest daily audiences for network television are in the prime hours of evening viewing (roughly, between 7 and 11 p.m.). Most programs during these hours are designed to attract the overall family audience; audience profiles therefore do not differ substantially for most shows.

In the heyday of network radio every sponsor sought to establish a close identification with his program and its leading personality. Although this was also the case during commercial television's first decade, television advertisers today generally have the objective of diffusing the largest possible number of messages in order to reduce the unit cost of an advertising "exposure" or "impression" (defined as the delivery of a message within the range of an individual's sight or hearing). The desire to combine cost efficiency with maximum "coverage" (or presentation of the message at least once to the largest possible number of people) has led to the growth of spot-television (which now accounts for 34 percent of advertisers' total television expenditures). The number of national spot-television advertisers increased from 1,306 in 1956 to 2,194 in 1967—an 82 percent increase. By contrast, there were 321 network advertisers in 1956; in 1967 there were 379—an increase of only 18 percent. Spot-television requires a smaller minimum investment and therefore offers greater flexibility to the medium-sized and smaller advertiser.

The spot advertiser must negotiate a position for each commercial with each individual station, placing it within a locally-originated program or sandwiched between network programs during the stationbreak. The same considerations in network television advertising have brought about the widespread adoption of "scatter plans" or "participation buys," in which an advertiser's commercial announcements are spread among a number of different programs. The advertiser thereby minimizes the otherwise inevitable concentration of his impact among the faithful viewers of any particular show, and thus scatters his message more widely to prospective customers. However, by participating in many programs he thereby identifies complete with none. Only 4 percent of network television advertising is represented by single-sponsorship of a program and another 3 percent by the shared sponsorship of two regular advertisers; the remaining 93 percent of network advertiser expenditures is "scattered." This has had important implications.

In the mid-fifties, decisions on programming content were strongly affected by powerful program departments in the advertising agencies, which dealt directly with the independent program "package producers." In many instances agencies themselves initiated or even produced shows. By the late 1960's this responsibility had passed largely to the network program departments, whose principal concern has been to build a continuing pattern of viewership in the course of each evening. Each network program lineup has the objective of inducing viewers to stay with a given channel from program-to-program, thereby maintaining audience size at a high level and attracting the maximum amount of advertising revenue. A weak program, or one appealing to minority tastes rather than to the broad family audience, causes the viewer to turn his dial, and thereby hurts the succeeding shows.

Programs and periodicals are often produced to a format that is designed to provide advertisers with audiences and readers that correspond to particular marketing dimensions that match a desired consumer profile. Only secondarily do such formats fulfill the original expressive needs on the part of editors or producers themselves to give voice to ideas, share strong sentiments, or express a private view of the world.

E. Media: Model or Mirror?

Public tastes can be molded; they reflect what is familiar. People learn to accept and value the media content and style to which they have become accustomed. Mass media operators therefore bear a responsibility for shaping the tastes they seek to satisfy. It is inherent in their role that media operators should be sensitive to public taste. They have a natural urge to expand their audiences and their influence.

There is perhaps no greater body of evidence on the effects of mass communication than that represented by the experience of American practitioners of marketing and advertising. Every marketer knows that advertising by itself can have little effect if the product is not in the channels of distributions. With media messages as with merchandise, the product that is most readily available is the one with the greatest likelihood of being consumed. Ideally, perhaps, the mass media should be like an endless Oriental bazaar with booths of enormous variety grouped into specialized sectors. It would be impossible to see them all, just as it is humanly impossible to explore every shop and stall in the souks of Cairo. The visitor must either confine himself to the quarter of the rug merchants or the leather craftsmen, or else he may wander through the entire place with only occasional stops, sampling here and there to obtain the overall flavor. It is easier to reach some booths than others. Some are larger or more inviting in their displays of merchandise. Some are more crowded. It is usually the most popular places that attract the attention of those who are not yet committed, who have not yet decided where to shop.

People go where the action is. They like to walk along a crowded street. The inexorable economics of the marketplace leads to a restriction of choices as unpopular offerings become economically unviable and disappear. Compared with countries where broadcasting (or even the press) is a state monopoly, the American system of private media ownership tends to make a multiplicity of choices available, because new capital is always attracted to innovations in marketable products or technique. The competition of old and new ideas in a free market results in diversification and, after testing and trial, in the emergence of new mass tastes. (For this reason, fads and fashions in the popular arts change dramatically from year to year.) The array of choices is limited only by inertia and by the entrenched power of existing institutions.

The American mass communications system is not conducive to the widespread and easy diffusion of nonconformist tastes and opinions, even though it provides many outlets for those who make the effort to seek them out. "Little magazines," scholarly periodicals, and the journals of minority political opinion are easily accessible to only a fraction of the population. Serious bcok reviews are found in a few of the newspapers. There are comparatively few bookstores that sell serious books (2,081 independent stores, 858 book sections in department stores, and 1,815 college bookshops). Even in a metropolitan area of 20 million people like New York there is only a small number of first-class bookstores which carry a complete line of books beyond the current bestsellers.

In its selection of media experiences, as with other commodities, the public always has a restricted range of options. Accessibility is the first condition. One cannot watch a television program on UHF, however good it may be, if one's receiver is equipped only for VHF; but when UHF becomes standard equipment on new sets, the audiences suddenly increase. Even then, with a given number of choices, they will be smaller for the same program when the channel must be tuned in manually than when it can be had with a single click of the knob, as in VHF. Most media exposure decisions are trivial, originating as they do in human laziness.

Whatever content, good or bad, is available in movies, broadcasts, books, or publications, someone will watch or read it, simply because it is there, and many or most in the audience and among readers would not otherwise be impelled to seek it out if access to it were less convenient.

Once accessibility is increased, the audiences expand, although the media content remains unchanged. Most radio listeners (three out of four) keep their sets tuned to a particular station that they turn to because it is local or comes in loud and clear or because it speaks to the listener's special interests or tastes. Magazines build and maintain circulation through reduced-rate, long-term subscriptions and newspapers by home-delivery routes—both to facilitate ready access for readers. In a similar way, the success of a motion picture is dependent not only on its inherent ability to arouse and sustain public interest in the theme, actors and style, but also on its distribution (which in turn reflects distributors' judgments of what the public will want). Many people attend the movies more for the pleasure of going out rather than because of the particular film that happens to be playing.

The matter of availability assumes particular importance if certain elements in the media produce a different effect among children than among adults. The motion picture that attracts adult audiences in the theater is seen by the whole family when it is broadcast on television. Media content is not merely a reflection of public taste exercised freely with unlimited choice; it represents deliberate decisions made by media operators competing for audiences of maximum size and competing for them by the same ground rules.

There is an old controversy as to whether the mass media should simply mirror existing public taste or whether they should lead it in new directions. Many mass media operators seek to do both, but they practice uplift and reenforcement in widely varying proportions. Broadcast stations are required to operate in the "public interest, convenience, and necessity" by the terms of their franchises under the Federal Communications Act, and when they apply for renewal every three years, they are asked to report on the extent of their news and public affairs programming, both past and intended in the future. The Act makes it explicit that the FCC should not engage in censorship, and in practice the Commission has been reluctant to police closely the extent of compliance with the public service provisions of the Act or to evaluate the merits of the programming that stations report under the category of public affairs. (No station license has ever been revoked because of low-quality programming, although charges have been filed in cases of obscenity.)

The real issue in any evaluation of mass culture is not whether or not it is properly balanced by an output of a higher order within the same media. A far more serious question has been raised about the overall level of mass entertainment which is devised according to the traditional formulas. For example, the quality of television programming is limited by that of the pool of available talent from which broadcasters can draw. The number of talented persons writing, producing, or acting in television programs is hardly sufficient to produce material of high quality to feed the voracious appetites of the audience. Most television broadcasts are evanescent in character. Although a few classic series (Jackie Gleason's "Honeymooners" and Lucille Ball's "I Love Lucy") have been repeated over and over, programs generally are expected to disappear forever after they are discontinued, regardless of how good they are thought to be. Only rarely is there an opportunity for a viewer who missed a show to see it again at some later date. The absence of opportunity is also linked to an absence of demand, because of the paucity of sustained and sophisticated criticism. There is no existing mechanism through which those who control the media are continually confronted with a reflection of what they are doing and thus faced with the recognition of its effects.

Criticism includes both immediate responses to specific works, prepared from a short-term viewpoint, and also more reflective and comparative works done from a historical perspective. The worlds of painting, music, dance, and letters are dependent on such criticism to provide the web of discussion and common intellectural concerns that binds their adherents together. Filmmakers are constantly goaded, exhorted, commented upon. The flow of reactions comes to them through publications that reach the general public, and therefore that affect the immediate success of their current productions. More significantly, perhaps, it appears in specialized publications that are directed to their colleagues and peers, and which present them with a direct picture of their own accomplishments and failures. Such a picture is almost totally lacking for those who produce newspapers, magazines, and broadcasts. (The *Columbia Journalism Review* has sought to fill this gap, but its readership is modest relative to the need.)

Every community has its own local media critics, but their voices normally do not carry very far. Occasionally they find expression in some publication of the underground press (generally unprofessional in its writing and makeup and with little hope of long continuance). Criticism of the press generally comes from the political fringes rather than from a professional source whose seriousness and integrity give it validity and importance through the industry. Criticism of individual television programs is published *after* the broadcasts, and therefore does not affect the size of the audience except in those rare instances where favorable press notices lead to a rebroadcast.

In a free society control over objectionable content in mass communications is exercised primarily through the self-restraint of those who manage the media. It is generally understood that the dangers of a puritanical censorship are far greater than those wrought by offensive subject matter. Decisions over content are comparatively easy to control in the case of a medium like television, not merely because it is a regulated industry, but because it has a relatively limited output which it places before a vast audience. Comparable decisions are difficult to control in the case of publications that exist in great variety and, in many instances, reach only minor sectors of the public.

All media mechanisms for self-regulation are negative in nature. They aim to eliminate objectionable words or pictures rather than to raise the quality of output in any cultural or intellectual sense. Government interference with media operations is incompatible with freedom, and has been fought with fervor throughout American history. Yet media manage their affairs in a world where government rules and government functionaries are never very distant.[5]

Self-policing or censorship on the part of the media has been most commonly adopted where there has been the greatest danger of official censorship. For years the Hays Office (Motion Picture Association) rigidly interpreted a code of propriety which was effectively enforced as long as the leading motion picture producing firms and the leading theater chains had common or closely associated ownership. The old code lost its strength as a result of the forced divestiture of distribution facilities, the competition from television and foreign films, the rise of independent producers, and the shifting of judicial standards of obscenity. As the output of marginal films increased, and as "frank" or "adult" scenes became more common in routine Hollywood features, the fear of a renewed popular reaction led to the adoption of a new film-classification system designed to restrict juvenile attendance, rather than to modify content directly. Those mass media whose products enter the home and are readily accessible to the young have always been most self-consciously squeamish in controlling offensive material. In newspapers and magazines these controls have been exercised by individual editors. There is no record of any expulsions from the American Society of Newspaper Editors on the grounds of failure to comply with its Code of Ethics, which was adopted at the organizations' founding in 1922.

The broadcast media, since they are directly subject to Federal regulation, have been more alert to the need for policing their programs. The Code of the National Association of Broadcasters was adopted in 1937, modified to the requirements of television in 1952, and subsequently amended. It is currently subscribed to by 398 of the 665 commercial television stations and by 2,489 of 6,840 commercial radio stations. However, a station's agreement to abide by the Code is still subject to interpretation by its staff for specific program content. There are few instances of investigative or punitive action on violations by the NAB Code office, which can do no more than withdraw its seal from an offender. The individual networks all have offices that review the scripts of entertainment programs to assure compliance with the Code and with their own ground rules.

Media policy questions in the domain of taste and creative expression are in no way clearly distinguishable from similar questions in the domain of information and politics. There is no ready agreement on the standards that should prevail, and even less agreement as to how they should be applied. What is considered to be of importance or interest to the broad public differs with each community and with each country. Everywhere in the world news media tend to report the day's events from a local perspective. The same report filtered through the editing apparatus of a great news agency is reinterpreted in each country or region where it is received. This makes it all the more difficult to appraise the objectivity of news media in a worldwide perspective, because objectivity relates to the definition of what is newsworthy as well as to the interpretation that the facts receive.

The social class interests served by different media also commonly produce different emphases and treatments of the identical assortment of available news items. A newspaper that appeals to the business elite inevitably provides strong coverage of business and financial news and of cultural and social events. Is it therefore less objective, less accurate a reporter of the day's realities than its competitor, which directs itself to the interests of a working-class audience?

In broadcasting, FCC regulations (Sec. 315) require "equal time" for rebuttal of controversial statements made on the air. Because there are often a number of contradictory rival viewpoints, the interpretation of this rule sometimes has led to confusion, havoc, or avoidance of controversy altogether. This became particularly apparent during the 1968 election campaign, in which unsuccessful attempts were made to modify the FCC's equal-time formula to clear the way for a two-way debate between the two major presidential candidates. Under existing rules, any debate would have had to include minor political parties, giving them equal prominence.[6]

The direct confrontation of opposing political platforms or philosophies may, however, be of less moment than the live broadcasting of news events. Producers, directors, and cameramen, working under the pressure of time, combine to produce a vision of reality which is only one among many possible perspectives, none others of which can ever be recreated. The newsman's decision as to whether or how to report the violent, the base, and the politically eccentric must be made in the light of his responsibility to present a full picture of the significant events of the day. He suffers from an overabundance of choices. He can cover only a fraction of the potential stories. His input from wire or picture services gives him much more material than he has space or time for. His choices on what to use and how to emphasize it must be made in great haste and often under great pressure.

These conditions are the very opposite of those faced by the producer of mass entertainment, who suffers from a chronic shortage of material adequate to his highest aims. The entertainment producer's activities are more purposeful in nature and more thoughtfully planned. He works against deadlines that are not nearly as tight as those faced by the producer of the daily newspaper or the daily newscast, and he usually has a much more involved procedure for including other people in the collective judgments on script, casting, and direction which finally produce the finished product.

Political controls have always been exercised by the media through different channels from those that relate to censorship of the prurient or horrible. Fairness in the reporting of the news has always been the responsibility of editors or producers. Politically motivated and deliberate distortion is normally difficult to conceal, both because news reporting requires the cooperation of many different hands, and because truth that is suppressed in one channel usually will out through another. The question of objectivity becomes more acute when there is a reduction in the number of conflicting reports and interpretations available on the same events. In many single-ownership-newspaper cities a broad range of political opinions is expressed on the editorial page, by featuring columnists who do not necessarily share the editor's opinions.

Any media organization that truly serves the public interest, either in the realm of information or entertainment, must have independence of action for its professional personnel. If they are subject to direct political controls and directions, or even directly responsive to the size of their audience as the only yardstick of their achievement, they can never feel free in their own minds. And unless they feel free, they can hardly respond to their tasks at the full height of their capabilities. (For this reason, the news departments of the broadcasting networks report directly to the top management of the parent corporations rather than to the operating managements which have their eyes primarily on audience size and on advertising sales and profits.)

As in any human endeavor, there is a high degree of variability in the talents and human qualities of those who practice journalism or produce mass media entertainment. Can one rely on the professional objectivity of journalists to produce honest reports when they are themselves workers whose sense of occupational role or social class interest may be sharpened at moments of crisis which polarize loyalties and emotions? Can one repose one's trust in the sense of professional pride on the part of individuals who lack any common professional training and meet no official standards in order to practice their craft? The essence of professionalism resides in a recognition of the public interest, and this is the basis for the tradition of integrity in interpretative journalism.

Professional pride and morale, high standards of performance, and maintenance of the public interest—all are dependent on continuing diversity in the channels of expression. Where the pressure for improvement comes through the channels of government, there is an inevitable threat to independence and integrity and thus to professionalism, high standards, and the public interest. Herein lies the dilemma which must be faced in any effort to raise the level of the mass media and thus to improve the quality of life in America.

REFERENCES

1. These figures are based on a survey conducted by Opinion Research Corp. in 1967. Other surveys based on different methods show a substantially higher level of viewing. A. C. Nielson, for example, reports that the average adult spends 3 hours and 45 minutes a day watching television.
2. Another 11 percent of newspaper circulation is accounted for by suburban dailies which compete with metropolitan papers. If we include the suburban circulation of single-ownership, central-city newspapers, about half the circulation of the United States may be described as directly competitive.
3. Four magazine publishers and a book publisher each own three or more television stations.
4. This assumption is not necessarily correct, because the quality of communications is not merely a reflection of the frequency of contact. Some attempts at persuasion are more pleasing and convincing than others.
5. Modern communications technology involves innumerable practical considerations that bring mass media operations under close scrutiny by the state, if for no other reason than to regulate the allocation of a scarce-commodity like broadcast frequencies or the capacities of the postal system to handle large quantities of printed matter. Media profits are subject to taxation, and, like any other large enterprises with many employees, media are subject to labor laws.
6. Just as minority political candidates, with smaller budgets and no party machinery, are handicapped in their ability to attain a substantial part of the popular vote against major party candidates, so under normal circumstances is it difficult to create widespread acceptance for minority opinions, simply because their expression is normally relegated to media which are obscure and uninfluential rather than to those with broad audiences.

Appendix II-B

CONTEMPORARY FUNCTIONS OF THE MASS MEDIA

By Jack Lyle*

A. Mass Media as Institutions

The mass media are society's institutionalized channels of communication. Like all institutions, they must have a raison d'etre which is functional for the society. They must fill an existing need or a need that is created and, unless they are responsive to changing conditions within the society and the complex of interrelated institutions serving it, they may cease to be functional and will disappear.

Some of the dislocations that have occurred and are still occurring within the mass media as a result of changes in technology and in financial and political organization have been outlined in earlier chapters of this Task Force report. Our question here is: what are the functions of the mass media in contemporary American society and how do these relate to the members of our society, both as individuals and as members of groups within that society?

Basically, we communicate to exchange information in an attempt to reduce the uncertainty of the world about us and thereby increase our chances of survival. To paraphrase Harold D. Lasswell,[1] communication serves to: (1) provide a survey of our environment, (2) coordinate the society's collective response to the environment, and (3) achieve transfer of the society's culture from one generation to the next. The mass media came into being to perform these tasks as a specialization.

But from the beginning the content of the media has included items obviously aimed more at titillating rather than informing the public. Thus the media have developed a second category of functions, that of entertaining the public. The balance of these two functions between media and within each medium has been a frequent cause of concern both to the professional staffs of the media and to critics and others concerned with public affairs.

1. The Information Function

"What we don't know won't hurt us" is perhaps one of the most false of adages. To survive, individually or grouped into societies, we need continuing

---

* Associate Professor of Journalism, University of California, Los Angeles.

inputs of information both on changes in the physical environment and on the activities of other individuals and societies. The work of Allport and Postman[2] during World War II documented the uneasiness which people feel in situations where they lack information and where the normal communication media do not (or cannot) keep them sufficiently informed to allay such uneasiness. People then seek alternate sources of information and in such situations rumors flourish. These situations become more severe if the public loses faith in either the media or official spokesmen.

In recent decades the ability of one society to change the environment of another has been geographically expanded, thus extending the boundaries of our "critical" environment. As this has taken place, we have become increasingly dependent upon others, particularly the mass media, to provide us with a survey of a larger proportion of the environment relative to what we can personally observe. But concomitant with this has been an expansion of the ability of one society to communicate directly with members of another (or conversely, a diminution of the ability of one society to be kept psychologically isolated from others) through the modern mass media's potential for broad and rapid dissemination of information.

a. Implications for Democratic Society

Americans have perhaps a heavier responsibility in this regard than the citizens of any other society today, perhaps of any society in history. As citizens of a representative democracy, we have the responsibility to maintain a level of knowledge of conditions and events so that we can fulfill our role in making the system work. Democracy demands full dissemination of information together with free discussion, in contrast to those societies governed by elite individuals or groups. The extraordinary position of the United States in world politics today makes the entire world our critical environment. It is not surprising that such a situation produces great tension for individuals and the society as a whole.

Much has appeared in the media in recent years about a "credibility gap" between the Executive branch of government and the public (particularly as represented by media reporters). The justification of these charges is beyond the scope of this discussion, but remembering the work of Allport and Postman, the implications of the situation are quite obvious. What makes the situation far more serious is the fact that the major news media also are finding that a credibility gap exists between at least some members of their audiences and themselves.

Economic conditions have pressured the general media toward bigness and consolidation. This has produced within some segments of the public a perception of increasing uniformity and blandness in media content which these people feel reflects manipulation of the media by the agencies or persons in control. The truth or falseness of this perception is beside the point here, for the perception does constitute the "reality" on which these individuals base their assessment of and reaction to the media and the media's role in today's society. Having such a perception, it is understandable that these persons feel the "free and open marketplace of ideas" on which a democracy is predicated is diminishing. An increasing number of groups now feel the necessity to launch their own periodicals to present their side of the argument. Sizeable numbers of individuals, as individuals and as members of groups, express skepticism regarding the nation's regular news media. For example, one study has shown that among a sampling in a medium-sized California city the respondents discounted, on the average, a third of what they read in the newspapers and a fifth of what they heard on television newscasts.[3]

This type of outlook is frequently a result of strong political convictions (or strong convictions on any salient attitudinal or behaviorial continuum), and it is interesting to note that many of the same charges of bias are raised against the media by those at both extremes of the political spectrum. The charges, for example, made against the media by conservatives at the 1964 Republican Convention are very reminiscent of those made by liberal Democrats through the years.[4] The charges are also frequently heard among other strongly committed persons, whether they be "hippies", southern segregationists, or Black Panthers.

A 1963 study—two years before the Watts riots—showed that from a sampling of Los Angeles Negroes only 32 percent felt the metropolitan dailies would give a black candidate treatment equal to that given a white opponent, only 25 percent felt Negro churches and organizations had a chance equal to white organizations for getting publicity in the daily press, and 54 percent felt that the daily press was not fair in its treatment of race relation issues.[5] A 1960 study showed a much greater perception of political bias in the Dallas *Morning News* among Roman Catholic priests as compared to Baptist ministers, but perhaps more significant was the finding that among all clergymen the perception of political bias increased if the individual felt the paper was unfair to his own religious group.[6]

This latter fact underlines a conclusion drawn from a series of reader attitude studies; that the unfavorable attitudes toward the newspapers (and possibly the other news media) by the public are general.[7] From this it may also be concluded that if people find fault with a newspaper on some specific count, they tend to lower their estimation of the rest of the paper's performance in general. Hovland and Sherif[8] reported that their respondents tended to distort the location of other points of view as a function of the location of their own position on the continuum. Thus, those at either extreme are likely to ascribe the middle position to themselves and exaggerate the extremity of other positions, while putting the objective neutral position "on the other side" in their perception. We can accordingly see that a newspaper that attempts to follow a neutral course might be construed as biased by strongly committed persons.

While many blame distrust of the media on media consolidations, it seems equally plausible to postulate that the situation offers strong evidence of uneasiness within our society. The relationship between this uneasiness and the media-audience trust situation is undoubtedly circular. Perhaps this is most graphically illustrated in the matter of race relations. If, prior to a riot, the media report smoldering conditions, after the riot some persons will accuse them of sparking the violence; if they ignore the conditions, others will blame them for having failed to warn society of the threat.[9]

Knowledge has been called power, but there are stresses that can result from "knowing too much." From data on radio news listening among New Yorkers, Mendelsohn[10] developed the point that today's citizen lives in an age of anxiety based on real conditions. This, he reported, leads to "an almost desperate sense of urgency regarding 'the news.'" In its extreme forms, this anxiety can lead some persons to reject their responsibility as participants in a democratic society and to avoid the informational aspects of media content. In a 1962 audience and reader study in Los Angeles, a correlation was found between not reading the newspaper, not watching television news, and not listening to radio news, thereby showing that there are persons who almost totally ignore the informational media.[11] It has not been an uncommon experience of the author to encounter respondents in field surveys who state that they consciously avoid the news "because it just upsets me."

2. The Entertainment Function

With considerable insight, Cooley described early 20th century American newspaper content as "organized gossip."[12] Gossip does usually contain information that has pertinence for the listener, but it also contains details (factual or otherwise) that are included primarily to enhance the interest of the story itself. It is not surprising that professional reporters have long recognized that it is not sufficient in most cases to relate only the critical facts; effort must be expended to make the story interesting as well as important to the audience. (The ego requirements of the reporter are also a factor. It is certainly possible, even among professionals as well as gossips, to let the desire to attract and maintain attention cause the reporter to distort his presentation. This has obvious detrimental consequences for his success in fulfilling his obligation to report accurately.)

Another factor, however, is the balance of activities competing for the individual's time. In recent years the amount of leisure time available to the average American has been steadily growing. And as the time available for activities of one's own choosing has increased, so has the relative affluence to make possible a broader range of choices. This has created opportunities for people and agencies with ideas for providing leisure activity.

3. The Information-Entertainment Mix

All of the mass media can be and are used to provide entertainment as well as information and many have sought to benefit from the new opportunities offered by increased leisure time. Each medium has distinct advantages and disadvantages in various areas which have been demonstrated by empirical research.[13] The audio-visual have been described as having dominantly entertainment advantages, and the printed media as having predominantly informational advantages. But let us hasten to reaffirm that such a division of functions is anything but complete. Furthermore, as we shall show in later sections of this report, individuals differ in their personal orientation to and use of the various media. A basic point, however, remains that within any mass medium the information function generally is intentionally intertwined with some degree of entertainment. As Mendelsohn inferred from his New

York study, without such content to provide relief from the tension produced by factual reports of important events, anxiety levels might rise to an intolerable level and drive more persons to totally avoid the news.

The problem is to establish a proper balance between information and entertainment. Again, because of individual differences, there is no universal "proper" balance. Because these are mass media, the tendency generally is to attempt an optimal balance from the standpoint of the majority. This inevitably leaves a minority irritated.

4. Leader or Reflector of Society?

An examination of the social comment on contemporary society over the decades shows that whatever mass medium was predominant at the time was frequently accused of undermining the existing society and its values. This situation realistically reflects the potency of the media to influence, but it also reflects the fact that the extent to which the mass media are expected to assume leading roles in correlating society's action and in molding its culture remains unresolved. Too frequently the critics confuse manifestations of conditions and problems with the conditions and problems themselves. As was stated earlier, the media are institutions of society and as such reflect how the members of the society choose to use them.

As we have already seen, within the area of the information function, various factions raise charges of systematic bias in the media's performance. In the area of entertainment, some critics charge that the media are debasing values and cultural levels. A debate on the validity of these charges is not appropriate here; our point is that the charges themselves demonstrate what is perhaps a basic tension within a social organization—here, a democracy—that requires that its citizens permit and listen to opposing points of view and to be tolerant of them. Such behavior guarantees maximum freedom for society as a whole, but inevitably imposes some restrictions upon each individual. And, recalling the work of Hovland and Sherif, we should not be surprised that those who are most critical, who feel most oppressed, are frequently among the most doctrinaire and intolerant of other viewpoints.

As societal institutions, the mass media are inevitably involved in this problem. The news media have traditionally attempted to solve it by a distinction between "news" and "editorial comment." Increasingly it is being recognized that some degree of interpretation is inherent in the very act of reporting, regardless of the medium, and that interpretation inevitably reflects individual differences of physical perception and sociopsychological background. Furthermore, selective interpretation is exercised by each individual member of the audience and readership. Thus in situations where the society is highly polarized on one or several issues, it becomes increasingly difficult for the media to communicate effectively to all. The reactions to the television confrontations of John F. Kennedy and Richard Nixon in 1960 are an obvious example of how such selective perception and interpretation can operate within even a highly controlled format.[14]

As for entertainment functions, many if not most of those who deplore the quality of American television and what they perceive as its failure to raise national cultural levels are also among the strongest critics of the type of

Kulturpolitik reflected by boards of censorship and "official" art. The all-important question is: who is to make the decision as to what is "good" and in what direction society should move? This is a continuing source of tension within a democracy, and as institutions within a democratic society the media are inevitably a focal point of this tension.

B. Survey of General Media Content and Audience

In this section we will look at the broad outline of mass media content together with some measure of the media available to and their general use by the American public. Table B-1 presents the levels of use reported in a 1967 study of residents of a small city in the Midwest and provides a useful point of reference for this discussion.[15]

Following the discussion of the individual media we shall discuss some different patterns of media use which have been documented.

1. Books

Despite the alarms expressed about the possibility that television might have devastating effects upon book reading, book publishing is still a flourishing industry. Both dollar sales receipts and the number of new books published have shown a general upward trend during the past decade, although there have been year-to-year fluctuations in the latter category. In 1967, 28,762 new books were published in this country, of which 22,887 were new titles and 5,875 were new editions.[16]

The importance of books as a medium for furnishing specialized information is shown by the data contained in Table B-2. Of the total number of books published, fiction, biography, and juveniles accounted for only 23 percent, the arts for 14 percent, sports, recreation, and travel for 6 percent, while 57 percent of the titles were in areas of specialized interests or reference.

This is not to deny that books continue to play an important entertainment role in American society. The role of books has actually been expanded in the postwar years through the continued growth of paperback or "soft cover" publishing. Although their lower price means that they account for only 6 percent of the total dollar income of the publishing business (textbooks account for 51 percent, professional books for 10 percent, juveniles for 6.3 percent, book clubs for 9 percent, and trade books for 7.3 percent,) over 310 million copies were sold in 1966 and there were 42,500 titles in print in soft-cover editions.[17]

Although much of the consumption of paperbacks is for escape reading (Ian Fleming's "James Bond" adventures have sold a total of over 36 million copies and *You Only Live Twice* had a first printing of 2.7 million), some of the biggest sellers have been hard information books (Dr. Spock's *Pocket Book of Baby and Child Care* had sold over 16 million copies by 1965) and books of literary and historical merit (Lee's *To Kill a Mockingbird,* over 6 million copies, and Baldwin's *Another Country,* over 2.25 million). Accordingly, the major publishing houses have found that quality books may not attract a large readership in expensive cloth editions but will bring

Table B-1 — Typical Media Use in a Small City

Sample Size 206

	Percent
TV Time "Yesterday"":	
None	40.8
Under 4 hours	41.7
4 hours or more	17.1
Radio Time "Yesterday":	
None	29.1
Under 2 hours	39.2
2 hours or more	31.6
Read Newspaper Daily	77.2
Read a Magazine "Yesterday"	52.9
Attended Movie Within Past Month	29.6
Phonograph Listening "Yesterday":	
None	62.6
Under 1 hour	9.2
1 hour or more	14.0
(Remainder do not own a phonograph.)	

Table B-2 — Books published in 1967

Category	New Title	New Edition	Total
Fiction	1,981	1,099	3,080
Biography	783	261	1,044
Juveniles	2,390	321	2,711
Art	844	221	1,065
Literature	1,172	553	1,725
Music	165	52	217
Poetry/Drama	739	237	976
Sports/Recreation	391	110	501
Travel	769	321	1,090
Agriculture	218	69	287
Business	509	118	627
Education	781	124	905
General Works	426	128	554
History	1,015	472	1,487
Home Economics	203	53	256
Language	382	182	564
Law	392	135	527
Medicine	935	254	1,189
Philosophy/Psychology	633	230	863
Religion	1,502	362	1,864
Science	1,835	532	2,367
Sociology/Economics	2,761	850	1,232
Technical	1,051	201	1,232
Total	**21,887**	**6,875**	**28,762**

Source: *The Bowker Annual of Library and Book Trade Information 1968, p. 61.*

multimillion-dollar sales in lower priced soft-cover editions whose price range is from 95 cents to $2.95.[18]

In recent years advances in technology and marketing practices have made it possible for books to become a much more contemporary medium, in that they now capitalize quickly on important events. Thus we have seen the appearance of "new books," such as the variety of titles appearing within weeks of the assassination of President Kennedy, and within a matter of days following the Arab-Israeli war of 1967 and the murders of Dr. Martin Luther King, Jr., and Senator Robert F. Kennedy in 1968.

One problem faced by the book industry and the public is that the sheer number of titles makes it impossible for most bookstores to stock more than a small fraction of the total number of books in print, and proper display of even the books stocked also presents severe difficulties. The latter situation is perhaps most acute for paperbacks, because many paperback sales are a result of casual browsing by bookstore patrons. Personal checks of paperback displays at newsstands in various locations revealed a wide variety of titles. Escape content—westerns and crime, science, and erotic fiction—predominated in most cases, but there were also books on current affairs, good fiction, and history, as well as standard literary works.

2. Libraries

Not all book reading is a result of book sales, for, of course, books may also be obtained from a library. The importance of libraries as a communication channel is shown by the fact that 19 cities have libraries containing more than a million volumes, and that libraries in 65 cities circulate more than a million volumes per year. Seven libraries circulate more than 5 million.[19]

Most libraries find that their staff and space are pressed by growing operations and few are able to make systematic analysis of their patronage. The Los Angeles City Public Library, one of the nation's largest, keeps no regular detailed information on circulation on a citywide basis. However, library officials did collect and provide some statistics from several branches that were selected to reflect a socioeconomic cross section of the city, as shown in Table B-3. Because no firm relationship exists between branches and their "market area," and because these circulation figures are not related to number of users, interpretation of such figures from a sociological point of view is risky. However, at least two interesting observations might be pointed out. The first is that adult patronage relative to total circulation is considerably lower in poorer neighborhoods, particularly where Negroes predominate. The second is that nonfiction generally constititutes the larger share of adult books circulated, as it also does in the case of book sales (although not nearly to the same degree), while fiction is very predominant in child circulation.

3. The Book Public

Despite the fairly sizeable figures cited above, it must be admitted that book reading is not a common activity among the majority of the population. The sale and circulation of books, even more than that of magazines and

Table B-3. – Average monthly circulation at eight branches
of the City of Los Angeles Public Library

Branch and type of community	Total circulation	Total percent adult	Total percent juvenile	Percent of adult		Percent of juvenile	
				Fiction	Nonfiction	Fiction	Nonfiction
San Vincente (upper class) .	9,121	82	18	46	56	74	26
Hawthorne (industrial) . . .	31,853	68	32	32	68	61	39
Culver City (industrial) . . .	21,679	64	36	37	63	58	42
Holly Park (industrial) . . .	7,718	51	49	43	57	40	30
Woodcrest (welfare-middle class)	6,002		40	60	40	60	71
Lennox (transient)	5,581	54	46	51	49	65	35
View Park (Negro)	6,107	45	55	45	55	66	34
North Enterprise (Negro) . .	2,917	36	64	27	63	77	23

newspapers, suffers from the fact that the general level of reading skill is low. (One researcher has estimated that 60 percent of adult Americans have only limited reading skill.[20]) A national survey found that book reading "yesterday" was reported by only 5.8 percent of college-educated respondents and by only 0.9 percent of those with less than a high school education.[21] Indeed, according to *Los Angeles Times* Book Editor Robert Kirsch, book dealers estimate that their total trade is accounted for by no more than 11 percent of the nation's population. And in the question of public taste, no definitive information is available: such indices as "best seller lists" are based only on sales at selected book outlets, and accordingly are not an accurate measure of total sales.

It is perhaps worth noting that while television has often been considered a threat to book reading, some librarians report they find indications that it may actually stimulate reading.[22]

4. Magazines

The number of magazines published in the United States is astounding. The *Ayer Directory*[23] lists over 22,500 periodicals (not including newspapers). However, only 147 titles are listed in the "General Editorial" category, which includes current news, fiction, literary, and illustrated publications. Of these, 12 are primarily for children, 17 are comic groups, 49 are for men (including 18 adventure/detective/western types), 13 are movie magazines, and 41 are youth publications. There is a wide variety of categories, including many titles for women's interests and 21 categories under sports. But the great bulk of publications consists of those directed at special trade, technical, and class interest groups.

Of what might be considered general circulation magazines which have audited circulation, 52 had an average per issue circulation of one million or more in 1967 (table B-4).[24] It is worth noting that in the post-World War II years several Negro magazines have been started and have achieved considerable success. Best known is the largest, *Ebony,* with an audited circulation of just under a million. The same publishing firm also issues a weekly Negro news magazine, *Jet,* whose circulation is over 350,000, and a monthly service magazine for Negro women, *Tan,* with 122,000 circulation.

The content of magazines varies in both subject matter and quality. Perhaps the most straightforward way to deal with the topic of magazine content is to state that at the average newsstand the American of whatever age is offered an opportunity to indulge whatever his fancy of the moment might be: high-quality fiction and essays on contemporary affairs as well as violence and sex of every description. With a little searching he can obtain magazines that range from the sublime to the ridiculous, from the obscene to those that reflect nearly every political or philosophical viewpoint.

The number of titles available at a large newsstand makes it very difficult to make a comprehensive systematic survey of the magazines. The following is an admittedly cursory and subjective review of a sampling from some of the more exotic offerings at a large newsstand in the suburban San Fernando Valley section of Los Angeles, and is presented to give a general idea of the more extreme types of trash that are readily available to the public.

*Table B-4.—Magazines with ABC circulation of
one million or more in 1967*

(Source: World Almanac 1968, p. 161)

[in millions]

General

17.2 *Reader's Digest*
7.7 *Look*
7.4 *Life*
6.7 *Saturday Evening Post*

Women

8.6 *McCall's*
7.5 *Family Circle*
7.1 *Woman's Day*
7.0 *Better Homes & Gardens*
6.2 *Ladies Home Journal*
5.8 *Good Housekeeping*
4.3 *Redbook*
3.4 *American Home*
2.2 *True Story*
1.3 *Glamor*
1.3 *House & Garden*
1.0 *House Beautiful*

Men

3.9 *Playboy*
2.5 *True*
1.4 *Argosy*
1.0 *Esquire*

Sports

1.4 *Outdoor Life*
1.4 *Field & Stream*
1.3 *Sports Afield*
1.2 *Sports Illustrated*

Scholastic

2.0 *Senior Scholastic*
1.8 *Junior Scholastic*

News

3.5 *Time*
2.0 *Newsweek*
1.5 *U.S. News & World Report*
1.1 *Newstime*

Farm

3.0 *Farm Journal*
1.3 *Successful Farming*
1.3 *Progressive Farmer*
1.1 *Grit*

Juvenile

2.4 *Boy's Life*
1.8 *Scouting*
1.4 *Seventeen*
1.0 *American Girl*

Religion/Fraternal

2.5 *American Legion*
1.4 *Elks*
1.3 *VFW*
1.1 *Presbyterian Life*

Miscellaneous

11.3 *TV Guide*
5.0 *National Geographic*
2.0 *Parents*
1.5 *Popular Mechanics*
1.5 *Workbasket*
1.4 *Photoplay*
1.4 *Popular Science*
1.4 *Mechanics Illustrated*
1.1 *Columbia*
1.0 *Holiday*

Single Girl (50 cents), *Exciting Confessions* (25 cents), and *Real Secrets* (35 cents) are published by three different companies. Despite the lurid titles displayed on their colorful slick covers—"Save a Bad Girl for Me," "We Had More Than Fun That Night Our Beach Party Turned into a Bare Party," "I Learned the True Meaning of Sex Making Love to a Stranger"—the stories are surprisingly wordy and almost always end on a strongly moralistic note. Less moralistic and more explicit are the stories in *Action for Men* (40 cents) and *Man's World* (50 cents), where, for example, "The Girl Who Played Virgin" gives her virginity to her "uncle" on her wedding night and the victims of "The Mantrappers" are subjected to the nymphomaniacal lust of a female military horde.

Mixing sex and violence are the "crime" or "detective" magazines which suggest that the stories are actual cases. It might be noted, however, that of the two examined, *Confidential Detective* (35 cents) and *Detective Cases* (50 cents), one featured a number of foreign cases, and in both the accompanying photographs suggested that many of the stories took place some years ago. With titles such as "The Hippie Orgy and the Bludgeoned Nude Beauty," "Twisted Sex Provided a Pervert's Alibi," "The Oversexed Butcher Who Bathed in Blood," "Hit Her with a Jack-handle, Crush Her with a Rock," the stories in general are fairly explicit in describing what kind of violence was committed, how it was done, and to what effect.

"Girlie magazines" have long been familiar on newsstand racks, but other erotic publications are also common now. Some seem to be directed at homosexual males, others at lesbians. *RAM* ($3.50), for example, is simply a 54-page collection of full-page photos of nude males, with a focus upon the genital area. *Salute* ($3) states that its aim is "to illuminate the conviction that the unclothed human body is worthy of respect and deserving of increased acceptance in our culture." It mixes editorial matter ("Go-Go Guys of the Golden Gate," "Why I Model Naked") with front and back shots of nude males, singly and in groups. The issue examined was dedicated to the premise that "Youth will be served," and of the 69 photographs approximately half featured subjects who appeared to be in their midteens. The color cover of *Sapho* ($3) shows a photo of a bare-breasted, black-booted blonde flaying two nude companions who are trussed up in harnesses suspended from the rafters. The stories, illustrated with posed photos and drawings, include "Torture Chamber," "Leather Whipper," "Bobby-sox Spanker," and other items depicting sadistic/masochistic lesbianism.

(Unreleased) *Dynamic Films* ($2) is "for mature adults . . . a pictorial representation of phases and mores of our contemporary society," although its "editorial content is not to be construed as descriptive or to condone any action." It is heterosexual in its approach, but also features a heavy emphasis on sadistic sex, particularly the kidnapping of men for sexual purposes by groups of females. In "Under the Dum-Dum Tree" a "baddie gets it from three chicks"; in "The Bellboy Caper" the bellboy expected a tip, but was stripped for action instead, while in "Acid" a bearded hippie is shown kidnaped, stripped, chained, flogged, bitten, and force-fed by a motorcycle gang chick and a hairdresser who "is downright mean and likes to kick the hell out of men before beddy bye time . . ." The editorial attacks local censorship of erotic films, arguing "In an age when the viewing of violent murders, fictional or unreal, on television or in the 'legitimate' movie houses [is permitted], it seems incongruous that there should be such bias shown toward sex and the portrayal of it on film (*sic*) . . . Must sex be forced underground with dope and gambling, while war, violence, deceit, avarice and general debauchery remain on the surface for all to view as being acceptable, even to our children?" This general type of magazine is marked "adults only" and issues are either stapled or sealed in clear plastic envelopes to prevent their contents from being inspected prior to purchase.

As for the magazine readership, a great deal is known about the readers of the larger general-circulation periodicals—they tend to be better educated, white-collar, professional people. But with regard to those who might be termed marginal (or worse) within the general social mores, we have little more than speculation. In a study of children, it was found that the reading of pulp magazines did decline with the advent of television and that these children fit into a general pattern of immediate gratification use of the mass media.[25] But the very nature of the content of such magazines makes their readers reluctant in many cases to admit that they do indeed read them. Circulation figures are also difficult to obtain and often are not reliable. Furthermore, sales figures have drawbacks as a measure of magazine readership, for magazines often have a "life span" of weeks, months, or even years and during this time they may be passed from hand-to-hand, from family to family. The data in Table B–1 shows that of the respondents, two-thirds stated they had read a magazine of some sort within the past week.

5. Comic Books

Perhaps for most adults, the mention of comic books evokes an image of animal characters popularized by Disney and others, together with "Superman," "Batman," and their fellow superhuman fighters against evil. However, these represent only a few of the general types found today within the comic book selection on most large newsstands. In gathering a sample for informal inspection for this paper, two dozen were selected from well over 100 titles on display (the practice of stocking several issues of the same series concurrently makes it difficult to establish an exact count). Most are 32-page issues that sell for 12 cents, but there are also "giant" 80-page "classics" series that sell for 25 cents.

The *Ayer Directory* lists 13 comic book publishing firms, each publishing a number of series. In addition, there are "illustrated magazines," such as *Creepy* and *Eerie,* which sell for 40 cents and more. Where circulation figures are provided in the directory, they are for the publisher's entire group rather than by individual title. Only seven publishers provided circulation information, and their total combined monthly circulation was 30.7 million.

Comic book reading appears to peak among children between the ages of 12 and 15. A study of San Francisco school children showed the median number of comic books read per month as 4.5 for boys and 3.3 for girls at the eighth-grade level, while at the sixth-grade level the figures were 3.3 and 1.4 respectively. In five Rocky Mountain towns reported medians were 8.5 for boys and 4.7 for girls in the sixth grade (eighth-graders were not studied). By the end of high school, reading has been discontinued by most students (in San Francisco, the median at the 12th grade was 0.9 for boys and 0.07 for girls).[26] Despite this decline with age, it is well known that there is an adult readership of comic books. The Armed Forces, for example, have capitalized on this by using the comic book format in some of their educational programs. Several comics publishers include in their group a series on the "true romance—true confessions" theme, such as *Career Girl Romances, I Love You, Just Married, Teenage Love,* and *Secret Hearts.*

The major categories of comic books appear to be: (1) the kiddie comics, such as the Disney characters "Tom and Jerry," etc.; (2) the action comics which break down into three subtypes of (*a*) *Superman, Captain Marvel, Space Adventures,* etc., (*b*) war comics such as *Fightin' Marines, G.I. Combat,* etc., and (*c*) the westerns such as *Bat Lash, Outlaws of the West,* etc.; (3) the teen scene set such as *Archie, Binky, Sooter,* etc.; and (4) the adult-aimed romance series mentioned earlier.

The action group are a glorification of superhuman violence in which, to use the words of "Stretcho" of the *Fantastic Four,* "every force for evil must fight a counter-force for good." There is seemingly an inexhaustible supply of evil forces and, in a large number of cases, the fight between good and evil is never quite brought to a resolution, although these books do include a certain amount of moralizing. "Iron Man" closes one sequence with the following speech: "Sometimes I grow overconfident in my super-powered armor! I must always remember President Johnson's favorite motto, 'Let us reason together'; for a man's *brain* is still his most potent weapon!" The all-American "Teen Titans" are forced in one sequence to work with "Starfire," a Russian teen superhero who sums up their mutual experience, ". . . all men, regardless of their belief, *must* learn to live together! For when your ideologies and mine have long since turned to dust, *man must still survive!*"

One of the newest series is *Brother Power, The Geek,* whose leading character is a tailor's dummy which has been given life and superpower by a bolt of lightning and who both protects the hippies of San Francisco and exhorts them to be productive contributors to society. Issue number 2 projects an exceedingly ambivalent picture of the hippies in what appears to be an attempt to use the hippie image to attract young readers in order to preach against the general hippie ethos.

6. Newspapers

The term "newspaper" covers a wide variety of publications. The *Ayer Directory* lists over 10,000 entries under this title. However, we generally use the term to describe the some 1,760 daily general-circulation publications whose function is to provide a record of current events. Although we think of news coverage as the raison d'etre of the daily press, this is actually only one of its activities. In an early media study, Berelson analyzed the responses of New Yorkers when he asked them what they missed during a period when the presses were shut down because of a strike. From these he concluded that the daily paper not only provided information about public affairs, but also that, through its advertising, it was an aid in shopping, that it gave its readers a feeling of prestige and facilitated business and social contacts, and finally that, as a source of entertainment, it was a welcome respite from the chores of the day.

If we look systematically at the content of any newspaper it becomes obvious that the staff tacitly, if not explicitly, recognizes these functions. In post-World-War-II years advertising's share of space has steadily increased, and today it is not uncommon for it to fill up 70 percent of a paper. Of the remaining 30 percent, "hard news" seldom occupies more than one-third of the paper (or 10 percent of total space). One study of Sunday editions showed that while the average number of pages had increased from 118 in 1939 to 193 in 1959, the space allocated to news had actually decreased. The growth of special sections, particularly those devoted to leisure activities, together with increased advertising was blamed for this decrease.[28] It should be noted, however, that advertising is an important attraction for the papers and that it plays an important part in a paper's role as "a tool for daily living."

Table B-5 points up the fact that there is considerable variation from paper to paper in the balance of "hard news" and entertainment-type content provided, and that even within the same paper quite different emphases may be given from day to day, and from edition to edition within the same day. For example, even the comparatively staid Los Angeles *Times* changes to a sensational makeup featuring the more sensational news of the day for its street editions. Such a treatment is almost standard for street editions because of the fact that they must catch the eye of the passersby and literally shock them into buying the paper. It will be noticed in Table B-5 that the last four categories, which constitute the more sensational/entertainment types, account for over a third of the news and editorial space in five of the eight papers.

Most children are introduced to the newspaper through the comic pages and readership of the comics remains high through the adult years.[29] Most papers include a wide variety of comics, ranging from "soap opera" types such as "Mary Worth" and "Gasoline Alley," to kiddie strips such as "Donald Duck," to satirical strips such as "Lil' Abner" and "Pogo," to strips of violent action. Indeed, the general level of mayhem maintained over the decades in one of the most popular of all strips, "Dick Tracy," would be hard to match even in comic books. Nor are the comics free from political and ideological propagandizing, as evidenced by the conservatism espoused by "Little Orphan Annie" and the liberalism of "Pogo."

In earlier decades, when even small cities had competing dailies, individual newspapers frequently developed—by design or by chance—a pattern of content that appealed to specific audiences. Today, however, only 3 percent of the nation's cities have competing dailies under separate ownership. As newspaper consolidations have decreased the variety of daily papers available to the urban public, the survivors have been faced with the task of trying to provide coverage to fit the needs of the public at large. At the same time the population growth and increased organizational complexity of society have made the job of reporting news more difficult. In trying to serve the broad needs of the community, it is inevitable that some individuals and groups will feel slighted and will consider the coverage as biased. The fact that the daily press has been neither able nor inclined to provide adequate coverage of the problems of ethnic communities has led to the establishment of periodicals that focus on these groups. A variety of such papers will be found in most larger cities, some in foreign languages, others in English, others bilingual.

*Table B-5—Division of news and editorial space
by 8 Midwestern dailies**
[In percent]

News category	Paper							
	1	*2*	*3*	*4*	*5*	*6*	*7*	*8*
War/defense	15	20	19	26	22	22	26	25
Economic activity	11	21	14	12	8	15	12	12
Education/ classical arts	15	5	12	13	12	10	12	9
Public health/ welfare	4	3	2	7	3	3	4	5
Science/invention	1	1	3	3	2	1	2	2
Public moral problems	1	1	2	1	2	1	2	2
Crime	3	6	5	3	4	4	7	6
Accidents/disasters	4	10	6	3	3	2	5	6
Popular amusements	25	6	12	10	21	17	10	9
Human interest	16	14	14	9	15	13	13	11

*From Guido H. Stempel III. "Content Patterns of Small and Metropolitan Dailies," *Journalism Quarterly,* 39, 89 (1962).

Because black citizens have been the victims of severe and prolonged segregation in the American community, it is not surprising that the Negro press is particularly widespread. The 1968 *Editor and Publisher Yearbook*[30] lists 148 Negro newspapers publishing in 102 cities in 34 states and the District of Columbia. These include two dailies (in Atlanta and Chicago), each with 30,000 circulation, six biweeklies with a combined circulation of 117,000, and 140 weeklies whose circulation totals 1,508,500. And this list is not complete.

The Negro press has a long history that dates back to before the Civil War. These papers have been frequently criticized by black militants and sociologists alike as being dysfunctional for the advancement of Negro rights and Negro living conditions.[31] As recently as 1963 it was asserted that the black press was declining, at least partly as a result of advances in the integration of black Americans into the general stream of American life.[32] However, with the burgeoning of the black power and black pride movements, there has been some evidence of a new militancy and life in Negro papers, as manifested either through change of editorial tone in older papers or the establishment of new publications.

7. The Underground Press

Despite the relative decline in general daily newspapers in the post-1930 decades, a considerable number of new papers have continued to appear. In several ways, these papers are reminiscent of the publications that were the forerunners of today's press: they are unabashedly journals of opinion, crusading to defend and advance particular points of view. Their content is directed not to the general public but to the "believers." Furthermore (and as a result of this situation), they are generally small, financially pressed, and must be published spasmodically on uncertain schedules. However, a few of them have grown into relatively fat and prosperous publications.

Among these, much public interest and attention has been focused upon the self-labelled "underground press," which serves primarily to express the frustrations of groups within the society—particularly among the young—who question aspects of established values and institutions.* Such papers have appeared in most of the larger urban centers and, although they cling to the "underground" label, they are sold openly and at least some have qualified for and use second class mailing permits.

There are certain parallels between the "underground press," which is generally oriented to the "new left," and the publications of the radical right. These shared characteristics distinguish both groups from the mainstream of ethnic-minority publications. The latter were (and are) seldom intended to be the sole information source for their readers, and they generally sought to promote the assimilation of their readers into the national society while maintaining ethnic traditions in harmonious relationship to the larger society. But in many papers of both right and left, and in the publications of some of the more militant Negro groups, there is both active rejection of the existing society and a concerted attempt to discredit the general information media. In this respect, they are symptomatic of the centrifugal conditions within our contemporary society.

The first reaction of those members of the general public who may come in contact with a copy of an "underground" paper is probably shock at the frequency with which sexual words, figures of speech, and pictures are used. News stories and features are frequently written in the earthiest language with little regard for grammatical niceties. It is difficult not to suspect that some readers of such papers as the *Los Angeles Free Press*, the *Berkeley Barb*, or The *East Village Other* buy the paper primarily for the titillation found in the sex section of the classified ads. And it is somewhat depressing to note that in the smaller, weaker papers the bulk of the advertising is devoted to promoting erotic books and products.

An informal survey of twelve such papers available at The Free Press Bookstore in Westwood (near the Los Angeles campus of the University of California) shows a wide variation in content and treatment, from the highly esoteric printed psychedelia of *Oracle* (including articles such as "Unique

---

*In the Editorial Writing section of the 1967 "High School Journalism Day" at UCLA, about half of the participants stated that "underground," i.e., unsanctioned, paper had been published on their campuses. Many implied that the staffs of the official school paper had been involved in the clandestine enterprise because they were repudiating what they thought was overly strict supervision of the official paper by school authorities.

vocal abilities of certain Tibetan Lamas") to what are, in effect, "community" papers containing articles with news announcements and features of special interest to the hippie element and even to militant crusaders such as *Movement* and the *Barb*. Many of the papers do concentrate on exposing what the staff perceives to be discrimination against and persecution of minorities within the society generally, but more particularly, discrimination against "their own." Thus they are reminiscent of the turn-of-the-century "Muckrakers." The quality of writing varies, even within the same paper, and may range from well-written and researched articles of high journalistic merit to blatantly propagandistic and emotional essays and to what seems to be little more than "dirty word exercises."

As was previously stated, many of these papers operate on an exceedingly informal and financially precarious basis, which in part is a reflection of the attitudes of their audience. It is an ironic fact that if a paper reaches a point of financial stability, it is likely to be accused of having surrendered to the "Establishment" ethos of materialism. This charge has been raised by other papers against the *Los Angeles Free Press,* but its editor, Art Kunin, states that only by becoming economically sound can such papers be assured of continued ability to present their viewpoints, and that conformity to "Establishment" business practices need not be accompanied by acceptance of "Establishment" social practice and principles.[33]

Circulation figures for these publications are difficult to ascertain, because they do not participate in the usual inventories of periodicals, such as the *Ayer Directory*. A study of the four major underground papers in the Los Angeles area that reported claimed individual circulations as high as 68,000 and combined circulations of 166,000. The same study showed that the Underground Press Syndicate has 39 member papers in 23 cities in 12 states and the District of Columbia (plus five Canadian and English members).[34]

8. Movies

Of all the mass media, the movies felt perhaps most strongly the impact of television's competition. There were cities in the nation whose movie theaters did not close their doors in the years immediately following television's local debut. And while the number of feature films released in the United States has actually increased in the post-television years, the nature of these films has changed. For example, in 1945, 93 percent of all films released (377) were produced in this country. In the following years American production declined while foreign imports increased, and in 1958 American productions were in the minority for the first time. This trend continued until the early 1960's, with American film production falling to as low as 28 percent of the total. However, in recent years there has been an upturn, and by 1967 American films accounted for 39 percent of the 462 new features.[35]

The variation in the availability of movie features is pronounced as one moves from urban areas to smaller cities and towns. It is only in the largest cities that the public has access to all or most of the total output. Thus it is very difficult to establish any conception of the "average" motion picture content available for the American public. Although there is no systematic content analysis to support this contention, most observers feel that movies have become increasingly "adult" in recent years, and certainly American studios now put great emphasis on the "spectacle" pictures. These trends have been related to increased ticket prices. First-run picture tickets in the cities generally cost $2.50 to $3 and the price is still rising. These factors make it difficult to think of movies today as "family entertainment," although there are some productions obviously aimed at child and family group viewing. Some indication that movies are not primarily intended to be a family activity is shown by an inspection of the films offered in any major city. For example, the *Los Angeles Times* "Calendar" section of October 6, 1968 listed 48 major engagement films currently showing in the city. Of these, 13 were recommended for "adults only" (most containing explicit erotic scenes and/or exceptional violence), 27 for "mature audiences" (including teenagers), and only eight for "families." These eight included "Camelot," "Paper Lion," "The Secret War of Harry Frig," "The Two of Us," "2001—a Space Odyssey," "War and Peace" (Russian production), and the new wide-screen print of "Gone With the Wind."

Various minority interests are catered to by selected movie houses in most larger cities. Just as in literature, it is often difficult to determine where the line should be drawn between art and pornography. Most cities do have movie houses advertising "a warehouse of wild and wooly adult entertainment," "male film festival," "for unshockable adults." Such films can claim little in the way of redeeming artictic value. With regard to ethnic minorities, imported films have provided attractive fare for most ethnic groups. The one segment of the population that has not had film fare of its own is the largest minority group, the Negroes.

Weekly attendance at the movies averages 45 million.[36] The Michigan study on which Table B-1 was based reported that only 7 percent of the respondents had attended a movie during the previous week.[37] Post-television period studies on teenagers have reported that the median monthly movie attendance by teenagers in a large city was about 1.5 and just over twice monthly for teenagers in several smaller cities and towns.[38]

9. Radio

As with the movies, radio was seriously hurt by the advent of television and has survived only in a drastically revised form. Yet the number of radios in the country continues to increase, particularly the number of transistorized portables and car radios, for radio is truly the medium that goes wherever we go. It is no longer so much an entertainment medium as a companion or background to our activities. Several studies have documented that most radio listening today is a "secondary activity."[39] It emits a continuous stream of music and chatter to accompany other activities, whether it be doing homework or housework or fighting traffic on the freeway. In 1966, there were 262 million radios in the United States and of these 64 million were car radios.[40] The *1968 Broadcasting Yearbook* gives a national estimate of 147 minutes of radio listening per day by those who some time during the day use television. In fact, the report states that the percentage of adults who listened to the radio each day in comparison with those who watched television was 75 percent and 66 percent, respectively.[41]

While the most prevalent type of programming today is some variation of the music/chatter format, "all-talk" programming is appearing in some urban areas, and several cities now have "all-news" stations. One of the most interesting types of programs is the "open-line" format, in which is broadcast the telephone conversation between the program host and the listeners who call in. These programs provide an opportunity for persons of diverse outlook to express their opinions publicly.

The abundance of radio stations relative to television outlets, particularly with the expansion of Frequency Modulation (FM) broadcasting, coupled with comparatively low production and operating costs, has made it possible for many radio stations to establish a format for specific-interest groups rather than for the general mass audience. This has included specialization not only in music categories, but also for ethnic groups. Most larger cities have at least one station which seeks to appeal to the Negro public. There is also a scattering of stations operated by public agencies and private foundations which attempt to provide intellectual and cultural fare for an acknowledgedly small audience.

10. Phonograph Recordings

The phonograph has become an increasingly important mass medium in recent years. Today there are over 48 million phonographs in this country, and the number has increased 33 percent in the last 5 years.[42] The development of compact, transistorized disk-and tape-playing machines has increased the flexibility of the medium and, indeed, phonographs are beginning to pose a challenge to radio as a car-carried medium. Table B-1 shows that about a fourth of that sample of adults had listened to records the day before being interviewed.

Phonograph recordings might be thought of as the "books" of the electronic media, in terms both of flexibility offerred and of selection of content and time of use. The variety of titles, as with books, is immense. The *Schwann Catalogue*[43] recently stated that there were approximately 35,000 titles currently on the market. During a single year over 7,000 "singles" and 3,500 long-play titles may be released.[44] The biggest sales have always been in popular music, but in recent years the youth market has become increasingly important to the record industry. Reflecting this is the fact that the long-time champion of record sales, Bing Crosby, has now been supplanted by "The Beatles," whose records sold over 210 million copies in only 4 years.[45]

Songs have been used in many cultures not only to entertain, but to inform and propagandize as well. This is true in the United States today, as careful listening to the lyrics of many of the widely played records will reveal. However, there are other phonograph recordings that are much more explicitly designed for this purpose. The "Spoken and Miscellaneous" section of the *Schwann Catalog* contains not only a long list of humor records, of which many contain social commentary, but also a wide variety of recorded propaganda and information, from "Bipartisan Treason" and "The Case Against Flouridation" to the "Quotations of Mao Tse-Tung" and "Two Fists of Communism."

11. Television

Although it is the newest of the mass media, television holds undisputed mastery of the field. The amount of time spent watching television relative to that spent with other media and leisure activities will vary, but television is the medium that receives the largest share of the public's free time. According to the *1968 World Almanac,* 94 percent of American homes today have television and 25 percent have two or more sets. A 1967 Roper survey reported that the average time spent by adult Americans watching television each weekday was about 2 3/4 hours. [46] Of the 66 percent of adults who do watch some television on a given day, the *1968 Broadcasting Yearbook* estimates an average daily viewing time of just over 3 1/2 hours.[47] The *Nielsen National TV Rating* report for the second half of January 1968 estimated that the average daily operating hours per set varied from a low of 4.8 hours in midsummer to a high of 6.8 hours in January. In January, the estimated percentage of households watching television rose from 55 percent at 6 p.m. to a high of 68 percent in the 8-10 p.m. "prime-time" period, after which is gradually declined. But 22 percent of the households were estimated as still watching at midnight. About a fifth of the households had their sets on by 10 a.m. and by midday the figure rose to one-third.

A leading show, such as "Here's Lucy," may be viewed by over 40 million persons, and NBC's "Saturday Night Movie" may have an audience equal to two-thirds of the total paid attendance for all the nation's movie houses during the entire week. The President's "State of the Union" address in January 1968 was estimated to have had an audience of over 52 million viewers. Although the late afternoon hours on weekdays are generally thought of as the "children's hours" on television, the largest number of children are actually watching in the early evening hours. For example, 14 evening shows had a larger number of 2-to5-year-olds watching than did any daytime program in the same Nielsen report, and these evening programs ranged from "The Avengers" and "Batman" to "The Beverly Hillbillies" and "Disney's Wonderful World of Color." Furthermore, according to the Nielsen projections, children continue to be watching by the millions up to as late as 11 p.m. on weekdays. Over 5 million children under the age of 12 and almost 6.4 million 12-to-17-year-olds were still watching between 10:30 and 11 p.m. on one Monday in the period covered. Returning to the "children's hours," programming in this period frequently consists of little more than a parade of old movie cartoons interspersed with toy and cereal commercials.

The content of television varies from community to community, reflecting both the number of channels available and the programs selected by the local network affiliates for broadcasting. The major input, of course, comes from the three major networks, and this is particularly true in the prime evening hours. During the day, affiliated stations have more freedom to fill their schedule at their own discretion. However, a large portion of daytime programming by these stations and of all programming by nonaffiliated stations is filled with reruns of old network series and movies.

Table B-6 shows a breakdown of the 35 hours of evening programming (6-11 p.m.) provided each week by each of the three network-owned and-operated stations in Los Angeles during their normal schedule for the 1968 fall season (which includes the actual network schedule plus locally supplied materials in several periods, primarily between 6 and 7 p.m., when no network service may be provided).

It is interesting to note the prominent place given to movies even during prime-time network programming. Actually, in terms of total program

Table B-6.—Breakdown of fall season programming between 6-11 p.m.
on network-owned stations in Los Angeles for a typical week

[In hours and minutes]

Category	ABC	CBS	NBC
News	0:00*	9:00	8:30
Information	0:00	2:00	0:30
Adventure	2:00	1:00	1:00
Mystery/detective	7:30	2:00	3:30
Western	2:30	3:00	4:30
Situation comedy	4:00	6:00	2:30
Serial drama	1:00	0:00	0:00
Family variety/family adventure	0:00	2:00	2:30
Variety	4:30	6:00	5:00
Movies	12:30	12:30	4:0
Quiz/games	1:00	0:00	0:30
Unspecified film	0:00	0:00	0:30

*The ABC station schedules its early evening news hour at 5 p.m. and its late evening news at 11 p.m.

schedules of all stations, most communities are provided with a larger number of movies each week on television than in their local movie theaters. To cite an extreme example, in a single week the seven VHF stations in Los Angeles showed five musical, 15 science fiction, 18 western, 18 comedy, 29 detective, and 73 dramatic films, for a total of 158 different full-length feature films. In former years the films shown on television tended to be older features, but today this has been somewhat modified. Of this 158, 33 were made in the 1960's and nine were less than 3 years old. Among the films were not only all-time classics (as well as potboilers), but art films of critical acclaim. The importance of films is shown by ratings cited earlier, which reported that feature films had the largest average audience of all program categories. Both type of film and audience are broken down in Table B-7.

There are numerous "specials" on each network during each season. For the fall of 1968, ABC scheduled 17, CBS 20, and NBC 34. These included a wide variety of content, from sports and musicals to public affairs, documentaries, and children's features.

The relative scarcity of avilable television channels and the medium's high operating costs generally have made it the most "mass" of all the media. The gradual expansion into UHF still has not provided much specialization although there are a few Spanish-language stations operating. An all-Negro station was attempted in Los Angeles in the early 1960's, but due to a number of factors (a UHF allocation and an attempt to have all-black programming for which there were no sources except local production, were important handicaps) it survived only about half a year. (It would be interesting to know whether or not, with a wider distribution of UHF-receiving sets and the new spirit of black pride now evident, such a station could survive today.) However, in recent months the networks and some local stations have presented programming that focuses on Negro problems and features Negro entertainment.

Table B-7.—Average audience estimates according to
Nielsen's second report for January 1968

	Average percent of TV Households
Evening:	
General drama:	
30 minutes length	19.7
60 minutes length	16.3
Suspense/mystery:	
30 minutes length	18.1
60 minutes length	17.0
Situation comedy	19.6
Western	18.1
Adventure	18.0
Science fiction	17.0
Variety	20.4
Feature films	21.2
Dinner-hour news	12.5
Daytime:	
Serials	9.9
Situation comedy	8.6
Quiz	8.0
News	6.7
Weekend:	
Children	7.3
Sports	7.1

12. Educational Television

One type of "minority" station that has appeared in many communities is the noncommercial "educational" station. There are now over 140 such stations in operation, the majority being affiliated with the National Educational Television (NET) organization, which facilitates the exchange of programs between stations and the supply of a few special productions. The programming of these stations is varied, with heavy emphasis placed on public affairs discussions, programs of practical information and a few of formal instructional content, and the arts. During the day on weekdays, many transmit instructional programs for the local school systems.

These stations supply a highly contrasting alternate choice to the viewing public. However, many of their programs deal with highly specific subject matter and appeal primarily to a limited audience of those interested in that particular subject. It is therefore not surprising that the audience of these stations at any given hour is generally too small to be reflected in the major audience measurement services, but there are a few programs which have won sizeable audiences both locally and nationally through NET distribution. Over the course of a week most of these stations that operate on a VHF frequency will attract the attention of 10 to 25 percent of the households in their area at least once.[48]

C. Different Patterns of Media Selection and Use

The discussion of educational television with its limited, specialized audience serves to bring into focus the fact that the mass media do not have a single mass audience. Individuals do differ both in their choice of media and in their selection of content within each medium. Some of these differences reflect differences in the practical needs of the individual. Thus the person who owns stocks is more likely to read the financial section of the newspaper than one who does not. Other differences reflect differences in the means available to individuals. Thus low-income families may have to rely upon the "free" entertainment of television rather than upon entertainment, such as the movies, that carries an admission price. Still other differences reflect social and psychological factors that vary not only from individual to individual, but the balance of which may vary within the same individual from time to time. Thus as children mature they begin to seek information and content that conform to their sex role expectations. Or the person who is troubled or physically fatigued may seek "escape" content from the media, whereas under normal conditions he might reject the same content as puerile and seek instead more informational, edifying content.

The overall situation is further complicated by the fact that the same content may have different value for the various individuals who do give it their attention. For example, a psychiatrist working with institutionalized disturbed children might say that these children were upset, not by television shows that were heavy in violence, but by those situation-comedy shows that portrayed happy families. Thus Dr. Benjamin Spock is quoted as deploring the sadism in Disney's feature film, "Snow White," and another writer reported hysterical reactions to Pinocchio being swallowed by the whale in the Disney feature film of the same name.[49]

Although the situation is complex, there are some patterns that have been traced out in empirical research and that provide some insights into the relationship between the media and the public. The following paragraphs are only a brief survey of some of these relationships.

1. Demographic and Ecological Factors

Choice of media and of content within media has been found to differ in systematic relationship to a variety of demographic and ecological factors. For example, one study of media behavior in children reported relationships between sex, religious affiliation, and social class, and whether or not the child was primarily oriented to "pictorial media" (boys, Catholics, and blue-collar workers' children were more apt to be so oriented than their opposites).[50] One of the earliest qualitative audience analysis studies documented the importance of age, sex, and socioeconomic status on the choice of newspaper content. (The reading of "hard" news comes in the late teens, whereas comics reading peaks early, remains at a plateau, and gradually declines with age; blue collar readers tend to read sensational and entertainment content at the expense of "hard" news; the reading of society and sports news is sex-related, as one would expect, etc.)[51]

One of the best indications of a person's orientation to media use is his socioeconomic status, usually measured by type of occupation, income, and education (singly or in combination). The Michigan study of audience behavior included comparison of poor whites and poor blacks with the general population. The results are summarized in Table B-8. Similar patterns have been reported by other studies. Generally speaking, those in the lower socioeconomic categories are more likely to be heavy users of pictorial media, particularly television, while those in the upper socioeconomic categories use a wider range of media. Poor blacks are even more extreme in this respect than poor whites. This television-orientation is further reflected in the preference of television over the newspaper for news by these latter groups. Accordingly, it is not surprising that both the "CBS Evening News" with Walter Cronkite and NBC's "Huntley-Brinkley Report" draw a larger proportion of blue-collar than white-collar viewers.[52]

Because of a combination of pressures, those who have had relatively more education and are in white-collar or professional occupations need and desire more information from the media than is the case among the lower income, blue-collar groups. The differences in media use between the groups partly reflect differing levels of competition for the individual's time. Unemployed people, for example, have more free time than those with jobs, but they also obviously have fewer means to avail themselves of a wide range of activities.

The professional has the financial resources to exercise a wide range of options. He also is under pressures that require him to participate in a wide variety of activities, not only civic and social, but professional as well "to keep up with his field." Within the limits of present technology, this type of professional information is still most efficiently provided by the printed media, so that the professional man must maintain a high level of literacy. A result of this is that the act of reading is less demanding for him than for the blue-collar worker, so that it probably has for him an intrinsic pleasure value in itself. One study has documented that the orientation toward all the media increases with education, but also that the demands connected with education preempt time that otherwise might be spent with the media. Use of other media further preempts the time that the educated man might like to spend watching television.[53]

Turning again to the question of choice of news sources, the pattern shown in Table B-8 has been reported in many studies together with the further finding that the level of trust placed in the different media also differs. For example, studies in Los Angeles showed that the poor, and particularly the Negro poor, were much more suspicious of the newspaper (including Negro papers) than they were of television, whereas white-collar workers were moderate in their trust of television.[54] A variety of other factors have also been found to be related to different patterns of media usage, some of which seem to be a reflection of changing patterns in American living. For example, interest in community news in comparison with interest in metropolitan area, national, and international news has been found to be lower among more mobile families (and in some metropolitan areas 20 percent or more—in Los Angeles 25 percent of the families change residence within a calendar year), among apartment dwellers, and among those who commute to other areas for work or shopping. These factors also appear to be related to the selection of media in a number of complex ways, even to predicating the choice of competing daily newspapers.[55]

Studies have also documented differences in interest in and selection of

Table B-8.—Differences in media use patterns
according to income and race*
[In percent]

	General Population	Poor Whites (150)	Poor Blacks (131)
TV time "yesterday":			
None	40.8	22.7	25.2
Under 4 hours	41.7	25.3	19.8
4 hours or more	17.1	52.0	55.0
Radio time "yesterday":			
None	29.1	40.0	36.7
Under 2 hours	39.2	32.7	25.9
2 hours or more	31.6	26.0	35.9
Read newspaper daily	77.2	69.4	58.8
Read a magazine "yesterday"	52.9	38.3	38.2
Attended movie within past month	29.6	12.0	16.0
Do not own phonograph	13.6	29.3	16.0
Phonograph listening "yesterday":			
None	62.6	24.7	13.0
Under 1 hour	9.2	33.3	48.1
1 hour or more	14.0	12.7	22.9
Medium preferred for world news:			
Television	34.9	65.3	65.6
Radio	25.7	12.0	19.8
Newspaper	31.5	18.0	10.7
People	4.4	4.7	3.1
Medium preferred for local news:			
Television	20.4	32.7	26.7
Radio	31.0	34.0	32.1
Newspaper	40.3	25.3	18.3
People	„6.8	6.7	21.4

*From Bradley S. Greenberg and Brenda Dervin, *Communication Among the Poor* (East Lansing: Michigan State University Press, 1967-1968).

media content, particularly news. Crime news has been found to be of greater interest not only to the poor in comparison with the middle class, but also to city dwellers in comparison to suburbanites.[56] The fact that the *Nielsen Television Index Market Section Audiences Report* provides a breakdown of individual program audiences by such factors as size of family, size of community, and section of the nation, as well as a variety of socioeconomic indicators, reflects that the composition of the audience does vary from program to program.

2. Sociopsychological Factors

There is some evidence that lower income groups are more concerned with seeking immediate solutions and pleasures, whereas higher income groups are frequently willing to undergo intermediate discomfurture and to expend effort if by so doing they see the possibility of a greater ultimate reward.[57] This is felt to constitute a difference in the mores of socioeconomic groups that extends into many types of behavior, including media use.

Data to support this generalization has been reported in a number of studies. For example, white-collar-working parents have been found to have "guilt feelings" about watching television and permitting their children to do the same.[58] Some authors have hypothesized that certain media—the pictorial media and television in particular—have a greater potential for providing "immediate" gratification, while other media such as books and magazines are more efficient for providing the type of detailed information frequently required for "deferred" gratification. Such studies as those of Schramm *et al.*[59] have graphically demonstrated the importance of parental example and guidance in influencing the child's acquisition of values and their application to media behavior. Another study presented evidence suggesting that blue-collar workers who do not conform to their class mores concerning media viewing (i.e., they are high users of print and low users of television) exhibit other behavior and attitudes suggesting that they are striving for upward mobility.[60] Intelligence is another factor that has been found to be strongly related to media orientation, with the more intelligent persons more frequently selecting media and content that offer deferred gratification than is the case with those of average and lower intelligence. [61] These factors are frequently interrelated, but each has been found to operate independently as well as in combination with others in influencing media usage.

There are also other factors that may intervene. The media are at times used to enhance the image we wish to project to others. It will be recalled that Berelson's study showed that many of the respondents indicated that social prestige was a factor in their reading of the newspaper. Emotional factors have also been shown to be an important variable. Again, Berelson's study showed that some newspaper reading was predicated on combating "anomie" or loneliness. Another early study reported that radio soap operas often served a similar purpose in combating isolation for housewives.[62] Children's use of comics was found to vary similarly, with lonely children using them for fantasy while other children put the story content to creative uses, such as providing ideas for play activity.[63]

Still another factor which has been found to be important in influencing the amount of use of media for fantasy is the degree of personal stress or tension felt by a person at a given time. One adult study reports that "escape" television viewing increased among adults when they were under high stress.[64] Surveys of child and teen media use have found that children who reported conflict with their parents and/or peer groups showed increased media use for fantasy. Such media use was also found to accompany high scores on antisocial aggression scales.[65]

It should be pointed out that, in these studies, use of the media as a means of escape from social isolation and/or personal tension is higher among white-collar working families. This is inevitable because the normative use of immediate-reward media is so high among blue-collar workers that it leaves little room for them to use increases of such behavior to relieve personal stress. The general fact remains, however, that people are likely to take their problems to the media, and in extreme cases it appears that the gratification found therein may lead to a circular situation resulting in "addiction" to this "mechanical friend." The question of the extent to which this may also lead them to active antisocial behavior, e.g., violence, is a question that will be treated in later sections of this Task Force's report.

D. Some Problems Related to the Mass Media's Nature

One frequently hears complaints from a wide variety of sources about today's "mass society." Population growth and increasing population density create a multitude of tensions within our society, and being institutions within that society it is inescapable that the media are intertwined with these tensions and complaints. Given the existing economic and technological conditions, the general media must seek large audiences to survive. At the same time, technology has extended the immediate accessibility of content to everyone. This accessibility has its dysfunctional aspects. Much of the great artistic heritage of our culture contains elements of violence and sex. Recognizing this, society has generally sought to provide some safeguards regarding the use of such content. Thus, for example, various types of literature are introduced to children at what is considered an appropriate period in their maturation. It is significant that many collections of Bible stories for children omit a considerable number of details contained in the original.

As the media grow both in the bulk of their content and the ease with which people may generally gain access to that content, such controls are increasingly difficult to maintain. Furthermore, these same characteristics of universal accessibility mean that the persons responsible for the media do not have the means to guarantee that their content reaches those for whom it was intended and that it does not become accessible to those for whom it might be harmful. This creates great strains within all the media. Some critics, for example, complain that television is generally puerile and that more adult cultural fare should be presented. Yet if the programmers attempted to provide more adult fare, they would then hear complaints from others that they were perverting youth. One can argue that the media can never be made totally "safe," simply because content which is harmless or actively beneficial for the vast majority of the population may trigger violently harmful reactions in some few members of the audience.

In conclusion, let us return to a consideration of the media's role as institutions of communication within society and the impact of the increasing mass use of the media on the functions they are supposed to perform.

The massiveness of the audience is a particular problem for news media, for as the size and diversity of a given medium's audience increase, so do the difficulties of communicating effectively to all segments of the audience. This, then, makes it increasingly difficult to maintain a high level of satisfaction and trust among the members of a society that places a high value upon individual rights and identity. The media today can transmit more information to more people more quickly than ever before. In doing this they can help to reduce anxiety within the public. However, there is also the less happy possibility that they can be used, inadvertently or intentionally, to increase anxiety. As institutions, the media consist of professional staffs made up of fallible human beings who are using a potent technology under an implicit mandate of the society. Just how potent that technology is has still not been determined, but as the technology is developed and improved its ability to effect good and evil becomes stronger, more immediate, and far-reaching. But in the final analysis, technology is only the tool; it is the members of society who must determine the manner of its use.

REFERENCES

1. Harold D. Lasswell, *The Structure and Functions of Communication in Society,* Institute for Religion and Social Studies of New York City (1948).
2. Gordon W. Allport and Leo J. Postman, "The Basic Psychology of Rumor," in Wilbur Schramm, *Process and Effects of Mass Communication* (Urbana: University of Illinois Press, 1955).
3. Richard F. Carter and Bradley S. Greenberg, "Newspaper or Television: Which Do You Believe?," *Journalism Quarterly,* 42, 29 (1965).
4. See, for example, pp. 39-42 in Jack Lyle, *The News in Megalopolis* (San Francisco: Chandler, 1967).
5. *Ibid.* p. 171.
6. *Ibid.* p. 44-45.
7. See James E. Brinton et al., *The Newspaper and Its Public* (Stanford: Institute for Communication Research (undated)).
8. See Muzafer Sherif and Carol I. Hovland, *Social Judgement* (New Haven: Yale University Press, 1961).
9. See, for example, pp. 29-30 in Jack Lyle, *The Black American and the Press* (Los Angeles: Ward Ritchie Press, 1968).
10. Harold Mendelsohn, "Socio-Psychological Perspectives on the Mass Media and Public Anxiety," *Journalism Quarterly,* 40, 511 (1963).
11. Jack Lyle and Walter Wilcox (editors), *A Community Daily in a Changing Metropolitan Press Environment* (Los Angeles: UCLA Department of Journalism). (See p. 27.)
12. Charles H. Cooley, *Social Organization* (Glencoe: Free Press, 1956).
13. See, for example, Joseph T. Klapper, *The Effects of Mass Communication* (Glencoe: Free Press, 1960).
14. Several studies illustrating this phenomenon are contained in *The Great Debates* edited by Sidney Kraus (Bloomington: University of Indiana Press, 1962).
15. Bradley S. Greenberg and Brenda Dervin, *Communication Among the Poor* (in three volumes) (East Lansing: Michigan State University Press, 1967-68).
16. These figures and those in Table 2 are from *The Bowker Annual of Library and Book Trade Information 1968* (New York: R. R. Bowker, 1968).
17. *World Almanac 1968* (New York: Newspaper Enterprise Association, 1967).
18. Figures in this paragraph are from Charles A. Madison, *Book Publishing in America* (New York: McGraw-Hill, 1966). See pp. 547-56.
19. *World Almanac 1968, op. cit.,* footnote 17.
20. Philip Converse, "Information Flow and Stability of Partisan Attitudes," *Public Opinion Quarterly,* 26, 592 (1962).
21. *News Research Bulletin* (of the American Newspaper Publishers Association), No. 2, dated Feb. 7, 1968.
22. See, for example, Frances L. Spain and Margaret C. Scoggins, "They Still Read Books," *in The Eighth Art* (New York: Holt, Rinehart and Winston, 1962).
23. *1968 Ayer Directory* (Philadelphia: N.W. Ayer and Son, 1968).
24. *World Almanac 1968, op. cit.,* footnote 17.
25. Wilbur Schramm, Jack Lyle, and Edwin B. Parker, *Television in the Lives of Our Children* (Stanford: Stanford University Press, 1961). See p. 101.
26. *Ibid.* p. 261.
27. Bernard Berelson, "What 'Missing the Newspaper' Means," *in* Paul F. Lazarsfeld and Frank Stanton, *Communication Research 1948-1949* (New York: Harper, 1949).
28. William A. Hacten, "The Changing U. S. Sunday Newspaper," *Journalism Quarterly,* 38, 281 (1961).
29. Schramm, Lyle, and Parker, *op. cit.,* footnote 25, pp. 247-248.

30. *1968 Editor and Publisher Yearbook* (New York: The Editor and Publisher Co., Inc., 1968). See pp. 316-317.
31. See, for example, Franlin Frazier, *Black Bourgeoisie* (Glencoe: Free Press, 1957).
32. See, for example, "Negro Press: Victim of Negro Progress," on p. 50 of the Aug. 26, 1963, issue of *Newsweek*.
33. Quoted in Gaye S. Smith, "The Underground Press in Los Angeles," unpublished report for the Department of Journalism, UCLA (1968).
34. *Ibid.*
35. *The Film Daily Yearbook of Motion Pictures* (New York: The Film Daily, 1968).
36. *Popular Photography*, June 1967.
37. Greenberg and Dervin, *op. cit.*, footnote 15.
38. Schramm, Lyle, and Parker, *op. cit.*, footnote 25 pp. 252- 253
39. For example, see converse, *op. cit.*, footnote 20 and Schramm, Lyle, and Parker, *op. cit.*, footnote 25, pp. 243, 251.
40. *World Almanac, op. cit.*, footnote 17.
41. *1968 Broadcasting Yearbook* (New York: Broadcasting Publications, Inc., 1968). See pp. 22-24.
42. *World Almanac, op. cit.*, footnote 17.
43. "Preface," *Schwann Catalog* Dec. 1968, p. 4.
44. *Billboard International Buyer's Guide*, Aug. 6, 1966.
45. *World Almanac, op. cit.*, footnote 17.
46. Burns W. Roper, *Emerging Profiles of Television and Other Mass Media: Public Attitudes 1959-1967* (New York: Television Information Office, 1967).
47. Broadcasting Yearbook, *op. cit.*, footnote 41.
48. Wilbur Schramm, Jack Lyle, and Ithiel de Sola Pool, *The People Look at Educational Television* (Stanford: Stanford University Press, 1963). See p. 50.
49. Carey McWilliams, *The California Revolution* (New York: The Grossman Publisher, Inc., 1968). See p. 137.
50. Lotte Bailyn, "Mass Media and Children: A Study of Exposure Habits and Cognitive Effects," *Psychological Monographs*, 73, 1 (1959).
51. Wilbur Schramm and David M. White, "Age, Education, Economic Status: Factors in Newspaper Reading," *Journalism Quarterly*, 26, 149 (1959).
52. See, for example, the March *1968 Nielsen Television Index Report.*
53. Merrill Samuelson, Richard F. Cater, and Lee Ruggels, "Education, Available Time, and Use of Mass Media," *Journalism Quarterly*, 40, 491 (1963).
54. See Chapters 8 and 9 in *The News in Megalopis, op. cit.*, footnote 4.
55. *Ibid.*, Chapter 8.
56. Roy E. Carter Jr. and Peter Clarke, "Suburbanites, City Residents, and Local News," *Journalism Quarterly*, 40, 548 (1963).
57. See, for example, Ken Geiger and Robert Sokol, "Social Norms in Television Watching," *American Sociol.*, 65, 174 (1959). Also see Chapter 6 in Schramm, Lyle, and Parker, *op. cit.*, footnote 25.
58. Gary Steiner, *The People Look at Television* (New York: Knopf, 1963).
59. Schramm, Lyle, and Parker, *op. cit.*, footnote 25, pp. 47-48.
60. Jack Lyle, "Educational Television and Social Mobility," unpublished paper read to Association for Education in Journalism convention,. 1962.
61. Schramm, Lyle, and Parker, *op. cit.*, footnote 25, p. 105.
62. Herta Herzog, "Motivations and Gratifications of Daily Serial Listeners," in Paul Lazarsfeld and Frank Stanton, *Radio Research, 1942-1943* (New York: Duell, Sloan and Pearce, 1944).
63. Katherine M. Wolfe and Marjorie Fiske, "Why They Read Comics," in Lazarsfeld and Stanton, *Communication Research, 1948-1949, op. cit.*
64. L. I. Pearlin, "Social and Personal Stress and Escape Television Viewing," *Public Opinion Quarterly*, 23, 255 (1959).
65. See Chapter 7 of Schramm, Lyle, and Parker, *op. cit.*, footnote 5.

Appendix II-C

MEDIA CODES, GUIDELINES, AND POLICIES FOR NEWS COVERAGE

A. *Need for Guidelines*

The need for guidelines is recognized especially by the television medium, which advertises its presence at the scene of violence with cameras, lights, and, sometimes, special mobile trucks, in order to make a vivid, instantaneous transmission of the event. This presence can serve as a catalyst for those involved in the violence to create "incidents" specifically for the camera, and the ability to transmit instantaneously makes balanced coverage inherently more difficult.

Concerning these problems, Dr. Frank Stanton, president of CBS, has said:

> Like no other medium in history, television catches the flavor, the immediacy, the excitement, the tension and the confusion, too, of the moment. This is the great strength of television, but also, in a way, its weakness.
> The problems related to the news media's coverage of insurrections ... while they can never be wholly eradicated ... can be minimized by the use of responsible and intelligent guidelines. Setting up such guidelines ... seems to us to be our responsibility and obligation as journalists and editors and we cannot delegate this to anyone else.

The National Advisory Commission on Civil Disorders, in March 1968, urged news organizations to discuss among themselves the special problems of covering riots and to "formulate and disseminate directives based on the discussions." The Community Relations Service (CRS) of the Department of Justice has also encouraged the news media to discuss with city and police officials the promulgation of community-wide guidelines for covering racial disturbances; but it does not recommend or endorse any specific set of guidelines. Rather, it believes, as did the Kerner Commission, that discussions on this subject *within* the news organizations are as important as the establishment of formal guidelines.

Many news editors and their staffs seem willing to rethink and redefine their procedures for reporting disorders; but they always jealously safeguard their rights, citing the freedom of the press, the right of the public to know and make its own decisions, and the responsibility of the "fourth estate" to report fully, fairly, and responsibly without prior restraint by any public authority. To paraphrase one newspaper editor: any code established by the media itself is a policy; any code imposed from the outside is censorship.

The news media have growing misgivings about outside restrictions on news coverage of controversial public events—and not without reason. Only last year, the Ohio House of Representatives considered denying newsmen access to scenes of riots and other emergencies. Congressional committees have announced hearings on news practices. And some city officials have, without consulting the media, issued riot coverage policies.

These pressures, coupled with the media's own sense of responsibility, have resulted in the adoption of self-determined guidelines. While the daily press, with the belated exception of the wire services, has been reluctant to formulate specific formal guidelines for riot coverage, the case is considerably different in the broadcasting media. All three of the major television networks, ABC, CBS, and NBC, and their 15 owned-and-operated stations, 11 of 14 commercial television stations, and 13 of the 17 commercial radio stations, responding to the Violence Commission's five-city survey, have adopted some form of policy or guideline for the coverage of violence.

But many of the news editors, both broadcast and print, strongly emphasized that their policies, with respect to coverage of inflammatory or violent events, are simply formalizations of good reporting practices, have evolved over long periods of time, and undergo constant review and revision when necessary. In cases where the stations, wire services, or newspapers reported the date they initiated their formal written policies on coverage of violence, it occurred most frequently during the past 3 years—in *all* cases, including the networks, it actually occurred during the past 5 years.

1. Characteristics of Guidelines

Much similarity exists among the "guidelines" of all media:

Language.—Caution extreme care in the use of language (e.g., avoid inflammatory descriptions), catchwords (such as "police brutality" and "angry mob"), and stereotyped phrases; use moderate language; avoid words such as "riot" and "racial" (often until officially designated); caution in characterization of crowd, disturbance, etc.; care not to exaggerate in headlines.

Equipment and lights.—Designation or warnings against use of certain equipment and lights, e.g., use unmarked cars; use certain microphones, cameras, and lights.

Conduct and safety of personnel.—Provision of police escorts, special equipment, special credentials; be a "moderating" influence.

Procedures and assignments.—Most experienced newsmen to field and command posts, special liaison with police.

Reporting practices.—Emphasis on traditional good reporting practices, e.g., confirmation, good sources; balance and fairness in story, avoidance of reports that might inflame or incite to violence; report causes, as well as effects; accuracy, restraint, strict attribution.

Many of the guidelines simply extend normal news procedures, but several pertain only to the unusual circumstances surrounding riots and other violent disorders:

Provisions for helmets, police escorts, etc.; cautions against use of certain terms and characterizations, e.g., "riot," "racial"; procedures for use of only certain equipment and lights; embargoes on live reports and use of "bulletins"; policy of delay; avoidance of giving exact location and descriptions of weapons.

2. Effectiveness of Guidelines

Just how effective have these policies, or guidelines, been? From the responses, the media have found them, without qualification, to be useful and workable. These are some representative comments:

". . . useful so far as it describes a management philosophy to which one entire news staff can and does subscribe."

—WWDC-FM, Washington, D.C.

". . . such guidelines keep various personnel . . . alert to consequences, alert to overemphasis, and cause of unrest and violence."

— Evening Tribune, San Diego, Calif.

". . . guides to good judgment . . . particularly at times when quick decisions must be made."

—WRC-TV, Washington, D.C.

Above all, the formulation and establishment of guidelines appears to have increased the sensitivity of news personnel to the problems of covering violence.

3. Operation of Guidelines

In all types of journalism, many people take part in shaping stories, and they all hold some decision-making power. Reporters, camera and sound men, researchers, rewrite men, writers, film editors, desk editors, regional and state editors, station managers and executive editors—all assume responsibility, in part, for the way a story is reported. This shared responsibility argues most strongly for the formulation of a common policy.

Although the news editor on duty usually bears direct responsibility for administering a policy, every person on the staff must know and abide by its meaning, in both letter and spirit, to make it effective. Several responding stations noted closer management supervision in times of disorder. Sanctions that enforce station policy include criticism, suspension, or discharge.

B. *Specific Media Guidelines*

1. The Networks

All three of the major commercial networks—ABC, CBS, and NBC—subscribe to the NAB Code and have *general* broadcast news policies and standards to guide their news operation and personnel.

ABC has five "considerations" for news scripts:

(1) Good taste;

(2) Avoidance of obscene, indecent, and profane language;

(3) Avoidance of defamation;

(4) Compliance with government regulations during times of emergency; and

(5) Competent news authority.

In addition, "the news shall not be broadcast in a manner that might create alarm or panic."

The November 1963 "Policies and Procedures" statement of NBC sets out broad but specific standards for the conduct of news personnel and the treatment of program subjects. Pertinent to the issue of violence is clause 5:

> In the factual presentation and in the analysis of news, sensational treatment will be avoided. News may never be presented in a manner which would create public alarm or panic. News items relating to crime or sex in particular must be handled without morbid or sensational detail and must be treated with the judgment required in presentation to a family audience.

For many years, CBS and NBC have reflected in their public statements, in their internal memoranda, and in directives to their news personnel at the network and at owned-and-operated stations, a strong sense of responsibility in their broadcast news operation. All three networks have adopted, and now have in effect, policy guides specifically for coverage of riots. The genesis of these policy guidelines at CBS and NBC go back to 1963 in both cases, and they have been augmented periodically in the intervening years. ABC's guidelines were formalized at least as early as July 1967.

Public events and demands have precipitated a revaluation of policies at the three networks, which has often resulted in a redefinition of news policies and practices. It should be noted, however, that CBS and NBC have often anticipated the special conditions and challenges of the events of these last few turbulent years and have reiterated or modified their policies accordingly. At CBS, Richard Salant, president of CBS News, sent a memorandum to news personnel in June 1963, in anticipation of the disturbances in Selma, Alabama. He warned of "the unsettling effect on a stimulated crowd that the presence of TV cameras has," and requested that personnel and equipment be as unobtrusive as possible and that cameras be turned away or capped whenever there was a danger that they might exacerbate an event. In handling "racial crises and other confrontations throughout the country," Salant urged news personnel to conduct themselves with restraint and care.

In August 1963, after Selma and after he had appeared before the House Subcommittee on Communications and Power, NBC President Robert Kintner "reiterated" in a memorandum to all news personnel four points for the handling of controversial issues and events, using as an example a demonstration in connection with segregation: accuracy, judgment in selection of air material, avoidance in taking sides by manner or tone or presentation, and balancing.

Both CBS and NBC elaborated upon these basic statements over the years, and by mid-1967 both networks had formally codified a set of guidelines for coverage of riots and civil disturbances. In May 1967, after Watts—but before the widespread summer riots of that year—NBC had set 13 guidelines for handling civil disturbances, which were "not designed to curtail coverage, but to insure its responsibility." NBC reiterated points which it said "are journalistic basics we all know but may forget in the heat of covering a big story." During the summer of 1967, CBS defined seven specific "precautions" for its news personnel. (The first CBS document referring to their existence was Dr. Frank Stanton's letter of Aug. 10, 1967, to Senator Hugh Scott.)

Early in June 1968, NBC restated its policy with some updating, and on August 20, 1968, a few days before the Democratic National Convention, CBS News President Richard Salant amplified on the policy guidelines of CBS—cameras are to be capped if they are aggravating the situation, the exact location of the disturbance is not to be revealed, reportage should concern itself with the underlying issues of the disorder—and warned about the especially troublesome circumstances awaiting the news media in Chicago. After Chicago, CBS adopted two new policies for the coverage of riots and civil disorders: extreme care in the use of lights, and a general prohibition of live television (not radio) coverage.

The following is a checklist that highlights the points of overlap and difference in the written policy guidelines of ABC, CBS, and NBC in reporting disorders:

	CBS	ABC	NBC
Use unmarked or camouflaged cars and equipment	X		X
Avoid using lights	X		
Obey all police instructions	X		
Caution in characterizing and estimating size, intensity, and mood of crowd or disturbance	X	X	X
Confirm all rumor and eye-witness, wire service, reports, strict attribution	X		X
Balance all statements by rioters, responsible officials	X	X	
Avoid catchwords and stereotyped phrases (such as police brutality, angry mob), play news straight, without emotion	X	X	X
Cap cameras if contributing to situation	X		
Avoid giving exact location, specifics about weaponry, etc.	X		X
Report underlying issues and causes	X	X	X
Do not reenact, simulate, stage, or aid demonstration		X	X
No live TV coverage	X	X	
Advise affiliates when network coverage may conflict with local voluntary restrictive agreements			X

	CBS	ABC	NBC
Do not describe disturbance as "riot" or "racial" until officially designated		X	X
Specific editing cautions			X
Swift dispatch of reporters to scene of disturbance			X
Avoid interviews with participants, self-appointed leaders			

The written guidelines of the networks differ in two important respects:

ABC and CBS have prohibited live coverage of civil disturbances—a policy that implies delay, and

CBS recommends obeying all police instructions, whereas the policy set by NBC to advise the affiliate when network coverage may conflict with local voluntary agreement implies a situation wherein NBC coverage may be in opposition to police wishes. ABC has no policy that applies.

2. Television Stations

Eighteen of the 22 television stations in the five cities surveyed completed and returned the Violence Commission's questionnaire. Of these 18 stations, four were public television stations. Eleven of the 14 commercial television stations completing the questionnaire said they had adopted specific written or unwritten guidelines for the reporting of "inflammatory or violent news events." None of the public television stations had adopted specific guidelines, but, with the exception of WETA-TV, Channel 26 in Washington, D.C., which broadcasts on-the-hour wire-service reports, the public television stations also did not carry any "hard news" programs.

Although the television station guidelines tended to be similar, the codes ranged over a wide spectrum in detail and specifics. Several stations—WMAL-TV, an ABC owned-and-operated station in Washington, D.C., and KOGO-TV, an NBC-affiliate Time-Life station in San Diego, Calif.—had set very detailed, stringent plans and guidelines for their staffs, as well as general directives, and also alternative emergency plans and procedures. The policies of WSAV-TV, an NBC/ABC affiliate in Savannah, Ga., as enunciated by the president in a memorandum to the news department, related only to pretaping and delaying inflammatory film and the prerelease of information about demonstrations. Other notable specifics in codes were the following:

Only a few of the 11 stations had any specific policy for delaying the news.
Only one or two stations recommended against live coverage.

Several stations were concerned with the use of "bulletins."

Here are some representative examples given by reporting television stations of stories affected by their standards or codes:

Editing of, or decision not to carry, film accounts of inflammatory remarks by Stokely Carmichael, Eldridge Cleaver, and angry whites.

Deliberate downplaying of riots in Washington, D.C.

Decision to report the event fully, but without a film of the rioting.

Long, general shots of disturbances rather than closeups of angry rioters, flaming building, etc.

Delay in broadcasting of the melee.

Delay in broadcasting the occasion of integrating a theater until after the fact.

Edited film of hippie dispersal by police to show the causes for the action.

The most frequent complaints reported by stations came from viewers who accused the station or its network of showing a pro-Negro bias in its news coverage. Two stations, WKRC-TV and WLWT-TV, both in Cincinnati, reported their listeners complained that their policy of delay might be harmful and ill served the public interest. The stations surveyed also seemed to have received their share of protest mail about network coverage of the 1968 Democratic National Convention.

3. Radio

Because the radio stations in the five communities surveyed were selected arbitrarily (every other one was listed in *Broadcasting Yearbook,* including FM stations) and because only 17 of the 35 stations solicited, or 50 percent of them, returned a completed questionnaire, this sampling of responses cannot be considered as representative either of the radio service in these communities or of radio guidelines in general.

However, a few observations on the returns are important and interesting. Of the 17 responding commercial radio stations—including seven FM stations—13 have adopted some form of guidelines. In two communities, Washington, D.C., and San Diego, all four commercial radio stations that responded to the questionnaire from each community have adopted some form of policy for reporting of inflammatory events and civil disturbances.

The two most frequently mentioned guidelines adopted by radio were: an avoidance of live broadcasts from scenes of turmoil; and an intentional delay in broadcasting reports, with holdbacks ranging from a half-hour (WKRC, Cincinnati) to as much as 12 hours duration (KEYN, Wichita, Kan.).

Two apparently Negro-oriented stations answering to the questionnaire—WOL, Washington, D.C., and KEYN, Wichita—have evaluated their role with special care. Each had provisions for delay in broadcasting reports of incipient violence in order to refrain from drawing a crowd. Each responded in unique ways during times of racial turmoil in their communities: WOL, in the April 1968 riots in Washington, broadcast gospel music in the hope of quieting the Negro community; at the request of the police, KEYN in Wichita stayed on the air beyond its usual signoff time during civil disorders to play soul music with Negro announcers—during that evening they did not report news events.

As with television stations, agreement prevailed among radio stations that had adopted guidelines that these were helpful to their news operation. But although a number of radio stations have given considerable thought to their role in time of disorder, they nevertheless heavily depend—especially the smaller stations—upon wire-service reports and often lack a well-trained and experienced news staff.

4. Newspapers

There is little evidence that many newspapers have adopted any specific codes of guidelines for the coverage of inflammatory events or civil disturbances. Although three of the four papers responding from four cities in the five-city survey indicated they have some policy for the coverage of "inflammatory or violent news events," only two of the papers, the *Evening Tribune* in San Diego, and The *Washington Post* in Washington, D.C., had codified their guidelines for riot coverage.

A survey of editors of riot-torn cities that was done by William Ware, Editor of the *Cleveland Plain Dealer*, for the Freedom of Information Committee of the Associated Press Managing Editors Association, emphatically concluded that there was no need for a code of voluntary self-restraint. But while editors expressed reluctance about a "code"—in the words of one editor, a "kind of journalistic sleeping sickness"—many did say that they had exercised voluntary restraint and learned several things from their experience: (1) to exercise extreme caution to avoid inflammatory and exaggerated copy, headlines, and pictures; (2) to take measures to protect their staffs; (3) to make preparations for riot coverage; and (4) to fully print stories about what is going on as the best way to scotch rumors.

5. Wire Services

The wire-service reports of demonstrations and riots have come under severe criticism from many sources. Because all of the rest of the media—radio, television, and newspapers—depend to a great extent upon their accounts, their influence is immediate and widespread; and their errors and misjudgments compound many times over. This concern for inflammatory language and inaccurate descriptions in wire service reports has persuaded the networks and several radio and television stations to specifically provide in their guidelines that wire stories be rechecked before use.

Both UPI and AP have now issued basic instructions on the handling of stories involving racial violence. The AP had formed a racial task force in 1965 to set down some guidelines based on staffers' experience. These guidelines were recirculated again in 1967 and substantially updated in 1968 to take into account the Riot Commission Report. The AP guidelines are considerably more detailed than those of UPI, which were only set on August 3, 1967. Local UPI bureaus may have entered into community-wide agreements that are respected in times of emergency.

Appendix II-D
THE CANONS OF JOURNALISM

(American Society of Newspaper Editors)

The primary function of newspapers is to communicate to the human race what its members do, feel, and think. Journalism, therefore, demands of its practitioners the widest range of intelligence or knowledge and of experience, as well as natural and trained powers of observation and reasoning. To its opportunities as a chronicle are indissolubly linked its obligations as teacher and interpreter.

To the end of finding some means of codifying sound practice and just aspirations of American journalism, these canons are set forth:

I

Responsibility. The right of a newspaper to attract and hold readers is restricted by nothing but considerations of public welfare. The use a newspaper makes of the share of public attention it gains serves to determine its sense of responsibility, which it shares with every member of its staff. A journalist who uses his power for any selfish or otherwise unworthy purpose is faithless to a high trust.

II

Freedom of the Press. Freedom of the press is to be guarded as a vital right of mankind. It is the unquestionable right to discuss whatever is not explicitly forbidden by law, including the wisdom of any restrictive statute.

III

Independence. Freedom from all obligations except that of fidelity to the public interest is vital.

1. Promotion of any private interest contrary to the general welfare, for whatever reason, is not compatible with honest journalism. So-called news communications from private sources should not be published without public notice of their source or else substantiation of their claims to value as news, both in form and substance.
2. Partisanship, in editorial comment which knowingly departs from the truth, does violence to the best spirit of American journalism; in the news columns it is subversive of a fundamental principle of the profession.

IV

Sincerity, Truthfulness, Accuracy. Good faith with the reader is the foundation of all journalism worthy of the name.

1. By every consideration of good faith a newspaper is constrained to be truthful. It is not to be excused for lack of thoroughness or accuracy within its control, or failure to obtain command of these essential qualities. 2. Headlines should be fully warranted by the contents of the article which they surmount.

V

Impartiality. Sound practice makes clear distinction between news reports and expressions of opinion. News reports should be free from opinion or bias of any kind.

1. This rule does not apply to so-called special articles unmistakably devoted to advocacy or characterized by a signature authorizing the writer's own conclusions and interpretation.

VI

Fair Play. A newspaper should not publish official charges affecting reputation or moral character without opportunity given to the accused to be heard; right practice demands the giving of such opportunity in all cases of serious accusation outside judicial proceedings.

1. A newspaper should not invade private rights or feelings without sure warrant of public right as distinguished from public curiosity. 2. It is the privilege, as it is the duty, of a newspaper to make prompt and complete correction of its own serious mistakes of fact or opinion, whatever their origin.

VII

Decency. A newspaper cannot escape conviction of insincerity if while professing high moral ,purpose it supplies incentives to base conduct, such as are to be found in details of crime and vice, publication of which is not demonstrably for the general good. Lacking authority to enforce its canons, the journalism here represented can but express the hope that deliberate panderings to vicious instincts will encounter effective public disapproval or yield to the influence of a preponderant professional condemnation.

Appendix II-E

CODE OF BROADCAST NEWS ETHIC

The following Code of Broadcast News Ethics for RTNDA was adopted January 2, 1966.

The members of the Radio Television News Directors Association agree that their prime responsibility as newsmen—and that of the broadcasting industry as the collective sponsor of news broadcasting—is to provide to the public they serve a news service as accurate, full and prompt as human integrity and devotion can devise, To that end, they declare their acceptance of the standards of practice here set forth, and their solemn intent to honor them to the limits of their ability.

Article One

The primary purpose of broadcast newsmen—to inform the public of events of importance and appropriate interest in a manner that is accurate and comprehensive—shall override all other purposes.

Article Two

Broadcast news presentations shall be designed not only to offer timely and accurate information, but also to present it in the light of relevant circumstances that give it meaning and perspective. This standard means that news reports, when clarity demands it, will be laid against pertinent factual background; that factors such as race, creed, nationality or prior status will be reported only when they are relevant; that comment or subjective content will be properly identified; and that errors in fact will be promptly acknowledged and corrected.

Article Three

Broadcast newsmen shall seek to select material for newscast solely on their evaluation of its merits as news. This standard means that news will be selected on the criteria of significance, community and regional relevance, appropriate human interest, service to defined audiences. It excludes sensationalism or misleading emphasis in any form; subservience to external or " interested" efforts to influence news selection and presentation, whether from within the broadcasting industry or from without. It requires that such terms as "bulletin" and "flash" be used only when the character of the news justifies them; that bombastic or misleading descriptions of newsroom facilities and personnel be rejected, along with undue use of sound and visual effects; and that promotional or publicity material be sharply scrutinized before use and identified by source or otherwise when broadcast.

227

Article Four

Broadcast newsmen shall at all times display humane respect for the dignity, privacy and the well-being of persons with whom the news deals.

Article Five

Broadcast newsmen shall govern their personal lives and such nonprofessional associations as may impinge on their professional activities in a manner that will protect them from conflict of interest, real or apparent.

Article Six

Broadcast newsmen shall seek actively to present all news the knowledge of which will serve the public interest, no matter what selfish, uninformed or corrupt efforts attempt to color it, withold it or prevent its presentation. They shall make constant effort to open doors closed to the reporting of public proceedings with tools appropriate to broadcasting (including cameras and recorders), consistent with the public interest. They acknowledge the newsman's ethic of protection of confidential information and sources, and urge unswerving observation of it except in instances in which it would clearly and unmistakably defy the public interest.

Article Seven

Broadcast newsmen recognize the responsibility borne by broadcasting for informed analysis, comment and editorial opinion on public events and issues. They accept the obligation of broadcasters, for the presentation of such matters by individuals whose competence, experience and judgment qualify them for it.

Article Eight

In court, broadcast newsmen shall conduct themselves with dignity, whether the court is in or out of session. They shall keep broadcast equipment as unobtrusive and silent as possible. Where court facilities are inadequate, pool broadcasts should be arranged.

Article Nine

In reporting matters that are or may be litigated, the newsman shall avoid practices which would lend to interfere with the right of an individual to a fair trial.

Article Ten

Broadcast newsmen shall actively censure and seek to prevent violations of these standards, and shall actively encourage their observance by all newsmen, whether of the Radio Television News Directors Association or not.

Appendix II-F

BROADCAST GUIDELINES
FOR COVERAGE OF CIVIL DISORDERS

The following suggestions are to be considered as guidelines for voluntary use by broadcast newsmen during possible or actual widespread civil disorder. They are the product of a committee of the Northern California Chapter of the Radio and Television News Directors Association formed to consider carefully the sensitive and influential role of the electronic news operation in its coverage of such disorders and recommend ways and means in which broadcaster may better serve the public interest, safety and welfare.

Voluntary acknowledgment of these suggestions is based on the following factors:

1. A majority of broadcast news directors in this region must indicate they feel such a set of guidelines is necessary in this one area of coverage because an instance of widespread civil disobedience, particularly one involving racial strife, is entirely unique from any other kind of story in that its coverage could affect the direction of its development and intensity, its duration and outcome and therefore demands exceptional treatment.

2. The civil disorder must be of such size, or indicate a potential for developing into such size, that it could be a considerable threat to the community.

3. Competition between broadcasters in coverage of such disorders should continue to be vigorous but, in this one volatile area, more thought should be given to changing the focus from dynamic impact to authoritative and calm reporting of vital information to the public with maximum assistance in the re-establishment of control as the primary goal.

4. Law enforcement authorities should take the necessary steps to ensure that adequately informed staff members will be on duty at command posts who will be readily available to supply properly identified broadcast newsmen with pertinent information concerning the disorder.

A. Guidelines
(Prior to reaching the scene)

1. Stories of civil disorder, particularly when the disorder is in its early stages, should not be over-emphasized nor should a "scare" approach be taken by the broadcasters in their initial reporting.

2. The official designation of the incident should be used by the broadcasters, employing the term "riot" only after authorities do.

3. At the outset of the disorder, broadcast newsmen should be dispatched to law enforcement command posts, rather than directly to the scene where their presence may heighten the disturbance or interfere with efforts to establish control. An authoritatively staffed command post will undoubtedly be in communication with the scenes of disorder and be capable of providing newsmen with any desired information.

4. Determination of when newsmen may be sent to the scene without danger of inflaming or inciting further discord is the individual responsibility of each broadcast news director and his outlet.

(From the scene, command post, and studio)

5. Broadcasts which might tend to inflame or incite further violence should not be aired.

6. Emphasis should be on the steps being taken to restore order, advisements to the public to keep out of the general disturbance area and, if a curfew has been invoked, of obeying that curfew.

7. Reports should be calm, objective and present the "overall picture" and should be devoid of sensationalism, speculation and rumors which could incite or further extend the disturbance or stir a new outbreak in a controlled area. It should be emphasized that reports from the field are describing only those segments of the disorder that are being witnessed by that particular newsman.

8. Caution should be taken against over-emphasizing isolated and, for the most part, trivial incidents. Such incidents should be incorporated into the "overall picture" and their importance fully explained, thus avoiding inflammatory editing of audio tape and film.

9. Exact locations of intersections, street names and addresses of flareups should not be revealed by the broadcaster until authorities have announced order has been established and control being maintained in that particular area.

10. Avoid broadcasting interviews with obvious lawbreakers in the disorder who are on the side which opposes law and order when the interview could be considered inflammatory and may add further

problems to the disorder. Whenever possible, the broadcast newsman should seek out a responsible spokesman for the community in which the disturbance occurs.

11. Broadcast newsmen should avoid creating further disturbances through the indiscriminate use of cameras, lights or microphones; i.e., avoid filming a milling crowd if it does not add to the story and might inspire a disorder by that crowd. When possible, cameramen should attempt to film with a long lens so as not to expose the presence of a camera and should use natural lighting whenever feasible. In short, use good taste and common sense.

12. Unless and until a situation reaches the point of martial law , all Constitutional guarantees are deemed to be in force and applicable. Hence, the aforementioned constitute guidelines for voluntary conduct designed to provide the greatest assistance to the public and law enforcement agencies in the treatment of civil disorders and, at the same time, provide essential information to the public.

13. Therefore, the basic goal of all broadcast newsmen participating in the coverage of civil disorder should be to encourage, by exemplary performance, responsible reporting that will produce an even greater fulfillment of their obligation to serve the public interest and safety, as well as defend the aims of duly constituted law and authority.

(Endorsed by the membership at a meeting on February 23, 1967, for submission to station management and law enforcement officials.)

Appendix II-G

EMPLOYMENT DATA

Professionals on TV and Radio News Staffs —
Network Owned and Operated Stations

CBS:

Total professional staff 1,123
Total number of Negroes 51

Number of years on staff as of Oct. 1968:

6 mos. or less	6 mos to 1 yr.	1 yr. to 18 mos.	18 mos. to 2 yrs.	2 yrs. or more
31	2	1	5	12

Percentage of Negroes on staff: **4.5%**

ABC:

Total professional staff 672
Total number of Negroes 26

Numbers of years on staff as of Oct. 1968:

6 mos. or less	6 mos to 1 yr.	1 yr. to 18 mos.	18 mos. to 2 yrs.	2 yrs. or more
14	2	3	0	7

Percentage of Negroes on staff: 3.9%

NBC:

Total professional staff 718
Total number of Negroes 29

Number of years on staff as of Oct. 1968:

6 mos. or less	6 mos. to 1 yr.	1 yr. to 18 mos.	18 mos. to 2 yrs.	2 yrs. or more
14	3	5	2	5

Percentage of Negroes on staff: **4.0%**

PART III

TELEVISION ENTERTAINMENT AND VIOLENCE

Parts I and II contained an examination of the past and present characteristics and context of the mass media in America. Part III examines one key facet of mass media activity and production entertainment programming and presentations. The major focus will be on television.

Mass media organizations spend countless hours producing and presenting entertainment, and the American public spends a comparable amount of time in consumption of such productions. The specific focus of attention here is on the effects of mass media portrayals of *violence* upon audiences. The specific effects of violence cannot be isolated from the effects of total entertainment fares, the role of the mass media in society, or the characteristics of mass audiences and their social environment. Thus, the analysis of such effects must be presented in the context of the overall effects of mass media entertainment upon audiences.

Although violence is one of the most discussed topics in America today, it is used in so many different contexts, that it is necessary to make clear what the term does and does not mean in this analysis. Violence is here defined as: "The threat or use of force that results, or is intended to result, in the injury or forcible restraint or intimidation of persons, or the destruction or forcible seizure of property."

It is necessary to distinguish violence, as here defined, from other phenomena, such as crime, conflict, and aggression. For example, the definition of violence used in this Report does not completely coincide with a common definition of crime. Crime necessarily involves the breaking of a law, while violence does not. Crime usually connotes disapproved behavior, while violence in American society can be approved or disapproved. For example, the primary characteristic of war is the use of violence by one nation against another; yet some American wars have received broad public approval and have been legal acts of violence. Another example of widely approved and legal violence is found in contact sports. Often, the most violent individuals in contact sports, as in war, are called heroes, while an individual committing a violent crime is labelled "criminal."

In a discussion concerned with the effects of media portrayals of violence, distinctions between violence and conflict are particularly important. Conflict is a natural social process and one of the most central and enduring themes of all forms of literature, drama, and other arts. Conflict, as presented in the arts or experienced by human beings, occurs both within and between individuals and groups. Violence, on the other hand, requires at least two individuals in direct or indirect relation to one another.

The battle between passion and reason provides an illustration of the differences between conflict and violence. An individual can experience severe conflict between the dictates of passion and reason. Such conflict may be resolved in a variety of ways which may or may not involve violence. The relationship between the more general psychological or social phenomenon of conflict and the inter-personal or inter-group phenomenon of violence is complex. Conflict can be one, but not the only, cause of violence, and violence can be one, but not the only, cause of conflict or mode of conflict expression and resolution.

The necessity of conflict in drama, including mass media entertainment, has often been noted by the authors. Because some defenders of mass media presentations appear to rest their defense of violence on the necessity of conflict it is especially important to note that violence, as defined, bears no absolute relation to conflict. Some persons, for example, have pointed to Shakespearian plays such as *Hamlet* to illustrate and justify the necessity of violence in entertainment programs. The issues are only clouded by such arguments. They fail to distinguish conflict from violence. For example, if all the violence (as here defined) visibly portrayed in *Hamlet* were deleted, essential elements and messages of the story would still remain. It is doubtful that the same can be said for most mass media dramatic presentations.

Much of the research relevant to the issue of violence and mass media entertainment has been carried out by psychologists interested in testing theories of aggression. Therefore, it is important to consider the similarities and differences between violence, as defined in this Report, and aggression.

One can act aggressively without becoming violent. Furthermore, aggression within an individual can take the form of a feeling, drive, or motive, and can lie dormant without becoming manifest in aggressive behavior. Aggression, then, encompasses both feeling and behavioral states of one or more individuals, while violence most commonly refers to *manifest behavior* between individuals.

All acts of violence can be called aggressive, while all instances of aggression cannot be called violence. As a result of the partial conceptual overlap between violence and aggression, research findings obtained from laboratory studies can be informative on the effects of exposure to both inter-personal behavioral aggression and violence portrayed in the media.

Chapter 10

POSING THE PROBLEM OF EFFECTS*

The individual and social effects of mass communication must depend in in some way upon: (1) the pattern of content offered by the mass media; (2) the opportunities for access to the media; and (3) the credibility attributed by audiences to media content attributes to mass media exposure.

Numerous studies from both commercial and academic research centers clearly support what has long been the contention of many concerned citizens about these elementary points: (1) the menu offered by the mass media is heavily saturated with violent content, including incidents of persons intentionally doing physical harm to one another; (2) more and more people have ready access to the media, with the average American spending between one-quarter and one-half of his waking day attending to the mass media; and (3) for most persons, but particularly for the poor in American society, television is perceived as the most credible and believable source of information on the reality of the world.

These points add up to a statement of one simple effect: *mass media portrayals of violence attract large audiences.* This also implies a much more troublesome question: If models for violent behavior are repeatedly presented with few competing notions, and people, particularly children, repeatedly expose themselves to such materials, what could be a more favorable arrangement for learning *about* violence, if not learning *to do* violence? However, merely to ask this question is not enough. The abundance of violent media content, and the frequency of exposure to the same, do *not* suffice to prove that the mass media can modify attitudes or induce violent behavior.

When expressed in this manner, such questions can hardly be unequivocally answered. Indeed, many of the questions that concern us most intensely involve both fact and value-judgment. More than this, their answers depend on *relations between* different kinds of facts, connections between these relations, and certain value-judgments implicit in the thoughts of the questioner. It is not difficult, for example, to catalog the portrayals of violence on television. It is more difficult to relate such tabulations to personality and behavioral traits of viewers. It is still more difficult to show that such a relation is one of cause and effect, and if this can be established,

---

*Prepared for the Media Task Force by Otto N. Larsen, Professor of Sociology, University of Washington.

the effects produced must still be evaluated. When any one of these steps is omitted, basic policy decisions cannot readily be made about the desirability of continuing or changing the existing pattern of media performance.

Mass media, moreover, do not operate alone; they are embedded in a social system which has many other facets. Whatever may be their effects upon the members of their audience, these must be assessed in relation to the way *other* aspects of this larger system affect these same persons.

To speak meaningfully of the role of mass communications media in such critical concerns as the formation of personality, the induction of violent behavior, or in value formation, it is necessary to seek out and chart the main outlines of what is known *in general* about relevant processes of social learning. Because human personality is developed largely through a process of interaction in primary groups (such as the family), and because the various mass media can more or less simulate such primary interaction, they can play a real part in this process. Furthermore, they may do so unintentionally when they only seem to be entertaining or informing, because audience members are engaged in a process of "observational learning" and the mass media contribute to this through "symbolic modeling."

As a child matures physically, he also undergoes a process of social preparation for adult roles. Much of this preparation ordinarily takes place in the family, while some of it occurs in play groups and some of it involves formal education. It occurs all the time the child is awake and active, even when he and the persons with whom he interacts are not consciously concerned with shaping his character. He becomes a residue of what he has done and experienced, which in turn depends on his genetic endowment and the social heritage into which he was born.

As each child grows up, he has a wide range of skills to learn. He has values and customs to embrace, amend, or reject. He has to discover for himself what kind of world he lives in; he gets clues to this from the way others act toward things, toward each other, and toward him. He has to discover who and what he is, and how his identity relates him to the world; again his clues come from the interactions of others with him. He has to find out where he will be going in life, how he will go, who will accompany him, and how they can get together.

It would be surprising indeed if in our society the ubiquitous mass media did *not* play some part in this complex process. And yet until recently, not only has the potential involvement of mass media been relatively neglected, but even the fact that the process is social has sometimes been forgotten.

The mass media enter into this process mainly by providing material for "observational learning," defined as "imitation" in experimental psychology and as "identification" in personality theory. The common denominator for all three terms is a recognition that human beings in certain circumstances tend to reproduce the actions, attitudes, or emotions they perceive in other persons. These other persons may either be live or symbolized models (e.g., a character in a story). As knowledge of the principles of observational learning accumulates, more can be said about *how* groups shape the personalities of their members. The clearer our understanding of these mechanisms, the firmer the ground on which to base statements about the possible effects of symbolized groups, such as those depicted in a television drama.

If the content of mass communications is being widely discussed, perhaps this indicates that it has other effects. One contention is that symbolic violence, whether portraying fantasy or reality, will arouse aggression or increase aggressive behavior, hardening persons to human pain and suffering and leading them to accept violence as a way of life and as a solution to personal and social problems. Another school of thought contends that such exposure has precisely the opposite effect. This view holds that exposure to violence will allow the media user to discharge in fantasy what he might otherwise act out. Thus, watching *Gunsmoke* or reading a *Superman* comic will provide a safe and harmless outlet for human frustrations and aggressive-hostile impulses in much the same manner as hitting a punching bag. A third position holds that violent content has little or no effect. Proponents of this view suggest that in a controlled and relatively secure society, the passive recipient can vicariously live bravely and dangerously through the video hero with no enduring impact on his feeling, attitudes or behavior in life.

It is, of course, the first point of view which has aroused the concern and interest of vast sectors of the general public. However, little is accomplished if one merely notes the presence of undersirable features of some communication medium or art form, and then lets his aversion to both be transmuted into an assumption that the one disliked thing must be caused by the other. Much criticism of the mass media, and especially television, seems to reflect this kind of non-sequitur. This is unnecessary. There are research findings which afford a more objective basis for assessing the situation.

To understand the full implications of the research, it is important to keep in mind just how recent man's experience is with the pervasive presence of mass media. Even now, a decade into the space age, the majority of the world's human beings are illiterate. In our own advanced society, many citizens have first-hand memories of the pre-television and pre-radio era. Some can even remember a childhood in which there was no such thing as a movie theater. Daily newspapers, in fact, have been around for a mere five generations. Since mass communications are so relatively new, it is not surprising that men are not agreed as to the social impact of the various media.

Despite their tender age, mass communications have indeed become a pervasive aspect of our way of life. The media form the core of our leisure time activities, and television is the heart of this core. For the average American, mass media usage occupies almost as much time as does work, and for some, appreciably *more* time is devoted to mass communications. For children, television alone occupies almost as much time as school in their first sixteen years of life. Time-expenditure data by themselves do not prove any of the charges leveled against the media, nor do such data validate the praise the media have received. It is clear that the controversy over the effects of television is unlikely to be the only result of this deluge.

The fact that time devoted to one activity cannot be used in some other way means that the large amount of time allocated by Americans to mass communications must have entailed some redirection of their lives. Although casual radio listening can be done in conjunction with other (presumably inattentive) activities, and newspapers can be read on the commuter train, the mass media must in general have displaced other pursuits.

There are more direct and less incidental ways in which exposure to the mass media could influence persons, and these may have either immediate or long-range impact. Immediate effects include the emotional reactions of a person while he is viewing, listening, or reading, and the ensuing repercussions of these in defensive reactions, fatigue, excitement, dreams, and so on. The long-range effects concern the learning that is produced: both the content (vocabulary, items of information, beliefs) and the strengthening or weakening of personality traits, such as aggressiveness, passivity, and the like. Beyond the psychological level, concern must also be directed to the impact of the media on interpersonal relations, the development of norms, and the acquisition of values. The possibility of a change in behavior without a change in values must also be considered.

These are some of the dimensions of the effects of mass media violence that must be coped with. As with most significant social issues, seemingly straightforward questions become, upon analysis, acutely challenging and do not yield simple solutions. Thus, the following guideline must be set up: when we ask about the effects of the mass media, we must not phrase the question simply in terms of whether the media have an effect; rather, we seek to know under what conditions, how much, and what kind of effect the media are likely to have within specified populations.

We do not underestimate the enormity of the task, nor the necessity of its continuing pursuit. The impact of television in America is difficult to measure because very few people remain unexposed to it, and those few tend to act differently, in ways that pre-date the television era. One solution is to study the way television and other mass media fit into the life cycles of those who use them, without hoping for a comparison group of non-users. We all breathe air, after all, and the unavailability of a control group of non-breathers does not preclude our learning what air does for us.

Present Approach

In seeking answers to guide policy recommendations, the Violence Commission, given its short life-span, could not undertake or sponsor new research other than producing the relevant materials reported in Chapters 15 and 16. Instead, the Media Task Force approached the problem of effects by turning to acknowledged leaders of research in the behavioral sciences. They were asked to prepare papers on media effects by critically examining for their discipline what is known, what inferences can fairly be drawn from that knowledge, what needs to be known through further study, and what procedures are required to discover the relevant information.

Chapters 11-14 organize and present these efforts to convey an understanding of the effects of media violence, based on objective evidence.

The research literature emerges from many sources and flows in many directions. It is crowded with complex issues, marked with incomplete efforts, and subject to various interpretations. However, the research effort is substantial enough to merit close scrutiny both for delineating what is known and for marking out promising territory for further inquiry The problem of communicating these assessments is a demanding one. The reader may prefer a statement of simple findings which state unequivocal action implications. However, research is, of necessity, conditional in nature. A presentation devoid of qualifications may achieve clarity, but at a cost of essential validity. While we have asked our authors to phrase their reports with scientific fidelity, we have also encouraged them to *interpret* and *evaluate* the implications of the inquiries reviewed.

A few consultant papers are presented to convey the full flavor of the research-interpretive enterprise. The bulk of the reports, including the more technical statements, are presented in the appendix. To guide the reader through all these selections, a further distillation of issues is presented briefly below. The general question before us is "what issues concerning the effects of mass media violence have been addressed by researchers? What have been the main thrust and chief contributions of empirical inquiry, particularly as they pertain to the "entainment" realm of mass media performance?

A. Menu and Diet—Communicator Intent versus Audience Use

Mass communicators attempt to attract and hold the attention of large audiences by providing material they deem of interest to their audience. Indeed, communicators often proclaim that their central concern is to give the audience "what it wants." Accordingly, a great bulk of their material is designed to be entertaining. That is often the major effect they seek to achieve.

However, what is *given* may not be all that is *taken* by the audience. The kind of research on effects concerned with the intent of the mass media menu-makers might produce quite different results than that directed toward the diet and digestive processes of the mass media audiences themselves. This is particularly the case, since the social setting for audience experience of mass media content is itself undergoing rapid change of the type envisioned in the concept of "growing urbanism."

In what ways have researchers found it fruitful to think about the nature of effects? In Chapter 11, Professor Catton carefuly traces the evolution, the findings, and the implications in the shift from research on effects of mass media on audiences toward a model concerned with how audience members receive and use mass media content. In the process, he reviews past and contemporary classifications of effects, notes the importance of "intervening variables" in the mass communicative process, and sensitizes us to new conceptions of effects by referring, for example, to the "opportunity cost" by the abundance of violence portrayed by the media. In this latter connection, he asserts that the presentation of violence by mass media does effect the behavior of mass media audiences: it keeps them from using in their own ways whatever other kinds of content might have been presented in the same time of space.

Chapter 11 thus alerts us to the following critical conclusion: research has shown the mass media do not easily and inevitably produce intended effects. To say that intended effects do not automatically occur is not to say, however, that unintended effects do not occur. Data in support of this important conception will appear in several places throughout the Report.

B. What is the Message? Medium or Content as the Basis for Social Learning

The development of the technology of mass communication has rapidly transformed the nature of receiving impressions and information in modern society. When does the medium become the message? How does the form of transmission affect the perception and learning of the content being offered? What does technology do to the distinction between fantasy and reality?

In Chapter 12, these and other questions about the effect of exposure to mass media violence on the social behavior of children are asked. Professor Siegal opens by noting several trends in the history of the development of techniques for transmitting information to the human senses. These trends include a diminishing reliance on written forms, the integration of appeals to several senses, the increased rapidity of communication, the increased availability of mass media material, and the increased fidelity in communication techniques. To illustrate the latter point, the correspondense between the printed word "fire" and an actual fire is low, but between a color film about a fire and the actual event, it is much closer. In a word, their trends add up to a characterization of television.

The significance of these trends is addressed in a discussion of the distinctions that have traditionally been made between the entertainment and information functions of the mass media. For children at least, Professor Siegal senses that television, because of its vividness and fidelity, blurs this distinction. She argues that both fact and fancy have a certain inherent authenticity when presented on television. Supporting illustrations and research data are then presented to show that since children view these presentations as authentic and credible, and assume that the world is really the way it appears on television, it is natural for them to take the behavior they observe as a model for their own.

The studies cited by Professor Siegal are important because they represent a consistent set of findings based on observations of behavior, not merely self-reports of attitudes or actions. The conclusion is dramatic: although it is not governed by a board of education, television does teach. And what is being taught? Under a wide range of conditions, children learn aggressive behavior which they then enact in their play under suitable circumstances. One study from this review which deserves special notice demonstrated that children mimic the aggressive behavior of adults, whether they observe this behavior in the flesh or on film, and that this imitation was drawn equally from realistic and cartoon-like films. The conclusion is that the fantasy-reality distinction on which adults pin so much hope seemed of little significance for the children of this particular research effort.

C. Stimulating versus Cathartic Effects of Media Violence

Does witnessing mass media violence tend to facilitate or purge the impulse to aggression?

For many, this is the central question of effects. Convincing evidence one way or the other could help resolve many policy issues. If the catharsis effect was clearly dominant, anxiety about symbolic violence would be greatly relieved. Indeed, one implication could be that the media would be serving a healthy function or performing a public service by portraying violence, since such portrayals would tend to control or inhibit the acting out of aggressive impulses. The appeal of the catharsis effect is thus evident. It stands in positive support of free expression by the media.

The concept of catharsis has been at the center of considerable intellectual debate since the time of Aristotle. Only recently, however, have there been systematic attempts to test the notion through research by seeking out the conditions under which it might have some validity. A large and growing number of laboratory experiments have addressed the issue. The advantage of these studies is that they isolate and control relevant conditions and afford reasonably clear causal interpretations. Their disadvantage is that they are often based on small samples, have a restricted time-dimension, and involve conditions that are not closely comparable to natural exposure to the media.

In Appendix III-D Professor Goransen provides a thorough review of the evidence from laboratory studies on the catharsis issue. His general conclusion is that this line of research has *not* supported the idea that the probability of aggressive behavior is reduced by observing the kind of violence seen in the mass media. He adds that the vast majority of experimental studies on this issue have reported media aggression as stimulating rather than providing aggression catharsis.

Some of the more specific findings from laboratory studies also merit attention because they suggest the variety of conditions under which the observation of violence tends to increase rather than decrease subsequent aggressiveness. For example:

(1) The stimulation of aggressive responses is more likely to occur when aggression anxiety is experimentally minimized rather than induced prior to exposure to filmed aggression. That is, where subjects are not frustrated, insulted, or otherwise angered before seeing a film, they tend to increase their willingness to inflict physical pain as a result of exposure to filmed aggression.

(2) The stimulation of aggressive responses from exposure to filmed aggression is more likely to occur when the witnessed aggression occurs in a *justified* rather than in a *non-justified* content. (This point is ironic in light of current media programming policies. In showing that "crime does not pay" by depicting the hero's successful and righteous use of violence against the "bad guys," the media may be creating those very conditions most conductive to the instigation of aggression.)

(3) Novel, aggressive behavior is learned by children through exposure to realistic portrayals of aggression on television or films. A large proportion of these behaviors are retained over long periods of time if they are practiced at least once. The likelihood that such aggressive behaviors will be performed is determined, in part, by the similarity of the violence observed from the media and the cues (e.g., names, social characteristics, etc.) present in actual later situations.

(4) The actual performance of aggressive behaviors learned from the media is largely contingent on the child's belief in the effectiveness of aggression in attaining his goals while avoiding punishment. (The mass media typically present aggression as a highly effective form of behavior).

(5) Frequent exposure produces an emotional habituation to media violence. There is suggestive evidence that this results in an increased likelihood of actually engaging in aggression.

(6) Aggressive impulses may be held in check if the viewer has been made especially aware of the suffering that may result from violence. (Production codes for most of the media include prohibitions against the portrayal of physical agony and suffering and too much punishment. Question: When this kind of *de facto* self-censorship operates to "sanitize" violence by "prettying up" or entirely omitting the real consequences of aggression, is the result again an unwitting creation of the very conditions found most conducive to the instigation to aggression? Laboratory research suggests that it is.)

In general, then, an extensive program of laboratory research mounts a strong indictment of media performance not only with respect to the amount of violence portrayed but, more particularly, with the manner in which violence is portrayed. From this research perspective, there is no evidence in support of the credibility of a catharsis effect. Indeed, under laboratory conditions, the bulk of the evidence indicates that vicariously experienced violence tends to serve as a triggering mechanism and increases the probability of more aggressive behavior.

It should be emphasized that some studies from the laboratory setting do show a reduction of aggressiveness resulting from exposure to symbolic aggression. However, it is the contention of the researchers that this can be explained without reference to any cathartic "draining off" of aggressiveness. Such inhibition to acting out aggressiveness occurring from exposure to media violence results from the reminder that aggression is morally wrong (especially in the case where media violence is portrayed as unjustified), and when the subjects were made aware of the painful aftermath of aggression.

A further interpretation in a broader context of sociological factors is presented by Professor Catton in Chapter 14. He contends that the eliciting effect is far more likely than the cathartic effect. In doing so, he remind us that evidence that media operators are good people and have no desire to promote violence cannot suffice to prove the mass communications either cannot or do not produce increases in violent behavior. By providing cues that violence is socially acceptable, mass media may inadvertently both elicit and disinhibit violent behavior.

Despite the evidence from laboratory studies, the question of stimulating versus cathartic effects remains as an issue in the literature of mass media research. This comes forcefully to our attention when we turn to research involving more natural conditions of exposure to the mass media in field situations. Here we have more limited research experience to draw from, but available evidence suggests caution in dismissing the possibility of catharsis as a major effect. The prime exhibit of such research is porvided in Appendix III-E where excerpts from a recent study by Professor Feshbach are presented.

Going beyond earlier survey research in the field setting, Professor Feshbach has launched an experimental study involving relatively prolonged (six hours a week for six weeks) exposure to television by prep-school boys in seven residential schools located in California and New York. In each school, boys were randomly assigned to witness either aggressive television programs depicting fighting, shooting, or other forms of physical violence, or non-aggressive programs from regular television fare offered during the evening and weekend hours. The programs were classified along this dimension, with a high degree of agreement, by three independent raters.

A number of personality tests and attitude scales were administered at the beginning and end of the six-week experimental period. In addition, daily behavior rating forms were completed for each boy over the experimental period. By these means the investigator was able to measure and compare not only overt aggressive behavior such as fighting and swearing but also the mediating cognitive ideas, the hostile-aggressive attitudes, and the preferences and the fantasies experienced by both sets of boys.

What were the major findings? This study failed to reveal any evidence that exposure to aggressive content in television stimulates or facilitates the acting out of aggressive behavior. Furthermore, this study did yield evidence suggesting that exposure to aggressive content in television serves to control or reduce aggressive behavior in pre-adolescent boys from low socio-economic backgrounds with aggressive tendencies.

The investigator is properly cautious in interpreting the findings of the study. He would not, for example, advocate, on the basis of this research, that boys should be encouraged to watch aggressive television programs. He also recognizes the conditional nature of his research and is aware of some methodological shortcomings. Nonetheless, these findings clearly contradict the weight of evidence from the laboratory setting. Here the investigator acknowledges the problem of comparing the results from the two settings. The laboratory experiments deal with highly restricted situations, with dependent measures that are often play-like and vulnerable to the suggestive properties of the immediate stimulus situation. On the other hand, while the field studies have been more naturalistic, they have not experimentally controlled exposure to aggressive content in television as closely as would be desired. For these reasons, he concludes, there is an acute need for comparable field investigations and replication of the present findings. While new knowledge has been gained, the question of stimulating versus cathartic effects still remains a salient issue for researchers and policy makers.

While the present state of knowledge on this important issue does not easily lend itself to policy formulation, enough is known to alert the mass media to a more sensitive, cautious, and creative approach in using violence in entertainment programming. Grave risks are run in a continued policy of an indiscriminate use of violence where other options are open. While the burden of proof lies with the researchers, the burden of risk lies with the daily activities of the mass media.

D. Mass Media Effects on Norms, Attitudes, and Values

Up to this point, attention has primarily been directed to research bearing on the question of whether exposure to symbolic violence directly triggers violent acts. We must also be concerned with how the media portrayal of violence might build a climate of attitudes, norms, and values as conditions that lead to or support actual violence, or prevent the abandonment of it in society. This suggests a concern with questions of the following broad order:

(1) Does mass media content cultivate acceptance of the idea that this is a violent world where there is nothing one can do but accept violence as a norm?

(2) Does mass communication tend to teach its audience that they live in a kind of world against which they must take up arms?

(3) Even if the mass media focus on violence does not instigate violent behavior, is there an opportunity lost because the media do not promote alternatives to violence by the audience?

This level of questioning suggests research not unlike the study of climate or ocean tides. Such study may not tell us what given persons will do or where they will go, but it could tell us in which way the cultural winds blow or the cultural tide flows. And much can move with that.

To put it another way, research on effects is also concerned with the aspects of life, values, and means the informal schooling of mass communication provides. Careful studies of television entertainment fare has revealed one dominant theme for all types of programs. That value theme is the *the end justifies the means,* and the most prominent means for achieving goals in television stories is by violence.

To be concerned with values is to suggest that whether or not such messages directly encourage violence may not be as important as the cultivation of the assumption that *that is the way life is.* The critical possibility is that the acceptance of violence can make those who accept it a party to the occurrence of violence by making those who are inclined to engage in violence act in ways they sense to be socially tolerated, approved, or even expected.

There is still a critical need for concerted research effort by students of mass communication in this area. Such work as does address the issue is partial and scattered. So vital is the concern, however, that we present in Chapter 14 an integration of approach, findings, and implications from the field by Professor Catton. In Appendix III-F, a further statement by this author may be found under the title of "The Worldview Presented by Mass Media." Here the author speculates on the possible degradation of values that occurs as a result of the intimate linkage of the entertainment content of the mass media with commercial messages.

Chapter 11

MASS MEDIA AS
PRODUCERS OF EFFECTS :
AN OVERVIEW OF RESEARCH TRENDS*

During the last several decades, the trend in research and theory on mass communications has been away from the attribution of great potency to the media, and toward regarding them as relatively impotent (or at least innocuous). The media were initially viewed as insidious shapers of consent; their audiences were initially seen   as atomized and defenseless targets of deliberate or inadvertent propaganda. Research findings, and the interpretations given to them, have changed this image. The media have come to be seen by many social scientists as components in an elaborate social system. Their audiences have been found to be less atomized than had been supposed, and there has accordingly been a change of direction. Instead of asking "What effects do mass media produce?," the question now is, "How do people and groups in the audience use mass media?"

This analysis will attempt to show that this trend does not suffice to prove that there is no cause for concern. If it has not been demonstrated that mass communications can regiment the population, or that these media *have* corrupted our society, neither has it been proven that they are inherently (or at least under our free enterprise system) harmless.

A. *Decline and Fall of the "Hypodermic" Image*

The early supposition that mass media can "inject" effects into a passively recipient audience was based on a supposition about the nature of modern societies. It was assumed that western civilization had become a "mass" society, in which individuals were relatively detached from each other and from a social fabric, and therefore homogeneously susceptible to stimuli from impersonal media. It was supposed that the urban way of life, in which primary group relations had been largely displaced by secondary group relations, made this so. The traditional basis of solidarity had been undermined, it was assumed, the family had lost its place in the social order, and the neighborhood as a social entity was disappearing.[1] Segmentalization

*Prepared for the Media Task Force by William R. Catton, Jr., Professor of Sociology, University of Washington.

of human relations was seen as characteristic of but not confined to cities. The heterogeneity of urban populations, the sheer numbers of people, and increased mobility all tended to detach people from stable groups and to foster increased reliance on formal mechanisms of norm enforcement.[2] Kinship ties, it was assumed, lose their effectiveness in urban environments, and territorial units such as the residential neighborhood cease to function as a basis for social solidarity The city becomes "a series of tenuous segmental relationships superimposed upon a territorial base with a definite center but without a definite periphery."[3]

In the early 1950's, LaPiere sternly rebuked his fellow sociologists for swallowing the dichotomous classification of societies into two types, *Gemeinschaft*, and *Gesellschaft*, the former emphasizing homogeneity and primary group living, and the latter emphasizing heterogeneity or social differentiation and secondary group or impersonal contractual relations. The assumption of an inexorable trend toward *Gesellschaft* had originally been set forth by Tonnies in 1887.[4] LaPiere's rebuke was part of a rather widespread trend toward rethinking the sociological image of the urban way of life. Family and neighborhood ties were found to be still functioning in varying degrees in all parts of even the largest cities. Astronomical numbers of people did not alone turn a community into a mass society where individuals were psychologically isolated from one another.[5] There was diminishing acceptance of the assumption that a kind of social pathology called *anomie*, wherein human beings lose their capacity to relate to each other effectively, was the necessary result of over-elaboration of the division of labor.[6] Thus there was growing skepticism among social scientists about the notion that a functionally heterogenous population produces such a segmentalized life that in relation to mass media, the people are uniformly submissive.

Propaganda efforts during World War I were based on a relatively simple theory that was consistent with the *Gesellschaft* image. This theory assumed that cleverly designed stimuli would reach every individual member of the mass society via the media, that each would perceive it in the same general manner as his fellows, and that this would provoke a more or less uniform response from all."

As research accumulated, it became necessary to introduce more and more "intervening variables" into this simple stimulus-response model. It became necessary to recognize significant variations in the desires and inclinations of audience members, in the way they received media stimuli, and in their socially-shaped opportunities to respond.[8] The upshot of all these complications was that it began to seem as if the answer to the question, "What effects do mass media produce?" had to be, "It all depends . . .", and it was only a short step from that to a feeling that the media really don't *produce* effects at all. The contingent nature of mass media impact made it seem that the effects ought to be attributed to the intervening variables instead of (rather than in conjunction with) to the mass media stimuli.

Thinking was moved in this direction by research that established the selective nature of perception. Individuals with different values, or whose other personality characteristics differ, perceive the same stimuli differently. At first, this discovery resulted merely in a modification of the "hypodermic" concept of mass communication: media may produce different effects with different kinds of people, but if people can be put in categories, the effects of mass communications injections into a particular category may still be predictable and powerful.[9] Later the emphasis on perceptual selectivity led to outright disparagement of the notion that media have effects at all. For example, DeFleur writes: "When communication 'effects' are a focus of research attention, the assumption that the media are in some way 'causes' of these effects is a natural one. Even if it is granted that intervening processes of some sort can soften or otherwise modify this relationship, the underlying cause-effect conceptualization is not different, only more complicated."[10] He implies that conceptualizations in terms of cause and effect are inherently misleading.

Skepticism regarding the "mass society" concept increased after the 1940 voter study in Erie County, Ohio. It was found that a significant role in the mass communication process was played by informal social relationships. The personal influence of "opinion leaders" was found to mediate between radio or newspaper presentations on the one hand and the resulting attitudes of voters on the other.[11] A 1953 article in the *American Sociological Review* articulated the realization that had grown from this study and its successors that the behavior of mass media audiences is "distinctly social" and hardly conforms to the previous sociological views on "collective behavior." This article made it clear that the old "hypodermic" model was inappropriate not only because people in different categories perceive the stimuli differently, but also because people in different groups use the media differently; not that they get different injections from the same needle, but they often seem to get no injection at all; they get material for use in their own group- and self-determined activities. Being a member of the local audience of mass communications "is a distinctly social activity in which interaction with others before, during, and after any single occasion of spectatorship has created definite shared expectations and predisposing definitions. These in turn have a determinate effect, in conjunction with the institutionalized character of the activity, on what members of the audience select or do not select, and how they react or do not react.[12]

But this does not logically indicate that mass media have *no* effect on their audiences. At most it might imply that mass media seldom if ever have any altogether independent effect. This idea has been constructed, however, as the basis for pious rebuttal to the worried critics of the media. Sociologists as well as media spokesmen have taken this change in theoretical orientation of mass communications research as warrant for some complacency about media effects.[13]

B. *Contemporary Assumptions and Theoretical Views*

The assumptions people make about a topic are often implied by the kinds of questions they ask about it. Several kinds of questions can be asked about mass media. According to DeFleur,[14] most sociological inquiry about mass media has thus far addressed itself primarily to the question, "How do mass media affect society and its members?" Similarly, he says, most of the criticism of mass media has been phrased in terms of this question. The question implicity assumes that mass media *produce* distinguishable effects (both on people and on societies), and DeFleur and others are critical of this assumption. He suggests two other kinds of questions each of which implies somewhat different assumptions; (1) How does mass communication work, and is it in principle any different from direct interpersonal communication process? Mass communication stimulates primary interaction in varying degrees. Its capacity for socializing members of its audiences and shaping their communication simulates primary interaction in varying degrees. Its capacity for socializing members of its audiences and shaping their values and personality characteristics has some striking resemblances to, and some important differences from, real primary interaction. DeFleur also asks, (2) What political, economic, or cultural conditions have led mass media to operate as they do?

In the earliest days of cinema, the sheer fact that pictures moved was enough to attract an audience. The customers in the penny arcades soon began to choose among different kinds of film content, however. According to DeFleur, "Such films as *Beavers at Play* or *The Surf at Dover* brought in fewer pennies than the brief but exciting *Dane du Ventre,* or the titillating *What the Bootblack Saw.* Efforts toward the filming of more serious or artistic subjects were not received with enthusiasm. Film content aimed at more elementary gratifications was what brought in the money."[15] Thus, when mass media are commercial enterprises, content is shaped by considerations of what brings in the money. The mass media operate as they do partly because of the kind of enterprise they are in the kind of society they are in.

Mass communication differs from other communication in some ways and resembles it in other ways partly from purely technical considerations. But the similarities and differences arise partly from the kinds of use people in the audience have learned to make of the content provided. What is needed to understand the impact of television, for example, on children is to ask not only what television presents to them, but also what do they do with what they take from it?[16] Television is often used as a babysitter, and the child is often completely absorbed in the program. Some children seem addicted to it, watching a great deal, and becoming restless when the set is not turned on or is unavailable to them. Perhaps this medium has not made children generally more passive, since it has only displaced an average of about half an hour a day of active play (out of a two- or three-hour quota). The remainder of television time is a displacement of other mass media, or of sleep. For children who, for other social or temperamental reasons, might be inclined toward passivity and withdrawal, television does afford them a clear opportunity in that direction.[17]

Adolescents, and younger children as well, seem to seek satisfaction of a hunger for contact with the adult world from television. They have a desire to know about it, to participate in it (which they can do vicariously with television), and to acquire status in it. [18] This is the socialization process, so there is inherent in the medium a potential for socializing youngsters who bring to it an attention motivated by this sort of appetite.

If television provides information (and misinformation) about the adult world, it may extend the limited opportunities the child or adolescent would otherwise have for contact with that world. However, this extension is always only an imitation, not a direct interpersonal relation. [19] For this reason, as children grow older, some of them at least tend to shift their mass media use from a fantasy-oriented type to more reality-oriented usage; for some, this means less television and more reading. This trend is more pronounced in the middle class than in the working class. [20] It may reflect a shift from vicarious to real social relationships as the child matures. Televised simulation of primary group life is partly abandoned as real primary group experiences accumulate and as skills are acquired for secondary interaction. Again, however, discovery of this trend does not indicate that television or other mass media have no effects; they are used by viewers seeking to be affected in one way or another. Usage changes in relation to desires as the alternative sources of various desired effects are changed.

Sociologists have probably erred as much in downgrading the notion of mass media effects as they had previously erred in elevating it. To say, as Klapper does, that mass communications effects are mediated by a complex nexus of social and psychological factors, and that mass media are thus not the necessary or sufficient causes of various audience effects,[21] is not the same as saying mass media are ineffectual (and hence harmless). Klapper maintains that there is strong indication from communications research that the mass media are more likely to reinforce than to change existing opinions. He bases this conclusion on the findings about perceptual selectivity, group processes and normative influences on audience members, the interpersonal network that is superimposed on the communication link between medium and audience member, the allegedly "super-normative" characteristics of opinion leaders in this network, and the need of commercial mass media to comply with audience desires so as to retain large (and thus lucrative) audiences.[22] If existing opinions are reinforced by mass media when they would otherwise have been changed by other factors, the mass media have produced an effect; pointing out the conservative nature of this effect cannot argue it out of existence.

Klapper acknowledges that field and laboratory studies have shown that "communications are extremely effective in creating opinions on matters about which the audience is unlikely to have preexisting opinions."[23] Children are born with no opinions at all (unless their innate preference for comfort over discomfort is dubbed an "opinion"). They begin acquiring them as soon as they begin to be socialized. The trend in sociological thought toward the "little or no effect" view of mass communication was developing during the decades when television was being technically perfected and socially adopted. Research has shown how television now dominates children's mass media experience. If it once might have been true that the previous types of mass media produced little or no effect on audience members, and if this was only belatedly recognized, in the meantime the idea has ceased to be applicable. This new electronic audiovisual medium represents a significant jump over its less versatile predecessors in ability to simulate primary interaction, and it is avidly attended by the most nearly opinionless segment of the population—children.

Attitude changes do occur, and Klapper acknowledges that special circumstances occasionally enable mass media to convert people from one view to another view, even an opposing one. These special circumstances can include any reduction of the strength of the factors that ordinarily cause the media to be conservative and reinforcing in their influence. They can also include the fact that people vary in their susceptibility to persuasion. Some people can be persuaded of anything; Klapper cites research which indicates that the extremes of persuasion are "topic free." [24] But again, these considerations do not necessarily divest the mass media of responsibility for audience effects; they indicate that the average impact of communications cannot be regarded as the only impact. The social acceptability of the average impact is no warrant for disregarding the special effects which may or may not be so socially acceptable.

Klapper also notes the capacity of the mass media to confer status on the persons or ideas to which the media give attention.[25] This is an effect, inasmuch as there is no basis for believing that status would be allocated to exactly the same people and in exactly the same proportions by agencies other than mass media and by means other than the sheer giving or withholding of attention. Moreover, this can have other effects. Status can be instrumental; people who have been accorded status by the mass media can do things they could not otherwise do, and the effects of their actions are due to the mass media.

Finally, Klapper discounts the assumption made by mass media critics that the abundant portrayal of violence stimulates socially undesirable behavior.[26] Content analysis studies have repeatedly shown how abundantly the mass media do portray violence, both real and fictional. Logically, the data produced by content analyses can be said to fall short of the demonstration of a causal link between communications content and audience behavior. But if we remind ourselves that mass communicators strive to attract and retain large audiences, analyses of mass media content tell us something about what those who control the media think about their audiences, even if they do not explain what the audience members think or do as a result of exposure to the content. Content analyses do measure an effect, then—the way media men have been affected by their relative freedom to choose alternative means of attracting audiences and by their perceptions of audience interests. Mass media time, space and resources devoted to the portrayal of violence are not available for presentation of other kinds of content. There is thus a clear opportunity cost to the abundance of violence even if (as hopefully alleged) it entails no such social cost as the perpetration of violent behavior. Presentation of violence by mass media does affect the behavior of mass media audiences: it keeps them from using in their own ways whatever other kinds of content might have been presented in the same time or space. Moreover, recalling the alleged conserving effect of mass media, and recognizing certain traditions of violence in American history, it follows that abundant portrayal of violence by mass media may have helped prevent abandonment of violence by the audience. If it is true that violence is valued by at least some Americans, then the very argument that has been used by media apologists cuts the other way; this value, like any other, would be subject to the value-conserving influence of the mass media.

C. Contemporary Classification of Effects

The trend away from considering what mass media do to audiences and toward considering how audience members receive and use mass media content does not seem to have weakened the relevance of Lasswell's now classic categorization of mass media "functions."[27] He suggested in 1948 that mass media perform three kinds of social (as distinct from private) functions. (1) They carry on a *surveillance* of the environment, keeping audiences informed of opportunities and threats to which they may need or wish to respond individually or collectively. This is a social effect because different kinds of social order are dependent on populations with different degrees of informedness. (2) The media tend to bring about some *correlation* of the components of society for effective, organized response to the environment. The arguments about the limited persuasive capacity of the media, and about the involvement of intervening variables in the persuasion process leave this function intact, for the leaders of a modern community or society do turn to the mass media as aids in exercising their leadership, and the audience expects mass media to be used in the process of organizing social action. (3) The mass media help in *transmission* of the social heritage from one generation to the next. Studies of the occurrence of incidental learning show that this function is served (appropriately or not) even when this may not be the intent of the communicator. Studies of vicarious learning, from observing both the behavior of models and the consequences accruing to the models, have revealed one of the processes by which this takes place.

Clearly, the second of Lasswell's types, and especially the third, are closely related to the socialization process which occurs apart from the mass media. Both pertain to the imparting of values.

It is important to remember that these functions are very often subordinated to two other purposes, more private than social, in our system. This fact itself has value implications. A great deal of the content of mass communications is presented as entertainment. The purpose of the audience members in exposing themselves to the mass media is very often to be entertained. [28] If they are informed, if their activities are correlated with those of others, and if they absorb something of their social hertage, it is largely incidental to being amused or distracted. It is also largely incidental to the communicator's quest for monetary gain. Movies bring in revenue from admission tickets, and that is why they are produced. Books yield revenue by being sold, and that is why they are published. Reading is incidental. Magazines and newspapers yield negligible revenue from their subscribers; their profit depends on income from advertising. the latter provides virtually the entire base for radio and television. In any of these sponsored media, the volume of advertising revenue depends in part on the size of the audience. The advertiser ostensibly buys time or space, but his real interest is in buying audience attention. He exchanges entertainment or otherwise interesting communication for the audience attention required to give him opportunity to sell his product.

D. *Mass Media Incompletely Exonerated*

Many good things can properly be said about the mass media in general and about television in particular. Granted the validity of much of this commendation, and granted that the imaginable harm television might conceivably do to a child who is already warped or deprived of good social relationships will not usually be done to children with warm and secure family lives, nonetheless many of the severest criticisms remain at best simply unproved rather than disproved. [29] As Bandura notes in reference to a number of widely circulated survey studies that have been construed as showing that television violence neither harms nor helps its viewers, "It is surprising how this view has won uncritical acceptance," based as it is on opinion studies of parents or people who work with children rather than on studies of children's actual behavior and attitudes. [30]

Studies of the impact of audiovisual stimuli on children's behavior have, of course, been made. To discount the implications of these experimental studies because laboratory conditions do not duplicate real life situations, Bandura points out, is to misunderstand the manner in which knowledge is advanced. "Indeed," he says, "experiments are not designed to reproduce the stimulus events that occur in real-life situations and they would be superfluous if they were,"[31] An experiment deliberately controls some of the factors which vary in real life so as to be able to discern the relations between certain specific variables which can be manipulated as they might not be outside the laboratory.

To ensure development of principles of social learning, for example, laboratory experimentation must involve dependent variables that overlap the social responses to which the tester wishes to generalize the conclusions drawn from his experiment. However, ethical considerations preclude some of the conceivable manipulations of some variables. Accordingly, laboratory methods must be supplemented by field studies. By the same token, field studies take on different meanings when supplemented by laboratory experimentation. Some of the behaviors whose causes are sought by social scientists have resulted from such an interplay of multiple socializing agents and compound effects of any single agent that it is often necessary to begin with field studies that are purely correlational. These can generate hypotheses about relations between antecedents and consequents which then require testing in rigorous laboratory studies. Without the latter, the statements of correlation derived from field studies cannot properly be taken to represent causal relations.[32] The finding in a field study that two variables seem to be uncorrelated cannot be taken as proof that there is no causal relation between them; two or more causal relations that could be disentangled in careful experimentation may mask each other in the field.

The optimistic mass media theorists, Wilenksy says, "seem always to come to the same punch line: the burden of evidence indicates that the media are not omnipotent; they are absorbed into local cultures via the two-step flow from media to local group to person; and this absorption involves a self-selection of exposure corresponding to previous attitude."[33] The advances in theories of mass communication may be characterized as a progressive modification of the image of anomic mass society by the increased recognition of a host of mediating factors intervening in the previously oversimplified stimulus-response link between communicator and audience member. While the trend in theory and research has been toward greater recognition of such influences, the trend in modern society at the same time apparently has been toward the weakening of the actual influence of these intervening social variables. Society has been moving closer to being the way we once thought it was, while we have been abandoning that once inappropriate image of it.

In the United States in recent decades there has been growth of structural differentiation and increasing cultural uniformity. In this or any other country undergoing rapid social change, the characteristics of mass society can be found to some degree.[34] Blumer's and Wirth's classic statements of those characteristics may have exaggerated the extent to which they applied to American society at the time they were written, but forces have been at work tending to detach people from their local cultures and weaken local group affiliations. People have been thrust into a new and broader world by migration and by exposure to mass media. They have had to adjust to this changed world somewhat independently of traditional values. So Blumer was not really wrong in saying that "Under conditions of modern urban and industrial life, mass behavior has emerged in increasing magnitude and importance."[35] The trend has been extended since he wrote about it.

According to Wirth, urbanites characteristically (he did not say always) interact with one another in terms of segmentalized roles. City life is characterized by depersonalized or secondary group contacts, rather than primary group contacts. There are, to be sure, face-to-face encounters, but these commonly are segmental and impersonal. Urbanites accordingly develop a reserve and indifference toward one another which serve as immunization against personal claims and expectations of others.[36] A single ride on a New York subway will show what he meant, and the so-called "rediscovery of primary groups" by sociologists does not invalidate his statements. Certainly there are primary groups in large cities; but they embrace a lesser proportion of the human interactions occurring in urban than in preurban societies.

Blumer said the mass "consists of an aggregation of individuals who are separate, detached, anonymous, and thus, homogeneous as far as mass behavior is concerned. . .the individual in the mass. . .acts in response to the object that has gained his attention and on the basis of the impulses that are aroused by it."[37] Sociologists recognize today that this description fits society less well than they once thought it did, but that recognition is not inconsistent with the contention that it fits more closely today than it did when it was more naively accepted.

Larsen has defined mass communication in general terms as "the relatively simultaneous exposure of a large, scattered, and heterogeneous audience to stimuli transmitted by impersonal means from an organized source for whom the audience members are anonymous."[38] Normally the devices we refer to as mass media do indeed reach a large, scattered, and heterogeneous audience roughly simultaneously, and the research on intervening psychological or social variables does not refute this. The means of transmission are impersonal, and audience members are usually anonymous to the communicator, if not to each other. That is all the definition specifies, so all the research on group affiliations as mediators of communications and all the theorizing about audience use of media content in no way turn mass communication into something that would have to be called by another name.

Mass media audience members may not be anonymous to all other members of the audience, but they are anonymous to *most* others, as well as to the communicator. This is what influences the nature of the communication. They are socially involved in a direct way with only a very small fraction of the total audience. Therefore, assertions that the collective behavior concept of the "mass" is inapplicable to mass media audiences are as serious overstatements as are the earlier views these statements were intended to counter.

If television, and to a lesser extent other media, serve some people as substitutes for primary interaction, these people are thereby made less available to others as primary group associates. The need to turn to mass media for substitute primary group experiences is thereby increased. The detachment of people from intimate relationships which Blumer associated with mass behavior and the reserved and indifferent attitude toward others which Wirth associated with urbanism need not be assumed to exist before effects can be attributed to the mass media. The mass media, when they have become as omnipresent as they are in the lives of Americans, can foster detachment, reserve, and indifference.

The concept of the mass is naturally associated with the concept of urbanism. Cities are, sociologically speaking, relatively large, dense, and permanent settlements of socially heterogeneous people. The characteristics of the urban way of life become more pronounced the larger, the denser, and the more heterogeneous the city happens to be.[39] Most of our cities have been growing, and a growing fraction of our population have become city dwellers. Modern cities have as their economic base, as Wirth noted, the concentrative force of mechanized industry. Factories mass produce for impersonal markets. This leads to product standardization, which, together with the essential anonymity of customers in relation to producers, further results in a largely pecuniary social nexus. Products and services are purchasable by persons who possess the requisite dollars, whatever may be their other characteristics.[40] Thus, as a result of the continued intensification of urbanism and industrialism, our occupationally, ethnically, and culturally heterogeneous population has acquired a good deal of the psychological lowest-common-denominator kind of homogeneity that was presupposed by the hypodermic model of mass communications.

To understand what continued urbanization means for the impact the mass media may have in our lives, it is important to spell out the conditions that would be required for mass communication to "be effective." After reviewing four examples of explicit mass media attempts to influence audience behavior—Kate Smith's marathon bond-selling broadcasts in World War II, a 1947 radio effort to curb juvenile delinquency ("The Eagle's Brood"), a New York TV station's effort to mobilize civilian defense workers, and the televised hearings of the Kefauver Committee—Wiebe asked whether radio and television can sell social objectives as they sell soap? The answer ventured was this: "Given a reasonable amount of receptivity among audience members, radio or television programs can produce forceful motivation. The sponsor of the social objective must tell us to what social mechanism the motivation is to be directed. He must see to the existence, adequacy and compatibility of the mechanism and he must consider the distance of audience members from this mechanism in formulating his expectations of results."[41] Then Wiebe, who was Research Psychologist for CBS Radio, added: "To the extent that he finds these factors in good order, he is in a situation comparable to that of a commercial sponsor, and he can reasonably expect results comparable with those of a commercial sponsor."[42] It is of course assumed that commercial sponsors do sell their products as a result of their advertising efforts.

Advertising on radio or television is intended to accomplish limited objectives. Given smokers in the audience and cigarettes in the stores, cigarette commercials merely seek to bring the two together. The intent is to cause the potential customer to take whatever steps separate him from actually making the purchase. In principle, such effects should be expected to occur even in cases where there was no intent to produce them. A Camel commercial may help sell Marlboros, and vice versa, simply by arousing the viewer's urge to smoke (whatever may be his brand preference). In the same manner, televised violence should be expected to arouse violent behavior in viewers with violent habits who may be harboring a grudge and who happen to have accessible targets.

Opportunities for the inadvertent "advertising" of violence to succeed are increasing. As our cities have grown, certain areas in them have visibly deteriorated. Other parts of them have changed in ways which may not represent deterioration, but which cause regrets, in people with value-commitments to previous conditions. Many of the newer residents of urban areas have not reaped the rewards anticipated. The very presence of some may be resented by persons who were there before them, who react to their social differences ethnocentrically, and who see their intrusion into the area as a threat. These people are variously experiencing an accelerated pace of living which has led some sociologists to expect that adaptations to new situations are likely to be made increasingly violently. Change is coming at unprecedented speed and tradition and custom hardly prevail as constraints on human behavior. People are now living in megalopolis without benefit of previous personal or ancestral familiarity with this kind of environment. It is a new kind of world.[43]

Thus, our cities contain increasing numbers of people with violent attitudes and habits, smouldering grievances, and easy access to targets of hostility. To televise violence into such an audience without expecting to arouse violent behavior seems sharply inconsistent with the belief that broadcasting cigarette commercials to an audience that includes smokers can increase sales.

Consider the simple fact that in forty years the percentage of the U.S. Negro population which lives in urban areas has more than doubled.[44] In just twenty years, the percentage of Southern-born non-whites residing outside the South has almost doubled.[45] These two facts point to an increasing abundance of contacts between persons who are more or less strangers to each other—the prior residents of a city and the recent immigrants—who are products of somewhat unlike subcultures, and who have a color difference that can visibly symbolize both their cultural differences and their social distance. In many of these encounters, both parties must be expected to harbor a sense of frustration, for various reasons. An increasing proportion of such contacts take place in large metropolitan environments, where, for all the reasons cited previously, informal means of norm-enforcement are attenuated. In the face of these circumstances it takes some strong and questionable assumptions to support the supposition that televised violence will not produce violent behavior.

Apologists for the television industry are fond of asserting that fictional violence on the screen will not cause normal children in happy families and stable communities to behave violently. But today they can hardly avoid knowing that there are a good many children (and adults) whose sociopsychological normality is dubious, whose family life is less than happy, and who are living in communities that are far from stable. There is ample reason for concern about the probable behavioral impact of broadcasting to audiences of this sort such programs as *Mannix, Rat Patrol, High Chaparral, Mod Squad,* or *N.Y.P.D.,* just to mention a few.

As Wilensky points out, mass media may have considerable effect under conditions of rapid social change because this condition includes persons without the usual cultural and social anchorages. When norms are in flux, mass media may reach their audiences more directly than usual, unfiltered by the intervening variables sociologists and others have so laboriously discovered.[46] Crisis—social, economic, or political—puts extra burdens on mass media.[47] Crisis conditions can also open the way for mass media impacts that would be restrained by non-critical circumstances.

Even if crises were unknown and social change always occurred at a snail's pace, the possibly cumulative effects of mass media would require attention. If a single act of violence on a single television drama could be shown to cause no discernible behavioral response, this would not demonstrate that a continuous exposure to such stimuli over long periods will not affect behavior or values in profound ways. Moreover, if many audience members are exposed to the same stimuli repeatedly, and are also recurrently exposed to each other, a sort of "multiplier effect" is possible. Distorted images of the real world that are obtained from the fantasy world of television are less likely to be set straight by interaction of real human groups if all the members of these groups have also been absorbing the same distorted images. Just as people sometimes have the impression they "confirmed" a rumor when they hear it from a second or a third source, the very abundance of mass communications, and the universality of the population's exposure to television in particular, tend to foster the illusion of "consensual validation" of whatever values are thus absorbed.

To sum up, research has shown that mass media do not easily and inevitably produce intended effects. To say that intended effects do not automatically occur is not to say, however, that unintended effects automatically do not occur. Yet the apologists for the media, and some of the social scientists who have been unduly impressed with exceptions to the mass society concept, have left this distinction unstated. Serious investigation is needed now to determine what long-range unintended consequences will occur from the way we have organized our lives around the mass media, and especially around that simulator of primary groups, television.

REFERENCES

1. Louis Wirth, "Urbanism as a Way of Life," *American Journal of Sociology,* 44 (July 1938), pp. 20-21.
2. *Ibid.,* p. 1.
3. *Ibid.,* p. 23.
4. Richard T. LaPiere   *A Theory of Social Control* (New York: McGraw-Hill, 1954), pp. 3-24.
5. Melvin L. DeFleur, *Theories of Mass Communication* (New York: David McKay, 1966), p. 111.
6. *Ibid.,* pp. 109-110.
7. *Ibid.,* p. 114.
8. *Ibid.,* p. 115.
9. *Ibid.,* p. 127.

10. *Ibid.,* p. 122.
11. Paul F. Lazarsfeld, Bernard Berelson, and Hazel Gaudet, *The People's Choice* (New York: Columbia University Press, 1948); Elihu Katz and Paul F. Lazarsfeld, *Personal Influence* (Glencoe, Ill.: The Free Press, 1954); Elihu Katz, "The Two-Step Flow of Communication: An Up-to-Date Report on an Hypothesis," *Public Opinion Quarterly,* 21 (Spring, 1957), pp. 61-78.
12. Eliot Friedson, "Communications Research and the Concept of the Mass," *American Sociological Review,* 18 (1953), pp. 313-317.
13. LaPiere, *op. cit.* note 4, pp. 518-522.
14. Defleur, *op. cit.* note 5, pp. 6-7.
15. *Ibid.,* p. 36.
16. Wilbur Schramm, Jack Lyle, and Edwin B. Parker, *Television in the Lives of Our Children* (Stanford, Calif.: Stanford Univ. Press, 1961), p. 169.
17. *Ibid.,* pp. 159-160.
18. Robert Lewis Shayon, *Television and Our Children* (New York: Longmans, Green, 1951), pp. 26-29.
19. Schramm, Lyle, and Parker, *op. cit.* note 16, p. 145.
20. *Ibid.,* pp. 105-109.
21. Joseph T. Klapper, *The Effects of Mass Communication* (Glencoe, Ill.: The Free Press, 1960), p. 8.
22. *Ibid.,* pp. 49-51.
23. *Ibid.,* p. 60.
24. *Ibid.,* pp. 94-97.
25. *Ibid.,* p. 129.
26. *Ibid.,* Ch. VI.
27. Harold D. Lasswell, "The Structure and Function of Communication in Society," in Lyman Bryson (ed.), *The Communication of Ideas* (New York: Harper & Bros., 1948), pp. 37-51.
28. See Douglas Waples, Bernard Berelson, and Franklyn R. Bradshaw, *What Reading Does to People* (Chicago: Univ. of Chicago Press, 1940), pp. 123-124.
29. Cf. Schramm, Lyle, and Parker, *op. cit.* note 16, p. 175.
30. Albert Bandura, "What TV Violence Can Do to Your Child," reprinted from *Look,* Oct. 22, 1963, pp. 46-52 in Otto N. Larsen (ed.), *Violence and the Mass Media* (New York: Harper & Row, 1968), p. 124.
31. Albert Bandura and Richard H. Walters, *Social Learning and Personality Development* (New York: Holt, Rinehart & Winston, 1963), p. 41.
32. *Ibid.,* p. 39.
33. Harold L. Wilensky, "Mass Society and Mass Culture: Interdependence or Independence?" *American Sociological Review,* 29 (April 1964), p. 175.
34. *Ibid.,* pp. 177-179.
35. Herbert Blumer, "Elementary Collective Groupings," Ch. 21 in Alfred M. Lee (ed.), *New Outline of the Principles of Sociology* (New York: Barnes & Noble, 1946), p. 187.
36. Wirth, *op. cit.* note 1, p. 12.
37. Blumer, *op. cit.* note 35, pp. 186-187.
38. Larson, *op. cit.* note 30, p. 6.
39. Wirth, *op. cit.* note 1, pp. 8-9.
40. *Ibid.,* p. 17.
41. G. D. Wiebe, "Merchandising Commodities and Citizenship on Television," *Public Opinion Quarterly,* 15 (Winter, 1951), p. 691.
42. *Ibid.*
43. Roy G. Francis, "Problems of Tomorrow," *Social Problems,* 12 (1965), p. 331.
44. C. Horace Hamilton, "The Negro Leaves the South," *Demography,* 1 (1964), p. 277.
45. *Ibid.,* p. 281.
46. Harold L. Wilensky, "Social Structure, Popular Culture, and Mass Behavior: Some Research Implications," *Studies in Public Communication,* 3 (1961), pp. 15-22.
47. Waples, Berelson, and Bradshaw, *op. cit.* note 28, p. 3.

Chapter 12

THE EFFECTS OF MEDIA VIOLENCE
ON SOCIAL LEARNING*

A. The Media, the Senses, and Information Transmission

The media differ in the senses to which they appeal and in the amount of training that is necessary before they can be used. Thus, personal oral communication is perhaps the primary human medium of communication. It appeals to audition and secondarily to vision (lip reading), and the training needed to understand it is given universally to all children in the early years of life.

Graphic communication appeals to vision. Since it is directly representational, little training is needed for understanding. (Research findings about blind people who are given vision surgically after childhood reveal that these individuals are unable to grasp the meaning of graphic representations. Because of this we know that some training is necessary for a child to be able to decode such representations.)

Written communication also appeals to vision, and extensive training is needed for comprehension. As is noted above, that training has in the past been offered to only selected human beings. Moreover, the production of written communications has in times past been a slow process. Until the invention of printing, a written communication could be reproduced only by a human copier. In the medieval period, many individuals devoted their lifetimes to copying texts. With the invention of printing, mass production of printed texts became possible, and thereafter the written (printed) word became increasingly important in human affairs. Still, the impact of printing as a mass medium of communication was limited by a technology in which paper was rare, binding was done by hand, and distribution of printed materials was slow and inefficient. It took centuries for our society to develop the means to benefit from the invention of printing, and only by the late nineteenth and early twentieth centuries did we have the technology to support this invention—the ability to produce paper, to produce printing machines, to distribute printed paper rapidly and widely, etc. Only then did we have a mass base of consumers able to benefit from this technology—people who could read and understand the printed word. Thus

* Excerpt from a larger paper prepared for the Media Task Force by Alberta Engvall Siegel, Associate Professor of Psychology in Psychiatry, Stanford University.

261

the printed word became increasingly important to mass culture.

The twentieth century has witnessed the invention and promulgation of several new modes of communication. One of these, the telephone, appeals exclusively to audition. Communication is entirely by hearing, and in fact even the audio fidelity of the telephone is grossly limited. The special appeal of this mode is that it enables contact between individuals who are not within hailing distance of each other. The telephone is an extension of the ear, and thus of the voice. Very little training appears to be needed for its use, although there are folk tales about adult immigrants to America who could never learn to use the telephone effectively, who never got over the habit of shouting into the receiver, and who were perplexed by the babble in the receiver. Infants are fascinated by telephones, and young children go through a period when they appear to understand the speech that they hear through the phone receiver but do not respond to it. (Every doting parent has had the experience of telling his two-year-old to "say hello to grandma" and of then standing by with growing exasperation watching his child listen mutely to grandmother's voice saying "hello, Danny," and "are you there, Danny?") By age three or four, the child is able to carry on the give and take of a telephone conversation, and as soon as he understands numbers he is able to dial the phone to get his intended party. (The ability to dial comes much earlier, and in these days of direct dialing many of us have had the experience of answering the phone's ring to find ourselves chatting haltingly with an adventuresome three-year-old in another state.) The school-age child is an accomplished telephone user, and by adolescence the telephone seems to be the preferred mode of social interaction.

Radio is another modern medium that appeals exclusively to audition. In contrast to the telephone, it is a one-way rather than a two-way system, putting the communications receiver in a totally passive role. (The recent renaissance of radio has occurred in part because of "call-in" techniques which remove the listener from that passivity and use the telephone to transform radio into a two-way communications system.) Radio contrasts with the telephone also in fidelity. It is capable of transmitting a very wide range of sounds, and may be used for music as well as for human speech. Little or no training is needed to enable an individual to comprehend radio communication, and very little is required to acquire the skill of turning it on and tuning it in. Children are able to receive radio communication as soon as they are able to attend to sounds, and many mothers find that their young infants are soothed by music from radio or by an announcer's mellifluous tones. Children are able to understand spoken communications by radio almost as soon as they can understand face-to-face speech; there is some lag, because in face-to-face speech the spoken word is augmented by detailed non-verbal communications which reinforce it. The child "gets the message" not only from the words but also from the speaker's facial expression, body position, etc. These modalities are absent from radio, and for this reason radio is less effective in communicating with the very young child. By age three or four, however, children are "tuned in" to radio, and in years past it was a preferred communications medium for many school-age children. Just as their mothers listened to the soap operas during the morning and early afternoon hours, school-age children listened to their serials during the late afternoon and early evening hours.

Comic books are a form of visual communication, although they have esthetic appeal through touch and smell as well—most adults are able to remember how the books felt and how they smelled as well as what they looked like. Their central device is redundancy between the verbal message and the accompanying graphic message, which is typically vivid and simple. The books hold some appeal for children who cannot read at all, an indication of how much is communicated directly by the pictures. Their central appeal is to the partly-literate reader, child or adult, and for this reason the comic book format has been widely imitated—in manuals to train hard-core unemployed workers, in appeals to voters in underprivileged communities, etc. In contrast to the telephone and the radio, the comic book has almost no appeal to the infant and young child, and children become interested in this format only after they are relatively mature and sophisticated as communications-receivers (usually in their fifth year or later). Another contrast between the radio and the comic book is that the pacing of the former is outside the receiver's control; the radio listener cannot adjust the rate at which the announcer speaks. However, the comic book reader can control the pace at which the information on the page comes to him. Adults who watch children read comic books are struck by the children's absorption, their deliberateness in plodding from square to square, their turning back pages for rereading, and their return to the same comic book for another exposure on another day. Comic books offer these possibilities for a slow pace because they are permanent embodiments of the communication.

The wax recording was also a permanent embodiment, this time of an auditory rather than a visual message. Despite initial low fidelity, records won a wide audience, and they continue to be a popular form of mass communication. Like the comic book, they can be controlled by the consumer, and the child can play the same record over and over. Very young children can listen to records, but their access is controlled by the difficulties in playing them: the task of getting the needle into the groove is too difficult for a child until he is three or four years old. Special records for children have a wide audience among the young, and of course records for adolescents are the mainstay of the industry.

The film was a dramatic innovation in communication technology. Like the comic book and the record, and in contrast to the telephone and the radio, it involves the permanent embodiment of a message. Film provided a means of recording, preserving, and transmitting visual images which is infinitely more faithful to the source than any comic strip could be. Both rely on sequences of still graphics, but the film sequence is so rapid that it creates the illusion of movement and of temporal continuity. The silent film appealed exclusively to vision, but did so in a way which has much greater impact than that of the earlier visual media—print, graphics, and the print-graphics combination we know as the comic book. This impact occurs because of the film's fidelity to its source and its minimal reliance on conventional symbolization. It occurs also because the film embodies motion, and the human visual system is especially tuned to the perception of motion. The audience for a silent film does not need to know how to read in order to enjoy the film, although that ability is necessary for understanding the subtitles. As with comics, the subtitles in a silent film are largely redundant. Children respond to and enjoy films from a very young age. Their access to films has been controlled by the economics of the motion picture industry, rather than by any constraints in their own sensory or intellectual endowment. The expense of owning and operating projection equipment, the need for a darkened room in which to show the film, and the expense of renting commercial films, have combined to keep movies in commercial theatres, with access blocked by an admissions booth collecting tolls. The importance of the box office in controlling access is attested to by the ingenuity of youngsters in dreaming up ways to circumvent it, and also by the fact that many American youngsters habitually spent all of their weekly allowances at that box office during the heyday of the movies.

The printed page became a mass medium of communication only when the system of education created a mass audience of readers. Thus books and newspapers represented the "first wave" of the mass media. The telephone stands apart from this history, differing from the other communications media in the particularity of both sender and receiver. Although there is mass ownership of telephones in the United States today, the telephone is not presently used for mass communication. Radio, comic books, records, and silent films were the "second wave" of modern communications media. They were techniques of communication that required little sophistication on the part of the receiver. Unlike books and newspapers, these media did not require reading ability of their audience. Each technique in this second wave was beamed to one sense modality—radio and records appealing to audition, and comic books and silent movies to vision.

The "talkie" was such a major innovation that it deserves to be thought of as "the third wave," a medium that provides an integrated appeal to eye and ear. The audience for a talking film needs no special training nor special skills; they need only the capacity for visual information-processing and for language-understanding or sound-decoding which is universally characteristic of the human species. By being a normal member of the human race, and by paying the price of admission, one is able to receive communication from sound motion pictures. Only the grossly handicapped—the deaf and the blind—are excluded from full participation. For the rest of us, the communication from sound films comes to us in the senses which are most acute and discriminating—seeing and hearing. The sound motion picture seemed to be "the ultimate" in mass communication, and it seemed so not only to the masters of hyperbole who were paid to advertise Hollywood. Some suggested adding scents to the stimuli in order to sensitize the audience olfactorily as well as visually and auditorily, but the "talkies" were so satisfactory that the proposal to replace them with "smellies" was never seriously considered. Refinements—wider screens, curved screens, three dimensions, color, and stereophonic sound—were but minor embellishments on the basic technique of reaching the viewer through eye and ear with a vivid and integrated message. Children were delighted by the talkies, usually preferring them to any other medium of communication. Even the youngest child could be held in rapt fascination by a movie, and the amount of information children learned effortlessly from films was prodigious. As with the silent films, limitations on children's use of movies were external to the child, created by the technology and economics of the movie—the need for a darkened room, expensive equipment, and money to rent the expensive film.

These limitations were bypassed by the next major innovation in mass communication, television. Like the movies, television beams simultaneous signals to both eye and ear. Unlike movies, TV does not require a darkened room, expensive equipment, or rental payments. In the American economy, the receiver is inexpensive and television programs are free. The child need not pay to enjoy television; his access is limited only by his ability to switch on the set, and most children can do that as soon as they can stand, i.e., by the end of their first year. Television also lends a sense of immediacy to the action, as opposed to the "canned" film one sees in movie theaters.* Differences between movies and television justify our calling the advent of television a separate wave in the development of mass communications.

Several trends are evident in the history of the development of techniques for transmitting information to the human senses. One trend is diminishing reliance on written symbolization. To enjoy a book, one had to be a skilled reader. To read a newspaper, less skill was required. Even less reading ability yet was needed for access to comic books and to silent films. And no reading ability at all is needed to be able to "get the message" from sound movies, radio, records, and TV.

A second trend is the integration of appeals to several senses. The early media reached one sense, but the newer media reach two senses simultaneously with an integrated message. The two senses which movies and television reach—vision and audition—are the most highly developed senses in man, those on which he relies most heavily for gaining useful information from his environment. Further, movies and television embody motion. In the deployment of attention, the human visual system is especially vigilant to movement.

A third trend is toward rapidity of communication. In the days when the only way to get information across distances was to send a courier with a hand-written document, information travelled slowly. The invention of printing signalled the development of more rapid means of communication, but generations passed before supporting technology developed sufficiently to use printing in the production of newspapers. Early newspapers appeared monthly or weekly, and dailies are a relatively recent innovation. Simultaneous transmission of information is achieved by the newer media—radio, telephone, and television—with only a split second elapsing between the occurrence of an event and its perception by the communications-receiver at a distant spot.

Fourth, there is a trend toward increasing availability of mass communications. Printed communications such as books and journals were in former times available only to an educated elite. Today such communications reach a mass readership. Newspapers are widely available. Radio has reached into almost every American home. Movie theaters exist in the remotest hamlet. Most Americans, even the poorest, own television sets and in many homes more than one set is in use.

Finally, there is a trend toward increased fidelity in communication techniques. The "fidelity" of a communication is the correspondence of the transmission to the event itself. Today's telephone is a much higher fidelity instrument than its predecessors, but the correspondence between the voice one hears over the telephone and the voice of that person when present is still

---

*With the advent of videotape, almost everything (except movies) on television appears to be "live," whether or not it actually is.

not exact. Radio has higher fidelity than the telephone, and today's radio is notably higher in fidelity than its ancestor, Similarly, phonograph records and tape recordings have improved in audio fidelity over the years. The color movie, like the color television, is more "hi-fi" than its black-and-white counterpart.

B. Fidelity, Vividness, Credibility, and Authenticity

Every member of a society must learn about that society, its values, and its habits. All children achieve this learning through trial and error, reward and punishment, observation, imitation, oral instruction, and attending to graphic representations. Children in literate societies such as ours also may learn about their society and its culture via the written word. To what extent are children likely to learn also from the even newer media—from radio, movies, and television? We have reviewed the characteristics of these media, showing how they reach different senses and how accessible they are to children. Now we consider how much is learned from these media.

"Fidelity" is an engineering concept, readily definable in terms of the correspondence between an event and its reproduction by a communications medium. The fidelity of a phonograph or a tape player may be of considerable importance to its owner. More interesting to the social scientist than a medium's fidelity is its credibility; he wonders how "credible," "believable," "compelling," or "authentic" the medium is.

The mass media have historically been used for two main purposes: to entertain and to inform, and every medium of communication has been used for both purposes. The book, for example, provides entertainment in the form of novels, poetry, albums of photographs, etc., and it provides information in the form of textbooks, encyclopedias, biographies and histories. Radio entertainment comes in the form of comedy skits, radio dramas, and the like, and information is distributed in news reports, bulletins about traffic conditions, weather reports, and interviews. Comic books have been used principally to entertain, but this format has also been adapted for political propaganda and in how-to-do-it manuals. Motion pictures provide entertainment in dramas, comedies, and musicals, but its informational capacity has been exploited in instructional films, documentaries, and news films. Television broadcasts both entertainment shows and informational presentations such as news reports, and the newspaper contains crossword puzzles, comic strips, horoscopes, and humor columns as well as informational news columns. Thus the distinction between entertaining and informing is not related to a particular medium—all the media perform both functions.

We all believe that presentations meant to inform should be authentic. A factual error in an encyclopedia is harmful to the reputation of that publication. A distortion of fact in the news columns of a newspaper can provide the basis for a libel suit and public demands for a retraction. A textbook is judged by the accuracy and completeness of the information it conveys to the student. A historian's account of a sequence of events is judged above all by its authenticity, and the notion of changing history to make it conform to ideology or political convenience is abhorrent to our tradition. A biography will draw sharp criticism, even ridicule, if it misspells the name of a principal, places his birth incorrectly, or misrepresents a date.

On the other hand, authenticity is not an issue when the object is entertainment. We do not criticize a comic strip about spacemen because the rockets portrayed move more quickly than any known propellant could power them. A soap opera is no less enjoyed because in reality no person could endure such an unending succession of reversals and still remain full of good cheer. A comedy skit may be improved, not debased, if a comedian wears outsize shoes, a ridiculous necktie, and a zany hat. We do not reject a children's story because it says that all the characters "lived happily ever after." Part of the creativity of fiction is the use of fantasy, imagination, and dramatic distortion.

In short, we do grant poetic license not only to the poet, but also to the novelist, the comic strip artist, the soap opera dramatist, the comedian, the children's fiction writer, and the television dramatist; we do not grant such license to the educator, news broadcaster, reporter, biographer, historian, or encyclopedist.

The distinctions between fact and fiction, news and entertainment, and reality and fantasy, are not new. They antedate all the media, including print. Sophisticated and literate adults find these distinctions both useful and easily discernible. They can be applied to each of the media—to the textbook in contrast with the novel, to the news broadcast as opposed to the war movie—but in making this distinction, we may be in danger of ignoring the authenticity or credibility inherent in that medium.

For the intellect of the child, and for the less sophisticated aspects of intellect which adults share with children, there may be another distinction which cuts across the familiar reality-fantasy distinction. Perhaps each medium of communication has its own intrinsic authenticity or credibility, and perhaps this feature lends itself to all the communications from that medium.

At the outset, it seems that this intrinsic authenticity is simply the fidelity and the vividness of the communication. We have already defined "fidelity" as the psychophysical correspondence between the communication and its source. The "vividness" of a communication is defined in terms of the senses to which it appeals. Since sight and hearing are the primary modes of information-processing in man, a medium which appeals to these senses is especially vivid. Thus, it is possible to present the symbols of our language through touch, as is done in Braille print. Obviously, this is especially useful to the blind person, but is unlikely to be chosen by anyone who has the option of receiving symbolic communication through vision. It would be possible for the average housewife to locate the vegetables she wishes to buy in the supermarket solely by smell, since each vegetable has a distinctive fragrance. Simply by relying on smell and touch she *could* choose the particular vegetables that correspond to her standards of freshness and crispness, but no normal housewife selects vegetables this way; it is much more efficient for her to rely on vision in locating the ware she wants. This is the sense in which a visual communication is especially vivid.

Media which appeal to more than one sense are more vivid than those reaching only one. We have already shown that talking movies and television are in a class by themselves as effective media because of their vividness as here defined.

A medium's intrinsic authenticity is a joint function of its vividness and fidelity. Both print and film appeal solely to vision, but film has more intrinsic authenticity because its fidelity is higher. Similarly, although black-and-white and color film appeal solely to vision, color film is more authentic because its fidelity is higher. If a communication technique is both vivid and of high fidelity, as is the color film or the color television image (high fidelity representations reaching the two most important senses), its intrinsic authenticity is especially high.

Certain media lend an air of veracity to any message presented. Because of the characteristics of the medium, the presentation comes across as authentic. We may "know better," but still there is part of us that gullibly accepts the vivid evidence of our senses. The psychologist might apply the term "face validity" to describe the intrinsic authenticity of a television presentation. The vividness and fidelity of a presentation provide an implicit internal validation of its content.

Every moviegoer has had the discomfiting experience of being unable to enjoy a musical precisely because the film does not come across as fantasy. This makes it difficult to accept the "unreal" actions of the characters in a musical, who break into song while embracing or tap dance down a factory assembly line. The success of animated cartoons in portraying fantasy, on the other hand, rests precisely on the fact that they circumvent the inherent authenticity of photography.

When movies and TV are used to report and inform, their inherent authenticity works to impress the news on the viewer in a forceful and compelling way. Most observers of the contemporary American social scene are struck by the significant effect television news reporting has on the public's involvement in political issues, understanding of current affairs, and preferences among public figures. Through television coverage of a national catastrophe and its aftermath, the tragic assassination of our President in 1963, a single mood of shared grief and mourning was sustained throughout the entire country.

A newspaper reporter made a typical comment on the impact of television news reporting in his account of the 1968 presidential election contest in rural Iowa. He noted that the farmers whom he interviewed seemed less preoccupied with political issues immediately affecting their livelihood and their communities than with those they had learned about through television and the other mass media:

Other issues have become so overriding as to obscure the farmer's problems, even in his own mind. Through some miracle of modern communication and repetition, the farmer lives in rural solitude and dwells upon crime-filled city streets, fiery demonstrations, bloody riots, bearded campus protestors, the frustrating war in Vietnam. And all indications are that those are the images that will fill the farmer's mind when he walks into the voting booth November 5.[1]

Today, the commonplace observation that television news reporting influences people's concepts of reality and thus their behavior is being supplemented by the feeling that dramatic shows may have the same effect. The same television set that brings news into the living room is also bringing realistic dramatic presentations. Russell Baker, commenting on the nation's response to the assassination of Senator Robert F. Kennedy, noted the mixed emotions evoked by the fact that information about this event came to the viewer on the same set that purveys entertainment and sports:

> "Gradually, grouped together around the social center of the TV screen with its humdrum evocation of the shared boredom of idle evenings and endless Sunday afternoons, we struggle to suppress the horror.[2]"

Perhaps the fact that news and entertainment appear through the same medium is helping to blur the distinction between fact and fantasy. This was suggested by Clive Barnes when he remarked that the author of a Broadway play is—"against the moral blindness that permits million of people to treat [the war in Vietnam] as a kind of spectator sport to be watched on TV until we are no longer completely sure whether we are seeing our sons and brothers being killed on a newsreel or a few Hollywood actors biting the dust on the Late Late Show.[3]

We must consider the possibility that the inherent authenticity which characterizes television leds credibility to fictional presentations. George Willey has raised his own doubts about the distinction between reality and the producers' make-believe: "The growing concern is that what they make, many believe."[4] He argues that the problem with violence in the mass media is not that it is emotionally upsetting or aesthetically displeasing, but that it is accepted as a representation of the way things really are. In one column, he reviewed the difficulty which producers have encountered in attempting to edit violence from programs already in production. His example is a producer who cut out some of the gorier aspects of a violent scene—a lady sniper fires a rifle at a young man driving through Black Rock Town—"What will not be seen . . . is a part of the same sequence which had been filmed in the original version: a close-up shot of the windshield shattering and the young man, face bleeding, collapsing over the steering sheel. This of course, is missing the point altogether. The objection to violence is not directed so much to the effect of violence but to the constant use of violence and the implicit suggestion that it should be anticipated wherever one goes."[5]

This account shows one response to the assassination of Senator Kennedy, an effort by the television and advertising industries to cut down on the amount of violence beamed over the airways. Other comments on that effort also touched on the blurred distinction between reality and fantasy. For example, a newspaper column related that the Association of National Advertisers was urging its members to select television scripts that avoid excessive or unnecessary violence. The column concluded by stating: "Yesterday an agency media guy made a valid point about television violence. 'What do you do about the news programs?' he asked."[6]

The same intution was the basis for a column that appeared after the Democratic Convention in Chicago in August, 1968:

Has the campaign against violence in TV programs, which started after the killing of Dr. Martin Luther King, Jr., and Sen. Robert F. Kennedy, suffered a setback as a result of the riots attending the Democratic National Convention?

All three networks have been seriously examining ways of diminishing violence in dramatic entertainment and in children's cartoons partly as a result of the widespread belief that television's example can influence the impressionable for good or evil. But the way network spokesmen look at it at the moment there isn't much point in cutting out the shooting in a Western or the pistol-whipping in an underworld drama if the viewer can switch to a news program and see citizens and the police locked in a bloody real life no-holds-barred conflict. No network would have dared stage in make-believe anything as violent as the battle in Chicago.[7]

The argument imputed to the network spokesmen makes sense only if one lumps together both fiction and news presentations in evaluating their effects on behavior.

No doubt the cues as to a communication's authenticity are important. A television presentation identified on the screen as "news," and discussed by someone called a "newsman," provides internal cues that its pictures of mayhem and destruction are to be understood differently from similar photographs identified as "drama."

The comfortable and well-understood old distinction between truth and fiction is blurred by a medium that presents truth and drama alternately, in the same frame, with the same sharp fidelity, and with the vividness that only a medium appealing to eye and ear simultaneously can invoke.

C. Media Content and Social Learning

Is social behavior affected by the media? Do children who have grown up on a steady diet of television behave differently than they would if it did not exist?

These questions lie at the heart of our current concern about the media and violence. Serious and disinterested observers differ as to how to frame the best answer on the basis of our present knowledge. Observers with a stake in the media capitalize on our ignorance to reassure one another that the *status quo* will hold.

Behavior is guided by belief. People act in a context of convictions about the meaning of their acts, what acts are appropriate in particular settings, and what responses may be expected from others. Action emerges from beliefs about the world and how one should respond to it.

Human social behavior is learned. Much of this process occurs through trial and error, especially in the earliest years of life. It does not seem likely that television and other non-interactive media play a great role in such learning, since they cannot provide differentiated "feedback" to an individual. Whether an infant is crying or quiet, awake or asleep, hungry or full, walking or sitting, behaving well or mischievously, the television drones on and on, uninfluenced by the infant's behavior. Such an unresponsive communications system does not enter into trial and error learning.

A great deal of human social behavior is also learned through observation and imitation. As the years pass, children acquire the ability to model their behavior after certain others, and this ability seems to be independent of rewards and punishments. To explain a child's behavior, we inquire about the observational learning opportunities which have been available to him—"Where in the world did he learn to do *that*?" We know that children watch television. Do they also imitate what they observe there? The inherent authenticity of television and movies makes it easy to believe that they do. Children understand such presentations as authentic and credible, and assume that the world is really the way it appears there. It is natural for them to take the behavior they observe on television as a model for their own. An amusing illustration of this comes from Britain:

> Presenting a resolution urging the Government to consider a code of conduct to guide people responsible for selecting television programs, Fred Armstrong [a member of the Rural District Councils Association, speaking at its annual conference] said that during one half-hour program the word "bloody" had been used 30 to 40 times.
>
> Was it surprising, he asked, when a 6-year-old boy told a woman in a shop she was a "bloody silly old moo" because his favorite candy was sold out?[8]

Although Americans might differ with this Briton as to the seriousness of the behavior he described, most would agree with him that the child's use of the proscribed word "bloody" probably resulted from his watching shows in which it was used by characters he subsequently imitated. At the other extreme is another account of imitative behavior in Britain, this time about a 12-year-old boy who was found dead at his home in Leicester, in the English Midlands:

> Television chiefs issued a warning to millions of youngsters today after an inquest on a boy who died while imitating his masked and cloaked hero, "Batman"...His father...told the inquest yesterday he thought his son, hanged while wearing a homemade Batman-style outfit, had been leaping from a cabinet in the garden shed when his neck caught in a nylon loop hanging from the roof. The inquest verdict was misadventure.
>
> After the inquest [the father] said that he hoped the Batman show would be taken off British television. "It is far too dramatic and hair-raising," he said. "It encourages children to attempt the impossible." A television company spokesman said:
>
> "We regret that the death of Charles Lee should be attributed to his viewing of Batman. Young viewers are cautioned that they should make no attempt to imitate Batman's activities.
>
> "Before each episode young viewers are reminded that Batman does not in fact fly and that all of his exploits are accomplished by means of his secret equipment."[9]

What are we to think of this event? In what sense is television "responsible" for this child's violent death? Is this twelve-year-old's imitative behavior in the same category as the six-year-old's remarks about "a bloody silly old moo"?

Adult behavior, as well as children's, may be imitative. On December 13, 1966, the National Broadcasting Company presented a filmed drama entitled "The Doomsday Flight."

> The plot of the film centered on the placement of a bomb on a transcontinental airliner...The plane emerged safely because it landed at an altitude above that at which the bomb was triggered to go off. The supposed suspense lay in tracing the deranged man who kept teasing officials with information on his deadly act.[10]

While the film was still on the air, a bomb threat (which turned out to be a hoax) was telephoned to one U.S. airline. Within twenty-four hours of the show, four more had been phoned in. Within the week following the show, eight such hoax calls in all were received by various U.S. airlines, including American, TWA, Eastern, Pan-American, and Northwest.[11] These eight bomb threats in one week equaled the number of such calls that had been received in the entire previous month, according to the Federal Aviation Agency.[12]

Before the film was shown, the Air Lines Pilots Association had urged NBC to keep the program off the air in the interest of air safety. They advised NBC that experience had shown that "the mentally unstable are highly responsive to, and easily provoked by, suggestion."[13] The pilots indicated that they feared the program could cause an irrational person to commit an act of sabotage. Telegrams were sent by the president of the pilots' association to the author of the script, to an NBC vice president, to the West Coast publicity director for NBC, and to the producer of the film at a Hollywood studio.[14] When no response was received, another representative of the pilots' association telephoned another NBC vice president in a further attempt to convince the network to call off the program.

These efforts proved unsuccessful. The film was shown and the feared rash of bomb hoaxes did ensue. Fortunately, there is no record that a bomb was in fact placed on any plane. Unfortunately, we have no information on the identities of the individuals who translated screen behavior into acts in their own lives. We do not know their ages, their social histories, nor whether they were "disturbed," "unstable," or "impulsive." Probably some of them were. Many such individuals do exist in our society, and in our concern for the effects of television, we must consider them as well as the "balanced," "stable," and "restrained" persons for whom such a ready translation from drama to reality may be unthinkable.

For many years, black citizens have objected to the stereotyped representations of Negroes in the mass media. They have resented the fact that blacks were almost always portrayed in subordinate and menial roles, such as servants, shoeshine boys, fieldhands, and ne'er-do-wells. They have felt that these condesending and two-dimensional portrayals would influence the way Americans felt about black people, even the way black Americans would feel about themselves. This argument rests on the assumption that people "accept" and "believe" the fictional representations in the media. The depth of the objections of black citizens lends seriousness to this assumption. It has not been sufficient to reply, "but it's only a story" or, "that's only fantasy." Even the media men themselves have finally accepted the validity of this argument, and serious efforts are now being made to portray blacks in dignified and admirable roles, to represent in the media the true variety of the human condition among black as well as white Americans. They have taken seriously the notion that for some Americans the media constitute their only acquaintance with blacks, and that therefore it is important for the media portrayals to be fair and realistic. Should we take seriously the notion that for some Americans the media constitute their principal acquaintance with violence and aggression, and that they learn about these phenomena and how to deal with them solely through the media?

Several research studies have addressed this question. One examined the influence of violence in the mass media upon children's role expectations.[15]

An effort was made to study young children's impressions of a taxi driver—a role chosen because taxi drivers are not widely sterotyped in our society. One group of second graders heard a series of radio dramas about taxi drivers. In each "thrilling episode," the taxi driver got into trouble with another person and extricated himself by being violently aggressive against the other person. A second group of children in the same grade heard a series which differed from the other only in the endings. In this series, the endings were not violent—instead, the taxi driver found a constructive way to resolve the problem.

To determine whether the children's reality conceptions had been influenced by these fictional presentations, the researcher gave each child a newspaper test. The child was shown a copy of the local newspaper and was asked to explain what a newspaper is. Only those who understood that a newspaper reports reality were in the final analysis. The individual who showed the newspaper to the child had not been involved in the earlier playing of the dramas on radio, nor did she acknowledge any acquaintance with them. She asked the child to tell her how certain newspaper stories ended. The first stories presented to the child concerned current local news—the current weather, the fact that Lincoln's Birthday was approaching and that it would be a school holiday. Then the child was read stories about local taxi drivers, and asked to finish the story. One of these stories related an episode very similar to one the children had heard enacted on the radio. The children who had heard the violent endings to the radio drama gave very different responses to this newspaper story than did those who had heard the non-violent series. The responses were categorized according to whether the child attributed high, intermediate, or low aggression to the taxi driver in completing the newspaper account. In this Pennsylvania community, taxi drivers are helpful and friendly, so it is not surprising that the children who had heard the non-violent radio dramas tended to finish the news story in a way that attributed no aggression (two-thirds of the cases) or only intermediate aggression (in the other one-third) to the taxi driver. The children who had heard the violent series, on the other hand, apparently thought that taxi drivers in their own town would behave the same way as the fictional ones, for half of them finished the news account in a way that attributed "high" aggression to the local taxi driver, and only one-third attributed no aggression.

This small study would need to be duplicated with various children, roles, and media before we could generalize from its findings. In the meantime, it warns us that the distinction between reality and fantasy may be blurred for normal young children.

A striking series of studies by Professor Albert Bandura and his colleagues at Stanford University has demonstrated that children learn aggressive behavior from television and that they enact this behavior in their play under suitable circumstances. In earlier studies, Bandura had already shown that children will imitate the specifics of aggressive behavior they observe in an adult.[16] He and his colleagues then conducted a study to determine whether children will imitate aggression they observe in a film as readily as they will imitate aggression they observe performed by adults.[17]

The study included ninety-six nursery school children, ranging in age from less than three to nearly six, with an average age of four and one-half. He assigned the children arbitrarily to four categories. A child in the first category, the "Real-Life Aggressive condition," was brought to a room and given some materials to play with at a small table. After the child settled down to play, an adult in another part of the room began playing with several toys, including a mallet and a five-foot inflated plastic Bobo doll. The adult was aggressive toward the Bobo doll in highly novel and distinctive ways, and performed each of these aggressive acts—like pummeling the Bobo on its head with a mallet—several times in the course of the session. The child, of course, observed this aggressive adult behavior occurring in his presence. A child in the second category was brought to the same playroom, set to playing with the same toys, and then shown a color film on which the same adult model displayed the same sequence of novel aggressive behaviors to a Bobo doll. This was called the "Human Film-Aggression condition." A child in the third category was shown a cartoon film showing an adult costumed as a cat, playing against a fantasyland backdrop of brightly colored trees, butterflies, etc. On this film, the cat was similarly aggressive towards the Bobo doll. Finally, children in the fourth category were reserved as a comparison group, with no exposure to aggressive models in the course of the study.

Immediately after the experience described above, the child was taken to an anteroom containing a variety of highly attractive toys. The experimenter told him he might play with them, but once he had begun, the experimenter purposely frustrated the child by saying she had decided to reserve the toys for some other children. She indicated that instead he could play with some toys in another room. They went to that room, where the adult busied herself with paperwork at a desk, while the child played with the toys. These included toys typically used in aggressive play and others associated with unaggressive activities. Among them was a Bobo doll and a mallet. The child played for twenty minutes, while his behavior was observed and scored by judges watching through a one-way mirror from an adjoining room.

The main finding of this study was that children who had observed adult aggression prior to being frustrated were more aggressive in their subsequent play than those who had been frustrated, but had not observed any adult aggression. The average total aggression score for the control children was 54, while the average was 83 for children in the "Real-Life Aggressive" category, 92 for those in the "Human Film-Aggressive" category, and 99 for those in the "Cartoon Film-Aggressive" category.

The second finding was that the aggression of the children who had observed adult models would be imitative. The child's behavior during the play session was rated as imitative, partially imitative, or non-imitative. An imitative act was one which directly copied the adult behavior the child had seen earlier, with the child exhibiting the very acts he had observed or speaking the very words the adult had spoken. In the "Real-Life" and "Human Film" categories, eighty-eight percent of the children exhibited varying degrees of imitative aggression, and in the "Cartoon Film" condition, seventy-nine percent did so. Not only were these children more aggressive as a whole, but, more significantly, the character of their aggressive behavior was closely modeled on the behavior they had observed in adults, whether live or on film. Scores for imitative aggression were significantly higher for the children who had observed models than for the control children, and the same was true for scores of partially imitative aggression. On the other hand, aggressive gunplay was displayed equally by the various groups. This is an example of aggressive behavior which had not been modeled by the adults in the experiment.

This study holds special interest not only because it demonstrates that children mimic the aggressive behavior of adults, whether they observe this behavior in the flesh or on film, but also because it demonstrates that the kind of film seen does not seem to affect the mimicking process significantly. The fantasy-reality distinction in which adults believe seems to have little significance for the bright middle-class pre-school children Bandura and his colleagues studied.

One reason that Bandura's work is so widely respected by other psychologists is that his conclusions do not rest on a single study. He has conducted a series of investigations over the years, using different children and different films. Each study adds to the strength of the conclusions we can draw.

A second study meriting close consideration here used nursery school children whose ages ranged from three to five years, with an average of just over four years.[18] They were assigned at random to different categories. A child in the first category was taken to a playroom where the adult experimenter worked at a desk while the child watched a five-minute film projected on a TV console. This film concerns two adult men, Rocky and Johnny. At the beginning, Johnny is playing with his highly attractive collection of toys. Rocky asks to play with some, and Johnny refuses. Rocky then behaves aggressively toward Johnny and his possessions, enacting a series of highly unusual and distinctive aggressive behaviors while making hostile remarks. (These unusual and distinctive acts of aggression were employed in this series of studies to enable observers to distinguish imitative acts of aggression in the child's subsequent play from other stereotyped acts common to the play of many children.) Rocky is the victor as the result of his aggressive behavior, and "the final scene shows Johnny seated dejectedly in the corner while Rocky is playing with the toys, serving himself generous helpings of 7-Up and cookies, and riding a large bouncing hobby horse with gusto. As the scene closes, Rocky packs the playthings in a sack and sings a merry tune."[19] A commentator announces that Rocky is the victor.

Another film was used which also involved aggression between Rocky and Johnny, but was rearranged in sequence so that the aggression behavior shown by Rocky results in his being severly punished. "Rocky is thoroughly thrashed by Johnny. As soon as he succeeds in freeing himself, Rocky flees to a corner of the room where he sits cowering, while Johnny places his toys in the sack and walks away. The announcer comments on Rocky's punishment."[20]

After viewing one of these films, the child was taken to a room for a twenty-minute play session which was observed and scored by judges behind a one-way vision screen. This room contained some toys similar to those in the film, and others as well—the latter being present to avoid loading the dice. The child's imitative aggressive acts and his nonimitative aggressive acts were recorded.

The total aggressive scores of the children in the "Aggressive Model-Rewarded" category were 75.2, which is significantly higher than the total for children in the "Aggressive Model-Punished" category (53.5). In contrast, children who had seen neither film but who simply were brought to the playroom for a twenty-minute play session had total aggression scores that were intermediate (61.8). Most of the aggression was not sufficiently close to that exhibited by Rocky and Johnny to be called imitative, but the imitative aggression that was observed occurred more commonly among the Model-Rewarded children than among the Model-Punished children, and both showed more imitative aggression than the controls, who had never observed the distinctive adult behaviors.

After the play session was over, a child was asked to evaluate the behavior exhibited by Rocky and Johnny, and to select the character he preferred to emulate. Among the children who had seen Rocky emerge the victor because of his aggressiveness, 60 percent preferred him, 5 percent preferred Johnny, and 35 percent voiced no preference. Among those who had seen Johnny triumph despite Rocky's aggressiveness, 20 percent preferred Johnny, 20 percent preferred Rocky, and 60 percent had no preference.

Almost without exception the children who said they preferred Rocky as a model were nonetheless critical of his behavior. They preferred him despite his infamy, siding with the winner: " 'Rocky is harsh, I be harsh like he was,' 'Rough and bossy,' 'Mean,'. . .'Rocky beat Johnny and chase him and get all the good toys.' 'He come and snatched Johnny's toys. Get a lot of toys' . . . 'He was a fighter. He got all good toys.' "[21] Bandura's comment on the meaning of this finding deserves to be quoted:

> The finding that successful villainy may outweigh the viewers' value systems has important implications for the possible impact of televised stimulation on children's attitudes and social behavior. The present experiment involves only a single episode of aggression that was rewarded or punished. In most televised programs the "bad guy" gains control over important resources and amasses considerable social and material rewards through a series of aggressive maneuvers, whereas his punishment is generally delayed until just before the last commercial. Thus children have opportunities to observe many episodes in which antisocially aggressive behavior has paid off abundantly and, considering that immediate rewards are much more influential than delayed punishment in regulating behavior, the terminal punishment of the villain may have a relatively weak inhibitory effect on the viewer.[22]

These two studies demonstrate that young children imitate the specific acts of aggression they have observed in the behavior of adults on film or television. This imitation occurs whether the dramatic presentation is realistic or fantasylike. Imitation is enhanced if the aggression brings rewards to the adult who is observed and minimized if the aggression brings punishment.

A third, more recent study by Bandura again confirms the finding on imitation. However, it is somewhat more ominous in its implications, for it shows that children acquire from watching television the capability of performing imitatively many more acts of aggression than they spontaneously exhibit—that children learn more from television than their spontaneous behavior reveals.

The sixty-six children who participated in this third study were again of nursery school age, averaging just over four years of age.[23] They were assigned at random to three categories—"Model Rewarded," "Model Punished," and "No Consequences." A child in the first category began his participation by watching a five-minute television show in which an adult exhibited physical and verbal aggression toward a Bobo doll. In the closing scene of the Model Rewarded film, a second adult appeared, bearing an abundant supply of candies and soft drinks, informed the model that he was a "strong champion," and that his superb performance of aggression clearly deserved a treat. He then gave the model various desirable foods, and while the model consumed these he continued to describe and praise the model's feats.

A child in the "Model Punished" category saw a performance which was identical to the above in its initial sequences, but concluded with a second adult's reproving rather than praising the model:

> "Hey there, you big bully. You quit picking on that clown. I won't tolerate it." As the model drew back he tripped and fell, and the other adult sat on the model and spanked him with a rolled-up magazine while reminding him of his aggressive behavior. As the model ran off cowering, the agent forewarned him, "If I catch you doing that again, you big bully, I'll give you a hard spanking. You quit acting that way."[24]

Finally, a child in the "No Consequences" category saw a performance involving only the initial section of the above film, the part showing the adult's aggression toward the Bobo doll.

Each child was then observed in a ten-minute play session while alone in a room containing a variety of toys, among which were some similar to those used by the adult model on the film. Judges observed through a one-way screen and recorded the occurrence of imitative aggressive responses. Then the experimenter returned to the playroom, bringing an assortment of fruit juices and booklets of sticker pictures to be presented to the child as rewards. She then asked, "Show me what Rocky did in the TV program," and "Tell me what he said," promising to reward the child for each imitation performed.

The findings of this study have to do with how much imitative aggression each child performed spontaneously in the ten-minute session as compared with how much imitative aggression he showed himself capable of performing when offered an incentive.

As might be expected from the earlier studies, the children in the "Model Rewarded" and the "No Consequences" categories mimicked the adult model in their own free play, doing so more frequently than those in the "Model Punished" category. Again we have a demonstration that children imitate aggression they observe on television and again the finding that punishment of the adult in the television show serves to inhibit the children's tendency to imitate spontaneously.

When requested to imitate the adult's behavior and offered an incentive, each group of children performed more imitative acts of aggression than had been performed spontaneously in free play. This demonstrated that the children were capable of more imitative aggression than they had initially shown. Further, those in the "Model Punished" category could imitate aggressive acts just as efficiently as those in the "Model Rewarded" and "No

Consequences" categories. Remarkably, the girls in this study (as had the girls in the other two) exhibited less imitative behavior in their own free play than the boys, but when offered an incentive for imitating aggression, the mimicked essentially as many aggressive acts as the boys.

Thus, this third study of Bandura's reinforces the theory that children learn some of the behavior they observe. Some sequences of their learning are exhibited spontaneously in their play, and others can be elicited if the setting is right. This is equally true whether the observed behavior was condemned and had painful consequences, was rewarded and had positive consequences, or was neither rewarded nor punished and had no known consequences. The study suggests that the observed consequences of behavior have some influence on the spontaneous mimicking of that behavior, but none on the retention of the capability to imitate the behavior when offered an incentive for doing so.

A related study deserves brief mention. The participants were seventy-two children, ages six to eight, from a lower-middle-class neighborhood.[25] Every child saw the same four-minute color film showing an adult performing a series of novel acts with various toys. For example, when he first came on stage, the adult had his right hand cupped over his eyes. Later, he tossed bean bags at a target, but instead of standing erect, he bent over with his back to the target and threw the bean bags through his legs.

Children were assigned at random to three categories. Some simply observed the film. Others were instructed to verbalize every action of the model as they watched the actions unfold on the TV screen. Those in the third category engaged in competing symbolization, counting aloud while they watched the TV film: "1 and a 2 and a 3 and a 4 . ."

Each child was then taken to a room containing the toys the adult had used in the film. The experimenter asked him to demonstrate every one of the model's actions he could recall. She praised and rewarded each correct response. She also prompted the child with a standard set of cues, asking him to show the way the adult behaved in the opening scene, to demonstrate what the adult had done with the dart gun, the Bobo doll, and the bean bags, and to portray the adult's behavior in the closing scene.

The children did very well in mimicking the adult they had just observed. Those who had simply watched the four-minute television show were able to reproduce an average of fourteen sequences of behavior. Not surprisingly, those children who had verbalized the sequences as they watched the same film could reproduce even more—an average of seventeen. As expected, completing verbal activity interfered with the child's retention of the film content—the children who had counted aloud during the film could reproduce only nine of the sequences afterwards.

Again we have a demonstration of the child's powers of observation and retention. Such demonstrations have interested other psychologists, and a number of them have conducted studies providing independent confirmation of this phenomenon.[26] What is especially significant about these studies is their concern with the child's behavior. Many questionnaire and interview studies report what people say they think and what they say they might do or not do, but these report what the subjects actually do.

D. Conclusions

Every civilization is only twenty years away from barbarism. For twenty years is all we have to accomplish the task of civilizing the infants who are born into our midst each year. These savages know nothing of our language, our culture, our religion, our values, or our customs of interpersonal relations. The infant knows nothing about communism, fascism, democracy, civil liberties, the rights of the minority as contrasted with the prerogatives of the majority, respect, decency, ethics, morality, conventions, and customs. The barbarian must be tamed if civilization is to survive. Over the centuries, man has evolved methods of accomplishing this.

Our methods of "socializing" the barbarian hordes who invade our community every year rely on their remarkable learning abilities. The infant learns by trial and error, and man has capitalized on this ability by rewarding infants for acceptable behavior and punishing them for unacceptable behavior. The infant develops a close attachment to one or two persons who care for him and meet his needs, and because of this he desires to conform to their wishes and expectations. Man has capitalized on the infant's propensity to make attachments by assigning special educative responsiblities to mothers and fathers. The young child learns through observation and imitation, and throughout the ages man has provided opportunities for young people to learn from their elders in apprentice relations—the girl learning housewifery by watching her mother, the boy learning farming skills by working alongside his father, the youngsters learning hunting skills by observing the experienced hunters. The young child learns through oral instruction, and man makes use of this opportunity by talking to children about the social group and its values and ideals, by relating legends, telling tales, gossiping, sermonizing, lecturing, conversing, explaining, scolding, and moralizing. The young child learns from graphic representations, and for many years parents have created pictorial representations of the culture, its religious symbols, its heroes, and its workers. All of these age-old techniques of socialization have enabled man to teach most of the young barbarians how to behave as members of the group if civilization is to flourish.

In the modern era, these techniques continue to be very important, but they have been joined by others whose impact is less well understood. At first, the new methods of teaching were available only to a privileged few. Thus, the method of teaching through written instruction reached only those who had been taught to read and who could gain possession of rare scripts. As the technology of printing and distribution of printed materials advanced, more and more individuals had access to the printed word, and more and more were taught the literacy skills needed to gain meaning from print. Thus the printed word became important in socializing the young. Any educated person is impressed with the extent of this importance, and perhaps it is worthwhile to remind the reader that the ability to read is acquired late in a child's life, long after his basic social learning has been accomplished, and the ability to read efficiently comes even later. The child is well advanced before he is so skillful in reading that the printed page can modify his behavior or alter his beliefs.

The newer forms of communication circumvent this difficulty. As we have discussed, they are meaningful to the illiterate as well as to the tutored. The most powerful of these new forms, movies and television, communicate with the individual both audibly and visually. The most powerful medium of all, television, accomplishes this feat in the individual's own home, bringing into that arena instantaneous reports of events in the world around him, not only in his neighborhood and city, but in his nation and other nations.

The fact that we do not think of the new media as being instructors for our young does not affect their teaching ability. Although it is not governed by a board of education, TV does teach. We think of radio, movies, and TV as "entertainment," but in fact children learn efficiently from them. Our media-saturated college students, born eighteen or twenty years ago, just as television was coming into prominence, get their kicks from playing "Trivia," a campy game of inconsequential questions and answers about radio, TV, movies, comic books, and popular songs in which the effectiveness of these media as teachers is demonstrated by the young people's ability to answer questions like "Who was Bob Hope's radio announcer?" "What was the consolation prize on 'The $64,000 Question'?" and "Who was the singer of 'Come on-a My House'?" A Trivia Contest was held at Columbia University in 1967, with teams from Princeton, Yale, Pennsylvania, Barnard, and other elite schools battling it out, and with the winner receiving a trophy while a chorus sang the Mr. Trivia song—"There he goes, think of all the crap he knows." The proud winner declared, "You have to get your basic training from the time you are six until perhaps 12 or 13," and credited his success to "my garbage-filled mind."[27]

The new media speak directly to the child's two best developed senses, conveying a reality which is not very different from the other realities he experiences. A child who has seen President Johnson on television would recognize him instantly if he should encounter him; a child who has only read about Mr. Johnson or heard his name spoken would not recognize him on sight, but instead would need to be told, "That's our President, Mr. Johnson." It is precisely the direct correspondence between reality and the television representation of reality—with no need for reliance on verbal labels for encoding and decoding—that makes television so powerful.

American children spend many hours a week watching television. They begin watching at a very young age, and are faithful to the set on weekdays and weekends, throughout the summer, and during the school year, with the result that at age sixteen, the average American child has spent as many hours watching television as he has spent in school. Is it a fair bet that the two sources of information have affected his social learning equally?

Perhaps, but one might lean toward television. The child turned to "the tube" at a younger and more impressionable age, and he attended the television school on his own initiative and volition, not because of the combination of social pressures, parental expectations, and truancy laws which enforce school attendance. One hears a great deal about school dropouts, but very little about those who do not watch television. The ability of television to hold its audience better than our schools can hold their students may tell us something about its superior effectiveness as a communicator and thus as a teacher.

What is this electronic mechanism teaching the child? The *Christian Science Monitor* completed a survey of TV programming six weeks after the assassination of Senator Kennedy. In 85½ hours of programming in prime evening hours and on Saturday mornings, 84 killings were observed. Both acts of violence and threats of violence were recorded.

> The survey found that the most violent evening hours were between 7:30 and 9, when, according to official network estimates, 26.7 million children between the ages of 2 and 17 are watching television.
>
> "In those early evening hours, violent incidents occurred on an average of once every 16.3 minutes. After 9 p.m., violence tapered off quickly, with incidents occurring once every 35 minutes, " the paper said.
>
> "In the early evening, there was a murder or killing once every 31 minutes," the survey reported. "Later, once every two hours."[28]

Everything that social scientists know about human learning and remembering tells us that this carnage is being observed and remembered by the audience. If children can remember and reproduce fourteen or fifteen sequences of behavior from one of Bandura's amateurish five-minute films, how much do they remember from hour after hour of professionally-produced TV?

The fact that a student can recall the 1946 singing commercial, "Use Ajax, boom, boom, the foaming cleanser" when playing Trivia does not mean that he *will* use that foaming cleanser when he grows up and has to scour his toilet bowl. Similarly, the fact that children watch TV "pictures of mayhem, mugging, and murder"[29] does not mean that they *will* perform comparable acts of violence in their own lives. This is obvious from our crime statistics, which show that children are among the least violent of our citizens, and that violence is most characteristic of the adolescent and young adult male.

However, television time is sold to sponsors on the conviction that although the Ajax ad will not guarantee that the viewer will buy the product, it raises the probability that he will. Social scientists would simply make the same claim for filmed or televised violence, whether fictitious or real. Viewing the carnage does not guarantee that the viewer will "go forth and do likewise," but it raises the probability that he will.

Media spokesmen make much of the fact that as yet social scientists have no convincing proof for this hypothesis.[30] They minimize the fact that the evidence for it is accumulating year by year and at an accelerating rate. They also ignore the fact that there is no convincing scientific evidence for or against most of our social practices and policies.

To the media spokesman, one is tempted to reply "Media man speaks with forked tongue." The television industry exists and reaps its profits from the conviction that television viewing does affect behavior—buying behavior.

Is it fanciful to imagine that there may be a relation between the Trivia game at Columbia in 1967 and the violence at Columbia in 1968? Where did the students learn the attitudes and the aggressive behaviors that they vented against the police? Where did they learn the implicit values that seemed to justify their expressing what may be entirely legitimate grievances in such profoundly antisocial ways? They acknowledge that their minds are "garbage filled" by the media, and we may wonder whether they are "aggression stuffed" by the same sources.

The evidence that we do have indicates that films and television are profoundly educative for their viewers, teaching them that the world is a violent and untrustworthy place, and demonstrating for them a variety of violent techniques for copying with this hostile environment. Whether this message is beamed as fact or fiction, it is accepted by young children. They incorporate in their own behavior patterns all the sequences of adult behavior they observe on television.

Whether they will ever employ these aggressive behaviors in their interpersonal relations depends on many complex factors. Every individual is capable of more different behaviors than he has occasion to display. Many of us remember our high school French, and although years pass without presenting us with any occasion to speak it, we continue to retain some capability of doing so when the occasion does arise. The analogy to television violence is not exact, for television as a school for violence enrolls adult viewers as well as high school students, and has them in class for many more hours than any French teacher ever did. When the occasion arises that calls for violence, one does not have to cast his mind to his high school classroom, but only to last night's or last week's "thrilling episode."

What else will he remember from that episode? There was a murder every half hour during prime viewing time on 1968 network television. How many instances are there of constructive interventions to end disagreement? What other methods of resolving conflict are shown? How many instances of tact and decency could an avid televiewer chronicle during the same hours? How often is reconciliation dramatized? How many adult acts of generosity are provided to children for modeling? What strategies for ameliorating hate are displayed? How many times does the child viewer see adults behaving in loving and helpful ways? What examples of mutual respect does he view? What can he learn about law and order? How many episodes of police kindness does he see? How frequently does the glow of compassion illuminate the screen?

References

1. Douglas E. Kneeland, "Pocketbook Issues Secondary in Rural Iowa," *New York Times,* Oct. 18, 1968, p.34.
2. Russell Baker,"Nightmare out of the Attic," *New York Times,* June 6, 1968.
3. Clive Barnes, "Heller's 'We Bombed in New Haven' Opens," *New York Times,* Oct. 18, 1968, p. 36.
4. George Willey, "Does Happy Ending Justify Violence?" *Palo Alta* (Calif.) *Times,* June 10, 1968, p. 22.
5. George Willey, "Editing out Violence Poses Problems," *Palo Alto* (Calif.) *Times,* Oct. 8, 1968, p. 16.
6. Philip H. Dougherty, "Putting a Damper on Violence," *New York Times,* July 12, 1968, p. 38.
7. No reference 7.
8. "Children in Britain, 13 to 14, called Rulers of the TV Set," *New York Times,* July 17, 1967, p. 12.
9. "Young Britons Told Not to Copy Batman," *New York Times,* Aug. 25, 1966, p. 42.

10. Jack Gould, "The Doomsday Flight," *New York Times,* Dec. 15, 1966.
11. Jack Gould, "A Bomb Backfires," *New York Times,* Dec. 16, 1966.
12. "TV Show Blamed by FAA For Rise in Bomb Hoax Calls," *New York Times,* Dec. 21, 1966, p. 69.
13. "Air Bomb Threats Follow TV Drama," *New York Times,* Dec. 15, 1966, pp. 35-56.
14. *Ibid.*
15. Alberta E. Siegal, "The Influence of Violence in the Mass Media Upon Children's Role Expectations," *Child Development,* 1958, vol. 29, pp. 35-56.
16. A. Bandura and Althea C. Huston, "Identification as a Process of Incidental Learning," *Journal of Abnormal and Social Psychology,* 1961, vol. 63, pp. 311-318; A. Bandura, Dorothea Ross, and Sheila A. Ross, "Transmission of Aggression Through Imitation of Aggressive Models," *Journal of Abnormal and Social Psychology,* 1961, vol. 63, pp. 575-582.
17. A. Bandura, Dorothea Ross, and Sheila A. Ross, "Imitation of Film-Meditated Aggressive Models," *Journal of Abnormal and Social Psychology,* 1963, vol. 66, pp. 3-11.
18. A. Bandura, Dorothea Ross, and Sheila A. Ross, "Vicarious Reinforcement and Imitative Learning," *Journal of Abnormal and Social Psychology,* 1963, vol. 67, pp. 601-607.
19. *Ibid.,* p. 602.
20. *Ibid.*
21. *Ibid.,* p. 605.
22. *Ibid.,* pp. 605-606.
23. A. Bandura, "Influence of Models' Reinforcement Contingent on the Acquisition of Imitative Responses," *Journal of Personality and Social Psychology,* 1965, col. 1, pp. 589-595.
24. *Ibid.,* p. 591.
25. A. Bandura, Joan E. Grusec and Frances L. Menlove, "Observational Learning as a Function of Symbolization and Incentive," *Child Development,* 1966, vol. 37, pp. 499-506.
26. Mary A. Rosenkrans and W.W. Hartup, "Imitative Influence of Consistent and Inconsistent Response Consequences to a Model on Aggressive Behavior in Children," *Journal of Personality and Social Psychology,* 1967, vol. 7, pp. 429-434; Deanna Z. Kuhn, C.H. Madsen, and W.C. Becker, "Effects of Exposure to an Aggressive Model and 'Frustration' on Children's Aggressive Behavior," *Child Development,* 1967, vol. 38, pp. 739-745.
27. "Triviaddiction," *Time,* March 10, 1967, pp. 69-70.
28. "84 Killings Shown in 85½ TV Hours on the 3 Networks," *New York Times,* July 26, 1968, p. 29.
29. Morris Ernst, quoted by George Gent in "Human Life Seen as Devalued by Violence in the Mass Media," *New York Times,* Sept. 17, 1968, p. 78.
30. Joseph A. Loftus, "CBS Man Doubts Violence Theory: Tells Panel Studies Fail to Establish Links to TV," *New York Times,* Oct. 17, 1968, p. 87. This is an account of the testimony of Joseph T. Klapper before the National Commission on the Causes and Prevention of Violence.

Chapter 13

VALUE MODIFICATION
BY MASS MEDIA*

Before turning to research data that indicate modification of values by exposure to mass media, some clarification of concepts is required.

Values may be briefly defined as conceptions of the desirable.[1] Most values can be stated in words, but for some this is difficult and even impossible. Even when people can verbalize their values, it is not clear how effective such values are as determinants of behavior. People may behave as they do because they hold certain values, but there are many other factors that shape almost any human act.

Values can sometimes be stated by the people who hold them.

Values can sometimes be inferred, even when not explicitly stated, from what people do, from rules that say what people should do, or from things people say.

Values can change. Since the link between values and actions is problematic, however, a change in values does not necessarily entail changed behavior. Nor does changed behavior necessarily presuppose changed values. To be specific: a population might differ from its ancestors in the degree to which it admires certain forms of violence and the degree to which it abhors other forms, yet it might behave in the same violent ways on the same kinds of occasions as before.

Some of the ways in which behavior may change without a corresponding change in values will be examined in the next section. The present analysis simply assumes that there is such connection between values and behavior that the fact that people behave in one way instead of another can sometimes be regarded as an expression of preference, and can thus be taken as a basis for inferring their values. If people interact with each other, for example, in situations where it would be possible for them to inflict physical injury upon each other, and if they seem to strive to avoid inflicting these injuries, it might be inferred that they value the lives of others. Perhaps each values only his own safety and behaves non-violently toward others to avoid retaliatory

*Paper prepared for Media Task Force by William R. Catton, Jr., Professor of Sociology, University of Washington.

violence: even then, the expectation of retaliation would imply a norm enforced by sanctions. The existence and enforcement of the norm would seem to imply that the secured condition is valued. "Live and let live" is preferred to "kill or be killed."

Thus values can sometimes be inferred from norms. It will be assumed that values can be inferred from verbal expressions of preference. Patrick Henry's rhetorical question, "Is life so dear, or peace so sweet, as to be purchased at the price of chains and slavery?" was an implied expression of preference. At least on the verbal level, precarious liberty was being declared preferable to enslaved security; he was declaring the value of freedom.

It should not be assumed that values inferred from verbal expressions of preference will necessarily be congruent with values inferred from non-verbal behavior. For example, men have not always responded affirmatively to the challenge to "Put your money where your mouth is."

The process of inferring values from preferences, either verbal or non-verbal is not a simple one. If, on a certain stretch of road, we observe that most drivers of high-powered cars keep their speed under thirty miles per hour, we cannot simply infer that they value moving at a leisurely pace. More likely, they value avoidance of speeding tickets and accidents, and have seen signs indicating a twenty-five-mile-per-hour speed limit. The posted speed limit does not indicate that some legal authority assigns a negative value to speed as such; the negative value -may again be attached to the risks of accident, injury, or death which would be made excessive in this congested area by speeds that would be tolerable elsewhere.

A. Acquisition of Values

Values are acquired in the socializing process. To the extent that the mass media are involved in socializing human personalities, there is an inherent possibility that these media can affect the way people acquire values and the kinds of values they acquire.

LaPiere speaks of a category of "fugitive" values, which people impute temporarily to certain acts or objects because of their newness. Group status is determined partly by sharing in these fugitive values. All groups assign such values.[2] For teenagers, there are slang expressions, popular songs, and hair styles. For academicians, there are intellectual fashions. For motorists, there is the value assigned to owning the latest model car. Mass media, of course, have the power to create or implement such fugitive values. This is indicated by the role of the radio disc jockey. The play he gives a particular record on the air affects its "popularity" far more than the frequency with which he, or any other private individual, plays it at home. This is why "payola" was considered scandalous, because people who have a fondness for music did not want to feel that the frequency with which a piece was played on the air was induced through monetary considerations.

There are various ways in which different media can affect or have affected values. When a new medium first comes into existence, the mere fact that some people have access to it and some do not may give one group an advantage over another. In the ancient and medieval worlds, only a select segment of the population, distinguished by status and education, constituted the reading public. Literacy was at first associated with membership in a ruling elite.[3] Now that literacy is so nearly universal in a number of lands, the ability to read no longer has that special value, although in a sense it has greater utility than ever because of the continued multiplication and diversification of written materials. Similarly, when the electronic media were new, social distinctions arose between set owners and non-owners. Quite apart from the impact of broadcast content upon audience values, set ownership had a social value that is now lacking. Both radio and television came on the scene after literacy was nearly universal in our society, and set ownership, especially of television, has now reached the same status.

The transition from non-literacy to nearly universal literacy took several thousand years. The elite status of literate people in the early centuries of that transition was not a "fugitive" value. In the United States, it took less than one generation for radios to become standard household fixtures, and the corresponding transition for television took about a decade. Since universal literacy already prevailed at the beginning of these latter two transitions, it was never possible for early access to either of these electronic media to have the powerful stratifying effect that early access to literacy had had. Early television ownership did have some kind of "fugitive" value, but this seldom gave anyone access to a fund of information from which non-owners were totally and hopelessly cut off: newspapers and other media were always available. Consequently, what mattered to the television viewer was the subtler difference between the eye-witness quality of membership in the television audience versus the quality of indirectness inherent in membership in the audiences of the printed media. The difference between membership in the viewing audience of television and in the listening audience of radio was even less, though it was great enough to stimulate the rapid adoption of television by a nation already equipped with radios.

The invention of printing increased the importance of literacy because there was more available to read. As literacy became more universal, it took on a different kind of value; the ability to read lost its aura of religious and political power. The spread of literacy provided the social context for the invention of new kinds of printed media, including the daily newspaper. A century ago relatively few people really needed to keep abreast of current events, but as newspaper publication began to make this more possible, the knowledge of current events acquired a social value (and a lack of this knowledge implied a loss of social status).

The value of being "informed" was further enhanced with the advent of radio newscasting. It was now possible not only to know what had occurred, but to be involved in it in a new way. One did not just read about the President's "State of the Union" address; it could be heard on the radio, and this gave the message a great deal more immediacy. Accordingly, the value of audible events and experiences was enhanced.

The advent of television did not reduce the number of radios, but did bring about a drastic change in radio programming. The audiovisual medium improved on some of the innovations that the sound-only medium had been performing rather well. Most drama, and a good deal of the news, were even more interesting when experienced through the audiovisual medium. Programmers soon realized that radio was at a distinct disadvantage in comparison with the sound-and-sight combination, and radio programming became largely confined to music and abbreviated news, and some special events coverage and sportscasting aimed at people only temporarily out of touch with television.

Just as radio newscasting discovered that the distinctive things it *could* do it *must* do (e.g., replay recorded excerpts of a president's speech rather than just a newscaster's descriptive summary), so the networks have found that because they *can* show interesting events, they *must*.[4] The visual aspects of the news event or a drama thus acquired new values. During a radio broadcast of a presidential address, the listener is allowed to form his own opinions about the speech and the various points in it. Television, on the other hand, must (because it can) show which senators or congressmen are or are not applauding, and must show any disturbance in the gallery, or any cabinet member who happens to be dozing during any part of the speech. Because television *can* make eyewitnesses of its audience, it *must* and must therefore go out of its way to present interesting and unusual visual aspects. There is thus an inherent tendency for television to introduce a visual bias into our value system.

Because television allows its audience to see and hear, its socializing power should be appreciably greater than that of radio, which in turn has somewhat more socializing power than most printed media. The power of visual broadcasting to change attitudes and behavior is well-illustrated in an experiment by Bandura and Menlove.[5] Children in nursery school at Stanford who were afraid of dogs showed a significant reduction in this behavior (on a test consisting of a graded series of actual acts of approach) after they had been exposed to eight three-minute films, two per day on four alternate days. The films showed a child making progressively bolder approaches to a dog. Two different treatments were tried in the experiment. One group saw a series of films which all used the same five-year-old male model and the same cocker spaniel. Another group saw a series in which the same single-model sequence was interspersed with scenes in which models of both sexes and of various ages approached different dogs in a graded series of increasing size and fearsomeness. Both groups showed significant and lasting reduction in their fear of live dogs in comparison with a control group of equally apprehensive children who were shown neutral films (Disneyland and Marineland scenes).

Television programs frequently portray actions which most viewers would have some inhibition about performing—from switching cigarette brands or using a hair color rinse for the first time, to killing an adversary. The viewing these events could be expected to reduce inhibitions to some degree, in much the same manner as the dog-approaching inhibitions of the children. Before the films were shown, the children had a negative attitude toward dogs; after seeing the films, in which approach behavior was exhibited without adverse consequences to the model, these values (as expressed in overt behavior) had been shifted in a positive direction. The children not only learned to approach the dog used in the experimental test, but their learning was generalized to include other dogs.[6]

It seems to be well established that differential vicarious reinforcement can produce differential amounts of imitative behavior. There is no reason for assuming that human actions described or depicted in the mass media will not function as models in this manner. Berelson and Salter, after performing a content analysis of a magazine fiction sample and finding majority-type Americans overrepresented among the characters and especially among the favorably portrayed ones (whereas minority members were underrepresented numerically and unfavorably treated in the stories), commented on the "presumable effects" of such images. They had not actually studied reader behavior before and after exposure to the stories, but their comments are significant in the light of subsequent experiments on observational learning. They wrote:

> These stories are probably offered and accepted purely as entertainment. Their typical effect upon readers is . . . respite . . . from daily routines and daily cares . . . but it is certainly not the only one. Many communications have other than their intended effects upon readers or listeners and this is probably such a case . . . . Readers with latent tendencies to assign the usual stereotypic descriptions to groups whom they do not know, or toward whom they are unsympathetic, or with whom they do not come in personal contact, can find support for their convenient tags, labels, and aggressions in such magazine fiction. Thus the condition and behavior of fictional characters can readily be used to "prove" that the Negroes are lazy or ignorant, the Jews sly, the Irish superstitious, the Italians criminal, and so on.
>
> The nature of these stories, then, tends to perpetuate the myth of the "100% American" by differentiating subtly and consistently between *The Americans* and the representatives of other groups.[7]

A key idea here is that people are influenced in serious ways even when they seek only entertainment (or "respite") by exposure to mass media. This was also found to be true in the case of those who listened to the radio daytime serials, or "soap operas." From a study of one hundred intensive interviews, Herzog noted three major types of soap opera listener gratification: (1) emotional release—a "chance to cry," or derivation of comfort from sensing that "other people have troubles, too;" (2) opportunities for wishful thinking—exposure to happy episodes which offset one's own problems; and (3) a chance to obtain usable advice. The third type was considered something of a surprise, and was further studied in a poll of 2,500 serial listeners who were asked whether these programs helped them deal better with their own everyday problems. Forty-one percent claimed to have been helped, 28 percent said they had not been helped, and 31 percent had not thought of it that way, did not know, or did not reply.[8]

The propensity to take advice from radio serials varied inversely with education, directly with the perceived amount of worry, and directly with the number of soap operas listened to. The kind of advice obtained consisted mainly of: (1) learning "how to take it" (acquiring what might be termed "stoical values" and absorbing the conviction that "things come out all right"); (2) learning to project blame on others (because the interpersonal problems portrayed are attributable to another's character defects); and (3) acquiring ready-made formulas of behavior (e.g., don't slap your children, deprive them of something; take things calmly, don't get excited).[9]

In England, Himmelweit and his associates found that, even with regard to values that are implicitly rather than explicitly preached editorially, television does have some measurable impact on children despite their exposure to many other sources of values. The influence of television depends on repetition in dramatic form and is most possible where views are not firmly fixed. The optimal age of responsiveness varies for different topics and depends on emotional and social maturity as well as mental or chronological age. The more emotionally responsive the child is to television, the greater its influence.[10]

B. Crime and Viloence

Several content analyses of television programming have shown the steady diet of crime shows available to viewers, many of which present recurrent acts of violence. Schramm and his associates asked a sample of parents, "If you could prevent certain TV programs from being seen by your children, what kinds would you try to prevent?" Almost two-thirds answered that they would like to eliminate programs of crime, violence, and horror. Then they were asked why they objected to these programs. The respondents thought that: (1) these programs tended to frighten children; (2) the children tended to dwell on and dream about them; (3) some children tended to re-enact some of the dramatic scenes; or (4) such programs might induce delinquency. These apprehensions were more common among college-educated, middle-class parents than among lower-class parents.[11] One interesting implication of the study is that the wish that children be insulated from such programs, and the fear that such programs would have harmful effects, did not seem to be accompanied by a conviction that parents actually could eliminate these programs from their children's television diet.

These apprehensions and parents' implicit resignation to the pervasiveness of these unwanted influences are important. From several kinds of tests, Himmelweit demonstrated that—

> ... under certain conditions, ideas and values which form part of the underlying entertainment pattern do influence children's attitudes, not because they differ from the content of other mass media, but because they are repeated and seen much more often. We have no reason for assuming that respect for violence and aggression—a basic feature of the popular dramatized programmes under review—should have a smaller effect than other scenes on television.[12]

Wertham has suggested several kinds of effects that might result from exposure to abundant television violence. Whether or not the viewer actually learns to value violence, Wertham suggests that viewing could conceivably reinforce a pro-violence value. Television could demonstrate violent methods or how to escape detection after a violent act, or the viewer's awareness of the undesirability of violence may merely be dulled. He sees television as a school for violence, and says, "In this school young people are never, literally never, taught that violence is in itself reprehensible. The lesson they do get is that violence is the great adventure and the sure solution, and he who is best at it wins."[13]

There is violence, for instance, in westerns. Some people assume that if these shows are regarded as teaching anything, it is that good wins out over evil. However, it can also be suggested that "good triumphs over bad *through violence*—the manly, as well as the only, course of action."[14] There are other values presented (and perhaps taught to some viewers) by the westerns:

> .... regard for justice, life, and property. A whole range of values, however, never finds expression in Westerns—those to do with family, work education, and manners. The characters do not need them in their way of life; they are rarely encumbered by parents, wives, or children, and seldom eat or go into their homes; most of the indoor action takes place in the sheriff's office or in the saloon.[15]

A number of studies have shown that exposure to violent or aggressive models can increase the propensity for aggressive behavior. Lövass conducted three experiments with preschool children who were exposed to five-minute movies and then allowed to play with a lever-pressing toy which can cause one doll to beat another on the hand. Exposure to a film that portrayed aggressive behavior increased the child's indulgence in this symbolic kind of aggression; exposure to a film of non-aggressive behavior did not.[16] Mussen and Rutherford carried out an experiment with thirty-six first-grade children of middle-class origin. A third of them were exposed to aggressive fantasy in an animated cartoon, another third to a non-aggressive cartoon, and the remainder to no cartoon. Those who viewed the aggressive cartoon manifested an increased subsequent preference for the prospect of bursting a balloon (or having it popped) over the prospect of merely playing with it.[17] Balloons are trivial objects, and balloon popping may be a relatively minor form of aggression, but keeping in mind that values are conceptions of the desirable which we infer from preferences, the demonstration that viewing a single animated cartoon which portrays aggressive behavior can arouse a preference for even such mildly destructive behavior seems to indicate that visual media can influence values.

In a sample of 354 sixth-to eighth-grade boys in the schools of Adelaide, Australia before television was available, Lovibond found that exposure to comic books and frequency of cinema attendance were positively correlated with scores on a scale designed to measure acceptance of a fascist-like admiration for use of force by the strong to dominate and exploit the weak. In a sample of ninety-three sixth-and seventh-graders, after television became available, this same scale was found to be positively correlated with the number of hours viewed per week. Moreover, preference for crime and violence programs was positively associated both with the scale scores and with high amounts of television exposure.[18] The attitude scale was constructed on the basis of a content analysis of crime and war comic books which found that these seem to express an ideology amounting to "idolatry of force and violence."

Most of the people who write and draw for the comic-book industry presumably have little intention of instilling a set of values or an ideology in those who read their material. Certainly few of them are employed on the basis of credentials signifying that society has certified their qualification for transmission of values to children. However, an investigation of comic-book readership by children (similar to the study of women who listened to soap operas) reveals that such media do function as socializing agents.

Developmental, as well as entertainment, needs of children are served by comic-reading.[19] How well is another question.

Zajonc found that radio programs could persuade children "to admire and identify with a model who bears striking resemblance to the so-called 'authoritarian personality,' and who represents a system of values more typical of autocratic than of democratic societies."[20] The structure of the experiment showed that the acceptance of the values implicit in the model's behavior depended primarily on the success rather than on the conventionality of the behavior.

Berkowitz and Geen demonstrated that the inhibitions of male undergraduates at Wisconsin against aggressive behavior could be reduced by showing a filmed episode of "justified aggression." Their aggressive responses toward another experimental subject were also increased when the name attributed to that person tended to associate him with the target of the justified aggression in the film.[21]

In the light of such studies, it is somewhat ironic that the various self-regulatory media codes of good practice insist that violence should not be shown *unless germane to the dramatic development of the story.* One test of relevance is that it produces a desired outcome; another is to have the violence directed toward a character who is defined as "deserving it." In either case, as the studies have shown, the conditions for effective observational learning through vicarious reinforcement have been ensured. To the child who views television for entertainment, but is also available for incidental learning (although this is unintended so far as the media people are concerned), violence that contributes to "dramatic development" accomplishes something. What is to prevent the child from learning that violence is an acceptable means to ends he may have learned or will subsequently learn to value? When the codes forbid "senseless" violence, but permit violence that leads to some end, perhaps they simply create the impression that violence is usually sensible—an unintentional imparting of pro-violence values.

In the very process of seeming to preach that "crime does not pay," the media may actually undermine the moral restraints against violent and anti-social behavior. Screenplays based on the precept of "an eye for an eye and a tooth for a tooth" can lead to "socially harmful consequences. If the criminal or 'bad guy' is punished aggressively, so that others do to him what he has done to them, the violence appears justified."[22] There is always the possibility that precisely those aspects of the dramatization which convey the sense that the violence was justified can stimulate some previously-angered person to violence.[23]

There is another danger worth noting. Even if mass media violence does not induce pro-violence values among the audience, it could so define violence as to make certain values seem inapplicable. By repeated exposure to stylized violence on television, for example, children may come to regard all violence, even in news broadcasts, as unreal or unimportant.[24] This might be the effect on some viewers, even while others were learning to admire the uses of violence and still others were learning to abhor violence. The existence of perceptual selectivity, so commonly cited in defense of the harmlessness of mass media, must also preclude any easy assurance that everyone in the audience will respond in a desirable way.

Wertham is not necessarily exaggerating when he says, "Many modern children fail to see the evil in horror and the wrong in violence and have lost their natural sympathy for the suffering of others. The trouble is not that they get frightened, but that they do not get frightened."[25] Crime dramas, in addition to portraying the value that crime—because it does not pay—is bad, also portray other values: (1) What you do does not matter so much as which side you are on; the "good guys" do many of the same things the "bad guys" do, and are admired for it. (2) Good appearances more often mask an evil character than vice versa.[26]

As a horizon-broadening experience, exposure to television affects the values of viewers in other ways. In England, more viewers than non-viewers in a children's sample disagreed with the statement "My own country is always right."[27] Evidently exposure to television can reduce ethnocentrism; some may desire and others may regret such an effect. Viewers in the same sample showed slightly more interest in other countries than did non-viewers. In describing six categories of foreigners, viewers made more objective and fewer evaluative statements that non-viewers.[28] The BBC policy of presenting programs about foreign countries for children had the effect of leading many viewers toward a more detached view of foreigners.

C. Family and Sex

In the same British sample, viewers and non-viewers did not differ significantly in the proportion wishing to marry when they grow up, or in percentage disagreeing with the expectation that marriage assures happiness. There was some difference in their impressions of what makes a good husband (the viewers were more inclined to stress personality attributes and the non-viewers gave proportionally more stress to role performance), but none in the impressions of what makes a good wife. Since television portrayals of family life are quite varied, their effects may tend to cancel one another out in an overall sampling of opinions. Moreover, for viewers and non-viewers alike, their own families still seem to function as the major source of children's ideas about family life.[29]

There is one important exception. Children usually have little opportunity (at least in American society) to observe adult sexual behavior directly, save for its milder or peripheral forms. Due to norms of privacy, children can hardly model their own sexual behavior after that of their parents. Characters portrayed in the mass media afford some additional opportunity for observational learning and may thus be of considerable importance. By contrast, children in some other societies have abundant opportunities to observe all phases of sexual behavior; in such societies there is a considerable amount of imitation by children. It is sometimes encouraged, and often fully accepted.[30] Similar imitative behavior occurs when opportunities do arise for children to observe adult sex activity in normally nonpermissive societies such as the United States. Such situations occur in crowded slum housing, for example, where parents have little privacy from their children.[31]

To the extent that sex is presented in the mass media, there is a pressure upon children to learn from these presentations because of the paucity of other opportunities for observational learning. Walters, Bowen, and Parke conducted an experiment which produced results suggesting that sex values can be acquired from such experiences. Male college undergraduates were shown a series of photos of erotically posed nude or nearly nude males and females. A moving spot of light on the film was said to indicate the eye movements of a previous viewer. Half of the subjects saw a version of the film in which the spot of light (ostensibly "the previous viewer's eye") was on the background most of the time, and the other half was a version in which it was on the breast or genital area a high proportion of the time. An eye-marker camera attached to the subject's head recorded his own eye movements while he subsequently looked at a series of similar pictures, presented on slides. The group which was shown the second film spent significantly more time than the other group inspecting the nude or nearly nude bodies and significantly less time looking at the background features.[32]

Questions can be raised as to the validity of the sexual learning available to mass media audiences. Apart from the readers of the limited array of serious books about sex, what image of the sexual nature of human beings is obtained by the audiences from such media as movies, television, radio (and the popular songs it presents), and magazines? The balance between mutually rewarding marital sex and exploitive, obsessive, casual, or brutal sex varies from medium to medium. Again, as in the case of other kinds of communications, most of the people involved in preparing these images probably have little intention of instilling one kind of sex value or another in their audience. They are providing entertainment or some other supposedly effectless commodity, but their intentions may be an inadequate guide to their impact.

D. Occupational Values

In a study of television's version of the labor force, not only was the frequency of occurrence of various job types tabulated, but a listing was also made of the number of times each character, whatever his or her occupation, (1) gave an order to be carried out; (2) obeyed an order an order given by someone else; (3) gave permission to another person; (4) received permission from someone; (5) was addressed by a term of respect, such as "sir" or "your honor;" or (6) used such a term of respect in addressing someone else. From these tabulations, indexes of "power" for each occupational category were calculated by subtracting the number of submissive acts from the number of dominant acts and dividing the difference by the sum.[33] The ranking of jobs depicted in the analyzed programs (which was reasonably realistic) is not so important here; what is of interest is that the tabulations could be made with such facility. This showed that readily discernible acts of interpersonal dominance and submission are built into television portrayals of human interaction.

Power or lack of it is not always a highly salient aspect of occupational roles in real life. As indicated before, the characteristics of television as a communication medium influence the kinds of material that will be selected for presentation.. In a television drama, the episodes in which employed people interact with each other may be easier to portray and more germane to development of the story than other aspects which are more characteristic of job performance. The pencil-pushing acts of a powerful occupational category may, in real life, consume more time than the people-pushing acts, but they are unlikely to occupy a proportionate amount of the time in a television dramatization of that role. As a result, it is possible that television viewers come to assign greater importance to the visible signs of power, or even to the power aspects of positions, than they would in the absence of this influence.

Himmelweit did find that the importance of viewers attached to jobs differed from that of non-viewers. Viewers were more ambitious and more "middle-class" in their job preferences, and often stressed the need for self-confidence as one of the factors contributing to personal success.[34] Perhaps this was due, in part, to the repeated witnessing of dramatic symbolizations, where dominance is an indication of self-confidence, while deference indicates humility.

E. Gratification Deferment

The training of the maturing human being to defer certain activities until a more appropriate time is a necessary part of the socialization process. There are situations in which foregoing an immediate reward will facilitate the attainment of a larger reward later, such as studying rather than playing, or investing some of one's money rather than spending it all as it comes. Since immediate gratification is more appealing, it takes prolonged and intensive training to overcome the innate reluctance to defer gratification. The ability to defer gratification is generally considered an aspect of maturity, and is demonstrably useful. How is it affected by the mass media?

Schramm and his associates made a study of 198 tenth-graders in Denver. They divided the group into categories of "high" and "low" users of print, and "high" and "low" users of television. On the premise that printed media and television differ in the presentation of fantasy versus reality, they formed four types: "Low users" (low TV, low print), "fantasy-oriented" (high TV, low print), "reality-oriented" (low TV, high print), and "high users" (high TV, high print). On a questionnaire, 83 percent of the "reality-oriented" disagreed with the statement that "The best way to live is to enjoy today and not think about tomorrow," while only 43 percent of the "fantasy-oriented" disagreed. In response to the statement, "The best way to be happy is to plan ahead," 58 percent of the "reality-oriented" agreed, and only 36 percent of the "fantasy-oriented" agreed. In response to the statement "It's a good idea to work hard today so you can enjoy tomorrow more," 56 percent of the "reality-oriented" agreed, as compared with only 40 percent ·of the "fantasy-oriented." Both the low-users and the high-users tended to fall between the other two categories in response to these statements.[35]

The reality group was thus most in favor of deferred gratification and the fantasy group least so. In other words, high exposure to print favored and high exposure to television disapproved gratification-deferring values. The study did not show the extent to which the differences in media exposure might be responsible for the differences in gratification-deferment preference, or vice versa. Assuming that a preference for immediate gratification would tend to point one toward television as a fantasy-laden medium, and a preference for deferred gratification would tend to point one toward the reality-laden printed media, the differential exposure thus produced would hardly tend to undo the value difference, and seems likely to strengthen and increase it.

The most common reason given by children for watching television is the pleasure of being passively entertained, having vicarious thrills, and living a fantasy. In their teens they begin to express this differently—it keeps them from getting bored.[36] The implication that without television they would be threatened with boredom could be symptomatic of a television-bred inability to find other means of entertainment for themselves.

Children acknowledge that they learn from television, but they generally prefer that such learning be incidental to the entertainment value of the medium. They consciously learn manners and customs, hair styles, clothing fashions (for both sexes), athletic and other techniques, ideas for school themes, conversational topics, etc. They are often loath to view educational programs where learning is *not* incidental to entertainment.[37] It would seem that this attitude, repeatedly reinforced by years of exposure to commercial television, would carry over into school, making them unreceptive to learning which, in those formal educational contexts, is quite clearly not incidental to immediate pleasure. The modern college student's restless complaint that his classes "don't seem relevant" (usually without specification of what he wants them to be relevant *to*) may be a direct symptom of retarded development of the ability to defer gratification. College classes usually are not as relevant *to immediate pleasure* as are television programs, and the solutions to real-life problems that might be derived from higher learning will seldom be as simple and immediate as the familiar perpetration of violence upon the personal sources of problems in televised fantasy.

On the basis of testimony by parents and teachers, Himmelweit concluded that television does not seem to have either diminished or enhanced the importance children attach to school, and he seemed to find no difference between viewers and non-viewers in respective interest in school work and extracurricular activities.[38] However, the children in Schramm's studies felt, in large numbers, that school is dull by comparison with television. The proportion who felt this way was highest among eighth-graders, and higher for boys than for girls.[39] Perhaps there is a greater difference in the attachment to male roles on TV as opposed to real life than in the case of female roles. In any event, as children enter their teens and pay increasing heed to their peers and less to their parents, they are acutely conscious of the contrast between entertainment by commercial television and education by noncommercial television. They tend to disparage the latter as being for "squares." Television is regarded as part of the non-educational portion of their day's routine.[40] This almost implies that school would be viewed as part of the non-pleasurable portion of the day.

F. "Sleeper" Effects

When exposure to mass communication can be shown to produce little or no immediate effect on attitudes, but an appreciable delayed effect shows up, this is called the "sleeper effect."

Such an effect occurred in the study cited earlier in which children's fear of dogs was reduced by watching films of a child playing harmlessly with a dog. The increment in dog-approaching behavior was significant in the group which saw the series of films always showing the same child making a graded series of approaches to the same dog; this improvement lasted with virtually no diminution when remeasured a month later. However, in the group exposed to the films showing a variety of persons interacting with a variety of dogs, while the immediate increment was comparable, there was no loss over the ensuing month, and there was actually some further gain.[41] It seems likely that this was due to an enhancement of stimulus generalization by the fact that both the humans and the dogs shown in the films were diverse enough to provide a generalized model. Equipped with a more general pro-dog frame of reference, these children were more likely to perceive subsequent real-life encounters between persons and dogs as continuations of the film-viewing experience. Thus they could continue to learn that fear of dogs was usually unnecessary and that pleasure from playing with dogs was possible, whereas the other group's learning was completed when it stopped seeing films on the subject.

Knowledge of the sleeper effect began to accumulate from systematic research as far back as 1933, when studies of movies as stimuli for attitude change began to question the permanence of the change. It was soon apparent that increments of further change were possible.[42] During World War II, in studies of the effects of indoctrination films used in troop training, clear cases of sleeper effects were found; factual information would be forgotten as time passed, but opinion changes often grew. Several explanations were suggested: (1) individuals pre-disposed to accept an opinion who had not yet done so might be won over slowly; (2) forgetting the source while retaining the ideas might make them more acceptable; (3) forgetting specifics while retaining generalities might produce cumulative attitude change; and (4) implications might be retained while the specific bases were forgotten.[43] Later research indicated the possibility of another mechanism: (5) exposure to mass communication could provide the audience member with a new cognitive frame of reference by which he would perceive subsequent events in a changed manner.[44]

Whatever the explanation for sleeper effects, it is clear from the fact that such phenomena do occur that mass media produce long-range changes in values that would escape notice in short-range studies. It should be clear, too, that previous exposure to the mass media may be among the factors which shape the perceptual selections which in turn shape the effects of subsequent exposures to mass media. Thus, the fact that perceptions are selective is no warrant for complacent assumptions that the impact of mass communication upon values is either negligible or necessarily benign.

REFERENCES

1. See also William R. Catton, Jr., "A Theory of Value," *American Sociological Review,* 24 (June 1959), pp. 310-317; Douglas Waples, Bernard Berelson, and Franklyn R. Bradshaw, *What Reading Does to People* (Chicago: Univ. of Chicago Press, 1940), pp. 21-22. For a somewhat different but compatible definition, see Richard T. LaPiere, *A Theory of Social Control* (New York: McGraw-Hill, 1954), p. 133.
2. LaPiere, *op. cit.* note 1, p. 142.

3. Waples, Berelson and Bradshaw, *op. cit.*, note 1, p. 103.
4. Wilbur Schramm, Jack Lyle, and Edwin B. Parker, *Television in the Lives of Our Children* (Stanford, Calif.: Stanford Univ. Press, 1961), pp. 22-23.
5. Albert Bandura and Frances L. Menlove, "Factors Determining Vicarious Extinction of Avoidance Behavior Through Symbolic Modeling." *Journal of Personality and Social Psychology*, 8 (1968), pp. 99-108.
6. *Ibid.,* p. 106.
7. Bernard Berelson and Patricia J. Salter, "Majority and Minority Americans: An Analysis of Magazine Fiction," *Public Opinion Quarterly*, 10 (Summer, 1946), pp. 168-190.
8. Herta Herzog, "Motivations and Gratifications of Daily Serial Listeners," reprinted from Paul Lazarsfeld and Frank Stanton (eds.), *Radio Research, 1942-1943* (New York: Duell, Sloan & Pearce, 1944) and in Wilbur Schramm (ed.), *The Process and Effects of Mass Communication* (Urbana, Ill.: Univ. of Illinois Press, 1954), pp. 50-55.
9. *Ibid.*
10. Hilde T. Himmelweit, A. N. Oppenheim, and Pamela Vince, *Television and the Child* (London: Oxford U. Press, 1958), pp. 260-261.
11. Schramm, , Lyle, and Parker, *op. cit.* note 4, p. 55.
12. Himmelweit, Oppenheim, and Vince, *op. cit.*, note 10, p. 216.
13. Fredric Wertham, "School for Violence," in Otto N. Larsen (ed.), *Violence and the Mass Media* (New York: Harper & Row, 1968), p. 39.
14. Himmelweit, Oppenheim, and Vince, *op. cit.*, note 10, p. 184 (emphasis added).
15. *Ibid.*
16. O. Ivar Lövass, "Effect of Exposure to Symbolic Agression on Aggressive Behavior," *Child Development*, 32 (1961), pp. 37-44.
17. Paul Mussen and Eldred Rutherford, "Effects of Aggressive Cartoons on Children's Aggressive Play," *Journal of Abnormal and Social Psychology*, 62 (1961), pp. 461-464.
18. S. H. Lovibond, "The Effect of Media Stressing Crime and Violence Upon Children's Attitudes," *Social Problems*, 15 (1967), pp. 91-100.
19. Katherine M. Wolfe and Marjorie Fiske, "Why They Read Comics," reprinted from Paul Lazarsfeld and Frank Stanton (eds.), *Communications Research, 1948-1949* (New York: Harper & Bros., 1949); and Wilbur Schramm (ed.), *The Process and Effects of Mass Communication* (Urbana, Ill.: Univ. of Illinois Press, 1954), p. 49.
20. Robert B. Zajonc, "Some Effects of the 'Space' Serials," *Public Opinion Quarterly*, 18 (1954), pp. 373.
21. Leonard Berkowitz and Russell G. Geen, "Stimulus Qualities of the Target of Aggression: A Further Study," *Journal of Personality and Social Psychology*, 5 (1967), pp. 364-368.
22. Percy H. Tannenbaum and Bradley S. Greenberg, "Mass Communication," *Annual Review of Psychology*, 19 (1968), pp. 372-373.
23. Leonard Berkowitz, "The Effects of Observing Violence," *Scientific American*, 210 (Feb. 1964), p. 5.
24. Himmelweit, Oppenheim, and Vince, *op. cit.*, note 10, p. 216.
25. Wertham, *op. cit.*, note 13, p. 38
26. Himmelweit, Oppenheim, and Vince, *op. cit.*, note 10, p. 190.
27. *Ibid.*, p. 256.
28. *Ibid.*, pp. 253-254.
29. *Ibid.*, pp. 247-248.
30. Albert Bandura and Richard H. Walters, *Social Learning and Personality Development* (New York: Holt, Rinehart & Winston, 1963), p. 65.
31. *Ibid.*, p. 66.
32. *Ibid.*, pp. 76-78.
33. Melvin L. DeFleur, "Occupational Roles as Portrayed on Television," *Public Opinion Quarterly*, 28 (Spring, 1964), pp. 68-69.
34. Himmelweit, Oppenheim, and Vince, *op. cit.*, note 10, p. 18.
35. Schramm, Lyle, and Parker, *op. cit.*, note 4, p. 114.
36. *Ibid.*, pp. 57-58.
37. *Ibid.*, pp. 58-59.
38. Himmelweit, Oppenheim, and Vince, *op. cit.*, note 10, p. 246.

39. Schramm, Lyle, and Parker, *op. cit.*, note 4, p. 91.
40. *Ibid.*, pp. 93-94.
41. Bandura and Menlove, *op. cit.*, note 5, pp. 102-103.
42. See Ruth C. Peterson and L. L. Thurstone, *Motion Pictures and the Social Attitudes of Children* (New York: Macmillan, 1933), pp. 65-66; and Perry W. Holaday and George D. Stoddard, *Getting Ideas from the Movies* (New York: Macmillan, 1933), pp. 78-79.
43. Carl I. Hovland, Arthur A. Lumsdaine, and Fred D. Sheffield, *Experiments on Mass Communication* (Princeton, N.J.: Princeton Univ. Press, 1949), ch. 7.
44. William R. Catton, Jr., "Changing Cognitive Structure as a Basis for the 'Sleeper Effect,'" *Social Forces,* 38 (May 1960), pp. 348-354.

Chapter 14

MASS MEDIA AS ACTIVATORS
OF LATENT TENDENCIES*

From what has been said in the preceding chapters, it should be abundantly clear that good intentions are not enough. Evidence that media operators are good people and have no desire to promote violence cannot suffice to prove that mass communications either cannot or do not produce increases in violent behavior.

It is not necessary to assume that the mass media would have to change people's values, either, in order to change their behavior. Values and behavior are not that tightly linked. Making audiences value violence is not the only conceivable way in which mass media could promote violent actions. For various reasons, people do not always do what they would value doing, and they sometimes undertake actions that are markedly inconsistent with the values they hold.

It is likewise not necessary to assume that the mass media would have to produce deviant motivation in order to foster deviant behavior. Deviant behavior may be either intentional or unintentional. People with deviant motivations may not behave in a deviant manner, for any of several reasons. Blake and Davis have listed five reasons why deviant motivation may not result in deviant actions: (1) A person tempted to deviate in certain ways from one norm may be inhibited by other norms and values which he has also internalized. (2) People generally desire approval by others and the temptation to deviate from some norm may be offset by the recognition that it will result in disapproval. (3) The temptation to deviate may also be offset by anticipation of formal punishment. (4) The anticipation of mere nonreward, even without actual anticipation of disapproval and punishment, may keep a person from deviating in spite of temptation to do so. Nonreward, unlike punishment, affords no glamour or heroic status to the deviant. (5) Deviant behavior may be inhibited by lack of opportunity even when a person is motivated toward it.[1]

To the extent that deviant motivation may already exist, and to the extent that the mass media may inadvertently alter any of these preventives of

*A paper prepared for the Media Task Force by William R. Catton, Jr., Professor of Sociology, University of Washington.

deviant behavior, the media can thus indirectly and unintentionally foster deviant actions.

A. Changing Behavior Without Changing Values

The same values do not always produce the same behavior, and different values do not always give rise to different behavior. There are several reasons for this. If different people with the same values have different kinds or different amounts of knowledge about the characteristics of various potential goals, the knowledge differences will cause the same values to lead to different actions. Even if the values and the knowledge are alike for various people, these persons may act differently if they are at different distances from the goals in question. Proximity to a potential goal tends to make it a stronger motivator. Not many people will literally "walk a mile for a Camel," especially if another brand is available only a few feet away.

Each person has many values. At any given moment, only one or a few of his values are salient. Two persons with the same sets of values, then, may behave differently because different ones of their values are activated at a given moment.

If all these things are kept in mind it should be clear that overt adoption of some action which has been persuasively advocated through mass media is by no means the only kind of "effect" mass media may have. Audience behavior can be influenced without any change of attitudes or values. Mass communications may convey new knowledge about goals already sought, thus altering the goal-pursuing behavior of the audience. Or, mass media may indicate to audience members that their proximity to (and hence motivation to strive for) a goal they already desire is greater than they had supposed. Mass media content may alter the momentary salience of the various values already held by the audience member, showing him that another of his values applies to a given situation to a greater degree than the one he had been invoking.

In all of this, the fact that incidental learning does occur must also be borne in mind. Sheer entertainment content, not intended to affect either values or behavior, may influence what audience members do if, in an incidental way, it modifies any of the kinds of conditions set forth in the last several paragraphs.

Apologists for mass media, especially television, have argued that the provision of substitute satisfactions or vicarious experiences can serve to prevent overt actions that would be socially undesirable. According to this line of reasoning, the mass media serve a socially useful "cathartic" function; by displaying violence they provide harmless outlets for the violent impulses of audience members. But this is apparently not the way it works, according to a series of experiments summarized by Berkowitz.[2] These studies have shown that catharsis is less likely than arousal of aggressive behavior, as a result of observation of aggression. In particular, watching "justified movie violence" does not discharge the anger of previously antagonized viewers but rather makes them feel freer to attack the person who had antagonized them.

It has become clear from a considerable body of research that televised or filmed violence affects viewers in one or more of the following ways: (1) It may reduce their inhibitions against behaving in violent and aggressive ways. (2) It may teach them forms of aggression, by giving them information about how someone they may want to attack could be attacked when an occasion presents itself. (3) The customary ethical ending, which supposedly shows that crime or other wrongdoing does not pay because the villian gets punished, may *delay* any tendency by viewers to reproduce the actions they have seen, but such endings do not always suffice to eliminate effects (1) and (2).[3]

In more general terms, studies of the effects of observing models have experimentally demonstrated that (1) the observer may learn novel responses—and this is what is meant by the "modeling effect;" (2) the observer may have existing responses strengthened or weakened—"disinhibited or inhibited;" or (3) the observer may be stimulated to do something he has already learned to do—the "eliciting effect."[4] The eliciting effect is far more likely than the cathartic effect. By providing cues that violence is socially acceptable, mass media may inadvertently both elicit and disinhibit violent behavior.[5]

Consider the fact that military training, which teaches men to use weapons, can only be effective by expecting the trainees to apply their training at a later time under motivational conditions that differ from those prevailing during training. If the military trainee can generalize what he has been taught to a motivationally different situation, so can the mass media audience member. A child observing use of such a weapon as a switch-blade knife (either in face-to-face play or in mass media entertainment, or both) acquires a greater likelihood of inflicting injury later if three things happen to be present: appropriate motivation for using such a weapon, the weapon itself, and a person whom he defines as an object of his hostility. One who had not observed the weapon's use would lack one learning ingredient fostering the act.[6]

Berkowitz described an experiment with male college students which shows that the several ingredients for hostile behavior can be acquired at different times. Subjects in that experiement were led to expect an opportunity to retaliate after receiving electric shocks from a supposed partner, but they were then denied this opportunity at the time it was expected. They retaliated more aggressively later when another opportunity was given than did subjects who had not originally been led to expect to be able to retaliate.[7] It is possible that one effect of the traditional "ethical ending" of crime shows is to teach the idea that opportunities to retaliate against offenders are usually forthcoming. If the viewer doesn't absorb this expectation of the right to retaliate from this source alone, he is also in a position to acquire it from observing the recurrent exchanges of violence berween the "good guys" and the "bad guys."

It is not necessary to continue making the assumption that audience "persuasion" by mass media consists in so modifying the individual audience member's internal psychological structure (e.g., his values) that "the psychodynamic relationship between latent internal processes and manifest overt behavior will lead to acts intended by the persuader." Such mass media persuasion efforts as charity appeals, chest X-ray drives, political campaigns, and efforts toward prevention of littering have apparently operated on such an assumption.[8] In the several other ways already enumerated, behavior can be changed without changing values—and the mass media are no more automatically exempt from producing such effects than any other agent to which people devote so much of their time and attention.

B. *Communication and Social Contagion*

Is it only coincidence that the crescendo of campus unrest, street demonstrations, etc.—so uncharacteristic of American life in the past—has come in the years when the first generation to have been wholly socialized within a society saturated with television were graduating from adolescence into adulthood? To raise such a question is not merely to "blame" television indiscriminately for diverse social problems. It is to suggest simply that the ubiquity of this medium in our lives is a fact of some social importance. People ordinarily learn in the process of being socialized that they can check doubtful impressions of the world around them which they have obtained from one source by seeking information from other, independent sources. The ubiquity of television, together with the degree to which people depend on it both as a prime news source and as a means of entertainment from which—with their guard down—they derive incidental learning, tends to undermine the independence of anyone's alternative sources.[9] If one viewer derives from his exposure to TV crime shows the notion that police are often stupid and brutal, and if he asks his acquaintances, "Do you think the cops are stupid and brutal?" they may "confirm" his impressions because they have been watching the same shows. But, having thus obtained the same image from several sources which seem independent to him, this viewer's impression hardens into a conviction. Worse yet, the conviction may cause him so to act in some subsequent encounter with a law enforcement official, as to elicit a hostile response which he will then regard as the final "confirmation."

The ubiquity of the medium can cause problems in other ways, too. It is common to ask whether *viewing* violence on TV tends to make the viewer more prone to commit acts of violence. It is often assumed that the answer is affirmative, and mass media research findings have been interpreted both ways—in opposition to the assumption and in support of it. But it is not so commonly asked whether the expectation or hope of *being shown* on television in the act of committing violent acts increases the probability of so acting. There are at least two reasons for believing the medium may have this effect. The "status conferral" function of the mass media generally, combined with the "visual bias" of television, previously discussed, can operate to favor violent behavior. When people want attention, whether just for the sake of some non-instrumental sort of status, or because they want to say something to an audience, they are under some pressure to do the things that will get them the attention they want. One way to get attention from the television cameras is to behave in a "newsworthy" way, which can mean to engage in acts of disruption or violence which the television news people are likely to film for showing on the air.

Along with recognition of the status conferral function, it has been supposed that mass media can perform an "ethicizing" function by strengthening social control and prevention of deviance through the publicizing of deviant behavior.[10] There is no sufficient reason, however, for believing that publicity is necessarily unwanted by everyone engaged in actions which someone may regard as deviant. Publicity may be precisely what is desired, especially by people of strong convictions who feel themselves denied a hearing through conventional channels. Such people may include: Negroes still suffering deprivations and injustices a century after the nominal ending of slavery; white urban residents who are resentful of assorted changes in their urban environments—including the influx of black population; college students perturbed about the depersonalized nature of modern, large-scale campus life and angry about the prospect of having to leave even this to serve in the military in a war they disapprove of and which they believe their country improperly stumbled into; or policemen who feel beleaguered by each of the previous categories and earnestly desire increased public support for their own profession. Whether the publicity any of these groups can obtain for themselves by acting in ways that cater to television's visual bias will actually serve their more ultimate ends is somewhat beside the point. One thing they all have in common is the feeling that they are being overlooked, and by relieving them of at least *that* sense of deprivation, the attention their actions obtain from television cameras provides reinforcement of whatever kinds of actions receive such attention.

There is another, and perhaps even subtler, way in which the television display of various forms of behavior that had generally been regarded as anti-social can tend to foster more of it. The word "contagion" may not be too inapplicable. People who have felt certain impulses but have not acted them out may be more likely to do so when they become aware that others are doing so. This would be especially so when the impulses are strong and when the other people have similar identity so that they function as a positive reference group. Students at the Free University of West Berlin, after staging a sit-in demonstration, were reported to have asked an American on the scene, "Is this the way it was done at Berkeley?" The implication is that definitions of the student role are not confined to a single campus. When students on one campus are aware of the way the role is defined elsewhere, under some circumstances they may feel some obligation to adopt behavior that was previously alien to them because it now appears to be part of the very role to which they feel committed. And again, because of television's visual bias, the aspect of campus life most likely to attract the cameras and microphones (other than intercollegiate athletics) is more likely to be protest demonstrations, especially when disorderly, than quiet and serious work in classrooms, libraries, and laboratories.

In many languages, it is said, "teach" and "show" are completely synonymous. Children in many societies learn a good deal of their society's culture by learning to do what they see adults doing, rather than just what adults may tell them to do. Learning from models, live or symbolized, is common to the socialization process in all cultures.[11] Development of the mass media has hardly exempted the technologically advanced societies from these principles.

"Behavioral contagion" has been observed in a number of species. It refers to processes that include the release of a well-established pattern of behavior in other members of a species when they witness that pattern's occurrence in one of them. One familiar example is the "social facilitation" of yawning in a group of humans.[12] In the absence of mass media, one person's yawn is unlikely to release similar responses in more than a few other individuals. But television can make common role models available to a worldwide (or nationwide) audience of potential players of the same role. Television can provide reference groups and a knowledge of their norms and values. For example, in pre-mass media days, a farm girl might have few role models for feminine behavior beyond her own mother, sisters, and the occasionally encountered relatives and neighbors who happened to be female. Today, her descendent can model her behavior as a woman after glimpses she has had of "womanly" behavior all over the world, in many walks of life. Similarly, learning to be Negro in a white-dominated society meant one thing to the socially isolated sharecropper's child; it means something else to the child in the urban ghetto with access to a television set, and its new meaning can easily include violent rejection of anything regarded as a token of continued white dominance. The ghetto dweller's child has abundant opportunities to see whites in roles other than landlord and overseer, and he has abundant opportunities to see how other Negroes are going about the business of breaking down racial barriers. If television gives him more glimpses of the violent ways than of the non-violent ways, he must be expected to learn accordingly.

C. Identities, Reference Groups, Information, and Action

There are some rather clear techniques by which a mass communicator can exert persuasion. He can relate an object of persuasion to a role with which audience members are known or expected to identify, and he can stress a definition of that role which involves use of the object, implying that non-users are *deviant*. The communicator may portray or imply social sanctions which can or will be brought to bear upon such deviants, or he can describe or allude to the social rewards and social approval likely to accrue to the adopter of the communicator's goals. Congruence of the suggested act with group approved values, or with values known to be already accepted by the audience, may be asserted and emphasized. This will tend to show how compliance by the individual audience member with the patterns of action the communicator is trying to persuade him to accept will be good for the audience member's own group.[13]

The skill of a communicator in deliberate persuasive efforts depends on the correctness of his assumptions as to the identities of members of his audience (as they perceive themselves), the reference groups to whose values they are attracted or committed, and the kinds of information they already have and the kinds they need in order to act out their identities in the way he desires and to invoke their reference groups' values along lines he intends. All of these considerations apply in a modified way to unintended persuasion, to incidental learning, or to inadvertent symbolic modeling.

In an experiment by Maccoby, Wilson, and Burton, observations of subjects' eye movements showed that during romantic movie scenes involving just two characters—the male lead and the female lead—male viewers had their eyes on the male actor more of the time than did female viewers, while the latter spent more time than did male viewers watching the female player.[14] Reasoning purely from the sex interests of the viewers, it might have been expected that boys would watch girls, and vice versa, so the actual results which were contrary to this strongly suggest a predominance of the process of identification. Each subject watched the movie character whose actions were most likely to resemble his own. To the extent that the subject might be inclined to take the movie character as a model, then, he might change his own actions in similar situations to change the degree of resemblance. For a model he defined positively, the observer would tend to increase the resemblance between his own behavior and the model's; for a model defined negatively, the tendency would be to decrease the behavioral resemblance.

Maccoby and Wilson also showed a "class B" movie to seventh graders and tested them for retention of its content. Boys were found more likely to remember aggressive content, and girls were found more likely to remember romantic content. But boys remembered proportionately more of the aggressive acts of male characters than of female characters, and girls remembered proportionately more of the romantic acts of female characters than of male characters.[15] If observation and retention were thus selective along sex lines (and presumably further tests would show other identity lines of selectivity), then observational learning can be expected to depend on the matching of identities between model and observer.

Waples, Berelson, and Bradshaw cited the kinds of satisfactions housewives obtained from reading women's magazines to illustrate enhancement of readers' prestige as a social effect of reading. Housewife readers received implied prestige from emphasis placed in such magazines upon "the complexities of domestic life, on the skills required to be parent, dietitian, decorator, chauffeur, politician, and economist at the same time." They added that,

> When fiction plays up the important role of women whose husbands stray from the marital fold only to be retrieved by the tact of the wife, or whose children go mildly astray and are rescued, the prestige effects are further intensified. Where the mother considers divorce or ventures into business, calamities crowd the pages, and the reader eventually decides that husband and home are the true sources of happiness. Match this with readers who fear that their husbands and children will err, but who want to believe that women can hold the home together, and the effect is a sense of pride at what a woman can do and security that this reader can do as well as a fiction character.[16]

The possible effects of magazine fiction were also discussed, as noted earlier, by Berelson and Salter.[17] They made an analysis of the characteristics and roles of all speaking characters portrayed in 198 short stories published in sample issues of eight of America's most widely circulated magazines in 1937 and 1943. Their analysis revealed abundant stereotyping and clearcut discrimination. Minorities were numerically underrepresented, and were usually assigned to unimportant or unfavorably described roles, and often stereotyped. Common stereotypes included "the amusingly ignorant Negro," "The Italian gangster," "The sly and shrewd Jew," "The emotional Irish," etc.

Berelson and Salter studied magazine stories, not readers of magazine stories. To the reader who identifies with majority characters while reading such stories, the story treatment of minority characters could become a model which could affect his subsequent behavior— particularly if that is the way the minority characters are treated in the story by the characters with whom majority readers identify, and if such majority character behavior is rewarded in the story. Such considerations as these partially offset the lack of data directly revealing reader reactions. Berelson and Salter asserted that an ethnic group stereotype in such fiction "operates socially as a stimulus of xenophobia."[18] They attributed no mal-intent to the stories' writers, and they recognized that minority stereotypes facilitate the filling of stock roles with stock characters, thus meeting the need of this category of fiction for brief, compact plots, in which the action develops quickly and with clarity. Considerations of business success and audience heterogeneity help perpetuate formula writing, they noted. But such writing, they went on to suggest, actually activates prejudice in its readers, who use the discriminatory fictional portrayals of certain minorities as "proof" of the validity of stereotypes already held by the readers.

What do minority readers of such fiction learn? This question is seldom asked. It seems unlikely that the majority reader identifies with a majority character solely because of their common majority status; writers have a variety of more sophisticated techniques which they use to induce reader identification with certain characters around whom the story revolves. Accordingly, minority readers may experience an ambivalence not felt by majority readers, for they will be affected by these deliberately used identification-provoking techniques but will, because of their minority status, also identify with some of the unfavorably depicted characters.

Regardless of internal psychological predispositions, people acquire definitions of appropriate behavior and interpretations of reality from their organizational memberships, their work roles, reference groups, cultural norms, and primary group expectations. This has been made clear by a substantial body of research and theory in sociology. DeFleur cites these matters in the context of showing why mass media should not be considered hypodermically omnipotent,[19] but it can also be noted that people acquire definitions of appropriate behavior and interpretations of reality from the mass media.

In one experiment, six groups of six children apiece were shown a movie in which an adult did various simple acts with various objects. Three of the groups were told beforehand that they would be tested afterward on their ability to do the same things with such objects. Three were not told this, but were also tested afterward. One group from each set was instructed to verbalize what they saw as they watched the four-minute film. Another group from each set was told to count as they watched (thereby distracting them from even covertly verbalizing what they were watching). The remaining groups just watched. Verbalizing what was seen increased ability to reproduce the acts later, while counting somewhat reduced it, in comparison with the control groups. Advance warning that this ability to reproduce the acts would be tested afterward somewhat diminished the spread that was wrought by verbalizing versus counting.[20] The various manipulations of the subjects in this experiment can be interpreted as having altered the degree to which the children in the various groups watched the adult in the movie as a role model—i.e., as a person who either could be or should be identified with and imitated. Thus, the results of the experiment support the principle that observational learning depends on perception of the model in terms of common identity.

The effects of reference groups (or reference persons) and the way such effects can be modified are evident from an experiment in which seven to eleven-year-old subjects played a sort of bowling game and rewarded their own performances by taking plastic tokens from a bowl, after watching an adult model or a peer model, or both, play the game and reward their own performances in this manner. When children saw the adult model set high achievement standards for himself, reward himself according to such standards and receive social recognition for adhering to such norms, these children subsequently imposed higher performance standards on themselves than did children who had seen models doing exactly the same but without getting social recognition for it.[21]

In an experiment with 84 boys whose mean age was just under six, exposure to a three-minute color movie (silent, but with backgound music) was shown to affect subsequent tendencies to play with available but forbidden toys in the experimental room. The movie depicted a child playing with similar toys. Three versions of the film differed in their endings. When the child in the film was rewarded for his actions, or incurred no consequences, the subjects deviated more (and more promptly) than when the movie ended with a punishment scene, or when the subject saw no movie at all.[22] What happens to the model as a consequence of his behavior, then, clearly affects the model's influence on the behavior of an observer.[23]

In another experiment subjects were "frustrated" at the beginning by being shocked several times by an accomplice who purported to be another subject in the experiment. They then viewed either a boxing film in which one character takes a brutal beating, or a neutral film showing no such aggression. Afterward, the subjects were given a chance ostensibly to administer shocks to the accomplice. If the accomplice had been originally introduced by a name resembling either the beaten character in the boxing movie or the actor portraying him, the subject tended to give more shocks than when the accomplice was otherwise introduced or when the neutral film was shown. The number of shocks given was not increased by having introduced the accomplice by a name associating him with the movie character who did the beating.[24] Thus, aggressive responses by the subject were patterned according to variable relationships among the apparent identities of film models, subject, target, and whatever preexisting values provide standards of "justification" for aggression.

REFERENCES

1. Judith Blake and Kingsley Davis, "Norms, Values, and Sanctions," in R.E. L. Faris (ed.), *Handbook of Modern Sociology* (Chicago: Rand McNally, 1964), pp. 456-484.
2. Leonard Berkowitz, "The Effects of Observing Violence," *Scientific American*, 210 (Feb. 1964), pp. 1-8.
3. Albert Bandura, "What TV Violence Can do to Your Child," reprinted from *Look*

(Oct. 22, 1963), pp. 46-52 in Otto N. Larsen (ed.), *Violence and the Mass Media* (New York: Harper & Row, 1968), p. 130.

4. Albert Bandura and Richard H. Walters, *Social Learning and Personality Development* (New York: Holt, Rinehart & Winston, 1963), p. 60.

5. Larsen, *op. cit.* note 3, p. 117.

6. Bandura and Walters, *op. cit.* note 4, pp. 116-117.

7. Leonard Berkowitz, "On Not Being Able to Aggress," *British Journal of Social and Clinical Psychology*, 5 (1966), pp. 130-139.

8. Melvin L. DeFleur, *Theories of Mass Communication* (New York: David McKay, 1966), p. 123.

9. Melvin L. DeFleur, "Occupational Roles as Portrayed on Television," *Public Opinion Quarterly*, 28 (Spring, 1964), p. 74.

10. Paul F. Lazarsfeld and Robert K. Merton, "Mass Communication, Popular Taste and Organized Social Action," in Lyman Bryson (ed.), *The Communication of Ideas* (New York: Harper & Bros., 1948), pp. 95-118.

11. Bandura and Walters, *op. cit.* note 4, pp. 47-49.

12. W? H. Thorpe, *Learning and Instinct in Animals* (London: Nethuen, 1956), pp. 120-122.

13. DeFleur, *Theories of Mass Communication*, pp. 136-137.

14. Eleanor E. Maccoby, W. C. Wilson, and R. V. Burton, "Differential Movie Viewing Behavior of Male and Female Viewers," *Journal of Personality*, 26 (1958), pp. 159-167.

15. Elenor E. Maccoby and W. C. Wilson, "Identification and Observational Learning from Films," *Journal of Abnormal and Social Psychology*, 55, (1957), pp. 76-87.

16. Douglas Waples, Bernard Berelson, and Franklyn R. Bradshaw, *What Reading Does to People* (Chicago: Univ. of Chicago Press, 1940), pp. 127-128.

17. Bernard Berelson and Patricia J. Salter, "Majority and Minority Americans: An Analysis of Magazine Fiction," *Public Opinion Quarterly*, 10 (Summer, 1946), pp. 168-190.

18. *Ibid.*, p. 179.

19. DeFleur, *Theories of Mass Communication*, p. 134.

20. Albert Bandura, Joan E. Grusec, and Frances L. Menlove, "Observational Learning as a Function of Symbolization and Incentive Set," *Child Development* (Sept. 1966), pp. 199-506.

21. Albert Bandura, Joan E. Grusec, and Frances L. Menlove, "Some Social Determinants of Self-Monitoring Reinforcement Systems," *Journal of Personality and Social Psychology*, 5 (1967), pp. 449-455.

22. Richard H. Walters and Ross D. Parke, "Influence of Response Consequences to a Social Model on Resistance to Deviation" *Journal of Experimental Child Psychology*, 1 (1964), pp. 269-280.

23. Bandura and Walters, *op. cit.* note 4, pp. 15, 103, 107; Richard H. Walters, Ross D. Parke, and Valarie A. Cane, "Timing of Punishment and the Observation of Consequences to Others as Determinants of Response Inhibition," *Journal of Experimental Child Psychology*, 2 (1965), pp. 10-30.

24. Leonard Berkowtz and Russell Geen, "Name-mediated Aggressive Cue Properties," *Journal of Personality*, 23 (1966), pp. 456-465..

Chapter 15

THE TELEVISION WORLD
OF VIOLENCE

Since the advent of mass communication which are owned and operated by increasingly complex and profitable corporations, there has been a growing concern on the part of citizens and public officials about the effects of mass media programming on audiences. Before these effects can be assessed in an objective and systematic way, it is necessary to know what the media are presenting to their audiences. The most effective way to determine this is through content analysis.

Analyses of mass media content vary considerably in their scope, focus, and information value for the problem of evaluation of the effects upon exposed audiences. The most common type is the familiar procedure of counting the number of times persons are shot, attacked, or killed in a given program or series of programs. However, this type of analysis provides very little information about the effects of the programming. For example, this knowledge does not tell us (a) if the killings were justified or unjustified; (b) if killers were rewarded or punished; (c) if the killings were presented in a bloodless and sanitized way, or in a "blood and guts" portrayal; and (d) whether or not the killings occurred sadistically, as a means to a desired end, or during the course of self-defense, law enforcement, or war.

The Media Task Force was directed by the Violence Commission to investigate the relationship of mass media programming and violence. Several initial decisions made by the Task Force led eventually to a contract with Dean George Gerbner and his staff at the Annenberg School of Communications. The Task Force first made the decision to concentrate on media *entertainment* programming. After a review of content analyses available, it was clear that no single or multiple research was sufficient.

The second decision concerned the selection of a mass medium for analysis. Studies of media availability, preferences, and use led to the selection of commercial television entertainment programming. Television has a virtual corner on the mass media entertainment market. No other single mass medium of communication approaches its claim on massive audiences composed of all sectors of American society.

Our findings show that 43 percent of adult Americans (eighteen years and older) picked television as the mass medium they use most of the time for entertainment. The next most chosen medium was books, a distant second with 19 percent.

At least two other considerations influenced our selection:

(1) Young children use television to an even greater extent than adults.[1] Most young children cannot read with sufficient proficiency to use newspapers, books, or magazines for daily entertainment, and they cannot or do not attend movies as a daily or weekly form of entertainment.[2] Radio will not hold their attention for any great length of time. Television, then, is uniquely equipped by its audiovisual properties to sustain children's attention. It is unique among the mass media for children's use because of its availability in the home and because advanced reading skills are not a prerequisite for use.

(2) Television is the only mass medium whose entertainment content at any point in time is very much the same regardless of locale. The three national networks, ABC, CBS, and NBC, through their owned stations and affiliates, are responsible for the vast majority of all entertainment broadcasting. Hence, when an analysis is made of television entertainment broadcast by these three networks, there is a high probability that audiences are being exposed to the same content.

We next had to decide what time periods to research and how to construct a content analysis that would provide useful information for the general research problem—the relationship of mass media entertainment programming and violence. The week of October 1 through 7 was selected as typical, and in order to assess possible changes in programming, the same week (October 1-7) was analyzed for both 1967 and 1968. It was further decided to analyze only prime-time viewing hours.

In the simplest of terms, the research aim was to provide an objective and reliable analysis from which the Task Force could deduce the messages about violence which were communicated to the audience. How violence is portrayed is at least as important as the amount presented. Knowledge of the incidence and intensity of violence in television programming can tell us, among other things, how often audiences are exposed to messages about violence and what opportunity audiences have to view programs which do not contain violence.

Finally, the Task Force had to decide who was best suited to perform the content analysis. We felt it essential that such an analysis should provide new and directly relevant information, and meet all the criteria of scientific objectivity and systematic thoroughness. Thus it was necessary that the task be undertaken by trained social scientists who had expertise in the methods of content analysis and mass media effects research. It was also important to find a group which had the necessary equipment (the capability to analyze video tape and film materials), and the ability to form an expert research team on extremely short notice.

We were fortunate to be able to contract the project to Dr. George Gerbner, Dean of the Annenberg School of Communications at the University of Pennsylvania. Dean Gerbner is a well-known expert on content analysis, and was keenly interested in conducting the type of research proposed by the Task Force.

It was also necessary to seek the cooperation of the three major television networks in this endeavor. The networks were most helpful in compiling and sending all the requested programs to the Annenberg School.[3]

The multitude of specific details involved in translating a research project aim into a viable research effort were carried out by Dr. Gerbner and his staff. In a remarkably short time, this group completed the analysis and submitted their report to the Task Force. Significant portions of the total report are presented in the following pages.

A. Dimensions of Violence in Television Drama: Summary[4]

In September of 1968, the Mass Media Task Force of the National Commission on the Causes and Prevention of Violence contacted Dr. Gerbner to inquire if a study of violence in television drama could be completed in less than two months. The study was to be based on a week's prime-time network programming from 1967. The purpose of the study was to yield objective and reliable indicators of the extent and nature of violent presentations shared by all classes of the American viewing public.

1. Challenge and Difficulties

The scope and significance of the challenge were matched by its difficulties. Some of these were conceptual. What are useful indicators of violence in fictional dramatizations? How could a study based on 1967 material reflect the impact upon television programming, if any, of the tragic series of violent events that shook the conscience of the nation and the world in 1968? It was felt that the study was worth attempting only if it could yield multiple indicators which would be useful for a variety of investigative and policy purposes, if it contained dimensions salient to problems of social communication theory and practice, and if it could include 1968 material relevant to the tendencies and dynamics of television programming.

Other difficulties were logistical. A team of research analysts had to be recruited immediately. Physical facilities and program material had to be obtained and organized. Instruments of analysis had to be constructed and tested with no opportunity for pilot studies. It was anticipated that much information would fall below acceptable standards of reliability and would have to be discarded. Therefore, several simultaneous approaches had to be employed to assure corroboration of results and sufficient useful information even after eventual elimination of much that had been assembled.

2. Accomplishments

The decision to proceed with the study was taken in the understanding that this would be a "bare bones" report, one with little interpretation. Its purpose would be to extend the factual basis for a consideration of one aspect of television programming and for the further exploration of the role of fictional violence in contemporary culture. Interpretation and analysis was to continue in a broader scope and context after the termination of the research reported here.

What follows, then, must be seen in light of these circumstances. The report overcame some of the difficulties and achieved some of the objectives, despite false starts, the elimination of much interesting material of questionable reliability, and unavoidable shortcomings. The principal lessons to be learned are (1) the confirmation of the adage that "haste makes waste," and (2) the clear conviction that if indices of mass cultural content have theoretical, social, and policy significance, only a systematic and continuous program of research will be adequate to the task.

A special debt is owed to wives and friends for many evenings and weekends of work, the ready assistance of an able clerical force, particularly Mrs. Kiki Faye, the support of the research staff of the Mass Media Task Force, and the full cooperation of the television networks.

B. A Bird's-Eye View of the Results

All network television programs transmitted during prime evening time and on Saturday morning during the weeks of October 1-7, 1967 and 1968, were monitored for this study. Regular television dramas, cartoon programs, and feature films presenting one or more plays were subjected to analysis. The analysts recorded observations about the prevalence and "seriousness" of violence in each play; rates and types of violent episodes; the role of major characters in inflicting or absorbing violence; the role different times, places, people, and "the law" play in the world of dramatic violence; the significance of violence to the plots; and, when violence was an integral part of the plot, the rates and characteristics of encounters between parties inflicting and suffering violence.

There are certain key terms used throughout this report, and they are defined as follows:

"Program" and "play" are synonymous unless otherwise noted, and denote a single fictional story presented in play or skit form. "Violence" means the overt expression of force intended to hurt or kill. A "violent episode" is a scene of any duration between the same violent parties. A story element, such as violence, "significant to the plot" is one that would be noted in a one-page general synopsis of the play. An "act of violence" or "encounter" is an action originating in a particular source and directed toward a particular receiver with no major shift in the style of action.

During the week of October 1-7, 1967, the three television networks transmitted 96 plays in 64 hours of broadcast time. During the same week in 1968 the networks transmitted 87 plays in 58½ hours. In the total of 183 plays or 122½ program hours analyzed, 455 characters played major parts, 241 of which were violent. These occurred in 149 plays (or 104.4 program hours), which contained a total of 872 violent episodes. Of all plays containing violence, 112 (or 78.9 program hours) portrayed violence significant to the plot. These plays included 1215 separate violent encounters.

1. The Extent of Violence

Some violence occurred in eight out of every ten plays. The average rate of violent episodes was five per play (ranging from three in a comedy to 7 in a cartoon or acting drama) and seven per program hour (ranging from five each comedy to twenty-four each cartoon hour).

Most violence was an integral part of the play in which it occurred. The average rate of acts of violence was eleven per play or fifteen per hour. Eight out of every ten violent episodes and acts were presented as serious rather than humorous occurrences.

There was no evidence of overall decline in the prevalence of violence from 1967 to 1968. Some indications of possible moderation come from slight and selective reductions in the rates of violent episodes per play, in the proportions of "serious" violence, and in the proportions of plays in which violence was significant to the plot. The rates of violent encounters in these plays indicated that, with some exceptions, the saturation of such programs with acts of violence remained in 1968 what it had been in 1967.

Programming on CBS generally featured the least violence, and moved in two different directions: the rate of violent episodes increased somewhat from 1967 to 1968, but the proportion of violence significant to the plots and the frequency of violent acts in such plays decreased. ABC, the most violent in many respects, maintained its share of violent programming but reduced the proportion of programs containing the most significant type and the highest rate of violent episodes. Violence on NBC, as prevalent in 1967 as on ABC, declined slightly in some respects in 1968.

2. The Nature of Violence

Violent acts were usually performed at close range. They were inflicted primarily through use of a weapon, half the time upon strangers, and, in the majority of encounters, upon opponents who could not or did not resist.

Those who committed acts of violence generally perceived them to be in self-interest rather than for some other reason. Violent encounters were usually between males, and almost as frequently between as within different national or ethnic groups. These encounters primarily engaged group leaders as initiators and group members as targets of violence.

Witnesses to scenes of violence were usually passive spectators. For every bystander who attempted to prevent violence, there was at least one who joined to assist or encourage it.

Pain was difficult to detect except when severe or fatal. Even so, some injury was evident in half of all violent episodes.The casualty count of injured and dead was at least 790 for the two weeks, and one in every ten acts of violence resulted in a fatality.

Most violence took place between the forces of good and evil. The "good guys" inflicted as much violence as the "bad guys," suffered a little more, but triumphed in the end.

3. The People of Violence

The two weeks of dramatic programming featured 455 leading characters. Of this number, 241 committed some violence, 54 killed an opponent, and 24 died violent deaths. The dramatic lead thus inflicted violence 50 percent of the time, became a killer ten percent of the time, and was killed five percent of the time. One-third of those killed were also killers, and one out of every seven killers died a violent death. Surprisingly, nearly half of all killers suffered no consequences for their acts.

The "typical violent" actor was an unmarried young or middle-aged male. At least one out of three characters in every age group committed violence, but the adolescent and the middle-aged perpetrated more than their share. They also played nine out of every ten killers and eight out of every ten fatal victims. Those in the middle-aged group were likely to be victims.

The forces of law and of lawlessness, each numbering about one out of every ten leading characters, accounted for one-third of all violent aggressors and half of all killers. Criminals were somewhat more likely to commit violence, but, when violent, agents of the law were as likely to kill as were criminals. Members of the armed forces were less violent than the other groups, but when violent, the most deadly; every second violent soldier killed an "enemy." More criminals than soldiers and none of the agents of the law died violent deaths.

There may be as many violent "good guys" as "bad guys," but those fated for a happy outcome (mostly "good guys") were slightly less likely to be violent than were those fated for a clearly unhappy outcome (mostly "bad guys"). Even though half of all "violents" and nearly half of all killers achieved a happy ending, those who did not were more likely to commit violence, to kill, and to be killed.

4. The World of Violence

The past, the future, and the far-away loom large in the world of violence. The settings of plays without violence tended to be contemporary, domestic, and civilized. By comparison, then, the settings of violent plays was more global, more distant in time as well as in place, more mobile, and more exotic.

Foreigners and non-whites committed more than their share of violence, and, unlike white Americans, for nearly every life taken, they paid with a life of their own.

Violence rarely appeared to violate legal codes, and when it did, the law itself was likely to be violent.

To sum up—the prevalence of violence in about eight out of every ten plays did not decline from 1967 to 1968, despite some evidence of moderation in its rate and tone. Most violence was individual, selfish, and often directed against strangers and victims who do not resist. Violence stuns, maims, and kills with little visible pain. A count of casualties may find an average of five per play injured or dead. Those who inflict violence may be "good guys" or "bad guys," but they are not as likely to reach a happy ending as non-violent types. All major characters, especially males in the prime of life, have a better than even chance to commit violence, at least one chance in ten to kill, and still reach a happy ending nearly fifty percent of the time. Foreigners and non-whites are more violent than white Americans, but pay much more dearly for their actions. Television drama projects Americans as a violent country a world of many violent strangers, with a mostly violent past and a totally violent future.

C. *Dimensions of Violence*

Violence in drama, as in life, is a complex matter, the full implications of which were not the subject of this study. Our subject was the extent and nature of overt violence in television plays. Our purposes were (1) to extend the factual consideration of one aspect of television programming; (2) to make a contribution to the understanding of some dimensions of the dynamics of fictional violence; and (3) to suggest certain expectations about violent behavior and consequences that these presentations might cultivate.

In the following pages, we give a descriptive account of the "bare facts" relevant to the extent of violent representations during the 1967 and 1968 study periods and to selected manifestations of violent behavior, people, and circumstances in the fictional world of television drama.[5]

Selected findings will be discussed according to their relevance to these questions:

How much violence is there is television drama? Did the prevalence, significance, frequency, and "seriousness" of violent portrayals change between the 1967 and 1968 study periods?

What is the nature of violence in television drama? What characteristics of violent behavior and of its consequences do these portrayals present to the audience?

Who are the people of violence? What is the distribution of violent roles among various groups of the fictional population? What part does violence play in the fate of "good guys" and "bad guys"?

And, finally, how does the world of violence differ from the world of non-violent drama in historical time, place of action, nationality and ethnicity of the population, and some of its recurrent themes?

The analysis included all dramatic network programs transmitted in prime evening time and Saturday mornings for the weeks of October 1-7 in 1967 and 1968. The 1967 study period contained ninety-six plays and the 1968 period eighty-seven. It should be noted again that the basic program unit analyzed was the play, and the terms "program" and "play" are used interchangeably.

To correct for differences in playing time between short plays and skits and long plays or feature-length films, the time of a program was also measured. The 1967 study period included sixty-four hours of dramatic programming, and the 1968 period fifty-eight and one half hours.

Regualr drama programs produced for television comprised 60 percent of all plays in 1967 and 63 percent in 1968, or 62 percent and 69 percent of program hours, respectively. Cartoons accounted for 33 percent of program time. Six feature films were telecast each week, accounting for six and eight percnt of the plays, but twenty and 26 percent of program time.

Crime, western, and action-adventure style stories comprised about two-thirds of all television drama; comedies made up nearly half of all programs, with some changes in proportions and shifts in network share of each kind between the two study periods. Differences in the extent of violence between the 1967 and 1968 study periods and among the networks may be attributed to shifts in a few program categories, policies affecting most programs, or to a combination of both.

1. The Extent of Violence

How much violence was there in television drama? Did the three networks share equally in the amount? Did the proportions change between 1967 and 1968?

The four dimensions dealing primarily with the amount of violence are prevalence, significance to the story, rate, and extent of "seriousness."

Prevalence is the incidence of any violence on a program. It measures the number of programs in which at least one violent act occurs, regardless of frequency or other characteristics.

Significance to the story indicates the extent to which violence was an integral part of the plot.

The rate of violence was measured as the frequency of violent episodes and acts per play and program hour.

"Seriousness" involved the style and context of violent portrayals. How much violence was presented in a humorous vein, and how much was not?

a. *Prevalence*

Some violence occured in 81 percent of all programs and 85 percent of all program hours. The prevalence of violence in dramatic programming did not decline between 1967 and 1968. If anything, there was a slight (four percent) increase.

Violence was more prevalent on ABC and NBC than on CBS. However, CBS increased its percentage of violent programming between the 1967 and 1968 study periods.

b. *Significance to the Story*

Violence may be either an incidental or integral part of the story. The measure of significance was used to ascertain the proportions of these two types of presentations. (It was also employed as a screening device to select those plays in which violent encounters and acts were to be subjected to further analysis). The criterion used to measure "significance to the plot" was whether or not the violence, regardless of type or amount, would have to be noted in a one-page summary of the story of the play.[6]

Most plays containing any violence met this criterion. Eight out of every ten violent programs in 1967 and seven out of ten in 1968 contained violence significant to the plot. Whether this slight change represents a real decline or merely reflects shifts in the proportion of different types of plays in uncertain; but at least the overall significance of violence did not increase.

c. *Rates of Violent Episodes and Acts*

Violent *episodes* are defined as scenes of violence involving the same parties, and violent *acts* as actions by each party in violent encounters on programs where violence was judged to be significant to the plot.

During the 1967 study week, a total of 478 violent episodes were observed. During the 1968 study week, 394 such episodes were observed. This decline of 18 percent, compared to the 10 percent decrease of all dramatic programs analyzed, indicated the possibility of a slight reduction in the overall number of violent episodes.

Violent episodes ranged from three per comedy to seven per cartoon or crime, western, and action-adventure play, and from five per hour of all comedy programming to 24 per hour of cartoons. The overall rate of violent episodes was five per play or seven per program hour. Programming which contained any violence at all contained an average of six violent episodes per play and eight per hour. Reductions in these rates by less than one point per play and per hour indicate that the frequency of violent episodes might have declined slightly from 1967 to 1968. The overall reduction, if any, was not evenly distributed.

CBS programs generally contained somewhat lower rates of violent episodes than did those of the other two networks. However, although ABC and NBC reduced their frequencies of violent episodes, CBS increased theirs.

Of all the violent episodes on the networks for both years, 35 percent were transmitted by ABC, 37 percent by NBC, and 28 percent by CBS. Although 1967 figures show ABC leading (41 percent). NBC second (36 percent, and CBS third (23 percent), in 1968, NBC led (37 percent), CBS was second (35 percent), and ABC third (28 percent). A reduction in the number of cartoon, crime, and other action programs and perhaps in the general level of violent spisodes on ABC and an increase in cartoon violence on both CBS and NBC appear to have been the major sources of these relative shifts.

The rate of violent *acts* per play was 11.1 in 1967 and 10.5 in 1968. The only substantial change was a reduction of the rate of violent acts from 10.9 to 7.1 per play on CBS programs. In other words, although CBS increased its share of dramatic violence, it reduced the frequency of violent acts on those programs.

d. *The "Seriousness" of Violence*

It can be argued that violence is always relevant to personal existence, well-being, and integrity. To that extent, violence is always serious. Whether presenting it in a humorous way makes it more or less acceptable or part of a given framework of knowledge are issues that measures of presentation alone cannot resolve.

Measures of "seriousness" can indicate dramatic convention, convenience, and intent. They show that even when we include cartoons (which are saturated with violence), the great bulk of all violence occurs in a serious or sinister context.

Three-fourths of all violent programs and nearly nine out of every ten violent episodes were found in the crime, western, or action-adventure categories. Nearly all such programs contained some violence. Separate observations in all program categories showed that eight out of every ten violent episodes occured in a serious or sinister context. Eight out of every ten violent acts were also judged as "serious." In other words, overtly humorous (slapstick, sham, satirical) intent was apparent in only two out of every ten violent episodes or acts in all program categories. However, there appeared to be a shift (of perhaps one in every ten) toward a higher proportion of "humorous" types of violence between the two study periods.

2. The Nature of Violence

What happens in violent incidents, and how? What are some personal and social characteristics and consequences of violent behavior in television drama? The portrayal of violence may be at least as relevant to the cultivation of public assumptions as the amount of violence presented. We turn, therefore, from general questions of amount to more specific questions about the nature of violent representations.

Two different approaches were focused on selected characteristics of violent behavior. One was the observation of violent episodes in all plays, concentrating on the agents and means of violence, witnesses and group relations among violent opponents. Another set of observations dealt with *acts* of violence in plays in which violence was significant to the plot (112 out of 183). The focus here was on the nature of the interaction between sources and receivers of violence.

Any reference to persons involved in violent episodes and acts is not to individuals as such, but to their participation in the incidents observed. A single individual may participate in several capacities. Participation as both source and receiver tends to equalize figures in those categories and lends greater significance to such differences as may occur.

Three-fourths of all violent episodes involved human agents (both "live" and cartoon). The rest involved "humanized" (speaking) and other animals, creatures (a robot), and "accidents" (which, in fiction, are of course not accidental). There was no "act of nature" found as an agent of violence.[7] All violent acts involved human or human-like sources and receivers.[8]

a. Means and Personal Aspects

Weapons were used in at least six out of every ten violent episodes and acts. Small instruments were used to commit one-third of all violent acts, and more complex instruments, ranging from machine guns and explosives to elaborate devices of torture or mass destruction, were used in 26 percent of the acts.

In the majority of acts (six out of ten), those who committed violence perceived it as in their own personal self-interest rather than as a service to some other cause.

Was it effective? In terms of immediate response, yes. Six out of ten violent acts evoked no response from their victims; they could not or did not resist. Counter-violence was the response 36 percent of the time and non-violent resistance six percent of the time.

Was it personal? In seven out of ten acts the violent opponents were close enough to speak to one another, 24 percent of the time, they were more distant but still within sight; and in four percent they were out of sight of each other.

Violent encounters occurred primarily at close range, but rarely among intimates. Half of all violent acts took place between strangers.

In at least eight out of every ten violent acts, both the source and the receiver was male. The source of violence was female in seven percent of all acts and the receiver was female six percent of the time. The rest were indeterminate or mixed as far as the sexes of sources and receivers were concerned. A sexual aspect to the relationship between sources and receivers was noted in four percent of all violent acts.

b. *Group Aspects*

Nationality, ethnicity, or family membership of the opponents was observed in two-thirds of all violent episodes. Approximately one-third of the time violent opponents were from the same ethnic background. Violence between different national or ethnic group members was observed in 28 percent of all violent episodes. Violence between members of the same family was rare (two percent).

An analysis of acts coded separately by sources and receivers gives an indication of the group structure of violent encounters, and of the effect of group membership upon chances of generating or suffering violence. Isolated individuals, group leaders, and groups themselves each generated about one-fifth of all violent acts, and individual group members generated more than one-third. On the receiving end, however, group leaders suffered less and group members more than their share. Group leaders generated 21 percent and received eighteen percent of all violent acts while group members committed 37 percent and suffered 40 percent of all violent acts received. If there is any pattern in these slight differences, it suggest that, among those involved in violence, there is greater safety in isolation from, leadership of, or total immersion in a group than in being an identifiable group member. Group members committed sixteen percent more of all violent acts than did the leaders, but became the targets of 22 percent more than did the leaders.

C. *Witnesses to Violence*

Is violence presented as acceptable in the social context of the portrayal itself? One approach is to observe witnesses and their reaction or relation to the violence.

It is difficult to pinpoint witnesses on television. Frequent closeups and medium shots tend to exclude them. The presence and reaction of witnesses in drama is not an independent occurence, but part of the whole structure and intent of the play. Even if witnesses are assumed to be present, showing them and their reactions adds to the cost and complicates the scene; this is done only to make a specific point in the story.

Half of all violent episodes did not show any witnesses. When witnesses were shown, they were usually passive. In thirty three percent of all violent episodes, witnesses were present but did not or could not react. In eight percent, witnesses attempted to prevent violence. In nine percent, witnesses assisted or encouraged violence. On the whole, violence is rarely overtly objected to or punished by witnesses in the world of television drama.

d. *Physical Consequences*

At least three-fourths of all violent acts had no permanent physical effects upon the victims. Some incapacity was observed in seven percent of the acts, and death in nine percent. Focusing on acts rather than on individuals tends to emphasize the more repeatable (and, therefore, less serious) consequences; a victim may suffer several acts of violence, but only one fatality.

A study of violent episodes revealed that half of all episodes resulted in physical injury or fatality. The average rate was almost two casualties per violent episode. Three-fourths of all episodes with any injury resulted in a single casualty, thirteen percent in two casualties, another eight percent in three to eight casualties, and six percent in eight or more (including mass) casualties.

Gory details of physical injury (blood and wounds) were shown in fourteen percent of all programs,

e. *"Good" vs. "Bad" and "Winner" vs. "Loser"*

In at least eight out of every ten violent acts, the opponents were clearly recognizable as "good" or "bad" and as ultimate "winners" and "losers." On the receiving end, the "good guys" suffered in five out of every ten acts, while the "bad guys" suffered in only three out of every ten. The difference between "winners" and "losers" as targets of violence was less pronounced, but in the same direction; "winners" were subjected to violence in 35 percent and "losers" in 31 percent of all acts received.

The pattern remained the same with "good guy winners" and "bad guy losers." Violent acts tended to engage the two combined types equally as sources, but not as receivers. Violent virtue suffered more than violent evil, but triumphed in the end.

3. The People of Violence

Violence is a form of conflict in which lives are at stake, and force governs the outcome. Who is given the power to inflict violence upon whom in television drama? What are some characteristics of the killers and their victims? What roles do the forces of law or lawlessness play in the distribution of violence? What part does violence play in the fate of the fictional characters?

These questions guided the analysis of all major characters in all plays, both violent and non-violent. A total 455 such characters were found in the plays analyzed for both 1967 and 1968. Nearly one out of every four (23 percent) were cartoon characters; nearly nine out of every ten (89 percent) were human (both "live" and cartoon); the rest were "humanized" (speaking), other animals, and a robot.

Unmarried white males in the prime of life were cast in the majority of dramatic leads and violence was the dominant theme of life in their fictional world.

a. "Violents," Killers and their Victims

At least half of all characters inflicted some violence upon others. The proportion of these "violents" was 56 percent in 1967 and 50 percent in 1968.

At least one out of every ten leading characters (twelve percent) was a killer. More than one in every five (22 percent) of those who committed any violence was a killer. The proportion of killers remained unchanged from one study period to the other.

Widespread victimization was evident, but again difficult to specify unless resulting in death. At least five percent of all characters, eight percent of all violent characters, and fifteen percent of all killers met violent ends.

Most of those who were killed also committed violence, but most killers did not die violent deaths. Of the 25 major characters killed in all television plays, twenty inflicted violence upon others and eight were killers. Of all 54 killers, 46 did not pay for their acts with their own lives.

b. *Males and Females*

Male characters dominated the world of television drama by a four-to-one ratio, and committed six times more violence than females. Males killed eight times more frequently than females, and were killed seven times as often. To look at these figures another way, 58 percent of all male leading characters and 33 percent of all female leading characters committed some violence. 23 percent of violent males, (or, of all males, 13 percent) were killers. Finally, 6 percent of all males and 3 percent of all females suffered violent deaths.

c. *Age and Marriage*

The average character had 50 percent chance of committing some violence. The likelihood increased with age, but declined in old age. Middle-aged characters and those of indeterminate age (mostly cartoon characters) were the most probable "violents." More specifically, "violents" comprised one-third of all preschool and primary school-age characters, 45 percent of secondary school-age characters, 48 percent of young adults, 56 percent of middle-aged character , 42 percent of those in old age, and 65 percent of indeterminate or "ageless" characters.

Young adults and middle-aged characters portrayed nine of every ten killers and eight of every ten victims of fatal violence. Each of these age groups had a greater share of killings than their proportion of the total population might suggest. The adolescent was less likely than the middle-aged to play violent roles, but more likely to commit fatal violence. However, the older characters were much more likely to be killed than the younger.

Of all violent young adults, one-third became killers, while only 24 of all violent middle-aged characters did so. However, most fatal victims (60 percent) were middle-aged. The violent fatality rate among young adults was 3.4 percent, but among middle-aged characters was 7.3 percent.

Marriage reduced the chances of violent involvement. Married characters played 29 percent of all major parts, 22 percent of "violents," nineteen percent of violent killers, and twelve percent of fatalities. The bulk of "violents," killers, and their victims came from among the unmarried characters or those whose martial status could not be determined. More single than married people engaged in violence (58 percent against 40 percent), turned killers (fourteen percent against eight percent), and died violent deaths (seven percent against two percent).

d. Forces of Law and of Lawlessness

The forces of law and of lawlessness together made up one-fourth of the total lead population of television drama, one-third of all violent characters, and half of all killers.

Criminals numbered 10 percent of all characters, 15 percent of violent characters, 20 percent of killers, and 24 percent of those killed. Arrayed against them were public and private agents who portrayed nine percent of the total lead populations, 11 percent of the "violents," 13 percent of the killers, and none of the killed.

Two of every ten violent acts included criminals, and one out of every ten public and private law agents. While criminals inflicted 22 percent of all violent acts and suffered in only 17 percent, the agents were equally balanced at both ends of the scale. The imbalance between virtue and evil on the receiving end may be due, in part, to the fact that criminals suffer less frequent but more lethal violence than others.

Most criminals (82 percent) engaged in some violence; 25 percent of all criminals and 31 percent of violent criminals were killers, and 14 percent of all criminals were killed.

Police and other law enforcement agents were almost as violent but they rarely, if ever, paid with their own lives. Seven of every ten agents committed violence and 20 percent of these actions resulted in a fatality. Those who committed violence were as likely to kill as were violent criminals.

Fewer private agents were violent (67 percent), and they rarely killed or were killed.

The armed forces of various nations made up six percent of the total lead population, about the same percentage of "violents," 15 percent of the killers, and 12 percent of the fatal victims.

A somewhat smaller percentage of members of the armed forces (60 percent) committed violence than did either agents or criminals. However, when they did, they killed more often and suffered fewer casualties. Half of all soldiers involved in violence killed, but only one in ten was killed.

e. Outcome: "Happies" and "Unhappies"

Most of the "good guys," usually also the "winners," are by definition those who achieve a happy outcome. "Bad guys—losers" come to an unhappy end. Six of every ten major characters reached an unmistakably happy end, and two of ten an unhappy end; the rest were mixed or indeterminate. 58 percent of all characters achieved "happy" endings, while only 52 percent of "violents" did; 20 percent of the total achieved "unhappy" endings, as opposed to 25 percent of the "violents." The figures did not vary significantly for those whose ending was uncertain.

The pattern extends to killers. The proportion of "happies" among all killers declines by another six percentage points, and the proportion of "unhappies" among killers increases by 5 more percentage points.

Although more than half of all "violents" and nearly half of all killers may be destined for a happy ending, violence and killing each make a happy outcome less likely for one out of every ten major characters.

Nearly half (147 percent) of the "happies" commit violence, nearly one in ten (nine percent) turns killer and not one "happy" was killed; the proportions are only slightly below those for the total lead population. For the "unhappies," the proportions are much higher: seven of every ten commit violence, two of ten become killers, and three of ten die violent deaths.

4. The World of Violence

What is the setting of the fictional world in which violence is prevalent? What kind of people inhabit that world? How is the law enforced in that world? Dimensions of the analysis addressed to these questions compared violent and non-violent television plays with respect to the time and place of action, nationality and ethnicity of population, and aspects of law enforcement portrayed.

a. *Time of Action*

Most television plays were set in contemporary America, and 80 percent contained some violence. The "present" (the sixties) was the setting in 85 percent of the non-violent plays, but only 55 percent of the plays that contained violence. The past was the setting in only a negligible portion (three percent) of non-violent plays, but 26 percent of the violent plays. The future (the setting in ten percent of the plays) was never shown without violence, and the time of action was indeterminate in one out of ten plays regardless of violence.

Ninety-eight percent of all plays set in the past contained violence, the future was always violent, only 74 percent (less than average) of plays set in the present contained violence, and the plays set in several or no identifiable time periods contained an average share of violence (79 percent).

b. *Places and People*

Violence tended to shift the action toward other places, as well as to other times. The location was varied, indeterminate, or totally outside the United States in 38 percent of violent, but only fifteen percent of non-violent plays.

Other countries and foreign or minority groups were significant themes in four out of ten violent plays, but only two out of ten non-violent plays.

Space travel was twice as frequent in violent as in non-violent plays. Uninhabited or mobile settings provided the locales of 44 percent of violent, but only 21 percent of non-violent plays. Urban and rural settings, on the other hand, were the primary locales of the great majority of non-violent plays.

In other words, whenever the place of action was *not* limited to the United States alone or *not* localized to a city, town, or village, or whenever foreign themes or people other than majority-type Americans were significant elements in the story, violence prevailed in nine out of every ten plays.

We have noted before that intergroup violence was nearly as frequent as ingroup violence. Now we see that foreign themes and people are more frequent in the fictional world of violence than of non-violence. It is not surprising, therefore, to find that a violent world of other times and places also involved in violent action a disproportionate number of "others."

Major characters playing violent roles included half of all white Americans, six out of every ten white non-Americans, and nearly seven out of every ten non-whites.

While all "others" were more violent, white foreigners killed more, and non-whites less, than white Americans. Both foreigners and non-whites suffered proportionately higher fatalities than did white Americans. Twenty-eight percent of all violent whites inflicted fatal violence, and white killers outnumbered whites killed two-to-one, but only two of the twenty violent non-whites were killers, and for each non-white killer there was a non-white killed.

c. *Law and Its Enforcement*

Legality was seldom portrayed as being violated unless criminal themes were involved. Such themes were featured as significant elements in one-third of all and less than half (45 percent) of violent plays. When crime was featured, however, the plays nearly always involved violence.

Due process of law (legal apprehension or trial) was indicated as a consequence of major acts of violence in only two out of every ten violent plays. Official agents of law enforcement, (seven percent of all major characters), were thus confined to a small segment of the population of the fictional world of violence. These agents played a discernible role in one out of every ten violent episodes. When they did play a part, it was violent on two of every three occasions. The violence was initiated by agents of law 40 percent of the time. Agents of law responded to violence in a violent manner on three of every ten occasions. Police restraint in the face of violence was rare (one out of every ten such episodes), and law agents suffered violence but could make no response in two of every ten such episodes.

The level of violence employed by agents of law appeared to be no more than that necessary to accomplish their objectives on eight out of every ten occasions. Their actions were portrayed as justifiable on seven of every ten occasions.

In conclusion, television drama presents a lawless world in which due process plays a small part. It is a wild world of many violent strangers, with a mostly violent past and a totally violent future.

D. *The World of Television Entertainment: 1967 and 1968*

This section will be devoted to interpretation of the findings reported in the previous section. The content analysis research carried out by the Gerbner research team provides us with information about the extent, nature, and presentation of violence on television. This information permits us to decipher the messages about violence being sent to television audiences on the basis of factual, objective, and reliable information. Thus, we do not have to rely on selective impressions, biased opinions, or subjective judgments about the nature and extent of violence on prime-time television.

1. Extent of Violent Programs

The first issue to be considered is the extent to which violent programs appear in the total entertainment package offered by the three major television networks during prime-time viewing hours (4 p.m. - 10 p.m. Monday through Friday and Sunday, and 8 a.m. - 11 a.m. Saturdays).

Table 1—programs containing violence
[Percent of total programs presented] *

	All Networks		ABC		CBS		NBC	
	N	Percent	N	Percent	N	Percent	N	Percent
1967	(78)	81.3	(31)	88.6	(21)	65.6	(26)	89.7
1968	(71)	81.6	(20)	90.9	(27)	77.1	(24)	80.0
Total	(149)	81.4	(51)	89.5	(48)	71.6	(50)	84.7

*N=Number of violent programs

The figures presented in Table 1 are conservative estimates of the extent of violent programming. This is because (a) only explicit threats or acts of violence were included, and (b) the number of programs counted by Gerbner exceeds the actual number of programs as defined by half-hour segments.

If television is compared to a meal, programming containing violence clearly is the main course being served. The total volume of violent programming on the three networks did not decrease from 1967 to 1968. ABC programming contained the second highest percentage of violent programs in 1967 (88.6 percent) and the highest in 1968 (90.9 percent). A person tuned to ABC who wished to avoid programs containing violence[9] would have had a difficult time in 1967 and even more trouble in 1968.

CBS had the lowest percentage of programs containing violence in both 1967 (65.6 percent) and 1968 (77.1 percent). However, the percentage of violent programs increased from 1967 to 1968. Dr. Frank Stanton, president of CBS, indicated shortly after the assassination of Senator Robert Kennedy that the extent of violence in CBS programs would be reduced (in a letter to Dr. Milton Eisenhower, Chairman of the Violence Commission).

If CBS had reduced the amount of violent scenes in the following months, it would have affected the results of the 1968 content analysis. It is difficult to know how much higher the percentage of CBS programs containing

328 Mass Media and Violence

violence might have been if the 1968 content analysis had been conducted before instead of after Senator Kennedy's assassination. In any case, a regular viewer of CBS would have trouble finding non-violent programs.

NBC had the highest percentage of programs containing violence in 1967 (89.7 percent), and the second highest in 1968 (80.0 percent), and was the only network to show a decrease in the percentage of violent programs. Despite this fact, a regular NBC viewer who seeks to avoid violent programs for his or his children's viewing during prime-time is in the same situation as ABC and CBS viewers.

On the other hand, if a person seeks to watch programs containing violence, as is entirely conceivable, he would probably be able to do so during all of prime-time television. Those who wish to avoid violent programming have an extemely difficult task, while those who seek it have little trouble.

2. The Incidence of Violence for Different Types of Programs

Within the total entertainment programming package, different types of programs vary in terms of the presence or absence and frequency of violence. All entertainment programs were classified into three general categories (for the purposes of this section of the report): (1) Comedy Tone, (2) Crime-Western-Adventure Style, and (3) Cartoons Format.[10]

a. *Programs with a Comedy Tone*

Comedy programs constituted 45.8 percent of all entertainment programming analyzed for 1967, and 48.3 percent of that analyzed for 1968. In Table 2, the extent and intensity of violence in comedy programs in 1967 and 1968 is presented.

Table 2.—Violence in programs with a comedy tone

	1967	1968	Total
Percent containing violence	65.9	66.7	66.3
Average number of violent episodes:			
Per program	2.8	3.2	3.0
Per program containing violence .	4.2	4.8	4.5

Of the three program types, we might expect to find the least violence in comedy programs. While this expectation is supported, approximately two-thirds of all comedy programs analyzed contained some violence.

A viewer of comedy programs broadcast during prime-time hours can expect to see an average of three violent episodes per show, and if he is watching a comedy program containing violence, he will see an average of four violent episodes per show. The percentage of comedy type programs did not change significantly from 1967 to 1968, although the average number of violent episodes increased slightly. Thus it appears that violence plays a significant role in television comedy.

b. Crime-Western Action-Adventure Style Programs

When the topic of violence on television is raised, people customarily think of the crime-western action-adventure type of program. The content analysis findings show that the majority of all television entertainment program types during prime-time hours contained violence, but the crime-western adventure style does indeed contain the highest percentage of violent programs. The findings are presented in Table 3.

Table 3.—Violence in crime, western, action-adventure style

	1967	1968	Total
Percent containing violence	95.3	98.1	96.6
Average number of violent episodes per program	6.5	6.3	6.4
Per program containing violence	6.9	6.4	6.7
Per hour	8.8	8.7	8.7

This kind of program constituted a large portion of the total presented during prime-time hours, in 1967 (66.7 percent), and again in 1968 (62.1 percent).

According to Table 3, crime-western, action-adventure type programs: (1) almost always contain violence; (2) did not decrease in the percentage containing violence from 1967 to 1968; and (3) have a high incidence of violent episodes, the intensity of which decreased slightly from 1967 to 1968. In other words, little change occurred in the extent of violence in these programs between 1967 and 1968.

Entire battle scenes, as well as all other instances in which a group was involved in violence, were counted as only one violent episode. In light of this fact, the methods used to count the number of violent episodes are certainly conservative. Had individual acts of violence in a war, gang fight, or other scenes been counted, the overall incidence of violent episodes would certainly have been much greater.

c. Programs with a Cartoon Format

Of all of the types of television entertainment, cartoon programs are the most specifically directed toward an audience of children. For example, the Saturday morning (8 a.m. - 11 a.m.) programming format, regardless of which network is being watched, is almost exclusively cartoon-type programs, and a large part of the advertising presented during cartoon programs is specifically directed toward children.

In almost every public or governmental expression of concern about the effects of television entertainment programming, a primary focus is on the possible effects upon children. Recent studies of childrens' media habits show strong indications that children are viewing more and more prime-time programming.[11] Thus, the decision was made not to do separate content analyses of child and adult programming. However, the extent and intensity of violence contained in cartoon programs can give a clear indication of how often and how much violence is presented when the known and expected audience is almost exclusively composed of children. We can thus get a reasonably clear indication of the emphasis placed upon violence for child audiences by network personnel.

Table 4—Violence in programs with a cartoon format

	1967	1968	Total
Percent containing violence	94.3	92.8	93.5
Per program	4.7	6.5	5.5
Per program containing violence	5.0	6.7	5.8
Per hour	21.6	23.5	22.5

The findings in Table 4 are underestimates of the extent and intensity of violence occurring in a fifteen-minute or half-hour cartoon show, because a cartoon program, as defined for purposes of this content analysis, means a single cartoon story (e.g., one "Bird Man" cartoon).

Cartoon programs made up 33 percent of all programming analyzed for 1967, and 29 percent for 1968. Though there is a decrease in the percentage of cartoon programs from 1967 to 1968, the largest increase in intensity of violence occurred in cartoon programming. Violence was pervasive and intense in cartoon programs broadcast in prime time hours for the periods studied.

Some observers may discount these findings on the grounds that: (1) cartoon programs are fantasy, not reality; (2) children know the difference between fantasy and reality; and (3) fantasy programs can have no harmful effect upon child viewers.

Without going into the crucial question of the messages being sent via cartoon and other program types, the following points should be made in regard to the real or potential effects of violence presented in cartoons and other programs which are thought to fall within the realm of fantasy.

1. There is no conclusive evidence that children can differentiate between fantasy and reality in television programs.
2. It remains to be proven that fantasy programs have no effect upon child viewers—harmful or otherwise.
3. Some psychologists suggest that television, with its capacity to stimulate audiovisual senses, has properties of perceptual reality which blur the distinction between fantasy and reality.[12]
4. For many children, the first contact with violence probably occurs while viewing television. For many children, their only contact with several types of violence may be from exposure to television programs.

3. Do Television Audiences Get What They Want?

For many years the claim has been made that the extent and nature of violence in television entertainment programming prevails because it is what the public wants. In support of this claim, the television networks point to studies of audience size. It is not easy to determine just how these studies are carried out, thereby making it difficult to assess the scientific validity of the sampling process.

Two important points should be made which bear directly on audience preferences:

a. *Manifold Functions of Television*

Social scientists have noted that the mass media do more than merely fulfill the desire for acquisition of information and entertainment. In the case of radio, soap operas give many female listeners[13] lessons in family-related problem-solving; lower income persons often think they are learning the style and etiquette of middle-class society from television programs.[14]

Television also serves as a baby-sitter. Almost all American families own a television set. It is a fair guess that many harried parents are relieved when their children are busy watching television, and some parents encourage this so that parental work and other activities may be accomplished in relative peace and quiet.

Television also serves a "companion function." For many persons who are alone for long periods of time, television can act as a substitute for the presence of loved ones or the company of other people.

The point to be made is that many persons may not watch television solely for the inherent appeal of its entertainment or informational content. For them, television viewing may result directly from a variety of factors essentially unrelated to program content.

b. *Habitual Nature of Television Viewing*

Television viewing, like newspaper reading, may be a habitual activity. When some subscribers do not receive their newspaper, they become irritated and upset.[15] The irritation does not result solely from the inability to keep up with current events, but also from the disruption of a habitual daily routine. Given the numbers of hours of television that Americans watch daily, it appears reasonable to speculate that television viewing, regardless of the content, may be a habitual activity for some Americans. This hypothesis could be tested by measuring people's reactions when their set is out of order, or by systematically preventing some communities from watching television for various lengths of time.

c. *The TV Public's Choices*

Regardless of the merits of audience appeal studies, network officials claim that these studies represent what the viewing public chooses to watch from what is available.

What are these choices? First of all, the public can decide whether or not to watch television at all. We know that most American families have at least one set, and that most of them watch some television. The question remains, however, as to why these persons choose to become members of the television viewing public.

One obvious reason is that it seems wasteful not to use a television once it has been purchased. Many may choose to watch television simply because it is an inexpensive form of entertainment. Sports and news programs, which were not included in the content analysis, often provide the viewer with a better vantage point than persons who are actually on the scene.

Another possible factor may be termed the "Jones' effect": "If everyone else is watching television, why should we be different?" Sometimes, a television serial becomes a topic of discussion at social gatherings or even a full-fledged fad. In these instances, some persons, especially children, may watch that program in order to know what people are talking about or to be able to participate in discussions related to the program.

In any case, many factors probably affect the decisions of persons to become members of the viewing public.

The television public also makes choices about which channels and programs to watch. For the viewer whose criterion is the absence of violence, choice is limited to less than nineteen percent of all programs broadcast during prime-time hours, according to our study. By way of contrast, viewers, seeking to watch programs containing violence have little difficulty.

d. The Public's Views on TV Violence

In view of the above discussion, it is important to know how Americans view the amount and kinds of violence they find available in television entertainment programming. Two items bearing directly on this question were included in the Violence Commission National Survey. The first inquired:

> How do you feel about the amount of violence portrayed in television programs today, not including news programs—do you think that there is too much, a reasonable amount, or very little violence?

A representative sample of adult Americans gave the following responses to this question: (1) fifty-nine percent said there was *too much* violence, (2) thirty-two percent said there was a *reasonable amount,* (3) four percent said there was *very little,* and (4) four percent were not sure.

Thus a majority of adult Americans think there is too much violence on television.

A second item was asked of the same sample:

> Apart from the *amount* of violence, do you generally approve or disapprove of the *kind* of violence that is protrayed on TV?

	Responses (Percent)
Approve	25
Disapprove	63
. . . .	12
	100

Americans may not be getting what they want in television programming when the issue is the kind of violence portrayed.[16]

e. *Summary*

Whether audiences get the programming they want is an issue which should be assessed in light of all the relevant factors associated with television viewing and program selection. It has been suggested that the inherent appeal of television programming is not the only factor affecting conscious or unconscious decisions to watch television in general or a given program in particular.

With regard to violence, our findings indicate that a majority of adults are not getting what they want with respect to the amount and kind of violence on television. In addition, to the extent that the two weeks of entertainment programming analyzed are typical, the entertainment choices available to the viewing public appear to be reduced either to watching programs containing violence or watching very little television.

Major findings of the analysis include the following:

1. Violence is pervasive, occurring in eighty-one percent of all 1967 programs analyzed and eighty-two percent in 1968.
2. The extent of violence varies by type of program, but a majority of *all* types of programs contain violence. Programs with a crime-western-action adventure style have the highest proportion containing violence, with cartoons a close second, and comedies third.
3. Networks vary in the proportion of their schedule allocated to given types of programs. This largely accounts for the differences between networks, and changes from 1967 to 1968. However, no network had less than seventy-seven percent of all its programming (prime time, October 1—7) containing violence in 1968.
4. The majority of adult Americans not only think there is too much violence on television, but also disapprove of the kind of violence portrayed.

4. Messages for Violence Contained in TV Entertainment Programming

In order to investigate the real or potential effects of television violence, it is not sufficient to know only the extent of violence; these effects are most directly determined by the *messages* sent to the viewing public. To use a medical analogy, we might say that the extent of violence is the "dosage given and the message sent is the medication. So far we know the "dosage" is very high, but we need to know the nature of the medication.

Each of the norms for violence listed below has been inferred from one or more of the findings summarized in the preceding pages. This process involves identification of the substantive meaning of an event on the basis of incomplete information. For example, when a boy has received three consecutive refusals for a date from a girl, he may draw the inference that the girl is not interested in ever dating him. Although she has not categorically stated that she is not interested, her actions imply this meaning. Thus the boy "gets the message," and makes an inference made on the basis of incomplete information.

This procedure was involved in deciphering some of the norms for violence which are implied by television messages. The problem is to infer what the substantive meanings of these messages of violence could be (e.g., norms). It is likely that more than one norm could be inferred from the same message, and it is conceivable that an inference made by one investigator would not be made by another, or that contradictory inferences could be drawn from the same message.

The fact that inference does involve judgments means that there can be legitimate differences in judgment between two or more investigators within reasonable limits.

We can return to the boy-girl situation to illustrate this point. The boy who receives three consecutive refusals may make the inference that the girl is not interested in him. On the basis of exactly the same facts, he could also draw the inference that the girl is very popular, so that if he keeps trying, eventually he will get a date with her. However, there are practical, if not logical, limits to the inferences which he can make: for example, he could not infer that she has been eagerly waiting by the phone just for him to call and ask for a date.

Inference, then is not haphazard or whimsical. It is a process of attributing meaning on the basis of factual, but incomplete, data within the confines of logic and trained judgment.

The most frequent and relevant messages about violence contained in the programs studied are abstracted below. Accompanying each message are one or more norms for violence which have been inferred from that message. Messages are ordered from the most specific to the most general.

1. Message: Unmarried young to middle-aged males are usually violent.

   Norm: Expect unmarried young to middle-aged males to be more violent than others.

2. Message: Non-whites and foreigners are disproportionately more violent than whites and Americans.

   Norm: Expect violence more from non-whites or non-Americans than from whites and Americans.

3. Message: The vast majority of violence occurs between strangers who are within talking distance of one another.

   Norm: When anticipating violence, be wary of situations in which you encounter strangers at close physical range.

   Norm: Violence is to be expected more from strangers than from friends, acquaintances, or family members.

   Norm: If you want to avoid being involved in or the victim of violence, avoid strangers.

   Combining Messages 1–3: In the U.S., expect violence from unmarried young to middle-aged male strangers; if outside of the U.S., expect violence from non-white or foreign unmarried young to middle-age male strangers.

4. Message: Non-whites kill less often than do whites, but are killed more often.

   Message: Violent young males are more likely to kill than are violent middle-aged males, but less likely to be killed.

   Norm: The violent people, including killers, who should be the most concerned about getting killed are middle-aged men and non-whites.

5. Message: Law enforcement officers are frequently involved in violent encounters with segments of the American public.

   Message: A law enforcement officer's response to violence is more often violent, than non-violent.

   Norm: It is to be expected that law enforcement officers will be as violent as the most violent citizens.

6. Message: The future is pervasively violent.

   Norm: Although the past and present are heavily saturated with violence, the future will be more extensively so.

7. Message: Although violence can lead to death, physical injuries are not often accompanied by visible gore.

   Norm: Physical injury caused by violence can kill, but is sanitized and does not hurt.

8. Message: When there are witnesses to violence, the most typical reaction is non-reaction or passivity.

   Norm: If you are a witness to a violent episode, do not get directly involved by intervening, and do not publicly disapprove; just watch quietly.

9. Message: The use of violence, even killing, often goes unpunished by formal means of due process of law or by informal means of public or private expression of disapproval.

   Norm: If you use violence, do not be too concerned about being formally or informally punished.

10. Message: "Good guys" and "winners" use as much violence as "bad guys" and "loser."

    Norm: The use of violence has nothing to do with the distinction between "good guys" and "bad guys" and "winners" and "losers."

    Message: Violence is used by "good guys" and "bad guys" as means to an end, and "good guys" generally attain their goals.

    Norm: Violence is a legitimate and successful means of attaining a desired end.

    Norm: There is no inconsistency between achieving a desired goal through violence and being a "good guy."

The above messages and norms have been selected as the most relevant for the present discussion. The overall impression is that violence, employed as a means of conflict resolution or acquisition of personal goals, is a predominant characteristic of life. Cooperation, compromise, debate, and other non-violent means of conflict resolution are notable for their relative lact of prominence.

A general impression gleaned from the selected messages and implicit norms presented above is that violence often accompanies conflict, is a successful means of reaching personal ends (especially for individuals cast in the role of "good guy"), and is not usually punished. These findings are consistent with those obtained by Larsen, Grey, and Fertis in a content analysis of popular television programs.[17]

5. Research Implications

Even though findings and inferences from content analysis may give rise to serious concerns about the effects of exposure to television violence, they do not provide conclusive evidence about them. Exposure alone does not automatically mean that the viewer will be affected. The degree to which exposure is likely to have a direct effect depends, in large part, upon the type of effect being considered.

If our concern is solely to determine whether or not persons have an *emotional reaction* to television violence research shows that they do. We are dealing with a relatively direct and simple effect of exposure.[18] In this case, messages and implicit norms for violence have little, if any, bearing.

However, if we wish to determine what persons can and do learn from their exposure to television portrayals of violence, range of messages and norms for violence which can be inferred are a salient concern.

In chapter 12, experimental studies provide consistent evidence that people, especially children, can and do learn complex and novel acts of aggression from observation of television and film portrayals.[19] However, learning novel acts of aggression is less complex than the process involved in acquiring *implied norms* for violence. If a group was exposed to the same series of messages about violence for the same length of time, we would expect different individuals to perceive the portrayals of violence in relatively different ways. This expectation is based upon the well-established principle of selective. perception.

In some respects, the implications of selective perception are greater when the issue is learning norms rather than acts. Learning norms requires a complex symbolic process of attributing normative meaning to an observed event. To the extent that people differ in their perceptions of a television portrayal of violence, we would expect different normative inferences to be made. Differences in inferred norms would probably lead to differences in the nature of probable effects.

The inferral of the same norms by a group still does not prove that the process of making a normative inference has an effect. If audiences were to draw similar inferences, under what conditions will they incorporate the norms implied in that television program as their own norms for violence? The next question is: What are the behavioral implications for persons who incorporate television norms for violence as their own?

The questions which must be answered before we can definitively assess the effects of exposure to messages about violence on television are: (1) under what conditions does learning of norms for violence occur from exposure to television?; (2) under what conditions are inferred norms for violence adopted, once they are learned?; and (3) under what conditions are the norms for violence, when learned and adopted, acted upon?

Studies cited in Chapter 12 point to the following conditions in which learning of aggressive acts is demonstrated: (a) when a situation is encountered similar to the portrayal situation in which aggressive acts were learned; (b) when there is an expectation of being rewarded for performing the learned aggression or escaping detection;[20] and (c) when no disapproval of the portrayed behavior is shown by another person who is exposed to the same portrayal.[21]

These three conditions are by no means the only ones which must be considered, but they lend themselves most easily to evaluation through content analysis.

The likelihood that viewers who were exposed to the two weeks of TV programming analyzed would face similar situations is somewhat reduced by the fact that only fifty-five percent of all programs containing violence were set in the 1960's. Time of action, of course, is only one aspect of a portrayal situation. Thus, a different time of action does not remove the possibility that the portrayal situation could be quite similar to those encountered by persons in the 1960's.

For example, the portrayal of a teenage boy in frontier times encountering a situation where he must decide whether or not to resolve conflict with another teenager by the use of violence may influence a teenage boy living in the 1960's who encounters a similar situation.

To the degree that portrayal situations are different from those the viewing audience are likely to encounter, learning of violent acts and norms may occur, but are less likely to be acted upon than when such situations are similar.

The content analysis findings bear directly upon the second research condition; there is an increase in the likelihood that subjects in experiments will act upon their learning of aggressive acts when subjects expect to be or see actors in television portrayals rewarded for aggressive behavior. One of the clearest content analysis findings is that violent characters in television portrayals are often rewarded for their behavior. Reward comes most directly to "good guys," who often achieve success through violence. In addition, the use of violence is not often punished in the television world. Thus, if viewers infer from their exposure that violence not only goes largely unpunished but is rewarded, they may be more likely to transfer this inference into an expectation that they might be rewarded or go unpunished for using violence.

Although the rewarding and non-punishment condition does occur in the programs analyzed, it is not known whether this condition will have the same effect (significantly increasing the probability that learned aggression will be performed) on audiences who are not subjects in a laboratory experiment. In other words, we cannot assume that the effects occurring under the controlled setting of an experiment will also occur in home settings.

The importance of considering the social contexts in which television viewing typically takes place is pointed up in the third condition—whether or not approval or disapproval is expressed by one viewer in another viewer's presence. The content analysis research does not provide any information on the degree to which children view television in the presence of others, or how often others, when present, verbally approve or disapprove of portrayals of violent acts. Future research is required before we will know if the effect of this condition will be the same in a home as in laboratory experiments—i.e. increasing the probability of learned acts of aggression being performed.

Future research is also required to determine if the conditions which are found to increase the probability of persons performing learned aggression also increase the probability of persons acting in accordance with norms for violence learned from exposure to television programs. The present assumption is that it will, but future research is needed to corroborate or disprove the hypothesis.

E. Summary

The world of television violence is a place in which severe violence is commonplace. The main characters are unmarried young to middle-age males who became involved in violent encounters with strangers. Violent encounters are often unwitnessed, but when they are, the predominant reaction is passive observation and non-intervention. Violence, regardless of the identity of the initiator, goes largely unpunished. The central role played by violence in this cold world of strangers and passive observers is to provide a successful means for individuals or groups to resolve conflicts in their favor or self-interest. Forces of law enforcement are undistinguishable from others insofar as they also use violence as the predominant mode of conflict resolution. Legality, in many instances, is not a relevant dimension or concern.

An examination of some of the most frequent messages being sent to mass audiences and norms for violence inferred from these messages leads to a serious concern about the effects upon audiences of television entertainment programs. At the very least, it can be said that the messages being sent about violence are inconsistent with a philosophy of social behavior based upon involved cooperation, non-violent resolution of conflict, and non-violent means of attaining personal ends.

The next series of questions which needs to be addressed is (1) Are the messages which are sent actually received by TV audiences? (2) Are these messages learned? (3) Can norms for violence implied in these messages be learned and adopted as the audience's norms for violence? This series of questions lies at the crux of the issue of the social and psychological effects of mass media portrayals of violence.

REFERENCES

1. See Bradley Greenberg, "The Content and Context of Violence in The Mass Media," paper submitted to the Violence Commission, Fall, 1968. This paper can be found in Appendix II C.
2. Jack Lyle, "Contemporary Functions of the Mass Media," paper submitted to the Violence Commission, Fall, 1968.
3. We would like to thank ABC, CBS, and NBC for their cooperation.
4. A study of network programs transmitted October 1-7, 1967 and 1968, conducted in October and November 1968 for the Mass Media Task Force, National Commission on the Causes and Prevention of Violence.

Associate investigators: Marten Brouwer, visiting professor of communications; Cedric C. Clark, post-doctoral fellow in Communications; Supervisor of data processing: Klaus Krippendorff, Assistant Professor of Communications. Administrative Assistant and Staff Supervisor: Michael F. Eleey.

Technical Director: Vernon J. Wattenberger, Director of Facilities and Engineering Assistants: Barry Hampe, Supervisor of Film Laboratory Services; John Massi, Supervisor of Broadcasting Laboratory Services

5. Appendix K describes the selection of programs, terms, units, and other conditions of analysis, and the methods used to control and measure the extent to which unreliable observations or prior judgements might affect the usefulness of the results in providing a basis for fresh judgment. The structures of interpretation noted should be kept in mind in reading and using the results.

6. In other words, an accurate and meaningful capsule statement of the story requires one or more references to violent acts.

7. A category for an act of nature as the agent of violence was included, but none were observed.

8. Three-fourths of all sources and receivers were human beings, and one fourth were human-like (animals or human-like cartoon characters that can and did speak, and one robot who also could speak).

9. It is difficult to know how many viewers actually include the violent or non-violent nature of television programs as a criterion of program selection. However, if this criterion were employed, the range of available non-violent programs is quite limited.

10. In Appendix K, analysis is made of more detailed program types. Note that one program can be classified as one, two, or three types; e.g., a cartoon format with a comedy tone.

11. See Eleanor Macoby, *"Effects of Mass Media,"* in M. L. and L. W. Hoffman, (eds.), *Review of Child Development Research* (Russell Sage Foundation, 1964), pp. 323-348.

12. See Alberta Siegal, *"Effects of Mass Media Violence on Inter-Personal Relations,"* paper submitted to the Violence Commission, Fall, 1968.

13. Herta Herzog, "What Do We Really Know About Daytime Serial Listeners?" in P. F. Lazarsfeld and F. N. Stanton (eds.), *Radio Research* (New York: Duell, Sloan & Pearce, 1942), pp. 3-33.

14. W. M. Gerson, "Social Structure and Mass Media Socialization," Unpublished doctoral dissertation, University of Washington, 1963.

15. Bernard Berelson, "What 'Missing the Newspaper' Means," in Wilbur Schramm (ed.), *The Process and Effects of Mass Communications* (Urban, Illinois: Univ. of Illinois Press, 1954), pp. 36-47.

16. Social desirability could have affected these responses—i.e., some respondents may have felt that the expected or desirable response was to say that they disapproved of the kind of violence or that there is too much violence in television entertainment programming.

17. Otto Larsen, Louis Grey, and J. Fortas, "Achieving Goals Through Violence on Television," in O. N. Larsen (ed.), *Violence and the Mass Media* (New York: Harper & Row 1968), pp. 97-111.

18. For example, see Leonard Berkowitz, "The Effects of Observing Violence," *Scientific American,* vol. 210 (Feb. 1964), pp. 2-8.

19. See Chapter 12, for a review of research concerning observational learning from exposure to audiovisual portrayals of aggression.

20. See Chapter 12.

21. *Ibid.*

Chapter 16

THE ACTUAL WORLD OF VIOLENCE

A. *Norms for Violence*

Thus far it has been shown that (1) television programming is and has been saturated with violence; (2) the norms implicit in the television world of violence support the use of of violence as a means of conflict resolution and as a successful and legitimate means to an array of personal ends; (3) many social scientists conclude that audiences exposed to media violence over a period of time can absorb norms and attitudes of violence which are implicitly or explicitly contained in media entertainment programming; and (4) many social scientists conclude that the media can stimulate aggressive tendencies which, under some conditions, can lead to aggressive behavior.[1]

No scientists would argue that the media are the sole determinants of past or present violence in America. However, there appears to be a growing consensus of opinion that the mass media cannot be ignored when an attempt is made to explain the phenomenon of violence in contemporary America. Social and psychological phenomena are not caused by one and only one factor. Thus, the search for an explanation of violence must be directed at an investigation of many factors, including mass media presentations and practices.

The Commission staff did not restrict itself to an examination of the television world of violence; they also investigated the actual world of violence as experienced by Americans. This study is important as a basis for comparing real and fictional worlds of violence. It is, then, a factor which must be considered in an attempt to explain why some people are violent and others are not. Perhaps those who have had direct experience with violence are affected differently by exposure to violence as portrayed on television. Thus, experience with violence may be both an independent source of learning and an intervening factor between exposure to and the effects of violence on television.

Comparison of the two is extremely complex. The impetus for research on the actual world of violence stemmed in part from the fact that the effects of mass media portrayals of violence upon audience attitudes and behavior necessarily involve both (1) the nature of media portrayals of violence in this case, the television world of violence and (2) the nature of the norms of and direct experience with violence.

341

1. Survey of Adult and Teenage Americans

The Media Task Force portion of the national survey constituted approximately one-half of the questions given in a one-hour interview. Area probability samples of the adult (eighteen and over) and teenage (fourteen to nineteen) population of the United States were drawn by Louis Harris and Associates. [2] The samples of 1,176 adult Americans and 496 teenagers are broadly representative of the total adult and teenage population of this country.

The three major parts of the interview provide detailed information on (a) the respondent's norms for violence; (b) the extent and nature of his actual experiences with violence; and (c) his media habits and preferences. [3] A copy of the Media Task Force portion of the interview schedule is presented in Appendix I.

2. Norms for Violence: Adult and Teenage Americans

Norms set standards for behavior and define the limits between acceptable and unacceptable behavior. It is generally, assumed that most persons will seek to act in accordance with these norms in order to avoid disapproval. However, applicable norms in a given situation may not coincide either with personal norms or with norms of others, and therein lies the opportunity for deviance and conflict. Persons who deviate from their own norms may lose self-esteem. Persons who deviate from the norms held by others, such as friends and family members, may lose the respect of these people or be otherwise sanctioned or punished for their deviance. Thus, norms have an explicit control function over behavior; conformity is rewarded and deviance elicits punishment.

a. *Description of Findings*

Both samples were asked to respond to a series of questions, phrased as hypothetical situations, which were intended to ascertain their norms for violence. Sixteen of these situations, containing minor and major (low level and severe) instances of violence occurring between eight different assailant-victim relationships were presented to the respondents.[4] An example of the question format is presented below:

39a. Are there any situations that you can imagine in which you would approve of a public school teacher *hitting* a student?

Yes 1
No 2
Not sure 3

40a. Are there any situations that you can imagine in which you would approve of a public school teacher *punching* or *beating* a student?

Yes 1
No 2
Not sure 3

Thus, each role relationship, in this case teacher-student, was repeated twice—once with a relatively low-level or minor act of violence (hitting) and once with a relatively severe act of violence (punching or beating).

Adult and teenager general approval of violence patterns were assessed by this procedure for the following role relationships:

(a) Parent and Child (at least one year old and healthy).
(b) Husband and Wife*
(c) Wife and Husband
(d) Public School Teacher and Student
(e) Male Teenager and Male Teenager
(f) Man and Adult Male Stranger
(g) Policeman and Adult Male
(h) Judge and Citizen

The *adult* responses to the general question of "are there any situations that you can imagine in which you would approve of X doing B to Y?" are:

			Percent	
		Yes	*Not sure*	*No*
1.	Parent spanking his or her child assuming the child is healthy and over a year old	93	1	6
2.	Parent beating his or her child	8	1	91
3.	Husband slapping his wife's face	20	2	78
4.	Husband shooting his wife	3	0	97
5.	Wife slapping her husband's face	22	2	76
6.	Wife shooting her husband	4	(*)	95
7.	Public school teacher hitting a student	49	4	47
8.	Public school teacher punching or beating a student	5	2	93
9.	Policeman striking an adult male citizen	73	5	22
10.	Policeman shooting an adult male citizen	71	5	24
11.	Teenage boy punching another teenage boy	66	4	30

*In (b) the husband acts violently against his wife, while in (c) the wife acts violently against her husband.

Percent

		Yes	Not sure	No
12.	Teenage boy knifing another teenage boy	3	(*)	97
13.	Man punching an adult male stranger	52	5	43
14.	Man choking an adult male stranger	24	4	72
15.	Judge sentencing a person to one or more years of hard labor .	84	6	10
16.	Judge sentencing a person to death	53	7	40

Only two of the eight role relationships (policeman-adult male and judge-citizen) received approval from a majority of the American adult population, regardless of severity of the act of violence. Policemen and judges may engage in minor or severe acts of violence with the general approval of a majority of adult Americans. Parents, teachers, teenagers, adult males, husbands, and wives may engage in minor violence with varying degrees of approval, but severe acts of violence are disapproved by a majority of the adult population.

The major difference between policemen and judges and the other roles studied is that policemen and judges have institutionalized legal authority to use violence. The policemen is authorized to use whatever force, including violence, necessary to apprehend lawbreakers, while judges have the authority and responsibility to mete out punishment consistent with the dictates of the law, including punishments which may be acts of violence.

In light of the incidence of television programs in which policemen play a significant role and the apparent increases in domestic disorders which directly involve law enforcement agencies, it is important to understand the specific conditions under which adult Americans approve of the use of violence by policemen.

b. *Norms for the Use of Violence by Policemen*

Seventy-six percent of the adult sample and 78 percent of the teenage sample in general approved ("yes" and "not sure" responses) of a policeman shooting an adult male citizen. A series of specific hypothetical situations were presented to respondents who gave general approval in an attempt to discover what level of provocation was necessary before these respondents would approve of such an action. Percentages in this study are based only on responses of general approval (i.e., 32 percent here means 32 percent of the 76 percent who gave general approval).

42a. Are there any situations you can imagine in which you would approve of a policeman shooting an adult citizen?

*Less than one percent.

	Adult responses *(N=1176)* Percent		*Teenage responses* *(N=496)* Percent
Yes	71	Yes	74
No	24	No	22
Not sure	5	Not sure	4

42b. Would you approve if the citizen:

	Percent of persons saying *yes* or not sure above	
	Adults* Yes	Teens* Yes
Had said vulgar and obscene things to the policeman		2
Was demonstrating against the war in Vietnam and carrying a Vietcong flag	1	4
Was being questioned as a suspect in a murder case	2	2
Was attacking the policeman with his fists	32	28
Was attempting to escape from custody	55	59
Was threatening the policeman with a gun	96	90

An extremely small minority would approve of a policeman shooting a citizen for saying obscene things to the policeman, demonstrating against the war in Vietnam, or for being a suspect in a murder case. However, a sizeable minority of adults (32 percent) and teenagers (28 percent) would approve of a policeman responding to an assault in this manner. A majority of adults (55 percent) and teenagers (59 percent) approve of a policeman shooting someone who was attempting to escape, while the great majority approve of a policeman shooting someone who is threatening him with a gun.

Both class and race differences were found in this study. Those with higher income and more education approve of policemen using violence, more than those with lower income and less education. Non-blacks approve of police violence more than blacks.[5] One possible interpretation is that lower-class persons, especially blacks, have much more contact with policemen in a violent context, and hence, see themselves as likely recipients· of such violence.

It is particularly important to recall that police on television are very violent. In a later section of this report, norms for police use of violence held by adults and teenage Americans are compared with the norms for police use of violence implicit in television programming.

Adult and teenage responses to the question involving a policeman striking an adult male citizen are strikingly similar:

41a. Are there any situations you can imagine in which you would approve of a policeman striking an adult male citizen?

---

*N=894 adults, N=387 teens.

| Adult responses | Teenage responses |
| N=1176 | N=496 |

Percent	Percent
Yes 73	Yes 73
Not sure 5	Not sure 4
No 22	No 23

41b. Would you approve if:*

Yes responses
Percent

	Adults	Teens
Had said vulgar and obscene things to the policeman	27	21
Was demonstrating against the war in Vietnam and carrying a Vietcong flag	19	27
Was being questioned as a suspect in a murder case	8	9
Was attempting to escape from custody	83	84
Was attacking the policeman with his fists	97	97

*Asked only of persons saying "Yes" or "Not Sure" to general questions
(41a), Adults, N=917, teens, N=382.

In this case, as with almost all the questions, there is very little discrepancy between adult and teenage responses. Approximately three-fourths of the adult and teenage populations can imagine a situation in which they would approve of a policeman striking an adult male citizen.

A remarkable proportion of adults and teenagers approve of a policeman striking a citizen if he has said vulgar and obscene things to the policeman (adults, 27 percent; teens, 21 percent). Police use of violence thus is approved in response to strictly verbal deviance, which does not involve breaking a law.

Likewise, a substantial minority would approve of a policeman striking an adult male who was demonstrating against the Vietnam war. Again, the adult male is doing nothing illegal and is not endangering anyone's life or physical well-being. These respondents are approving of police violence as a means of punishing political deviance.

At one extreme, nearly one out of ten approved of "third degree" methods of dealing with suspects. At the other extreme, a sizeable minority of adults (22 percent) and teenagers (23 percent) do not approve of a policeman striking an adult male in any situation imaginable. Approximately the same percentage of adults (24) and teenagers (22 percent) cannot imagine any situation in which they would approve of a policeman shooting an adult male citizen. Thus, for a substantial minority of adult and teenage Americans police violence is normatively disapproved.

Thus, two sizable minorities are divided with respect to the use of violence by policemen. One group disapproves of police violence regardless of the provocation, while the other group gives almost unqualified approval to the use of violence by policemen. Certainly, as noted earlier in this Report, the norm that policemen should be non-violent is not being supported by the television world of violence.

The majority of Americans, however, are consistent with legal norms, approving of police use of violence only when the provocation is illegal, potentially threatening to the life of the policeman, or directly hindering law enforcement.

c. An Overview of Adult and Teenage Norms for Violence

Using just the "yes," "no," or "not sure" responses to the general question of "Are there any situations that you can imagine in which you would approve of X doing A to Y?," we can derive a summary profile of American norms for violence. As one approach to this problem, the hypothetical situations involving relatively low and severe violence have been ranked separately on the basis of the percentage approval given by the sample of adult Americans.[6]

Rank Order of Low Violence Situations: Adults

	Role relationship	Violence act	Percent Approval*	Rank
(a)	Parent-child	Spanking	94	1
(b)	Judge-citizen	1-year hard labor	90	2
(c)	Policeman-adult male	Striking	78	3
(d)	Teenage boy-teenage boy	Punching	69	4
(e)	Man-adult male stranger	Punching	57	5
(f)	Teacher-student	Hitting	53	6
(g)	Wife-husband	Slapping face	24	7
(h)	Husband-wife	Slapping face	22	8

*Approval includes "yes" and "not sure" responses.

Rank Order of High Violence Situations: Adults

	Role relationship	Violent act	Percent Approval*	Rank
(a)	Police-adult male	Shooting	77	1
(b)	Judge-citizen	Death sentence	60	2
(c)	Man-adult male stranger	Choking	28	3
(d)	Parent-child	Beating	9	4
(e)	Teacher-student	Punching or beating	7	5
(f)	Wife-husband	Shooting	4.5	6
(g)	Teenage boy-teenage boy	Knifing	4	7
(h)	Husband-wife	Shooting	3.5	8

Again, policemen and judges received high levels of approval regardless of the severity of violence. None of the other six role relationships receives approval from anywhere near a majority of the adults. Thus it seems that most adult Americans only approve of *institutionalized law enforcement officials* performing severe acts of violence. Furthermore, law enforcement officials receive approval from a majority of adults for the use of violence only when it is necessary to protect their lives or to carry out their legal responsibilities.

The least approved role relationship is the most intimate, the relationship between husband and wife. There is little difference between percentage approval of violence on the part of husbands and wives in the same situations,

---

*Yes and not sure responses.

regardless of the severity. The vast majority of American adults disapprove of violence between husbands and wives, no matter who was the instigator.

Perhaps the most relevant institutionalized aspect of family violence has to do with parents' needs, rights, or responsibilities toward their children. Physical punishment in the form of spanking is an act of violence, even though common sense and our findings tell us that this is approved by all but a small minority of adult Americans. However, when we consider beating, a more severe form of physical punishment, we find that only nine percent of adult Americans approve of this action in any imaginable situation.[7]

Another institutionalized relationship in which one party has authority over the other is the public school teacher-student relationship. A slight majority of adult Americans approve of corporal punishment in some situations. A majority of these do not approve of a teacher hitting a student for being noisy in class, but do approve if the student had been repeatedly disobedient and uncooperative, destroyed school property, or hit the teacher.

The vast majority of American adults (ninety-three percent) would not approve of a teacher punching or beating a student in any situation. Of the remaining seven percent, a majority approved only when the teacher has been hit by the student.

The teenage boy-teenage boy role relationship is an interesting one because there is no difference in authority between the two parties, and neither party has formal authority to use violence against the other. However, there does seem to be a prevalent dilemma for teenagers and their parents in this country, since two inconsistent norms apply here—one, that conflict should not be resolved with violence, and the other, that males should not back down from a challenge, even if it might result in violence. In America, violence is most often conceived as a male activity, whether the situation involves crime, war, or private conflict.

A majority of adult Americans feel that it is all right for one teenage boy to punch another, especially if the other boy has challenged him to a fistfight or actually hit him; but knifing is never approved behavior. However, a significant minority of adults (thirty-one percent) disapprove of violence between teenage boys, regardless of the level of violence or the nature of the situation.

The man-adult male stranger is especially interesting because the majority of television violence takes place between adult male strangers. This is similar to the above mentioned relationship in that both parties are equals with regard to authority. Both have the legal right to use violence only in self-defense or when the other is trespassing and all other possibilities have been exhausted.

The man-adult male stranger relationship may also involve a normative dilemma, which is evident in the two dictums that "men should not take the law into their own hands" and "men have a right to defend themselves, their loved ones, and their property."

The findings indicate that a slight majority of adults can imagine a situation in which they would approve of a man punching an adult male stranger, while a large majority cannot imagine a situation when they would approve of a man choking a stranger. Low-level violence (in this case punching), is approved, specifically in response to violent or illegal provocation.

45a. Are there any situations that you can imagine in which you would approve of a man punching an adult male stranger?

Adult responses
(N=1,176)
Percent

Yes . . . . .52 −1
No . . . . .43 −2
Not sure . . . . 5 −3

45b. Would you approve if the stranger:

Percent of persons saying
Yes or not sure above
(N=670)
Percent
Yes

Was in a protest march showing opposition to the other
man's views 2

Was drunk and bumped into the man and his wife on the street 8

Had hit the man's child after the child accidentally damaged
the stranger's car 59

Was beating up a woman and the man saw it 81

Had broken into the man's house 93

46a. Are there any situations that you can imagine in which you would approve of a man choking a stranger?

Adult responses
(N=1,176)
Percent

Yes . . . . .24 −1
No . . . . .72 −2
Not sure . . . . 4 −3

46b. Would you approve if the stranger:

Percent of persons saying
yes or not sure above
(N=329)
(Percent
Yes

Was in a protest march showing opposition to the other
man's views 0

Was drunk and bumped into the man and his wife on the street 2

Had hit the man's child after the child accidentally damaged
the stranger's car 27

Had broken into the man's house 71

Had knocked the man down and was trying to rob him 92

In general, adult norms for the use of violence by against a stranger support low level violence when the man is playing a protective role, but reject the use of high-level violence. Even the minority of adults (28 percent) who can imagine a situation in which they would approve of a man choking an adult male stranger, do so only when the stranger is beating up a woman, has broken into the man's house, or has knocked the man down and is trying to rob him.

d. *Adult and Teenage Norms for Violence: Comparison and Summary*

A simple method of measuring the degree of similarity between adult and teenage norms is to compare the percentage of approval each group assigns to the eight role relationships. Adult and teenage rankings of *low violence* items are almost idential.

Table 1 – Adult and teenage rankings of role relationships: low violence items

Role relationship	Act	Adult	Rank Teenage
Parent-child	Spank	1	1
Judge-citizen	1 year hard labor	2	2
Policeman-adult male	Strike	3	3
Teenage boy-teenage boy	Punch	4	4
Man-male stranger	Punch	5	5
Teacher-student	Hit	6	7
Wife-husband	Slap face	7	6
Husband-wife	Slap face	8	8

Spearman's rho=0.98.

Adult and teenage rankings of *high violence* items are also extremely similar. Although there are important differences between each group's norms for violence, the overall patterns of approval are very similar.

Table 2. – Adult and teenage rankings of role relationships: high violence items

Role relationship	Act	Rank Adult	Teenage
Police-adult male	Shoot	1	1
Judge-citizen	Death penalty	2	2
Man-male stranger	Choke	3	3
Parent-child	Beat	4	4
Teacher-student	Punch or beat	5	6
Wife-husband	Shoot	6	7
Teenage boy-teenage boy	knife	7	5
Husband-wife	Shoot	8	8

Spearman's rho=0.93.

The most notable aspect of adult and teenage American norms for violence is that only legally constituted authorities are given approval by the majority to use *high-level* violence. Judges and policemen may use high-level violence when legally permitted and when the situation warrants it. Low-level violence with the exception of the husband-wife role relationship is much more broadly approved by the majority of adult and teen Americans.

3. Black and Non-Black Comparisons

Although there are some important differences between black and non-black norms for violence (the most important is that a greater percentage of non-blacks approve of the use of violence by policemen than do blacks), there is a striking similarity between their rank orders of approval of the low-level and severe violence items. Spearman's Rho, a statistical measure which assesses the degree of similarity between two rank orders, is 0.84 between black and non-black rank orders of the low-level violence items, and 0.98 for severe violence items. In general then, black and non-black norms with respect to violence are similar.

In the following section, exploration will be made of the demographic and social characteristics of the minority of adult and teenage Americans who give the highest overall approval of violence.

4. The Approvers of Violence: Low-Level Violence

The first group consists of those who approve of low-level violence (slapping face) between husbands and wives.

Twenty-nine percent of the adults approved of a husband slapping his wife's face and/or a wife slapping her husband's face. This minority can be described in terms of four demographic characteristics which distinguish them from the rest of the adult population: (1) sex, (2) age, (3) residence, and (4) education. The most common group of high approvers of low-level violence consists of: (1) male, (2) eighteen to thirty-five years of age, (3) residing in cities having a population over 50,000 persons, and (4) without a college education.

Thirty-three percent of adult males and twenty-five percent of adult females are high approvers of low-level violence. Although more males than females are high approvers of low level violence, the demographic patterns for males and females are identical. High approvers are young city people who do not have a college education.

Teenagers are higher approvers (45 percent) of low level violence than either male or female adults. The same demographic characteristics were used to identify teenage approvers, with the exception that race was substituted for education, with a higher percentage of blacks expressing approval.

There is no variation between male and female teenagers with respect to percent approval of low level violence (45 percent of both males and females are high approvers). Teenagers were split into two age groups: 13 to 15 years old and 16 to 19 years old. There is no significant variation in percentage approval between age groups for males or females.

The two characteristics which do distinguish teenage high approvers of low-level violence from the rest of the teenage population are residence and race. A greater proportion of teenagers living in metropolitan areas are high approvers than teenagers living in rural, small city, or suburban areas. Of teenagers residing in metropolitan areas, a greater proportion of blacks are high approvers than non-blacks.

The subgroup of teenagers who are high approvers of low-level violence consists of those living in metropolitan areas, especially blacks. It should be noted that the majority of blacks live in metropolitan areas, especially northern blacks. It is difficult to compare black residents of northern suburbs with similar metropolitan residents, since there are too few suburban blacks to make a meaningful comparison.

5. The Approvers of Violence: High-Level Violence

High approvers of high-level violence are defined as those who approve of a high-level violence item which is approved by less than fifteen percent of the total population. These items are (a) parent beating child, (b) teacher beating student, (c) teenager knifing teenager, (d) wife shooting husband, and (e) husband shooting wife.

Twenty percent of the adult population fall into this category. There is variation in approval between the sexes, with twenty-five percent of the males and fourteen percent of the females defined as high approvers. The demographic group with the highest proportion of high approvers of severe violence is exactly the same as the group approving of low-level violence: (1) male, (2) eighteen to thirty-five years of age, (3) residing in a metropolitan area, and (4) with less than a college education.

The group with the second-highest proportion consists of males thirty-six to sixty years of age, living in metropolitan areas, and having less than a college education.

Only fourteen percent of adult females are defined as high approvers of severe violence, but an examination of their demographic characteristics reveals the same pattern found among males.

The teenage group with the highest proportion of high approvers of high-level violence is: (1) male, (2) between the ages of sixteen and nineteen, (3) residing in metropolitan areas, and (4) black. Male teenagers between the ages of thirteen and fifteen with the same residential and racial characteristics constitute the second most approving group of high level violence.

There is a greater percentage of high-approving teenagers (twenty-eight percent) than adults. Thirty-four percent of male and twenty-one percent of female teenagers are classified as high approvers of high-level violence. Black female teenagers living in metropolitan areas are the highest approving group among females.

The fact that black teenagers are consistently higher approvers of violence may be an indirect result of the fact that metropolitan residents are high approvers of violence. Social scientists have pointed to many aspects of urban living in an effort to explain why the rates of deviant behavior are higher in large cities than in suburbs, small cities, or rural areas. Cultural differences between blacks and non-blacks are probably less important than residential differences with respect to approval of violence.

6. Summary

Adult and teenage Americans have similar patterns of general approval of violence. The major characteristics of these patterns are: (1) the use of violence, regardless of severity, is never unconditionally approved by a majority of adults or teenagers; (2) low-level violence is approved behavior for all the role relationships, except the husband-wife relationship, where violence of any level is never approved by a majority of the respondents; (3) the situational bases of approval of low-level violence vary from punishment and control by parents of children and teachers over students, to self-defense and protection of property, loved ones, or masculinity for teenage boys and adult male strangers, and self-defense and law enforcement for policemen and judges; (4) high-level violence is approved by a majority of adults and teens only for the policeman-adult male and judge-citizen role relationships; and (5) policemen and judges may employ high-level violence with the approval of the majority of adults only when legally permitted (e.g., self-defense).

Two findings with particular relevance concern norms relative to the use of violence:

(1) Two significant minorities of adults and teenagers hold opposing views with regard to policemen using violence—one approves of police violence almost unconditionally, while the other never approves of it. This finding has clear implications for the study of political polarization. From the content analysis of the televison world of violence and the role played by law enforcement officials in that world, it is clear that the norms for police use of violence on television support the norms espoused by a minority who almost unconditionally approve the use of violence by police. Conversely, the minority who disapprove police use of violence receive no normative support from television programming. It is important to note television norms with respect to police violence are not supportive of those expressed by the majority of Americans who approve of police violence only when it is legally permitted and necessary, as well as the minority who never approve of it.

(2) A large proportion of teenagers are high approvers of violence, regardless of the level.

In both teenage and adult populations, the highest proportion of high approvers of violence was composed of metropolitan residents. High approvers among adults were most often males between the ages of eighteen and thirty-five residing in a metropolitan area and having less than a college education. Black male metropolitan residents had the highest proportion of high approvers in the teen population.

High approval of violence, then, is related to sex, age, residence, and perhaps to race, although race did not distinguish adult high approvers from the rest of the population.[8] However, when non-black and black metropolitan residents were compared, a slightly greater percentage of blacks were high approvers. In any case, race is not as closely associated with high approval among teenagers as are sex and residence.

An interpretation of these findings will be deferred until the actual experience of adult and teenage Americans with violence is examined.

B. *Actual Experience With Violence: Adults and Teens*

Adult and teenage respondents were asked if they had had direct personal experience with any of five violent encounters. Direct personal experience with violence was assessed by repeating the same series of violent encounters for three different types of experience: (a) as the victim, (b) as the assailant, and (c) as an observer.[9]

The series of violent encounters is listed below. Presented next to the series of violent encounters are the questions asked of respondents to assess their experience as victim and observer.

Victim: Have you ever been (repeated 1-5)	(1)	Slapped or kicked
	(2)	Punched or beaten
	(3)	Threatened or actually cut with a knife
	(4)	Threatened with a gun or shot at
Observer: Have you ever seen another person (repeated 1-5)	(5)	Choked

Measurement of experience with violence as an assailant required a slightly different procedure. It was strongly suspected that very few persons would be willing to admit that they had taken a severe act of violence against another person. The questions asked to assess assailant experience are presented below.

(1) Have you ever *slapped or kicked* another person?
(2) Have you ever *punched or beaten* another person?
(3) Have you ever been in the situation in which you had to *defend yourself with a knife?*
(4) Have you ever been in the situation in which you had to *defend yourself with a gun?*

Choking was deleted for the assailant role. The questions about use of a knife or gun are put within the context of self-defense, which should not have hindered the willingness of the respondent to give an honest answer. The use of a knife or a gun for reasons other than self-defense is not reflected by these questions.

The responses to the experience questions for all three types of roles are presented in Table 3.

*Table 3.—Percent of adults and teens who have had experience
with violence as the victim, assailant, and observer**

Violent acts	Adults			Teens		
	Victim	Assailant	Observer	Victim	Assailant	Observer
Slapped or kicked	0.54	0.30	0.57	0.72	0.49	0.83
Punched or beaten	.30	0.16	.45	.42	0.38	.64
Threatened or cut with a knife	.13	NA	.17	.11	NA	.19
Threatened or shot at with a gun	.12	NA	.16	.06	NA	.14
Choked	.08	NA	.13	.16	NA	.22
Self-defense: Knife	NA	0.05	NA	NA	0.03	NA
Self-defense: Gun	NA	0.09	NA	NA	0.01	NA

The most common violent experience for both adults and teens is in the role of observer. There seems to be a widespread opportunity for persons to learn about relatively low-level riolence by direct observation. However, less than one-fourth of the adult and teen populations have the opportunity to learn about relatively *severe* violence through observation.

The central concern here is based on the assumption that experience can be a source of learning as well as an intervening variable between exposure to television portrayals of violence and the effects of such exposure. However, the extent of experience with violence in the adult and teenage populations is surprising. Although there is no reason to doubt the veracity of the responses, it must be pointed out that the questions are significantly dependent upon the accuracy of the respondents' memory. It is difficult to tell whether errors in memory would lead to an underestimation or overestimation of overall levels of experience with violence. Middle-aged or elderly persons may have forgotten incidents where they were the victim, assailant, or observer of a violent-encounter involving slapping, kicking, punching, or beating. In this case, errors in memory would lead to underestimation. However, it does not seem reasonable to expect that many persons, regardless of age, would forget being the victim of a knifing or shooting.

In addition to errors that may have resulted from faulty memory, what social scientists have called "social desirability" may have affected the responses. Social desirability occurs when a subject responds to a question in a manner which he believes will be approved by the interviewer or by society at large. For example, it is possible that a young male may overestimate his

---

*NA=Not asked

experience with violence because he thinks others might question his masculinity if they knew his experience was limited. On the other hand, many persons may underestimate their actual experience with violence for fear of being seen by others as violent. The assailant role would most probably be affected by such concerns.

There are two reasons to believe that the findings reported in Table 3 are fairly accurate. The effects of faulty memory and social desirability are likely to result in such underestimations and overestimations that their effects may cancel out one other. Also, each respondent reporting an violent experience was then asked a series of questions about the most recent experience of that type. Thus, the fact that respondents were called upon to describe in some detail their violent experiences significantly decreases the likelihood of error.

A majority of adults and teenagers have been the victims of slapping or kicking, while a minority have been punched or beaten. It is surprising to find that approximately the same percentage of adults as teenagers have been threatened or cut with a knife. The extent of victimization by knives (thirteen percent adults, eleven percent teens) seems high, since knives are not commonly used weapons of violence in this society. Victimization by being threatened or shot at with a gun is virtually the same for adults (twelve percent), but much lower for teenagers (six percent). This percentage seems quite high, however, in view of the severity of such violence. Unlike adults, most teens will not have had any military experience as a victim, assailant, or observer of violence involving a knife or gun as the weapon.

In the assailant role, as well as for the victim and observer roles, a greater percentage of teens than adults have experienced relatively low-level riolence. A sharp dividing line is evident in all three roles between the sizable minority who have had experience with punching or beating and the small minority who have experienced violence involving the threat or use of a knife.

Members of the small minority who have had experience with severe violence have had a unique opportunity to learn about it from direct personal experience. For example, persons who have shot, been shot, or seen someone shot are more likely to realize the bloody reality of gunshot wounds. These persons may also develop attitudes and norms about the use of guns or violence as a result of their own experiences.

One finding is that the vast majority of Americans have not had direct personal experience with severe violence. Thus, direct personal experience is not a source of learning about severe violence for the majority of the American adult and teenage population.

It is worth noting that approximately the same proportion of blacks as whites have had experience with severe violence in the victim and assailant roles found in the total population. The only sizeable difference in experience with violence between blacks and non-blacks is the observer role, where forty-eight percent of black adults and sixty percent of black teens have observed severe violence, compared to twenty-one percent of the non-black adult population and twenty-six percent of the non-black teen population.

The fact that most Americans have not had experience with severe violence does not mean that those adults and teens who have had such experience should be forgotten. Most law enforcement officials and social analysts believe that only a small minority of Americans are actively engaged in violence. Typically, a small minority accounts for a majority of the violence committed, because the same individuals repeatedly engage in violence. It is, therefore, extremely important to identify this group.

C. The "Violents" in the Actual World of Violence

The "violents", or persons who have experienced severe violence, will be treated separately as, victim, assailant, and observer. A "violent" for the roles of victim and observer means anyone who been or seen someone: (a) threatened or cut with a knife, (b) threatened or shot at with a gun, or (c) choked. A "violent" in the assailant role is anyone who has found it necessary to defend himself with a knife or gun.

Are the "violents" in one role also "violents" in the other two roles? A simple way to answer this question is to compute a measure of association for each pair of roles (e.g., victim-assailant, victim-observer, observer-assailant).

The data indicate that if a person is a violent in one role, he is likely to be a violent in the other two roles.[10] In other words, many of the "violents" in the victim role are also "violents" in the assailant and observer roles.

The same procedures used to identify high approvers of violence were used for "violents". Consequently, it is possible to assess whether "violents" are also high approvers of violence.

Twenty-one percent of the adult population fall into the "violents" category in the role of victim. The demographic group of adults with the largest proportion of its membership as "violents" in the victim role is: (1) male, (2) 18 to 35 years of age, (3) residing in metropolitan areas, and (4) having less than a college education. The same demographic characteristics are true for "violents" in the observer and assailant roles. Twenty-six percent of the adult population are defined as "violents" in the observer role, while nine percent are "violents" in the assailant role.

In the adult population, the demographic group with the largest proportion of its members defined as "violents" also has the largest proportion of high approvers of violence. Thus, there is high congruence between adults who are high approvers of violence and those who have experience with severe violence.

An interesting variation occurs when examination is made of the teenage "violents." Twenty-four percent of the teen population were defined as "violents" in the victim role. The group with the largest proportion of its members labelled "violents" in the victim role consists of (1) males, (2) 16 to 19 years old, (3) residing in suburban areas, (4) who are non-black.[11] This same group had the highest proportion of "violents" in the observer role, where thirty-one percent of the teens were labeled "violents."

Teenage males between the ages of sixteen and nineteen residing in suburban areas have a slightly greater proportion of "violents" in the victim and observers roles than do males of the same age living in metropolitan areas. This finding indicates that experience with violence is not restricted to metropolitan areas, where many lower income and less educated residents are found. Experience with violence is slightly more common for teenage males who are suburban residents. Further evidence of the extent of experience with violence in the suburbs is found by noting that the adult group with the second largest proportion of its members being "violents" in all three roles is:

(1) males, (2) 18 to 35 years old, (3) residing in suburban areas, (4) having less than a college education.

The demographic group of teenagers with the second highest proportion of its members labelled "violents" in the victim and observer roles consists of (1) males, (2) 16 to 19 years of age, (3) residing in metropolitan areas, (4) who are black.

Only three percent of the teenage population meet the description of "violents" in the assailant role. The group of Negro teenage males living in metropolitan areas had the largest proportion of violents in the assailant role.

In general, both adult and teen demographic subgroups with the highest proportion of "violents" are strikingly similar to the adult and teen groups with the highest proportion of approvers of violence.

Another important aspect of experience with violence is a description of the context and situation in which violence is experienced.

D. *The Context of Violence*

All respondents who said that they had experienced an act of violence as a victim, observer, or assailant were asked the following questions: (1) "How many times would you estimate that this has happened to you?;" (2) "Did this happen to you as a child or as an adult?;" (3) "Considering just the most recent time this happened: (a) In what kind of a situation did it happen?" and (b) "What was your relationship to the other person?"

Analysis of responses to these questions suggests that two contextual aspects characterize the violent experience of our respondents: (1) the great majority took place in an anger or conflict situation with (2) friends or family members.[12]

Differences were found in social context between low- and high-level violence experience. For adults, a greater majority of high-level violence occurs in anger and conflict situations. As expected, high-level violence is experienced less frequently, and it is experienced more often as an adult than low-level violence. Differences between low and high-level violence are similar for teens, except that teenage high-level violence experience more often involves strangers.[13] Teenagers, in fact, report much more contact with strangers in both low-and high-level experience, especially in the victim role. Adults report more frequent experiences in the observer role, but the majority of both teens and adults have observed low-and high-level violence two or more times. These findings are summarized in terms of the most common context patterns for each violent act and experience role for adults in Table 4 and for teenagers in Table 5.

E. *Summary*

There is a striking similarity between the demographic characteristics of "violents" and high approvers of violence in the adult population. This fact supports the assumption that norms for violence are directly related to experience. Further evidence of the relationship between norms and experience is shown by their fairly strong statistical association.[14] Perhaps

TABLE 4

Table 4.—Two Most Common Context Patterns of Experience With Violence: Adults

Experience Role	Violent Act	Relationship	Context Pattern			Percent of Persons Having This Experience
			Situation	Age	Frequency	
Victim Role	Slapped or Kicked	1. Primary	Anger	Child	High	25
		2. Primary	Fun	Child	High	23
	Punched or Beaten	1. Primary	Anger	Child	High	26
		2. Primary	Anger	Adult	High	26
	Knifed	1. Primary	Anger	Adult	Low	30
		2. Primary	Anger	Adult	High	21
	Shot at	1. Primary	Anger	Adult	High	34
		2. Primary	Anger	Adult	Low	19
	Choked	1. Primary	Anger	Adult	Low	25
		2. Primary	Anger	Adult	High	19
Assailant Role	Slapped or Kicked	1. Primary	Anger	Adult	High	24
		2. Secondary	Anger	Adult	High	18
	Punched or Beaten	1. Secondary	Anger	Adult	High	31
		2. Primary	Anger	Child	High	13
Observer Role	Slapped or Kicked	1. Primary	Anger	Adult	High	47
		2. Primary	Anger	Child	High	12
	Punched or Beaten	1. Primary	Anger	Adult	High	52
		2. Primary	Anger	Child	High	12
	Knifed	1. Primary	Anger	Adult	High	52
		2. Primary	Anger	Adult	Low	22
	Shot at	1. Primary	Anger	Adult	High	47
		2. Primary	Anger	Adult	Low	25
	Choked	1. Primary	Anger	Adult	High	43
		2. Primary	Anger	Adult	Low	17

Table 5.—Two Most Common Context Patterns of Experience With Violence: Teens

Experience Role	Violent Act		Relationship	Context Pattern Situation	Frequency	Percent of Persons Having This Experience
Victim	Slapped or Kicked	1.	Primary	Anger	High	38
		2.	Primary	Fun	High	29
	Punched or Beaten	1.	Primary	Anger	High	30
		2.	Secondary	Anger	High	25
	Knifed	1.	Secondary	Anger	Low	35
		2.	Secondary	Anger	High	28
	Shot at	1.	Secondary	Anger	Low	53
		2.	Secondary	Anger	High	17
	Choked	1.	Primary	Fun	High	30
		2.	Primary	Fun	Low	17
Assailant	Slapped or Kicked	1.	Primary	Fun	High	36
		2.	Primary	Anger	High	34
	Punched or Beaten	1.	Secondary	Anger	High	31
		2.	Primary	Anger	High	27
	Slapped or Kicked	1.	Primary	Anger	High	37
		2.	Secondary	Anger	High	30
	Punched or Beaten	1.	Primary	Anger	High	44
		2.	Secondary	Anger	High	31
Observer	Knifed	1.	Secondary	Anger	Low	32
		2.	Secondary	Anger	High	30
	Shot at	1.	Secondary	Anger	High	26
		2.	Primary	Anger	Low	25
	Choked	1.	Primary	Anger	High	26
		2.	Secondary	Anger	High	18

the simplest way to state the nature of this relationship is that many of the "violents" in experience also are high approvers of violence and vice versa.

Norms relative to violence are, therefore, relevant to one's experience with violence. Norms obviously are not the single cause of experience with violence; indeed, it is inappropriate to attempt to draw a causal link between norms for violence and experience with violence on the basis of the present research because there is no way of determining which came first.

A more realistic view is that the relationship between norms and experience is reciprocal. That is, they are mutually reinforcing. Once this approach is taken, research on why some people are violent while others are not moves out of the narrow search for single causes. The search becomes more realistic by looking for factors which increase the *probability* of violent behavior. At this point in the present research, evidence has been presented which shows that norms for violence constitute one factor related to the probability of experience with violence.

The television world of violence and the actual world of violence have been described in terms of the extent and nature of violence. Having described these two worlds, attention can now be turned to the central problem of this research effort: the relationship between these two worlds. Does intensive and prolonged exposure to television increase the probability of violent behavior? Do the norms projected by the television world of violence affect the norms for violence held by audiences, in such a way as to increase the probability of violent behavior?

REFERENCES

1. For example, see L. Beckowitz, R. Corwin, M. Heironimous, "Film Violence and Subsequent Aggressive Tendencies," *Public Opinion Quarterly*, 1963, vol. 27, pp. 217-229.
2. See Appendix III−I for a more detailed discussion of the sampling procedures.
3. The major responsibility for question and questionnaire construction rested with Dr. Sandra J. Ball, Media Task Force Co-Director. Significant contributions were made by Mr. David Lange, Media Task Force General Counsel, Dr. Otto N. Larsen and Dr. Arline Sakuma, and Dr. Richard Nagasawa, consultants to the Mass Media Task Force.
4. See Appendix III−I for inspections of these questions (Q 33 through 48).
5. For example, forty-eight percent of black adults approve (yes responses) of a policeman striking, compared to 73 percent of the total adult population. Likewise, forty-six percent of black adults approve of a policeman shooting, compared to seventy-four percent of the total adult population.
6. "Not sure" responses were included with "yes" responses as the category of general approvers, because the frequency of "not sure" responses was low and a "not sure" response does not remove the possibility of approval in a specific provocation situation.
7. The effect of including "not sure" responses upon the rank orders (both low and high violence items) is minimal. The same rank orders are obtained for "yes" responses only for adults, while the only difference in teen rank orders of "yes" responses occurs in the "teenager punching teenager" item, which is ranked third with only "yes" responses are considered, and ranks fourth when "yes" and "not sure" responses are considered.

8. We suspect that "beating" has a different meaning for black Americans, from the meaning given to "beating" by non-black Americans. This suspicion arises from informal quiries of blacks who said that beating, to them, could mean anything from a hard spanking to being hit with a closed fist. The fact that twenty-four percent of black adults have general approval to a parent beating a child compared to nine percent of the total adult population, adds some further indication that "beating" probably means something less severe to blacks. In other words, our suspicion is that this difference results from different meanings attached to the word, beating, not from different norms for parental punishment of children.

9. Race does not distinguish adult high approvers from the total adult population when residence is held constant.

10. Refer to Appendix III—I for the complete series of these questions (Q's 26-31).

11. Gamma was computed as the ordinal measure of association. For victim-assailant: Gamma=0.84 for adults, and 0.82 for teens: for victim-observer: Gamma=0.75 for adults, and 0.70 for teens; and for observer-assailant: Gamma=0.74 for adults, and 0.69 for teens.

12. Only one black male, sixteen to nineteen years old, in our sample lived in a surburban area, making the racial comparison invalid.

13. Two other aspects of the social context of violence experience, intervention by a third party and the respondent's relationship to the intervenor, were also asked, but time did not permit analysis of these items.

14. Content questions were not asked for severe violence experience in the assailant role (self—defense with a knife or gun).

15. The adult-child distinction was not made in the analysis of the social context of teenage experience with violence.

16. Approval of high level violence and experience in the victim role: Gamma=0.43. Approval of high-level violence and experience in the assailant role: Gamma=0.43. Approval of high-level violence and experience in the observer role: Gamma=0.37.

Chapter 17

THE TWO WORLDS OF VIOLENCE:
TELEVISION AND REALITY

A. The Two Worlds of Violence: A Comparison

The claim that the television world of entertainment and violence is an accurate reflection of the real world of violence clearly is refuted by the research findings in chapters 15 and 16.

The norms for violence contained in the television world of violence are in stark contrast to the norms espoused by a majority of Americans.[1] The most notable contrasts bear upon the criteria which distinguish between approved and disapproved violence. Legality is a primary criterion of approved violence for the majority of adults and teens, while it is not in the television world of violence. In the television world, violence is used almost without restriction as successful means to individual ends. The majority of adult and teenage Americans place severe restrictions on the use of violence in such a manner. For example, low-level violence is approved as a means of punishment and control when a person is in a position of authority or when he is sufficiently provoked. Severe violence, on the other hand, can only be used as a means to law enforcement, or defense of self, others, or property, when the situation clearly necessitates its use.

The norms for violence espoused by a majority of Americans are virtually at polar opposites with those contained in the television world of violence. There is an even greater disparity between the minority of adults and teens who espoused norms of non-violence (persons who very rarely or never approve of violence in any situation) and the television world's norms for violence.

The least disparity between the television world and real world in norms for violence is found between the sizable minority of adults and teenagers who have been called the "violents." Their norms for violence are *less* restrictive than the majority of Americans, but are still *more* restrictive than implied norms in the television world.

The television world of violence does not accurately reflect the real world in many significant respects. The vast majority of all levels of violence experienced by adult and teenage Americans as victims, observers, and assailants occurs with persons who are friends or family members of the respondents.[2] In the television world, the majority of violence occurs between strangers. The most prevalent type of violence in the television world involves the use of a weapon; the great majority of adults and teenagers have never experienced this type of severe violence. The most common role in the television world of violence is the assailant, while the least common is the role of observer; in the actual world, the observer is most common and the assailant is the least common role.

The television world of violence is often set in a time and place other than contemporary America. Television may or may not inaccurately reflect the actual world of violence in the American past or in foreign countries; there is no evidence from present research which can prove or disprove this statement.

When comparing the actual and television worlds of violence, our concern lies with the kinds of implied norms that are projected by television. What can or do audiences, especially children, learn from short and long-term exposure to the television world of violence and what are the behavioral implications of such learning?

B. The Relationship of the Two Worlds of Violence

The viewing habits and preferences of American audiences is a vital link between the actual and television worlds of violence. One method of assessing the relationship between the two worlds is to compare the characteristics of those in our study sample who have been identified as "violents" with the characteristics of persons who use television as their primary mode of media entertainment. Characteristics of adult and teenage "violents" can also be compared with the characteristics of those who have strong preferences for media violence, especially on television.

1. Users of TV for Entertainment

Adults and teenagers were presented with a list of mass media (radio, newspapers, magazines, television, books, movies) and asked which one, if any, they most frequently choose when they wanted to relax and get away from daily tensions. The responses are presented in Table 1.

Table 1.—Adult and teen media choices for entertainment or relaxation [in percent]

Television	43	32
Books	19	22
Radio	12	26
Magazines	9	6
Newspapers	9	4
Movies	5	9
Other	1	1
None	2	
Total	100	100

Teenagers, in general, choose the electronic media (radio, television, and movies) more than adults. A larger percentage of adults choose television as the mass medium most frequently used for relaxation. Note that these figures do not represent all television users, but only those who prefer television as a method of relaxation.

The same demographic characteristics which best distinguished "violents" in norms for and experience with violence were used to describe groups who choose television.

The demographic subgroup of adults with the highest proportion of its members choosing television for relaxation is composed of adults (no difference between males and females) between the ages of eighteen and thirty-five having less than a college education. Age and education characteristics are the same both for this subgroup and the group of adult "violents."

The demographic group of teenagers with the highest proportion of its members choosing television for relaxation consists of males, between the ages of thirteen and fifteen who are black. Common characteristics between this subgroup and the teenage "violents" are sex, race, and, to some extent, age.

2. The Approvers of Television Violence

Twenty-eight percent of the adults said they approved of the kind of violence portrayed on television. The group with the largest proportion approving of television violence is composed of males, from eighteen to thirty-five years of age, residing in metropolitan areas, and having less than a college education. This group contains the largest proportion of adult "violents" in terms of norms and experience with violence.

Fifty-three percent of the teenage respondents approved of the kind of violence portrayed on television. The group with the greatest portion of approvers is made up of males, between the ages of thirteen and fifteen, living in metropolitan areas, who are black.

There is almost a complete overlap between this group of approvers and teenage "violents" both in terms of norms and experience with violence. Common characteristics are sex, race, and, to a large extent, age and residence.

3. Persons With a Strong Preference for Media Violence

Adult and teenage respondents were given a series of six paired alternatives, with each pair containing one violent media content choice and one non-violent choice. For each pair, the respondents were asked to pick the one that they would prefer. An analysis of the choices can be summarized into an index of overall preference for media violence.

Fifteen percent of the adult respondents express high media violence preference.[3] The demographic group with the largest proportion of its members having a high media violence preference consists of males, eighteen to thirty-five years of age, who have less than a college education. This group overlaps with adult "violents" in all respects except residence.

Thirty-three percent of the teenagers have a high media violence preference. The demographic group with the largest proportion of its membership having a high media violence preference consists of males between the ages of thirteen and fifteen. This group overlaps with teen "violents" with regard to sex and, to some extent, age, but not in terms of residence and race.

C. Limitations of Demographic Comparison and Survey Data

There are severe limitations upon the conclusions which can be made on the basis of survey data and demographic data analysis. The information potential of any data analysis is necessarily dependent upon the research prodecures employed to collect data and select respondents.

The data collection procedures employed was a series of interviews administered by trained personnel. There are a variety of factors which can affect the validity of the responses given to these interviewers. Two of these factors which were discussed in chapter 16 are social desirability (responses that are given in light of the respondent's perception of what is desirable to himself, the interviewer, or significant others) and errors of memory, which may occur when the respondent is asked to recall his prior attitudes or experiences.

Another factor which can reduce the validity of responses occurs when the dress, expressions, or general behavior of the interviewer affect the respondent's answers. Errors resulting from this factor are generally minimized by adequate training of interviewers.

There are other factors which can reduce the validity of responses. Whenever a method of data collection involves verbal or written responses, it is likely that some errors will occur. However, a variety of techniques have been utilized in this research to keep these errors at a minimum.

Data in the form of verbal or written responses, even when generally valid, is limited in terms of the inferences about actual behavior which can be made. For example, respondents who indicate on the basis of their responses a high media violence preference may not actually expose themselves to predominantly violent media content.

However, even if it were certain that the responses were valid, we still can only infer behavioral correlates. One method of assessing the validity of an answer is to conduct further research to determine whether or not people behave in a manner which is consistent with their verbal or written responses. For example, future research could be undertaken to see if persons classified as having a high media violence preference actually select and expose themselves to this violent media content.

Thus, the limitations of survey data should be kept in mind when evaluating the findings of this research.

The limitations of demographic data analysis should also be recognized. We have found that there is substantial overlap between the demographic groups of adults and teenagers who are "violents" with respect to norms and experience with violence and the demographic groups who choose television for relaxation, approve of the kind of violence on television, and prefer violent media content.

On the basis of this information, we cannot and do not draw any causal conclusions. For example, we cannot say that exposure to television content "causes" violent norms and behavior, or that having violent norms and experiences "causes" a preference for violent television content. Such conclusions can only follow controlled experimental assessment of causal hypotheses. Neither of these two conditions are present, for the implicit hypotheses of this research are not causal and the research procedures employed are not experimental.

Another important limitation of data analysis involving demographic comparisons is that the unit of analysis is a demographic group, not an individual. Thus, when the same demographic group has the largest proportion of its members classified as "violents," television users, and approvers of television violence and of violent media content, this does not mean that all or most individuals who have the same demographic characteristics also have the same norms, experiences, and preferences with respect to violence. It also does not mean that only those who have the same norms, experiences, and preferences are members of that demographic group.

Given these limitations, some relevant aspects of the two worlds of violence have been identified and described. We now turn to a discussion of the implications of these findings. The following discussion presents hypotheses about the effects of exposure to television portrayals of violence suggested by the research findings which suggest possible directions and problems for future research.

D. Implications of Demographic Comparisons

As previously noted, there is a substantial overlap between the "violents" in norms and "violents" in experience in both the adult and teenage populations. Thus, "violents" in norms are likely to be "violents" in experience, and vice versa. There is also a considerable overlap between the adult and teenage demographic groups of "violents" and the demographic groups of adults and teenagers who approve of the kind of violence portrayed on television and have a high media violence preference.

The fact that there is substantial overlap between these demographic groups and the adult and teen demographic groups who choose television for relaxation indicates that a substantial portion of the "violents," "approvers" of television violence, and "those who prefer media violence" are probably exposed frequently to the television world of violence.

What, then, is the empirical relationship between the television and actual worlds of violence? The present data cannot establish a clear cause-and-effect relationship. In fact, it is clear that whatever influence television' has, that power is not exercised uniformly across all sectors of its audience. However, our major concern is with a special section of that audience—those who are likely to support violent norms and engage in violent acts. Here our data provide a basis for concern and for reasoned estimation of effects.

The high degree of coincidence between preferences for media violence and experience with actual violence, coupled with norms in support of such acts, suggests that the television world of violence has the capacity to reinforce the "violents" in their beliefs and actions in the real world. To the extent that long-term exposure to the patterned world of television violence can provide models for learning norms and behavior, the implication of the present findings is that the effect on the "violents" would be in the direction of unrestricted approval of actual violence. Specifically, this group might be expected to act violently when in conflict situations, enforcing the law, and when attempting to achieve personal ends.

1. Adult and Teen Differences

A substantially greater percentage of teenagers than adults fit the definition of "violents" in the actual world of violence.

Several factors may be relevant to an explanation of this finding. One element may be long-term exposure to the television world of violence. If the norms for and extent of violence found in the content analysis of television programming reported in chapter 15 are typical of television programming of the last fifteen years, it is reasonable to consider the socialization role that television may have played. The vast majority of present-day teenagers were born into families who owned and frequently used television. Most of today's adults, on the other hand, had matured considerably before the advent of large-scale commercial television.

A significant aspect of the changing social environment in which these children were raised was an increasing reliance upon mass communication for recreation, education, and numerous other activities. The mass media, especially television, may have played a more powerful role in the earlier years of personality formation and character development in the lives of teenagers than for adults.

2. Identification and Learning

A factor which increases concern over the learning and socialization implications of television is the potential for identification. "Identification" occurs when an individual emulates another, seeking to be like that person in appearance and behavior. Psychiatrists and psychologists have noted the importance of the process of identification in personality and attitude formation.

In both the television and actual worlds of violence, young to middle-aged males predominate. The potential for identification with characters in the television world of violence is greatest for young males. One commonly noted problem in the male maturation process is the establishment of a male identity. If, in the search for masculinity, young males identify with the male "violents" in the television world, they may be more likely to imitate the attitudes and behavior found in the TV world of violence.

The phenomenon of identification, then, may act as an intervening factor between exposure to the television world of violence and the learning of violent attitudes and behavior from this exposure. Thus, young males are more likely than young females to learn violent attitudes and behavior from exposure to the television world of violence.

3. Socialization of the Non-Violents

Being taught by the television world of violence means learning the norms, techniques, and values for violence contained in the messages presented. Being effectively socialized by the television world of violence means adopting the television world's norms, attitudes, and values for violence as your own.

If television teaches, as the evidence indicates that it can, it teaches norms and attitudes which promote violence. If it can socialize, it socializes audiences, especially children, into norms, attitudes, and values which promote violent behavior and toleration of violence.

The implications of the present research extend past the active reinforcement of violent norms and behavior. The great majority of adults and teenagers in this country do not have violent norms or experience severe violence. The significant implications revolve around the question of whether or not further exposure to the television world of violence can act as one factor in concert with others that could alter their present norms or behavior.

In regard to socialization implications, some questions which are deserving of future research are: (1) what are the effects of continued exposure to the television world of violence on violent teenagers? (2) will future exposure affect teenagers who presently are not violent in norms or behavior? (3) are the millions of infants and young children in this country, most of whom are being exposed daily to television, learning the violent attitudes and behavior portrayed in the television world of violence?

REFERENCES

1.   References to television programming or the TV world of violence are based on the programs broadcast during the weeks of October 1-7 in 1967 and 1968 during prime-time hours 4 p.m. to 10 p.m. Monday through Friday and Sunday, and 8 a.m. to 11 a.m. and 7 p.m. to 10 p.m. on Saturday.

2.   The great majority of homicides (94 percent) occur within racial groups and in only twelve percent of all homicides were the assailant and the victim strangers. One-quarter of all homicides involve family members, and twenty-eight percent involve close friends. For further information, see Marvin Wolfgang, *Patterns in Criminal Homicide,* Philadelphia, Pa: University of Pennsylvania Press, 1948.

3.   A high media violence preference is defined as those persons who select four or more violent alternatives out of the six paired alternatives.

Chapter 18

DISCUSSIONS AND CONCLUSIONS

The edited papers presented and discussed in Chapter 12 and the research reported in Chapters 15, 16, and 17 are focused upon one effect of mass media presentations of violence, particularly in the entertainment realm. However, a thorough understanding of the effect of violent media presentations on individual and social behavior can further be enlarged through a brief review of: (a) the nature of the mass communications; (b) the unique properties of television; (c) the organizational and institutional role of the mass media; and (d) the general short- and long-term effects of media presentations which are known or thought to occur.

A. The Nature of Mass Communication

Communication involves the transmission and receiving of messages. Generally speaking, effective communication occurs when the meaning transmitted is the same as the meaning received.

In interpersonal communication between persons who speak the same language and share the same culture, immediate feedback is usually available to the communicator. This enables him to decide whether or not his messages have been interpreted as intended. Furthermore, those engaged in interpersonal communication can often directly assess other aspects, such as whether or not others are shocked or disturbed or whether or not their messages have influenced others' behavior or attitudes.

During interpersonal communication, one party usually has the opportunity to express forthright reactions to another's messages. In many cases, this reaction can directly affect the communicator's subsequent behavior or attitudes. Of course, the opportunity to honestly respond to another's message is frequently unused because of anticipated consequences.

Traditionally, the primary method of transmitting cultural values in any society has been interpersonal communications. Now, however, modern industrial societies are marked by the presence and widespread availability of mass communication. Accordingly we ask again, this time in the context of violence, what is the capacity of the mass media to influence audiences? What can mass communicators teach their audiences?

The socializing potential of the mass media can be detected by noting some significant differences between interpersonal and mass communication. Through messages in entertainment presentations, the mass media may have the capacity to teach and socialize audiences, but what is the "feedback" capability of the audience?

The flow of messages in mass communication is largely in one direction. The mass communicator transmits and the audience receives, sometimes passively, and sometimes with active effort and response. Thus, an important difference emerges between mass and interpersonal communication. In mass communication the roles of transmitter and receiver are distinct and separate. The responses of the receiver are not immediately visible to the transmitter. The roles of transmitter and receiver are often more integrated and mutually sensitive in interpersonal communication, where the initial receiver may, if he chooses, become a transmitter and respond directly to another's message. However, the mass audience cannot immediately affect what the mass communicator says, nor can the audience clarify the message or test the knowledge of the mass communicator by asking questions.

Some implications of the position of the audience in mass communication have been noted in regard to the effects of news, public affairs, and propaganda materials.   However, it is likely that these same characteristics have additional implications for messages sent in entertainment presentations.

A series of messages and inferred norms for violence projected by television programming was presented in Chapter 15. A major finding of the national survey reported in Chapter 16 was that the great majority of adults and teenagers reported that they have had little or no personal experience with severe kinds of violence, When these two sets of findings are linked to the more rigid nature of mass communication how, then, may concern for the effects of the television world of violence be stated? More specifically, what occurs if audiences gain the impression that violence in the television world, which occurs largely between strangers and members of different ethnic or racial groups, transfer this impression to the real world? There is little in the direct personal experience of the audience either to contradict or validate the impression that violence in the real world is similar to that portrayed on television. The nature of mass communications precludes major efforts to challenge media messages at the point of origin. There is much in the published statistics and public statements of criminologists which contradict media expression of violence, but the audience of criminologists is hardly a significant element of the total television audience.

The nature of mass communication also has important implications for the ability of the mass communicator to assess the effects of his messages upon all segments of his audience. The mass communicator cannot, without special effort, receive an immediate impression of audience reaction to this message. When he does get letters or telephone calls, they may be unrepresentative of the sentiments of the whole audience. Perhaps the most form of letters or phone calls voicing a negative response to the use of certain words, characterizations of certain groups, or dramatization of sensitive social topics.

The most common type of media-initiated audience feedback is, no doubt, the rating of audience size and composition, as well as audience-consumer practices. This type of audience feedback may indicate to what certain segments of the audience, and may provide some information on the effectiveness of advertisements. Mass communicators responsible for entertainment programming have displayed a sensitivity to this feedback by eliminating programs which precipitate negative feedback or fall below certain audience size levels.

The feedback process in mass communication is generally more selective and delayed than in interpersonal communication. However, there is nothing inherent in the nature of mass communication which would prevent enlarging the scope of present feedback practices. The mass media, or other interested agencies, could devote the necessary money, skill, and energy to extend present feedback mechanisms, or create new ones which could substantially increase the ability to assess the short-run and long-term effects of media entertainment presentations.

1. The Unique Properties of Television

Television is the most frequently used mass medium in America. Data from the Violence Commission study support other surveys to show that television is selected by a majority of both teens and adults as the mass medium they most frequently use for urban, national, and international news and entertainment. (Newspapers were selected by the majority for local news.) Furthermore, there is some evidence which suggests that persons who relied on a variety of media for entertainment have increased the amount of time devoted to television viewing and decreased the time devoted to other forms of mass communications.

Television is uniquely appealing and accessible to children, and to some extent, adults because: (1) reading ability is not required; (2) it is commonly available in the home; and (3) audio-visual presentations have more fidelity and thus a greater capacity to create the appearance of authentic and realistic presentations. This capability has probably increased with the advent of color television. Television then, has characteristics which make it readily accessible and highly appealing. The fact that a broad spectrum of the population uses television more frequently than any other mass medium places television in the position of having the greatest potential of all the mass media to affect audience attitudes and behavioe.

Current commercial television programming practices also enhance the possibility of effects and actually are an aid to the scientific study of such effects. As was pointed out in Chapter 15, television content is highly patterned. In basic themes involving problems and their solutions, television probably has the least variability in content at any one point in time of all the mass media.

These special properties are enough to warrant the heavy emphasis placed upon television entertainment programming in the research initiated by this Task Force. However, the decision to focus on television was largely a product of time limitations. The heavy emphasis given to television in the effects portion of this report does not reflect a conviction that the effects of other mass media entertainment presentations are necessarily less important or of a totally different nature.

2. The Organization and Institutional Role of the Mass Media

The mass media in this country are primarily oriented towards the goals which are common to businesses in a private enterprise system. They are, like any other business, oriented toward economic well-being dependent upon financial gain.

The various forms of mass communication tend to join together in large systems. For example, the movie industry sells some of its products to television; radio stations, television networks, newspapers, and some magazines subscribe to the same wire services; and a few popular novels are transformed into movies.

Perhaps more important are the organizational links between the mass media and non-media organizations. One organizational link, not addressed by the present research, is the relationship between advertising organizations and various mass media. We need to know more about the role played by advertising agencies in affecting mass media entertainment content, decisions to interrupt a program for an advertisement, and the effects of advertising content.

There are also significant institutional ties to television which, if studied in future research, would illuminate issues of effects. Many of these institutional links, such as between the mass media and the political institution, fall within the primary realm of news, which is treated elsewhere in this Report.

One example of an institutional tie within the realm of entertainment programming may be seen in the relationship between mass media and recreation. Two questions which could be explored are: (1) what psychological and social effects occur, if any, for persons who spend the majority of their leisure time being entertained by the mass media? and (2) how have sports, especially professional sports, been affected by extensive coverage on television, and what are the effects, if any, of media sports presentations themselves?

B. Orientation to the Study of the Effects of Mass Media Presentations

For a number of years, representatives of the mass media and some social scientists have argued that the primary, if not the only, effect of media entertainment is reinforcement. In these discussions, reinforcement has taken on the unique meaning of "no effect." Thus, it is argued that mass media presentations do not create audience attitudes, norms, or values; they merely support or reinforce the attitudes, norms, or values already held by audience members. The logic of this argument rests upon the assumption that the family, church, schools, and other institutions are "the" socializers, teachers, and influencing agents in American society. These institutions, the argument continues, determine what people think, feel, and do, and, as such, act as insulators against any effect from exposure to the mass media.

For equally as many years, some critics have been arguing that the mass media are the most important cause of the social problems of the day. In recent years, both television and movies have been the primary targets of such allegations.

The accuracy and usefulness of both arguments are unsatisfactory in the light of recent research and the growing sophistication of social science approaches to effect problems.

It may now be suggested that it is more realistic and productive to look at the effects of mass media presentations from a probablistic and multiple factor orientation. In the case of short-run effects of television portrayals of violence, a probablistic approach means that the investigator hypothesizes that exposure to specific portrayals of violence significantly increases the probability of violent attitudes or behavior. It can also mean that "significantly" greater proportions of persons who have been exposed to violent media content will behave violently than persons who have not been exposed. The claim made in short-run effects research are that the effect would be exhibited for a short time after exposure.

A multiple factor approach usually coincides with a probablistic approach to permit a closer approximation of a causal analysis. Not everyone exposed to violent content is expected to subsequently behave violently; other factors are significant. For example, personality differences or different prior experience with violence may cause some people to react non-violently to exposure to violent content.

In the case of learning and long-run effects, it is particularly important to avoid the assumption that exposure to mass media violence alone causes behavior or attitudes. For example, the discussion in Chapters 15, 16, and 17 is centered around what audiences can learn from exposure to messages about violence. Common sense and observation refute the claim that exposure alone makes all people think and act violently. We know that millions of adults and children are exposed daily to television entertainment programming, but a majority of them do not espouse violent norms or behave violently.

Thus, in the continued search for answers about effects, we must look to other relevant conditions in the social environment of television audiences to identify either violent segments of the population or those sets of conditions in which mass media entertainment programming is an important actual or potential contributor to violent attitudes and behavior.

For the present, we know that the mass media and mass media entertainment are significant aspects of the daily lives of most Americans. While the evidence is incomplete, we can also assert the probability that mass media portrayals of violence are one major contributory factor which *must* be considered in attempts to explain the many forms of violent behavior that mark American society today. The following section spells out the conclusions and the conditions that underlie this assertion.

C. Conclusions: Effects of Mass Media Portrayals of Violence

1. General Conclusions

1. The weight of social science stands in opposition to the conclusion that mass media portrayals of violence have no effect upon individuals, groups, and society.
2. To the extent that mass media portrayals of violence have effects upon individuals, groups, and society, it is a variety that most persons would deem costly and harmful to individuals and society.
3. The direction of effects of mass media portrayals of violence is to extend the behaviorial and attitudinal boundaries of acceptable violence beyond legal and social norms currently espoused by a majority of Americans.

a. Short-Run Effects

1. Exposure to mass media portrayals of violence stimulates violent behavior when—

    (a) Subjects are either calm or anxious prior to exposure, but more so when they are not frustrated, insulted, or otherwise angered.
    (b) Aggressive or violent cues are presented (e.g., weapons of violence).
    (c) Subjects are exposed either to justified or unjustified violence, but more so when justified violence is portrayed.

2. The weight of relevant research evidence throws doubt on the tenability of the "catharsis" hypothesis.
3. Audiences exposed to mass media portrayals of violence learn how to perform violent acts.
4. Audiences who have learned violent behavior from the mass media are likely to exhibit that learning (i.e, engage in acts of violence) if they encounter a situation similar to the portrayal situation, expect to be rewarded for violent behavior, or do not observe disapproving reactions to the portrayed aggression from another person in the viewing situation.

b. Long-Run Effects

The following statements contain hypotheses which are clearly consistent with and suggested by established research findings and by the most informed social science thinking about the long-run effects of exposure to mass media portrayals of violence.

1. Exposure to mass media portrayals of violence over a long period of time socializes audiences into the norms, attitudes, and values for violence contained in those portrayals. The probability of socialization increases as—

    (a) The duration of exposure increases;
    (b) The intensity of exposure increases (e.g., number of hours per day);
    (c) The age of the viewer decreases;
    (d) The number of other sources of socialization into violence decreases;
    (e) The number of senses stimulated by the medium increases (e.g., sight or sound);
    (f) The primacy of the part played by violence in media presentations increases.

2. Persons who have been effectively socialized by mass media portrayals of violence will under a broad set of precipitating conditions, behave in accordance with the norms, attitudes, and values for violence contained in media presentations. Persons who have been effectively socialized into the norms for violence contained in the television world of violence would behave in the following manner:
    (a) They would probably resolve conflict by the use of violence.

(b) They would probably use violence as a means to obtain desired ends.

(c) They would probably passively observe violence between others.

(d) They would not be likely to sanction or punish others' use of violence.

(e) They would probably use a weapon when engaging in violence.

(f) If they were policemen, they would be likely to meet violence with violence, often escalating its level.

3. Persons exposed to mass media portrayals of violence over a long period of time are influenced by their exposure, especially when:

(a) The mass media are the sole or major sources of information about violence.

(b) There is ambiguity in the communities' norms for violence.

(c) There is ambiguity in audience members' minds about the violent or relatively non-violent character of groups which are portrayed.

4. Persons influenced by the television world of violence would be influenced in at least the following ways:

(a) Development of more positive attitudes toward violence as a means to fulfillment of individual ends.

(b) Support and extension of the attitude that young men can enhance their masculinity by displaying proficiency in the use of violence.

(c) Lowering the value of non-violent means of problem-solving.

(d) Development of the attitude that it is not the responsibility of individual citizens to help each other out of violent situations.

(e) Development of and support for the belief that policemen are as violent as criminals.

(f) Development of and support for the attitude that successful people may or may not break the law as they please.

5. Distinctions between fantasy and reality presentations of media violence are not consistently perceived by child audiences.

6. Appearance in the media confers status upon those appearing, regardless of their portrayed behavior.

7. Long-term exposure to mass media portrayals of violence may make audience members insensitive or emotionally neutral in response to real acts of violence.

8. Long-term exposure to mass media portrayals of violence in which the physical, psychological, and social effects of violence are not realistically shown can lower inhibitions against the use of violence.

9. The effects of long-term exposure to goreless, unrealistic portrayals of violence and gory realistic presentations are probably both conducive to lowering emotional reactions to violence, making the audience more likely to use violence and to passively tolerate violence by others. There is some reason to suggest that periodic presentations of gory, realistic, violence would have more salutary effects than either completely unrealistic and goreless or realistic and gory portrayals.

10. The extent and intensity of mass media portrayals of violence, especially in the case of television, probably have the effect of creating and/or supporting a view of the world as totally violent. Such a world view tends

to promote widespread toleration of violence, a feeling that it is hopeless to try to control violence, and the belief that individuals must be violent in order to survive in a violent world.

11. The high value placed upon action, immediacy, and simple resolution of problems in the mass media works against the idea that one should react to problems and conflict by deliberation and communication.

12. To the extent that mass media portrayals of violence contain rigid "good-guy"-"bad-guy," right-wrong, and other either-or distinctions, young audiences are likely to develop and maintain psychological rigidity characteristic of adolescence.

13. Inaccurate portrayals of class, ethnic, racial, and occupational groups in mass media presentations retard productive communication between groups. To the extent that certain groups are portrayed as violent, members of those groups may emulate their portrayal, while non-members may react with fear, hatred, and other emotions conducive to intergroup conflict and violence. The effects of these portrayals are especially potent when members of those groups have no direct personal contact with one another.

2. Television and Violence

1. Of all the mass media, television portrayals of violence have the greatest potential for short and long term effects upon audiences.
   (a) The combined properties of audiovisual stimulation and the home-viewing environment make television the most authentic appearing of the mass media.
   (b) Commericial television is the most frequently used mass medium for entertainment.
   (c) Television plays a more central and pervasive role in the total communication of modern society than any other mass medium.
   (d) Television more than any other mass medium, is re-shaping the traditional definitinal and socializing activities of political, economic, educational, recreational, and religious institutions.

2. The television world of violence:*
   (a) Is not an accurate reflection of the real world of violence as experienced by adult and teenage Americans;
   (b) Is not what the majority of adult and teenage Americans want;
   (c) Is the primary source of exposure to severe acts of violence for the majority of Americans;
   (d) Constitutes the vast majority of network entertainment (eight-one percent of all programs analyzed for 1967, and eighty-two percent of all programs analyzed for 1968 contain violence), the majority of every type of programming (e.g.

*The Television World of Violence consists of all programs containing violence which were broadcast during the week of October 1-7, in 1967 and 1968 during prime-time viewing hours. This week of programming has been shown to be typical of all weeks of programming in both 1967 and 1968. (See Michael Eleey, "Variations In Generalizability Resulting From Sampling Characteristics of Content Analysis Data: A Case Study," unpublished master's thesis, Annenberg School of Communications, University of Pennsylvania, 1964.)

cartoon, comedy), and has not significantly changed from 1967 to 1968;

(e) Is deminated by norms for violence which are inconsistent with those espoused by a majority of adult and teenage Americans;

(f) Explicitly and implicitly portrays norms for violence which are most similar to a minority of adult and teenage Americans who—

    i. Have the experience with violence as a victims, assailants, and observers;

    ii. Have the strongest preference for violence in mass media presentations;

    iii. Use commercial television more than any other mass medium for entertainment;

    iv. Are the most similar in age and sex to violent characters in the television world of violence (young to middle-aged males).

A representative sample of adult Americans was asked whether or not television violence has a series of effects. The series contains an equal number of "positive" and "negative" effects, and these six represent the best-known hypotheses concerning the effects of mass media.

The responses given by adult Americans are presented in table 1.

Table 1.—Adult American judgments on the effect of TV violence

In Percent

	Likely or possible	Unlikely	Not sure
1. Plays a part in making America a violent society	75	20	5
2. Triggers violent acts from people who are maladjusted and mentally unstable	86	8	6
3. Makes people insensitive to real acts of violence that they hear about or see	60	31	9
4. Allows viewers to blow off steam by watching violence, thus decreasing the likelihood of their being violent	44	45	11
5. Provides entertainment and relaxation without harmful or bad effects	62	32	6
6. Supports and strengthens traditional American values	34	52	14

The judgments of a majority of adult Americans are in substantial agreement with the conclusions drawn by the Mass Media and Violence Task Force concerning the effects of mass media portrayals of violence. These judgments do not validate or add any scientific support to the findings and conclusions presented, but they do demonstrate the widespread concern that adults express about the effects of television violence.

REFERENCES

1. C. I. Hovland, I. L. Janis, and H. H. Kelley, *Communication and Persuasion* (New Haven: Yale University Press, 1953).
2. J. T. Klapper, *The Effects of Mass Communication*, (Glencoe, Ill: Free Press, 1960).
3. See G. W. Allport and L. Postman, *The Psychology of Rumor* (New York: Holt, Rinehart, Winston, 1947,) and T. Shibutani. *Improvised News: A Sociological Study of Rumor* (New York: Bobbs Merrill, 1967).
4. See L. Berkowitz, "Aggressive Cues in Aggressive Behavior and Hostility Catharsis," *Psychological Review*, 71 (1964), pp. 104-122; and L. Berkowitz and R. Guen, "Film violence and Cue Properties of Available Targets," *Journal of Personality and Social Psychology*, 3 (1966), pp. 525-530.
5. S. Feshbach, "The Stimulating Versus Cathartic Effects of a Vicarious Aggressive Activity," *Journal of Abnormal and Social Psychology*, 63 (1961), pp. 381-385.
6. See A. Bandura, D. Ross, and S. Ross, "Imitation of Film-mediated Aggressive Models," *Journal of Abnormal and Social Psychology*, 66 (1963) pp. 3-11; and A. Bandura and F. L. Menlove, "Factors Determining Vicarious Extinction of Avoidance Behavior Through Symbolic Modeling," *Journal of Personality and Social Psychology*, 8 (1968), pp. 99-108.
7. A. Siegal, "Film-Mediated Fantasy Aggression and Strength of Aggressive Drive," *Child Development*, 27, (1966), pp. 355-278.
8. See A. Bandura and A. Huston, "Identification as a Process of Incidental Learning," *Journal of Abnormal and Social Psychology*, 63 (1961), pp. 311-312 and E. Maccoby, and W. C. Wilson, "Identification and Observational Learning from Films," *Journal of Abnormal and Social Psychology*, 55 (1957), pp. 76-87.

Chapter 19

RECOMMENDATIONS

A. Effects and Effects Research

1. Given the following facts:
   a) The broadcast media are given the right to use public airwaves.
   b) A major criterion for receipt of a broadcasting license is the serving of the public interest.
   c) There is sufficient evidence that mass media presentations, especially portrayals of violence, have negative effects upon audiences.
   d) The majority of the American public believes that there is too much violence of which they disapprove, and believe that television portrayals of violence have undesirable effects.
   e) The commercial television industry is one of the most profitable industries in the world.
   Then:
   > It is recommended that the burden of research and proof be placed squarely on the mass media, especially commercial television, to carry out meaningful research on the psychological and social effects of mass media portrayals of violence.

2. The statement that the only point at which public concern and media responsibility for the effects of media presentations need be aroused is when media presentations are proven to be "the single cause" of violence or any other behavior should be recognized as faulty assertion. The public, the media, and policy makers should be made aware that a single factor causation approach is rarely employed in modern social science. Rather, if mass media portrayals of violence are "a" cause or "a" contributing factor to the creation, support, or stimulation of violent behavior and attitudes, then public and private concern is warranted.

3. The mass media should appraise their role in American society and take a responsible attitude toward the effects of their products. The major source of media profits in the realm of news and entertainment comes from advertising, the cost of which is dependent upon how many thousands of Americans can be expected to be exposed to the

advertising message. Advertisers would not use the mass media unless they were convinced that their advertising has the desired effects upon the purchasing behavior of audiences. Intricate rationalization is necessary to claim that mass media advertising has effects, but that extensive and long-term exposure to violence in media entertainment presentations has no effects upon audiences. This sort of rationalization, which has been common, is unproductive at best.

4. Social scientists should turn to the question of the mass media, mass communications, and violence, incorporating them into theoretical frameworks and developing research methodologies for their examination.

5. The effects of news media should be researched with the same concern and research questions posed for entertainment media, as well as a variety of other questions relevant to the news media.

6. Policy makers, media personnel, and the public need to enlarge their perspective on the range of possible desirable and undesirable effects of media presentations, and clearly specify what effects are and what effects are not desired.

7. A permanent research institute should be established for long-term cummulative research on the short- and long-run effects of mass media presentations. This institute should be completely free from governmental and media control.

8. The public, media, and government should recognize that the most important and primary effects of mass media entertainment presentations cannot be corrected or prevented by hit-and-miss deletions of certain scenes, slight and temporary reductions in the number of certain types of episodes, or any other minor alterations of extent and intensity of certain types of content. With regard to violence and other effects, the crux of the issue and concern should lie with the substantive messages sent by mass media presentations to audiences. For example, reductions in the extent of violent episodes or alterations in how those violent episodes are portrayed will not alter the primacy that violence has in mass media entertainment or the messages about violence sent to child and adult audiences.

National commissions have addressed the issue of effects of mass media presentations before, but the most significant result of their work and existence may have been to sooth public concern. No significant and enduring changes in mass media content have occurred in the direction suggested by former commissions and other concerned agencies though some have occurred in the opposite direction. The message sent by television entertainment programming to child and adult audiences have been objectively and reliably determined and reported (II). There is some reason to suspect that these messages are fairly accurate reflections of the messages sent by other mass mediums, but research needs to be carried out on the entertainment content of all major mass mediums.

If the public, the media, and politicians are satisfied that these messages and their effects are desirable, there is no problem. On the other hand, if these messages and their effects are undesirable, television networks must fundamentally alter the messages sent to audiences before the effects of this entertainment content can be altered.

Some suggested guidelines for the alteration of messages sent dealing with violences are:

a) The assumption that violence, per se, is bad and should, therefore, be entirely removed from media entertainment content, should *not* be made.

b) The phenomena of violence and conflict should not be confused; rather, their essential differences should be recognized as well as the different roles that conflict and violence play in drama.

c) Thorough appreciation of the fact that simple reversal of the meaning of present messages (e.g. reversing the message that violence is the most successful means to the attainment of individual ends to the message that nonviolence is the most successful means to the attainment of individual ends) is not sufficient and may result in other effects which are equally undesirable. Alteration of messages should be carried out with the consultation of experts on effects of mass media content, and continuous research should be conducted on the effects of present and future messages contained in media content.

d) In no way should concern for the effects of mass media presentations or actions taken to correct undesirable effects open the door to government censorship of mass media content or government intrusion on the First Amendment rights of all Americans. In the last analysis, the mass media themselves must be the changers of media content. The unfortunate fact is that so far, the mass media have failed to respond meaningfully to legitimate public concerns in more than superficial ways. The public has tremendous powers to bring about changes in mass media content that are held by no governmental agency. The source of the public's power derives directly from the fact that modern mass media organizations are economic in nature and orientation, and are directly dependent upon the public for their economic welfare. If the mass media public refuses to buy, and more importantly, use mass media products, until changes are made in mass media presentations, then these changes would be made.

B. General Recommendations

1. Alternatives to commercial mass media, especially television, should be actively and seriously promoted and supported by local, state, and federal agencies. For example, the Corporation for Public Broadcasting or National Educational Television offer an alternative or choice to viewers who are dissatisfied with commercial television.

2. A thorough examination should be made of the institutional and organizational reciprocity between the mass media and the advertising business, politicians, and policy makers in local, state, and national governments. Two of the questions that could be examined are: a) How does advertising directly and indirectly affect programming policy and content? and b) What is the effect of the dependence of politicians upon the media to win elections, publicize issues, influence public

opinion and other related activities upon their policy decisions, including media-related issues?

3. The question of why violence is such a predominant aspect of mass media presentations should be examined from an economic point of view. Specifically, is violence predominant because it is the least expensive type of content to produce and the least demanding in terms of creative skills?

4. A complete examination should be made of what happens to a television program once it is taken off a network. A review of program logs of the major commercial and independent stations suggests that programs that are sold by one major network to another or to an independent station are largely violent programs which are shown during non-prime-time hours when large child audiences can be expected (late afternoon), or during late night hours when adult audiences would be expected.

5. The American public, especially parents, should become informed about the established and tenable effects of their own and their children's intenst and prolonged exposure to mass media portrayals of violence. The public, too, has a responsibility, and should exert its rights to have a voice in what is broadcast on their public airways.

6. The Federal Communications Commission, which has the power to renew broadcasting licenses, should publish each renewal request and dissemenate the basis of their decision to renew or not renew each broadcasting license.

7. Pressure should be exerted from the public to make mass media self-regulation work. In order for self-regulation to be an effective and meaningful means of regulating media content, at least the following things are required and recommended:

a) A permanent vehicle of feedback and communication between the mass media and their audiences should be created so that the public can accurately and effectively register their opinions on media content.

b) A permanent vehicle of dissemenation of research findings on mass media effects and content to the public should be established.

c) Research on the mass media, especially long-term mass media effects, should be promoted and financed by the mass media and private and public funding organizations.

C. A Center for Media Study

The public should be able to ask the media to improve when they falter, but responsible criticism, like responsible media operation, requires information about the subject matter in order to be accurate and effective. Until now, the media have not been quick to divulge information about their practices. As a result, review and criticism of the media are based on little information or misinformation. One solution, we believe, is to provide for continuing systematic collection of data about media performance, practices, values, and effects.

The idea of some continuing review of the media is not new. The recent history of such proposals dates back almost twenty-five years.

1. Earlier Proposals

Twenty-two years ago, the Commission on Freedom of the Press (the "Hutchins Commission"), first advocated "the establishment of a new and independent agency to appraise and report annually upon the performance of the press."[1]

Professor Harold Lasswell, a member of that Commission, has made by far the most comprehensive articulation of the Hutchins Commission's proposal. Lasswell has suggested a private, non-profit "Commission on Public Communications," structured along dual functional lines and governed by twin bodies: (1) a Policy Board to "take responsibility for the statement of the criteria to be applied in appraising the media, and for periodic interpretations of available research data;" and (2) a Research Board to be "responsible for translating statements of goal or objectives in research terms, and in obtaining research indices."[2] Lasswell expressed the hope that the initiative for the establishment of such a Commission would come from a private foundation or major university, with funding to be provided by foundations, the communications industry, or other businesses.

The National Advisory Commission on Civil Disorders urged the establishment of an "Institute of Urban Communication on a private, non-profit basis," with "neither governmental ties nor governmental authority."[3] Such a governing board would consist of both professional journalists and "distinguished public figures." Again, the Kerner Commission looked to private foundations for initial funding, with subsequent support from the media. Functions of the Institute, as conceived by the Kerner Commission, would include the review of media performance on riots and racial issues; the training and education of journalists in urban affairs; recruitment, training, and placement of Negro journalists; the stimulation of improved police-press relations; the development of an Urban Affairs News Service; and research on the impact of the media on race relations.

Harry S. Ashmore, former editor of the *Arkansas Gazette*, has advocated the creation of an "independent agency, without powers of legal enforcement, but armed with great prestige, to appraise and report annually on the performance of mass communication." Similarly, Jack Gould, the television critic of the *New York Times*, urged the Carnegie Corporation, following its report on Public Television, to "set up a National Commission on Television" to make "periodic assessments of all forms of the media, a variation of a British Royal Commission."

In testimony before the Violence Commission, Dr. Otto Larsen suggested the creation of an "Institute" to conduct a "continuing, systematic, objective, comparative surveillance of mass media contents, located . . . in the universities," with the support of industry and "encouragement, if not support, from proper places in the government."

A detailed contemporary recommendation for such an institute came from Commissioner Nicholas Johnson of the Federal Communications Commission during his testimony before the Violence Commission. He proposed a Citizens Commission on Broadcasting, "completely free from any suggestion of government or industry influence."[4]

A series of related proposals for monitoring media performance patterned on such models as the British Press Council, bar associations and medical societies, would, if implemented, encompass certain of the functions of an independent agency. Thus, William L. Rivers supports the creation of a "Committee on Public Communication operating much as the British Press Council does . . . composed entirely of representatives of the mass media."[5] Former Federal Communications Commissioner Lee Loevinger has urged the broadcasting industry to establish an "American Broadcasting Council on Fairness and Accuracy in Reporting" to function in the same manner as the grievance committee of any professional association.

These proposals, while national in scope, are essentially innovative forms of self-regulation. The authority, membership, financing are to be drawn from the media themselves. However, the proposal for local Press Councils made by Barry Bingham, editor and publisher of the *Louisville Courier-Journal*, contemplates a council composed of three to five local community leaders, rather than media representatives, who would hear and judge complaints. The media would present their case to the local council in response to public criticism. Bingham's objective—to provide a foundation of public trust in the media[6]—is the same as ours.

2. The Task Force Proposal

The report and proposal of the Hutchins Commission was received with widespread public scorn and bitter media indignation.[7] That scorn has now abated, for the critical needs which gave rise to that Commission's proposal remain substantially unsatisfied.

We believe that there is a clear need for a national Center for Media Study, independent of both media and government, and responsible to the people. We also recommend the immediate establishment of the Center to bring to life the proposals made by the many astute and concerned observers of the media.

The case for an independent agency rests upon two basic judgments: (1) that the recurring conflict between media commercial interest and the public interest distorts both the performance of the media and their capacity for self-evaluation and self-criticism; and (2) that the media, through industry self-regulation, are capable of improving their performance under the stimulus of responsible criticism.

The harsh responses to the Hutchins Commission's and comparable later proposals were based on a perceived threat to freedom of the press which many journalists see as inherent in any form of external observation of media performance. Yet the "independent agency" was conceived and articulated as a discreet alternative to governmental surveillance; it would be as independent of political influence as any private institution, and would be completely devoid of any regulatory authority. These conditions are of paramount importance. Nevertheless, we do not believe that the financing of the operations of an organization so basic to our society should be left to the willingness of a foundation to underwrite its substantial costs, nor the ability of a university, sufficiently free of economic pressures, to undertake so strenuous a responsibility. No university or foundation has undertaken such a program in the years since the Hutchins Commission's proposal was advanced.

We think the known and potential effects of the media are so critical that we cannot wait another quarter-century.

In our judgment, the requisite permanence, independence and status for an organization capable of constructive impact upon media performance can best come from a non-profit corporation, organized under the laws of the District of Columbia. This organization should be granted such additional powers as may be required (provided by legislation on the pattern of the Public Broadcast Corporation); without any continuing responsibility to report to Congress or other government agency or official; with a financing mechanism independent of the political processes; and with clearly delineated powers of monitorship, evaluation, and publication, but without sanction. The Center for Media Study would be independently administered, maintained, and financed, and should have the requisite national standing and absolutely essential independence to insure that its findings and judgments would be subject to minimum influence by the media or government.

We suggest that the operations of the Center be governed by three distinct boards: a Governing Board with overall supervisory responsibility and policy-making powers; a Research Board to devise and execute continuing research and analysis of media practices and effects; and a Media Advisory Board. To provide the impetus necessary to begin the Center, we suggest that initial three-year appointments to the Center's governing boards be made by the President of the United States.

To assure the political as well as the economic independence of the Center, the President should select a Governing Board of prominent non-political and non-media public figures, with significant social and economic minority representation. To insure that the Center has access to the specialized knowledge and competence available in the media, the President should also select a Media Advisory Board from nominees submitted directly by the media themselves. Finally, the President should appoint a Research Board from among distinguished academic specialists in such diverse but relevant disciplines as communications research, social psychology, sociology, cultural anthropology, communications technology, law, psychiatry, economics, and management.

We have considered numerous possible methods of funding the operations of the Center. Our primary concern has been to insure that the Center will be subject neither to government nor media pressures. We also have sought methods of financing which would involve individual participation across the widest possible spectrum of the public.

If the media are to be responsible directly to the people, as Dr. Stanton of CBS and others have suggested, we believe it appropriate for the people to be asked to participate directly in a proposal to examine how well the media discharge that responsibility. We suggest that individual contributions be solicited through a nationwide advertising campaign, planned as a public service by the Advertising Council, and carried as public service advertising in all of the mass media. Supplemental advertising space or time could be purchased either from funds provided initially by a foundation or from contributions received from the public. As an incentive for individual contributions, there would be the usual Federal income tax deduction. A more viable alternative, however, would be a direct Federal tax credit of up to five dollars per person. If contributions exceed the amounts needed to operate the Center, the excess funds could be invested in government securities, with a set percentage of the proceeds used, for example, to endow additional scholarships, to supplement mid-career training programs, or to be added to the Center's endowment.

Supplemental means of financing would include a dedicated tax on advertising or the sale of radio and television receivers, on gross receipts of the media, or on foundations. One disadvantage of the dedicated tax is that the money passes through government control. The objection could be partially met by placing the funds in a trust account, free from the annual appropriations process.

Still other funding sources could include contributions from universities or corporations. Grants from the media industry would also be accepted. Within broad categories, funds provided by the industry would be employed wholly at the discretion of the Center's Governing Board.

In summary, several financing possibilities are available and should be explored. The criteria for ideal funding are: widespread and direct individual participation, freedom from government or industry control, sufficiency, and stability.

3. Tasks for the Center

The Center should be authorized by its charter to perform a broad spectrum of related tasks. Its basic functions would include collecting, studying, storing, and disseminating information about the performances, practices, and values of the mass media of the United States.

Among other tasks, the Center would undertake the following investigations:

a. The Analysis and Evaluation of Media Standards

The processes and substance of voluntary media standards, both internal and industry-wide, would be subjected to continuing consideration.

b. Collection of Data Concerning the Media

The Center would conduct or fund continuing collection of data on national media fare. Moreover, the Center could conduct spot surveys of local media fare. The availability of such data would encourage further experiments, surveys, and study by interested researchers.

c. The Monitoring and Evaluation of Media Performance

In the broadcast media, the Center could evaluate the degree of adherence to standards as well as measure the extent to which broadcasters meet their commitment (in licensing applications to the FCC) to provide specified amounts of public interest programming. The Center should also examine from time to time the accuracy, integrity, and relevance of the broadcast rating services.

In the print media, the Center could monitor standards for inclusion of news in newspapers and magazines and standards for the national wire services and syndicates. In all media, standards for granting access should be evaluated.

d. The Evaluation of Media Grievance Machinery

The Center might well contribute to the development of workable procedures to insure access to the media for significant dissident groups.

The responsiveness of the media to complaints and requests for the opportunity to present alternative views on public issues could be monitored and evaluated by the Center. To the extent that the media undertake to develop professional grievance machinery such as Press or Broadcasting Councils, the Center could contribute to their development and effectiveness by evaluating their responsiveness. Consideration could well be given to a "right of reply" for redressing grievances.

e. Analysis of the Institutional and Economic Structure, Trends within, and Practices of the Media

A thorough examination should be made of the relationship between the mass media and the advertising business, politicians, and policymakers in local, state, and national governments. The impact of economic concentration should be an intensive, continuing concern of the Center.

f. Analysis of Media Employment Practices

The Center should monitor practices and trends in media employment. As the Kerner Commission and others have observed, the quality of reporting on minority group problems is directly related to the extent to which minority group members are employed in substantive journalistic capacities.

g. The Evaluation of the Effectiveness of Government Agencies Charged with Media-Related Responsibilities

Certain government agencies are charged with the responsibility of overseeing specific aspects of the media's activities. These agencies in turn would benefit from a continuing examination of the performance of these functions.

h. Development of Standards and Programs for Ameliorating Community-Press Relations

As the Kerner Commission suggested, "the Institute could undertake the task of stimulating community action" and "could serve as a clearinghouse for an exchange of information on Police-Press Relations."

i. The Conduct or Funding of Journalism Training in Areas of Critical Social Significance

The Center should be authorized to conduct or fund programs for the training of minority group journalists, as well as for the training of non-minority group members in techniques for reporting on minorities and on social, economic, and environmental problems generally.

j. The Stimulation of Public Interest Coverage Through Grants and Awards

The Center's impact should not be limited to the negative sanctions of critical evaluation and condemnation. To the extent that its resources permit, the Center should engage in affirmative programs to stimulate media coverage in the public interest through grants. Such grants may be particularly appropriate for local media projects which may lie beyond the resources of local newspapers or commercial broadcasters to perform without financial assistance.

In addition, the Center might appropriately develop a program of awards for outstanding public interest coverage or other performance.

k. Long-Term Study of the Social Effects of Media Entertainment and News Practices

The Center should study and evaluate the social effects of media entertainment content to the benefit of both the media and society: a reasoned and dispassionate analysis could overcome much of the hyperbole that has attended accusations and denials that the effects of the media injure society.

In addition, the Center should conduct studies in three major areas of the news media to determine, much as in the case of the entertainment media, (a) news media content, (b) the effects of news content, and (c) the ways in which the news media function. Content analysis would include the decision-making process in news operations. Effects analysis would emphasize group effects, but would also include individual effects. Functional research should include research on the mechanical and business aspects of news, and would also deal with both the internal and external regulatory mechanisms applicable to the media.

l. The Conduct and Funding of Research

The Center should conduct a modest research program with its own research staff. Most research under the aegis of the Center, however, should be done by others, encouraged and supported by Center grants and contracts. The Research Board of the Center would provide advice and counsel to the Center Director in research matters.

4. Powers

In Section 6 we include detailed suggestions for the organizational structure of the Center. In addition to these suggestions, the Center should be granted certain minimal powers:

a. Authority to Publicize Findings and Conclusions

The Center would be expected to seek the widest possible dissemination of its statements and reports. While the Center should be authorized, if necessary, to purchase media time or space to publish its findings, the media would normally be expected to provide adequate coverage for Institute releases.

b. Authority to Request Data and Reports Through Government Agencies

The center should have access to relevant data from such agencies as the Securities and Exchange Commission, The Federal Communications Commission, the Department of Health, Education, and Welfare, and the Federal Trade Commission.

Finally, to provide a check on its own activities, as well as a formal occasion for evaluation of overall performance of trends within the media, the Center should be required to prepare and make available to the public an annual comprehensive report detailing its activities and rendering its judgments.

5. Summary

In summary, we recommend:

a. That a non-profit corporation be chartered under the laws of the District of Columbia and that the Congress enact such additional legislation as the tasks set forth here may require and legislation to permit a direct Federal income tax credit for individuals who contribute to its support.

b. That the President appoint three groups of distinguished Americans to assist in the birth and life of the Center for Media Study:

(1) A Governing Board,

(2) A Research Board, and

(3) A Media Advisory Board.

c. That the mass media of this country support the Center for Media Study with funds, cooperation and participation in its work and appropriate publicity for its reports.

d. That the people of the United States support the Center for Media Study by providing it with criticism and praise of the media, and by contributing the funds to give it life.

The Center should be a conduit for neither unwarranted attacks on the press nor whitewashes. It should strive to insure, however, in the words of Professor William L. Rivers, "that a reporter, an editor, a publisher, or a broadcaster who abuses the canons of journalism will at least be tested by pitiless publicity to determine whether he is incapable of chagrin."[8] The Institute should also try to meet Rivers' goal of a "Committee which praises as well as damns, which defends as vigorously as it attacks."

In short, we believe that the Center for Media Study will help to insure mutual confidence between press and public. By cooperating in establishing and operating the Center for Media Study, the press can demonstrate to the people that it is concerned with its defects and will do something about them.

6. The Boards

a. General

All three boards (Governing, Media Advisory, and Research) should be appointed by the President. Board members should serve three-year terms, and may be reappointed to a second term, but not to a third. Members appointed when the Center is established should be appointed to staggered terms, such that one-third of the membership of each board expires in each year.

b. Governing Board

This is to be composed of nine members. This board has directive power over the operations of the Center for Media Study, through the Director of the Center. Its members may all be non-media and non-governmental, or a small number may be from the media; in any event, all should be distinguished public-spirited citizens. At least two should be from social or economic minorities. There are two possible formulas for composition of the Governing Board;

a. All members are non-media and non-governmental. This should be construed to mean that none is presently active full-time in the media or the government, in order to avoid precluding the appointment of distinguished citizens with former service in these fields.

b. Seven members are non-media and non-governmental, as in "a," and the other two are recommended to the President by the Research Board and the Media Advisory Board from among their members.

c. Media Advisory Board

This is to be composed of eleven members. This Board provides advice direct from the various mass media to the Center for Media Study. Its members are appointed by the President, following recommendations mady by the organizations listed below. Recommendations should be selected from:

1. American Society of Newspaper Editors
2. American Association of Advertising Agencies
3. American Newspaper Publishers Association
4. Comics Magazine Association of America
5. Magazine Publishers Association
6. Motion Picture Association of America
7. National Association of Broadcasters
8. Underground Press Syndicate
9. U. S. Student Press Association
10. Radio and Television News Directors Association
11. Writers Guild of America

d. Research Board

This is to be composed of seven members. This board provides research advice and counsel to the Center for Media Study. Its members are appointed by the President, following recommendations made by the organizations listed below. Recommendations should be selected from:

1. Association for Education in Journalism
2. American Association of University Professors
3. National Academy of Sciences
4. American Psychological Association
5. American Sociological Association
6. American Association for Public Opinion Research
7. American Council on Education for Journalism

REFERENCES

1. *A Free and Responsible Press* (Chicago: University of Chicago Press, 1947), p. 100.
2. Harald Lasswell, *The Future of Commercial Television* (Stanford: Stanford University Press, 1965), p. 108.
3. *Report of the National Advisory Commission on Civil Disorders* (Washington: Government Printing Office, 1968), p. 212.
4. December hearings, p. 214.
5. William L. Rivers, *The Opinionmakers* (Boston: Beacon Press, 1965), p. 196.
6. *Ibid.*, p. 195.
7. *Ibid.*, p. 196.
8. *Ibid.*, p. 197.

Appendix III-A

A REVIEW OF RECENT LITERATURE ON PSYCHOLOGICAL EFFECTS OF MEDIA PORTRAYALS OF VIOLENCE*

by Richard E. Goranson

Although great social concern has periodically been expressed over the harmful social effects of the violence and aggression depicted in the mass media, only recently has an appreciable volume of empirical and experimental research been systematically directed toward the problem. Reviews of commentary and research findings on this topic have been published in Bandura and Walters, 1963; Berkowitz, 1962; Klapper, 1960; and Maccoby 1964. Going beyond these reviews, the last few years have seen the development of several new lines of research which have defined some of the complex issues involved, and provided partial answers to some of the questions that have been raised.

A. The Issues

Much of the recent work on the psychological effects of media violence has been devoted to a limited number of central issues. Discussion of this research will be organized around the following basic issues and questions:

(1) *Effects on learning*: Are children likely to learn and remember *new forms* of aggressive behavior by watching the kind of violence presented in the mass media? What are the conditions, if any, that encourage the actual performance of aggressive acts learned through the media.

(2) *Emotional effects*: Does the repetition of violence in the mass media result in a decreased emotional sensitivity to media violence? Is a decreased emotional sensitivity likely to have any implications for the probability of actual aggressive behavior in real-life situations?

(3) *The question of catharsis*: Does watching the kind of aggression shown in the media result in "aggression catharsis"—a "draining off of aggressive energy"? Does the observation of pain, horror, and suffering result in catharsis?

*A section of this paper, addressed to the issue of catharsis, has been deleted. It now appears as Appendix III-D

(4) *Effects on aggressive behavior*: Are there any conditions of observed violence that can serve either to inhibit or to facilitate aggression?

B. The Relevance of Psychological Research

Before going into the recent research on these questions, it is first necessary to confront some of the fundamental issues underlying the relevance of psychological research on media violence effects.

1. The Definition of Aggression

In the course of this review, it will become apparent that various investigators have employed quite different measures and operational definitions of aggression. To avoid confusion, some distinctions between these different usages should be made clear at the outset. While some researchers have used paper and pencil, or "verbal" measures of aggression (perhaps better called hostility), most have concentrated on behavioral measures. A major distinction can be made between two types of behavioral definitions: the *harm intent* definition, and the *response form* definition.

a. Harm Intent Measures

A *harm intent* definition is based on the measurement of the *intentional inflicting of pain or injury on another person*. Much of the research using this type of definition has measured the number, intensity, or duration of electric shocks that subjects have been willing to give to another person. Verbal responses or ratings which are potentially capable of causing harm to the target person have also been used as measures of aggression. The *harm intent* type of definition corresponds to one common use of the word aggression, and some writers have expressed a strong theoretical preference for this kind of measure, (Hartley, 1964; Weiss, in press).

b. Response Form Measures

The *response form* type definition, on the other hand, is based on the *physical characteristics of aggressive actions*: hitting, kicking, striking with a hammer, etc. These responses have a *form* which is, by another common usage, "aggressive" even when the responses are directed toward non-human targets. Bandura and Walters (1963) have argued for the appropriateness of this type of definition, particularly in research on the learning of aggressive acts by children. They point out that aggressiveness is not really a directly measurable quality of an act, but rather, aggression is a *label* applied on the basis of a social judgment. Furthermore, when "harmless" responses having an aggressive form are learned and later transferred to interpersonal situations, they can be very *harmful* indeed (Walters and Brown, 1963).

These various definitions and measures are not, of course, mutually exclusive. In fact, there is some justification for thinking of each one as a representative measure for a whole *class* of aggressive responses. The results of a number of empirical studies have indicated the essential comparability of a variety of different kinds of aggression (Berkowitz, 1962, 1965; Williams, Meyerson, and Eron, 1967; and Walters and Brown, 1963). The important implication of these studies is that the results obtained with laboratory measures of aggression can have implications for other, perhaps more serious, kinds of aggression occurring outside the laboratory.

2. Individual Differences

There is no question that the same kind of experience can have quite different effects on different people. This is surely the case for the effects of violence witnessed in the mass media. The primary purpose of psychological research on media violence effects, however, is *not* to analyze completely the reactions of specific individuals. Rather, the main interest of research in this area is focused on the *likelihood that a substantial proportion of the audience will be* influenced, regardless of the identity of the particular persons making up that proportion. For this reason, little attention will be given in this review to the matter of individual differences in reactions to observed violence.

3. The Generality of Research Findings

The problem of the *generality* of research findings refers to the degree to which the results of an experiment can be directly applied to situations occuring in everyday life. For present purposes, the question of generality centers on two main points: (1) the representativeness of the sample of subjects studied and, (2) the representativeness of the research setting.

a. The Representativeness of the Subjects

Typically, the subjects studied in a given experiment have been drawn from a relatively narrow group—few psychology experiments are conducted with a completely representative sample of subjects drawn from all areas of the general population. It is dangerous then, to generalize too freely on the basis of results from a single study. However, our confidence in a particular research result is greatly increased when a number of experiments, each using a different kind of subject sample, produce similar patterns of results. When the same kind of findings are obtained from different experiments using children, teenagers, and male or female adults, there is good reason to assume a high degree of generality for the results.

b. The Representativeness of the Research Setting

Much the same kind of argument holds true for the problem of the generality of results obtained from a particular *research setting*. The results from a *single* laboratory study might well depend on some peculiar feature of the experimental procedure. However, when the same kind of findings are obtained in a number of different studies, using widely different research techniques and measures, our confidence in the general validity of the conclusions is greatly increased.

Furthermore, while the laboratory situation may not represent in detail the ordinary movie theater or living room, certain important aspects of the real-life setting may be represented in the laboratory—the television set or film screen, the audience, etc. Other features of the living room such as table lamps or drapes on the wall, for example, may be quite unimportant in determining whether the findings obtained in the laboratory will hold for the American home. In other words, it isn't really necessary to duplicate the home or theater in complete detail in order to have *some* degree of generalization from the laboratory to the real world.

Frequently, however, there will be real limitations on the generality of specific research findings. These limitations should be clearly recognized, especially when a result has been repeated only one or two times. To be realistic in the present case, we should recognize that no amount of experimental research can ever provide *complete* certainty about the *exact* effects of media violence; the conclusions drawn from research findings must always be taken as probability statements about the likelihood of these effects, rather than as statements of absolute truth.

C. *Learning Aggression Through Observation*

An issue of great concern to both parents and social theorists alike stems from the possibility that *young people may learn new techniques and strategies of aggressive behavior through their exposure to media violence.* The teaching potential of the media, particularly the visual media, has led some critics to speak of television as a "school for violence" (Wertham, 1954), and as a "preparatory school for delinquency" (Banay, 1955). In contrast to this kind of alarm, psychologists and learning theorists have not, until quite recently, focused much attention on learning via the mass media. Learning researchers have traditionally been preoccupied with the role of reward and punishment during the active practice of overt responses—the absence of these factors in the passive viewing situation has, no doubt, served to divert their attention from the media.

Recently, however, a dramatic series of experiments by Albert Bandura and his co-workers has clearly demonstrated how complex and novel behavior sequences can be learned directly through observing the actions of others. Since much of this work has dealt with the learning of *aggressive* behaviors, it is particularly relevant here. Discussion of this research can be conveniently divided into (1) factors affecting the learning and retention of aggressive acts, and (2) post-observational factors determining the actual performance of these acts.

1. Conditions Affecting the Learning of Aggressive Behavior Through Observation

a. *Acquisition*

Since a similar set of basic procedures have been employed in a number of the experiments to follow, it will be worthwhile to look at the methods of at least one representative study in some detail—an experiment by Bandura, Ross, and Ross (1963) provides a good example.

Nursery school children, both boys and girls, were individually given the opportunity to observe an adult perform a series of novel aggressive actions. In this particular study, the adult model's behavior was presented in one of several alternative forms; some children saw a live model perform the aggressive acts, others saw a film of the same sequence, and still others saw the model costumed as a cartoon character with the sequence presented on a television set. In each case, the model punched a large inflated doll in the face, kicked the doll, and struck it in the face with a hammer. In addition to these physical acts, the model made a variety of aggressive verbal comments such as "pow...kick him...socko." A fourth set of subjects who saw no model at all serves as a control group (a control group is usually made up of subjects who do not receive any of the experimental treatments, and thus it served as a baseline against which the other groups can be compared).

Following exposure to one of these conditions, the children were subjected to a mild frustration—they were first given some attractive toys to play with, and then the toys were arbitrarily taken away. Each child was then allowed to play for twenty minutes in a room containing, among other things, the inflated doll previously attacked by the model. During this period, an observer kept a record of the child's responses, noting the acts of *imitative* aggressions (including kicking or punching the figure, or striking it in the face with a hammer), as well as *partially imitative* aggression, and *non-imitative* aggressive responses. Results from this study showed that aggressive behavior was sharply higher in each of the model conditions in comparison with the control, and further, that most of this difference was due to the direct imitation of the model's aggressive behaviors. Differences between the various viewing conditions—*live, film and television*—were negligible.

Before looking at a number of additional studies which have supported and clarified these findings, we should consider how far such findings can be applied in the field of the mass media. It is clear, of course, that no single experiment can provide results which will hold true for all people, in all situations.

The results of the preceding study, like any other, were obtained under a highly specific set of circumstances: (1) the children were frustrated just prior to testing, (2) they were tested in a situation which was highly similar to the one in which they had seen the model perform and, (3) they were tested right after they had observed the model. The results then must be considered with these qualifications in mind. What the study does clearly demonstrate, however, is that, under the specified circumstances, children *can* perform new sequences of aggressive behaviors after watching someone else carry out similar actions, even when the model is seen only in a single short session. Whether or not children *will* perform these behaviors is another question, one to be considered below. The frustration treatment, for example, may have facilitated the expression of the newly acquired aggressive acts—non-frustrated subjects might well have inhibited some of these responses. It is clear, nevertheless, that observation alone was sufficient to add the aggressive responses to the subject's behavioral repertoire. There is reason to believe, then, that novel techniques of aggression (such as karate chops or knife throwing, for example) may be acquired by young children merely by observing these actions on television or in the movies.

b. *Retention*

The effect of the lapse of time between the observational learning and the performance of novel responses is an important issue, and one which has not been completely answered by research done to date. Two studies by David Hicks have been directed toward this matter. One experiment (Hicks, 1965) used films of aggressive models presented to children in a simulated television program. All subjects were observed and rated in a procedure similar to that described above. Again, those subjects who observed the aggressive model showed much more imitative aggression than the no-model control subjects. Subjects in this experiment, however, were tested a second time, without further exposure to the model, after an interval of six months. Again the experimental subjects were much more aggressive than the controls, although the level of spontaneous imitation was much lower than on first testing.

A second study (Hicks, 1968) also dealt with the long term retention of aggressive behaviors learned through observation. Children saw a filmed model perform a number of novel acts, some of which were clearly aggressive. After an interval of two months, the behaviors were shown again and subjects were given an opportunity to perform the responses. The tests for immediate retention given at this point showed that better than sixty percent of the aggressive responses were recalled. A final test for retention was conducted after an interval of eight months. By this time, about forty percent of the behaviors were still recalled.

The interpretation of the results of these two studies in terms of the "long term" retention of observation-learned aggression must, however, be tempered by the recognition that the second testing in each of these studies was, in fact, a *retest* rather than a delayed test—that is, the experimental subjects had each been given what amounted to a "practice trial" immediately after having observed the model. Thus, recall and reproduction of these responses may then not have been based on the initial *observation* alone, but also on the subjects' recall of their previous *performance* of the acts. This distinction is important for the assessment of the social effects of media aggression, since violent actions in films and television programs are not likely to be "practiced" immediately after they have been seen. Research comparing the retention of practiced versus unpracticed responses is needed in order to determine the relative permanence or transience of aggression learning by observation in the media.

The research findings on observational learning of aggressive behavior discussed up to this point can be briefly summarized as follows: novel, aggressive behavior sequences are learned by children through exposure to aggressive actions shown on television or in films; and a large proportion of the aggressive behaviors learned by observation are retained over long periods of time if the responses have been practiced at least once, although the length of retention for unpracticed aggressive responses is not known.

2. Post-Observational Conditions Affecting the Performance of Aggressive Behavior

a. The Similarity Factor

When children observe aggressive models, in a modelling experiment or in the mass media, the aggression is always seen in a particular setting containing a variety of cues. In the research situation the child is given an opportunity to imitate the aggression in a highly *similar* testing setting, one containing practically all of these cues. Following exposure to media aggression, however, the child may or may not later encounter a situation similar to the original observation setting. The level of similarity, then, between the initial viewing situation and the later behavioral setting is an important factor to be considered in evaluating the likely effects of media violence.

The importance of this variable is suggested by the results of several experiments in which the similarity factor was quite low. Studies by Lovaas (1961) and Siegel (1956) employed animated *cartoon* films depicting a large number of highly aggressive behaviors. After seeing the films, the children were observed in settings which contained few if any of the cues present in the cartoons. In only one of the four studies reported by these investigations was there any reliable indication of heightened aggressiveness induced by the film. These borderline results of course contrast sharply with Bandura's findings, and the factor of inter-situation cue similarity may well account for the difference. An experiment reported by Meyerson (1966) was conducted specifically to examine this possibility. Children in this study were exposed to the filmed aggressive performance of a model and were then observed in a test situation having either high, medium, or low similarity to the observed setting. The results showed that the level of imitative aggression increased with increasing similarity between the film and the post-film settings. The importance of this similarity factor is not restricted to children alone, as a recent study by Greenwald and Albert (1967) has shown. The speed with which adults learned complex motor responses was also found to vary directly with the proportion of stimulus elements common to both the observed performance and the later testing situation.

To summarize then, we can say that the availability of aggressive responses in the post-viewing situation is determined, in part, by the level of similarity between (1) the observed setting in which the aggressive action occurs, and (2) the real situations that the viewer later encounters. The overall implication of these studies is that aggressive behaviors learned from media violence portrayed in highly realistic, "everyday" settings will be more available on later occasions than those learned from fantasy settings. The implications of the similarity factor, however, are bound closely together with the question of the permanency of unpracticed, observational learning. If observational learning tends to fade rather quickly, then the aggressive responses may be lost before the appropriate stimulus situation arises. If, on the other hand, observational learning is more permanent than this, the likelihood of encountering an appropriate cue situation while the aggressive responses are still available will be greatly increased.

b. The Effects of Observed Rewards or Punishments to the Aggressor

Research discussed so far has dealt mainly with the *acquisition* of aggressive responses through observation. However, the fact that the potential for making a response has been acquired (i.e. that it has been learned) does not imply that the response must be performed. Failure to distinguish between the *acquisition* and the *performance* of aggressive behaviors has been a frequent source of confusion in discussion of learned aggression. The importance of this distinction can be seen in several recent studies of aggression learning by observation.

Bandura (1965), for example, conducted an aggression modeling experiment essentially similar to those already described. In this study, however, following the initial test for spontaneous imitation, children were offered positive incentives (food and trinkets) for performing the behaviors that they observed. With this explicit promise of reward, the children produced roughly twice as many imitative aggressive responses than they had shown before. Clearly, the subjects had learned far more than they had demonstrated spontaneously at the first testing. Hicks (1965), in the study of retention of observational learning cited earlier, also gave positive incentives for imitative aggression following the delayed retest for spontaneous imitation. Again there was a highly significant effect due to introduction of the incentives, showing that, even after an interval of six months, there were still far more aggressive, imitative responses available to the subject than were spontaneously performed.

Keeping in mind the distinction between acquisition and performance, one may ask, "what are the features of the film or television presentation that will inhibit or facilitate the later performance of aggressive responses which have been acquired through observation?" One likely feature of this sort is the observed *consequences* for the aggressive model. An experiment by Bandura, Ross and Ross (1963) approached this question directly by showing a televised model either being lavishly rewarded or harshly punished for his aggression. Subjects in two control groups saw either a non-aggressive model or no model at all. The subjects who had seen the aggression rewarded subsequently showed reliably more imitative aggression than did the children in the other groups.

A more recent study by Bandura (1965) also looked at the effects of observed reinforcement. Models in this study were again either rewarded or punished for their aggressive behavior. In comparison with a control group that saw the model neither rewarded nor punished, the model-punished group later showed much less aggression. The no-consequences control group was almost as aggressive as the model rewarded group, however, suggesting that children may be just as likely to imitate an aggressive character who "gets away with it" as they are a model who is explicitly rewarded for his aggression.

Putting these studies into some kind of perspective, the imitation of observed aggression may be seen as part of the child's strategy in reaching his goals—the obtaining of rewards, and the avoiding of punishments. It is the observed sequence of events that teaches him a lesson about the use of aggression as an effective means of achieving his goals.

What then, is the relation between the use of violent methods and successful goal achievement as typically portrayed in the mass media? A detailed thematic analysis of the content of popular television programs conducted by Larsen (1968) indicates that (1) violent methods are the single most popular means employed by characters to reach desired goals, and (2) that socially disapproved methods are more frequently portrayed as being successful than are approved methods. These relations were found to be particularly strong for programming directed specifically toward children. If we are justified in putting these two lines of research together, we might then conclude that young viewers are constantly being given the message that aggression "works". They are taught that aggression is a highly effective means of achieving one's goals even though it may be socially disapproved. The perceived effectiveness of aggressive actions may thus serve to encourage young viewers to actually use some of the techniques of aggression that they have learned from the media.

c. *Effects of the Social Context*

Subjects in most of the studies cited so far have been left by themselves while they watched the model's televised or filmed performance. Children's everyday exposure to violence in the media, however, frequently occurs when the child is with others—often older children, adults, or other important socializing agents. The attitudes expressed by these other people in the audience may be an important factor determining the child's view of the appropriateness of the observed aggression.

Hicks (1968) investigated this possibility by having children watch a televised, aggressive model while in the presence of an adult "co-observer". the co-observer appeared to be involved in the program and spontaneously made a variety of positive evaluative comments ("Boy look at him go"..."He sure is a tough guy") for one set of subjects, and a number of negative comments ("He shouldn't do that"..."That's awful") for another group. In a control group, the co-observer remained silent. The effect of these evaluative comments appeared when the subjects were put into the test situation along with the co-observer; under the watchful eye of the co-observer, those children who had heard the positive comments showed a high level of imitative aggression, while those who heard the negative comments showed a reduced level of aggression in comparison with the controls. Three additional groups in this experiment were given the same three treatments except that the co-observer was absent in the testing situation. Interestingly, this variation caused the condition differences to be washed out. Thus the co-observer's comments proved effective only when children were under the surveillance of this same co-observer. In a somewhat similar experiment reported by De Rath (1963) the model provided more explicit verbal prohibitions against specific aggressive acts shown in the film. These prohibitions later served to inhibit aggressive behavior both in the presence of the adult who had invoked the prohibitions, and in the presence of another "neutral" adult.

Extrapolating from these results to the media viewing situation, the implication is that parental evaluation or instruction regarding the permissibility of aggression seen in the media can be effective in controlling aggression imitation, but this communication may be irrelevant when adults are not later present to monitor the child's behavior.

d. *Other Factors*

There are other features of the observed material that also operate to elicit or inhibit imitation. Liking for the model, established by the prior experience of warm, nurturant interaction, has been shown to facilitate the imitation of non-aggressive behaviors, although *aggressive* behaviors are likely to be imitated regardless of the quality of the model-child relationship (Bandura, Ross and Ross, 1961). In the case where more than one model is presented, there is some evidence that children will be most likely to imitate the model who is perceived to have the greatest social power (Bandura, Ross and Ross, 1963b).

An entirely different line of research, that will be covered in greater detail below, suggests the importance of the stimulus properties of available targets in determining the level of post-film aggression. Adults who have seen an aggressive film presentation have been found to be especially willing to attack a victim who has had some prior association with violence (Berkowitz, 1965a). This effect has been shown to hold even when the association has been established on the basis of information contained within the film itself (Berkowitz and Geen, 1966; Geen and Berkowitz, 1966; and Berkowitz and Geen, 1967).

D. Emotional Effects

1. The Blunting of Emotional Responses

A number of writers have expressed concern that the *abundance* of violence and brutality in the mass media has the effect of blunting viewers' emotional sensitivity. In attempting to assess the validity of this contention, it is necessary first to establish that people do, in fact, initially show some special emotional reactions to observed violence; available research suggest that this is the case. A sizeable proportion of the children in a well known survey study of media effects (Himmilweit, Oppenheim and Vince, 1958) reported that they were upset by watching the killings on television. In the study by Siegel (1956) mentioned earlier, an aggressive film did not increase aggressive behavior, but it did produce a highly significant increase in the level of rated anxiety. With adult subjects, several studies by Berger (1962) have demonstrated physiologically that intense emotional reactions are produced in persons watching someone else receiving an electric shock. Taken together, these experiments leave little doubt that people do show a special emotional responsivity to observed violence.

a. *The Habituation of Emotional Responses to Observed Violence*

What happens, however, when these emotional responses are evoked again and again? A general principle, long accepted by psychologists and physiologists, is that the repeated elicitation of an emotional response results in the progressive decrease in the strength of this response. The phenomenon has been given various names: habituation, adaptation, satiation, and accommodation. There is good reason to believe that this process of habituation takes place with emotional responses repeatedly evoked by the observation of violence. Adult subjects in several of Berger's (1962) experiments saw a victim receiving an extended series of electric shocks. The strength of the observer's galvanic skin response (the "GSR" is a standard physiological measure of emotional arousal) decreased progressively through the series. This habituation occurred even when the victim was observed to jerk convulsively on each shock trial. Several studies by Lazarus and his colleagues (Lazarus, 1966; Lazarus and Alfert, 1964; and Speisman, Lazarus and Mordkoff, 1964) have measured the physiological responses of adult observers watching a film dealing with a primitive tribal ritual called subincision. A series of different victims were shown with each one being subjected to bloody and painful genital mutilation. Again the process of habituation was apparent as the emotional reactions showed a marked progressive diminution throughout the series. Although none of these studies was designed specifically to investigate emotional habituation to observed violence, it is safe to conclude that this process also occurs during the repeated presentation of violence in the mass media; the viewer becomes progressively less emotionally responsive to the repeated scenes of violence that he observes.

b. *Some Possible Implications of Emotional Habituation*

While the viewer may become habituated to *media violence*, it is quite another thing to assert that he will lose his aversion to *actual violence* when it occurs in real-life, face to face situations. There is some indirect evidence, however, that just such a process may occur.

Desensitization, one of the techniques of modern behavior therapy, involves the progressive introduction of anxiety provoking stimuli, again and again, to patients who are relaxed in otherwise non-threatening surroundings (Wolpe, 1958; Eyesenck, 1964). For example, a patient with a phobic fear of snakes may be placed in a relaxed situation and then exposed to stimuli associated with snakes (the word "snake," pictures of snakes, or rubber "snakes,"). As long as the patient remains relaxed, the intensity of the stimuli is increased. Finally, sometimes after hundreds of repeated presentations, the patient may be "cured" of his phobia; he can remain in close proximity to large snakes without anxiety, and may even be able to touch or handle snakes.

In more general terms, the effect of such a procedure is that phobic patients gradually become less and less anxious with repeated presentations of the anxiety evoking stimuli; they are finally able to tolerate direct confrontation without the aversion they previously experienced. Transfer of this tolerance from the therapy situation to real-life, face-to-face behavior is often quite complete. "Cured" patients are frequently able to engage freely in behaviors that were previously difficult or impossible because of intense anxiety (Krassner and Ullman, 1965).

Sears, Maccoby and Levin (1957) argue that members of our culture "...do not tolerate aggression comfortably, neither their own nor that displayed by others. It evokes too much anxiety...". The parallel between the abovementioned behavior therapy procedures and the situation of the media viewer who is repeatedly exposed to violence while relaxing at home or in the theater suggests the possibility that viewers are being "*cured*" of this kind of aggression anxiety. If this sort of process is going on, viewers may increasingly be willing to accept real-life acts of extreme violence without attempting to interfere (Rosenthal, 1964), and may themselves be less reluctant to engage directly in aggression when provoking circumstances arise.

The research which is most relevant to this possibility comes again from Bandura's laboratory at Stanford University. Several studies by this investigator and his co-workers have dealt with the extinction of phobic behavior with observational treatment techniques. Children, in one of these studies (Bandura, Grussec and Menlove, 1967), were selected because they showed consistent fearful avoidance behaviors towards dogs. Subjects, in the course of a number of brief sessions, saw a peer engaged in a variety of interactions with a brown cocker spaniel. Control groups were either shown the dog alone or were given no special treatment at all. When subsequently tested, the subjects in the experimental groups showed a sharp reduction in avoidance behavior. Many were now able to engage in intimate and potentially fearful interactions not only with the dog they had seen before, but also with an unfamiliar dog. Reduction of avoidance in the experimental groups was statistically very significantly lower than in the control groups, and these differences were maintained in a follow-up test a month later.

A second study along these same lines (Bandura and Menlove, 1968) employed motion picture films. Over a period of time, groups of children who were initially fearful of dogs were shown a number of different films depicting a peer playing with a single dog, or, alternatively, "numerous dogs varying in size and fearsomeness." A control group of dog-phobic children was shown a parallel series of non-threatening films containing no dogs at all. Again, there was a striking reduction of fearful avoidance behavior in the experimental groups. The untreated subjects in the control group, however, continued to be fearful and maintained their avoidance at a high level.

Repeated observation of the anxiety provoking activity, then, in both of these studies, served to eliminate the subjects' initial anxiety-based avoidance responses. If results from these studies can be generalized to the effects of aggressive episodes repeatedly presented in the mass media, the repetition of media violence may have the effect not only of reducing emotional reaction to fictional violence, but also it may make viewers more willing to actually involve themselves in aggressive actions when provoking circumstances arise. It must be emphasized again, however, that none of these experiments were directed specifically toward the investigation of media-violence effects per se. Experiments using media-type violence materials along with direct measures of aggression are needed before these conclusions can be drawn with confidence.

E. The Inhibition and Facilitation of Impulsive Aggression

In looking previously at the results of modeling studies done with children, we found that the observed consequences for the aggressor could serve either to inhibit or to facilitate the expression of aggressive behavior. The likelihood of post-film aggression was determined by the perceived effectiveness of aggressive behavior as a means of goal attainment. No doubt human behavior is very often guided by such utilitarian, goal-oriented strategies, but we should recognize that sometimes aggressive behavior is determined by far less rational motives; under some circumstances, an angered person may respond with *impulsive aggression*, never considering the long-range implications of his actions. A complete analysis of media violence effects must take into account some of the conditions affecting the expression of this kind of impulsive aggression.

1. The Inhibition of Impulsive Aggression

In the earlier discussion of research on the question of catharsis, some of the features of observed violence that serve to inhibit aggression were covered, so a few brief comments can be made without going into the details of the work on this topic.

The inhibitory effects found to result from the perception of *unjustified* aggression presumably arose because subjects were reminded that aggression is morally wrong. Thus, we should not assume, just because impulsive aggression is irrational, that it cannot be modified or inhibited by an awareness of one's ethical principles. Again we should note that aggressive action in the media is often performed by the "good guy" under provoking circumstances that minimize the likelihood that the viewer will be reminded of his own principles regarding the immorality of violence.

Research on the revised catharsis hypothesis has identified another feature of observed violence that serves to inhibit the aggressive impulses of the viewer. Recall that when subjects were made aware of the bloody, painful aftermath of aggression, they were then inhibited in their willingness to inflict harm on others. In the typical media presentation, however, the action is rarely designed to remind the viewer of aggression's horrible consequences. Critic Robert Warshaw (1962), in discussing "Western" movies, has noted that "...our eyes are not focused on the sufferings of the defeated, but on the deportment of the hero." It is just these painful sufferings of the defeated victim, however, that may allow the provoked viewer to "think twice" about acting out his own aggressive impulses.

2. The Facilitation of Impulsive Aggression

a. *The Cue Properties of Available Targets*

Berkowitz (1965) has argued that when aggressive responses have been aroused within the individual, his hostility may remain in "low gear" unless the appropriate aggression-evoking cues are present in the environment. Only when these cues are introduced do the person's aggressive impulses become translated into actual aggressive behavior. Appropriate cues of this sort may be based on the stimuli in the post-observation situation that have some association with previously observed violence. "Thus, a person who sees a brutal fight may not himself display any detectable aggression immediately afterwards, even if his inhibitions are relatively weak, unless he encounters stimuli having some association with the fight" (Berkowitz, 1965, p. 300).

The role of the association between the victim of the observed violence and the target of the viewer's aggression has been investigated in a series of experiments by Berkowitz and his co-workers at the University of Wisconsin psychology laboratories.

An experiment reported by Berkowitz (1965) used college students who were initially either insulted or not insulted by a confederate posing as another subject. The confederate was introduced either as a speech major, or as a college boxer. Subjects then watched a film clip of a violent boxing match or of a neutral control film. After the film, all subjects were given an opportunity to give electric shocks to the confederate within the context of a learning experiment. For the insulted subjects, the largest number of shocks were given in the condition where the boxing film had been shown and the confederate had been represented as a boxer. The association between the target and the characters in the observed violence could be seen as "drawing out" the aggressive responses from the angered subjects. A follow-up study by Berkowitz and Geen (1966) sought to clarify this relationship by establishing the association on the basis of the target's name. The design of the study was similar to the previous one except that half of the subjects seeing the boxing film were introduced to a confederate having the same name as one of the boxers. In this study the control film was based on a track race and was thus a highly exciting, though non-violent, control. When subjects were given an opportunity to administer electric shocks to the confederate, they were most aggressive in the condition where they had been angered by someone having the same name as the character in the aggressive film. Here again, the victim's association with aggression-related stimuli apparently served to produce more intense attacks.

A further extension of this line of experimentation (Geen and Berkowitz, 1966) found that the highest level of aggression was obtained when the person to be shocked was associated by name with the filmed *victim* rather than the filmed *victor*. An additional study (Berkowitz and Geen, 1967) found similar results even when the name-mediated association was formed *after* the film.

Generalization from these results to real-life social problems must, by necessity, require a certain amount of speculation. One possible, though speculative, implication that might be drawn from this area of research is that when members of minority groups having distinctive cue characteristics are repeatedly portrayed in the media as targets for aggression, there may be an increase in the likelihood that some member may, because of this association, become the victim of violence. Although, again, caution must be exercised in extrapolating from the results of laboratory experiments, this possibility lends credence to the outcry of some Italian-American interest groups against a once-popular television series featuring a weekly "war" against Italian Mafia villains.

b. *The General State of Arousal of the Aggressor*

A variety of studies have shown that when subjects have been attacked and then exposed to film violence, they later aggress against a victim more than subjects who have not been attacked (see Berkowitz, 1965; and Geen, 1966, for example). Other studies have shown similar effects following emotional arousal due to *frustration* (Geen and Berkowitz, 1967; Geen, 1968). These results are consistent with the idea that attack or frustration produces a general state of physiological arousal, which, in turn, increases the probability of aggression resulting from observed aggression (Berkowitz, 1968).

A recent study by Geen (1968) sought to examine the role of arousal more directly. Male college students, in his experiment, were shown either an aggressive boxing film or a film depicting a nonaggressive sport and then put in the position of giving electric shocks to another student. While they gave the shocks, half of the men in each film group were put in a state of somewhat stressful arousal by having to listen to a loud continuous noise over a pair of earphones.

The highest level of aggression, in terms of the number and the intensity of shocks given, was shown by the students who received both the aggressive film and the stress producing noise. One interpretation of this result is that the stress produced arousal may have served to activate or "energize" latent aggressive responses produced by aggressive cues in the film.

Physiological arousal may arise from a variety of causes, such as drugs, personal crises, or even extreme temperature conditions. In light of this, a possible implication of Geen's study is that the aggression triggering effects of media violence may be particularly serious during periods of continuing stress (fear of nuclear war, long uncomfortable "hot spells" of weather, and the threat of the military draft are some contemporary sources of stress. Under such conditions, violence observed in the media might serve to trigger off acts of impulsive aggression that would otherwise have remained latent.

Once more, it should be emphasized that generalizations from these laboratory studies of impulsive aggression should be taken as *hypotheses*, or possible explanations, rather than as "proven facts." One serious limitation of the research on impulsive aggression stems from the fact that the influence of the passage of time has not been investigated. As in the studies of behavior modeling discussed earlier, the implications of the present experiments are much more serious if the aggression arousing effects are more than just transitory.

Even if such heightened aggressiveness is very short-lived however, it has been pointed out (Larsen, 1968, p. 288) that when there are as many as 20,000,000 people viewing a televised scene of brutal violence, there is a real increase in the likelihood of someone being hurt because of it.

F. Summary

In summarizing the results of the studies reviewed here, it should again be pointed out that the conclusions drawn from research findings must always be, to some degree, tentative. A truly complete understanding of the exact effects of violence portrayed in the mass media is a goal for researchers to aim for, but, realistically, it is a goal that will probably never be reached. With this caveat in mind, the following conclusions seem to be warranted on the basis of available research evidence.

1. Learning Effects

Novel, aggressive behavior sequences are learned by children through exposure to realistic portrayals of aggression on television or in films. A large proportion of these behaviors are retained over long periods of time if they are practiced at least once. The likelihood that such aggressive behaviors will be performed is determined, in part, by the similarity of the setting of the observed violence and the cues present in later situations. The actual performance of aggressive behaviors learned from the media is largely contingent on the child's belief in the effectiveness of aggression in attaining his goals while avoiding punishment. The mass media typically present aggression as a highly effective form of behavior.

2. Emotional Effects

Frequent exposure produces an emotional habituation to media violence. There is suggestive evidence that this results in an increased likelihood of actually engaging in aggression.

3. Impulsive Aggression

Aggressive impulses may be held in check if the viewer has been made especially aware of the "wrongness" of aggression or of the suffering that may result from violence. The target person's prior association with media violence serves to heighten the intensity of aggressive attacks on him.

Going beyond the work that has been done to date, there are a number of specific research questions that remain to be answered.

The permanency of media violence effects is a central issue. When novel, aggressive behaviors and techniques are learned by observation, are they quickly forgotten or is this learning more permanent? Does the permanency of this learning depend on the "practice" of aggressive responses immediately after they are observed? When media violence arouses aggressive impulses, are these impulses very short-lived or not?

The effects of different observed outcomes of violent episodes should be studied in greater detail. When the hero guns down the villain, do children really learn that "crime does not pay" or do they learn that it is *good* to kill "bad people"? When media violence is cleaned up by removal of the bloody and horrible aftermath of violence, does this make real-life aggression seem more acceptable?

The possibility that emotional habituation may make people less reluctant to actually commit violence needs further investigation.

Apart from these specific research questions, it is important to know, more generally, just how far the results of these experimental studies can be applied to everyday media effects. We need additional research methods and experimental designs that will allow the necessary element of experimental control in natural, everyday media viewing situations.

G. Bibliography

Bandura, A. "Influence of Models' Reinforcement Contingencies on the Acquisition of Imitative Responses." *Journal of Personality and Social Psychology*, 1965, V. 1 589-595.

Bandura, A. "Vicarious Processes: A Case of No-trial Learning." In L. Berkowitz (ed.) *Advances in Experimental Social Psychology*. Vol. 2. New York: Academic Press 1965.

Bandura, A., Grusec, J.E., and Menlove, F.L. "Vicarious Extinction of Avoidance Behavior." *Journal of Personality and Social Psychology*, 1967, *5*, 16-23.

Bandura, A., and Huston, A.C. "Identification As a Process of Incidental Learning." *Journal of Abnormal and Social Psychology*, 1961, 63, 311-318.

Bandura, A., and Menlove, F.L. "Factors Determining Vicarious Extinction of Avoidance Behavior Through Symbolic Modeling." *Journal of Personality and Social Psychology*, 1968, *8*, 99-108.

Bandura, A., Ross, D., and Ross, S.A. "Transmission of Aggression Through Imitation of Aggressive Models." *Journal of Abnormal and Social Psychology*, 1961, *63*, 575-582.

Bandura, A., Ross, D., and Ross, S.A. "Imitation of Film-mediated Aggressive Models." *Journal of Abnormal and Social Psychology*, 1963, *66*, 3-11.

Bandura, A., Ross, D., and Ross, S.A. "A Comparative Test of the Status Envy, Social Power, and Secondary Reinforcement Theories of Identificatory Learning." *Journal of Abnormal and Social Psychology*. 1963, *67*, 527-534.

Bandura, A., Ross, D., and Ross, S.A. "Vicarious Reinforcement and Imitative Learning," *Journal of Abnormal and Social Psychology*, 1963, *67*, 601-607 (c).

Bandura, A., and Walters, R.H. *Social Learning and Personality Development*. New York: Holt, Rinehart and Winston, 1963.

Banay, R.S. Testimony before the Subcommittee to Investigate Juvenile Delinquency, of the Committee on the Judiciary, United States Senate, Eighty-fourth Cong. S. Res., April, 1955, 62, Washington, D.C.: Government Printing Office.

Berger, S.M. "Conditioning Through Vicarious Instigation." *Psychological Review*, 1962, *69*, 405-456.

Berkowitz, L. *Aggression: A Social Psychological Analysis*. New York: McGraw-Hill, 1962.

Berkowitz, L. "Some Aspects of Observed Aggression." *Journal of Personality and Social Psychology*, 1965, *2*, 359-369.

Berkowitz, L. "The Concept of Aggressive Drive: Some Additional Considerations." In L. Berkowitz (Ed.), *Advances in Experimental Social Psychology*. Vol. 2. New York: Academic Press, 1965.

Berkowitz, L. "The Frustration-aggression Hypothesis Revisited." In L. Berkowitz (ed.) *Roots of Aggression: A Re-examination of the Frustration-Aggression Hypothesis*. New York: Atherton Press, 1968, in press.

Berkowitz, L. and Geen, R. "Film Violence and the Cue Properties of Available Targets." *Journal of Personality and Social Psychology*, 1966, *3*, 525-530.

Berkowitz, L. and Geen, R. "The Stimulus Qualities of the Target of Aggression: A Further Study." *Journal of Personality and Social Psychology*, 1967, *5*, 364-368.

Berkowitz, L. and Rawlings, E. "Effects of Film Violence on Inhibitions Against Subsequent Aggression." *Journal of Abnormal and Social Psychology*, 1963, *66*, 405-412.

Berkowitz, L., Corwin, R. and Heironimous, M. "Film Violence and Subsequent Aggressive Tendencies." *Public Opinion Quarterly, 1963*, 27, 217-229.

Bramel, D., Taub, B. and Blum, B. "An Observer's Reaction to the Suffering of His Enemy." *Journal of Personality and Social Psychology*, 1968, *8*, 384-392.

De Rath, G.W. The Effects of Verbal Instructions on Imitative Aggression." Unpublished Doctoral Dissertation, Michigan State University, 1963.

Feshbach, S. The Stimulating Versus Cathartic Effects of a Vicarious Aggressive Activity." *Journal of Abnormal and Social Psychology*, 1961, *63*, 381-385.

Geen, R.G. "Effects of Frustration, Attack, and Prior Training in Aggressiveness on Aggressive Behavior." *Journal of Personality and Social Psychology*, 1968, in press.

Geen, R. and Berkowitz, L. "Name-mediated Aggressive Cue Properties." *Journal of Personality*, 1966, *34*, 456-465.

Geen, R.G., and Berkowitz, L. "Some Conditions Facilitating the Occurrence of Aggression After the Observation of Violence." *Journal of Personality*, 1967, *35*, 666-667.

Geen, R.G., and O'Neal, E.C. "Activation of Cue-elicited Aggression by General Arousal." *Journal of Personality and Social Psychology*, 1968, in press.

Goodman, P. Letter to the Editor. *Scientific American*, 1964, *210*, No. 6, 8.

Greenwald, A. and Albert S, S. "Observational Learning: A Technique for Elucidating S-R Mediation Processes." *Journal of Experimental Psychology*, 1968, *76*, 267-272.

Hartley, R. "The Impact of Viewing Aggression." Office of Social Research, CBS, Multilithed, 1964.

Hartmann, D. "The Influence of Symbolically Modeled Instrumental Aggression and Pain Cues on the Disinhibition of Aggressive Behavior." Unpublished Doctoral Dissertation, Stanford University, 1965.

Hicks, D. "Imitation and Retention of Film-mediated Aggressive Peer and Adult Models." *Journal of Personality and Social Psychology*, 1965, *2*, 97-100.

Hicks, D. "Short- and Long-term Retention of Affectively Varied Modeled Behavior." *Psychonomic Science*, 1968, *11*, 369-370.

Himmilweit, H., Oppenheim, A. and Vince, P. *Television and the Child: An Empirical Study of the Effect of Television on the Young.* New York: Oxford University Press, 1958.

Hoyt, J. "Vengeance and Self-defence as Justification for Filmed Aggression." Unpublished Masters Thesis, University of Wisconsin, 1967.

Klapper, J.T. "The Social Effects of Mass Communication." In W. Schramm (ed.), *The Science of Human Communication*. New York: Basic Books, 1963.

Krassner, L., and Ullman, L. *Research in Behavior Modification.* New York: Holt, Rinehart and Winston, 1968.

Larsen, O., Gray L., and Fortas, J. "Achieving Goals Through Violence on Television." In O.J. Larsen (ed.)., *Violence in the Mass Media*. New York: Harper and Row, 1968, 97-111.

Lazarus, R.S., *Psychological Stress and the Coping Process.* New York: McGraw-Hill, 1966.

Lazarus, R.S., and Alfert, E. "The Short-circuiting of Threat." *Journal of Abnormal and Social Psychology*, 1964, *69*, 195-205.

Lovaas, O.J. "Effect of Exposure to Symbolic Aggression on Aggressive Behavior." *Child Development*, 1961, *32*, 37-44.

Maccoby, Eleanor E. "Effects of Mass Media." In M.L. Hoffman and L.W. Hoffman (Eds.), *Review of Child Development Research*. New York: Russell Sage Foundation, 1964.

Meyerson, L. "The Effects of Filmed Aggression on the Aggressive Responses of High and Low Aggressive Subjects." Unpublished Doctoral Dissertation, University of Iowa, 1966.

Rosenthal, A. *Thirty-eight Witnesses.* New York: McGraw-Hill, 1964.

Sears, R., Maccoby, E. and Levin, H. *Patterns of Child Rearing.* New York: Harper, 1957.

Siegel, A., "Film-mediated Fantasy Aggression and Strength of Aggressive Drive." *Child Development*, 1956, *27*, 365-378.

Speisman, J.C., Lazarus, R.S., Mordkoff, A.M., and Davidson, L.A. "Experimental Reduction of Stress Based on Ego-defence theory." *Journal of Abnormal and Social Psychology*, 1964, *68*, 367-380.

Walters, R., and Brown, M. "Studies of Reinforcement of Aggression III: Transfer of Responses to an Interpersonal Situation." *Child Development*, *34*, 563-571.

Walters, R., and Thomas, E., "Enhancement of Punitiveness by Visual and Audio-visual Displays." *Canadian Journal of Psychology*, 1963, *17*, 244-255.

Walters, R., and Thomas, E., and Acker, C. "Enhancement of Punitive Behavior by Audiovisual Displays." *Science*, 1962, *136*, 872-873.

Warshaw, R. *The Immediate Experience.* Garden City, N.Y.: Doubleday, 1962.

Wertham, F.S. *Seduction of the Innocent*. New York: Holt, Rinehart, and Winston, 1954.

Weiss, W. "Effects of Mass Media on Communication." In *Handbook of Social Psychology*, G. Lindzey, and E. Aronson, (eds). Boston: Addison-Wesley Press, in press.

Williams, J., Meyerson, L. and Eron, L. "Peer-rated Aggression and Aggressive Responses Elicited in an Experimental Situation." *Child Development*, 1967, *38*, 191-189.

Wolpe, J. *Psychotherapy by Reciprocal Inhibition*. Stanford: Stanford University Press, 1958.

Appendix III-B

OUTLINE OF RESEARCH REQUIRED ON EFFECTS*

Several things are clear from the research that has been done up until now. Media characteristics do influence audience values, even though the impact of any single mass communication is likely to be unimpressive because it depends so much on various social and psychological factors in the intricate relations between communicator, medium, and audience. Some of the mass media are especially adept at simulating primary interaction. For this reason, and in line with principles of symbolic modeling, it is possible for content presented purely as entertainment to have cumulative socializing effects, and unintended effects can be as real as intended ones. When anti-social characters and violent actions are portrayed in abundance, the media can hardly hope to avoid any contribution to observational learning by some portions of the audience.

Degradation of values tends to result from the commercial operation of the mass media in the United States. There is no basis for assurance that a portrayal of a breakdown of social norms in the mass media does not contribute to anomic public attitudes and behavior; on the contrary, experimental evidence supports the opposite inference.

These conclusions can be stated with some confidence in spite of difficulties that have impeded adequate research assessment of the social and psychological effects of mass media content dealing with crime and violence. Such difficulties arise from several sources: (1) Mass media operate as part of a complex network of reinforcing and counteracting psychological, economic, social, and cultural factors. Isolation of the independent contribution of any one component to the total effect is not always possible and is seldom easy. (2) It has thus far been impossible to make adequate studies of the cumulative effects of exposure to mass media over long periods of time. There can be little doubt that some effects are cumulative; it is important to discover what they are. However, it is usually more difficult to organize, fund, staff, and conduct long-term studies than short-term ones. (3) It is increasingly difficult, as the media saturate this society, to find the degrees of variation in exposure which would be required for needed research designs. It is often virtually impossible to set up adequate control groups of unexposed

*Paper prepared for the Media Task Force by William R. Catton, Jr., Professor of Sociology, University of Washington.

persons who are otherwise comparable to groups with high exposure. People with low amounts of direct exposure often experience a great deal of indirect exposure through their peers. Thus, degree of exposure remains an uncertain and unclear variable, important as it may be in many studies.[1]

A. Need For Long-Term Studies

These difficulties must be overcome, however. To continue with short-term, piecemeal studies of single-medium effects on single aspects of small audience behavior and attitudes would be useless. Society may have little need to fear that any single magazine article, radio broadcast, movie, or television program will wreak psychological havoc with the majority of the population. But, as Merton suggested even before the age of television, "a society subjected ceaselessly to a flow of 'effective' half-truths and the exploitation of mass anxieties may all the sooner lose that mutuality of confidence and reciprocal trust so essential to a stable social structure."[2]

The research to date has fallen largely into two types, and further research along both lines is needed. These are: (1) large-scale surveys and field experiments such as the studies by Schramm, Lyle, and Parker in the United States and by Himmelweit, Oppenheim, and Vince in Great Britain; (2) laboratory experiments dealing with an isolated moment in the viewers' lives, when small samples are presented with specific and carefully controlled stimuli and their responses are carefully measured, such as the various experiments by Bandura, Berkowitz, Walters.

In addition, there is a need for such inquiries as (3) the long-term intensive panel study, absent thus far from the scholarly literature on television and children; and (4) frank epidemiological studies of the associations between media exposure and a host of other variables in a variety of real social contexts.

Short-term laboratory studies have an extremely important contribution to make to our understanding of media impact. Even in the laboratory, however, an effort must be made to ensure that every opportunity is afforded for the *cumulative* effects of exposure to the experimental stimuli to show up. Conclusions drawn from responses to brief exposures may not coincide with data from an experiment which were prolonged to show equilibrium relationships between the stimuli, the setting, and the experimental subjects.[3] Various writers have recognized that the long, slow effects on values, on the world view, on the general culture, and on broad response patterns are likely to be the most important consequences of television. Short-term research is thus at a serious disadvantage.[4]

Schramm and his associates have expressed concern about the effects of prolonged exposure of children to television violence. Year after year, for several hours a day, children are absorbed by material that ceases after the first few years to provide much intellectual stimulation and which depicts a fantasy world with rules quite unlike those which apply in real life. It will take a long time to measure the effects of this exposure adequately, and, if they turn out to be quite undesirable, it will be too late to rescue a whole generation of children. One implication is that broadcasters need to concern themselves with new, difficult, and vexing questions about what they are doing.[5] Another is that it is important to launch some long-term studies without further delay. To know just how much vicarious experience children gather from television, with its sustained level of excitement and fantasy, which dulls their sensibility, and makes them bored with more mundane forms of education and reluctant to submit to real-life routines, it is suggested that we should observe closely for a number of years a very large number of children of the television generation.[6]

One clue which already indicates the limitation of children's imagination is their almost total inability to suggest really novel alternatives in television programming. Most children seem unable to do anything more than suggest that television should carry more of the same programs.[7] The effect of continued reliance upon television fantasy on a child's imaginative capacity is unknown.

B. Experimental Studies

A series of experimental designs predicated upon certain assumptions will be sketched out in the following paragraphs. First, it will be assumed that sufficient funds are available. Second, it will be assumed that media men can become sufficiently concerned about the possible social impacts of their media that they will, as responsible citizens, take certain economic risks in order to bring about a definitive assessment of such impacts. For example, that media men would be willing to eliminate advertising (under a research subsidy, of course) in order to see whether advertising-dominated media have indeed been inducing major value degradations. The economic risk in this case would be that such a finding would jeopardize continuation of a system which has heretofore been profitable.

The mass media can and do play a part in the socialization of personality. Perhaps they can also play a part in the enforcement of certain norms accepted by the communities they serve. It has been claimed that by according publicity to deviant acts, the media can help curb deviance. The hazard inherent in attempts to do so has already been examined—the publicizing of deviant acts may encourage rather than discourage them by conferring status of a kind.

Suppose the cooperation of newspaper editors in a number of communities could be secured. The entire set of communities might be randomly divided into a number of subsets, each to be accorded a different "treatment," consisting of implementation of a specific editorial policy regarding news treatment of all acts of delinquancy, vandalism, etc. In several sets of towns, the editors might be asked to give maximum publicity to all such acts. In another set of towns publicity consistent with reporting essential community news would be accorded to such acts. In some of the high publicity sets of towns, names of offenders, names of their parents, and addresses would be explicitly and prominently mentioned. In one set, the eventual punishment would be given prominence in the news stories. This information would be omitted or played down in the other high publicity towns. In one set of towns, the offenders' names would be mentioned, but there would be no mention of parents' names or addresses. In one set of towns, pictures of offenders might be used, but not in the other sets of towns. Careful attention would be paid to police, school, and other public records over an extended period of time (several years) to ascertain the effects of these various mass communication treatments on community-wide delinquency rates and other related indices, and on the subsequent acts of specifically publicized offenders.

Somewhat similar experiments might be designed and carried out with other media besides newspapers—local radio and TV stations, for example. In these cases, it would be important to gather whatever data might be required to determine whether deviant acts were committed *for the sake of obtaining attention* from the media. The nature and changes in the peer group relationships of publicized offenders after they had received publicity should also be studied, along with the social relationships of their parents.

Other large-scale experiments are also conceivable, but might depend for their feasibility on a spontaneous "ripening" of circumstances. Knowledge about the function of newspapers in the lives of readers has been acquired during major newspaper strikes.[8] Perhaps the same could be done with television.

Many useful experiments could be designed to assess the effects of exposure of a population to television, using any of a number of different dependent variables—assorted attitudes and actions in assorted combinations and contexts. However, such experiments could not be carried out in a society such as ours, with ubiquitous television. The few communities in which no television is available even now, or in which its reception is so poor as to be almost negligible, would doubtless differ fundamentally from any of the television-receiving communities with which they might be intended to be experimentally compared. But if, in some area smaller than the entire country, there were a prolonged interruption of television broadcasting due to, say, a one hundred percent strike of television engineers throughout a several-state region, researchers could swing into action if an appropriate experimental design were already available and if funds, staff, and appropriate instruments were ready on a standby basis. Just as social science disaster research teams have been poised in the past to descend upon a community as soon as it happens to be stricken by a natural disaster, so a mass communications research team could be poised to begin immediate comparisons between TV-interrupted communities and TV-continued communities for the duration of the strike.

The mores of society set stern limits on the manipulations of people's lives by social scientists. Even so, it may be useful to devote some effort to thinking about manipulations that might fall within such limits. Could a whole community be persuaded, for example, to turn in all of its televisions for a year or so (to see how the people's lives would adapt to the absence of TV) by providing some sort of remuneration either to the community or to individual householders, or both? Could a group of similar communities be asked to participate in a potentially valuable social experiment by choosing from a list some one thing (a different thing in each community) to be removed from an otherwise standard American pattern of living? Just as Mackinac Island, Mich., chooses to do without automobiles to preserve a certain charm and quietude, some town might be persuaded to do without television (and yet be no more atypical because of its choice than the other towns). After the change had been implemented, all the communities would be studied in depth to determine the comparative effects of the various missing ingredients.

Could two comparable communities be persuaded to experiment upon themselves by offering rewards to citizens of one town in direct proportion to their hours of television viewing, and to citizens of the other town in inverse proportion to their hours of television viewing? The social scientists might study a number of facets of human behavior in both towns during this period.

It also would be useful to study the effects of television advertising by selecting two sets of communities with comparable television programming and deleting all commercials from two signals sent into one. This might be accomplished in the following manner: select a number of towns in the mountain areas of the West, where topography makes ordinary TV reception poor or useless. Divide these into two comparable groups, A and B. Make cable television available for both sets of towns. Arrange to show all network broadcasts by tape-delayed transmission; this would permit clock times in this time zone to correspond with clock times of original transmission in the East. It would thus be possible to edit all commercials out of the tapes going to towns in set A, leaving them in the tapes for towns in set B. For local-origin telecasts, subsidies would be provided to cover programming costs for towns in set A equal to the local advertising revenues raised in set B. Over a period of years, several kinds of differential data would be collected—behavioral, attitudinal, educational, criminal, legal, and sales—to permit measurement of the effects of presence versus absence of commercial advertising.

C. Epidemiological Studies

The term "epidemiological" is used here to refer to studies that strive to account for natural *variations in the rates of occurrence* of some behavior in assorted contexts which are not artificially created.[9] For example, Tumin found differences in the disposition of white Southerners toward desegregation according to whether they had high or low exposure to mass media.[10] Favorable disposition toward desegregation was associated with high media exposure.

Media exposure could also be treated as a dependent variable, and explanations could be sought for the fact that certain categories of people have higher rates of media exposure than do others. An effort to relate crime rates to media exposure rates, for example, taking the latter as an independent variable, would be an epidemiological study, but a rather crude one.

As an example of a somewhat more refined type of epidemiological study, consider the following problem: has television contributed to dissent in America during the Vietnam war? The question might be tentatively answered by assigning persons in a nationwide survey sample to categories according to whether they reported having viewed "many" or "few" World War II movies or television documentaries during the Vietnam war. The same persons would also be classified according to whether they had viewed "a great deal" or "a little" Vietnam combat news film footage. Finally, they would be classified as "hawks" or "doves" on Vietnam, on the basis of answers to relevant questionnaire items. Rates could then be computed for the various combinations of categories of television exposure, indicating the percent in each category who were "hawks." One could then determine whether "hawkishness" was more or less probable if one had been exposed abundantly to scenes of violence from *both* wars, from one war only, or from neither war.

An epidemiological study could attempt to ascertain the variance of anomic attitudes among population categories with different amounts of television exposure. A useful refinement would be to go beyond the raw correlations and try to determine what additional variables account for the differences between persons with high exposure and low anomie as opposed to those with high exposure and high anomie, etc.

Some light could probably be shed by epidemiological studies on the over-all social impact of accepted (or tolerated) misrepresentations in mass communications. A number of these are so common many people hardly recognize them as such. What are the social ramifications of such non-recognition? Examples of accepted or tolerated misrepresentations would include: postdated publications (e.g., the "November" magazine issue that appears on newstands early in October, or the Christmas advertising in a magazine that says "January" on the front cover); feigned giveaways that are actually sales gimmicks; magazine or book covers which are not representative of the contents; canned laughter on television comedy programs; studio response to a performer by command from a stage director; deceptive promises of immediacy, as in the newscaster's "I'll have that story next, right after this 'message' ..."; television commercials for automobiles showing them only in uncongested environments, never in heavy traffic; and the "fresh air" theme in cigarette commercials. Is there a negative correlation between abundant exposure to these in the various media and ability to discriminate between scrupulously honest statements and "white lies"?

A public opinion survey could ascertain certain public values by relating both a content analysis-derived typology of commercial sponsors and another content analysis-derived typology of commercial message styles to a typology of program content. Which types of commercial sponsorship and which types of advertising interruption are deemed appropriate, permissible, tolerable, or in bad taste when associated with which types of program content? What do mass media audience members feel should be done about the objectionable combinations?

The studies showing the types of persons who prefer crime and violence in television shows are largely of the epidemiological type. Such studies are no substitute for experimental inquiries, but they help identify problems for the latter kind of investigation, and provide additional kinds of data for extending the implications of experimental studios.

Epidemiological methods could be employed to compare the effects of color and black-and-white television on values, behavior, and perceptions. These methods could also determine what categories of people most readily shift over from black-and-white to color, and what other changes tend to be associated with this switch. How much difference does color make in program preferences, and how does it contribute to the kind of work view obtained by viewers from their exposure to television? Is the "visual bias" of color television any different from the "visual bias" of black-and-white television? Can any subtleties that were missed during the period of conversion from radio to television be belatedly discovered now in the conversion (at a somewhat slowed down pace) from black-and-white to color?

D. Mixed Studies

Some studies have the attributes of experimentation, but involve no manipulation of stimuli, and thus resemble the epidemiological approach. A general design for such studies has been worked out by Parker. He calls it the "ex post facto before-after design with switching replication." He contends that it offers a way to test cause-offect hypotheses regarding the mass media.[11] Retrospective data are obtained from a number of communities, some of which can be classified as "early adopters" and others as "late adopters" of some phenomenon, such as television. Data are obtained for two different time periods. If the study were on the effects of television on crime rates, the average of the crime rate difference between the two periods in the two sets of communities would equal the average of the crime rate difference between the two sets of communities in each of the time periods, and would be an estimate of the "effect" of TV on crime rates.

Perhaps by using data on such matters as Boy Scout activities, sales of various recreational goods, attendance by adults and children at various out-of-home activities, use of tennis courts and golf courses, and restaurant patronage during various hours of the day and evening, it would be possible to ascertain what priority television occupies in people's lives. It might also be possible to discover how the overall constellation of socializing agents is adjusted to make a place for television in the socializing of children and what effects the adaptation has on the child's personality development process.

Parker himself used the design to study library circulation changes as a result of television. In fourteen matched pairs of towns in Illinois, compared for three different years during the time television was being adopted, he found an overall increase in library circulation. However, he also found a clear indication that television had the effect of depressing library circulation relative to what it would have been in the same setting with no television.[12] Perhaps the same set of towns could be mined again for additional data in public records—e.g., school attendance figures and absenteeism rates, crime and delinquency statistics, hospital admissions and discharges, bank deposits and withdrawals, postal records, church and Sunday school attendance, participation in civic events, voter registration and turnout, hunting and fishing licenses sold, etc. The more variables that could be obtained and analyzed in terms of design, the more the total picture of the impact of TV on the lives of people in these communities could be filled in.

Finally, in a nationwide sample of adults and children, subdivided into high-and low-exposure subgroups, a series of hypothetical television story plots could be adminstered, in the manner of the psychologist's Thematic Apperception Test, with the respondent asked to suggest probable story endings. Various combinations of approved and disapproved goals and legal and illicit means could be presented. Some plots would involve violence, others not; in some the violence would be "justified," but not in others. After statistically controlling for various characteristics, high-and low-exposure respondents could be compared in regard to the percentage of their projected story outcomes which reflect anomie. In conjunction with other measures of anomic attitudes, this kind of comparison could give a clear indication of the extent to which this medium does or does not tend to produce anomie by presenting a fantasy world.

The purpose of this section has been merely to sketch a few research possibilities with a view to showing that experimental studies need not be small scale and short run, and that important knowledge about mass media impact can be generated with available or obtainable data of other kinds. There is much yet to be learned, and there are feasible ways of accomplishing this research. The social importance of continued and intensified inquiries cannot be understimated.

REFERENCES

1. S.H. Lovibond, "The Effect of Media Stressing Crime and Violence Upon Children's Attitudes," *Social Problems*, 15 (1967), p.91.
2. Robert K. Merton, *Mass Persuasion* (New York: Harper Bros., 1946).
3. See Robert L. burgess, "Communication Networks: An Experimental Reevaluation," *Social Psychology*, (July 1968), pp. 324-337.
4. Wilbur Schramm, Jack Lyle, and Edwin B. Parker, *Television in the Lives of Our Children* (Stanford, Calif.: Stanford Univ. Press, 1961), p. 137.
5. *Ibid.*, pp. 175-176.
6. *Ibid.*, p. 150
7. *Ibid.*, p. 154
8. Bernard Berelson, "What 'Missing the Newspaper' Means," reprinted from Paul Lazarsfeld and Frank Stanton (ed.), *Communication Research, 1948-1949* (New York: Harper Bros., 1949), and in Wilbur Schramm (ed.), *The Process and Effects of Mass Communication*, (Urbana, Ill.: Univ. of Illinois Press, 1954), pp. 36-47; Charles F. Cannell and Harry Sharp, "The Impact of the 1955-56 Detroit Newspaper Strike," *Journalism Quarterly*, 35 (Winter, 1953), pp. 26-35; Penn Kimball, "People Without Papers," *Public Opinion Quarterly*, 23 (Fall, 1959), pp. 389-398.
9. Cf. Donald R. Cressey, "Epidemiology and Individual Conduct: A Case from Criminology," *Pacific Sociological Review*, 3 (Fall, 1960), pp. 47-58.
10. Melvin M. Tumin, "Exposure to Mass Media and Readiness for Desegregation," *Public Opinion Quarterly*, 21 (Summer, 1957), pp. 237-251.
11. Edwin B. Parker, "The Effects of Television on Public Library Circulation," *Public Opinion Quarterly*, 27 (1963), pp. 578-589.
12. *Ibid.*

Appendix III-C

THE CONTENT AND CONTEXT OF VIOLENCE IN THE MASS MEDIA*

A. Introduction

This paper has three goals: (1) to synthesize available research on mass media content in terms of the time and/or space allocation to violent programs, acts, and news; (2) to examine the context or nature of violent content when it does appear in the mass media; and (3) to provide some rationale as to why such content is made available. Other papers commissioned by the Mass Media Task Force of the President's Commission deal specifically with the question of effects of violent content in the mass media. This paper specifically excludes information and research on the question of effects. We are concerned with the relative existence of violent content, its emphasis, the way it is portrayed, and secondarily, why it exists to the extent it does.

Two reasons appear to be foremost as to why such information will be useful in the deliberations of the Commission. These have been working assumptions in the preparation of this paper. First, there could be no effects from violent content in the mass media were there no such content available. There is a corresponding general belief that a considerable amount of mass media content concerns itself in one form or another with violence or acts of physical conflict. Without any prior disposition that there is too much, too little, or just enough, it is necessary to determine what exists and in what amount before the question of potential effects can be a viable one.

Second has been the assumption that for the typical citizen in the United States, *direct* exposure to physical violence is a rare event. Few of us have ourselves been robbed, mugged, or punched in the nose. More, but still few of us, know people to whom these things have happened. And few of us know people who have committed such acts. Probably the most prominent type of violence to which there has been more direct exposure than any other is car accidents. Even here the most frequent incident is one of fender bumping. Therefore, the second-order assumption is that the vast majority of our exposure to violent acts has been indirect, as communicated through the mass media. What we have seen in the way of violent acts, what we know of violence and its general consequences has occurred primarily through an indirect, mediation process.

---

*A paper prepared for the Media Task Force by William R. Catton, Professor of Sociology, University of Washington.

Given this rationale for the present undertaking, let us briefly describe the premises and the limitations of content analytic methods, before presenting the major results of such analyses.

Descriptive content analysis attempts to characterize a body of message content at a given point in time. When one is dealing with the message content of mass medium, let alone several media, the body of messages analyzed is generally some subsample of the total universe of content available. That is, there never has been, nor need there be, a complete census of newspaper content. The procedure most normatively used consists of sampling newspapers from among those available, then sampling issues (or days) for each of the sampled papers, and subsequently sampling sections or pages for each issue in the sample. This procedure is generally a reliable one, and is similar to the method by which one would obtain a sample of people, for example, to be interviewed in a market study or a public opinion poll. One must maintain, however, the recognition that content may vary greatly across time periods—or that any given analysis of media content is *timebound*. One must then look for the relative consistency of content patterns for a given medium across time and space.

To describe media content also implies that one has some predetermined categories into which various aspects of content are going to be assigned. The category in which we are most concerned here is that of violent content. But different investigators will use different category definitions for that aspect of media content. Some have chosen to assign entire programs to a violence category. Violence, as they define it, is a major theme; others have counted and assigned individual acts of violence regardless of program type to categories of different kinds of violence; still others have dealt separately with physical and verbal violence. This makes it most difficult to closely compare two different analyses of television programs; for example, in one study the unit of analysis may have been the program and in a second study the unit of analysis may have been an individual act of violence. However, for the present purposes, both approaches seek to describe some aspect of the violent content phenomenon and thus warrant presentation here, even if direct comparisons become relatively untenable.

Inferential content analysis attempts to go beyond sheer description of a given medium's content emphases. It attempts to draw inferences from the content itself about states of either the sources of those messages or the receivers of them.

Through an examination of the message output of a mass media institution, investigators have attempted to characterize the producers of those messages, whether they be individual producers or the institution itself. Those characteristics of the sources one attempts to infer about have included—

(a) The personal interests of the source; e.g., his political preferences or bias; his preoccupations with certain topics.

(b) The source's perception of the interests of the receivers; e.g., his beliefs as to the nature of entertainment which will draw the largest possible audience; his notions about the level of audience intelligence.

(c) Group and institutional pressures on the source; e.g.,

responsiveness to demands for better coverage and presentation of civil rights issues, urban problems, employment of Negroes.

(d) The social values of the source; e.g., what he perceives as the society's mores, or what he finds acceptable/unacceptable for presentation in such areas as drugs, sex, and, of course, violence.

By determining what messages are made available to receivers in great quantity, investigators have attempted equally to draw conclusions about audiences. Such inferences have dealt with—

(a) The interests of the typical audience member; e.g., the more messages of a given type, the more the interest of the audience in that type assuming that amount of display corresponds to level of consumption.

(b) The attitudes of the receiver; e.g., he attends to those content areas which he most generally approves of, and to those media which provide him with the most exticing or rewarding messages.

(c) The knowledge of the receiver, e.g., he comes to know most about those areas he receives the most messages about.

(d) The comprehension of the receiver; e.g., he attends to those messages which require the least effort on his part to understand, the least exertion to comprehend.

(e) The actions of the receiver; e.g., he is most likely to behave or model or act in accord with the values he receives a preponderance of.

(f) The social needs of the receiver; e.g., attention to messages reflects what the audience member thinks he has to know about and what he has to believe in order to get along best with those formal and informal allegiances he values most highly.

These represent some of the areas of inference which have led to many studies of mass media content. All such inferences are extremely risky, without estimates of their validity which are independent of content. That is, to make any of the kinds of inferences noted above without separate assessments of the sources themselves, or of audience members, reduces the conclusions of such content analyses to a speculative level. Nevertheless, it seems possible to obtain some degree of face validity from such efforts to the extent that independent investigators studying the content of the mass media at different times and with different measures come to the same conclusion.

With this general background, let us turn to the analyses of mass media content. An exhaustive search of the literature from communication, sociology, psychology, journalism, and broadcasting was made for the period 1950 to the present. We shall present this information for each of the three media categories where sufficient data were available to warrant an attempt at synthesis—magazines, comic books, and paperbacks; newspapers; and television. No substantial analyses of radio content were found. Since the advent of television, radio has virtually eliminated its dramatic output, and current analyses would have to focus on the content themes of popular music, or of its news programming. None were found for those two principal functions of contemporary radio. The lack of any recent analyses of movies precludes an analysis of that medium's content.

B. Magazines, Comic Books, and Paperbacks

This initial section might better have been titled, "A visit to the local newsstand—or drugstore—or discount house—or grocery store"—but the obvious implication is that it may be meaningful to examine content themes in part in terms of where they are available. Today, where one finds magazines, there usually is a section of comic books and paperback books to choose from also. And the number of places with such displays is growing so large as to make the alternative title as cumbersome as indicated. In addition one finds some marked similarities in the themes available and the content depicted across these three print and pictorial media.

Magazines of course run the gamut from the most general of family-oriented publications to those very specialized publications for the intellectual, the hobbyist, the food faddist, the girl-watcher, the crime devotee, etc.

Herbert Otto[29] has done the most comprehensive examination of magazines in terms of their propensity for sex and violence content. Analyzing a group of 55 magazines—the total available at a major newsstand on a given day in 1961—he grouped the magazines into five categories: police and detective (n =11); romance (n=14); family (n=10); men's (n=17); and intellectual magazines (n=3).

This set of magazines contained some 2,524 violent incidents, as well as another 1261 incidents in which sex was predominant. Almost 300,000 words were given to these subjects. If one uses family magazines as the baseline against which to compare the other types of generally available magazines, the police magazines contained seven times the amount of verbiage devoted to violence as the family magazines, and the men's magazines had three times as much. If one looks at frequency of violent incidents, rather than total space, the police and detective magazines had some 77 violent incidents per issue, the men's magazines 63, and the romance 33 before dropping to a dozen each for the intellectual and family magazines. The romance magazines, the obvious leader in sex incidents, tended to collate sex and violence, such that both appeared together and at roughly equal levels.

Physical torture, as a specific form of violence, was treated heavily in both the men's and police/detective magazines, and secondarily in the romance content.

Otto suggests that these are conservative estimates, inasmuch as the magazine distributor for this newsstand indicated that about 100 magazine titles had been specifically censored off the newsstand because of their "objectionable" content and emphases. Thus, this analysis deals with the more acceptable of the universe of magazines available.

In an even more recent study, Otto[28] examined more intensively the content of men's "girlie" magazines and men's physique magazines. Again taking all available magazines of these two types from a major newsstand (a different one), he analyzed separately the pulp magazines (inferior, coarse paper) and the slicks (smooth, quality paper, usually with large color illustrations). Each of the pulps had more than 100 incidents of sex and/or violence, with roughly equal frequency of violence stemming from physical assault, war, murder, and whippings. The slicks had far less violence in them, but far more obvious sex; e.g., fully, rather than partly naked women. And the pulps uniformly put their violence-sex combination on the covers, women being tortured, assaulted, or killed. The men's physique magazines were of a different genre, very little reading material; 95 percent of the content were photos of male poses.

An analysis of the nature of the characters presented in detective magazines by Hughes and Jefferson,[23] provides some additional insight. They compared the typical characteristics of fictional murderers, victims and detectives with available statistics on such individuals. Whereas two-thirds of the fictional murderers had gone to college, none were identified as only completing some portion of elementary school; in fact three-fourths of the real murderers had stopped with grade school and virtually none had completed college. Many of the fictional murderers were divorced; almost none of the real ones. Many of the fantasy killers were professional people; almost none of the real murderers.

As for the fantasy victims, they were far more likely to be men, single, and more advanced in education and job than their real-life counterparts. And the fantasy detectives were a dozen years younger, all unmarried, and far more likely to be private citizens rather than professional police—again in comparison with real detectives. And Negroes were neither victims, nor detectives, nor murderers in the fiction.

Several other analyses of magazine content have focused on the values being emphasized. Some of these deal with violence-related themes and others do not. Capsule summaries of their main findings appear in order at this point.

... Mental health content in popular magazines suggests that the mentally ill look and behave in ways different from normal, stresses of the immediate environment can drive people insane, physical factors frequently cause mental disease, and bad emotional habits learned while growing up make a person liable to mental breakdown. Principal treatments suggested by magazine fiction were that a change in personality is required, or change to a new environment with less stress. But for every two magazines (of 91 analyzed) there was only one article on mental health (Taylor).

... About one-fourth of the heroes in magazine fiction stories as were found in *Ladies Home Journal, Post, True Story,* had no visible occupation. About 10 percent of the story themes in these most general magazines dealt with crime, corresponding closely to Otto's findings for his family magazines. And the portrait of women indicated that the loving housewife was the ideal; employed women suffered from lack of love.[24]

... Among the same family-type magazines, white Americans carry virtually all the major roles, and generally are attractive individuals. Minority group members are minor and stereotyped, and far more likely to portray criminal roles. They are cast as less-educated and in lower status jobs. Whereas the white American can deal with lofty goals, the minority American is shown as dealing with mundane, often calculating goals.[5]

... In terms of trends over time among the most general magazines, *Life* showed a sharp upswing (between 1947 and 1957) in its preoccupation with crime. Virtually absent in the earlier period, crime was its most predominant topic by 1957. Across nine such general family magazines (e.g., *Readers's Digest, Saturday Evening Post, New Yorker, Ladies' Home Journal*) for the same time period, biographies diminished in number, to the same extent that crime biographies or crime narratives increased.[13] Stewart[42] analyzed a set of magazines designed primarily for the 13-19 age range. She reported that the predominant content categories were articles about entertainment heroes, teenage problems (with answers), and fashion and beauty sections. Only two magazines contained material she thought might be objectionable to parents. However, in terms of magazine readership, she found a sample of teen-agers was far more likely to read adult magazines, particularly *Life* and *Post* than the teen-age magazines.

Of even greater relevance, Goodrich[15] analyzed a set of magazines, among other mass media, to determine their fictional protrayal of crime and violence. In general, he found that the magazine fiction provided primarily an unemotional portrayal of crime and romance—again the subtle, but meaningful link between sex and violence noted earlier by this writer in several studies of media content. But more important, the virtual neutrality of the portrayal was Goodrich's main finding. In addition, he found little presentation of societal weaknesses as a possible contributor to violence. Goodrich stated that most such fiction presented obvious good guys and obvious bad guys, with little shading of characters between such polarities.

The role of one extremely popular magazine type—comic books—has been undergoing radical content alterations in the past 10 years. In response to public demands, self-regulation was imposed by the comics industry about a decade ago. In the last 4-5 years, however, a vastly increased sales of comics has accompanied a spawning of new heroes, monsters, rogues and related characters which appear to depart greatly in substance and intent from that earlier self-administered code. Let us here summarize one comprehensive study of comic books made just prior to the self-regulation period.

Graalfs[16] analyzed 351 comic books during the first three months of 1954, a set of all those available for general distribution. One-third of the comic books were humorous, 27 percent were crime themes, and twenty percent were romance stories. She found that *(a)* one in every seven frames or pictures portrayed a violent physical act; *(b)* one-fourth of all frames in western and war stories were such incidents and one-fifth in other crime-oriented comics: and *(c)* no war stories showed American soldiers dead or injured. She also found that plots and settings contributed to horror portrayals even in frames from which a specific violent act was absent. That is, many non-violent frames were set up to heighten the impact of the violent frame when it did appear. And the use of language by characters also served to describe the violent acts, perhaps more strikingly than the visual portion themselves.

A few years after this study, the self-regulation code of the comics industry was enacted. Horror, weird situations, crime and violence dropped sharply. One needs further analysis of the comics available today, however, inasmuch as there has been a seeming trend to replicate the kind and quantity of comic books that Graalfs found—after a brief hiatus with the regulatory code.

Let us turn to the third contributor to the display case, that of paperback books. In 1955, two-thirds of all paperbacks available (nearly 5,000) were reprints of already successful hard-cover books, and three-fourths were fiction. Most originals were unknowns, and were mysteries, westerns, science fiction and sex stories. The non-fiction originals tended to be higher in price and more readily available in bookstores than on newsstands.

Two major analyses have been made of such paperbacks a decade apart, and both have dealt primarily with the covers, titles or synopses of the books. Hanley[17] analyzed a sampling of 100 paperbacks available in December 1950. He found that sex and violence very frequently were found together, and that 40 percent of the paperbacks portrayed scenes of death and violence on their covers. As for context, the predominant locale for violence was out-of-doors, and the bed or its counterpart was the most favored indoor scene. More than a fourth of the covers featured one or more firearms.

Otto,[29] in 1961, sampled 296 paperbacks from eight topic categories. Three researchers independently coded the material to establish the reliability of the procedures. Of the paper covers, 44 percent were illustrations of seduction, sadism, or general violence. Another six percent featured the military or weapons, without actual violence, but in which the implication was the same. When Otto collated the book topics with the illustrations, he found that 60 percent of the detective stories displayed female seduction and another twenty percent showed other aspects of violence: 40 percent of the general fiction featured the female seduction cover. Of the westerns, 40 percent had violent cover scenes. Analysis of pocketbook titles showed the same trend. Some 30 percent of the titles were classified as either of violent or seductive language.

In a separate study, Otto[28] analyzed specifically a set of paperbacks generally referred to as "sexies," and commonly found in what is known as "dirty book stores." Here, more than half the books were concerned entirely with prostitution, orgies, nymphomania and/or gigolos. Of these, more than half had a minimum of 100 incidents of sex behavior, usually deviant—in books that averaged 160 pages in length.

To attempt to summarize our hypothetical visit to the American newsstand today, one can find satisfaction for virtually any appetite that exists. If one is at the magazine rack display, an orientation to family magazines—the biggest sellers in terms of individual magazine titles—provides a world that is relatively crime-and violence-free, in terms of the fictional content contained therein. That fictional world does not necessarily correspond closely to any real-world phenomena of violence. But these titles may be hidden on that rack in comparison with all other magazines available, which cumulatively have even more buyers. These are heavily oriented to sex problems and violence, and are readily available in greater numbers. The largest circulation magazines deal with violent incidents in about 10 percent of their fictional content. These lesser magazines will range from that figure to some three-fourths or four-fifths of their space.

If one moves then from the magazine rack to the paperback displays, then one locates a more pervasive violence and sex focus. One in every two covers, and one in every two titles will feature violence, with and without sex as a bonus. This of course, is only looking at the package for the product, but until further research analyzes the product itself, we may assume that the package does much of the selling.

Dropping down about 24 inches at the display counter we have been examining, and elbowing aside youngsters thumbing through comic books, this lower world is not too dissimilar a reflection of what we encountered in the other two areas of the store. Cheaper in price, smaller in size, and simpler in language, the comic book story is direct, active, and designed to accommodate a relatively shorter attention span. Until more recent studies are available, a very similar emphasis on violence seemingly exists as at the adult counter. One wonders to what extent this serves to nurture later interests at the newsstand.

C. Newspapers

Analyses of content in the U.S. newspaper have dealt with four general questions, and this section will abstract and summarize those studies which seem to have dealt most appropriately with those questions. The questions are: (a) What is the general distribution of content in the newspaper across topics areas; (b) What is the specific nature of news about crime; (c) What topics receive maximum attention from the readers; and (d) What are the content themes and values of the comic strip?

Stempel [41] analyzed the content of the four largest and four smallest daily newspapers in Michigan for a 6-day period in 1961. Considering only the largest newspapers, because of their disproportionate audience size, one finds this distribution of content in terms of allocation of total space:

	Percent
War and defense news	23
Crime news	5
Accident and disaster	4
Popular amusement	15
Human interest	13
Economic activity	12
Politics and government	10
Education and arts	11
All others	7
Total	100

Although differences were noted among individual papers, that proportion of content specifically reporting on crimes and accidents ranged from six to twelve percent of the total news content. One may note that this corresponds quite closely to the fictional crime and violence content of the most general family magazines described in the preceding section.

Two years earlier, Deutschmann [12] had used the identical news categories in an analysis of 30 days of the seven daily New York City newspapers that existed at that time, plus five Ohio daily newspapers. His categorical breakdown showed the following:

	Percent	
	New York City	Ohio
War and defense news	20	13
Crime news	15	10
Accident	7	5
Popular amusement	20	22
Human interest	19	23
Economic activity	24	15
Politics and government	20	14
Education and arts	14	18
All others	19	19

These proportions within each group of papers sum to more than 100 percent inasmuch as Deutschmann's technique assigned stories to more than one category if they dealt with more than one topic. Stempel had assigned space on the basis of which topic category was predominant for a single story. To make the figures more comparable then, one might index the crime/accident news in New York City papers by dividing the total given to those two categories (22 percent) by the total allocation to all categories (14 percent) and determine that the overall ratio of crime/accident news was 14 percent; a similar ratio for the Ohio papers puts the crime news at a 10 percent level. These two figures may now be compared more directly with Stempel's 9 percent figure for the major Michigan dailies.

Perhaps as intriguing as these overall estimates is the variance that one finds associated with individual newspapers. For example, Deutschmann reported that crime news occupied 7 percent of the space in the *New York Times,* but 28 percent of the *New York Daily News.* A breakdown of the dozen separate papers examined in that study shows:

	Percent	
	Crime/accident	War and defense
New York Times	10	36
Herald-Tribune	18	26
World-Telegram-Sun	17	12
Post	23	11
Journal-American	23	13
Daily News	45	12
Mirror	41	12
Cleveland Plain-Dealer	13	14
Cleveland News	14	8
Cleveland Press	13	10
Cincinnati Enquirer	18	19
Cincinnati Post-Times-Star	15	14

Thus, there was great variability among the New York City papers, and great similarity within each of the two Ohio cities.

Further confirmation of this basic trend in newspaper content comes from Otto.[29] Analyzing the content of ten major dailies for a single day (April 11,

1962), he found a total of five percent of the total column inches (not stories) dealt with violence. And he also found the *New York Daily News* as the largest single deviant—it carried four times as much violence as the next largest carrier of violent content, and it carried seven times as much sex news.

An even more recent analysis has been made by Stott.[43] For the week of April 10, 1967, the Stempel categorical scheme was applied to four Ohio papers, with the following results:

	Percent	
	Crime/accident	War and defense
Cincinnati Enquirer	14	14
Dayton Journal-Herald	13	28
Columbus Citizen-Journal	14	33
Cleveland Plain-Dealer	11	31

Thus, the 1967 figures for crime news correspond closely to those obtained in 1959 by Deutschmann and 1961 by Stempel. A moderate increase in crime news is found, of the order of a few percent. The New York City tabloid newspapers carried some two and one-half times as much news of this type, and corresponded closely to the level of the police/detective magazines in their presentation of violent content.

Of some passing interest at this point, Stott also analyzed the content of the 6:30 p.m. CBS and NBC network news programs for the same week in 1967. Five percent of the CBS news and six percent of the NBC news reported crime/accident content, and each of the networks devoted 50 percent of their news to war reports.

Part of the difference in emphasis of crime news among the New York papers may be attributable to the more intense competition situation (and/or the quest for different kinds of readers). Rarick and Hartman [31] analyzed the content of a daily newspaper for a two-month period during three eras of that paper's history. The first was in 1948-49, when there was no competition at all; the second was in 1953-54, a period of intense competiton with the circulation of the competing paper equal to that of the studied paper; and 1962-63, when the competition had dwindled to a minimal level. They found that intense competition led to two content phenomena; (1) significantly more of the non-advertising space was given to local news; and (2) significantly more of the non-advertising space was given to "sensational" news, i.e., news that dealt specifically with crime-vice, accidents-disasters, and human interest features.

In an earlier study, Nixon and Jones [27] had confirmed the first of these conclusions. In comparing the content of 53 competitive papers with 44 non-competitive papers (single issues of each between 1939-51), they found that the non-advertising content was larger in the non-competitive papers. In a second analysis of 13 matched pairs of daily newspapers for two weeks in 1955 (matched in terms of time of publication, population, circulation, geographic region), the news space in the competitive papers was 44% and in the noncompetitive ones, it was 40%. Although Nixon and Jones indicated that amount of crime content did not differ between competitive and noncompetitive situations, a reexamination of their data shows that: (a) crime, vice and accident content in the earlier period was 4 percent for the competitive papers and 5 percent for the noncompetitive ones; (b) the same content categories by 1955 showed 8 percent for the competitive papers and 6 percent for the noncompetitive ones. Thus, their data show an overall increase in space given to crime content over time, and the more recent tendency for the more competitive situations to give more overall space to crime news.

The content of stories by the Associated Press wire service has been similarly analyzed by Van Horn.[50] For a week in 1950, nine percent of the Wisconsin State AP wire stories were concerned with crime, vice and accidents. Thus, by this type of analysis, we continue to find a baseline of approximately one and one-tenth of both potential (wire service stories) and actual newspaper coverage deals with stories of crime and violence. Deviations upward from that figure exist among particular kinds of newspapers.

Cony [9] approached newspaper content in a somewhat different manner. Looking only at news stories in which the focus was on individual and group activities requiring contact with other individuals, he classified the nature of that interaction as either a conflict or a cooperation situation. In this manner, he examined (in six days of five major dailies) conflict and cooperation in political, economic, governmental, social (which included crime news) and international news stories.

For the newspaper content examined, 53 percent of the stories fell primarily into the conflict news category. Then, of the space given to conflict, more than one-fourth resided in crime stories. Crime plus partisan politics accounted for half of all the conflict situations presented, and no other category accounted for more than eight percent of the conflict. Of the stories in the cooperation category, social welfare (another social topics subcategory) and war (international category), together accounted for 25 percent of the cooperation stories. Finally, crime stories accounted for six-tenths of one percent of the cooperation stories, in comparison with accounting for 27 percent of the conflict stories.

Cony's study should reemphasize that the other analyses of content categories dealt only with space allocations—not with prominence, or treatment.

Studies of the treatment of violence or crime news in the American press are scanty and/or anecdotal. One rather intriguing study of crime news in Colorado newspapers was made by Davis. [10] He used three sources of data: measurement of crime news in four newspapers over sample issues from a two-year period, categorized into crimes of stealing, rape, and other violent crimes; e.g., murder, assault; FBI crime reports for the same period for the state of Colorado; and a statewide public opinion poll on public perceptions of criminal activity.

Davis found that there was no relationship between the changes in total crime rate in that state, and the changes in newspaper reporting of crime. For example, a +20 percent change in crime rate in a given category was reflected in newspaper coverage changes that ranged from, +10 percent to +159 percent from the prior time period, varying greatly from paper to paper.

Further, public opinion about crime in the state followed more closely the newspaper coverage than the actual crime rate. This was particularly so for violent crimes and for theft. It was not so for rape, but the incidence of rape was far less than for crimes of the other two types.

Bird has provided a qualitative analysis of newspaper attitudes toward lawbreaking. [6] From the way four daily Midwest newspapers wrote about crime in their editorials, Bird speculated that the papers downplayed economic causes of crime, e.g., low-income, but did focus on social causes, principally that of broken homes. Newspapers do not talk about criminal instinct.

At this point, given that we have begun to portray the presence and quantity of newspaper content that deals with violence, it would appear worthwhile to delve into the extent to which the newspaper reader is likely to choose that content from among all else available. The average American spends at most a half an hour with his daily paper and is selective in what he attends to. Violent content is high on the list of those things he is most interested in and those things he reads most regularly. Studies by Haskins [18] and Swanson [44] provide the evidence for that assertion.

Haskins reported a study conducted by the American Newspaper Publisher's Association Bureau of Advertising. A national sample of adults was asked to express their degree of interest on each of 120 different news items. The items were a sample of newspaper topics during late 1966 which were classified according to the degree of violence portrayed. It was found that the more violence in the item, the more interested the readers were. The supporting data were:

Items depicting:	Average interest index
High violence	52.2
Some violence	49.9
No violence	37.2

Haskins also indicated the extent to which the different mass media are preferred as sources of violent news content. Among the sample of media news items which contain some or high violence, 53 percent preferred the newspapers; 30 percent preferred television; 11 percent said radio, no one said magazines, and 6 percent did not choose. Among those items which contained no violence, 53 percent preferred the newspaper as the source, 20 percent preferred television, 15 percent radio, 12 percent magazines, and 14 percent did not choose. This of course refers to news items, alone, and not to entertainment material.

Swanson analyzed readership data for 130 daily newspapers which had been gathered over an 11-year period, 1939-50. For more than 40,000 items analyzed across the 130 newspapers, the average item was read by 20 percent of the readers. For crime news in particular, major crime stories, constituting 3 percent of the total items elicited a readership rate of 24 percent; minor crime stories, 2 percent of the total items, drew 13 percent readership, and accident/disaster stories, 3 percent of the total items, had 24 percent readership.

After comics and pictures, the 10 most read news categories of content were: war stories, defense, fire-disaster, human interest, weather, individuals, major crime, social significance, consumer information and science invention, in order. Although this represented 25 percent of all items in the papers, it accounted for 42 percent of total readership. Thus, although content presentation is necessary for readership, many content areas, crime news among them, receive far more attention from readers than indicated by the space allocation.

This is further supported in terms of evidence available about readership of photographs in newspapers. The average photo was looked at by one-half the readers. Photos about crimes, 2.5 percent of all photos, were read by 64 percent of the readers; accident photos, 1.4 percent of all photos, were read by 63 percent. Similar evidence existed in an earlier study of reader interest in pictures by Woodburn. [52]

The final aspect of newspaper content we shall examine is that of comic strips, read regularly by more than one half of all newspaper readers, with no other newspaper content category within 15 percent of that figure, according to Swanson.

Barcus [4] analyzed the trend of comics in Sunday papers for the period 1900-59, focusing on those syndicated by United Features, Chicago Tribune and King Features. Principal in the development of comic strips was the creation of the continuity or continuing story strip. Accompanying this new form of comic, Barcus found the major trends to be an increase in action and adventure stories, principally those portraying crime and romantic stories. In terms of characters, he reported a steady decline in the use of children and animals as central characters.

Goals and means to goals employed by comic characters have been extensively examined by Speigelman and Terwilliger. [39, 40] Using 52 comic strips as the data base, they looked principally at differences between male and female characters, and between socioeconomic classes portrayed. Major findings may be summarized in this manner:

(a). There are twice as many men as women; the men have quite active roles; the women are usually decorative.

(b). The men seek power and justice primarily, using violence as a p comfort using personal charm.

(c). Altruism is of major importance, but there is general conflict between group-oriented and self-oriented goals.

(d). As for class difference, lower-class people are portrayed in a less approved manner than higher classes; the chief difference between the lower and other classes is the former's greater concern with what the author termed "pleasure-seeking" goals, and their greater propensity to accept the decisions of fate, rather than using active methods to overcome such accidents.

(e). Seventy-seven percent of all settings were urban; but the characters of whom three-quarters were U.S. citizens, included no Negroes, no Mexican-Americans, no Oriental-Americans.

These findings may be supplemented by those from Saenger [34] through his analysis of the strips in nine New York city papers. One-half of the comic strips dealing with domestic situations were set in the lower middle-classes, with the other half in higher strata. Two-thirds of the male characters were white-collar workers. In these domestic situations, the male was the master if the situation was premarital, and the women the stronger in the post-marriage context. Between domestic situations and adventure strips, the female in terms of general activity threefold, but the domestic male is no more active than his female counterpart. Finally, the male in the domestic strip is usually unsuccessful in his goals; the male in the adventure strip succeeds.

In general, then, newspaper content consists of approximately 10 percent devoted to crime and accidents plus a negligible portion to photographs of violence. Both the written and the visual content of this type draw above-average attention and interest from readers. Individual newspapers deviate sharply from these levels, presenting far more in the way of such sensational content. Some of this increase may be attributable to the more competitive newspaper situations or to appealing to a special segment of the audience. Further, public perceptions of crime are likely to be related to extensiveness of newspaper coverage, rather than to actual changes in the incidence of crime. This would seem to provide some additional support to the notion that violence as we have come to know it, has been learned primarily through media expressions about violence, rather than through direct contact with violent acts, or realistic estimates of violence rates.

D. Television

Much has been written about the content of televison by social critics and philosophers—more than by quantitative researchers. For this reason, among others, the Mass Media Task Force commissioned from Professor George Gerbner of the Annenberg School of Communication, University of Pennsylvania, a quantitative analysis of contemporary television program content. This writer has taken as his task then the summary of the available research on the same question. This section is primarily intended to supplement Professor Gerbner's more comprehensive examination of this issue, to indicate how others have approached the problem, and also as background perspective for interpreting Professor Gerbner's work.

The studies we have surveyed deal with television in two principal ways. One has been to consider programs as units of analysis; the second has been to look at particular acts between people on programs. We shall deal with both outlooks, and urge the reader to be aware of the distinction.

Also, the question as to definition of what is violent content is as appropriate for this section of the Report as for others. Inasmuch as there tend to be as many definitions as there are investigators, we again choose not to quibble with the definitions used in the several studies. We have taken as given whatever was considered by a particular researcher to be violent content, or violent incidents, or violent acts, and have presented their findings. Given that no one will be completely happy with another person's definition, we have chosen to include studies which appear to be most informative, without attempting to find wholesale correspondence among them in the definition of content categories.

Much of the most relevant evidence on television content exists in testimony presented to the U.S. Senate Subcommittee to Investigate Juvenile Delinquency in hearings held in 1955, 1961 and 1964. [46, 47, 48, 49] We have abstracted liberally from those hearings, which dealt with an interest that parallels that of this Presidential Commission.

Let us begin this section with a summary of evidence presented at those male was predictable in the former because of his weakness, and predictable in the latter because of his strength. The adventure strip male outdoes the Senate hearings, and then relate that evidence to other studies which examined TV content and the context of particular types of programs.

The Senate hearings were concerned primarily with the viewing possibilities for youngsters. But there is ample evidence that children watch more televison than do adults, and they watch more in the way of adult programming than children's programs. [37]

From a 1955 subcommittee study of 9 cities for 1 day each (from 4 p.m. until 10 p.m.), plus a solid week of programming on four Washington, D.C., stations, the investigators found—

> (a). Thirty-nine hours of programs featuring crime and violence on the four Washington stations, of a total of 168 hours analyzed.
>
> (b). Thirty-eight hours devoted to crime and violence shows for the other nine cities, from a total of 192 hours analyzed.

Thus, they found from one-fourth to one-fifth of the programming available featured similar content, both within a city, and across the nation's largest cities.

For trends across time, the National Association of Educational Broadcasters reported to the Senate subcommittee on studies done in 1951 and 1953. In New York City, they found a 15 percent increase between those two periods in the number of acts or threats of violence within a single week of viewing. For that week of watching in 1953, they isolated 3,241 acts or threats of violence; the number of such acts had increased per one-hour program from 5.8 to 6.2. Further, the violence found during the children's hours (5-7 p.m. on weekdays, sign-on to 7 p.m. on weekends) was twice the amount visible during the remainder of the programming day.

These two studies already point out the difficulty of comparisons across studies where some count acts and others count hours. The next few studies, also analyzing time trends, used still a third measure—proportion of programs of a given type.

In the 1962 Senate hearings, a presentation was made that examined the percentage of prime time programs that featured "action and adventure." These findings are summarized in the following table:

		Percent 4–10 p.m.	7–10 p.m.
Washington:	1954	22	17
	1961	34	51
Denver:	1954	26	23
	1961	52	58
Atlanta:	1954	17	16
	1961	44	67
Seattle:	1954	17	11
	1961	44	67

This table shows a striking increase in shows of one type—and the investigators applied the same criteria for the two time periods. Further, for 1954, the programming for the two time slots was remarkably alike; for

1961, there was considerable difference. Action/adventure shows had gone from a minority level of programming to a majority situation. In looking at the offerings available in a given city, one must recognize that most programming may be network programming, with little option for the individual station. To check this, an analysis was made of network shows for 1961–62. Of those programs totally owned by the networks, 68 percent of the ABC offerings, 65 percent of NBC, and 54 percent of CBS were in the "action/adventure, crime, detective, or western" category. Of those partly owned by the networks, 77 percent from ABC, 86 percent from NBC and 44 percent from CBS were of that type.

At the 1964 Senate hearings, still another analysis of TV content was presented determining the then current proportion of programs falling into the action/adventure category, as discussed above. The 1964 levels were virtually identical to that determined in 1961; e.g., 49 percent of the programs on Washington, D.C., television stations were of the action/adventure type. Further comparisons between 1961 and 1964 for New York, Chicago, and Los Angeles (not in the 1954 study) indicated no changes between those two time periods for those cities—all at approximately the 50 percent level of programs of that single type. Thus, there was a significant increase between 1954 and 1961, with no further increment in 1964.

For the 1962 hearings, a monitoring was made of 80 programs in the action/adventure category on Washington, D.C., stations for a week in 1961. For that aspect of the study, the coders looked at incidents of aggressive behavior, in comparison with protective behavior. Rather than count each blow or gunshot as aggressive acts, each episode; e.g., gunfight or fistfight, was counted as a single event. They found:

> In the television drama analyzed, a total of 319 episodes of violent assaultive behavior occurred, an average of four such episodes per picture. In marked contrast is the occurrence of protective and affective behavior. This falls just under an average of one episode per picture. In other words, the ratio of assault to affection is 4 to 1.

A survey done a year earlier (one week of programs in Los Angeles, 1960) elicited the following incidents before 9 p.m.: 144 murders (with multiple or mass murders counted only once), 52 justifiable killings, thirteen kidnapings, seven torture scenes, eleven planned murders (unsuccessful), and four lynchings, in addition to some more miscellaneous incidents.

A few years earlier, estimates of violent content were made using the (then) seven New York City television channels as the source of information. [32] In three successive years, 1952–54, increases in acts of violence were obtained. In those studies violence is defined to include physical or psychological injury, hurt, or death, addressed to living things. For one week in 1954, the investigators coded 11 acts and threats of violence per hour, compared to 6.2 in 1953. And violence in news, sports, public events, etc., was specifically excluded from the analysis. Eighty-one percent of these acts were committed by humans and half of them with weapons.

These analysts also looked at violence by time of day. From sign-on to 5 p.m. was referred to as domestic programming, 5–7 p.m. as children's time; and after 7 p.m. as general programming. Although the majority of violence occurred during the last of these time segments (70 percent), the two-hour block for children yielded 29 percent of all acts. They then examined the context of the violence, using three basic contexts: thrilling or tension-producing (ominous music, lighting, suspense devices), neutral (realistic, but without sinister plots), and humorous or sham context. More than half of the violent acts during the children's hours were presented in a humorous context, with only nine percent in a thrilling context. In contrast, 27 percent of all violence during the general programming period was thrilling in nature, with 53 percent neutral. There appears to be some expectation that violence, when humorously presented, diminishes whatever implications raw violence might have. This assumption remains specifically an untested one.

Perhaps one more study of this straightforward counting variety will suffice, and we may then look to other ways of examining the portrayal of violence on television. Head[19,20] examined 209 programs for a thirteen-week period, finding, by his criterion, about four acts of aggression and moral transgression per program. The crime-aggression ratio was highest for children's programs where the most common act was physical assault. Among acts of aggression, violent ones predominated (56 percent), and half of those involved guns. For the 209 programs, there were 110 homicides, with the story line emphasizing the killer, not the victim; e.g., nine of ten killers, but only one-half of the victims were major characters. This latter trend was pervasive throughout the program; i.e., three-fourths of all criminals were major characters in comparison with one-half of noncriminal characters.

All of the studies reported to this point have been designed primarily to give some index of how much violence there is on television. A few have dealt with the manner, style, and/or context of that violence. Head's study, for example, was as concerned with the nature of the portrayal of violence as with its incidence. This is not to denigrate the counting of violent scenes, programs or incidents. Had that procedure not led to large numbers of happenings, then it would not have been useful for more recent investigators to focus more fully on qualities of violence, rather than their quantity. The principal aspect of these more recent studies has been the means by which problems are solved in television drama.

In an unpublished study made available to the writer, Stempel analyzed one week of 60- to 90-minute programs on the three networks. This was for the current (1968) season, between 7:30-11 p.m. All of the "problems" posed in the programs were recorded, and the analysts then examined the means by which such problems were solved—violent solutions, non-violent solutions, or unsolved problems. For the week, 202 story problems were identified. Of these, 58 percent were solved by violent tactics, 33 percent in a non-violent fashion, and 9 percent remained unresolved.

A further analysis was made of the 118 violent solutions used in the programs—was the violence verbal, physical, or mechanical (with weapons)? If more than one means of violence was used in obtaining a particular solution it was multiply coded. The results indicated that verbal, physical and mechanical means were used with approximately the same incidence. But this equality in means hid large and systematic differences in use of violence among the three major networks:

Percent

Means of violent solution:	ABC	NBC	CBS
Verbal	19	50	26
Physical	37	34	42
Mechanical	44	16	32

For this period of analysis, at any rate, ABC emphasized weapons as the means to a violent end, NBC was heavy on tongue lashings, and CBS gave more equivalent time to the three forms of violent solutions.

The point is that the main avenue of problem solution or conflict resolution in network programming for the current season is that of violence.

Larsen, Gray, and Fortis[25] examined this problem in an even broader context. They classified program goals (any verbal act or behavior indicating a desire or wish for an identifiable state of affairs, including preservation of status quo); e.g., property, self-preservation, affection, power. Then they examined what methods were used to obtain these goals; e.g., legal, economic, nonlegal (short of violence), violence, escape or avoidance, among others. They applied these categories to a sample of adult shows (less than 15 percent child audience), "kidult" shows (30-38 percent child audiences) and shows where children exceeded 38 percent of the audience.

In terms of program goals alone, the predominant adult show goals were self-preservation and affection (30 percent each) the kidult goal was sentiment (justice, revenge, advocacy of personal belief) in 40 percent of the instances, and the children's major goal was property acquisition (25 percent).

In terms of means for obtaining such goals in the programs analyzed, violent means predominated for each of the age-show groupings. For the adult programs, violent means were employed 32 percent of the time (with non-legal means and escape contributing an added 24 percent of all means); for the kidult shows, violence was the means twenty percent of the time (with nine percent from the other two means categories mentioned); for the children shows, violent means were used 47 percent of the time (with fifteen percent from the other two means categories).

If one considers those three means—non-legal, violence, and escape—as socially disapproved methods, then examining the relationship between program goals and means reveals one consistent pattern. Socially approved methods of achieving goals have the least likelihood of success across all the program types, as well as across all the goals.

These data suggest that children would be exposed to essentially similar material regardless of which viewing categories a particular program would fall in, at least in terms of the means used to achieve whatever goals are advanced in that program. Further, to the extent that the television industry argues that its medium supports common values or reinforces the existing values of its culture, these data dispute the validity of that contention.

Further dispute of that last argument is available from a number of studies which do not focus specifically on the question of violence, or means for achieving goals. Main findings from those studies would appear to be relevant as a concluding segment of this analysis of television content.

DeFleur[11] examined occupational portrayals on television drama (i.e., a person who for three minutes or longer was performing some recognizable occupational activity). Jobs, according to television, were of this order:

> One-third of the labor force was involved in law enforcement or administration; unskilled laborers did not exist.
>
> More than one-half the men held jobs high in occupational prestige; e.g., lawyers, doctors, judges.
>
> The proportion of workers shown in televised portrayals bore no correspondence to the proportion of workers actually in the labor force when TV jobs were classified into the twelve U.S. Census occupation categories.
>
> Certain occupations were consistently placed in relatively luxurious settings; e.g., personal servants, lawyers, while other consistently received more humble presentations; e.g., owners of small businesses, private detectives, artists and writers.
>
> Certain occupations were consistently characterized by good clothes, social skills, intelligence, and handsome people; e.g., doctors, educators and executives, while occupations of lesser prestige showed the eccentric, slovenly and ugly people.
>
> Occupations were generally stereotyped; e.g., lawyers were clever and unorthodox.

Some 10 years earlier, Smythe[38] noted the predominance of male characters to female characters in a ratio of 2-1. White, native-born Americans accounted for 80 percent of all characters with Negroes contributing 2 percent. More than half of all jobs were of a managerial or service nature, in comparison with 11 percent in reality (DeFleur found 46 percent in these two categories, compared with 14 percent in census data 10 years later).

Head examined thirteen weeks of drama shows, 209 programs in all. He found:

> 70 percent males as major characters.
>
> Seventeen percent of the jobs were police or protective work; Seventeen percent were criminals.
>
> Excluding the criminals, one-half of all jobs were in upper social groupings.
>
> Non-whites portrayed were most frequently domestic workers or service workers, infrequently in police work or white collar jobs.

Let us attempt some conclusions from this section on analyses of television content.

(1) From a wide variety and even wider manner of estimating how

much violence exists on television, one is hard pressed to offer a concise answer. The overriding impression, however, is that there is a great deal of violent content available, at all times of the day, for all manner of intended audience.

(2) The trend, if anything, through 1964 was not for decreasing amounts of violence, but for greater availability.

(3) The presentation of violence is typically as a means of achieving virtually any type of goal.

(4) The use of violence, whether sanctioned or not, is likely to be a successful means of obtaining such goals.

(5) Violence is the predominant means of conflict resolution suggested in television drama, as of 1968.

(6) General character presentations in television drama do not closely resemble in distribution any basic demographic characteristics of the population.

(7) Character depictions are stereotyped, emphasize the unusual behavior, and promote (through both emphasis and absence) certain behavioral values, a majority of which are socially disapproved, or undesirable.

E. Correlates of Exposure to Violent Content

In our search of the literature of analyses of mass media content, we found several studies which had looked not so much for trends in content, but for characteristics of audiences which were correlated with using particular kinds of content. This does not stipulate any cause-effect relationship; the investigators do not make any claim that exposure to violent content has caused these characteristic differences, nor that these characteristic differences have caused a particular affinity for violent media content. To this point in the state of theory and research, one can only say that each of these characteristics relates to or clusters with a marked preference for violent content. To wit:

1. Among Young People

1. Juvenile delinquents (10-17 years old) read more comic books than non-delinquents. The particular type of comic book read by delinquents indicates a marked propensity for those dealing with violent scenes and situations.[22]

2. Boys rated as more aggressive in school (but not delinquent) were far more likely to have violent-oriented television programs as their favorites. Further, the more aggressive the boy, the more the amount of violent TV programs he watched regularly. This relationship was not found among girls.[14]

3. TV addicts among children in Great Britain tend to be less intelligent, more insecure, more maladjusted, and with a high degree of weak social contacts and friendships.[21]

4. TV addicts among children in the United States are generally slower,

with more frequent family troubles and/or unsatisfactory social relationships.[37]

5. Frustrated middle-class children watch more television than less frustrated ones.[26]

6. Those children who do not belong to peer groups and do not enjoy satisfactory peer relationships watch more television content that is violent in emphasis than youngsters with more satisfactory peer group memberships.[33]

7. The aggressive hero type of television program is more often preferred by boys who are rebellious or rebelliously independent, those with lower IQ's and those who are more frequently spanked for misbehavior. In other words, those boys who are themselves more aggressive have a marked preference for aggressive content.[3]

2. Among Adults

1. Hostile patients in a VA hospital found hostile cartoons funnier than non-hostile patients in the same hospital; they were also more able to correctly identify hostile cartoons.[8]

2. Newspaper content that is more immediate in reward; i.e., whose manifest content provides vicarious pleasure, excitement, or lessening of anxieties, is more frequently read by less-educated, lower-income persons.[35]

3. Overall movie attendance is positively related to an individual's vicarious interests in eroticism, violence, luxury, and mishaps-disaster. Moviegoing is negatively related to vicarious interests in achievement and adventure. Among these relationships, the largest single association is between vicarious interest in violence and movie attendance (0.34). Moviegoing also correlates highly with the individual's perceived similarity between life as portrayed in the movies and real life.[1]

4. Television and movies are the most preferred media among individuals who are particularly "sensation-oriented" and least preferred among more "intuitive" personality types. The opposite is true for novels and non-fiction.[2]

5. The primary viewers of television programs which have been classified as "escape" shows are those adults who reported that their aspirations about their "getting ahead" and their opportunities in their jobs were heavily frustrated.[30]

6. Adult men and women who are heavy viewers of violent programs on network television tend to be over 35, of lower-income groups, of less education, in households with children, non-white and in smaller population counties. Those who view more of the violent shows also tend to be heavier viewers in general. However, when overall viewing is controlled, this same profile of those who more regularly watch violent programs is maintained.[51] Drivers with more poor driving records also watch more violent programs more regularly.[53]

3. Some Reasons for Violent Content in the Mass Media

The Mass Media Task Force asked us to reflect on our analysis of media content and to prepare as a final part of this paper some set of plausible explanations for the presence and nature of violent content in the mass media, particularly in television. This section represents that effort, and is speculative in the form of stated or implicit hypotheses. It comes in small part from our analysis of the research literature summarized earlier in this Report.It comes more, however, from conferences we have had with a variety of broadcasters and educators who have convened in two-to-four-hour seminar sessions. From these discussions, certain patterns or trends emerged which appeared to be of sufficient consequence to relate here. Although this section is mainly a commentary on television, certain points apply to other mass media as well, and we hope their relevance is clear. Further, the specific conclusions and suggestions made are the responsibility of the writer.

First, let us distinguish between two terms—conflict and violence—which often are used interchangeably, and which we choose to consider as conceptually different. Where references are made to conflict, the concern is with the establishment of problem situations, the interaction of antagonistic forces. This is central to virtually all dramatic presentations. In contrast, violence is considered as one particular means of problem solution, of conflict resolution. There are many alternative means of conflict resolution; principal among them are compromise, persuasion, arbitration, and fate or magical resolution. This essay will examine possible reasons for the predominance of violent solutions to conflict situations in media content.

This section has been organized around three discussion points or "theories." They are:

    (a) The "what makes for interesting drama" theory;
    (b) The "how has society changed" theory; and
    (c) The "what can we expect from TV" theory.

All three are presented as sources of information or arguments about what we perceive to be dominant media values which contribute to the emphasis of violent solutions to conflict situations.

4. What Makes for Interesting Drama

Conflict has always been the keystone of the dramatic form of entertainment, whether it be from television, the movie, or the stage. Whereas such conflict may exhibit either mental or physical manifestations, the nature of the medium will often determine which of these receives chief emphasis. Thus, the play or movie, with its two or three hour sequences, has an opportunity to examine motivations leading to conflict, and often the consequences of it. Television, in contrast, uses a more abbreviated dramatic style, which tends to limit dramatic development of motivations leading to conflict and the end results of different means of solving conflict. More effective, then, for immediately grabbing the attention of the audience member is some 'socko' situation, action, impact, movement.

Conflict in drama typically places man in a position of insecurity, some predicament, danger, threat, etc. The format then becomes one of intensification of insecurity, leading to crisis, and finally to climax. Man must take decisive actions to mitigate the immediate threat.

Television in particular tends to be a post-problem medium. It concentrates on chase and on solution. The problem is assumed, or given. The neophyte television writer usually starts too far back in the story, and must learn to use other techniques; e.g., flashbacks, for establishing whatever background is felt to be necessary, usually minimal. This makes for relatively simple problems and plot situations. The classic plot in modern pop fiction consists of (1) a sympathic hero (2) struggling (3) against great odds or problems (4) to obtain (5) some worthwhile goal.

The nature of the struggle that one takes to subdue those antagonistic forces may well depend on expectations as to the nature of the audience. Drama, in general, is considered to be an emotional experience, not designed for intensifying intellectual abilities, but for stimulating the audience to some emotional levels or states. So long as some kinds of drama, particularly contemporary TV drama, are intended for the masses, and not for select audiences, then drama is likely to present things happening, action. This implies physical action, action which is likely to be swift and sudden. This likely leads to a situation where the means used to resolve conflict is physical violence—the most intense type of physical solution to conflict. This is not mandatory in the dramatic form, but it is likely in television. It is likely to the extent that (a) there is little time to develop background, plot and climax; (b) there is strong competition for the mass audience; (c) visual presentation of non-violent conflict resolution is undeveloped; and (d) external stimuli compete for the attention of the audience member at any given time; e.g., losing one's self in a movie theater versus the TV drama interrupted by noise, commercials, etc.

Drama often presents a straightforward conflict between good and evil, black and white—with little of the shading that might otherwise characterize conflict. And this is all the more frequent when the situation is structured in terms of sudden and decisive acts. Some characters are evil, and they typically instigate violence as primary means of problem solving. Then violence is used to combat the violence instigated by the evil doer; i.e., violent retribution. This is the fairly typical portrayal of moral justification or rationalization for what is generally immoral behavior from the evil one. And without belaboring the point, the extent to which the drama can establish the preconditions for the good one to behave badly becomes crucial for evaluating his behavior. Such evaluation must focus on a consideration of whether the means used to obtain some goal are indeed worth the ends used. The conscious development of criteria within drama for that decision may serve as a basis to differentiate among dramatic presentations.

Conflict in dramatic situations, as in real life, may find solution through non-physical and/or non-violent means. Chief among these may be compromise and persuasion. These involve not only a great deal of verbal behavior for extended periods of time, but they also demand a necessarily higher level of information for the audience member. Such forms of conflict resolution pre-suppose that much background for current scenes is available, in terms of the characterizations and the storyline. In drama intended for the masses, it is not often profitable nor sometimes technically feasible to explore those alternative means of conflict resolution. It is easier to use the more direct means of physical violence as the remedy. Yet much thought might be given to their development in dramatic forms specifically intended for the largest of audiences.

There are some dramatic means to solving problems other than physical violence that are in widespread use in TV. Chief among these are (a) fate, flukes, magical or accidental solutions to problems, and (b) deviousness, or cunning. Perhaps fairy tales constitute the most primitive form of problem-solution through means over which the protagonist usually has no direct control. Here, one depends principally on faith in external forces, rather than on rational or violent means. The solution which depends on cunning or somebody getting fleeced rests on the assumption of audience identification. Everybody gets taken at one time or another, and they well enjoy seeing it happen to someone else. Thus, the villian gets put on, himself gets swindled, and again the means to punish are isomorphic with those which the villian himself would have used.

5. How Society Has Changed

Here it is useful to consider two historical perspectives. One deals with changes in the American environment which have shifted some basic values and eliminated others, leaving a partial vacuum. The second is to consider significant alterations in the history of the television industry itself—and to relate those changes to changes in the behavior of the American man.

The stereotyped picture of the American character is based on the concept of the frontiersman. That picture is one in which the individual was expected to make quick decisions, to decide things for himself, to be an individualist. Such actions were often beyond the constraints of the law, but there was supposedly little in the way of legal constraints, anyhow. The frontiersman was a doer in an era of doers. He was out-of-doors, physically active.

If such characteristics would have led to direct action by the individual, other values served to temper his action. Principal among these were the notions of being a good Christian, being a good neighbor, and a pervasive work ethic as a means of validating his existence. Religious values and the social and psychological implications of residing in a small community were features that presumably served to stabilize behavior.

Today, man is largely sedentary. He infrequently expresses himself physically. If one assumes he is tired of being inert, but still holds some of the values of the frontiersman, then he must seek other means of obtaining those values. We argue that he opts for vicarious expression of them explaining his appetite for the conflict in drama. Such conflict as presented is typically physical in emphasis, and that physical depiction is one of violence. Contemporary man can live dangerously without personal risk, without apparently sacrificing any aspect of his own well-being or safety by focusing those interests in available TV content.

Further, contemporary society tends to limit goals of becoming a hero, of outstanding individual deeds. Indeed, these goals and their countervailences in religious and social beliefs have been seen by many as deteriorating or at least changing, with little in the way of new myths or ideals supplanting them.

Through film and through television, man finds his access to the out-of-doors. Through such mediation, he finds certain forms of realism and freedom of action not readily available to him in his urban environs. He can easily find others to exercise for him.

Further, contemporary man through involvement and identification with fictional heroes can avoid responsibilities and soothe other potential guilt feelings by not directly taking part in asocial arts; i.e., physical violence. There is a certain disassociation, particularly in home viewing, of drama that serves to limit the nature of identification that may take place. There is no personal danger in watching others kill. An interesting hypothesis which may be developed from this line of reasoning is that as an audience for a particular medium increases, then individual assumption of responsibility decreases. One need not be overly concerned with the justification or the consequences of particular acts involved in dramatic presentations, if involvement is partial and identification minimal. Thus, one would feel least guilty about acts of physical violence in television presentations, and probably more so from novels, or even the movie situation, where the immediate involvement is probably more concentrated.

The stresses on man today are different in nature although similar in origin to those of a century ago. He still strives for individual gains, in job, income and other aspects of personal development, but an overriding work ethic is largely absent. Those goals appear more difficult in a more impersonal world. Competition, rather than cooperation is the key. Each man competes with the pluralistic system. Winning remains the criterion, but the means to winning emphasize physical acts less in real life. Contemporary drama provides some solace: you can win easily with guts. The violent solution becomes a credible, if only a fantasized one. Further, the adversary is highly visible, not a technological structure of management and government.

One may also consider a certain kind of ethnocentrism in America today. Traditionally, since before the frontier, we have been the toughest country, the one that can get things done directly. There may be more longing for that situation today, in the face of conflicting information as to whether we remain the toughest. There is the continued seeking of simple, direct solutions to complex, longitudinal problems. We require more information to handle complex problems, perhaps more than we have been trained to accommodate. Violent solutions to those problems are more visible, more immediate, and perhaps better understood, than non-violent ones.

A final contrast which we see between the men of the 19th and 20th centuries is in terms of their exposure to the consequences of violent acts. In drama today, victims tend to be mere objects for the most part. There is little identification with the loser, and the ultimate loser is the dead one. Death is largely impersonal and fantasy or dramatic death is usually swift and painless. Perhaps the basis for this particular notion can best be found in terms of changing death styles. To a considerable extent in contemporary America, people no longer die at home; they are in hospitals or nursing homes. The family no longer gathers around the bedside for the final moments and actually sees what death looks like. The repose of the funeral parlor is in marked contrast to the trauma of the bedside. Thus, adults are directly exposed to death infrequently and if so, probably much later in their own lifetime. Thus, what death consists of may largely be learned through dramatic presentations. In recent years, it may well have been the assassinations which were the first death exposure for many Americans. And there the deaths looked pretty much like any evening's entertainment. More of the 20th-century adults, although really a relatively small proportion, have had firsthand contact with war situations and its violence. Perhaps TV fare is pretty dull stuff compared to the real thing; or perhaps given direct contact with war violence, there is even greater appetite for that continuing interest.

The second historical perspective we wish to provide—before examining contemporary television values—is of relevant changes in the television industry.

There is considerable feeling today that more violence, and/or more extreme forms of violence, exist in dramatic conflict situations on television than did in the early 1950s. Further, this is perceived to be more "realistic" violence in comparison to the ritualistic violence of the classic western. One can make a case that a significant portion of this change took place at the time of the ABC-Paramount merger in the 1950's. ABC became the "action" network. This presumably led CBS and NBC to alter their programming concepts and worry about the competition of such ABC shows as the "Untouchables." Their worries led them into programming competition with copies based on the ABC prototype. Whereas CBS and NBC had been more conservative in what they chose to include as action or violence scenes, a sharp surge in violent content was the consequence.

A second, perhaps larger factor contributing to such perceived alterations in programming emphasis came from the appetite of the television medium. Original productions and old, old movies could not satisfy the programming schedules that had to be maintained. This led to increased dependence on Hollywood-produced television programs. In early days, networks would not even run film; later, they would run little else. The Hollywood-produced television programs were to be based on what had been a success in the movie theatre in pretelevision days. The producers operated on the basis of "what does it take to get them into the movie house." New criteria replaced old ones:

(*a*) To get crowds, you need action; the more the action the bigger the crowd; the most visual action is physical, and the best available is blood and thunder.

(*b*) Let's go on location; getting outside the studio makes it possible for even more action, more conflict, more interesting and more varied violence.

(*c*) What has worked before ought to work again, at least until the audience stops turning out. Thus, greater reliance on the formula script which can be knocked off fast enough to satisfy television's appetite.

(*d*) Let's keep an eye out for market syndication; now that we're on film (later on tape), duplicate sales and residuals are of great importance.

(*e*) Foreign sales are important; thus, the show has to be simple and easily understood, even without dubbing.

(*f*) Longevity makes for more profits. If the series is not too contemporary, then it ought to be reusable in 10-15 years.

(*g*) Don't innovate unless you can't help it. It costs too much; it's too risky; too much capital gets tied up. A decent pilot costs $100,000, so if you have to make a pilot, make it a feature film. Then we can get our costs back, even if the series doesn't sell.

These may be the major criteria used by the contemporary television producer, and those which have had the most profound impact on changes in television content.

F. What Can We Expect From Television

The propositions we wish to offer with respect to violent content on television can better be expressed in statement than in narrative form. This way, the statements become more obviously amenable to research which might test them as propositions, rather than as value statements only to be argued.

1. The information output of contemporary society is so great, and increasing, that the competition for people's time will induce even greater stress within the industry to obtain and hold audiences to overcome distractions. Such stress will manifest itself in increasing the arousal ability and level of dramatic programs. Thus, there will be an increase in conflict content with violence as the means of problem solving.

2. Conflict is more of a common denominator among the mass audience than is humor. Humor is more likely to segment the audience. Further, TV comedy today emasculates the American male; action, adventure, violence, strengthen him. He avidly seeks out the latter.

3. Films precede television in terms of acceptable trends. What may be avant garde in movie theaters today; e.g., "Bonnie and Clyde," will be the television staples of the 1970's. Moviegoing is no longer a significant activity of the lower classes; at $2-$3 a show, it has become a distinctly middle-class activity, and its original demise in the face of television was only overcome when it deviated from its old format (adopted wholesale by TV) to one of large-scale violence and sex.

4. The occupational milieu of the television business might well be studied. Writers, producers, directors operate under conditions of high tension and high aggression. Their high rewards are accompanied by high punishment in face of failure. They must fight to get to the "top." Some of this aggression and frustration may have as correlates aggressive content, and inhibitions against deviating from what has been succeeding. This may lead successively to more of the same—but at more intense levels of dramatic output; e.g., more and harder violence.

5. Audiences are being conditioned to higher and higher violence levels, given that the programmers feel a need to intensify what it takes to attract and maintain audience interest. Satiation occurs, so that today's violence is tomorrow's humdrum. Very little is fantastic or unbelievable today. Adult discount of the fantastic may well be going at a lower rate. Indeed, much news may be perceived as more fantastic than what is found on the entertainment schedule.

6. Violence in entertainment feeds into the news department. Television executives know what sells in entertainment programming, and the desire exists to get it into the news, to "spice up" the news. The same corporate criteria exist for news programs—size of audience, cost of production, return on investment. All this may occur without conscious awareness on the part of news personnel and certainly without explicit approval. But if there is some belief that the audience is angry about the Vietnam war—whatever the source of that perception—then that anger may well be fed. If a confrontation is expected in Chicago, then it may well be sought out to be nourished.

7. Television is primarily an entertainment medium, even when operating in an information-giving capacity. The response set brought to television news is an entertainment set. News people are celebrities in much the same way as program heroes. They are expected to deal with similar content, and they do. The emotional tone of news is the tone of the drama, of the conflict.

8. There is increasingly less differentiation by viewers between dramatic violence and news violence, less ability to divorce the real from the fantasy. Assassinations, Oswald, Chicago, Vietnam, were hard to believe as real, but they were just like what had always been seen on prime time. Violence in drama is all the more realistic, and violence in the news is perhaps all the more fantastic, thus merging the two in perceptual contexts.

9. News values for television demand immediacy, being first, and presenting visual action. Thus, the obvious event becomes the criterion; e.g., the fire or accident in contrast to the monetary crisis. Swift, decisive acts make the best visual news presentations, exactly as they make the most enticing drama.

10. Finally, audiences attribute news values to entertainment programs. People may well think they know how the police operate, how the government functions from what they get through their entertainment programs. And they may certainly expect the news content to confirm these expectations.

REFERENCES

1. Anast, Philip, "Differential Movie Appeals as Correlates of Attendance," *Journalism Quarterly*, vol. 44, 1967, pp. 86-90.
2. Anast, Philip, "Personality Determinants of Mass Media Preferences," *Journalism Quarterly*, vol. 43, 1966, pp. 729-732.
3. Bailyn, Lotte, *Mass Media and Children; a Study of Exposure Habits and Cognitive Effects. Psychological Monographs,* vol. 73, No. 1, (Washington: American Psychological Association, 1959).
4. Barcus, F. E., "A Content Analysis of Trends in Sunday Comics, 1900-1959," *Journalism Quarterly*, vol. 38, 1961, pp. 171-180.
5. Berelson, Bernard, and Salter, Patricia, "Majority and Minority Americans: An Analysis of Magazine Fiction," *Public Opinion Quarterly*, vol. 10, 1946, pp. 168-190.

6. Bird, G. L., "Newspaper Attitudes in Lawbreaking," *Journalism Quarterly*, vol. 15, 1938, pp. 149-158.
7. Blum, E., "Paperback Book Publishing," *Journalism Quarterly*, vol. 36, 1959, pp. 447-454.
8. Byrne, D., "The Relationship Between Humor and the Expression of Hostility," *Journal of Abnormal and Social Psychology*, vol. 53, 1956, pp. 84-89.
9. Cony, Edward R., "Conflict-Cooperation Content of Five American Dailies," *Journalism Quarterly*, vol. 30, no. 1, 1953, pp. 15-22.
10. Davis, F. J., "Crime News in Colorado Newspapers," *American Journal of Sociology*, vol. 57, 1951, pp. 325-330.
11. DeFleur, Melvin, "Occupational Roles as Portrayed on Television," *Public Opinion Quarterly*, vol. 28, No. 1, Spring, 1964.
12. Deutschmann, P.J., *News-Page Content of Twelve Metropolitan Dailies* (Cincinnati: Scripps-Howard Research, October 1959).
13. Ellison, J., and Gosser, F. T., "Non-Fiction Magazine Articles: A Content Analysis Study," *Journalism Quarterly*, vol. 36, 1959, pp. 27-34.
14. Eron, L. D., "Relationship of T.V. Viewing Habits and Aggressive Behavior in Children," *Journal of Abnormal and Social Psychology*, vol. 67, 1963, pp. 193-196.
15. Goodrich, H., "Man and Society in Mass-Media Fiction: The Pattern of Life in the Mass Media as Revealed by Content-Analysis Studies," *Dissertation Abstracts*, vol. 25, 1965, p. 4851.
16. Graalfs, Marilyn, "Violence in Comic Books," *Violence and the Mass Media*, Otto N. Larsen, ed. (New York: Harper & Row, Publishers, Inc., 1968), pp. 91-96.
17. Hanley, Edward, "Give Me Sex—Or Give Me Death," *Studies in Mass Communication (1950-1951)*, Martin S. Allwood, ed. (Geneva, N.Y.: Dept. of Sociology, Hobart and William Smith Colleges), pp. 34-35.
18. Haskins, Jack B., "Stories of Violence Get High Readership," *Editor & Publisher*, Oct. 19, 1968, p. 38.
19. Head, Sydney W., "Content Analysis of Television Drama Programs," *Quarterly of Film, Radio and Television*, vol. 9, 1954, pp. 175-194.
20. Head, S. W., "Television and Social Norms: An Analysis of the Social Content of a Sample of Television Dramas," *Dissertation Abstracts*, vol. 13, 1953, p. 606.
21. Himmelweit, Hilde T., Oppenheim, A. N., and Vince, Pamela, *Television and the Child* (London: Oxford University Press, 1958).
22. Hoult, T. F., "Comic Books and Juvenile Delinquency," *Sociology and Social Research*, No. 33, 1949, pp. 279-284.
23. Hughes, Norman, and Jefferson, Douglas, "Census of Murder," *Studies in Mass Communication (1950-1951)*, Martin S. Allwood, ed. (Geneva, N.Y.: Dept. of Sociology, Hobart and William Smith Colleges), pp. 26-27.
24. Johns-Heine, Patrick, and Gerth, Hans H., "Values in Mass Periodical Fiction," 1921-1940, *Public Opinion Quarterly*, vol. 13, 1949, pp. 105-113.
25. Larsen, Otto N., Gray, Louis N., and Fortis, J. Gerald, "Achieving Goals Through Violence on Television," *Violence and the Mass Media*, Otto N. Larsen, ed. (New York: Harper & Row Publishers, Inc., 1968), pp. 97-111.
26. Maccoby, Eleanor E., "Why Do Children Watch Television?" *Public Opinion Quarterly*, vol. 18, No. 3, 1954, pp. 239-244.
27. Nixon, R. B., and Jones, R. L., "The Content of Non-Competitive Vs. Competitive Newspapers," *Journalism Quarterly*, vol. 33, 1956, pp. 299-314.
28. Otto, H. A., "The Pornographic Fringeland on the American Newsstand," *Journal of Human Relations*, vol. 12, 1964, pp. 375-390.
29. Otto, H. A., "Sex and Violence on the American Newsstand," *Journalism Quarterly*, vol. 40, 1963, pp. 19-26.
30. Pearlin, L. I., "Social and Personal Stress and Escape Television Viewing," *Public Opinion Quarterly*, vol. 23, 1959, pp. 255-259.
31. Rarick, Galen, and Hartman, Barrie, "The Effects of Competition on One Daily Newspaper's Content," *Journalism Quarterly*, vol. 43, No. 3, 1966, pp. 459-463.
32. Remmers, H. H., *Four Years of New York Television:1951-1954* (Urbana: The National Association of Educational Broadcasters, June 1954).
33. Riley, John W., Jr., and Matilda, W., "A Sociological Approach to Communication

Research," *The Process and Effects of Mass Communication,* Wilbur Schramm, ed. (Urbana: University of Illinois Press, 1954), pp. 389-401.

34. Saenger, Gerhart, "Male and Female Relationship in the American Comic Strip," *Public Opinion Quarterly,* vol. 19, 1955-56, pp. 195-205.

35. Schramm, Wilbur, "The Nature of News," *Journalism Quarterly,* vol. 26, 1949, pp. 259-269.

36. Schramm, Wilbur, Lyle, Jack, and Parker, E. B., "Patterns in Children's Reading of Newspapers," *Journalism Quarterly,* vol. 37, 1960, pp. 35-40.

37. Schramm, Wilbur, Lyle, Jack, and Parker, E. B., *Television in the Lives of Our Children* (Stanford, Calif.: Stanford University Press, 1961).

38. Smythe, D. W., "Reality as Presented by TV," *Public Opinion Quarterly,* vol. 18, 1954, pp. 143-156.

39. Spiegelman, M., and Terwilliger, C., and Fearing, F., "The Content of Comics: Goals and Means to Goals of Comic Strip Characters," *The Journal of Social Psychology,* vol. 37, 1953, pp. 189-203.

40. Spiegelman, Marvin, Terwilliger, Carl, and Fearing, Franklin, "The Content of Comic Strips: A Study of a Mass Medium of Communication," *Journal of Social Psychology,* vol. 35-36, 1952, pp. 37-57.

41. Stempel, G.H., III, "Content and Readership of Teen Magazines," *Journalism Quarterly,* vol. 39, 1962, pp. 88-90.

42. Stewart, Janice S., "Content and Readership of Teen Magazines," *Journalism Quarterly,* vol. 41, Summer, 1964, pp. 580-583.

43. Scott, Michael, "A Content Comparison of 2 Evening Network Television News Programs With 4 Morning Ohio Daily Newspapers," unpublished M.A. thesis, Ohio State University, 1967.

44. Swanson, C. E., "What They Read in 130 Daily Newspapers," *Journalism Quarterly,* vol. 32, 1955, pp. 411-421.

45. Taylor, Wilson L., "Gauging the Mental Health Content of the Mass Media," *Journalism Quarterly,* vol. 34, 1957, pp. 191-201.

46. U. S. Congress, Senate. *Effects on Young People of Violence and Crime Portrayed on Television,* Part 10, hearings before the Subcommittee to Investigate Juvenile Delinquency, Committee on the Judiciary, 87th Cong. (Washington, D.C. U.S. Government Printing Office, 1963).

47. U. S. Congress, Senate. *Effects on Young People of Violence and Crime Portrayed on Television,* Part 16, Hearings before the Subcommittee to Investigate Juvenile Delinquency, Committee on the Judiciary, 88th Cong., 2d sess. (Washington, D.C.: U.S. Government Printing Office, 1965).

48. U. S. Congress, Senate. *Television and Juvenile Delinquency,* Hearings before the Subcommittee to Investigate Juvenile Delinquency, Committee on the Judiciary, 84th Cong., 1st sess. (Washington, D.C.: U.S. Government Printing Office, 1955).

49. U.S. Congress, Senate. *Television and Juvenile Delinquency,* Interim report of the Subcommittee to Investigate Juvenile Delinquency, Committee on the Judiciary, 88th Cong., 2d sess. (Washington, D.C.: U.S. Government Printing Office, 1965).

50 Van Horn, G. A., "Analysis of AP News on Trunk and Wisconsin State Wires," *Journalism Quarterly,* vol. 29, 1952, pp. 426-32.

51. *Which Shows, Who Watches, What Else Will They Watch?,* anonymous *Media/Scope,* vol. 12, No. 8, August 1968.

52. Woodburn, B. W., "Reader Interest in Newspaper Pictures," *Journalism Quarterly,* vol. 24, 1947, pp. 197-201.

53. Smith, James R., "Relationship Between Preferences for Violent Television Programs and Motor Vehicle Driving Behavior," unpublished M.A. thesis, Michigan State University, Department of Television-Radio, 1968.

Appendix III-D

THE CATHARSIS EFFECT:
TWO OPPOSING VIEWS*

The concept of catharsis has been with us for literally thousands of years; Aristotle wrote of the "purging" of audiences' feelings of fear and pity through watching these emotions portrayed on the stage. Some more contemporary theorists arguing by analogy, have speculated that the impulse to aggression might likewise be "purged" through the observation of aggression in the mass media. Only recently, however, have there been any serious attempts to empirically validate this notion of "symbolic catharsis." Despite some early supporting evidence, the more recent evidence has *not* supported the idea that the probability of aggressive behavior is reduced by observing the kind of violence seen in the mass media—in fact, the vast majority of experimental studies on this issue have reported aggression *stimulating* effects rather than "aggression catharsis."

A. Research on the Original Catharsis Formulation

In a study which has produced a good deal of subsequent research, Feshbach (1961) had college men assigned to one of several experimental conditions. Some men were initially insulted with "a number of unwarranted and extremely critical remarks." Subjects then saw either an extremely aggressive film sequence of brutal prizefight, or a neutral control film on the spread of rumors. Following the film, subjects were given a questionnaire on which they could evaluate the insulting experimenter (their ratings were supposedly to be used by the chairman of the department to judge the experimenter's competence). Comparison of ratings from the insulted groups showed a lower level of punitiveness in the group that had seen the fight film. Two parallel groups of non-insulted subjects showed no difference on this measure. The difference that was found among the two groups of angered subjects was interpreted as being due to the "cathartic" effect of the aggressive film.

Symbolic catharsis, however, is not the only explanation for this result. An alternative interpretation (Berkowitz and Rawlings, 1963) stresses the idea that the extremely brutal film aroused aggression anxiety and guilt feelings in

---

*Excerpt from a larger paper prepared for the Media Task Force by Richard E. Goranson, University of Wisconsin.

the angered subjects. The aggressive actions in the film (and perhaps the subjects' own emotional reactions to them) may have served as cues reminding the subjects of their own socially disapproved hostile reactions. As a result of their awareness of these internal responses, subjects were then careful not to display any overt hostility or punitiveness on the questionnaire. While the hypothesis may appear relatively complicated, the catharsis explanation is actually a good deal more complex than it may seem, making as it does, assumptions about the "building up" and "draining off" of aggressive energy and the process of "vicarious participation" in symbolic events. Later studies designed to test this matter more directly have consistently supported interpretations other than the original symbolic catharsis explanation (see Bandura, 1965).

A substantial number of studies have, in fact, shown that, under a variety of conditions, the observation of violence *increases* rather than decreases the viewer's subsequent aggressiveness. In the absence of any prior insult or "aggression arousal treatment," Walters, Thomas, and Acker (1962) found that subjects increased their willingness to inflict physical pain as a result of exposure to filmed aggression. Some of the details of their experimental procedure can be given since their method has served as a prototype for a number of more recent studies. The subjects (adult men) were lead to believe that they were participating in a study of the effects of punishment of association learning, and were asked to administer punishing electric shocks to a learner every time the learner made an association error. The errors were signalled on a display board in front of the subject and the signals were secretly pre-programmed so that fifteen out of the 30 trials were registered as errors. After each "error," the subject was to select one of the eleven intensity levels of the electric shock used as punishment. Following an initial series of 30 trials, subjects saw a film clip from a commercial movie showing two teenage boys engaged in a vicious knife fight. The remaining subjects saw a control film dealing with artwork. Everyone was then given a second series of 30 trials in which they again punished the learner's errors with electric shocks. Analysis of the pre-film to post-film changes in the average intensity of shocks showed that the group that had seen the aggressive film later shifted to a higher punishment level in comparison with the control group. Aggression scores based on shock duration showed a similar outcome. Walter and Thomas (1963) have used this same experimental paradigm with a number of different subject populations, and have consistently found the same pattern of results across groups of teenage males, male adults, and female adults.

The results obtained by Walters *et al.* (1962, 1963) were obtained under conditions where the subjects were not deliberately frustrated, insulted, or otherwise angered before seeing the film. A number of studies, however, have also found aggression inducing effects of observed violence in angered subjects under conditions designed to minimize aggression anxiety. One aspect of observed aggression that might be expected to influence the arousal of aggression anxiety is whether or not the witnessed attack is perceived as being warranted within the fictional context in which it occurs. Berkowitz and Rawlings (1963) investigated this factor in an experiment with college students by using two alternative introductory contexts to a highly aggressive boxing film. In one version, the boxer was represented as being a villainous character well deserving of the beating he received (justified version). Alternatively, he was represented as the victim of unfortunate circumstances, and an admirable, generally sympathetic character (unjustified version). The authors found that angered subjects expressed significantly less hostility toward their previous antagonist after they witnessed the scene of "unjustified" rather than "justified" aggression. The interpretation offered for this outcome is that the subjects seeing the justified aggression were temporarily convinced of the riteousness of expressing their anger toward their tormenters. In the less justified condition, however, the sight of the ethically unwarranted aggression aroused aggression anxiety which inhibited the expression of overt hostility.

Another study in this same vein employed dependent variables which can more clearly be interpreted as measures of overt hostility. Berkowitz, Corwin, and Heironimous (1963) extended the above design to include a control group shown a film on canal boats. Subjects were either insulted or not insulted by one experimenter and then were shown, by a second experimenter, the aggressive film. Subjects then responded to a number of questions, some of which were evaluations of the experimenters and their procedures (the evaluations again were to be delivered to the psychology department chairman). For the subjects who had not been angered, no reliable differences between conditions were obtained. Among those previously insulted, however, the group exposed to the justified version expressed significantly more hostility toward the insulting experimenter than the control group. The unjustified aggression group did not differ from the controls.

In a third study, Berkowitz (1965) used electric shocks as a measure of aggression toward a confederate posing as a fellow subject. Subjects were again either angered or not angered, and were shown a prize fight sequence preceded by the justified or unjustified introduction. The greatest aggression once more came from those subjects, who, according to the aggression-anxiety line of reasoning, should have been least inhibited. Both in terms of the number and the duration of shocks, the highest level of aggression was obtained from angered subjects who had been given the justified film version.

In this experiment, as in the two previous studies, the justified-nonjustified variable had no significant effect on subjects who had not previously been angered or insulted. Perhaps these subjects were simply not sufficiently aroused for inhibitory effects to have any influence on their behavior. On the other hand, it may be that the external cues provided by the aggressive film were only effective when they influenced the subject's interpretation of his own emotional state. Thus only previously aroused subjects would be led to interpret their own feelings as socially unacceptable hostility, and only these subjects would subsequently inhibit their aggression.

A recent study by Hoyt (1967) was designed to examine more closely some of the factors defining the justified-nonjustified dimension. College students serving in the context of a learning experiment were provoked by receiving an unfairly large number of electric shocks from a confederate posing as a naive subject. Following the presentation of the fight film, subjects were given an opportunity to give shocks to the confederate as punishment for the confederate's errors on a learning task. The experimental variations in this study centered on the type of introduction provided for the film sequence. Four conditions were formed by the combination of the presence or absence of two different types of justification. In one condition the justification was based on the vengeance motive—the eventual victor was seen as avenging an unfair beating that he had previously received. Justification in a second condition was based on the self-defense motive with the victor portrayed as defending himself in a "kill or be killed" situation. A third condition was formed by a combination of these two motives and a fourth condition served as a control with no mention of any justifying circumstances. The results, in terms of number and duration of shocks given, showed the lowest level of post-film aggression in the condition where no justification was provided. Subjects in the vengeance justification condition gave the confederate more shocks than did subjects give either the neutral introduction on the self-defense justification. Hoyt's interpretation of these results stresses the degree of similarity between the situation of the subject and the context of the observed aggression. In the two conditions which included the vengeance justification, the subject, who had himself been unfairly abused by the confederate, may have been influenced by motives similar to those portrayed in the film. This correspondence, of course, would be absent on the other two conditions. Thus, the aggression inhibiting or facilitating effects of filmed aggression may depend, in part, on the similarity of the context of the film and the viewer's perception of his own situation.

The findings of each of these studies then are generally consistent with the idea that inhibition of aggression may result when an angered viewer watches aggressive action in a context where the aggression is not justified.

Taken together, the results of all of the studies of emotional catharsis through vicarious participation in observed aggression provide little support for any simple conception of the aggression catharsis hypothesis. The few studies showing any reduction in aggressiveness can easily be explained without assuming that any cathartic "draining off" of aggressiveness has occurred (Berkowitz, 1964). Results have, in fact given a good deal of support to the opposite view. Again we must recognize the limits to any generalization from the laboratory to real-life situations, but the bulk of the studies of filmed violence indicate the presence of an aggression inducing effect rather than any cathartic effect. This aggression stimulating effect has been most evident when conditions for aggression anxiety are minimized, and specifically, when the witnessed aggression occurs in a justified context. This last point is particularly ironic in light of current media programming policies. In showing that "crime does not pay" by depicting the hero's successful and riteous use of violence against the "bad guys", the media may be creating those very conditions most conducive to the instigation of aggression.

B. *Research on A Revised Catharsis Formulation*

While a simple conception of vicarious hostility catharsis may no longer be tenable, several recent attempts have been made to test a revised catharsis hypothesis. This reformulation of the catharsis concept has been based on the idea that while a reduction in anger and aggressiveness may not arise from the observation of aggressive *attacks,* catharsis may obtain with the perception of the *results* of aggression—injury, pain, and suffering. An intriguing study by Bramel, Taub, and Blum (1968) employed such a revised catharsis concept in studying "an observer's reaction to the suffering of his enemy." Male college students were initially either insulted or not insulted by an experimenter. A second experimenter then took over and played a tape that purported to a recording of the reactions of the first experimenter while he was serving as a subject in a drug experiment. Three versions of the tape were prepared, each based on a different reaction to the drug: a euphoria reaction version, a neutral version, and a misery reaction version. The results of the experiment were somewhat complex and open to alternative interpretation, but, in summary, it can be said that subjects' punitiveness was reduced by observing the insulting experimenter suffer. Subjects were unaffected, relative to the controls, by observing him experiencing euphoria. The authors explain this outcome in terms of their revised catharsis hypothesis; the subject's desire to punish the antagonist was reduced by the perception of him undergoing an experience of extreme suffering.

The relevance of this study for the understanding of media effects is obviously limited by the fact that the viewer rarely if ever sees the suffering, in the media, of anyone who has just attacked or insulted him personally. An experiment by Hartman (1965), on the other hand, looked at a somewhat more general case. In this study, three versions of an experimental film were prepared. A control version showed a group of boys engaged in a vigorous, but non-violent basketball game. In the two other versions, the game was interrupted by an argument between two of the boys that quickly developed into a one-sided fist fight. In one version, the film focuses on the attacker's responses; his punching fists, kicks, angry facial expressions, and aggressive verbalizations. In another case, (the pain-cues version), the camera focuses on the plight of the victim including closeups of his face as he was knocked down, his groans, cries, and other expressions of distress. The effects of prior "aggression arousal" were also tested in this study. At the outset, the subjects, teenage juvenile delinquents, overheard their partner (actually a paid confederate) make either insulting remarks, or neutral comments about them. Following this, subjects were shown one of the three film versions, and then given a sanctioned opportunity, in the context of a learning task, to administer electric shocks to the confederate. In comparison to the control group, the effect of both aggressive film versions was to increase aggressiveness in terms of the intensity and duration of shocks given. This effect, however, was partially contingent on the pre-film "aggression arousal." On each of the measures, the aroused subjects were more aggressive after the pain-cues version. For the non-aroused subjects, however, aggressiveness was lower, though not significantly so, after seeing the pain-cues film. The overall effect then of the aggressive films was to stimulate rather than to reduce subsequent aggressiveness. Only for some subjects did the observation of suffering produce any suggestion of reduced aggressiveness. The results from these subjects, as well as the outcome of the preceding study, might be interpreted in terms of the revised catharsis hypothesis. Alternatively, however, the results can be seen as the result of an active inhibitory process. Exposure to cues of the witnessed suffering may have *sensitized* subjects to the possible serious consequences of their own punitive responses. The salience of this possible danger may then have functioned to inhibit their aggressive reactions. A recent, unpublished study by Tannenbaum and Goranson sheds some light on the relative validity of these alternatives. All subjects in this study were college men, and all were initially angered. Angering was achieved by having a confederate give them an unfairly large number of shocks as a judgment of their task performance as "learners" in a procedure disguised as an experiment in education. Each subject then saw a film of a highly aggressive boxing match with a taped ending given in one of three alternative versions. The first version stressed a *positive outcome* with the protagonist leaving the ring in good physical condition, and later going on to a life of success and fame. An alternate version depicted a highly *negative outcome* with stress on the defeated boxer's injuries, a cerebral hemorrage, extreme agony, and painful death. A *control* version merely recapitulated the events of the fight. When subjects were subsequently put in the position of giving shocks to a "learner," the number of shocks they administered was significantly reduced by exposure to the *negative outcome* version. In a follow-up study using very similar procedures, this inhibitory effect was obtained even when the horrible and bloody suffering of the protagonist was not directly attributable to the fight. Comparison of mood ratings, however, indicated that this reduced aggressiveness was not due to any pleasurable, cathartic reduction of anger or tension due to the perception of suffering. Changes in anger and tension ratings were roughly the same in the different outcome conditions, and the *negative outcome* group actually reported feeling significantly *less* happy following the film. The most reasonable explanation again seems to be that the perception of the horrible effects of the violence served to *sensitize* the subjects to the potential harm that they themselves might inflict. If this rather plausable explanation for the four preceding studies can be accepted, then this conclusion again runs directly counter to the current media programming policy. Production codes for radio, television, comic books, and motion pictures all include prohibitions against the portrayal of physical agony and suffering. A leading radio and television trade magazine (*Broadcasting,* Aug. 19, 1968, p. 23) quotes one television producer as saying "Anything that shows too much agony, too much punishment, or is too bloody, anything that could be too startling, whether it's in context or whether it was done for good and valid reasons, is being taken out or reduced, wherever possible." When this kind of *de facto* self-censorship serves to "sanitize" violence by "prettying up" or entirely omitting the real consequences of aggression, the result again is the unwitting creation of the very conditions found most conducive to the instigation to aggression.

C. The Status of the Symbolic Aggression Catharsis Hypothesis

In reviewing the evidence on symbolic aggression catharsis, we have found only a single study giving any support to this doctrine; a study using paper and pencil measures of hostility obtained after the presentation, without any justifying context, of a highly aggressive fight scene. The evaluation of the implications of this one experiment provides a good example of the dangers inherent in generalizing too freely from the results of a single piece of research. Additional experiments have indicated that the results of this study were very likely due to the arousal of aggression anxiety and the subsequent inhibition of overt hostility, rather than the result of symbolic catharsis. More recent experiments that have minimized the factor of aggression anxiety, have almost uniformly found that observed violence results in the *stimulation* of aggression. These results, along with the earlier mentioned findings of modeling experiments with children, all argue against the idea that observed violence results in a "cathartic discharge of aggressive energies."

A revised formulation has been proposed, based on the idea that aggression catharsis may result from the observation of pain, horror, and suffering. Although this formulation has not been as thoroughly tested as the original, the catharsis concept has, again, not been supported; while the observation of intense suffering may temporarily inhibit aggressive responses, this is probably not due to a cathartic process.

In light of the persistent belief in symbolic aggression catharsis, and the volume of research evidence against it, the time has perhaps come to recognize the extremely limited validity of the symbolic catharsis doctrine. This conclusion should not be too surprising. Bandura (1965) has pointed out that we would scarcely advocate that adolescents be shown libidinous films as a means of reducing sexual behavior, nor would we advise that a starving man observe the eating of a delicious meal in order to diminish his hunger pangs. Similarly, we should not expect that the outpourings of violence in the mass media will have the effect of reducing aggressive behavior.

Perhaps some of the persistence of the belief in the aggression catharsis notion has stemmed from a misapplication of Aristotle's original conception of catharsis. Goodman (1964) has noted that Aristotle's use of the word *catharsis* applied only to "tragic" feelings, the emotions of grief and fear which could be discharged through active expression by the audience. It is likely that, in the case of aggression, Aristotle would have predicted the very effects of observed violence that have so consistently been found—a facilitation, rather than a reduction, of aggressive behavior.

Appendix III-E

THE CATHARSIS EFFECT:
RESEARCH AND ANOTHER VIEW*

The question of the effects of viewing aggressive content on TV is very much an open one. On the one hand, there are survey data on the basis of which it is difficult to establish functional relationships and, on the other, laboratory studies with reasonably clear causal interpretations, based on small samples, whose generalizability and applicability to naturalistic TV exposure and real life effects are questionable. What appeared to be required was an experimental study involving prolonged and intensive viewing of TV aggressive versus non-aggressive content and measurement of effects on overt aggressive behaviors such as fighting and swearing, and mediating cognitive structure and covert behaviors such as hostile-aggressive attitudes, preferences and fantasies. It also appeared desirable to take into account individual differences in aggressive drive, overt aggressive expression, emotional control and related personality and demographic variables which might contribute to or modify the influence of TV exposure.

In order to gain control over the total TV viewing activities of the boys, it was decided that only boys who were living in a prep school, military academy, or other type of school or home for boys would be utilized in the study. In this way, the staff members of the schools and institutions and the experimenters would have complete control over the question of how much and what type of TV viewing would be engaged in by each boy. In addition, the use of residential settings would greatly facilitate the recording of the boy's behavior, especially in regard to aggressive incidents. Altogether, seven schools and institutions, five in the Greater Los Angeles area and two·in the greater New York City area participated in the research project.

A. Hypotheses

The investigator of this study has been associated with and has done previous research bearing on the catharsis hypothesis. He has demonstrated

---

*Excerpts from a larger paper, "Effects of Exposure to Aggressive Content in Television Upon Aggression in Boys" (review of literature, detailed data and analysis omitted) by Seymour Feshbach, Professor of Psychology, University of California, Los Angeles.

that when certain conditions are met, exposure to aggressive fantasy leads to a lowering of aggressive drive. He has also been instrumental in delineating the conditions under which aggressive drive can be increased by aggressive play and vicarious aggressive activities. On the basis of this research and the critique and evidence provided by other investigators, the following general hypotheses are proposed:

1. Children high on both overt aggression and covert hostility will show a cathartic effect and will show significantly less direct aggression and less fantasy hostility and related effects after long-term exposure to aggressive TV content as compared to similar exposure to non-aggressive TV content.

2. Children low on both overt aggression and covert hostility will experience disinhibiting and arousing effects and will show a rise in covert hostile fantasy and on related variables and, possibly, a rise in some aspects of overt aggression after exposure to non-aggressive TV content.

3. Children high on covert hostility and low on overt aggression will show a significant decrement in fantasy aggression and a significant increment in direct aggression after exposure to aggressive TV content as compared to similar exposure to non-aggressive TV content.

These hypotheses are based upon the following assumptions and arguments:

(a) High covert aggression is assumed to be indicative of strong aggressive drive, while low covert aggression is more ambiguous and may indicate either weak drive or strong inhibition.

(b) The high covert, low overt aggressive children are assumed to be relatively high in aggression anxiety while the children who are high in both forms of aggression are assumed to be relatively low in aggression anxiety.

(c) Covert aggression is assumed to be a more sensitive indicator of aggressive drive than overt aggression, whereas the latter is relatively more influenced by aggression anxiety and is probably a better index of the strength of the predisposition to respond with instrumental aggression.

(d) Displaced aggression (particularly where it takes a socially approved form) is a positive function of inhibition as well as of aggressive drive and aggressive habits.

(e) Exposure to aggressive TV content will tend to reduce the level of aggressive drive and aggression anxiety of the high covert, low direct aggressive children and, at the same time, tend to reinforce aggressive acts.

(f) Changes in aggression in children who are initially high in direct as well as covert aggression will primarily reflect the cathartic effects of sustained exposure to aggressive TV content since these children already freely express aggression.

(g) In the case of children who are initially low in covert and direct aggression, there is minimal opportunity for drive reduction to take place and the stimulating and reinforcing consequences of exposure to aggressive TV content will be paramount.

B. Methods

1. Subjects

Seven residential schools and institutions, five in the southern California area and two in the greater New York area, participated in the project. The California group consisted of three private schools—the Cate School, the Ojai Valley School, the Army and Navy Academy and two boys' homes: The McKinley Home for Boys and the Pacific Lodge Boys' Home. The New York institutions were both Catholic homes for boys: St. Vincent's Home and St. John's Home. Both the Cate School and the Army and Navy Academy are boys' schools. The Ojai Valley School is coeducational and, primarily for administrative reasons, a small number of girls were included in the experiment conducted at the school.

The three private schools all provide college preparatory programs, charge approximately similar sums for tuition and residence costs, and draw their children from primarily upper middle class homes. The Cate School offers a four-year high school curriculum while the Army and Navy Academy and Ojai Valley have junior high divisions. The latter also has an elementary program with the age range descending to eight, and also differs from the others in being coeducational. The atmosphere, goals, and population of the Cate School are very similar to those of the better New England prep schools. The Ojai Valley students are somewhat more heteogeneous in ability, and the atmosphere at the school tends to be more informal, and native Californian. The population of the Army and Navy Academy is still more heterogeneous than that of Ojai and the academy, being a military school, presents still another atmosphere as compared to Cate and Ojai. The Pacific Lodge Boys' Home is a charitable institution and is supported by the Los Angeles County United Way and various child placing agencies. The purpose of the institution, as is the case for each of the other boys' homes, is to provide general supervision, treatment and guidance to boys. Pacific Lodge focuses on adolescents, age at entrance usually being thirteen to fifteen, the boy being placed for reasons of social and personal adjustment difficulties or lack of adequate home care. The McKinley Home provides residential care and treatment for boys between the ages of eight and eighteen. They accept placements from parents and guardians as well as social agencies and have special fee arrangements with the former group. The children from both homes receive their education training at local public schools. St. Vincent's Home for Boys and St. John's Home for Boys have similar populations, except that the average age of the St. John's boy is younger, ranging within the junior high or high school level, while St. Vincent's has a number of high school age boys. Both institutions are run by the Archdiocese of Brooklyn and, like McKinley and Pacific Lodge, are intended for boys whose families are unable or unfit to take care of them.

In addition to boys at the participating institutions, the personality inventories were administered for normative purposes, at school to boys living with their families. One school, the Bishop Ford High School in Brooklyn, draws, by and large, on a lower middle-class population, with a minority of working class and upper middle-class families. The second school, a Queens junior high school, had children from chiefly working class families with about one-third lower middle-class.

2. Sample Size

The size of the experimental sample was subject to considerable fluctuation, depending upon the measures in question. There were 665 participants who were randomly assigned to the aggressive or control (nonaggressive) TV viewing groups, and for whom behavior observations are available. The number who took the premeasures and whose forms were legible was 516. This difference is largely due to 121 boys from the Army and Navy Academy who were not present at the pre-test for reasons of illness, lateness or submission of unusable forms, but who participated in the TV viewing. As Table 1 indicates, the number is still lower for the post-test and drops to 341 for the pre-test change measures. Differential absences on the pre-test and post-tests, unsigned questionnaires and one difficult to match, and some withdrawal from the experiment during the last few weeks were the major reasons for the smaller NUMBER available for the prepost change comparisons for the questionnaire data. Table 1 lists the NUMBER's for each of the participating institutions. For this table the following letter code was used for these institutions:

A. Cate School
B. McKinley Home
C. Pacific Lodge Home
D. Army and Navy Academy
E. Ojai Valley School
F. St. Vincent's Home
G. St. John's Home

3. Procedure

The experimental procedures and objectives were reviewed in detail with the headmasters and directors of the participating institutions. In two instances, the Army and Navy Academy and St. Vincent's Home, participation by the boys was compulsory. In each of the other five institutions, the boys volunteered for the project. The boys and the cottage supervisors and teachers who were to record and rate their behavior were told that the study was concerned with the relationship between the evaluation of different types of TV programs and the personality and attitudes of the viewer. They were further told that they would be assigned to a specific set of programs and that one of the conditions for participation in the experiment was that they stick to the specified set of programs. The reasons given for assigning individuals to particular program groups or "diets" were twofold: first, it would insure that there would be continuity in the

Table 1.—Number of subjects by school in the experiment and participating in the Premeasure and Postmeasure

			Schools				
	A	B	C	D	E	F	G
Ss participating (behavior observations available):							
Control	18	46	26	113	36	50	20
Aggressive TV	18	36	23	118	35	62	24
Total	36	82	49	231	71	112	44
N available for premeasures after absences and exclusions of illegible forms:							
Control	18	43	23	73	36	50	18
Aggressive TV	18	33	22	67	33	53	24
Total	36	76	45	140	69	103	42
N available after postmeasures after absences and exclusion of illegible forms:							
Control	1	39	26	83	36	50	18
Aggressive TV	7	24	22	81	32	54	23
Total	8	63	48	164	68	104	41
N available for prepost change questionnaire measures:							
Control	1	37	23	48	36	42	16
Aggressive TV	7	23	21	38	31	49	23
Total	8	60	44	86	67	91	39

A: Cate
B: McKinley
C: Pacific Lodge
D: Army & Navy
E: Ojai
F: St. Vincent's
G: St. John's

viewing and that we could get some information based on repeated viewing of the same program or same type of program; second, it was stated that we would get better evaluations of a particular program if the viewers were familiar with similar programs. Most of the boys and the supervisors appeared to accept these explanations as sufficient. Intensive interviewing of a sample of participants following completion of the experiment indicated that while several felt that the object of the project was to study the influence on children of exposure to aggression on television, a substantial majority accepted the explanation of the experimenters or else entertained some other hypothesis irrelevant to the main purpose of the study.

There were two procedures used for assignment of subjects to the aggressive or control (non-aggressive) TV diets. In the case of Ojai, Cate, and the Army and Navy Academy, the boys were randoming assigned to an aggressive or control treatment on an individual basis. The TV programs were viewed in classrooms and, in a few instances, in faculty homes. The boys' dormitory and room arrangements at these schools did not permit adequate centralized control in their dwelling area. The situation for the various boys' homes where the children were clustered in cottages or on floors with supervisors living with them, was quite different. Here it was best to have the TV sets located in the dwelling units. In the case of McKinley, individual cottages, initially paired for age, were randomly assigned to one of the two experimental treatments. At Pacific Lodge, random assignment of both individuals and clusters of boys was utilized. Half of a dwelling unit was assigned to the Aggressive and half to the Control treatment. At St. Vincent's and St. John's, the boys on one end of a floor were assigned to one of the two treatment conditions and those at the other end of the floor assigned to the other treatment. The size of the viewing groups at these different settings varied from 10 to 18.

The boys were required to watch a minimum of six hours of television a week for a period of six weeks. At St. Vincent's and St. John's, the minimum was closer to fourteen hours (two-hour viewing periods, seven days a week). The participants could view as much television as they wanted, provided they watched programs from the designated list. After each program they watched, the boys individually indicated the degree to which they liked the program and the effects it elicited, on a TV program rating form provided them. At St. John's and St. Vincent's, they were required to complete a form for only one program a day rather than after each program seen.

At three of the institutions, monitors or "captains" were appointed from among the boys to help the cottage mother, staff counselor or teacher collect the forms and regulate the TV viewing. To encourage the cooperation of the boys and to help make the experiment a positive experience for them, they were each promised and given a sum of ten dollars for completing the six week viewing period. This was not done at the Army and Navy Academy and probably should have been, in view of the number of boys at that school who managed not to take the pre-test and post-test. Every effort was made to reduce possible sources of frustration associated with the experiment. Thus, boys were permitted to drop out if they wished (even where participation was initially compulsory), since it was felt that resentment induced by forced compliance might override any experimental effect. When a number of boys in the control group at three of the institutions objected very strongly because Batman was not on their list, they were permitted to watch Batman. We were very conscious of the fact that, on the whole, the aggressive diet was more attractive to the boys and tried to minimize any frustration associated with being assigned to the control diet.

4. The Television Programs

The current programs on TV that appeared during the evening and weekend hours during which television was available to the boys, were categorized as aggressive or non-aggressive by three raters. Differences between raters occurred infrequently, the percentage of aggreement between pairs of raters varying from 90 to 96. Programs which depicted fighting, shooting, and other forms of physical violence were considered aggressive. These included cowboy, spy, detective, police and war themes. It is of interest that there are many more non-aggressive programs from which the control group could choose as compared to the choices available to the experimental group.

5. Measures

A number of personality tests and attitude scales were administered at the beginning and at the end of the six week experimental period. In addition, daily behavior rating forms were completed for each child for the experimental period and, in most instances, during the week before and the week after the six week TV viewing period.

C. Discussion and Conclusion

The experimental results are consistent and some of the findings, particularly those bearing on the acting out of aggression, are striking. The most modest conclusion that one can make from the data is that exposure to aggressive content in television over a six week period does not produce an increment in aggressive behavior. The only measure on which the Controls, as a whole, decreased relative to the Aggressive TV group was Fantasy Aggression. About all one can state regarding this latter finding is that boys who witness a great deal of non-aggressive content in television will make up fewer stories in which fighting takes place than boys who watch a greal deal of fighting on television. While there was some suggestion from the behavioral middle-class sample, the prepondersance of nonsignificant findings for this population renders occasional significant findings highly questionable.

The results in fact strongly indicate that witnessing aggressive TV programs serves to reduce or control the acting out of aggressive tendencies rather than to facilitate or stimulate aggression. This generalization requires qualification, particularly in regard to the populations to which it applies. This effect is pronounced in children with certain personality and social characteristics and is weak or absent in other personality constellations. We need also to examine the conditions of the experiment and consider possible alternative explanations of the findings. Nevertheless, what is most compelling about these data is the regularity with which the obtained differences in aggressive behaviors and changes in aggressive attitudes and values point to a reducing or controlling rather than to a stimulating or disinhibiting effect resulting from exposure to aggressive interaction in television programs.

In designing this study, it was decided to use as experimental materials standard television fare rather than specially constructed or selected programs. In doing so we sacrificed control of the structure, format, and precise content of the experimental stimuli but gained in representativeness and the extent to which the findings can be generalized to the kind of programs that are currently presented on television. This generalization also implies a restriction. The aggressive content which the boys witnessed by no means encompasses the full range of violence and brutality that is possible to depict on film or videotape. It may be that programs in which particular forms of aggression and brutality are rampant and are reinforced would have different effects than the programs observed by the Aggressive TV group. These data apply only to the type of aggressive material that is currently portrayed on television in this country, or to be more exact, in southern California and greater New York.

The generalization about the effects of these programs is further limited by the 6 week duration of the experimental period. A longer period could conceivably have resulted in the elimination of differences between the Experimental and Control groups and perhaps even a reversal. This latter possibility seems a most unlikely one, judging from the experimental data. There were no indications of a trend which, if extrapolated, would have resulted in the Aggressive TV group manifesting more aggression than the Control group. A longer duration might have exaggerated the differences between the Experimental and Control groups and would very likely have produced boredom and indifference in both. The question of the effects of the length of duration of the experimental period is a different question than that of the length of time to which children in this culture are exposed to violence in television. Our experimental sample is drawn from a population that has had a history of exposure to television and to other mass media. We have made only a brief intrusion into that history and our inferences are restricted to the consequences of this intrusion. We began with boys who have been already conditioned by their society and then considered the behavioral consequences of a systematic variation in their subsequent experiences. How this experimental variation would influence children from a completely different culture, children who are much younger, or children who have never been previously exposed to television or films is a question to which the present study was not addressed.

Within the restrictions of sample characteristics, range of stimuli utilized and the duration of the experimental period, there are two major conclusions indicated by the experimental findings:

   1. Exposure to aggressive content in television does not lead to a noticeable increase in aggressive behavior; and

   2. Exposure to aggressive content in television seems to reduce or control the expression of aggression.

The first conclusion is a weaker inference than the second. Although a negative assertion or statement of no difference tends to have little theoretical import, its application to social implications may have considerable significance. The major question that arises in evaluating any such assertion is methodological, particularly in regard to the reliability of the measures, their sensitivity to changes and the degree to which the "laboratory" procedure relates to the "real life" phenomena of interest. With respect to the first two criteria, it is evident that the measures employed were sufficiently reliable and sensitive to record significant effects of the experimental treatment, albeit these effects were in the direction of greater aggression in the Controls rather than in the Aggressive TV group. With respect to the third, a salient feature of the experimental design lies in the degree of representativeness achieved through incorporating experimental control in the context of a field setting. The manipulation of aggressive content was accomplished by controlling exposure to television programs that appear daily. The effectiveness of this controlled variation is reflected by the fact that the great majority of programs which each group watched were in accord with their experimental assignment. There is a gap between aggressive action and the measures of aggressive value and aggressive fantasy, although the former are still of great interest. However, the ratings of Peer and Authority Aggression were addressed to precisely the kinds of behaviors which are of social concern.

The second major conclusion, that witnessing aggressive content in TV serves to reduce or regulate the expression of aggression, while strongly supported by the data, may be objected to because of a design problem to which allusion has been made throughout this paper. We recognized from the very beginning of the study that boys preferred aggressive TV programs to non-aggressive ones, and were concerned about the possibility that boys might resent being assigned to the non-aggressive "diet." We were also concerned that there might be resistance to participation in the experiment regardless of diet. We implemented a number of steps designed to enhance the attractiveness of the study to the boys and to engage their interest. First, in most of the participating institutions, we used volunteers. Second, we met with the boys, reviewed the experimental procedures with them and their response was, for the most part, favorable and gratifying. In addition, with the exception of the boys in the Military Academy, we offered them ten dollars each for their participation. The boys were pleased by the prospect of receiving this money and were also pleased by the fact that new, large-screen television sets were placed in their respective dormitories, cottages, or selected schoolrooms. In the case of one school, Ojai (Institution E), we arranged to extend a TV cable to the school facilities from which TV had hitherto been absent. Finally, we maintained continuous contact with the participating institutions and, when an occasional problem arose, as in the case of the boys in the Control group wishing to see "Batman," we resolved it in favor of minimizing frustration. In terms of the design, it was essential that not all but the preponderance of programs witnessed be either aggressive or non-aggressive, depending upon whether the boy was in the Aggressive TV or Control condition. As the data indicate, this objective was achieved.

The responses of the boys to the TV programs they witnessed provide further evidence that the Control condition was not a frustrating one. The boys in this group liked most of the programs they saw and the difference between the Controls and Aggressive TV groups in the proportion of programs disliked is small, 15 percent versus 8 percent. The effective responses reported to these programs also reflected generally positive reactions by the Controls to the programs in their diet. Although their implications are indirect, the data based on the Like-Dislike ratings of the list of six aggressive and six non-aggressive programs that was included in the pre- and post-assessment are also of some relevance. While the mean ratings for the six non-aggressive programs were lower than the means for the aggressive programs, of the four institutions in which the Controls displayed significantly greater Peer Aggression than the Aggressive TV group, the initial mean rating for the non-aggressive programs was already high and two of the others showed significant increments in their mean ratings after the six week exposure period. Also to be noted is the positive correlation obtained between liking of aggressive programs and liking of non-aggressive programs, this correlation being considerably higher than the correlation obtained between the Like-Dislike ratings and the personality measures; and, as a final note, the correlations of the Like-Dislike ratings for the aggressive programs and non-aggressive programs with Peer and Authority Aggression were separately examined for the Control and Aggressive TV groups and in all instances were insignificantly different from zero.

There are no indications from these data of differential resentment. While the hypothesis cannot be completely discounted that resentment was elicited, and to a degree sufficient to account for the differences in Peer and Authority Aggression and the differential changes in the aggressive value measures, the data indicate that it is a highly improbable one.

We turn now to a consideration of possible mechanisms mediating the effects of exposure to aggressive and non-aggressive TV content. One possibility, and to us an unlikely one, is that the situation comedies seen as part of the non-aggressive diet tend to reduce restraint and thereby increase the aggressive and other behaviors which are normally inhibited. Why this process should result in an increase of the cognitive measures of aggressive value is unclear to us. More germane, however, is the fact that a number of the aggressive programs were also of this type; e.g., "Man from Uncle" and "Get Smart." Secondly, a primary characteristic of the aggressive shows is the reduced restraint in connection with the expression of aggression. This ready expression of aggression is more specific and salient than the reduction of inhibition sometimes depicted in the situation comedies. Of course, aggression as depicted in the Aggressive TV shows is frequently followed by punishment, a sequence which may serve to foster inhibition of aggressive expression. Increased inhibition of aggression would account for the tendency of the Aggressive TV group (in those institutions showing an experimental effect) to decline in Peer Aggression over the 6 week period, but is less satisfactory in accounting for the increments in the Controls on the change measures. Since these changes are at best relative, this objection is by no means crucial.

Because we did not attempt to control the stimulus properties of the TV programs seen within a particular diet, we cannot exclude the possibility that factors associated with aggressive and non-aggressive content may be responsible for the observed changes or may contribute, along with the variations in exposure to aggressive content, to the experimental effects. However, both theoretical considerations and data pattern suggest that a "binding" or substitute value function of exposure to aggressive content is a primary mechanism determining the experimental findings.

The findings are consistent with the view that vicarious aggressive experiences may serve to help regulate and partially satisfy aggressive tendencies. The term "experience" should be modified and restricted to "fantasy experience." The effect of vicarious experiences such as might be provided by observing actual aggressive incidents may be radically different from the effects of vicarious fantasy. The message of reality should be distinguished from the message of fantasy. They convey different information and the psychological relationship of the observer to each of these experiences differ.

There is now a fair degree of evidence that the cognitive activity of fantasy whether in the form of thoughts, dreams, stories or reveries, enables both child and adult to delay and control the immediate expression of impulses.

This proposition, initially formulated by Freud, has been expanded and applied by psychoanalytic ego psychology to a wide variety of phenomena. The present findings can be fruitfully viewed in this context.

Boys like to watch aggressive TV programs, at least boys raised in this culture. It seems plausible to assume that this experience has some functional value for them. One function may be vicarious satisfaction. A related but different function is cognitive support in controlling the expression of aggressive tendencies. The boys assigned to the Aggressive TV diet were provided with an opportunity for substitute satisfaction and additional cognitive supports. For the children in the boys' homes, the aggressive TV diet represented less of a change in their TV viewing behavior than was the case for the boys in the private schools who had less time and opportunity to watch television. Nonetheless, it was a change for the former group. Placing the boys on the Control diet had something of the quality of a deprivation experience, especially for the lower socioeconomic sample. The findings are reminiscent of the results of the effects of dream deprivation upon subsequent dreaming. Removal of the cognitive support and partial substitute that probably was provided by previous exposure to aggressive TV apparently resulted in increased acting out of aggressive behavior. This effect is most marked in boys who have strong aggressive tendencies and therefore a greater need for cognitive controls. The lack of an overall effect for the children in the private schools may be due to the availability of other outlets, enhanced cognitive skills, and less use of television.

The reduction in aggressive fantasy in the Controls is, in some respects, inconsistent with this explanation since one might have expected deprivation to have resulted in an increase in aggressive fantasy. However, the associative influence of the social interactions recently witnessed on television may have had an overriding influence on the thematic content of the stories given in response to the stimulus cards. In addition, it may be that TV and other media provide cognitive supports for the expression of aggression in TAT type fantasy, especially in children who do not habitually rely on this mode of control.

The findings for the boys initially above and below the mean in fantasy aggression and in overt aggression (based on peer nominations) are of interest in this regard. One possible explanation of these findings is that boys who are high in fantasy aggression but do not express their aggressive tendencies overtly may need the additional support provided by the TV fantasy experience to control their aggressive impulses. Boys who are low in aggressive fantasy but act out their aggressive tendencies may also need the support and substitute outlet provided by TV to control their aggressive behavior.

It must be acknowledged that these interpretations of the data are essentially *ad hoc* explanations although the hypotheses initially proposed did suggest that aggressive TV would have a cathartic or substitute function for certain personality constellations. The mechanisms suggested require further substantiation and it is in regard to the delineation of these processes that laboratory studies can make a unique contribution. Assertions regarding the behavioral consequences of aggressive content in television as contrasted to the mechanisms mediating those consequences are soundest when based upon direct assessment of the effects of TV exposure rather than extrapolation from laboratory experiments. Clearly, additional field investigations are needed both to confirm and to extend the findings of the present study.

Some of the factors responsible for conflicting results obtained in laboratory studies and many of these same factors (variations in initial level of hostility, nature of the dependent measure) pertain to differences between the outcome of some laboratory experiments and the results of the present study. An extensive review and critical analysis of this same area has been made by Hartley (1964) and theoretical issues germane to the frequently conflicting results have been considered elsewhere (Feshbach, 1964). As has been suggested in the formulation of the design of the present experiment, previous studies in this area are not directly comparable. The laboratory experiments deal with highly restricted situations, with dependent measures that are often playlike, and are vulnerable to the suggestive properties of the immediate stimulus situation. While the field studies have been more naturalistic, they have not experimentally controlled exposure to aggressive content in television. For these reasons, there is an acute need for comparable experimental field investigations and replication of the present findings.

Thus we would not advocate, on the basis of the present findings, that boys should be encouraged to watch aggressive TV programs. However, this study failed to reveal any evidence that exposure to aggressive content in television stimulates or facilitates the acting out of aggressive behavior, but did yield evidence suggesting that exposure to aggressive content in television serves to control or reduce aggressive behavior in lower socioeconomic status and aggressive preadolescent and adolescent boys.

Appendix III-F

THE WORLDVIEW PRESENTED
BY MASS MEDIA*

It is important to know not only the effectiveness of specific pieces of mass communication in promoting specific kinds of behavior or instilling specific kinds of values in specific categories of audience members, but also to try to understand the overall impact of the deluge of mass communication on the kind of worldview held by the exposed population. This problem has not been studied in the depth it requires, but one way to begin is by looking at various aspects of the worldview implicit in the long run patterns of media content.

A. *Anomie*

When there is a prevalent view that socially undesirable means are necessary to the attainment of socially desirable goals, a state of *anomie* may be said to exist. Some hypothetical examples: a belief that one has to cheat on his income tax return to avoid paying more than his fair share of the tax burden because "everyone else" is probably cheating; a belief that deceptive packaging of merchandise is necessary to keep up a sufficient sales volume to stay in business; or a belief that a politician has to make promises he knows he won't be able to fulfill because his opponent will anyway, and otherwise he can't get elected to do the good things his opponent has no intention of doing. *Anomie* represents, then, a condition of society in which means are not regulated by social norms as effectively as ends are prescribed by social values.

There is evidence that this is the kind of world depicted by at least some of the mass media. A content analysis by Larsen, Gray, and Fortis of eighteen television programs examined the way the stories paired off seven standard goals with eight recurrent methods of goal achievement. Six of the eighteen were adult programs, six were children's programs, and six were "kidult" programs—meant for both. There were few significant differences among the three categories in the combinations of ends-with-means they presented. Regardless of the type of programs viewed by children, then, they

---

*A paper prepared for the Media Task Force by William R. Catton, Jr., Professor of Sociology, University of Washington.

would be exposed to essentially the same sorts of means-ends combinations. The content analysis revealed a prevalent pattern of portraying socially disapproved means as the most effective in achieving socially approved ends. Thus, a condition of *anomie* is continuously and pervasively portrayed in the fantasy world of television, as represented in this sample of programs.[1]

These researchers pointed out the need for further studies to see whether the anomie implicit in the means-ends combinations commonly shown on TV is absorbed by viewers. Do viewers transfer this image from the fantasy world to the real world? Such studies, it was suggested, might best be carried out with school populations. If further inquiry were to reveal that belief in the necessity for using socially disapproved methods of goal achievement varies directly with the amount of exposure to television, then there would be the implication of a direct effect.[2]

But these are just stories, and the world they depict is just a fantasy world. Is there reason to suppose that most viewers even apply the image derived from these stories to the real world around them? Media apologists might ask such a question rhetorically, implying assurance that no such application occurs. But if the media can be completely exonerated from any responsibility for instilling anomic attitudes in receptive children by their portrayal of *anomie* in their dramatic content, then their efforts to sell products in the face of audience awareness of their intent and consequent audience sales resistance can hardly be assumed to be any more effective.

The fact is that media men and businessmen do assume that mass advertising sells goods. It is claimed that "The effectiveness of radio, and more recently of television, as advertising media requires no documentation beyond noting that American businessmen have invested hundreds of millions of dollars in radio and television advertising."[3] If such advertising is, as assumed, effective in selling goods, then mass communication of anomic images may sell *anomie,* whether this is intended or not. If the entertainment content of television can portray an anomic world without assuming any responsibility for the possible inculcation of anomic attitudes in its audience, then the validity of the assumption of the selling power of mass communication and television is implicitly practicing a fraud in selling air time to advertisers. To defend the television medium from this charge of fraud is to abandon the defense it would otherwise invoke against the charge of teaching *anomie,* and vice versa.

Faith that mass communication can and does persuade is abundantly expressed in the sponsorship of persuasion campaigns. These are not limited to the selling of merchandise. For example, the Dallas Citizens Council undertook to prepare the people of Dallas, for peaceful desegregation of schools in 1961, and made elaborate use of both interpersonal communication and the printed broadcast media. A film was produced, called "Dallas at the Crossroads," narrated anonymously by Walter Cronkite of CBS. The film was shown first, on request, to clubs, organized groups, labor meetings, Sunday schools, etc., in which it could be imbedded in a preliminary statement and a followup discussion. It was shown on television only at the close of the campaign.[4]

To take another example, there have recently been conspicuous increases in the use of Negro actors in various roles in TV drama and in commercials. This change implies the assumption that the presentation of Negroes in such roles will either (1) correct undesirable attitudes in white viewers, or (2) persuade Negro viewers that TV is non-racist. Such an assumption can hardly be reconciled with the claim that TV portrayal of crime, violence, and *anomie* has no effect on viewers' attitudes toward these things. If the latter claim is true, then the assumption that putting Negroes into dramatic and commercial roles will affect audience attitudes is questionable.

Major television program series have recently been aired for the obvious purpose of affecting audience attitudes and information. CBS, with Xerox sponsorship, showed the series, "Of Black America," with Negro comic and actor Bill Cosby as a narrator. ABC showed "Time for Americans," with Negro singer-actor Harry Belafonte. The assumption that these programs were worth showing was based partly on the expectation that they might change attitudes as well as enlighten the audience.[5] Yet this assumption is difficult to reconcile with the supposition that anomie in television drama will not affect attitudes. It would require us to suppose that viewers are *more* resistive to attitude change from entertainment programs through incidental learning and the modeling effect (when they're not on their guard) and *less* resistive to attitude change by documentary programs which make their "message" obvious.

Moreover, there is research which indicates that attitudes are affected by entertainment content, and specifically that anomic program plots may foster anomic attitudes. Zajonc compared two groups of children who listened to different versions of a radio "space" program, and a control group which responded to his questionnaire without exposure to either program version. He found an overwhelming tendency for a character's success, rather than the acceptability of his methods, to influence a child's desire to be like that character.[6] Bandura has described an experiment with two groups of nursery school children. One group was shown a film (projected through a TV console) showing a child aggressively seizing another child's favorite toys and kicking and hitting the other child. The other group saw the same film but with the villain receiving punishment at the end. After the showings, there was more imitation of the villain by the former group than by the latter. But even though they imitated his aggressive behavior, the children criticized him for it. Their imitation resulted from recognition that the villain's actions were successful, not from accepting them as decent.[7] In short, the film produced a tendency toward anomic behavior.

In describing the world of television drama, Himmelweit, Oppenheim, and Vince had some things to say which not only indicated anomic images of the world on British television, but also suggested the possible internalization of such images by viewers:

> Television plays teach that self-confidence and toughness are needed to achieve success—goodness of character is not enough; that life is difficult, especially for women; that marriages are frequently unhappy, and parent-child relationships often strained. Events rarely turn out satisfactorily and virtue seldom brings happiness in its train. Violence is an inevitable part of life, and good people often resort to it. For the adult observer a hackneyed view of life emerges, similar in many ways to that offered in films or in the theatre; for the child television may afford a glimpse of adult life which he would otherwise gain less often and only at a later age.[8]

Adolescent viewers were found to be, in comparison with non-viewers, more worried or even frightened about growing up, getting out of school, leaving their homes, getting their first jobs, and marrying. This was especially true of girls. The "anxiety-laden view of life" conveyed by adult plays on TV seemed to disturb adolescent girls, possibly because television offers few positive models for them, either in children's or adult's programs.[9]

As shown by responses of British children to the instruction to "Write down what sort of person you would like to be when you are 25 years old," television seems to increase viewers' interest in material things. The more they had been exposed to TV, the more likely children were to cite possession of specified material things (like cars and houses) as indicators of the kind of person they wanted to become.[10]

B. Dominance of Television

Television takes up time in the lives of today's children and adults that was not simply unoccupied a generation ago when there was no television. To have displaced other ways of spending time, television watching must have acquired value as an activity in its own right. But certain attributes of the medium contribute to its capacity to displace other things which, on some grounds, might be deemed more valuable.

In response to the question, "Do you like TV better than books?" Shayon quotes an 11-year-old boy as saying, "If there's really a terrific program, like a World Series game, I'd rather see it. I can read a book later. If the program isn't exciting, I'll take the book."[11] At least two implications can be drawn from this probably typical response. First, some programs may be ranked higher than some books (or other activities) on a child's value scale, and vice versa. Second, whatever the comparative value of a given television program and an alternative activity, the television program may take precedence simply because it is nonrecurrent. "I can read a book later" means "I may not have another chance to see this program." The individual television program has a "fugitive" value to the degree that it is expected not to be shown again, which enables it to displace other activities of greater non-fugitive value but lacking this special attribute of non-postponability.[12]

Compare television viewing with reading. Reading gives the appearance of inactivity, so people who are not reading commonly feel free to interrupt readers. Some readers may be annoyed when interrupted; few fully recognize the reason people unwillingly define reading as an activity which is permissible to interrupt; most will respond to the interruption without much overt indication of their annoyance, expecting to be able to resume reading in a moment. Since written matter is permanent, one can resume reading at the same point where one was interrupted. But this is not so for media like television. An interruption means an irrevocable loss, because the television program goes right on during the interruption. For adults, perhaps, there is sufficient awareness of this so that they may be somewhat more inhibited from interrupting another adult's television viewing.

In terms of the way values are inferred from preferential behavior, and are learned in part from inferring them in the behavior of persons with whom one identifies, any greater reluctance to interrupt television viewing than to interrupt reading could convey the impression that television is *accorded* more value than print.[13] Moreover, to the child, for whom the irrevocability of the loss experienced by his viewing parent when interrupted by the child is simply not comprehended, the parent's rebuke can convey the impression that watching television is more highly valued by the parent than interacting with the child. The parent seems to "defer" to the TV set more than to the child. It is not inconceivable that television thus has the power to create rifts between parents and children just by its very nature, quite qpart from disputes over what content is permissible or preferable for which members of the family to watch. Even the best-intentioned parents may be somewhat poorer parents because of television's power to dominate (at least in some degree) their lives and their interactions within the family.

C. Degradation of Values

The first generation of Americans wholly socialized within the era of nearly ubiquitous television has just come of age. For many of them, it is likely that this visual medium has greater apparent credibility than other media.[14] With this in mind, it is important to take account of the way values in any group tend to be organized around some value motif upon which the other values are more or less dependent.[15] With mass media, especially with television, the motif appears to be entertainment or fantasy. All else is organized around this and more or less subordinated to it—but conjoined to a second motif that is only subordinate to this one from the viewer's but not necessarily the broadcaster's point of view: salesmanship. Apart from what is known or believed about the audience effects of specific entertainment content, or specific acts of salesmanship, almost no scientific inquiry into the broadest effects of these two central value motifs has been attempted. But the issue is important enough to warrant some careful guesses based on general observation, and on applicable theoretical perspectives.

Bandura and Walters have pointed out that learned patterns of response tend to be generalized to situations beyond the one in which the pattern may have been learned. The extent of the generalization varies with degree of similarity between the learning situation and the other situations with their novel cues. It is also possible for responses to be "overgeneralized," which is to say, to be applied to other situations on the basis of similarity of irrelevant cues. In such cases, the behavior may be maladaptive.[16] To be effective, social learning must involve both adequate generalization and sharp discrimination or avoidance of inappropriate overgeneralization. When the reinforcements experienced in the learning process are haphazard, these two criteria of effective learning are unlikely to be met.[17]

In this theoretical framework, then, consider the following statement about the way television distorts its viewers' picture of the world. It does so

> ... by diminishing our opportunity to select and isolate the things to which we shall give attention. We grow accustomed to the weirdest of juxtapositions: the serious and the trivial, the comic and the tragic. . . . Here is a collapse of values, a fantasia of effects that resembles the debris left by a storm.[18]

This collapse of values and debris-like quality is illustrated daily by the

Mass Media and Violence

interpolation of singing commercials into the television newscasts in which all manner of events which have recently occurred are intoned in approximately the same portentous or somber voice, whether their consequences are of moment to the world, the nation, the state, the community, or only to some individual celebrity. Occasionally, however, the pattern is made flagrantly incongruous by the tragic content of the day's news.

Consider, for example the way the Huntley-Brinkley report began on June 5, 1968:

> *Chet Huntley*: Senator Robert F. Kennedy was shot in the head and gravely wounded early today before hundreds of people in his political headquarters in a Los Angeles hotel, a month and a day after the assassination of Dr. Martin Luther King in Memphis, seconds after he had made a speech celebrating his victory over Senator Eugene McCarthy in the California Democratic presidential primary. . . .

Continuing the reporting of this event, the scene was shifted to the hospital:

> *Jack Perkins*: The latest medical bulletin . . . says Senator Robert Kennedy remains in extremely critical condition. . . .

Frank Mankiewicz, the Senator's press secretary was then shown reading the medical bulletin. Perkins had some more to say, and then the camera returned to Chet Huntley for further reporting of certain aspects of the situation. He was followed by the face and clipped voice of David Brinkley.

> *David Brinkley*: . . . we have assembled some of the film from last night, beginning with the Senator's victory speech at the Ambassador Hotel, after he won the California primary.

The film, lasting several minutes, showed the speech, the cheers from the crowd, the moment of the shooting and the ensuing pandemonium and near-panic, the frantic and repeated requests for a doctor, the wounded Senator on the floor, police cars taking the suspect away to jail with crowd reactions as he is brought out and sirens fading into the distance, and then the grief-stricken crowd in the hall again. Then this:

> *Announcer*: The Huntley-Brinkley report is produced by NBC News and brought to you in color by Newport, the smoothest tasting menthol cigarette—Newport king size, and the new extra long Newport Deluxe 100's.

Then a filmed commercial showing a frivolous barbershop scene:

> Said a patron whose name was McNair,
> As the barber was trimming his hair;
> "This new cigarette has the roughest taste yet!
> Who's got a smooth one to spare?"
> Then up spoke a fellow named Dave
> Who had just finished having a shave:

"Newport, you'll find, is a much smoother kind,
With a taste about which you will rave."
Chorus: Ooooooh, Smoother Newport, Fresher Newport—
Smoother, more refreshing cigarette!

This was followed by a filmed commercial for tires sold by Phillips 66 dealers, concluding with the slogan, "At Phillips 66, it's performance that counts." Then:

> *David Brinkley*: The police are holding a young man charged with the shooting. . . .

No senator or presidential candidate need die in vain; his assassination can, after all, attract an audience to whom such commodities as cigarettes and tires can be sold. And children in the television audience can discover that that is what life and death are all about.

The intrusion of commercial sales pitches upon one's attention while one is trying to follow ostensibly non-commercial communication content is not limited to the broadcast media. It occurs in print as well. Consider the following striking example. In October 1968, the "November" issue of McCall's magazine appeared on the newsstands carrying the article by the late Senator Robert Kennedy entitled "Thirteen Days." The magazine proclaimed this to be an account of "the story about how the world almost ended." If there is anything that simply would not mix with product-peddling hucksterism, one might suppose it would be eschatology. Nevertheless it was virtually impossible to read continuously through this account of the unquestionably momentous decision-making processes by which the United States had coped with the Cuban missile crisis without having one's attention diverted to juxtaposed advertisements. The sequence of actions which had secured the removal of these weapons from Cuba, and which no single government could fully control or even predict, could not be followed by the reader without interruption. The precariousness of our lives, so evident in this backstage account of recent history, was offset by the advertiser's and makeup editor's skill in diverting the reader's eye from the text by the conspicuous placement of full-color advertising matter.

On the title page there was a photograph of Robert Kennedy's concerned countenance. On the first page of text there was one picture apiece of Chairman Khrushchev and President John Kennedy. Across the tops of the next two pages were small pictures of the faces of ten other principals in the story—Fidel Castro, General Taylor, Secretary McNamara, McGeorge Bundy, Secretary Rusk, Andrei Gromyko, Anatoly Dobrynin, Theodore Sorenson, George Ball, and Adlai Stevenson. There were no further illustrations germane to the story, not even any of the U-2 photographs by which the presence of the Soviet missiles in Cuba had been established, nor any pictures of the U.S. Navy ships carrying out the quarantine.

After the fourth page of text, the reader was instructed to "turn to page 148," in the center of which, surrounded by a narrow band of text, was a full color ad showing a block of cheese and a half an onion and proclaiming "Only Saran Wrap keeps them miles apart." On the next page there was even less text and an even larger ad, in color, urging the reader to "Invite your friends to munch ... Chex party mix" with Planters peanuts. Turning the page, the reader's eye was again deliberately distracted by a centrally placed color ad for Neo-Synephrine nasal drops, and on the right-hand page again, an even larger ad, in hard-to-ignore color of course, for feminine hygiene deodorant spray. Turning the page, one found three more columns of text next to one column of assorted black-and-white ads—for an anti-perspirant, an itch-relieving skin cream, a chapped lip remedy, hand lotion, a denture adhesive, and a proclamation of "cat week international" by the American Feline Society. On the facing page to the right was a full-page color ad for Christmas gift subscriptions to McCall's magazine.

Turning the page, the reader's eye might survey several more ads and read a line or two of text before discovering he had missed the fine print instruction at the bottom of the preceding page indicating that the continuation of the article was to be found on page 164, not page 154. The magazine makeup editor had not tried very hard to prevent the reader from making this error, and leafing ahead the reader would cover *twenty* pages before reaching the continuation, for the interval between page 154 and page 164 included ten additional unnumbered pages of virtually nothing but advertising, mostly in color.

Having arrived at page 164, then, the reader would find almost half of it occupied by a color ad for Kellogg's Rice Krispies, including a recipe for marshmallow treats, and more than half of the next page (facing, on the right) was devoted to a color ad for fresh almonds from California. Turning the page, one's eye was again drawn to a centered ad in color, surrounded by a thin margin of the late Senator's ominous text, used now to help sell facial tissues. To the right, on the facing page, a color ad taking up more than half the page showed an attractive young woman reclining in a bath tub to convince the "reader" of the merits of a certain brand of bath oil. Next page, a margin of text surrounding a graphic ad for Anacin, to relieve Nervous-Tension Headache—a malady less likely to have resulted from missile crises than from the would-be reader's chaotic eye movements, or even from such of life's problems as that depicted in the ad on the facing page: "How to get to the onion salt without knocking over the Worcestershire. Get a Rubbermaid turntable for 50¢ and 2 Del Monte labels" (color picture plus coupon). Next page, a centered ad, mostly black and white, for a denture cleanser. Right-hand facing page, a large color ad for continuous action cold capsules. Last page, half text, half color display (in two parts) advertising women's shoes.

Why, the reader might well wonder, *didn't* the world end?

When events of this sort are used unblushingly as bait to obtain an audience for attempts at selling products, there is need for research into the impact a lifetime of exposure to such mixtures of the momentous and the trivial will have on the values of readers, viewers, and listeners. But there is an immediate basis for inferring what has been happening to the value system of those who operate the communication media. They employ specialists whose assigned task is to make it as difficult as they can for the reader to get through an important article without being distracted by advertising, or to learn of the day's news on television without having his thoughts diverted to purchasable products. For the media operators, then, it is clear that there has already occurred an inversion of the relative significance of international crises and Saran Wrap.

Newspapers may seem relatively innocent of this degradation of values, insofar as for most American dailies the front page, at least, is all information and no advertising. But what effect does our profligate use of paper in the form of disposable daily newspapers have on our sense of the importance of any of the events and trends reported therein? Yesterday's paper is useful to most people only as fireplace kindling or as wrapping for garbage. An accumulation of last month's papers is merely a nuisance for which temporary storage must be found in basement or closet before eventual disposal to minimize both clutter and fire hazard. Does this make history itself come to seem a matter of momentary interest and long-run nuisance?

Another way in which the sense of values of mass media audiences may be degraded results from the very competition for attention. The sponsor system exerts competitive pressure on television broadcasters, for example. Sponsors and their agents "buy audiences" and are concerned with "cost per thousand" rather than with program quality as such or with television's effect on viewer's personalities. If one broadcaster doesn't give a sponsor the audience he seeks, another is willing to try. Such competition forces broadcasters to discard programs which draw small audiences. They must rely on proven formulas known to maximize audience size.[19] One effect of this is to reduce the choice available to the viewer in a multi-channel reception area. The several competing stations tend to offer essentially similar content at the same hour, so the options available to the viewer represent minor rather than major differences. Having to choose from what is available if they want to watch television at all, it becomes difficult for many viewers to imagine further alternatives.

Broadcasters themselves sometimes allude to these competitive economic processes as factors which prevent them from offering anything very much different from the material already being aired. Schramm and his associates have responded to this by suggesting that—

> ... if it is indeed to be the case that the commercial sponsorship and competitive bidding of television permit the industry to present no better opportunities for children than it does, then this seems to us a confession of failure of an entire system.[20]

One indication of the way commercial sponsorship has come to be so taken for granted that its possible sociocultural effects are seldom questioned is the way it is neglected in research. Tannenbaum and Greenberg, in an apparently exhaustive review of several years' research on mass communication processes and effects, make no mention of advertising and commercials.[21] They do offer a comment that can be related to the question of commercial sponsorship impact:

> McLuhan's central thesis can perhaps be best characterized as the Whorf hypothesis with a vengeance. He tends to see individuals and societies becoming conditioned to dominant modes or codes of communication. These, in turn, structure the way they perceive their

environment and carries the message imposes inherent constraints on form and content.[22]

The mass media as operated in the United States do appear to be impressing upon their audiences a worldview that is different from the worldview people would derive from exposure to other forms of information dissemination and entertainment. And serious questions can be raised about the long-range functionality of this worldview for society and its constituent groups.

D. *Undermining Directive Language*

Language, the basic medium of human communication, can be used for other purposes besides conveying *information*. One of these other uses is the attempt to make things happen, to influence the behavior of other persons either suggestively or imperatively. This is done in a number of ways.[23] One way is to give orders or instructions; another is to offer suggestions. These two differ only in the degree to which they imply that requested response is mandatory. But another way of using language to influence action is to assert or imply that the action desired of another by the speaker will result in certain consequences desired by the other. All of these ways constitute the *directive* uses of language, and the last form refers to direction by means of persuasion through implied promises. "Do this, and such-and-such will result."

The commercially sponsored mass media obviously use language directively in great abundance. In striving to sell products, implicit "promises" as to the gratifications to be derived from owning or using the products are offered. Many of these are so grossly exaggerated as to be almost pure fantasy—as in the implication that sexual gratification will follow the adoption of the sponsor's brand of toothpaste, or that one can experience the freedom of the open range by smoking a certain brand of cigarette. Others are not so implausible, and may be taken more or less seriously by the audience.

Knowledge of the social impact of the directive uses of language by mass media is badly needed. Evidence from various studies seems to indicate that television, as well as other media, can be effective in motivating specific purchases.[24] The principles by which mass media can be effective in this way are reasonably well understood. But what is still not clearly known is the range of unintended effects of directive mass communication. What *else* happens when a communicator persuades an audience member to buy a product?

One thing that is often overlooked in thinking about the possibilities in this area is the fact that commercial sponsorship of mass communications is not inevitable. When radio broadcasting began, it was not at first contemplated that it would be done on a commercially sponsored basis. This system evolved over a number of years, in spite of expressions of abhorrence at first and some active opposition all the way.[25]

Advertisers have sought, since television came into wide use, to make strong direct appeals to children. Children may themselves be customers for some products; for others, they can perhaps be persuaded to exert pressures on their parents, thus becoming the advertiser's accomplices. But there is mounting evidence which suggests that so much advertising is seen by even very young children that they have become as hostile as their parents to the hard-sell approach and are quite sophisticated about advertising.[26]

Television advertisements are variously evaluated by viewers. In the British samples studied by Himmelweit and associates, after BBC was supplemented with ITV, a commercial network, viewers were asked their opinions about the commercials. "I never notice them" was the response of less than three percent of the 13-14-year-olds, and of only six percent of the 10-11-year-olds. About half of the 13-14-year-olds either hated the interruptions or objected to having them come at such bad moments; only a third of the 10-11-year-olds gave these responses. About one-third of the 13-14-year-olds and one-fourth of the 10-11-year-olds welcomed the break afforded by advertisements, and about one-sixth of the older children and fully one-third of the younger ones said they looked forward to the advertisements.[27] But how well people like the commercials, or how strongly this dislike them, is only one indication of one aspect of the possible social impact of these procedures.

For social life to be possible, there must be willingness to rely on information obtained by others, based on others' observations. And it is equally imperative that people learn to report their own observations in such a way that others may rely on the reports. Insofar as the human species derives adaptive advantage from the capacity to communicate, it becomes essential that communication behavior be honest and that it be trusted.[28] Almost the same may be said of the directive uses of language. It is essential for the coordinated action that constitutes a society that men be able to use language directively, and this can be done only if people are willing to respond appropriately when others give directions. In short, excess gullibility and excess skepticism are twin perils to the effective functioning of social systems.

Sorokin was probably right in saying that the survival of mankind depends less on further great scientific or philosophical or artistic or technological achievements than on the reduction of egotism. He suggested the need for "a dynamic force effectively transfiguring individuals. . . ."[29] As presently operated, the mass media appear to be exerting a net force in the opposite direction. Ad writers who mask private interest in protestations of concern for public goals, and consistently make this kind of contribution to the deluge of directive communications in which the audience member is immersed may be contributing to the impression that there are no public goals which are sacred—which may persuade the audience member that there are no goals which are genuine. Many people readily see through inconsistencies between professed values and the values actually implicit in non-verbal behavior.[30] Spuriously altruistic values, whatever their effect on sales, may have seriously deleterious effects on the mutuality of trust that is apparently necessary to societal survival.

But again it might be supposed that there is little reason for concern because audience members respond with such obvious selectivity. If so many people ignore the commercial messages entirely, and others don't really find them objectionable, perhaps they do little social harm (and considerable good by keeping the wheels of commerce turning). The problem that remains unabated by this contention can be put in these terms: Other communication content is rather obviously subordinated to advertising, which has the observable privilege of interrupting *anything*. Yet advertising is something the audience member is free to ignore. (If he is a child, he will observe that his parents either begin to converse, or leave the room to do some errand, when there is a commercial break on television.) The inference of values is not difficult, then. The most obviously directive uses of language need not be heeded, and everything else in the communications world is subordinate to them, so everything is trivial! What else but this could be the composite message of the media?

Parents may try to teach their children to respect spokesmen for their cultural heritage, but postural and verbal cues are sometimes readily observable and easily interpretable. A person can often easily tell where a model is directing his attention, and the observer can thus imitate the model's perceptual responses.[31] When the child daily observes the way his parents ignore directive communications, he is likely to learn to ignore directive communications himself.

Parents often use non-response as a means of inhibiting behavior they disapprove. Actions of a child which evoke no parental response may soon be extinguished.[32] But the parents' ignoring of television commercials does not extinguish them. The child can observe this, and he can infer that there are adults somewhere "out there" who make the TV do what it does, and those adults persist in speaking directive language to his parents even when they ignore it. So the child fails to learn non-response as a technique of extinguishing unwanted behavior (because he has seen it not succeed), even though the child learns to ignore the commercials. Moreover, since the commercials are often louder than the content preceding and following them, the observant child may learn not only that the adults who operate the media hold values by which interruption of anything is permissible, but the interruptions may be loud and persistent.

Wertham deplores what he calls "sneering sadism" on television—by which he means the expression of cynical contempt by an aggressor for his victim.[33] His reference is to the content of crime shows, but the concept might be applied to some advertising, wherein housewives are depicted as imbeciles even though the presumed potential customers for the product being shown are also housewives. The inferences to be drawn by the child if his parents buy products advertised in this manner are obvious: (1) his parents approve of sneering sadism; (2) this is an effective means of persuasion—it has worked on them. If his parents do not buy the product in question, on the other hand, perhaps no inference will be drawn, unless they vocally denounce the particular commercial, in which case, once again the child is confronted with the implicit message that directive communications can be denounced. Yet behind it, he knows there are adults at the other end of the communication channel whose values endorse what his parents denounce.

When considered in these terms, it should take a considerable degree of obtuseness to prevent the suspicion that mass media have contributed (along with the way mixed adult and child audiences respond to them) to the behavior of today's youth which so perplexes some of their elders. The "generation gap" can be considered partly the result of inadvertent social training which has instilled in children values their parents did not mean to instill in them. Those youths who denounce or ignore all authority, who refuse to defer gratification, who seek to obtain speciously altruistic ends by violent or other antisocial means, who impose on the rights of others by interrupting and by shouting down opposition, and especially those who "drop out" and declare by behavior, appearance, and words that nothing is "relevant" or admirable, have perhaps shown an inordinate capacity for observational learning. *Anomie* is no monopoly of the younger generation, nor is value degradation.

REFERENCES

1. Otto N. Larsen, Louis N. Gray, and J. Gerald Fortis, "Goals and Goal-Achievement Methods in Television Content: Models for Anomie?" *Sociological Inquiry*, 33 (Spring, 1963), pp. 180-196.
2. *Ibid.*, p. 196.
3. G. D. Wiebe, "Merchandising Commodities and Citizenship on Television," *Public Opinion Quarterly*, 15 (Winter, 1951), p. 679; see also Otto N. Larsen, "Social Effects of Mass Communication," ch. 10 in R. E. L. Faris (ed.), *Handbook of Modern Sociology* (Chicago: Rand McNally, 1964), p. 364.
4. William R. Carmack, "Communication and Community Readiness for Social Change," *American Journal of Orthopsychiatry*, 35 (April 1964), pp. 539-543.
5. Press release from public relations office of Xerox Corp., May 23, 1968.
6. Robert Zajonc, "Some Effects of the 'Space' Serials," *Public Opinion Quarterly*, 18 (1954), pp. 367-374.
7. Albert Bandura, "What TV Violence Can Do to Your Child," reprinted from *Look*, Oct. 22, 1963, pp. 46-52 in Otto N. Larsen (ed.), *Violence and the Mass Media* (New York: Harper & Row, 1968), p. 128.
8. Hilde T. Himmelweit, A. N. Oppenheim, and Pamela Vince, *Television and the Child* (London: Oxford University Press, 1958), p. 17.
9. *Ibid.*, pp. 249, 259.
10. *Ibid.*, p. 248.
11. Robert Lewis Shayon, *Television and Our Children* (New York: Longmans, Green, 1951), p. 47.
12. Richard T. LaPiere, *A Theory of Social Control* (New York: McGraw-Hill, 1954), p. 142.
13. William R. Catton, Jr., "A Theory of Value," *American Sociological Review*, 24 (June 1959), p. 316.
14. Bradley S. Greenberg, "Media Use and Believability: Some Multiple Correlates," *Journalism Quarterly* 43 (1966), p. 669.
15. LaPiere, *op. cit.*, note 12, p. 143.
16. Albert Bandura and Richard H. Walters, *Social Learning and Personality Development* (New York: Holt, Rinehart & Winston, 1963), p. 8.
17. *Ibid.*, p. 9.
18. Shayon, *op. cit.*, note 11, p. 143.
19. Wilbur Schramm, Jack Lyle, and Edwin B. Parker, *Television in the Lives of Our Children* (Stanford, Calif.: Stanford Univ. Press, 1961), p. 180.
20. *Ibid.*, pp. 180-181.
21. Percy H. Tannenbaum and Bradley S. Greenberg, "Mass Communication," *Annual Review of Psychology*, 19 (1968), pp. 351-386.
22. *Ibid.*, p. 359; Marshall McLuhan, *Understanding Media: The Extensions of Man* (New York: McGraw-Hill, 1964); Benjamin Whorf, *Language, Thought, and Reality* (Cambridge, Mass.: The Technology Press, M.I.T., 1956).
23. S. I. Hayakawa, *Language in Action* (New York: Harcourt, Brace, 1939), ch. 7.
24. Thomas E. Coffin, "Television's Impact on Society," *American Psychologist*, 10 (1955), p. 638.
25. Melvin L. DeFleur, *Theories of Mass Communication* (New York: David McKay, 1966), p. 64.

26. Larsen, *op. cit.*, note 3, p. 356.
27. Himmelweit, Oppenheim, and Vince, *op. cit.*, note 8, p. 107.
28. Donald T. Campbell, "Variation and Selective Retention in Socio-Cultural Evolution," ch. 1 in Herbert R. Barringer, George I. Blanksten, and Raymond W. Mack (eds.), *Social Change in Developing Areas* (Cambridge, Mass.: Schenkman, 1965), p. 45.
29. Pitirim A. Sorokin, *Altruistic Love* (Boston: Beacon Press, 1950), p. v.
30. See the comment on this point by LaPiere, *op. cit.*, note 12, p. 134.
31. Bandura and Walters, *op. cit.*, note 16, p.79.
32. Richard H. Walters, Ross D. Parke, and Valarie A. Cane, "Timing of Punishment and the Observation of Consequences to Others as Determinants of Response Inhibition," *Journal of Experimental Child Psychology*, 2 (1965), p. 26.
33. Fredric Wertham, "School for Violence," in Otto N. Larsen (ed.), *Violence and the Mass Media* (New York: Harper & Row, 1968), p. 37.

Appendix III-G
CONSCIENCE FORMATION AND THE MASS MEDIA*

My first response to the charge that I should examine the relationship between mass media and violence from the point of view of a psychodynamically oriented psychiatrist was negative. Not much good can come of that, I said, and having advised against it, I proceeded to examine some of the issues. Now, the psychiatrist is a person who is concerned with the structure of a man's character. Where the experimental psychologist is concerned with the nature of a stimulus or a response, sometimes omitting consideration of what transpires in the mind between the former and the latter, the psychiatrist is prepared to assume that the man bears within himself a structure which produces a predictable response when the occasion arises. There is a very important distinction between these two points of view in that the experimental psychologist often looks for an immediate visible behavioral effect, dismissing concern with the unmeasurable aspect of how his subject might behave in the future, while the psychiatrist is prepared to accept the reality of an aspect of his patient's character which may never result in any behavior simply because the occasion does not present itself.

Now, these speculations bear a very real relationship to the problem of violence. There can be very little doubt that a violent act is the result of a complicated series of events which are not entirely predictable. The element of circumstance in any act of violence must be high. According to the Supplemental Studies for the National Advisory Commission on Civil Disorders,[1] 20 percent of Negro males declared themselves ready and willing to participate in riots as an act of protest. Yet only 3 percent actually had become involved in such an action. Obviously, one of the circumstances that would make a great difference in whether or not a person who believed in such forms of protest actually participated in a riot action would have to do with whether or not a riot occurred within a geographic vicinity which would allow the believer to participate. Similarly, whether the man, infuriated by his nagging wife, shoots her in an argument over who is to bring the milk inside, must be a function of whether or not there is a handy gun to shoot her with. It is true that some murders are premeditated, but these are in the vast minority, compared to the type of almost accidental happening outlined

*Paper prepared for the Media Task Force by Monica D. Blumenthal, Mental Health Research Institute, University of Michigan.

above. Since the nature of the precipitating event and the surrounding circumstances which allow an act of violence to occur must be regarded as somewhat accidental and having some quality of randomness, I believe it is important to ask what are the structural characteristics of a man that allow him to commit an act of violence, when such precipitating events occur. It is to this question that I wish to address myself.

In the usual psychiatric formulation, the soul is divided into three parts: (1) That primitive part of one's nature from which our earliest desires arise; the wish to be fed, loved, and to assert oneself; and wishes that as we grow older become complicated into desires to fulfill oneself in work, parenthood, and as a person. This part of the personality is technically known as the id. I do not wish to discuss this at length, but it is generally conceded the among these primitive wishes is the instinct to commit aggression. As the infant grows, the child becomes a man, this primitive instinct is modified into socially acceptable channels, so that while we decry manslaughter, we consciously encourage the young man to become an aggressive salesman, executive, or teacher, whatever the case may be. So aggression has its uses: (2) That part of a man which is able to perceive, to receive information, and to act. This part of the personality acts as an intermediary between the world and the driving desires of the id which seek expression. It is called the ego.

We spend a considerable amount of time and energy in our culture cultivating those aspects of our being which fall within the domain of the ego. Most formal education is directed in this area, and we spend large efforts to improve people's intelligence (a function of the ego), to cultivate skills, increase the sensitivity of a person's perception, increase the capacity for decision, judgment, and considered action of all kinds. Most of these capacities lie in the domain of the ego, or are mediated by it. When you consider the education of the average medical specialist, which may easily occupy the better part of a quarter of a century, it is probably realistic to say that the amount of the training which is directed at any part of the personality other than the ego could be measured in weeks, a very few weeks at that. Even much of what the social psychologists like to refer to as socialization, that is, what to do at the right time in the right place, is directed at the ego. We simply learn it: (3) That aspect of the personality which is an essential part of our being. This is that aspect of our personality that tells us what is right and what is wrong. It is also that part of us that fills us with warmth and satisfaction when we have done something that we believe to be good. It is to the relationship between this part of the personality, the superego, and the mass media that I wish to address myself.

Let me review with you very briefly some of the changes which occur in the superego between infancy and maturity. In the beginning there is none; obviously, the newborn has not the foggiest rudiments of anything within his personality that could conceivably be called a conscience. But while the infant is cuddled and loved, the toddler is the recipient of a constant series of "no, noes" and "you mustn'ts." So, the young child learns to see right and wrong from his mother's eyes. Often, he very concretely imagines that his mother knows everything that he has done, and behaves as though she were watching over him. Later the child incorporates his parents' beliefs into himself, through his wish to be like them, and then he begins to behave on the basis of his own beliefs, taken over from the parents. But the ethical propositions of childhood are very simple. Only in maturity can the full complexity of life be dealt with by the grown up conscience.

Piaget[2] has described in some detail the development of a child's system of morals. He regards morality as a set of rules, analogous to the rules of grammar, which are learned only slowly over time. Children hold primitive beliefs such as a belief in immanent justice, the idea that automatic punishments emanate from things themselves; and concepts like moral realism, that is the idea that an act should be punished in terms of the consequences of the act rather than the intent of the actor. In other words, a small child will regard an accidental act which causes substantial damage as more reprehensible than an intentional act which results in minor damage. At the same time, young children tend to see punishment as retributive, that is the emphasis in punishment seems to be on causing equal damage to the guilty party. This is an important concept which has cultural support in the Old Testament notion of an eye for an eye, a tooth for a tooth. As they grow older, children tend to move away from such primitive ethics; for example, an older child is likely to develop the notion that punishment should be restitutive rather than retributive, that is, the punishment should end in restoring the initial balance rather than in destroying the guilty party.

The earlier notions of psychiatry were that the formation of the superego was accomplished by the time the child had finished the process of identifying with his parents and resolved his Oedipal struggles, that is about age eight. The work of Piaget, however, indicates that the development of morality continues throughout childhood. There is very little information on what happens after childhood except for the work of Kolberg,[3] whose studies indicate that conscience formation continues throughout adolescence. I know of no studies that purport to examine the development of morality after adolescence in adulthood. But let us pause for a moment to reflect on the changes that we so typically observe in our young people and ourselves as we grow older. The adolescent, it is true, has lost the narrowness of interest and of scope in his moral considerations that characterizes the child. He announces his concern, often to our dismay, in a wide variety of issues. Characteristically, the teenager feels strongly, and indicates vigorous notions of right and wrong. But consider the nature of the adolescent's conscience. To begin with, he is most often convinced that he is right, and moreover, anybody who does not agree with him is not only an idiot, but clearly guilty of moral turpitude besides. It is the intolerance of adolescents for our weakness as human beings that so often makes those of us who are slightly older wish to cringe when we deal with them, or when they, condescendingly, deal with us. In spite of the high degree of ethical concern, the brightly waving standard of morals, the devotedness to a good cause, the adolescent often seems to have relatively little capacity to tolerate the majority of the members of the human race; and in the righteousness of his pronouncements, much of the world is dismissed as being unworthy of consideration. The capacity for compassion, which is based on empathy, is not yet fully developed. Moreover, in adolescence, there is either an inability or a lack of desire to deal with complexity. Complicated problems are easily solved on the basis of a single moral issue, all other matters being brushed aside. It seems possible for the teenager to easily characterize all problems and situations in terms of right or wrong. The in-between shades of gray seem not to be comprehended. Many persons seem to remain at this stage in their development of their consciences; the world is black or white, the actors in life's drama are good or evil, and punishment can and is assigned on the basis of retribution rather than restitution.

Fortunately, not all persons cease their development at this stage. Those of us who do not become petrified in our youth continue to grow, beginning a conscious struggle for achievement in morality. With increasing maturity we begin to be able to understand the complexity of the acts and actors. Together with an increased ability to understand and an appreciation for complexity, we begin to develop the capacity not only to see the other fellow for what he is, but also gain an ability to put ourselves in his shoes. And, at the same time, we begin a struggle to develop a moral consistency that allows us to act on the basis of the gratification we can derive from the strength of our own character. So we can base our morality not on a set of preconceived laws derived from our parents and the society around us, but on a creative ability that enables us to meet the new problems of our time with a maturity, characterized by love, compassion and understanding.

I think that you must all be aware that the development of a mature conscience, one that operates with mitigating empathy and compassion rather than solely from the strictures of a set of moral laws, is a relatively rare phenomenon. It is at this point that I believe that the mass media may be exerting a real and damaging effect on Americans. One of the aspects of conscience which is very much acted upon by the society rather than parents is the development of the so-called ego ideal, the image of the person that we would like to be. In the past, when communication was not as easy as it is now, the ego ideal must often have been some outstanding citizen of the town or some idealized hero learned about in school. Nowadays, with the intrusion into our lives for many hours each week of the stereotyped folk heroes of television, we must seriously consider that these characters may contribute to the formation of the individual's ego ideal. Let us consider for a moment the nature of many of the heroes presented on TV. To begin with they are always very "masculine" sorts of men. They are seldom portrayed as having any capacity for tenderness or love. They clearly and easily are identified as being in the "right." Never are these one-dimensional characters drawn in such a way as to portray the frailties of human existence that encumber us all. Moreover, not only are the heroes easily identified as being "right," it is also clear that the villain in the stories must be "wrong." Rarely are villains presented as people who might love their wives and children, be victims of circumstance, or nature's accidents. On the vast majority of occasions, villains are drawn as unidimensional characters representing a generalized personification of evil who deserve whatever unpleasant fate lies in store for them. Moreover, not only are these stories presented with a complete absence of all the ambiguities and complexities that make it so difficult to distinguish the good guys from the bad guys in real life, there is in most presentations the covert message that as long as a person is a bad guy, *it does not matter what you do to him.* In the pursuit of the good cause, any method of bringing the devil to bay is justified; so the marshal shoots the rustler, the policeman beats the murderer, the posse lynches the outlaw, and the secret service agent assassinates the spy. The ethical problems related to the idea that one human being is beating, maiming, killing another human being are never discussed. In fact, the idea that the criminal, spy, outlaw, enemy soldier, etc. is a human being is rarely presented.

It seems to me that this type of a story line represents a perpetuation and glorification of those characteristics of the adolescent superego that we would like to see young people abandon as they grow older. Over and over again, this plot line presents the same narrow ethnocentric dimensions which obviate the necessity of considering complexity in solving problems. Again and again, the intolerance of the adolescent for the other fellow is supported. Certainly, such stories do not in any way contribute to the capacity to develop empathy or real concern for the other fellow, and I believe that it is specifically the capacity for empathy that is essential in the development of the mature conscience. We need seriously to consider what characterological effect such sustained presentations adulating a primitive superego may have on the development of a mature personality.

If I could believe that these beliefs about the nature of good and evil were confined to the simple presentations given on television, I would not be so greatly concerned, but I think that these rudimentary notions of right and wrong are now a powerful part of the personality of many Americans. Moreover, such immature superego functions have very serious implications not only for the commission of acts of violence but also in the future of our political destinies. We have recently been engaged in some exploratory work on attitudes towards violence among Americans. This work has taken the form of small group meetings in which persons from a variety of walks of life are encouraged to discuss their notions of violence, its causes, and its cures. It has been a sad fact that of all the people we have talked to, only one took a moral stand against violence for all reasons. All others felt strongly that violence had its uses; some felt that it was necessary to use violence to change unjust laws, other felt it necessary to use violence to protect the law. What was especially interesting to us was that each man felt fully justified in using violence (and we were talking about death and serious bodily harm) in the name of his own good cause. Unfortunately, the good causes differed; and if all the people we had talked to were to act on their convictions, none of us would be alive to talk about it. So one group was ready to kill representatives of the "establishment" (for example, the police and the school board), and others wished to incarcerate, or shoot if necessary, those who protest against the establishment. This is not just a war between the black and white, young and old, haves and have-nots, it seems to be a war with any person (or any group) with whose opinions you disagree. But what has been appalling to me in these discussions is the righteousness with which each man holds his lethal convictions, and the utter incapacity of the various group members to look at their potential victims as fellow human beings.

If we are to take these considerations seriously, they suggest certain lines of action. In the first place, in addition to the excellent studies of the short term effects of the mass media on the human tendency to aggression and violence,[4] we need to begin consideration of the long-term effects of the media on the formation of the adult character. We need to develop measures of empathy, which are now missing from the set of tools available for making psychological measurements.[5] And, we need to begin some positive experiments with the media to see whether it can be used as a tool to expand the morality and insight of the American people.

There are some other kinds of consequences. The social sciences have been very much influenced by Adorno's *Authoritarian Personality* and there has been a great deal of effort expended in measuring and describing the characteristics of groups who deviate from the norm in terms of being given to prejudice or aggression.[6] In psychiatry, we have studied at length the traits of the abnormal individual, including those who for some reason or other appear to be unfettered by conscience or who have consciences characterized by large and observable gaps. But we have little information about the characteristics of the normal human being.[7] I think we now need to study those traits which go to make up a good human being and to begin to turn our attention to the nature of the developmental processes that lead to goodness. I have no very good ideas about how such studies should be conducted or what experimental designs lend themselves to such pursuits, but I have noticed that when scientists become truly interested in a problem, methods appear, and measurements become available. I see our present task as specifying the problem, and generating interest in it.

I believe, that if as a nation, we develop a genuine and honest concern about our goodness as human beings, we will find ways not only to assess ourselves from this point of view but also to create a better quality of life for this generation.

REFERENCES

1. *Supplemental Studies for the National Advisory Commission on Civil Disorders,* U.S. Govt. Printing Office, Washington, D.C., 1968.
2. Turiel, E. "On the psychology of moral development." Unpublished manuscript, Yale University, 1964.
3. Kohlberg, L. "The development of children's orientations toward a moral order." *Vita Humana,* vol. 6, 1963, p. 11.
4. Berkowitz, L. "The effects of observing violence." *Scientific American,* vol. 210, 1964, p. 35.
5. Gage, N.L., and Cronbach, L.J. "Conceptual and methodological problems in interpersonal perception." *Psychological Review,* vol. 62, 1955, p. 411.
6. Adorno, T.W., Frenkel-Brunswik, E., Levinson, D.J., and Sanford, R.N. *The Authoritarian Personality.* New York: Harper & Row, 1950.
7. Sabshin, M. "Psychiatric perspectives on normality." *Archives of General Psychiatry,* vol. 17, 1967, p. 258.

Appendix III-H

THE EFFECTS OF VIOLENCE IN THE PRINTED MEDIA*

A. Background

Monsieur L. J. G. Proal, a French criminologist, came to the definite conclusion around the turn of this century that Goethe, Shakespeare, Ovid and other writers of bygone days were directly responsible for murders and suicides committed by their readers (Muhlen, 1949). Regarding the current scene at the time, M. Proal "proved" with a few cases and newspaper clippings that crimes had been committed under the direct influence of novels by Dostoevsky, Paul Bourget, and others that the criminals had read.

Moving ahead, in time at any rate, if not methodologically, psychoanalyst D.S. Ferenczi commented in 1916 that perhaps horrifying fairy tales serve a useful purpose, since "a man may live in perpetual fear of attack . . . in the fairy tales a magic cap enables every transformation and makes us inaccessible." Not so, says British psychologist Nicholas Tucker in the enlightened year of 1968 (News item, Oct. 7, 1968); some nursery books are so terrifying they may do permanent harm—"Some great writers can create an overpowering effect with just one story."

In the late 1940's, psychiatrist Frederick Wertham turned to a different medium, comic books, but with essentially the same conclusion: the increase in juvenile delinquency, he asserted, has gone hand-in-hand with the distribution of comic books.

Intermittent attacks on newspaper sensationalism, magazine fiction and modern novels as lying at the root of undesirable behavior have led now in the 1960's to the "identification" of television as the primary culprit. Producers of the print media cannot rest entirely easy even yet, but. many a one must have said, "Thank God for television," in respect to the violence controversy at any rate.

The arguments over the years have been roughly the same: vicarious violence leads to real violence. If not a prime mover, say the more temperate, it at least aggravates existing tendencies.

The purpose of this paper is to dispense as much as possible with opinions pro and con which have repeated themselves endlessly over the years, and to (a) look at the evidence; (b) grade the evidence for quality, because much of it is faulty; and (c) determine what is really known, with evidence that will

---

*Excerpts from a longer paper prepared for the Media Task Force by Jack B. Haskins, Professor of Journalism, Newhouse Communications Center, Syracuse University.

stand the test of scientific validity, about the effects of media violence on real violence.

The emphasis throughout will be on *print media* (though some comparisons will be made with other media where appropriate), and on *causal evidence* (though much descriptive evidence will be admitted if for no other reason than that it is more abundant).

For those wanting an overview of opinions on the subject, professional and otherwise, the review by Larsen (1966) will serve the purpose.

B. *Summary of Evidence*

This summary of the evidence located in this review is stripped of opinions and reported as found—except that this investigator's evaluation of the *quality* of the evidence is appended to each finding as an opinion. Quality ratings are coded as follows: "A"—Highly reliable; "B"—Probably reliable; "C"—Questionable reliability; "D"—Probably unreliable; "E"—Definitely unreliable.

These findings are divided as follows:

Violence *content* in print media
Audiences for and exposure to violence in print media
Effects of violence in the print media

1. Evidence Regarding Violence Content in Print Media

(a) Newspapers
Printing names of juvenile offenders:

13 States: forbidden by law as of 1960. Among remaining States' daily newspapers:
    4 percent: Always print names if available.
    25 percent: Print all names except first offenders.
    26 percent: Print all names except minor offenses.
    18 percent: Print names only in case of top felonies.
    27 percent: Never print names, or hardly ever.

Quality: "C." Based on Steigleman and Jess (1960). A survey of editors' statements of policy rather than actual analysis of content.

Amount of violent content:

1913-15:	Violence as percent total news, all U.S. dailies; 23 percent (Garth, 1916) "C."
1929:	Violence as percent front page headlines, N.Y.C. dailies; 43 percent (Kingsbury et al., 1933); "B."
1939-50:	Violence as percent total news, all U.S. small and medium-sized dailies; 11 percent (text), 12 percent (photographs) (Swanson, 1955); "B."
1900-60:	"Crime and detective" as percent Sunday comic strips in U.S. dailies; from zero percent in 1900 to 16 percent in

1955-59 (high point, 23 percent in 1945-49)   Barcus, 1961); "B."

1950   Violence as percent of activity in syndicated U.S. Sunday comic strips; 18 percent for male characters, 9 percent for female characters (Spiegelman et al., 1953); "B."

1961-62:   Violence as percent total news, largest U.S. dailies; 5 percent, ranging from 2 percent to 34 percent by newspapers (Otto, 1963); "B."

Other evidence on newspaper content:

1967:   Empirically derived content categories for teenage boys, Washington State; speed and violence; science; teen news; sports; public affairs 'Clarke, 1968); "A."

1960   Unfavorable vs. favorable depiction of teenagers on front pages of South Dakota dailies; 40 percent favorable vs. 32 percent unfavorable, plus better display of favorable items (Stensaas, 1962); "A."

1954:   Sensationalism of coverage major murder trials in Cleveland *Press,* 1954 vs. past; equally sensational treatment 1954 vs. past (Sanders, 1964); "C."

Circa 1950's: Newspaper vs. radio news service treatments of sensational events; newspaper versions more violent than radio (Tannenbaum and Lynch, 1960a); "B."

Circa 1940's: Chicago, newspaper vs. radio coverage of famous murder trial; newspapers covered more prominently than radio (Gottlieb, 1947).

(b) Magazines

Relative incidence of violence by magazine types:

1961-62:   Comparison, number of violent incidents per issue in different magazine types in one city; family, 12; intellectual, 15; romance, 33; men's 63; police and detective, 77 (Otto, 1963); "B."

Circa 1960's: Negro vs. general magazines emphasis on interracial tension; Negro magazines more stress than general (Barcus and Levin, 1966); "B."

Amount of violent content: No evidence available.

(c) Paperback Books

Amount of violent content:

1961-62:   Sadism-violence as percent of total paperback covers on newsstands of a single city; 10 percent of titles, 11 percent of illustrations (Otto, 1963); "B."

1955:   "Mysteries" and "westerns" as percent of subject-matter;

19 percent mysteries, 14 percent westerns (among hardcover books, about 1 percent occurrence in each of those categories) (Blum, 1959); "C."

(d) Hardcover Books

Amount of violent content:

1955:   Mysteries and westerns as percent of subject-matter; 1 percent and 1½ percent, respectively (Blum, 1959); "C."

Circa 1950's: Best-sellers vs. worst-sellers content; no difference in incidence of anger, unhappiness and sensationalism (Harvey, 1953); "C."

(e) Various print media:

1900-60:   Asociality and amorality themes in fictional content of comic strips, magazines, movies, radio programs, TV drama; quantitative data unavailable (Goodrich, 1964).

(f) Weekly newspapers: No evidence at hand.

(g) Specialized periodicals (professional journals, house organs, etc.): No evidence at hand.

(h) Comic Books: No evidence at hand.

(i) Unusual print media (billboards, transit, direct mail, etc.): No evidence at hand.

2. Evidence Regarding Audiences and Exposure to Violence in the Print Media

(a) Newspapers:

1967:   Relative reading interest in "speed and violence" among teenage boys in Washington State; *Interest ratings (100 degree maximum):*

64	Speed and violence
60	Science
59	Teen news
51	Sports
27	Public affairs

(Clarke, 1968) "B."

1967:   Relative reading interest by degree of violence portrayed among national sample of U.S. adults

Items depicting	Mean interest index
High violence	52.2
Some violence	49.9
No violence	37.4

(Bureau of Advertising, 1967);"A."

1967:   Comparison of reader interest vs. editors' judgments of interest, national sample of U.S. adults:
Mean ranking of items by reader interest
(1=highest, 120 lowest=interest)

	Readers themselves	Editors predictions
Violent (death)	24.3	45.2
Violent (non-death)	54.3	46.8

(Editors underestimated public interest in violent death items, overestimated public interest in violent non-death. In particular, readers were more interested than editors predicted in remote, impersonal, large-scale death.) (ANPA, 1967); "A."

1939-50: Relative reading interest in violent and non-violent items by readers of 130 small and medium daily newspapers:

Mean readership (100 percent maximum)

	Text items			Photographs		
	Males	Females	Total	Males	Females	Total
Violence items	29.2	24.3	26.7	67.8	68.0	67.9
Non-violent	—	—	19.4	—	—	49.6

(Swanson, 1955); "A."

1950:   Reading interests among third to eleventh graders in Des Moines. Tables not available: Conclusions: Except for third graders, all grades and both sexes expressed high interest in reading about violence; boys were more interested than girls. These preferences extended across all media. (Lyness, 1952); "B."

(b) Comic Books:

Circa 1950: Relative reader interest in comic book themes among teenagers in Utica, N.Y. Tables not available: Conclusions: Crime and violence themes were highly interesting to boys, but were not major factors among girls. (Butterworth and Thompson, 1951); "B."

Circa 1940's: Reading interest associated with delinquency in children. Tables not available: Conclusions: Delinquents and non-delinquents were equally interested in "harmless" comic books; delinquents were more interested than non-delinquents in reading "questionable" and "harmful" comic books (the latter category including "crime"). (Hoult, 1949); "B."

Circa 1950: Reading interest associated with adolescent boy aggressiveness. Tables not available: Conclusions: No difference between "aggressive" and other boys with regard to anti-social role preference nor in liking for violent themes in comic books. (Karp, 1954); "A."

(c) Multimedia comparison:

1967:   Favored medium for violent and non-violent content among national sample of U.S. adults:

| | Percent of times each medium was chosen as most popular source | |
	Violent items	Non-violent items
Television	30	20
Radio	11	1
Newspapers	53	53
Magazines	0	12
No difference	6	14

(Broadcast media chosen more often as source for violent than for non-violent items, though in absolute terms newspaper was favored source for both violent and non-violent.) (Bureau of Advertising, 1967); "B."

Audience and exposure data for various other print media—magazines, books, etc.—were not available in time for the present analysis though such data are readily available given sufficient time (see "Conclusions and Recommendations").

C. *Evidence Regarding Effects of Violence in Print Media*

In order to truly measure the real effect of communication in the real world, a number of criteria must be met (Haskins, 1968):

1. Naturalistic communication conditions should prevail during the research in order that the results can be generalized to the real world. This is the *external validity* criterion.
2. The relationship between cause and effect should be clear, with irrelevant causal factors either controlled or held constant through appropriate experimental design. This is the *internal validity* criterion.
3. The measurement should be both unobtrusive and valid in the psychometric sense.

No evidence was encountered during this investigation that conformed to all three criteria. *Therefore, one must conclude that there is no rigorous evidence one way or another as to whether violence in the print media has beneficial, harmful, or no effect.* Nor was any rigorous evidence encountered regarding violence in the broadcast media or through any other means.

The best guess that one can make comes from laboratory experimental evidence, where internal validity is rigorous but external validity and unobtrusive valid measurement is questionable.

Rather than go into detail on the various laboratory experiments which have been summarized by Tannenbaum and Greenberg (1968), the general conclusion will simply be stated:

> Under laboratory conditions, the bulk of the evidence indicates the vicariously experienced violence tends to serve as a triggering mechanism and predisposes humans toward more aggressive behavior—at least among children and those with repressed inclinations toward hostility, under certain conditions.

D. *Conclusions*

These conclusions might better be called "what we think we know" or "reasonable hypotheses." They are based on direct evidence where available, and also on speculation with some basis of indirect evidence, or appropriate theory or logical projection (though the latter two are likely to be dangerous if acted upon, since everyone regards his own speculations as theoretically sound and/or logical).

These "reasonable hypotheses" are divided as follows:

Violence *content* in the print media

Audiences for and exposure to violence in print media.

Effects of violence in the print media.

1. Violent Content in the Print Media

Newspapers. —About one-tenth of the non-advertising content of U.S. dailies was "violence" in the 1939-50 period. Among the largest dailies, the proportion was somewhat lower in the early 1960's; however, there is great variations among individual metropolitan newspapers, ranging in one study from 2 percent to 34 percent. No reliable trend data were available, and one can only speculate as to the current situation.

Considering only the Sunday comic strips, the proportion appears somewhat higher than for news/editorial/feature material. In 1955-59, about one-sixth of Sunday comics were "crime and detective" topics, an apparent decline from the high of about one-fourth in the 1945-49 period. It may be significant to note that "crime and detective" comic strips were almost nonexistent until about 1930. The absence before that period may be a function either of reader interest or of editorial policy or both.

Regarding the printing of juvenile-offender names, the practice was forbidden by law in thirteen states (1960). In the remaining states, newspaper practices varied widely; about one-fourth of the dailies never printed juvenile-offender names, about one in 25 always printed such names, and the remainder practiced various in-between policies, some excluding only first offenders, others excluding only those charged with minor offenses, and so on.

The depiction of teenagers in the press is probably more favorable than unfavorable; at least that is the case if one can project nationally the results from the front pages of South Dakota dailies in 1960. The ratio of favorable/unfavorable depiction was 40:32 percent, the remainder being of a neutral tone.

In the 1940's and 1950's, newspapers probably had a more "violent" tone than radio news coverage of the same events. Among wire services, copy intended for newspapers was more sensationalized than that intended for radio stations. And in one large city, newspapers gave more prominent coverage to a murder trial than a local radio station.

Magazines.—No general statement of the incidence of violence in all magazines can be made.

Different kinds of specialized magazines probably give varying emphasis to violent topics. In one study of the early 1960's, the number of violent incidents depicted per issue ranged as follows: "family" magazines, 12; "intellectual" magazines, 15; "romance" magazines, 33; "men's" magazines, 63; "police and detective" magazines, 77. Negro magazines gave more emphasis to interracial tension than did general magazines.

Paperback books.—About one-tenth of paperback books emphasized the sadism-violence themes, in an early 1960's study of a single newsstand in a single city. An earlier study, however (1955) indicated that the "mysteries" category alone accounted for about one-fifth of paperback titles. The same study also showed that hardcover books are considerably less likely than paperbacks to be "mysteries," only about 1 percent fitting that category.

Other print media.—No evidence was available regarding the violence content of such other print media as weekly newspapers, specialized periodicals, comic books, billboards, direct mail, etc.

Comment regarding availability of evidence on content.—More studies have been done on the content of newspapers than of the other print media. Even for newspapers, however, the available evidence is very spotty—available only at haphazardly scattered points in time, on haphazard samples of newspapers not covering all available types or places, using noncomparable category definitions and different methodologies of widely varying quality. For other print media, the available data are much less adequate than for newspapers.

2. Audiences for and Exposure to Violence in the Print Media

There can be little doubt that topics of violence are of intense interest to the public and attract large audiences. This interest seems to extend across all media. It is somewhat stronger among boys than among girls. Among children, it seems to increase somewhat with age, particularly from the fourth grade on.

In a summary of 130 newspaper readership studies (1939-50), comparative readership of violent/non-violent news items was 27 percent/19 percent; comparative interest in violent/non-violent photographs was 68/50 percent. Men were somewhat more interested than women in reading about violence; women were equally interested in looking at "violent" photographs.

A recent national study of interest in a wide variety of topics (1967) showed that relative interest in topics graded according to degree of violence depicted was as follows: high violence, 52; some violence, 50; no violence, 37 (those are index numbers, not percentages). Public interest was higher for items dealing with large-scale, impersonal, remote death than for small-scale, personalized, close by accounts of death.

In that same study, it was demonstrated that editors underestimated reader interest in items dealing with "impersonal remote" death, and overestimated their interest in both "personalized" death and violent/nondeath items.

The same general pattern holds true for teenage boys in Washington. Among five empirically derived content categories in one study, "speed and violence" led in reading interest, followed in order by "science," "teen news," "sports" and—of extremely low interest—"public affairs."

Regarding comic books, one study showed that crime and violence themes were highly interesting among boys but not so among girls.

The best evidence is that "violent" comic books are equally interesting to "normal" and to delinquent-aggressive boys, particularly when other personal characteristics are held constant. However, when other factors are not held constant, then delinquents may be more interested in violent comic books than are nondelinquents.

There is some evidence that broadcast media may be chosen more often as a source for violent than for non-violent items. Newspapers are equally important as a source of violent and non-violent items, while magazines are chosen more often for non-violent than for violent items. Whether this is simply an image based on previous performance or a true indication of media usage is unknown.

Audience and exposure data for other print media were not available in time for the present analysis, though such data are readily available given sufficient time. A reasonably sound hypothesis, however, is that violence themes are highly interesting to a majority of the public regardless of medium.

3. The Effects of Violence in the Print Media

There is no rigorous evidence, one way or another, as to whether violence in the print media has beneficial, harmful or no effect—in the real world.

A "best guess" can be made from laboratory experiments but it must be kept in mind that the exposure and measurement processes in such tightly-controlled environments are not typical of the real world, and the results may not reflect what would happen in real life.

Best guess: It is more likely that media-depicted violence has an undesirable "triggering" effect than that it has a desirable "catharsis" effect. This triggering function is probably only operative among some small fraction of the population who have predispositions toward such violence in the first place, and even then only under certain restricted circumstances.

REFERENCES

American Newspaper Publishers Association. When people want to know, where do they go to find out? A.N.P.A. News Research Bulletin No. 21, Dec. 6, 1967.

Barcus, Francis E. A content analysis of trends in Sunday comics, 1900-1959. *Journalism Quarterly*, 1961, 38, 171-180.

Barcus, Francis E. and Levin, J. Role distance in Negro and majority fiction. *Journalism Quarterly*, 1966, 43, 709-714.

Blum, Eleanor. Paperback book publishing: A survey of content. *Journalism Quarterly*, 1959, 36, 447-454.

Bureau of Advertising A.N.P.A. *When People Want to Know, Where Do They Go to Find Out?* New York: Bureau of Advertising, 1967.

Butterworth, Robert F., and Thompson, George D. "Factors Related to Age-grade Trends and Sex Differences in Children's Preferences for Comic Books," *Journal of Genetic Psychology*, 1951, 78, 71-96.

Clarke, Peter. "Does Teen News Attract Boys to Newspapers?" *Journalism Quarterly*, 1968, 45, 1-3.

Garth, Thomas. "A Statistical Study of the Content of Newspapers," *School and Society*, 1916, v. 3 (56), 140-144.

Goodrich, Herbert. "Men and Society in Mass Media Fiction: The Pattern of Life in the Mass Media as Revealed by Content-analysis Studies" Ph.D. dissertation, University of Illinois, 1964. (Order No. 65-819.)

Gottlieb, Lillian. "Radio and Newspaper Reports of the Heirens Murder Case," *Journalism Quarterly*, 1947, 24 (2), 97-103.

Harvey, John. "The Content Characteristics of Best-selling Novels," *Public Opinion Quarterly*, 1953, 17 (1), 91-114.

Haskins, Jack B. *The Evaluation of Mass Communications: The Controlled Field Experiment.* New York: Advertising Research Foundation (In press, 1968).

Haskins, Jack B. "Public Interest in Violence Via Mass Media," *Editor & Publisher*, Oct. 19, 1968, p. 38.

Karp, Etta E. "Crime Comic Book Role Preferences," Ph.D. dissertation, New York University, 1954. (Pub. No. 10, 637).

Larsen, Otto N. "Controversies about the Mass Communication of Violence," *Annals of the American Academy of Political and Social Science*, 1966, 364, 37-49.

Lyness, Paul I. "The Place of the Mass Media in the Lives of Boys and Girls," *Journalism Quarterly*, 1952, 29, 43, 43-55.

Otto, Herbert A. "Sex and Violence on the American Newsstand," Jounalism Quarterly, 1963, 40, 19-26.

Sanders, Keith P. "The Cleveland Press Coverage of the Sheppard Murder Case in Relation to Sensational News Treatment," M.S. thesis, Ohio State University, 1964.

Spiegelman, Marvin, Turwilliger, Carl, and Fearing, Franklin. "The Content of Comics: Goals and Means to Goals of Comic Strip Characters," *The Journal of Social Psychology*, 1953, 37, 189-203.

Steigleman, Walter, and Jess, Paul. "Publication of Names of Juvenile Offenders," *Journalism Quarterly*, 1960, 37, 393-397.

Stensaas, Harlan S. "The Front-page Teenager: How 11 Dailies Treat Him, *Journalism Quarterly*, 1962, 38, 373-375.

Swanson, Charles E. "What They Read in 130 Daily Newspapers," *Journalism Quarterly*, 1955, 32, 411-421.

Tannenbaun, Percy H., and Lynch, Mervin D. "Sensationalism in Newspaper and Radio Wire Copy, *Journalism Quarterly*, 1960, 37, 590-591, 622.

Tannenbaum, Percy H., and Greenberg, Bradley S. "Mass Communication," *Annual Review of Psychology*, vol. 19, 1968, 351-386.

Appendix III-I
SAMPLING PROCEDURES USED
IN THE HARRIS POLL*

The total sample comprised 1,176 interviews with persons 18 years of age and older. Respondents were selected by means of an area probability sampling procedure which involved 100 sampling points, or "clusters," of approximately 12 interviews each. Instructions from the Harris home office directed interviewers to specific blocks or other geographical units and then designated systematic procedures for determining which individual within the household should be interviewed. No callbacks were employed; if no interview was obtained at an address, the interviewer attempted an interview at the next residence, following a prescribed route.

Coincident with the interview among adults, interviewers talked with teenage boys and girls (14-18) residing in the same localities. The interview with youngsters was considerably shorter, dealing only with media use, expressions of dissension, experience with violence, and approval of physical violence. One hundred and ninety-five teenager interviews were obtained along with the adult interviews; an additional 301 interviews were conducted one week later through the use of an identical sampling procedure, thus yielding a total of 496 interviews with teenagers.

Interviewing among adults took place October 1-8. The additional teenager interviews were made on October 10-12.

Analysis of the data from the adult sample involved the relationships between significant independent variables—some demographic, others attitudinal or behavioral—and all other data collected during the interview. Key variables are listed below:

---

*The American Public Looks at Violence, November 1968, a poll conducted at the request of the National Commission on the Causes and Prevention of Violence by Louis Harris and Associates, Inc. Other Task Forces also participated in the development of this Interview Schedule.

LOUIS HARRIS AND ASSOCIATES, INC.
1 Rockefeller Plaza, New York, N. Y. 10020

FOR OFFICIAL USE ONLY: Questionnaire No.
                                              5-6-7-8

Sample Point No. _____
                      10-11-12-13

Interviewer's Name _____

City/Town_____ State _____

TEENAGE INTERVIEW SCHEDULE

1. As you probably know, the Government in Washington has made many decisions and taken many actions during the past few years which have caused people to come out either in favor of the government's actions or against the government's actions. Could you tell me what action the government in Washington has taken during the past few years that you have *objected to* most? Any others?

2. Sometimes people feel so strongly about something that they take some action because of it and other times they do not feel strongly enough to take any action. Did you take any action because of your feelings about what the government has done?

Took action

No action taken

Not sure

2b. Do you happen to remember what that was?

3a. (HAND RESPONDENT SHOW CARD "A") When you want to find out what is going on in your local community, which *one* of the major forms of mass communications on that list do you use *most frequently* to get the news?

3b. Which one do you mainly *use* to find out about events in the nation and the world?

3c. More specifically, from which one have you gotten the clearest understanding of what's going on in Vietnam?

3d. Which one has been your main source of information concerning unrest in the cities and riots in the U.S.?

3e. Which one has contributed most to your understanding of the causes and meaning of student protest and uprisings in the U.S.?

3f. In your opinion, which one seems to emphasize news about crime and delinquency the most?

3g. Which one seems to you to dwell the most on accidents and national disasters?

3h. In your judgment, which *one* tends to emphasize the use of guns, knives, or other instruments of violence?

3i. From which one have you learned the most about the life and work of a policeman?

3j. Which one do you most frequently choose when you want to get away from daily tensions and just relax?

4. Now, I'd like to pose some more specific hypothetical or imaginary choices about the mass media to see about your preferences. (HAND RESPONDENT CARD "B") If you had to choose between *one* in each of the pairings on that card, which one would it be—a or b? (INTERVIEWER: GET ONE CHOICE FOR EACH PAIR)

    a. Read the editorial page
       OR
    b. Read the front pages of your daily newspaper.

    a. Read the comic strips
       OR
    b. Read the want-ad section.

    a. Go to a movie starring Bing Crosby
       OR
    b. Go to a movie starring John Wayne

    a. See a James Bond movie
       OR
    b. See a Walt Disney movie.

    a. Watch the Ed Sullivan Show on TV
       OR
    b. Watch Gunsmoke on TV.

    a. Read a detective story
       OR
    b. Read a love story.

5a. Imagine that for some reason you could only watch one television program a week. From all of last year's or this year's programs, what would be your choice?

5b. What's the main thing you like about that program?

5c. Imagine further that you had the power to eliminate one television program from the air of all last year's or this year's programs. Which *one* would you eliminate?

5d. What's the main thing you dislike about it?

5e. Of the three major television networks—ABC, NBC, CBS—do you detect any difference in the amount of violence they protray in their entertainment programs?
    Is a difference
    No difference
    Not sure

5f. How would you rank them from *most* to *least* violent? (RECORD ONLY ONE IN EACH CATEGORY)
    Most violent
    Medium violent
    Least violent

5g. How do you feel about the amount of violence portrayed in television programs today, not including news programs—do you think that there is too much, a reasonable amount, or very little violence?
    Too much
    A reasonable amount
    Very little
    Not sure

                                                                           Mass Media and Violence

5h. Apart from the *amount* of violence, do you generally approve or disapprove of the kind of violence that is portrayed on TV?
Approve
Disapprove
Not sure

6a. Now let's turn a moment to some other kinds of experiences. First, tell me if any of these somewhat dramatic things have ever happened to you: As a child, were you spanked—frequently, sometimes, or never?
Frequently
Sometimes
Never
Not sure

6b. By whom were you spanked? (MULTIPLE RECORD)
Mother
Father
Relative
Acquaintances
Other
Not sure

7. INTERVIEWER: ASK THE FOLLOWING SERIES OF QUESTIONS ABOUT EACH OF THE FIVE SITUATIONS LISTED BELOW, ALWAYS FOLLOWING THE SKIP INSTRUCTIONS AND RECORD ANSWERS BELOW' *ASK THE WHOLE SERIES OF QUESTIONS [7a-g] FOR EACH SITUATION BEFORE MOVING ON THE THE NEXT SITUATION.*

SITUATION 1. EVER BEEN SLAPPED OR KICKED BY ANOTHER PERSON
SITUATION 2. EVER BEEN PUNCHED OR BEATEN BY ANOTHER PERSON
SITUATION 3. EVER BEEN CHOKED BY ANOTHER PERSON
SITUATION 4. EVER BEEN THREATENED OR ACTUALLY CUT WITH A KNIFE
SITUATION 5. EVER BEEN THREATENED WITH A GUN OR SHOT AT

7a. Have you (READ SITUATION)?
Yes
No
Not sure

7b. How many times would you estimate that this has happened to you?
Once
Two or three times
Four or more times
Not sure

7c. Did this happen to you as a child or as an adult?
Child
Adult
Both (vol.)
Not sure

7d. Now let's just consider the most recent time that this happened. In what kind of situation did it happen?
Fun or play
Sports
Anger or conflict
Military combat
Other (specify)
Not sure

SITUATION 1. EVER BEEN SLAPPED OR KICKED BY ANOTHER PERSON
SITUATION 2. EVER BEEN PUNCHED OR BEATEN BY ANOTHER PERSON
SITUATION 3. EVER BEEN CHOKED BY ANOTHER PERSON
SITUATION 4. EVER BEEN THREATENED OR ACTUALLY CUT WITH A KNIFE
SITUATION 5. EVER BEEN THREATENED WITH A GUN OR SHOT AT

7e. What was your relationship to the person who (READ SITUATION)?
   Family member
   Friend
   Acquaintance
   Stranger
   Other (specify)
   Not sure

7f. Did anyone intervent to stop the action?
   Yes
   No
   Not sure

7g. Who intervened?
   Family member of one or both persons involved
   Friend of one or both persons involved
   Acquaintance of one or both persons involved
   Stranger to both persons involved
   Other (specify)
   Not sure

   8. INTERVIEWER: ASK THE FOLLOWING SERIES OF QUESTIONS ABOUT
EACH OF THE FIVE SITUATIONS LISTED BELOW, ALWAYS FOLLOWING THE
SKIP INSTRUCTIONS AND RECORD ANSWERS BELOW. *ASK THE WHOLE SERIES
OF QUESTIONS [8a-g] FOR EACH SITUATION BEFORE MOVING ON TO THE
NEXT SITUATION.* THIS SERIES OF QUESTIONS DOES NOT RELATE TO YOU
PERSONALLY BUT WHETHER OR NOT YOU HAVE SEEN THE FOLLOWING
SITUATIONS.

SITUATION 1. EVER SEEN ANOTHER PERSON SLAPPED OR KICKED
SITUATION 2. EVER SEEN ANOTHER PERSON PUNCHED OR BEATEN
SITUATION 3. EVER SEEN ANOTHER PERSON CHOKED
SITUATION 4. EVER SEEN ANOTHER PERSON THREATENED OR ACTUALLY
   CUT WITH A KNIFE
SITUATION 5. EVER SEEN ANOTHER PERSON THREATENED WITH A GUN
   OR SHOT AT

8a. Have you (READ SITUATION)?
   Yes
   No
   Not sure

8b. How many times would you estimate that you have (READ SITUATION)?
   Once
   Two or three times
   Four or more times
   Not sure

8c. Did you see this happen as a child or as an adult?
   Child
   Adult
   Both (vol.)
   Not sure

8d. Now let's just consider the most recent time that you saw this happen. In what kind of situation did it happen?
Fun or play
Sports
Anger or conflict
Military combat
Other (specify)
Not sure

SITUATION 1. EVER SEEN ANOTHER PERSON SLAPPED OR KICKED
SITUATION 2. EVER SEEN ANOTHER PERSON PUNCHED OR BEATEN
SITUATION 3. EVER SEEN ANOTHER PERSON CHOKED
SITUATION 4. EVER SEEN ANOTHER PERSON THREATENED OR ACTUALLY CUT WITH A KNIFE
SITUATION 5. EVER SEEN ANOTHER PERSON THREATENED WITH A GUN OR SHOT AT

8e. What was your relationship to the person?
Family member
Friend
Acquaintance
Stranger
Other (specify)
Not sure

8f. Did anyone intervene to stop the action?
Yes
No
Not sure

8g. Who intervened?
Family member of one or both persons involved
Friend of one or both persons involved
Acquaintance of one or both persons involved
Stranger to both persons involved
Other (specify)
Not sure

9a. Have you ever spanked a child?
Yes
No
Not sure

9b. What was your relationship to the child?
Parent
Other relative
Teacher
Babysitter
Acquaintance
Stranger
Other (specify)
Not sure

10a.Have you ever slapped or kicked another person?
Yes
No
Not sure

10b. How many times would you estimate that you have done this?
Once
Two or three times

Four or more times
Not sure

10c. Did you do this as a child or as an adult?
Child
Adult
Both (vol.)
Not sure

10d. Now let's consider just the most recent time that you slapped or kicked another person. In what kind of situation did it happen?
Fun or play
Sports
Anger or conflict
Military combat
Other (specify)
Not sure

10e. What was your relationship to the other person?
Family member
Friend
Acquaintance
Stranger
Other (specify)
Not sure

10f. Did anyone intervene to stop the action?
Yes
No
Not sure

10g. Who intervened?
Family member of one or both persons involved
Friend of one or both persons involved
Acquaintance of one or both persons involved
Stranger to both persons involved
Other (specify)
Not sure

11a. (ASK EVERYONE) Have you ever punched or beaten another person?
Yes
No
Not sure

11b. How many times would you estimate that you have done this?
Once
Two or three times
Four or more times
Not sure

11c. Did you do this as a child or as an adult?
Child
Adult
Both (vol.)
Not sure

11d. Now let's consider just the most recent time that you punched or beat another person. In what kind of a situation did it happen?
Fun or play
Sports
Anger or conflict

Military combat
Other (specify)
Not sure

11e. What was your relationship to the other person?
Family member
Friend
Acquaintance
Stranger
Other (specify)
Not sure

11f. Did anyone intervent to stop the action?
Yes
No
Not sure

11g. Who intervened?
Family member of one or both persons involved
Friend of one or both persons involved
Acquaintance of one or both persons involved
Stranger to both persons involved
Other (specify)
Not sure

12. Have you ever been in a situation where you had to defend yourself with a knife or a gun?
Yes
No
Not sure

13. Now I would like to get your judgment on some questions concerning the possible effect of television violence (REPEAT BEFORE EACH STATEMENT BELOW: "HOW LIKELY IS IT THAT TV VIOLENCE (READ STATEMENT. IS IT LIKELY, POSSIBLE, OR UNLIKELY?")
Plays a part in making America a violent society.
Allows viewers to blow off steam by watching violence, thus decreasing the likelihood of their being violent.
Makes people insensitive to real acts of violence that they hear about or see.
Provides entertainment and relaxation without harmful or bad effects.
Triggers violent acts from people who are maladjusted or mentally unstable.
Supports and strengthens traditional American values.

In this section, we would like to know if you would approve of disapprove or people taking certain actions in a variety of imaginary situations.

14. Are there any situations that you can imagine in which you would approve of a parent spanking his or her child assuming the child is healthy and over a year old?
Yes
No
Not sure

14b. Would you approve if the child (READ EACH STATEMENT):
Was noisy and getting on the parent's nerves.
Has been disobedient all day.
Had been expelled from school.
Had broken a law.

15a. Are there any situations that you can imagine in which you would approve of a parent beating his or her child?
Yes

No
Not sure

15b. Would you approve if the child (READ EACH STATEMENT):
Was noisy and getting on the parent's nerves.
Had been disobedient all day.
Had been expelled from school.
Had broken a law.

16a. Are there any situations that you can imagine in which you would approve of a husband slapping a wife's face?
Yes
No
Not sure

16b. Would you approve if (READ EACH STATEMENT):
The husband and wife were having an argument.
The wife had insulted her husband in public.
The wife had been flirting with other men.
The wife had been unfaithful.

17a. Are there any situations that you can imagine in which you would approve of a husband shooting his wife?
Yes
No
Not sure

17b. Would you approve if (READ EACH STATEMENT):
The husband and wife were having an argument.
The wife had insulted her husband in public.
The wife had been flirting.
The wife had been unfaithful.

18a. Are there any situations that you can imagine in which you would approve of a wife slapping her husband's face?
Yes
No
Not sure

18b. Would you approve if (READ EACH STATEMENT):
The wife and husband were having an argument.
The husband had insulted his wife in public.
The husband had been flirting.
The husband had been unfaithful.

19a. Are there any situations that you can imagine in which you would approve of a wife shooting her husband?
Yes
No
Not sure

19b. Would you approve if (READ EACH STATEMENT):
The wife and husband were having an argument.
The husband had insulted his wife in public.
The husband had been flirting.
The husband had been unfaithful.

20a. Are there any situations that you can imagine in which you would approve of a public school teacher hitting a student?
Yes
No
Not sure

20b. Would you approve if the student had (READ EACH STATEMENT):
   Been noisy in class.
   Been repeatedly disobedient and uncooperative.
   Destroyed school property.
   Hit.

21a. Are there any situations that you can imagine in which you would approve of a public school teacher punching or beating a student?
   Yes
   No
   Not sure

21b. Would you approve if the student had (READ EACH STATEMENT):
   Been noisy in class.
   Been repeatedly disobedient and uncooperative.
   Destroyed school property.
   Hit.

22a. Are there any situations you can imagine in which you would approve of a policeman striking an adult male citizen?
   Yes
   No
   Not sure

22b. Would you approve if the citizen (READ EACH STATEMENT):
   Had said vulgar and obscene things to the policeman.
   Was demonstrating against the war in Vietnam and carrying a Viet Cong flag.
   Was being questioned as a suspect in a murder case.
   Was attempting to escape from custody.
   Was attacking the policeman with his fists.

23a. Are there any situations you can imagine in which you would approve of a policeman shooting an adult male citizen?
   Yes
   No
   Not sure

23b. Would you approve if the citizen (READ EACH STATEMENT):
   Had said vulgar and obscene things to the policeman.
   Was demonstrating against the war in Vietnam and carrying a Viet Cong flag.
   Was being questioned as a suspect in a murder case.
   Was attempting to escape from custody.
   Was attacking the policeman with his fists.
   Was threatening the policeman with a gun.

24a. Are there any situations you can imagine in which you would approve of a teenage boy punching another teenage boy?
   Yes
   No
   Not sure

24b. Would you approve if the teenage boy (READ EACH STATEMENT):
   Didn't like the other boy.
   Had been ridiculed and picked on by the other boy.
   Had been challenged by the other boy to a fist fight.
   Had been hit by the other boy.

25a. Are there any situations you can imagine in which you would approve of a teenage boy knifing another teenage boy?
   Yes
   No
   Not sure

25b. Would you approve if the teenage boy (READ EACH STATEMENT):
    Didn't like the other boy.
    Had been ridiculed and picked on by the other boy.
    Had been challenged by the other boy to a fist fight.
    Had been hit by the other boy.

26. Are there any situations that you can imagine in which you would approve of a man punching an adult male stranger?
    Yes
    No
    Not sure

26b. Would you approve if the stranger (READ EACH STATEMENT):
    Was in a protest march showing opposition to the man's views.
    Was drunk and bumped into the man and his wife on the street.
    Had hit the man's child after the child accidentally damaged the stranger's car.
    Was beating up a woman and the man saw it.
    Had broken into the man's house.

27a. Are there any situations that you can imagine in which you would approve of a man choking a stranger?
    Yes
    No
    Not sure

27b. Would you approve if the stranger (READ EACH STATEMENT):
    Was in a protest march showing opposition to the other man's views.
    Was drunk and bumped into the man and his wife on the street.
    Had hit the man's child after the child accidentally damaged the stranger's car.
    Was beating up a woman and the man saw it.
    Had broken into the man's house.
    Had knocked the man down and was trying to rob him.

28a. Are there any situations that you can imagine in which you would approve of a judge sentencing a person to one or more years of hard labor?
    Yes
    No
    Not sure

28b. Would you approve if (READ EACH STATEMENT):
    The person is an atheist or believes that there is no god.
    The person is demonstrating after having been denied a demonstration permit.
    A man refused to serve in the Armed Forces of the United States.
    The person is an agitator who has incited people to riot.
    The person threatened to kill the President of the United States.

29a. Are there any situations that you can imagine in which you would approve of a judge sentencing a person to death?
    Yes
    No
    Not sure

29b. Would you approve if (READ EACH STATEMENT):
    The person is an atheist or believes that there is no god.
    The person is demonstrating after having been denied a demonstration permit.
    A man refused to serve in the Armed Forces of the United States.
    The person is an agitator who has incited people to riot.

The person has threatened to kill the President of the United States.
The person had been found guilty of first degree murder.
The person was proven to be a traitor.

FACTUAL:

F1. What is your age?

F2a. Are you married now and living with your wife (husband)—or are you widowed, divorced, separated, or single?
  Married
  Widowed
  Separated
  Divorced
  Single

F2b. (IF MARRIED) How long have you been married?
  5 years or under
  6 to 10 years
  11 to 15 years
  16 to 20 years
  21 to 25 years
  26 to 30 years
  31 to 40 years
  41 to 50 years
  50 or more

F3a. (ASK EVERYONE) Do you have any children under 18 years of age?
  Yes
  No

F3b. (IF CHILDREN) How many children under 6 hears of age do you have? How many children ages 6 to 13 do you have? And how many children ages 14 to 18 do you have?
  Under 6
  6 to 13
  14 to 18

F4. Record Position of Respondent in Household:
  Male head
  Female head (no male head)
  Wife
  Son
  Other male (specify)
  Daughter
  Other female (specify)

F5. What is the last grade of school you attended?
  4th grade or less
  5th grade to 8th grade
  Some high school
  High school graduate
  Some college
  College graduate
  Post-graduate

F6. Have you had any other schooling?
  Yes
  No

F7. What other schooling have you had;

F8. (ASK EVERYONE) Is the head of the household an hourly wage worker, salaried, or self-employed?
> Hourly wage worker
> Salaried
> Self-employed

> *None of the above:*

> Retired
> Student
> Military service
> Housewife
> Unemployed
> Other (specify)

F9. What type of work does the head of the household do? (PROBE FULLY—FIND OUT WHAT JOB IS CALLED, DUTIES INVOLVED, ETC.)

F10. (IF NOT HEAD OF HOUSEHOLD) Do you also work full or part-time?
> Full time
> Part time
> No

F11. There's quite a bit of talk these days about different social classes. Most people say they belong either to the middle class or to the working class. Do you ever think of yourself as being in one of these classes?
> Yes
> No
> Not sure

F12. Which class would you put yourself in—the middle class or the working class?
> Middle
> Working
> Not Sure

F13. Well, if you had to make a choice, would you call yourself middle class or working class?
> Middle
> Working
> Not sure

F14. What would you say your family was when you were growing up—middle class or working class?
> Middle
> Working
> Not sure

F15. What is your religion?
> Protestant
> Catholic
> Jewish
> Other
> Not sure

F16. What church is that?
> Baptist
> Methodist
> Lutherans
> Episcopalian
> Other (specify)
> Not sure

516   **Mass Media and Violence**

F17. (ASK EVERYONE) Would you say you go to church regularly, often, seldom or never?

    Regularly
    Often
    Seldom
    Never
    Not sure

F18. Where were you born?
    State
    Foreign Country

F19a. Were you brought up mostly on a farm, in a town, in a small city, or in a large city?

    Farm
    Town
    Small City
    Large City
    Not sure

F19b. Which city was that? In what state?

F20a. How long have you lived in your present house (apartment)?

    Less than one year
    One to four years
    Five to nine years
    Ten to nineteen years
    20 years or more
    All my life

F20b. How would you compare this neighborhood with the one you left? Is it less expensive, more expensive or about the same?

    Less expensive
    More
    About the same
    Not sure

F20c. What about the location of your present house (apartment)—is it closer to the center of the city, further out from the center of the city, or is it about the same as your old neighborhood?

    Closer to center of city
    Further out from center of city
    About the same
    Not sure

F21. For statistical purposes only, we need to know your total family income for 1967. Will you please look at this card (HAND RESPONDENT CARD "I") and tell me which letter best represents all the money the members of this household either earned or received from salary or wages or other sources, such as pensions, stocks and bonds, real estate, and other investments, in 1967 before taxes?

    A. Under $3,000
    B. $3,000 to 4,999
    C. $5,000 to 6,999
    D. $7,000 to 9,999
    E. $10,000 to 14,999
    F. $15,000 to 19,999
    G. $20,000 to 24,999
    H. $25,000 and over
    I. Not sure/refused

INTERVIEWER: IF NOT SURE OR REFUSED, ESTIMATE AND "X" THE LETTER "I" *PLUS* THE FIGURE YOU ARE ESTIMATING'

F22. Using the same scale tell me which letter represents the income of the head of the household only?

A
B
C
D
E
F
G
H
Not sure

F23. Do you own your own home here, or rent or what?

Own
Rent
Other (specify)

F24. What kind of work did your father do for a living while you were growing up?

F25. So far as you and your family are concerned, would you say that you are pretty well satisfied with your present financial situation, more or less satisfied, or not satisfied at all?

Pretty well satisfied
More or less satisfied
Not satisfied at all

F26. During the last few years, has your financial situation been getting better, getting worse, or has it stayed the same?

Getting better
Getting worse
Stayed the same
Not sure

F27. Now looking ahead and thinking about the next few years, do you expect your financial situation will stay about the way it is now, get getter, or get worse?

Stay the way it is
Get better
Get worse
Not sure

Appendix III-J

CONTENT ANALYSIS PROCEDURES
AND RESULTS

A. The Recording Instrument for Programs as a Whole

1. Recording Unit

The unit of observation for which this instrument is developed is the *program*, but it might more appropriately be called the play or story. Most dramatic television presentations (e.g., feature films) contain a single play or story and are therefore regarded as one program. When a cartoon show contains several separate stories or when general entertainment consists of several dramatic skits then each of these separate stories and skits is considered a separate program.

A "program" as listed in a television log or "program" schedule is not to be confused with the program as a recording unit in this instrument.

The duration is not a defining characteristic of the recording unit. Rather, the program length is considered as a variable of this unit.

Commercials are not subjected to the recording procedure described below; a log of commercials, however, is kept for further analysis.

2. Recording Procedure

The recording presupposes the viewing of the program as a whole, making necessary observations and, where necessary to complete the data sheets, reviewing of the details. A log of commercials is kept separately from the data sheets and any acts of products relevant to violence, weapons, war, etc., are noted.

The observer is instructed to record all items on the basis of explicit clues, clear verbal or other behavior, or other evidence. In order to decide on the category assignments of each program, evidence is to be obtained from the program itself, rather than from speculation.

Cover Page for Card No. 1

Column	Code	Description
1-3	2 5 5	Project number (bin number)
4	1	Deck number (unit = program)
5		Extent of violence

519

Column	*Code*	*Description*
6		Network
7		Year
8-9	0 1	Card number
10-12		Program identification
13		(Blank)
14-15		Coder identification
16		Month
17-18		Day
19		Audience
20		Format
21		Type
22		Duration
23-24		Program description

Variables and Categories

Program tone (25) . . . . . (1) The program is a comedy
(2) The program is serious, tragic or other; comic touch, if any, plays minor role

Time (26) of major action   (1) Before 1900
(2) Turn of century to World War II
(3) WW II to the 1960's
(4) The 1960's or general "present" (i.e., contemporary with time of production)
(5) Future
(9) Other (explain)

Note: State year if known on the coding sheet.

Location (27): Geographical location of major action.
(1) In U.S. (state location, if known)
(2) In a country outside of the U.S. (describe)
(9) Other (describe)

Setting (28) of major action (1) Urban or suburban setting
(2) Small town, provincial place, village, farm, rural
(3) Generally uninhabited area; desert, ocean, etc.
(4) Mainly mobile (ship, plane, train, etc.)
(5) Other planets
(9) Other or mixed (explain)

Religion (29) . . . . (1) Religion, church, clergy; also religious customs, rituals or any single term in the theme or aspect of life was part of the subject matter of the program *as a significant element.*
(0) Theme or aspect of life is not relevant to the subject or story.

Note: Use the following criteria of significance: code it (1) only if the theme or aspect would have to be noted in a one-page summary. This criterion applies to the following seven themes.

Animals-nature (30) . . . . (1) Animals, nature (jungle, mountains, ocean, rivers), forces of nature and the elements; exploration, discovery, and natural catastrophes; also agriculture, breeding, conservation of natural resources are significant elements of the program's subject or story.

(0) Theme is not relevant.

Mental illness (31) . . . . . (1) Mental illness, deficiency, abnormality, serious mental disorder; amnesia, phobias; cure, therapy, rehabilitation is significant to the subject or story.
(0) Theme is irrelevant.

Science (32) . . . . (1) Science and scientist (including social science); technology is significant to the subject or story.
(0) Theme is not relevant.

Minorities (33) . . . . . . (1) Minority groups and people; foreign countries and people; non-white religious and ethnic minorities are significant to the subject or story.
(0) Theme is not relevant.

Armed forces (34) . . . . . (1) Armed forces are significant to the subject or story.
(0) Theme is not relevant.

Crime (35) . . . . (1) Crime, corruption, rackets, "fixes," crime detection is significant to the subject or story.
(0) Theme is not relevant.

Education (36) . . . . . . (1) Schools, education, training, study, self-development are significant to the subject or story.
(0) Theme is not relevant.

Violence (37) . . . . (1) No violence.
(2) Violence incidental to the plot.
(3) Violence significant to the plot (defined as violence so germane that it would have to be noted in a brief [one-page] summary of the story).
(9) Other (explain).

Note: Violence is defined to include physical or psychological injury, hurt, or death, addressed to living things. Violence is explicit and overt. It can be verbal or physical. If verbal, it must express intent to use physical force and must be plausible and credible in the context of the program. IDLE, DISTANT, OR VAGUE THREATS; MERE VERBAL INSULTS, QUARRELS, OR ABUSE; OR COMIC THREATS WITH NO VIOLENT INTENT BEHIND THEM ARE *NOT* TO BE CONSIDERED VIOLENT.

Pleasure (38) . . . . (1) The program as a whole clearly supports or includes the proposition: there is pleasure, satisfaction derived from violence.
(0) The proposition is irrelevant to the program.

Note: In the following description of variables the theme is listed. It should be coded (1) if the program as a whole clearly supports or includes the proposition. Otherwise it should be coded (0).

CODING SHEETS

Part I

23-24. Write your answer to question 23-24 on this page.

Answer questions 25 through 55 on reverse side

25.	31.	37.	43.	49.
26.	32.	38.	44.	50.
27.	33.	39.	45.	51.
28.	34.	40.	46.	52.
29.	35.	41.	47.	53.
30.	36.	42.	48.	54.
				55.

Wealth (39) . . . . (1) Desire for money, wealth results in violence.
(0) Irrelevant.

Poverty (40) . . . . (1) Poverty, hunger, misery results in violence.
(0) Irrelevant.

Power (41) . . . . (1) Desire for power leads to violence.
(0) Irrelevant.

Alternatives (42) . . . . . . (1) There is an attempt to try alternative methods before resorting to violence; argument, negotiations, other ways are tried.
(0) Irrelevant.

Hero-ethnicity (43) . . . . (1) Features of enemy or villain are or resemble those of a race or ethnic group other than white Caucasian.
(0) Irrelevant.

Wounds (46) . . . . (1) Blood, wounds are actually shown on the screen.
(0) Irrelevant.

L. enf.-incompetence (47) (1) Agent of law enforcement is shown as incompetent, bungling, or inefficient.
(0) Irrelevant.

L. enf.-corruption (48) . . (1) Agent of law enforcement is shown as venal, corrupt, or criminal.
(0) Irrelevant.

Legal consequences (49) . . (1) Due process of law (legal apprehension or trial or both) is indicated as a consequence of major act(s) of violence.
(0) Irrelevant.

Negro-police (50) . . . . . (1) An agent of law enforcement is American Negro.
(0) Irrelevant.

Negro-criminal (51) . . . . (1) A criminal or alleged criminal is American Negro.
(0) Irrelevant.

"Police brutality"-used (52) (1) The phrase "police brutality" is explicitly used in the program (regardless of context).
(0) Irrelevant.

"Police brutality" ridiculed (53)	(1)	The phrase "police brutality" is ridiculed in the program.
	(0)	Irrelevant.

Nonenclosed spaces (54) .	(1)	Violence occurs in the streets or in nonenclosed spaces.
	(0)	Irrelevant.

Enclosed spaces (55) . . .	(1)	Violence occurs inside of a building or vehicle.
	(0)	Irrelevant.

Reliability of Variables

In the following the results of the final reliability estimates are listed for all variables that survived the pretest. The reliability is assessed on the basis of a random sample of 30 programs out of a total of 183 programs.

The information is listed in the following order:

Name of variable
Type of scale (N=nominal, I=interval)
Recoding whenever report differs from primary data
Reliability coefficient (1=perfect agreement and 0=chance)
Inclusion in the report (Yes=included, No=rejected)

Program tone (25)	N		0.861	Yes
Time (26)	N	(1, 2, 3) 4, 5, 9	.771	Yes
Location (27)	N		1.0	Yes
Setting (28)	N	1, 2 (3, 4, 5, 9)	.693	Yes
Religion (29)	N		.630	No
Animals-nature (30)	N		.788	Yes
Mental illness (31)	N		1.0	Yes
Science (32)	N		.856	Yes
Minorities (33)	N		.722	Yes
Armed forces (34)	N		1.0	Yes
Crime (35)	N		.931	Yes
Education (36)	N		.423	No
Violence (37)	I		.969	Yes
Pleasure (38)	N		.509	No
Wealth (39)	N		.583	No
Poverty (40)	N		-.017	No
Power (41)	N		.346	No
Alternatives (42)	N		.667	Yes
Hero-ethnicity (43)	N		.489	No
War (44)	N		1.0	Yes
Villain-ethnicity (45)	N		.255	No
Wounds (46)	N		0	No
Law enforcement-incompetence (47) . .	N		0	No
Law enforcement-corruption (48)	N		0	No
Legal consequences (49)	N		.760	Yes
Negro-police (50)	N		1.0	Yes
Negro-criminal (51)	N		.649	No
"Police brutality"-used (52)	N		0	No
"Police brutality" -ridiculed (53)	N		0	No
Nonenclosed spaces (54)	N		.700	Yes
Enclosed spaces (55)	N		.520	No

B. The Recording Instrument for Major Characters

1. Recording Unit

The unit of observation recorded by this instrument is a major character. Major characters are defined here as all leading roles representing the principal types essential to telling the story. This criterion applies equally to living and cartoon characters. How each character is portrayed in the context of the program as a whole, the role he assumes in the episodes of the play is the subject of detailed recording described below.

2. Recording Procedure

Observers must be familiar with the way each major character is portrayed in the play. They therefore must see the program at least once and may re-screen details if necessary.

In the first step, both observers in the pair must agree on which characters to record, and then record the characters' full names, with brief verbal descriptions of each.

In the second step, both observers *jointly decide* on the category assignments along the first 21 variables.

In the third step, each observer fills out a separate sheet, both sheets containing 27 identical semantic differential scales. For this, the observers are instructed as follows:

Place an X in the space closer to the end of each scale which fits the character better than the opposite. If one end of the scale seems *very closely associated* with the character, you would mark the first scale, for example, like this:

old   X   :   :   :   :   :   young or old   :   :   :   :   X   young

If one end of the scale seems *quite closely related* to the character, you would mark the scale like this:

old   :   X   :   :   :   :   young or old   :   :   :   X   :   young

If one. end of the scale is *only slightly related* to the character, you would mark the scale like this:

old   :   :   X   :   :   :   young or old   :   :   X   :   :   young

If both sides are *equally associated* with the character, or if you cannot decide which is more related to the character, or if the scale does not apply to the character, mark the center space. Mark each scale.

Cover Page for Card Number   (1st Semantic Differential)

Column	Code	Description
1-3	2 5 5	Project number
4-5		Total number of characters
6-9		Character ID for this card
10-11		Card number
12-13		Coder identification
14-15		(Blank)

(16-63)=Basic character data plus Semantic Differential for First Coder.

Cover Page for Card Number   (2d Semantic Differential)

Column	Code	Description
1-3	2 5 5	Project number
4-5		Total number of characters
6-9		Character ID for this card
10-11		Card number
12-13		Coder identification
14-36		(Blank)

(37-63)=Semantic Differential Data for Second Coder.

Program
Names of codes
Today's date

Part II: Character Analysis

16.	27.
17.	28.
18.	29.
19.	30.
20.	31.
21.	32.
22.	33.
23.	34.
24.	35.
25.	36.
26.	

B-5

Do Not Write in Boxes

Left					Right	Column	Code
old	:	:	:	:	young	37	
tall	:	:	:	:	short	38	
unusual	:	:	:	:	usual	39	
emotional	:	:	:	:	unemotional	40	
dull	:	:	:	:	sharp	41	
honest	:	:	:	:	dishonest	42	
feminine	:	:	:	:	masculine	43	
happy	:	:	:	:	sad	44	
repulsive	:	:	:	:	attractive	45	
tough	:	:	:	:	delicate	46	
moral	:	:	:	:	immoral	47	
predictable	:	:	:	:	unpredictable	48	
wholesome	:	:	:	:	unwholesome	49	
irrational	:	:	:	:	rational	50	
sensitive	:	:	:	:	insensitive	51	
bungling	:	:	:	:	efficient	52	
kind	:	:	:	:	cruel	53	
learned	:	:	:	:	ignorant	54	
dirty	:	:	:	:	clean	55	
free	:	:	:	:	restrained	56	
intuitive	:	:	:	:	logical	57	
bold	:	:	:	:	timid	58	
sociable	:	:	:	:	unsociable	59	
humble	:	:	:	:	proud	60	
rich	:	:	:	:	poor	61	
good	:	:	:	:	bad	62	
violent	:	:	:	:	non-violent	63	

Each analyst is to code scales independently

Coding Sheet

B-6

						Column	Code
Do Not Write in Boxes							
old	:	:	:	:	young	37	
tall	:	:	:	:	short	38	
unusual	:	:	:	:	usual	39	
emotional	:	:	:	:	unemotional	40	
dull	:	:	:	:	sharp	41	
honest	:	:	:	:	dishonest	42	
feminine	:	:	:	:	masculine	43	
happy	:	:	:	:	sad	44	
repulsive	:	:	:	:	attractive	45	
tough	:	:	:	:	delicate	46	
moral	:	:	:	:	immoral	47	
predictable	:	:	:	:	unpredictable	48	
wholesome	:	:	:	:	unwholesome	49	
irrational	:	:	:	:	rational	50	
sensitive	:	:	:	:	insensitive	51	
bungling	:	:	:	:	efficient	52	
kind	:	:	:	:	cruel	53	
learned	:	:	:	:	ignorant	54	
dirty	:	:	:	:	clean	55	
free	:	:	:	:	restrained	56	
intuitive	:	:	:	:	logical	57	
bold	:	:	:	:	timid	58	
sociable	:	:	:	:	unsociable	59	
humble	:	:	:	:	proud	60	
rich	:	:	:	:	poor	61	
good	:	:	:	:	bad	62	
violent	:	:	:	:	non-violent	63	

Each analyst is to code scales independently

3. Variables and Categories

Full name of the character and a one sentence description is required

(a) Demographic Characteristics and Relation to Violence

Sex (16) . . . .   (1)   Male.
                                     (2)   Female.
                                     (9)   Other (explain).

Humanity (17) . . . .   (1)   Human.
                                 (2)   Humanized (speaking) animal.
                                 (3)   Animal (not "humanized").
                                 (9)   Uncertain, other.

Age (18) . . . .   (1)   Infant, preschool age.
                                   (2)   Primary school age.
                                   (3)   Secondary school age; teens; adolescent.
                                   (4)   Young adult.
                                   (5)   Middle age (may play romantic part).
                                   (6)   Old.
                                   (9)   Ageless, several, other, cannot specify
                                          (explain on Coding sheet).

Marital status (19) . . . . . .   (1)   Unmarried or unknown, uncertain, other.
                                   (2)   Married, or has been married.
                                   (3)   Marries in story or expects to marry.

Occupation (20) . . . .   (1)   Housewife.
                                   (2)   Illegal (code for criminals, outlaws).
                                   (3)   Armed forces; militia.
                                   (4)   Entertainment, arts, mass media.
                                   (5)   Official law enforcement: police, FBI, T-men;
                                          marshal, sheriff.
                                   (6)   Agent working for private "client" in occupation
                                          that usually involve crime or violence; private
                                          detective, etc.
                                   (9)   Professional, other, uncertain, no visible means
                                          of support (explain on Coding sheet).

Note: If the character has several occupations simultaneously, consider only the major one.

Ethnicity (21) . . . .   (1)   White, Anglo-Saxon, native American.
                                   (2)   White, non-Anglo-Saxon, native American.
                                   (3)   White foreign-born American (speaks with accent, etc.).
                                   (4)   White non-American (other nationality).
                                   (5)   Non-white American.
                                   (6)   Non-white non-American.
                                   (9)   Uncertain, other.

Note: The nationality and ethnicity of the character must be judged as apparent on the screen.

Soc./Econ. status (22) . . . . .   (1)   Upper, elite, executive.
                                   (2)   Middle, average common, other, uncertain, mixed.
                                   (3)   Lower, poor.

Victim (23) . . . .   (1)   Not subjected to violence.
                                   (2)   Subjected to violence, not fatal.
                                   (3)   Dies violent death.
                                   (9)   Subjected, other.

Note: If several categories are appropriate for situations at different points in time consider the highest degree of violence to which he is subjected.

Aggressor (24) . . . .   (1)   Does not subject another to violence.
                                   (2)   Subjects another to violence, not fatal.
                                   (3)   Commits fatal violence.
                                   (9)   Subjects, other.

Note: If several categories are appropriate for situations at different points in time consider the highest degree of violence involved.

Final outcome (25) . . . . . .   (1)   Clearly happy, unambiguous success.
                                   (2)   Clearly unhappy; unambiguous failure.
                                   (3)   Mixed, unclear, ambiguous.

(b) Values Held by the Character

Sexual or amorous goals (26) .   (0)   If it was not explicitly desired
                                          or sought by the character at any
                                          time in the program (whether
                                          achieved or not).

	(1)	If it was explicitly desired or sought by the character at any time in the program.
Family, home (27)	(0) (1)	As above.
Respect for legality (28) . . .	(0) (1)	As above.
Money, material goods (29) .	(0) (1)	As above.
Ambition, will for power (30)	(0) (1)	As above.
Religious (31)	(0) (1)	As above.
Scientific (32)	(0) (1)	As above.
Artistic (33)	(0) (1)	As above.
Self-preservation (34)	(0) (1)	As above.
Vengeance (35)	(0) (1)	As above.
Evil, destructive, wanton goals (36)	(0) (1)	As above.

(c) Personality Characteristics of the Character

old	:	:	:	:	:	:	young
tall	:	:	:	:	:	:	short
unusual	:	:	:	:	:	:	usual
emotional	:	:	:	:	:	:	unemotional
dull	:	:	:	:	:	:	sharp
honest	:	:	:	:	:	:	dishonest
feminine	:	:	:	:	:	:	masculine
happy	:	:	:	:	:	:	sad
repulsive	:	:	:	:	:	:	attractive
tough	:	:	:	:	:	:	delicate
moral	:	:	:	:	:	:	immoral
predictable	:	:	:	:	:	:	unpredictable
wholesome	:	:	:	:	:	:	unwholesome
irrational	:	:	:	:	:	:	rational
sensitive	:	:	:	:	:	:	insensitive
bungling	:	:	:	:	:	:	efficient
kind	:	:	:	:	:	:	cruel
learned	:	:	:	:	:	:	ignorant
dirty	:	:	:	:	:	:	clean
free	:	:	:	:	:	:	restrained
intuitive	:	:	:	:	:	:	logical
bold	:	:	:	:	:	:	timid
sociable	:	:	:	:	:	:	unsociable
humble	:	:	:	:	:	:	proud
rich	:	:	:	:	:	:	poor
good	:	:	:	:	:	:	bad
violent	:	:	:	:	:	:	non-violent

4. Reliability of Variables

Below are listed the final reliability estimates for all those variables that survived the pretest. The reliability is assessed on the basis of a random sample of 30 programs out of a total of 183 and contained 66 characters out of a total of 455. In the case of personality characteristics, the scale values of the two observers were summed.

The information is listed in the following order:

Name of variable
Type of scale (N=nominal, I=interval)
Recoding whenever the report differs from primary data
Reliability coefficient (1=perfect agreement and 0=chance)
Inclusion in the report (Yes=included, No=rejected)

(a) Demographic Characteristics and Relation to Violence

Sex (16)	N		0.904	Yes
Humanity (17)	N		.903	Yes
Age (18)	N		.686	Yes
Marital status (19)	N		.939	Yes
Occupation (20)	N		.893	Yes
Ethnicity (21)	N	(1, 2, 3), 4, (5, 6), 9	.722	Yes
Soc./Econ status (22)	I		.651	No
Victim (23)	N	(1,2),3	.792	Yes
Aggressor (24)	N		.734	Yes
Final outcome (25)	N		.721	Yes

(b) Values Held by the Character

Sexual/amorous goals (26)	N	.482	No
Family/home (27)	N	.754	Yes
Respect for law (28)	N	.665	No
Money, goods (29)	N	.450	No
Ambition (30)	N	.573	No
Religious (31)	N	.484	No
Scientific (32)	N	.631	No
Artistic (33)	N	1.0	Yes
Self-preservation (34)	N	.624	No
Vengeance (35)	N	.573	No
Evil, destructive goals (36)	N	.716	Yes

(c) Personality Characteristics of the Character

Old-young (37)	I	.709	Yes
Tall-short (38)	I	.678	Yes
Unusual-usual (39)	I	.591	No
Emotional-unemotional (40	I	.525	No
Dull-sharp (41)	I	.434	No
Honest-dishonest (42)	I	.789	Yes
Feminine-Masculine (43)	I	.778	Yes
Happy-sad (44)	I	.652	No
Repulsive-attractive (45)	I	.565	No
Tough-delicate (46)	I	.572	No
Moral-immoral (47)	I	.760	Yes
Predictable-unpredictable (48)	I	.516	No
Wholesome-unwholesome (49)	I	.747	Yes
Irrational-rational (50)	I	.589	No
Sensitive-insensitive (51)	I	.657	No
Bungling-efficient (52)	I	.564	No

Kind-cruel (53)   I   .773   Yes
Learned-ignorant (54)   I   .567   No
Dirty-clean (55)   I   .252   No
Free-restrained (56)   I   .358   No
Intuitive-logical (57)   I   .484   No
Bold-timid (58)   I   .372   No
Sociable-unsociable (59)   I   .438   No
Humble-proud (60)   I   .253   No
Rich-poor (61)   I   .824   Yes
Good-bad (62)   I   .581   No
Violent-nonviolent (63)   I   .783   Yes

5. Current Form of Primary Data

Data are available in the form of IBM punchcards.

Card No. 1

Column	Variable	Code
1-3	Project number	225.
4	Recording unit	2=character.
5	Number of character in program	Exact number.
6		Blank.
7-9	Character identification	For a list, see the end of this appendix.
10-12	Program identification .	For a list, see the end of this appendix.
13	Card number	1.
14-15	Coder identification . .	For a list, see the end of this appendix.
16	Sex	(1) Male. (2) Female. (3) Other.
17	Humanity	(1) Human. (2) Humanized (speaking) animal. (3) Animal (not "humanized"). (9) Uncertain, other.
18	Age	(1) Infant, preschool age. (2) Primary school age. (3) Secondary school age; teens; adolescent. (4) Young adult. (5) Middle age (may play romantic part). (6) Old. (9) Ageless, several, other, cannot specify.
19	Marital status	(1) Unmarried or unknown, uncertain, other. (2) Married, or has been married. (3) Marries in story or expects to marry.

Column	Variable	Code	
20	Major occupation . . .	(1)	Housewife.
		(2)	Illegal (criminals, outlaws).
		(3)	Armed forces; militia.
		(4)	Entertainment, arts, mass media.
		(5)	Official law enforcement: police, FBI, T-men; marshal, sheriff.
		(6)	Agent working for private "client" in occupation that usually involves crime or violence; private detective, etc.
		(9)	Professional, other, uncertain, no visible means of support.
21	Ethnicity	(1)	White, Anglo-Saxon, native American.
		(2)	White, non-Anglo-Saxon, native American.
		(3)	White foreign-born American (speaks with accent, etc.)
		(4)	White non-American (other nationality).
		(5)	Non-white American.
		(6)	Non-white non-American.
		(9)	Uncertain, other.
22	Socio-economic status .	(1)	Upper, elite, executive.
		(2)	Middle, average, common, other, uncertain, mixed.
		(3)	Lower, poor.
23	Victim	(1)	Not subjected to violence.
		(2)	Subjected to violence, not fatal.
		(3)	Dies violent death.
		(9)	Subjected, other.
24	Aggressor	(1)	Does not subject another to violence.
		(2)	Subjects another to violence, not fatal.
		(3)	Commits fatal violence.
		(9)	Subjects, other.
25	Final outcome	(1)	Clearly happy, unambiguous success.
		(2)	Clearly unhappy; unambiguous failure.
		(3)	Mixed, unclear, ambiguous.
26	Sexual or amorous . . .		0=not explicitly desired. 1=explicitly desired.
27	Family, home		0=not explicitly desired. 1=explicitly desired.
28	Respect for legality . .		0=not explicitly desired. 1=explicitly desired.
29	Money, material goods		0=not explicitly desired. 1=explicitly desired.
30	Ambition, will for power		0=not explicitly desired. 1=explicitly desired.
31	Religion		0=not explicitly desired. 1=explicitly desired.

Column	Variable	Code
32	Scientific	0=not explicitly desired. 1=explicitly desired.
33	Artistic	0=not explicitly desired. 1=explicitly desired.
34	Self-preservation	0=not explicitly desired. 1=explicitly desired.
35	Vengeance	0=not explicitly desired. 1=explicitly desired.
36	Evil, destructive goals .	0=not explicitly desired. 1=explicitly desired.
37	Old-young	(Columns 37-63: score range from 1-7; 1 is assigned to the left term and 7 is assigned to its polar opposite on the right.)
38	Short-tall	
39	Unusual-usual	
40	Emotional-unemotional	
41	Dull-sharp	
42	Dishonest-honest	
43	Feminine-masculine . .	
44	Sad-happy	
45	Repulsive-attractive . .	
46	Delicate-tough	
47	Immoral-moral	
48	Unpredictable-predictable	
49	Unwholesome-wholesome	
50	Irrational-rational . . .	
51	Insensitive-sensitive . .	
52	Bungling-efficient . . .	
53	Cruel-kind	
54	Ignorant-learned	
55	Dirty-clean	
56	Restrained-free	
57	Intuitive-logical	
58	Bold-timid	
59	Unsociable-sociable . .	
60	Humble-proud	
61	Poor-rich	

Column	Variable	Code
62	Bad-good	
63	Violent-non-violent . .	

Card No. 2

Column	Variable	Code
1-3	Project number	225.
4	Recording unit	2-character.
5	Number of character in program	Exact number.
6		Blank.
7-9	Character identification	For a list, see the end of this appendix.
10-12	Program identification	For a list, see the end of this appendix.
13	Card number	2.
14-15	Coder identification . .	For a list, see the end of this appendix.
16-36		Blank.
37	Old-young	Columns 37-63: score ranges from 1-7; 1 is assigned to the left term and 7 is assigned to its polar opposite on the right.)
38	Short-tall	
39	Unusual-usual	
40	Emotional-unemotional	
41	Dull-sharp	
42	Dishonest-honest	
43	Feminine-masculine . .	
44	Sad-happy	
45	Repulsive-attractive . .	
46	Delicate-tough	
47	Immoral-moral	
48	Unpredictable-predictable	
49	Unwholesome-wholesome	
50	Irrelational-rational . .	
51	Insensitive-sensitive . .	
52	Bungling-efficient . . .	
53	Cruel-kind	
54	Ignorant-learned	

Column	Variable	Code
55	Dirty-clean	
56	Restrained-free	
57	Intuitive-logical	
58	Bold-timid	
59	Unsociable-sociable . .	
60	Humble-proud	
61	Poor-rich	
62	Bad-good	
63	Violent-nonviolent . . .	

C. The Recording Instrument for Violent Episodes

1. Recording Unit

The unit of recording for which this Instrument is designed is called a *violent episode*. A program may contain many violent episodes and in order to identify these units two definitions have been advanced as follows:

Violence is defined to include physical or psychological injury, hurt, or death, addressed to living things. Violence is explicit and overt. It can be verbal or physical. If verbal, it must express intent to use physical force and must be plausible and credible in the context of the program. Idle, distant, or vague threats: mere verbal insults, quarrels, or abuse: or comic threats with no violent intent behind them are not to be considered violent.

A violent *episode* is defined as a scene of whatever duration which concerns the same agent and the same receiver. Thus, a battle scene would be one episode; a chase scene with a posse pursuing a man would be one episode, even if interrupted by flashbacks to other scenes; an attack by one person on a second, in the course of which a third person attacks the first, would be two episodes.

2. Recording Procedure

The recording of violent episodes presupposes viewing the program as a whole, making necessary observations and, when necessary to complete the data sheets, a reviewing of the details.

A log containing notes pertaining to observed acts concerned with violence, weapons, war, etc., is compiled during the viewing. This record then provides the basis for identifying the program's set of violent episodes. Their actual number in the program is to be listed in the appropriate space on the data sheet. Then each violent episode (working across the respective rows on the data sheet) is to be judged independently according to the specified variables.

Cover Page for Card No. 3

Column	Code	Description
1-3	2 5 5	Project number
4	1	Deck number
5		Extent of violence
6-7		(Blank)
8-9	0 3	Card number
10-12		Program ID
13		(Blank)
14-15		Coder ID

Column	Code	Description
16-17		Number of violent episodes:
18-29		Episode 1
30-41		Episode 2
42-53		Episode 3
54-65		Episode 4
66-67		Episode 5

Cover Page for Card No. 4

Column	Code	Description
1-3	2 5 5	Project number
4	1	Deck number
5		Extent of violence
6-7		(Blank)
8-9	0 4	Card number
10-12		Program identification
13		(Blank)
14-15		Coder identification
16-17		Number of violent episodes:
18-29		Episode 6
30-41		Episode 7
42-53		Episode 8
54-65		Episode 9
66-77		Episode 10

Cover Page for Card No. 5

Column	Code	Description
1-3	2 5 5	Project number
4	1	Deck number
5		Extent of violence
6-7		(Blank)
8-9	0 5	Card number
10-12		Program identification
13		(Blank)
14-15		Coder identification
16-17		Number of violent episodes:
18-29		Episode 11
30-41		Episode 12
42-53		Episode 13
54-65		Episode 14
66-77		Episode 15

Cover Page for Card No. 6

Column	Code	Description
1-3	2 5 5	Project number
4	1	Deck number
5		Extent of violence
6-7		(Blank)
8-9	0 6	Card number
10-12		Program identification
13		(Blank)
14-15		Coder identification
16-17		Number of violent episodes:
18-29		Episode 16
30-41		Episode 17

Column	Code	Description
42-53		Episode 18
54-65		Episode 19
66-77		Episode 20

Cover Page for Card No. 7

Column	Code	Description
1-3	2 5 5	Project number
4	1	Deck number
5		Extent of violence
6-7		(Blank)
8-9	0 7	Card number
10-12		Program identification
13		(Blank)
14-15		Coder identification
16-17		Number of violent episodes:
18-29		Episode 21
30-41		Episode 22
42-53		Episode 23
54-65		Episode 24
66-77		Episode 25

Coding Sheet
Letter

Episode No.	a	b	c	d	e	f	g	h	i	j	k
1											
2											
3											
4											
5											
6											
7											
8											
9											
10											
11											
12											
13											
14											
15											
16											
17											
18											
19											
20											

3. Variables and Categories

Number of episodes . . . . . .   Exact number of violent episodes that occur
                                  in the program.

Agent (a) . . . .   (1)   Human (live or cartoon) individual(s).
                                  (2)   Humanized (speaking) animal (e.g. in cartoons).
                                  (3)   Animal (live or cartoon).
                                  (4)   "Thing," creature.
                                  (5)   Act of nature (widespread effect; not merely
                                             an accident).
                                  (6)   Accident (mechanical or other; mishap; chance).
                                  (9)   Other.

Weapons (b) . . . .   (1)   None; carried out by verbal or bodily means only.
                                  (2)   Weapon is used.
                                  (9)   Other.

Context (c) . . . .   (1)   Violence which occurs in serious or sinister
                                             contexts.
                                  (2)   Comic or sham violence.

Double context (d) . . . . . .   (1)   If the context is "1" above *and* if there is a
                                             comic element built into the presentation,
                                             despite its serious surface appearance. For
                                             example, canned (or real) audience laughter
                                             on soundtrack despite apparently real injury.
                                             Mark only if there is clear evidence of comic
                                             effect *in the context of serious presentation.*
                                  (0)   If no such double context is present or if
                                             irrelevant.

Witnesses (e) . . . .   (1)   The witnesses are passive; they do not or cannot
                                             react.
                                  (2)   The witnesses assist or encourage violence.
                                  (3)   The witnesses attempt to prevent, restrain, or
                                             seek alternatives to violence.
                                  (9)   Other, or no witnesses.

L.-enf. violent role (f) . . . . .   (1)   They play a non-violent role.
                                  (2)   They commit violence in the course of official
                                             duties.
                                  (3)   They commit violence, but not in the course of
                                             official duties.
                                  (9)   Other, or they play no role.

Note: Law enforcement agencies include only police, sheriff, marshal, official, deputies and detectives—not private detectives, agents, spies, armed forces, etc.

L.-enf. violence justified (g)   (1)   If violence is committed by law enforcement
                                             agencies, their actions are portrayed on the
                                             screen as justified.
                                  (2)   Their actions are portrayed on the screen as
                                             unjustified.
                                  (3)   Their actions are portrayed on the screen as
                                             both justified and unjustified (i.e., "mixed").
                                  (9)   Irrelevant (i.e., violence is not committed).

L.-enf. initiation/response (h)   (1)   If the agents of law enforcement play a role
                                             in violence, they initiate violence.
                                  (2)   They respond to violence in a violent manner.

(3)   They respond to violence in a non-violent manner.
(4)   They become victims of violence.
(9)   Irrelevant (i.e., they do not play a role).

L.-enf.-viol. necessary (i) . . (1)   If the agents of law enforcement play a role in
                                          violence, they commit only that level of violence
                                          which appears necessary to accomplish their
                                          objective(s).
                           (2)   They commit violence which appears to go beyond
                                          what is necessary (i.e., brutality, and
                                          recognized as such on screen).
                           (3)   Both, mixed.
                           (9)   Irrelevant (i.e., they do not play a role).

Relations-opponents (j) . . . (1)   Group relations among violent opponents are
                                          in the family.
                           (2)   Violent opponents are members of the same
                                          national or ethnic groups (but not in family).
                           (3)   Violent opponents are members of different
                                          national or ethnic groups.
                           (9)   Other.

Non-fatal casualties (k) . . . (0)   None
                           (1)   One
                           (2)   Two
                           (3)   Three
                           (4)   Four
                           (5)   Five
                           (6)   Six
                           (7)   Seven
                           (8)   Eight or more, but can be counted
                           (9)   Mass casualties; cannot be counted

Note: Count the number of persons or humanized animals hurt in the scene.

Fatal casualties (l) . . . . . .   (0)   None
                           (1)   One
                           (2)   Two
                           (3)   Three
                           (4)   Four
                           (5)   Five
                           (6)   Six
                           (7)   Seven
                           (8)   Eight or more, but can be counted
                           (9)   Mass casualties; cannot be counted

Note: Count the number of fatal casualties (bodies) in the scene. Include victims who are shown dead or who die as a consequence of injury in the scene.

4. Reliability of Variables

Below are listed the final reliability estimates for all those variables that survived the pre-test. The reliability is assessed on the basis of a random sample of 30 programs out of a total of 183 and contained 52 violent episodes out of a total of 873.

The information is listed in the following order:
   Name of variable
   Type of scale (*N*=nominal, *I*=interval)
   Recoding whenever the report differs from primary data
   Reliability coefficient (1=perfect agreement and 0=chance)
   Inclusion in the report (Yes=included, No=rejected)

No. of episodes	I		Not accessible
Agent (a)	N		.731 Yes
Weapons (b)	N	1 (2, 9)	.799 Yes
Context (c)	N		.736 Yes
Double context (d)	N		.729 Yes
Witnesses (e)	N		.677 Yes
L. enf.-violence role (f)	N		.819 Yes
L. enf.-violence justified (g)	N		.866 Yes
L. enf.-initiation/response (h)	N		.761 Yes
L. enf.-violence necessary (i)	N		1.0 Yes
Relations-opponents (j)	N		.915 Yes
Nonfatal casualties (k)	I		.995 Yes
Fatal casualties (l)	I		.514 No
Casualties, (k) and (l) summed	I		.710 Yes

D. The Recording Instrument for Violent Encounters and Acts and their Justification

1. Recording Unit

The units in terms of which violent encounters are transcribed are acts of violence. One TV program may have many acts of violence. Each has to be recorded as a separate entity. Acts of violence have to meet the following two defining criteria:

1. People, human groups or living things (including animals with human characteristics) are physically harmed, forcefully restrained or barely escape death, injury, pain, etc.

2. The harm is caused by or explained in terms of the behavior of other people. (Intention and motivation do not enter as defining criteria and entirely verbal threats are also excluded).

The two criteria for identifying acts of violence may be *distributed over a whole program*. Thus if an event is explained initially as an accident but linked to the behavior of another person at a later point in the drama it qualifies as an act of violence.

If harm, injury or physical confinement cannot be linked to individuals or groups of individuals then, by definition, it does not constitute an act of violence. Violence is a *form of interaction* involving at least two individuals or groups. The armed pursuit of a person constitutes an act of violence even though the bullet may miss its target. Forcing a person at gun point is an act of violence but just pointing a gun at someone may merely be regarded a threat and is therefore excluded as an act of violence. Acts of violence must have actual or potentially harmful consequences for their receivers. If one party physically attacks another party and the latter does not return the violence in defense, then the violent encounter has to be recorded as a single act. Acts of violence are distinguished on the number of bullets fired or how severe the kick may have been. Acts of violence mediate between a source of violence and a receiver.

However, if the receiver in turn *responds* with violence then the encounter has to be characterized by two acts of violence with the parties being interchangeably source and receiver of violence, though perhaps for different reasons. Lengthy shooting duels, fist fights and large-scale battle scenes would have to be regarded as two acts of violence provided that the exchange is actually shown (and not merely present in the fantasies of one party) and that this interaction is continuous, i.e., without significant interruptions and without significant changes in the way violence is exchanged.

If a prolonged exchange of violence is not continuous in the sense that major shifts in the style of interactions occur (e.g., a change in the means of fighting, a change in initiative or aims pursued, the introduction of a third party or a change in the original parties involved), then the violence has to be represented by more than two acts of violence. Shifts in the basic dimensions of violent interaction are indicative of transitions from one encounter to the next, differentiating between the acts (or pairs of acts) of violence to be recorded.

Two violent encounters may occur simultaneously on the screen. For example, two parties—who are relatively independent of each other, and whose behavior is not significantly coordinated, and hence cannot be considered a single group—may interact with different portions of a joint enemy. Or, when a third party becomes a source of violence without significantly affecting the nature of violent interaction between the first two parties, then the first encounter may be said to continue while a second encounter may have started at the point of the third party's entry.

For the purpose of analysis several basic components of an act of violence are distinguished each of which is subsequently characterized along several more specific variables.

By definition of an act of violence, the following three components must occur:

1. The *source* of violence, or that person or group which behaves in such a way that some second party is physically affected by it, whether intentionally or not.

2. The *receiver* of violence, or that person or group which is either directly harmed by the source's behavior or put in the immediate danger of being so affected regardless of whether the person or group is aware of the consequences of the encounter. Note that receivers are sometimes merely the vehicles through which an ultimate target is intended to be affected.

3. The *act* of violence, a causal link between the source's behavior and the receiver's harm or danger.

Moreover, there may be:

4. The *beneficiary* of the act or that individual, group or abstract idea in behalf of, or for the benefit of which the violent act is performed. The beneficiary need not appear on the screen but may appear in the source's justification of his behavior or may be asserted in the plot in order to

make his behavior consistent. Source and beneficiary may or may not coincide.

Sometimes the parties of violent encounters are single individuals (e.g., the lone hero or victim). But more often the role of the source and/or receiver of violence is assumed by a small group or an organization (e.g., a gang or an army). If a set of characters is referred to as a whole (e.g., the dynamic duo, Garrison's Gorillas, Charlie), if their behavior is highly coordinated (e.g., division of labor, the existence of formal organization) or if they lack individuality in the plot (e.g., same uniform, never shown isolated from others) then they should be regarded as one group. Conversely, if the characters are carefully distinguished, their behavior is relatively independent of each other and differences among their personalities is emphasized, they should be regarded as individuals. However, the recording of acts of violence should consider the fact that characters may act as individuals at one point in time and join a group as indistinguishable members at some other point in time. The witness of a violent encounter is always regarded as one component regardless of how many members it contains.

Beneficiaries are often perceived in terms of a hierarchy of increasing generality. A particular police officer may be seen as a member of a patrol and this patrol could be taken as an incident of the police in general which in turn is part of everything that is concerned with the preservation of law and order. Law enforcement agencies may have to fight on all levels. However, if it is the declared purpose of a detective to fight *his own* enemy then the beneficiary is the source itself. Generally, the beneficiary should be identified as that person, group or abstract idea which is thought to be gaining *most directly* from the acts of violence or which is *most explicitly* asserted in the source's justification for the act. The observer should avoid long chains of reasoning and describe the most obvious beneficiary and ultimate target.

2. Recording Procedure

The observer must *see the whole program* at least once (during which he may make informal notes regarding the acts of violence involved).

One cover sheet is provided for each program and one data sheet for each act of violence with cells into which the required information is to be inserted. No cell should be left blank.

The first step of the recording procedure is to *isolate the acts of violence* occurring in the program. The two defining criteria must be met in each case. It seems to be helpful to note the beginning and the end of the act of violence and to write this down on the data sheet for further reference. Then assign a serial number to this act, beginning with "01."

The second step of the recording procedure is to *identify the components* for describing the act in detail. The principal characters and groups involved in the violent encounter are to be assigned identification numbers. These are to be inserted in the appropriate cells for the source and the receiver on the data sheet together with a short description of the character or group.

The third step of the procedure is to *record* more detailed information along several variables. A set of questions are formulated that require an answer in terms of predefined *categories* and may call for a short *verbal description.*

TV - Violence/Part C - F/Programs

2 1
5 2
5 3
9 4
columns 5 through 9 BLAN]

Program

10
11
12
column 13 BLANK

Coders

14
15

3. Variables and Categories

(a) The *Source* of Violence

The verbal description of the source is required:

Ethnicity . . . .   (0)   Not identifiable.
   (1)   Identifiable.

If the source's ethnicity is identifiable give a verbal description (e.g., Negro, German, American Indian. Do not forget to include American white).

Sex . . . .   (0)   Indeterminate (like some cartoon characters).
   (1)   Male individual or group of males.
   (2)   Female individual or group of females.
   (3)   Mixed (if it is a group with both males and females).

Stardom . . . .   (0)   No visible role (only indirectly referred to).
   (1)   Minor part (role neither central nor extensive).
   (2)   Medium part (in between minor and major).
   (3)   Major part (role central and/or very extensive).

Note: Only the role in the plot has to be taken into account, not some actor's general fame.

Serial . . . .   (0)   Program is not a serial.
   (1)   Regular part (mostly announced as such).
   (2)   Guest part (mostly announced as such).

Group-belongingness . . . .   (1)   Isolated individual (no clear cut co-operation with or close ties to other individuals in the dramatic plot. *Note:* disregard information on ties to individuals not actually shown on screen.
   (2)   Group-leader (someone who actually has or shares the highest authority in the group he belongs to).
   (3)   Group member.
   (4)   Group (non-individualized collectivity).

Good-bad . . . .   (0)   Irrelevant (not clearly portrayed as good or bad; neutral).

(1)   Good (portrayed as belonging basically to the right side, even though he may on occasion act wrongly).

(2)   Bad (portrayed as belonging basically to the wrong side, even though he may on occasion act in the right way).

(3)   Good-bad (someone who switches from the right side to the wrong side, or the other way around; or someone with a complex role, as in Greek tragedy).

Relation to law . . . . (0)   No special relation to the law portrayed (e.g., ordinary citizen).

(1)   Law enforcement officer (e.g., policeman, national guard, etc., if portrayed in that role).

(2)   Semilaw enforcement (e.g., private detective working closely together with police; prison guard, executioner).

(3)   Criminal (if portrayed in that role).

Final outcome . . . . (0)   Neither gain nor loss shown; irrelevant; if a person or group does not appear in latest part of show, and is not by implication there, code 0 is appropriate.

(1)   Clear winner (e.g., gangster who gets away with the loot, the sheriff who killed the outlaw, etc.).

(2)   Winner - but (e.g., the man who got away, but lost a close friend; i.e., Pyrrhic victory).

(3)   Loser - but (e.g., the man who lands in jail but has a treasure hidden somewhere).

(4)   Clear loser (e.g., killed, or imprisoned without compensation).

(b) The Beneficiary of the Violence as Perceived by the Source

Beneficiary . . . . (0)   A designated individual.
(1)   A designated leader of a group.
(2)   A small group, a team.
(3)   An organization.
(4)   A large collectivity and/or an abstract idea as represented by the convictions and beliefs of many people.

Relation source-beneficiary . (0)   Identity (the source is the beneficiary).
(1)   Family ties and friendship, affection, communion and informal relations.

(2)   Formal social, occupational and economical grounds, on relations between well defined roles (e.g., employer-employee, officer-soldier or formal authority).

(3)   Ideological, ethnic and religious grounds or stems merely from possessing certain common or contrasting properties such as race, convictions, age groups, etc.

(4)   General rules of social conduct in public places, cutting across familial, formal social and ideological boundaries. (The encounter is typically accidental, e.g., with a stranger, but social norms are not absent.)

(c) The Act of Violence

A verbal description is required of both the act of violence and the instruments used by the source during the violent encounter.

TV-Violence 1 Part CF 1 Acts

Source

21 | 2 (ethnicity)

22 | 5

- 23 ethnicity
- 24 sex
- 25 stardom
- 26 serial
- 27 group-belongingness
- 28 good-bad
- 29 law
- 30 outcome
- 31 beneficiary
- 32 relation source-beneficiary

21 | 1 (nature of act)

21 | 3 (instrument)

- 33 complexity of instrument
- 34 degree of seriousness
- 35 distance source-receiver
- 36 prior relation source-receiver
- 37 amount of non-violent interaction
- 38 sexual aspect

Receiver

21 | 4 (ethnicity)

- 39 ethnicity
- 40 sex
- 41 stardom
- 42 serial
- 43 group-belongingness
- 44 good-bad
- 45 law
- 46 outcome
- 47 cognitive preparation
- 48 immediate response
- 49 consequences

Complexity of instruments . (1)   No instruments (e.g., fists).
(2)   Small devices, objects from everyday life (e.g., furniture, cars, small concealable firearms) including natural forces (e.g., leaving receiver in desert).
(3)   Somewhat more sophisticated and specialized machinery (e.g., torture chambers, specially prepared traps, machine guns, plastic explosives).
(4)   Elaborate organization and/or complex and specialized machinery (e.g., mass destruction devices, acts of James Bond's enemies).

Note: In the case of instruments of a mixed type, (e.g., fist fighting as well as shooting with a gun), always record the more complex of the instruments involved.

Seriousness . . . . (1)   Violence appears as an integral part of slapstick, (e.g., The Three Stooges, pie fights, cartoons).
(2)   Violence appears in the context of self satire, high camp.
(3)   Violence appears as scrimmage, friendly competition.
(4)   Violence appears as a real fight, serious combat.

Note: To decide how serious the violence is meant, consider the overall climate in which the violent acts take place. If removed from its contextual setting, the degree of seriousness may be distorted. If more than one category is appropriate, take the first one on this list.

Perceptual distance . . . . (1)   Direct, interpersonal, and of closest proximity, i.e., within natural talking distance (e.g., violence within a small room or small area).
(2)   Mediated in face-to-face contact, i.e., involving distances beyond the limits of natural conversation (e.g., sniper, cannon).
(3)   Mediated without sight (e.g., poisoning without observing the effects, sending the receiver into a fatal situation, dynamiting with a fuse).
(4)   Global and/or undirected (e.g., killing by push button, nuclear missiles, etc.) directed indiscriminately against a large population.

(d) Relations Between Source and Receiver

Prior relation . . . . (0)   None (strangers).
(1)   Husband and wife.
(2)   Direct family (parents, children, brothers, sisters).
(3)   Family, other.
(4)   Friends.
(5)   Neighbors.
(6)   Job colleagues, coworkers.
(7)   Competitors.
(8)   Enemies.
(9)   Other.

Note: Here the relationship between source and receiver, as existing prior to their first violent encounter, has to be coded. This applies also when entering the code for the second, third, etc., violent encounter.

Non-violent int   . . . . . (0)   No other than violent interaction.
(1)   Minor (only on one or two occasions, of short duration).
(2)   Medium (in between minor and major).

	(3)	Major (very frequent and/or of long duration).

Sexual aspect	(0)	No sexual aspect.
	(1)	Sex explicitly present (kissing, necking and other overt behavior).
	(2)	Sex implicitly present (as indicated by relevant verbal statements; by relationship husband-wife lovers, boy friend-girl friend, or by flirtation).

(e) The Receiver of Violence

A verbal description of the receiver is required:

Ethnicity	(0)	Not identifiable.
	(1)	Identifiable.

If the receiver's ethnicity is identifiable give a verbal description (e.g., Negro, German, American Indian. Do not forget to include American white).

Sex	(0)	Indeterminate (like some cartoon characters).
	(1)	Male individual or group of males.
	(2)	Female individual or group of females.
	(3)	Mixed (if it is a group with both males and females).

Stardom	(0)	No visible role (only indirectly referred to).
	(1)	Minor part (role neither central nor extensive).
	(2)	Medium part (in between minor and major).
	(3)	Major part (role central and/or very extensive).

Note: Only the role in the plot has to be taken into account, *not* some actor's general fame.

Serial	(0)	Program is not a serial.
	(1)	Regular part (mostly announced as such).
	(2)	Guest part (mostly announced as such).

Group-belongingness . . .	(1)	Isolated individual (no clear cut co-operation with or close ties to other individuals in the dramatic plot. *Note:* disregard information on ties to individuals not actually shown on screen.)
	(2)	Group-leader (someone who actually has or shares the highest authority in the group he belongs to).
	(3)	Group member.
	(4)	Group (non-individualized collectivity).

Good-bad	(0)	Irrelevant (not clearly portrayed as good or bad; neutral).
	(1)	Good (portrayed as belonging basically to the right side, even though he may on occasion act wrongly).
	(2)	Bad (portrayed as belonging basically to the wrong side, even though he may on occasion act in the right way).
	(3)	Good-bad (someone who switches from the right side to the wrong side, or the other way around; or someone with a complex role, as in Greek tragedy.

Relation to law	(0)	No special relation to the law portrayed (e.g., ordinary citizen).
	(1)	Law enforcement officer (e.g., policeman, national guard, etc., if portrayed in that role).
	(2)	Semi-law enforcement (e.g., private detective

working closely together with police; prison
guard, executioner).

(3)   Criminal (if portrayed in that role).

Final outcome . . . . . .   (0)   Neither gain nor loss shown; irrelevant if a
person or group does not appear in latest part
of show, and is not by implication there, code
0 is appropriate.

(1)   Clear winner (e.g., gangster who gets away with
the loot, the sheriff who killed the outlaw, etc.).

(2)   Winner - but (e.g., the man who got away, but lost
a close friend; i.e., Pyrrhic victory).

(3)   Loser - but (e.g., the man who lands in jail
but has a treasure hidden somewhere).

(4)   Clear loser (e.g., killed, or imprisoned without
compensation).

(f) State of and Consequences for the Receiver

Cognitive preparation . . .   (1)   The receiver is totally unaware, violence is not
perceived prior to occurrence (e.g., shooting
from back).

(2)   Recognizes the violence spontaneously, i.e.,
immediately before occurrence (e.g., stranger
draws gun on sheriff).

(3)   Anticipates the violence in general outline, i.e.,
expects violence before encounter takes place,
is warned.

(4)   Anticipates the violence in great detail (e.g.,
when elaborate plans of attack are known to
receiver).

Immediate response . . . .   (2)   Physically unable to respond (e.g., completely
confined, unconscious, dead), not responding
or the response is not clearly recognizable.

(3)   Withdraws from encounter, disengages.

(4)   Submits unconditionally.

(5)   Submits conditionally (e.g., intends to escape,
plans counter-violence or other measures of
retaliation).

(6)   Resists by other than violent means.

(7)   Responds with violence.

Note: All responses that are demanded by the source and are *willingly* executed by
the receiver should be regarded as "unconditional submission." If the receiver submits to
the source's demands in view of subsequent resistance or as a tactical means to counter
violence, the response should be considered "conditional submission."

Consequences . . . . . .   (0)   Are not shown or are not evident on the screen.

(1)   Are shown not to exist, i.e., the receiver
remains unaffected in the long run.

(2)   Somewhat impaired.

(3)   Severely incapacitated.

(4)   Dead or annihilated.

Note: Do not make long chains of inference. If someone is shown to be hurt and
subsequently disappears from the screen, ultimate consequence may not be known,
hence category "0" is appropriate.

Again note: If the receiver is a small group, an organization or a nation, judgments
should consider the severity of the permanent consequences. Thus, if a settler's raid on
an Indian tribe leaves half of its members dead, the tribe might be said to be

"severely incapacitated" though not "dead." If only a few are killed without significantly affecting the tribe's ability to defend itself, the permanent consequence might be "somewhat impaired."

4. Reliability of Variables

In the following the results of the final reliability estimates are listed for all those variables that survived the pre-test. The reliability is assessed on the basis of a random sample of 17 programs out of a total of 183 and contained 156 acts of violence out of a total of 1215. Where both the source and the receiver of violence are characterized by the same variables the observations are taken together.

The information is listed in the following order:

Name of variable
Type of scale (N=nominal, I=interval)
Recording whenever the report differs from primary data
Reliability coefficient (1=perfect agreement and 0=chance)
Inclusion in the report (Yes=included, No=rejected)

(a) The Source of Violence and (e) the Receiver of Violence

Ethnicity	N	0, (1, 2)	.656	No
Sex	N		.915	Yes
Stardom	I	(0, 1,), 2, 3	.652	No
Serial	N		.875	Yes
Group-belongingness	N		.844	Yes
Good-bad	I	1, (0, 3), 2	.886	Yes
Relation to law	N		.784	Yes
Final outcome	I	1, 2, 0, 3, 4	.792	Yes

b. The Beneficiary of Violence

Beneficiary	N	(0, 1), (2, 3, 4)	.650	No
Relation source-beneficiary	N	0, (1, 2, 3, 4)	.704	Yes

(c) The Act of Violence

Complexity of instruments	I	1, 2, (3, 4)	.678	Yes
Seriousness	N	(1, 2), (3, 4)	.827	Yes
Perceptual distance	N	1, 2, (3, 4)	.728	Yes

(d) Relations Between Source and Receiver

Prior relation	N	0, (1, 2, 3, 4, 5, 6, 9), (7, 8)	.460	No
Non-violent interaction	I		.753	Yes
Sexual aspect	N	0, (1, 2)	1.00	Yes

(f) State of and Consequences for the Receiver

Cognitive preparation	I		.616	No
Immediate response	N	(2, 3, 4, 5), 6, 7	.752	Yes
Consequences	N	0, (1, 2, 3, 4)	.473	No
Consequences	I	1, (2, 3), 4	.853	Yes

5. Current Form of Primary Data

Data are available in the form of IBM punchcards.

Column	Variable	Code
1-3	Project number	255
4	Recording unit	9=act of violence
5		Blank
6	Network	1=ABC 2=CBS 3=NBC
7-9		Blank
10-12	Serial number of program .	For a list, see the end of this appendix.
13		Blank
14-15	Observer identification . .	For a list, see the end of this appendix
16-18		Blank
19-20	Serial number of the act of violence	01 to 0.99 depending on the number of acts observed
21		Blank
22	Card Number	5
23	Ethnicity	0=not identifiable 1=identifiable
24	Sex	0=indeterminate 1=male 2=female 3=mixed
25	Stardom	0=no visible role 1=minor part 2=medium part 3=major part
26	Serial	0=program is not a serial 1=regular part 2=guest part
27	Group-belongingness . . .	1=isolated individual 2=group leader 3=member of a group 4=group, collectivity
28	Good-bad	0=neutral, irrelevant 1=good 2=bad 3=good-bad
29	Relation to law	0=none 1=law enforcement officer

Column	Variable	Code
		2=semi-law enforcement 3=criminal
30	Final outcome	0=neither gain nor loss shown 1=clear winner 2=winner - but 3=loser - but 4=clear loser
31	Beneficiary	0=a designated individual 1=a leader of a group 2=a small group or a team 3=an organization 4=a large collectivity
32	Relation source-receiver . .	0=identity, self 1=family and friendship 2=formal social 3=an organization 4=rules of conduct in public
33	Complexity of instruments	1=no instruments 2=small devices 3=somewhat sophisticated machinery 4=elaborate organization
34	Seriousness	1=slapstick 2=self satire, high camp 3=scrimmage, friendly competition 4=fight, serious combat
35	Perceptual distance	1=direct interpersonal 2=mediated in face to face combat 3=mediated without sight 4=global and/or undirected
36	Prior relation	0=none 1=husband 2=direct family 3=family, other 4=friends 5=neighbors 6=job colleagues, co-workers 7=competitors 8=enemies 9=others
37	Non-violent interaction . .	0=none prior to violence 1=minor 2=medium 3=major
38	Sexual aspect	0=no 1=explicitly present 2=implicitly present

Column	Variable	Code
39	Ethnicity	0=not identifiable 1=identifiable
40	Sex	0=indeterminate 1=male individual or group of males 2=female individual or group of females 3=mixed
41	Stardom	0=no visible role 1=minor part 2=medium part 3=major part
42	Serial	0=program is not a serial 1=regular part 2=guest part
43	Group-belongingness . . .	1=isolated individual 2=group-leader 3=group member 4=group
44	Good-bad	0=irrelevant 1=good 2=bad 3=good-bad
45	Relation to law	0=no special relation to the law portrayed 1=law enforcement officer 2=semi-law enforcement 3=criminal
46	Final outcome	0=neither gain nor loss shown 1=clear winner 2=winner - but 3=loser - but 4=clear loser
47	Cognitive preparation . . .	1=unaware 2=spontaneously recognized 3=anticipated without detail 4=anticipated in great detail
48	Immediate response	2=unable to respond 3=withdrawal 4=unconditional submission 5=conditional submission 6=active non-violent resistance 7=counter violence
49	Consequences	0=not shown 1=do not exist 2=somewhat impaired 3=severely incapacitated 4=dead or annihilated
50-80		Blank

List of Observers Using the Instruments

Column	Variable	Code
14-15 . . . . . . Observer identification . .		01=Cauley-Meadow
		02=Christianson-Hastrup
		03=Hastrup-Bryer
		04=Cauley-Javoronok
		05=Marcy-Hastrup
		06=Cauley-Bryer
		07=Cauley-Hastrup
		08=Travis-Gilbert
		09=Christianson-Fabian
		10=Meadow-Hastrup
		11=Gough-Meadow
		12=Bryer-Fulton
		13=Fabian-Gough
		14=Gandy-Fulton
		15=Belsky-Cauley
		16=Cauley-Fabian
		17=Fabian-Hastrup
		18=Gilbert-Cauley
		19=Christianson-Javoronok
		20=Christianson-Rothenberg
		21=Gough-Marcy
		22=Marcy-Javoronok
		23=Gough-Bryer
		24=Gough-Christianson
		25=Marcy-Belsky
		26=Bryer-Rothenberg
		27=Fabian-Burns
		28=Gilbert-Hastrup
		29=Christianson-Gilbert
		30=Cauley-Marcy
		31=Cauley-Christianson

List of Program Recorded by This Instrument

Column	Variable	Code
10-12 . . . . . . Serial number of program (1967)		004=Felony Squad
		006=Off to See the Wizard
		007=Ironside
		008=The Virginian
		010=Daktari
		011=Journey to the Center of the Earth
		014=Star Trek
		015=Man From U.N.C.L.E.
		016=Voyage to the Bottom of the Sea
		017=Hondo
		018=Custer
		020=Daniel Boone
		021=Maya
		022=Lost in Space
		023=The Invaders
		024=Bonanza
		030=Gunsmoke
		033=Super 6—Matzonuts
		034=Super 6—Man From TRASH

Column	*Variable*	*Code*
		046=Gentle Ben
		037=Magilla Gorilla I
		038=Casper
		039=Casper
		040=Casper
		042=Smothers Brothers
		043=Super President
		044=Super President
		045=Super President
		049=Fantastic 4
		050=Fantastic 4
		054=Spiderman I
		055=Second Time Around
		056=Tarzan
		057=NYPD
		059=Cimarron Strip
		060=Dragnet
		063=Garrison's Gorillas
		064=Walt Disney's World of, etc.
		065=Wild, Wild West
		069=Trouble with Harry
		071=Iron Horse
		074=Shazzan!
		075=Frankenstein, Jr.
		076=Frankenstein, Jr.
		077=Frankenstein, Jr.
		078=Flintstones
		079=Space Ghost I
		080=Herculoids
		081=Herculoids
		082=Samson and Goliath I
		083=Danny Thomas
		084=The FBI
		085=The Beagles II
		087=Get Smart
		088=Rat Patrol
		089=Guns of Will Sonnet
		090=Whatever Happened to Baby Jane
		091=Magilla Gorilla II
		092=Magilla Gorilla III
		093=Spiderman II
		094=Samson and Goliath II
		095=Space Ghost II
		096=Space Ghost III
	Serial number of program (1968)	103=Ugliest Girl in Town
		104=Outcasts
		107=The Mod Squad
		108=NYPD
		109=The Avengers
		111=Lancer
		112=Ironside
		113=The FBI
		114=Cat Ballou
		118=Spiderman II
		119=Spiderman I
		121=Gunsmoke
		122=Hawaii 5-0
		123=A Man Could Get Killed

Column   *Variable*   *Code*

124=Daktari
127=Land of the Giants
134=Wild, Wild West
138=Bonanza
140=Doris Day Show
145=Get Smart
148=Lassie
150=The Name of the Game
151=Felony Squad
155=Go-Go-Gophers Pt. I
156=Go-Go-Gophers Pt. II
157=Go-Go-Gophers Pt. III
158=Underdog
159=Wacky Races, Pt. I
160=Wacky Races, Pt. II
162=The Rare Breed
163=Batman/Superman II
   [9 Lives of Batman]
164=Batman/Superman II
   [Can a Luthor Change His Spots]
165=Batman/Superman III
   [Superham Forget Me Not Superdog]
166=Batman/Superman IV
   [In and Out Again Penguin]
167=High Chaparral
168=Fantastic Voyage
169=Super Six I [Thunder-8-Ball]
170=Super Six II [Ruin & Board]
171=Super Six II [Nursey Caper]
172=Herculoids I
   [Tiny World of Terror]
173=Herculoids II
   [Invasion of the Electrode Men]
174=Daniel Boone
175=Guns of Will Sonnett
176=Khartoum
177=Fantastic Four
178=Topcat
180=The Virginian
182=Banana Splits - "The Wizard
   Ramizer"
183=Banana Splits - "Danger Island"
184=Banana Splits - "The Plot of
   the Puppetmaster"

Table 1.—Programs analyzed, 1967

	Total N	Total Percent	ABC N	ABC Percent	CBS N	CBS Percent	NBC N	NBC Percent
All programs	96	100.0	35	100.0	32	100.0	29	100.0
(Percent of total)	(100.0)		(36.5)		(33.3)		(30.2)	
Program format:								
Cartoons	32	33.3	13	37.1	10	31.3	9	31.0
(Percent of total)	(100.0)		(40.6)		(31.3)		(28.1)	
TV plays	58	60.4	20	57.1	20	62.5	18	62.1
(Percent of total)	(100.0)		(34.5)		(34.5)		(31.0)	
Feature films	6	6.3	2	5.7	2	6.3	2	6.9
(Percent of total)	(100.0)		(33.3)		(33.3)		(33.3)	
Program style:								
Crime	10	10.4	6	17.1	0	0.0	4	13.8
(Percent of total)	(100.0)		(60.0)		(0.0)		(40.0)	
Western	9	9.4	4	11.4	3	9.3	2	6.9
(Percent of total)	(100.0)		(44.4)		(33.3)		(22.2)	
Action-adventure	45	46.9	15	42.9	15	46.9	15	51.7
(Percent of total)	(100.0)		(33.3)		(33.3)		(33.3)	
Other	32	33.3	10	28.6	14	43.8	8	27.6
(Percent of total)	(100.0)		(31.3)		(43.8)		(25.0)	
Program tone:								
Comedy	44	45.8	13	37.1	16	50.0	15	51.7
(Percent of total)	(100.0)		(29.5)		(36.4)		(34.1)	
Other	52	54.2	22	62.9	16	50.0	14	48.3
(Percent of total)	(100.0)		(42.3)		(30.8)		(26.9)	

Table 2.—Programs analyzed, 1968

	Total		ABC		CBS		NBC	
	N	Percent	N	Percent	N	Percent	N	Percent
All programs	87	100.0	22	100.0	35	100.0	30	100.0
(Percent of total)	(100.0)		(25.3)		(40.2)		(34.5)	
Program format:								
Cartoons	25	28.7	4	18.2	13	37.1	8	26.7
(Percent of total)	(100.0)		(16.0)		(52.0)		(32.0)	
TV plays	55	63.2	16	72.7	20	57.1	19	63.3
(Percent of total)	(100.0)		(29.1)		(36.4)		(34.5)	
Feature films	7	8.1	2	9.1	2	5.8	3	10.0
(Percent of total)	(100.0)		(28.6)		(28.6)		(42.8)	
Program style:								
Crime	8	9.2	4	18.2	1	2.9	3	10.0
(Percent of total)	(100.0)		(50.0)		(12.5)		(37.5)	
Western	11	12.6	4	18.2	3	8.6	4	13.3
(Percent of total)	(100.0)		(36.4)		(27.2)		(36.4)	
Action-adventure	35	40.2	8	36.4	14	40.0	13	43.4
(Percent of total)	(100.0)		(22.9)		(40.0)		(37.1)	
Other	33	38.0	6	27.2	17	48.5	10	33.3
(Percent of total)	(100.0)		(18.2)		(51.5)		(30.3)	
Program tone:								
Comedy	42	48.3	6	27.2	21	60.0	15	50.0
(Percent of total)	(100.0)		(14.3)		(50.0)		(35.7)	
Other	45	51.7	16	72.8	14	40.0	15	50.0
(Percent of total)	(100.0)		(35.6)		(31.1)		(33.3)	

Table 3.—*Programs analyzed, 1967 and 1968 totals*

	Total		ABC		CBS		NBC	
	N	Percent	N	Percent	N	Percent	N	Percent
All programs	183	100.0	57	100.0	67	100.0	59	100.0
(Percent of total)	(100.0)		(31.1)		(36.6)		(32.3)	
Program format:								
Cartoons	57	31.1	17	29.8	23	34.3	17	28.8
(Percent of total)	(100.0)		(29.8)		(40.4)		(29.8)	
TV plays	113	61.7	36	63.2	40	59.7	37	62.7
(Percent of total)	(100.0)		(31.9)		(35.4)		(32.7)	
Feature films	13	7.2	4	7.0	4	6.0	5	8.5
(Percent of total)	(100.0)		(30.8)		(30.8)		(38.4)	
Program style:								
Crime	18	9.8	10	17.5	1	1.5	7	11.9
(Percent of total)	(100.0)		(55.6)		(5.6)		(38.8)	
Western	20	10.9	8	14.0	6	9.0	6	10.2
(Percent of total)	(100.0)		(40.0)		(30.0)		(30.0)	
Action-adventure	80	43.7	23	40.4	29	43.3	28	47.4
(Percent of total)	(100.0)		(28.8)		(36.2)		(35.0)	
Other	65	35.5	16	28.1	31	46.2	18	30.5
(Percent of total)	(100.0)		(24.6)		(47.7)		(27.7)	
Program tone:								
Comedy	86	47.0	19	33.3	37	55.2	30	50.8
(Percent of total)	(100.0)		(22.1)		(43.0)		(34.9)	
Other	97	53.0	38	66.7	30	44.8	29	49.2
(Percent of total)	(100.0)		(39.2)		(30.9)		(29.9)	

Table 4.—Program hours analyzed, 1967

	Total		ABC		CBS		NBC	
	N	Percent	N	Percent	N	Percent	N	Percent
All hours	64.0	100.0	23.0	100.0	20.5	100.0	20.5	100.0
(Percent of total)	(100.0)		(35.9)		(32.0)		(32.0)	
Program format:								
Cartoons	7.0	10.9	3.0	13.0	2.0	9.8	2.0	9.8
(Percent of total)	(100.0)		(42.9)		(28.5)		(28.5)	
TV plays	44.0	68.8	15.0	65.2	14.5	70.7	14.5	70.7
(Percent of total)	(100.0)		(34.0)		(33.0)		(33.0)	
Feature films	13.0	20.3	5.0	21.7	4.0	19.5	4.0	19.5
(Percent of total)	(100.0)		(38.5)		(30.8)		(30.8)	
Program style:								
Crime	9.0	14.1	5.3	23.0	0.0	0.0	3.7	18.0
(Percent of total)	(100.0)		(58.9)		(0.0)		(41.1)	
Western	9.5	14.8	3.5	15.2	3.5	17.1	2.5	12.2
(Percent of total)	(100.0)		(36.8)		(36.8)		(26.3)	
Action/adventure	27.3	42.7	10.5	45.7	7.0	34.1	9.8	47.8
(Percent of total)	(100.0)		(38.5)		(25.6)		(35.9)	
Other	18.2	28.4	3.7	16.1	10.0	48.8	4.5	22.0
(Percent of total)	(100.0)		(20.3)		(54.9)		(24.7)	
Program tone:								
Comedy	24.8	38.8	6.0	26.1	8.0	39.0	10.8	52.7
(Percent of total)	(100.0)		(24.2)		(32.3)		(43.5)	
Other	39.2	61.2	17.0	73.9	12.5	61.0	9.7	47.3
(Percent of total)	(100.0)		(43.4)		(31.9)		(24.7)	

Table 5.—*Program hours analyzed, 1968*

	Total		ABC		CBS		NBC	
	N	Percent	N	Percent	N	Percent	N	Percent
All hours	58.5	100.0	17.5	100.0	20.0	100.0	21.0	100.0
(Percent of total)	(100.0)		(29.9)		(34.2)		(35.9)	
Program format:								
Cartoons	6.9	11.8	1.5	8.6	3.0	15.0	2.4	11.4
(Percent of total)	(100.0)		(21.7)		(43.5)		(34.8)	
TV plays	36.6	62.6	12.0	68.6	13.0	65.0	11.6	55.3
(Percent of total)	(100.0)		(32.8)		(35.5)		(31.7)	
Feature films	15.0	25.6	4.0	22.8	4.0	20.0	7.0	33.3
(Percent of total)	(100.0)		(26.7)		(26.7)		(46.6)	
Program style:								
Crime	6.5	11.1	3.5	20.0	1.0	5.0	2.0	9.5
(Percent of total)	(100.0)		(53.8)		(15.4)		(30.8)	
Western	13.3	22.7	4.5	25.7	3.0	15.0	5.8	27.6
(Percent of total)	(100.0)		(33.8)		(22.6)		(43.6)	
Action-adventrue	19.4	33.2	4.5	25.7	5.0	25.0	9.9	47.2
(Percent of total)	(100.0)		(23.2)		(25.8)		(51.0)	
Other	19.3	33.0	5.0	28.6	11.0	55.0	3.3	15.7
(Percent of total)	(100.0)		(25.9)		(57.0)		(17.1)	
Program tone:								
Comedy	20.2	34.5	6.0	34.3	7.9	39.5	6.3	30.0
(Percent of total)	(100.0)		(29.7)		(39.1)		(31.2)	
Other	38.3	65.5	11.5	65.7	12.1	60.5	14.7	70.0
(Percent of total)	(100.0)		(30.0)		(31.6)		(38.4)	

Table 6.—Program hours analyzed, 1967 and 1968 totals

	Total		ABC		CBS		NBC	
	N	Percent	N	Percent	N	Percent	N	Percent
All hours	122.5	100.0	40.5	100.0	40.5	100.0	41.5	100.0
(Percent of total)	(100.0)		(33.1)		(33.1)		(33.8)	
Program format:								
Cartoons	13.9	11.3	4.5	11.1	5.0	12.3	4.4	10.6
(Percent of total)	(100.0)		(32.4)		(36.0)		(31.6)	
TV plays	80.6	65.8	27.0	66.7	27.5	67.9	26.1	62.9
(Percent of total)	(100.0)		(33.5)		(34.1)		(32.4)	
Feature films	28.0	22.9	9.0	22.2	8.0	19.8	11.0	26.5
(Percent of total)	(100.0)		(32.1)		(28.6)		(39.3)	
Program style:								
Crime	15.5	12.7	8.8	21.7	1.0	2.5	5.7	13.7
(Percent of total)	(100.0)		(56.8)		(6.5)		(36.7)	
Western	22.8	18.6	8.0	19.8	6.5	16.0	8.3	20.0
(Percent of total)	(100.0)		(35.1)		(28.5)		(36.4)	
Action/adventure	46.7	38.1	15.0	37.0	12.0	29.6	19.7	47.5
(Percent of total)	(100.0)		(32.1)		(25.7)		(42.2)	
Other	37.5	30.6	8.7	21.5	21.0	51.9	7.8	18.8
(Percent of total)	(100.0)		(23.2)		(56.0)		(20.8)	
Program tone:								
Comedy	45.0	36.7	12.0	29.6	15.9	39.3	17.1	41.2
(Percent of total)	(100.0)		(26.7)		(35.3)		(38.0)	
Other	77.5	63.3	28.5	70.4	24.6	60.7	24.4	58.8
(Percent of total)	(100.0)		(36.8)		(31.7)		(31.5)	

Table 7.—Programs containing violence, 1967, 1968, and totals

	Total		ABC		CBS		NBC	
	N	Percent	N	Percent	N	Percent	N	Percent
All programs, 1967 (Percent of total)	96 (100.0)	100.0	35 (36.5)	100.0	32 (33.3)	100.0	29 (30.2)	100.0
Incidence of violence, 1967:								
No violence (Percent of total)	18 (100.0)	18.8	4 (22.2)	11.4	11 (61.1)	34.4	3 (16.7)	10.3
Programs containing violence (Percent of total)	78 (100.0)	81.3	31 (39.7)	88.6	21 (26.9)	65.6	26 (33.3)	89.7
All programs, 1968 (Percent of total)	87 (100.0)	100.0	22 (25.3)	100.0	35 (40.2)	100.0	30 (34.5)	100.0
Incidence of violence, 1968:								
No violence (Percent of total)	16 (100.0)	18.4	2 (12.5)	9.1	8 (50.0)	22.9	6 (37.5)	20.0
Programs containing violence (Percent of total)	71 (100.0)	81.6	20 (28.2)	90.9	27 (38.0)	77.1	24 (33.8)	80.0
All programs, 1967 and 1968 totals (Percent of total)	183 (100.0)	100.0	57 (31.1)	100.0	67 (36.6)	100.0	59 (32.3)	100.0
Incidence of violence 1967 and 1968:								
No violence (Percent of total)	34 (100.0)	18.6	6 (17.6)	10.5	19 (55.9)	28.4	9 (26.5)	15.3
Programs containing violence (Percent of total)	149 (100.0)	81.4	51 (34.2)	89.5	48 (32.2)	71.6	50 (33.6)	84.7

Table 8.—Program hours containing violence, 1967, 1968, and totals

	Total		ABC		CBS		NBC	
	N	Percent	N	Percent	N	Percent	N	Percent
All hours, 1967 (Percent of total)	64.0 (100.0)	100.0	23.0 (35.9)	100.0	20.5 (32.0)	100.0	20.5 (32.0)	100.0
Incidence of violence, 1967:								
No violence (Percent of total)	10.5 (100.0)	16.4	2.0 (19.0)	8.7	5.8 (55.2)	28.3	2.7 (25.7)	13.2
Program hours containing violence (Percent of total)	53.5 (100.0)	83.6	21.0 (39.3)	91.3	14.7 (27.5)	71.7	17.8 (33.2)	86.8
All hours, 1968 (Percent of total)	58.5 (100.0)	100.0	17.5 (29.9)	100.0	20.0 (34.2)	100.0	21.0 (35.9)	100.0
Incidence of violence, 1968:								
No violence (Percent of total)	7.6 (100.0)	13.0	1.0 (13.2)	5.7	4.0 (52.6)	20.0	2.6 (34.2)	12.4
Program hours containing violence (Percent of total)	50.9 (100.0)	87.0	16.5 (32.4)	94.3	16.0 (31.4)	80.0	18.4 (36.2)	87.6
All hours, 1967, 1968 totals (Percent of total)	122.5 (100.0)	100.0	40.5 (33.1)	100.0	40.5 (33.1)	100.0	41.5 (33.8)	100.0
Incidence of violence, 1967, 1968 totals:								
No violence (Percent of total)	18.1 (100.0)	14.8	3.0 (16.6)	7.4	9.8 (54.1)	24.2	5.3 (29.3)	12.8
Program hours containing violence (Percent of total)	104.4 (100.0)	85.2	37.5 (35.9)	92.6	30.7 (29.4)	75.8	36.2 (34.7)	87.2

Table 9.—Numbers and rates of violent episodes, 1967, 1968, and totals

	Total	ABC	CBS	NBC
Number of violent episodes, 1967	478	195	111	172
(Percent of total)	(100.0)	(40.8)	(23.2)	(36.0)
Rates per program, 1967:				
Average for all programs	5.0	5.6	3.5	5.9
Average for programs containing violence	6.1	6.3	4.3	6.6
Rates per hour, 1967:				
Average for all hours	7.5	8.5	5.4	8.4
Average for hours containing violence	8.9	9.3	7.5	9.7
Number of violent episodes, 1968	394	111	127	146
(Percent of total)	(100.0)	(28.2)	(34.8)	(37.0)
Rates per program, 1968:				
Average for all programs	4.5	5.0	3.9	4.9
Average for programs containing violence	5.5	5.5	5.1	6.1
Rates per hour, 1968:				
Average for all hours	6.7	6.3	6.9	7.0
Average for hours containing violence	7.7	6.7	8.6	7.9
Number of violent episodes, 1967, 1968 totals	872	306	248	318
(Percent of total)	(100.0)	(35.1)	(28.4)	(36.5)
Rates per program, 1967, 1968 totals:				
Average for all programs	4.8	5.4	3.7	5.4
Average for programs containing violence	5.9	6.0	5.2	6.4
Rates per hour, 1967 and 1968 totals:				
Average for all hours	7.1	7.6	6.1	7.7
Average for hours containing violence	8.4	8.2	8.1	8.8

Table 10.—All violence, violence significant to the plot, and rate of violent episodes, 1967, 1968, and totals

	All net programs			ABC programs			CBS programs			NBC programs		
	1967	1968	Both	1967	1968	Both	1967	1968	Both	1967	1968	Both
All programs (N)	96	87	183	35	22	57	32	35	67	29	30	59
All hours (N)	64.0	58.5	122.5	23.0	17.5	40.5	20.5	20.0	40.5	20.5	21.0	41.5
All violence:												
Percent of programs containing violence	81.2	81.6	81.4	88.6	90.9	89.5	65.6	77.1	71.6	89.0	80.0	84.7
Percent of hours containing violence	83.6	87.0	85.2	91.3	94.4	92.6	71.7	80.0	75.8	86.8	87.6	87.2
Violence significant to the plot:												
Percent of all programs	65.6	56.3	61.2	74.3	63.6	70.2	50.0	48.6	49.2	72.4	60.0	66.1
Percent of programs containing violence	80.8	69.0	75.2	83.9	70.0	78.4	76.2	63.0	68.7	80.1	75.0	78.0
Percent of all program hours	67.9	61.4	64.7	80.9	63.9	73.1	44.9	40.0	42.5	75.5	79.5	77.5
Percent of program hours containing violence	81.2	70.1	75.9	88.6	66.7	78.9	62.6	50.0	56.0	87.2	90.8	88.9
Network share of violence:												
Network share of all programs (Percent)				36.5	25.3	31.1	33.3	40.2	36.6	30.2	34.5	32.2

Table 10.—All violence, violence significant to the plot, and rate of violent episodes, 1967, 1968, and totals (continued)

	All net programs			ABC programs			CBS programs			NBC programs		
	1967	1968	Both	1967	1968	Both	1967	1968	Both	1967	1968	Both
Network share of programs containing violence (Percent)				39.7	28.2	34.4	26.9	38.0	32.2	33.3	33.8	33.5
Network share of all hours (Percent)				35.9	29.9	33.1	32.0	34.3	33.1	32.0	35.9	33.8
Network share of hours containing violence (Percent)				39.3	32.4	35.9	27.5	31.4	29.4	33.2	36.1	34.7
Violent episodes:												
Number of violent episodes (N)	478	394	873	195	111	306	111	137	248	172	146	318
Network share of all violent episodes (Percent)				40.7	28.2	35.0	23.2	34.8	28.4	36.0	37.0	36.5
Average number of violent episodes per program	5.0	4.5	4.8	5.6	5.0	5.4	3.5	3.9	3.7	5.9	4.9	5.4
Average number of violent episodes per hour	7.5	6.7	7.1	8.5	6.3	7.6	5.4	6.9	6.1	8.4	7.0	7.7

Table 11:- Violence by all programs and selected program types; all networks

	All programs			Cartoons			Crime, western, action–adventure			Comedy		
	1967	1968	Both	1967	1968	Both	1967	1968	Both	1967	1968	Both
Programs analyzed (N)	96	87	183	32	25	57	64	54	118	44	42	86
Programs containing violence (N)	78	71	149	30	24	54	61	53	114	29	28	57
Percent containing violence	81.2	81.6	81.1	93.7	96.0	94.7	95.3	98.1	96.6	65.9	66.7	66.3
Program hours analyzed (N)	640	58.5	122.5	7.0	6.9	13.9	47.6	39.1	86.8	24.8	20.2	45.0
Hours containing violence (N)	53.5	50.9	104.4	6.6	6.4	13.0	44.8	38.7	83.5	14.2	12.2	26.4
Percent containing violence	83.6	87.0	85.2	94.3	92.8	93.5	94.1	98.7	96.2	57.3	60.4	58.7
Number of violent episodes (N)	479	394	873	151	162	313	419	341	760	122	134	256
Average per program	5.0	4.5	4.8	4.7	6.5	5.5	6.5	6.3	6.4	2.8	3.2	3.0
Average per hour	7.5	6.7	7.1	21.6	23.5	22.5	8.8	8.7	8.7	4.9	6.6	5.7
Percentage share of program type out of all programs				33.3	28.7	31.1	66.7	62.1	64.5	45.8	48.3	47.0
Percentage share of program type containing violence out of all programs containing violence				38.5	33.8	36.2	78.2	74.6	76.5	37.2	39.4	38.3
Percentage share of violent episodes in each program type out of all violent episodes				31.5	41.1	35.8	87.5	86.5	87.1	25.5	34.0	29.3

Table 12:– Violence by all programs and selected program types, ABC

	All programs 1967	1968	Both	Cartoons 1967	1968	Both	Crime, western, action–adventure 1967	1968	Both	Comedy 1967	1968	Both
Programs analyzed (N)	35	22	57	13	4	17	25	16	41	13	6	19
Programs containing violence (N)	31	20	51	13	4	17	25	16	41	10	6	16
Percent containing violence	88.5	90.9	89.5	100.0	100.0	100.0	100.0	100.0	100.0	76.9	100.0	84.2
Program hours analyzed (N)	23.0	17.5	40.5	3.0	1.5	4.5	18.6	12.5	31.1	6.0	6.0	12.0
Hours containing violence (N)	21.0	16.5	37.5	3.0	1.5	4.5	18.6	12.5	31.1	3.5	6.0	9.5
Percent containing violence	91.2	94.4	92.6	100.0	100.0	100.0	100.0	100.0	100.0	58.3	100.0	79.2
Number of violent episodes (N)	195	111	306	70	26	96	170	99	269	452	77	
Average per program	5.6	5.0	5.4	5.4	6.5	5.6	6.8	6.2	6.6	3.5	5.3	4.1
Average per hour	8.5	6.3	7.6	23.3	17.3	21.3	9.1	7.9	8.6	7.5	5.3	6.4
Percentage share of program type out of all programs				37.1	18.2	29.8	71.4	72.7	71.9	37.1	27.3	33.3
Percentage share of program type containing violence out of all programs containing violence				41.9	12.9	33.3	80.6	51.6	80.4	32.3	19.4	31.4
Percentage share of violent episodes in each program type out of all violent episodes				35.9	23.4	31.4	87.2	89.2	87.9	23.1	28.8	25.2

Table 13– Violence by all programs and selected program types, CBS

	All programs 1967	1968	Both	Cartoons 1967	1968	Both	Crime, western, Action-adventure 1967	1968	Both	Comedy 1967	1968	Both
Programs analyzed (N)	32	35	67	10	13	23	18	18	36	16	21	37
Programs containing violence (N)	21	27	47	9	13	22	17	17	34	7	13	20
Percent containing violence	65.6	77.1	70.1	90.0	100.0	95.7	94.4	94.4	94.4	43.8	61.9	54.1
Program hours analyzed (N)	20.5	20.0	40.5	2.0	3.0	5.0	11.0	9.0	20.0	8.0	7.9	15.9
Hours containing violence (N)	14.7	16.0	30.7	1.8	3.0	4.8	10.8	8.5	19.3	3.0	3.9	6.9
Percent containing violence	71.7	80.0	75.8	87.5	100.0	96.0	97.7	94.4	96.5	37.5	49.4	43.4
Number of violent episodes (N)	111	137	248	44	77	121	99	107	206	16	61	77
Average per program	3.5	3.9	3.7	4.4	5.9	5.3	5.5	5.9	5.7	1.0	2.9	2.1
Average per hour	5.4	6.9	6.1	22.0	25.7	24.2	9.0	11.9	10.3	2.0	7.7	4.8
Percentage share of program type out of all programs				31.3	37.1	34.3	56.3	51.4	53.7	50.0	60.0	55.2
Percentage share of program type containing violence out of all programs containing violence				42.9	48.1	46.8	81.0	63.0	72.3	33.3	48.1	42.6
Percentage share of violent episodes in each program type out of all violent episodes				39.6	56.2	48.8	89.2	78.1	83.1	14.4	44.5	31.0

Table 14–Violence by all programs and selected program types, NBC

	All programs			Cartoons			Crime, western, action-adventure			Comedy		
	1967	1968	Both	1967	1968	Both	1967	1968	Both	1967	1968	Both
Programs analyzed (N)	29	30	59	9	8	17	21	20	41	15	15	30
Programs containing violence (N)	26	24	50	8	7	15	19	20	39	12	9	21
Percent containing violence	86.2	80.0	84.7	88.9	87.5	88.2	90.5	100.0	95.1	80.0	60.0	70.0
Program hours analyzed (N)	20.5	21.0	41.5	2.0	2.4	4.4	18.0	17.7	35.7	10.8	6.3	17.1
Hours containing violence (N)	17.8	18.4	34.7	1.8	1.9	3.7	15.5	17.7	33.2	7.7	2.3	10.0
Percent containing violence	86.8	87.6	87.2	90.0	79.2	84.1	86.1	100.0	93.0	71.0	35.7	58.5
Number of violent episodes (N)	173	146	319	37	59	96	150	135	285	61	41	102
Average per program	6.0	4.9	5.4	4.1	7.4	5.6	7.1	6.8	7.0	4.1	2.7	3.4
Average per hour	8.4	7.0	7.7	18.5	24.6	21.8	8.3	7.6	8.0	5.6	6.5	6.0
Percentage share of program type out of all programs				31.0	26.7	28.8	72.4	66.7	69.5	51.7	50.0	50.8
Percentage share of program type containing violence out of all programs containing violence				30.8	29.2	30.0	73.1	83.3	78.0	46.2	37.5	42.0
Percentage share of violent episodes in each program type out of all violent episodes				21.4	40.4	30.1	86.7	92.5	89.3	35.3	28.1	32.0

Table 15—Selected aspects of violent episodes, 1967, 1968, and totals

	1967	1968	Both years
Total number of violent episodes	478	394	872
Agents of violence:	Percent	Percent	Percent
Human (Whether live or cartoon character) .	75.7	77.7	76.6
"Humanized" (speaking) animal character ..	4.0	2.0	3.1
Animal character (live or cartoon)	3.8	5.3	4.5
Other creature or "thing"	6.7	4.8	5.9
Act of nature	0.0	0.0	0.0
Accident	5.0	7.9	6.3
Uncertain, other	4.8	2.3	3.7
Means of violence:			
Weapon is used	58.8	47.0	53.4
No weapon is used or uncertain	41.2	53.0	46.6
Seriousness of context:			
Violence occurs in serious or sinister context	87.0	73.9	81.1
Violence occurs in comic or sham context ..	13.0	26.1	18.9
Witnesses to violence:			
None; no evidence of any witnesses to violence	50.4	44.7	47.8
There are witnesses but they are passive; they do not or cannot react to violence ..	33.5	37.3	35.2
Witnesses attempt to prevent violence	7.7	7.4	7.6
Witnesses assist or encourage violence	8.4	10.7	9.4
Group relations among violent opponents:			
Members of the same family	2.5	2.0	2.3
Members of the same national or ethnic group	28.0	43.9	35.2
Members of different national or ethnic groups	29.9	26.1	28.2
Uncertain, other	39.5	27.9	34.3

Table 16—Casualties in violent episodes, 1967, 1968, and totals

	1967		1968		Both years	
	N	Percent	N	Percent	N	Percent
All violent episodes	478	100.0	394	100.0	872	100.0

Violent episodes in which—

Nobody appears to be physically injured or killed	250	52.3	202	51.3	454	51.8
Somebody appears to be physically injured or killed	228	47.7	192	48.7	420	48.2
Total number of casualties in all violent episodes was more than*	433		357		790	
Average number of casualties per violent episodes in which there were casualties was more than*	1.9		1.9		1.9	

Percent of violent episodes which the casualty count was—

	1967	1968	Both years
1	74.1	73.0	73.6
2	13.3	13.0	13.2
3	4.3	4.5	4.4
4	0.0	2.5	1.5
5	1.2	0.0	0.7
6	1.6	0.0	0.9
7	0.0	0.0	0.0
8 or more, including mass casualties	4.7	7.0	5.7

*For episodes in which there were 8 or more casualties, including mass casualties, only 8 were recorded.

Table 17–Major characters analyzed in 1967 programs

	All characters				Humans				Non-humans*			
	Total	Male	Female	Others	Total	Male	Female	Others	Total	Male	Female	Others
Cartoon	63	58	3	2	39	37	2	0	24	21	1	2
TV drama	158	124	34	0	147	117	30	0	11	7	4	0
Feature film	19	9	10	0	18	9	9	0	1	0	1	0
Crime	32	22	10	0	27	18	9	0	5	4	1	0
Western	24	24	0	0	24	24	0	0	0	0	0	0
Action/adventure	108	94	12	2	88	78	10	0	20	16	2	2
Other	76	51	25	0	65	43	22	0	11	8	3	0
Comedy	108	80	26	2	88	65	23	0	20	15	3	2
Other	132	111	21	0	116	98	18	0	16	13	3	0
Total	240	191	47	2	204	163	41	0	36	28	6	2

*Including "humanized" (speaking) animals, other animals, and other nonhuman characters (such as a robot).

Table 18–Major characters analyzed in 1968 programs

	All characters				Humans				Non-humans*			
	Total	Male	Female	Others	Total	Male	Female	Others	Total	Male	Female	Others
Cartoon	43	36	5	2	35	30	5	0	8	6	0	2
TV drama	145	113	32	0	140	109	31	0	5	4	1	0
Feature film	27	16	11	0	27	16	11	0	0	0	0	0
Crime	20	18	2	0	20	18	2	0	0	0	0	0
Western	38	32	6	0	38	32	6	0	0	0	0	0
Action/adventure	77	63	13	1	71	58	13	0	6	5	0	1
Other	80	52	27	1	73	47	26	0	7	5	1	1
Total	215	165	48	2	202	155	47	0	13	10	1	2

*Including "humanized" (speaking) animals, other animals, and other nonhuman characters (such as a robot).

Table 19—Major characters analyzed in 1967 and 1968 programs

	All characters				Humans				Non-humans*		
	Total	Male	Female	Others	Total	Male	Female	Others	Male	Female	Others
Cartoon	106	94	8	4	74	67	7	0	27	1	4
TV drama..........	303	237	66	0	287	226	61	0	11	5	0
Feature film	46	25	21	0	45	25	20	0	0	1	0
Crime	52	40	12	0	47	36	11	0	4	1	0
Western..........	62	56	6	0	62	56	6	0	0	0	0
Action/adventure ...	185	157	25	3	159	136	23	0	21	2	3
Other...........	156	103	52	1	138	90	48	0	13	4	1
Comedy	189	137	49	3	159	114	45	0	23	4	3
Other...........	266	219	46	1	247	204	43	0	15	3	1
Total..........	455	356	95	4	406	318	88	0	38	7	4

*Including "humanized" (speaking) animals, other animals, and other nonhuman characters (such as a robot).

Table 20.—"Violents," "killer," and "killed," 1967, 1968, and selected characteristics for both years

	Total		Those who commit violence against others							Those who die violent death		
			All "violents"			"Violent killers" only						
Age	N	Percent	N	Percent	Percent of total	N	Percent	Percent of total	Percent of violent	N	Percent	Percent of total
All characters-1967	240	52.7	134	55.6	55.8	30	55.6	12.5	22.4	17	68.0	7.1
All characters-1968	215	47.3	107	44.4	49.8	24	44.4	11.2	22.4	8	32.0	3.7
Both years	455	100.0	241	100.0	53.0	54	100.0	11.9	22.4	25	100.0	5.5

(Continued)

Selected characteristics for both 1967 and 1968

Column groups: **Total** | **Those who commit violence against others** (*All "violents"* and *"Violent killers" only*) | **Those who die violent death**

Characteristic	Total N	Total Percent	All "violents" N	All "violents" Percent	All "violents" Percent of total	"Violent killers" only N	"Violent killers" Percent	"Violent killers" Percent of total	"Violent killers" Percent of violent	Die violent death N	Die violent death Percent	Die violent death Percent of total
Sex:												
Males	358	78.7	206	85.5	57.5	48	88.9	13.4	23.3	22	88.0	6.1
Females	93	20.4	31	12.9	33.3	6	11.1	6.5	17.6	3	12.0	3.2
Other uncertain	4	.9	4	1.7		0	.0	.0	.0	0	.0	.0
	455	100.0	241	100.0		54	100.0		25	25	100.0	
Age:												
preschool and primary	9	2.0	3	1.3	33.3	0	0.0	0.0	0.0	0	0.0	0.0
secondary school age	20	4.4	9	3.7	45.0	1	1.8	5.0	11.1	0	.0	.0
Young adult	145	31.9	70	29.0	48.3	21	38.9	14.5	30.0	5	20.0	3.4
Middle age	206	45.3	116	48.1	56.3	28	51.9	13.5	24.1	15	60.0	7.3
Old age	26	5.7	11	4.6	42.3	1	1.8	3.8	9.1	2	8.0	7.7
Ageless, intermediate	47	10.7	32	12.3	65.3	3	5.6	6.4	9.4	3	12.0	6.4
	455	100.0	241	100.0		54	100.0			25	100.0	
Marital status:												
Unmarried, unknown	325	71.4	189	78.4	58.1	44	81.5	13.5	23.3	22	88.0	6.7
Married, marries	130	28.6	52	21.6	40.0	10	18.5	7.7	19.2	3	12.0	2.3
	455	100.0	241	100.0		54	100.0			25	100.0	100.0

(Continued)

Occupation:												
Housewife	25	5.5	10	4.2	40.0	0	0.0	0.0	0.0	0	0.0	0.0
Illegal occupation	44	9.7	36	14.9	81.8	11	20.4	25.0	30.6	6	24.0	13.6
Armed forces	26	5.7	15	6.2	57.7	8	14.8	30.8	53.3	3	12.0	11.5
Entertainment	35	7.7	12	5.0	34.3	2	3.7	5.7	16.7	1	4.0	2.9
Official law enforcement	30	6.6	21	8.7	70.0	6	11.1	20.0	28.6	0	.0	.0
Private agent	9	2.0	6	2.5	66.7	1	1.8	11.1	16.7	0	.0	.0
Other occupations	286	62.9	141	58.5	49.3	26	48.1	9.1	18.4	15	60.0	5.2
	455	100.0	241	100.0		54	99.9		25	100.0		

Nationality, ethnicity:												
White Americans	305	67.0	149	61.8	48.9	40	74.1	13.1	26.8	11	44.0	3.6
White non-Americans	46	10.1	27	11.2	58.7	9	16.7	19.6	33.3	7	28.0	15.2
non-whites	30	6.6	20	8.3	66.7	2	3.7	6.7	10.0	2	8.0	6.7
Certain, other	74	16.3	45	18.7	60.8	3	5.5	4.0	6.7	5	20.0	6.7
	455	100.0	241	100.0		54	100.0			25	25	100.0

(Continued)

     Mass Media and Violence

	Total		Those who commit violence against others							Those who die violent death		
			All "violents"			"Violent killers" only						
	N	Percent	N	Percent	Percent of total	N	Percent	Percent of total	Percent of violent	N	Percent	Percent of total
Outcome for character:												
Happy	266	58.5	126	52.3	47.4	25	46.3	9.4	19.8	0	0.0	0.0
Unhappy	89	19.6	61	25.3	68.5	16	29.6	18.0	26.2	25	100.0	28.1
Uncertain or other	100	22.0	54	22.4	54.0	13	24.1	13.0	24.1	0	.0	.0
	455	100.0	241	100.0		54	100.0			25	100.0	
Fatal victimization												
Do not die	430	94.5	221	91.7	51.4	46	85.2	10.7	20.8			
Die violent death	25	5.5	20	8.3	80.0	8	14.8	32.0	40.0			
	455	100.0	241	100.0		54	100.0					

Table 21—Time of action as a story element in violent and nonviolent TV drama: 1967, 1968, and totals

Story element and year	Occurrence of story element in all programs		percent of programs which— contain no violence		contain violence		Percent of violent programs out of all programs in which element occurs
	N	Percent	N	Percent	N	Percent=	Percent
Time of action, 1967:	(N 96)		(N 18)		(N 78)		
Past	21	21.9	0	0.0	21	26.9	100.0
Contemporary (1960's)	52	54.2	15	83.3	37	47.4	71.2
Future	8	8.3	0	0.0	8	10.3	100.0
Several, other	15	15.6	3	16.7	12	15.4	80.0
Time of action, 1968:	(N 87)		(N 16)		(N 71)		
Past	19	13.8	1	6.3	18	25.4	94.7
Contemporary (1960's)	59	67.8	14	87.5	45	63.4	76.3
Future	5	5.7	0	0.0	5	7.0	100.0
Several, other	4	4.6	1	6.3	3	4.2	75.0
Time of action, 1967 and 1968 total	(N 183)		(N 34)		(N 149)		
Past	40	21.9	1	2.9	39	26.2	97.5
Contemporary (1960's)	111	60.7	29	85.3	82	55.0	73.9
Future	13	7.1	0	0.0	13	8.7	100.0
Several, other	19	10.3	4	11.8	15	10.1	78.9

Table 22—Place of action as a story element in violent and nonviolent TV drama: 1967, 1968, and totals

Story Element and year	Occurrence of story element in—						Percent of violent programs out of all programs in which element occurs
	All programs		Percent of programs which—				
			Contain no violence		Contain violence		
	N	Percent	N	Percent	N	Percent	Percent
Place of action, 1967:	(N 96)		(N 18)		(N 78)		75.4
United States only	61	63.5	15	83.3	46	59.0	75.4
Several indeterminate, or outside United States	35	36.5	3	16.7	32	40.8	91.4
Urban setting	31	32.3	8	44.4	23	29.5	74.2
Small town, rural	21	21.9	7	38.9	14	17.9	66.7
Uninhabited, mobil, etc.	44	45.8	3	16.7	41	52.6	93.2
Place of action, 1968:	(N 87)		(N 16)		(N 71)		76.7
United States only	60	69.0	14	87.5	46	64.8	76.7
Several indeterminate, or outside United States	27	31.0	2	12.5	25	35.2	92.6
Urban setting	29	33.3	6	37.5	23	32.4	79.3
Small town, rural	30	34.5	6	37.5	24	33.8	80.0
Uninhabited, mobil, etc.	28	32.3	4	25.0	24	33.8	85.7
Place of action, 1967 and 1968 total:	(N 183)		(N 34)		(N 149)		76.0
United States only	121	66.1	29	85.3	92	61.7	76.0
Several indeterminate, or outside United States	62	33.9	5	14.7	57	38.3	91.9
Urban setting	60	32.8	14	41.2	46	30.9	76.7
Small town, rural	51	27.9	13	38.2	38	25.5	74.5
Uninhabited, mobil etc.	72	39.3	7	20.6	65	43.6	90.3

Table 23–Crime, science, and minority and foreign themes as significant story elements* in violent and nonviolent TV drama: 1967, 1968, and totals

Story element and year	Occurrence of story element in—						Percent of violent programs out of all programs in which element occurs
	All programs		Percent of programs which—				
			Contain no violence		Contain violence		
	N	Percent	N	Percent	N	Percent	Percent
1967	(N 96)		(N 18)		(N 78)		
Crime, corruption	31	32.3	2	11.1	29	37.2	93.6
Science, scientist	29	30.2	3	16.7	26	33.3	90.7
Minority, foreign	30	31.2	2	11.1	28	35.9	93.3
1968:	(N 87)		(N 16)		(N 71)		
Crime, corruption	39	44.8	1	6.3	38	53.5	97.4
Science, scientist	24	27.6	3	18.8	21	29.6	87.5
Minority, foreign	39	44.8	5	31.3	34	47.9	87.2
1967 and 1968:	(N 183)		(N 34)		(N 149)		
Crime, corruption	70	38.3	3	8.8	67	45.0	95.7
Science, scientist	53	28.0	6	17.6	47	31.5	88.7
Minority, foreign	69	37.7	7	20.6	62	41.6	89.9

*Significant element was defined as necessary for a 1-page plot description; i.e., of all programs containing violence in 1967, 37.2 percent featured crime, 33.3 percent featured science or scientists, and 35.9 percent featured minority of foreign groups or people as *significant* themes or aspects.

Table 24—Law and law enforcement as story elements in violent and nonviolent TV drama: 1967, 1968, and totals

Story element and year	Occurrence of story element in—						Percent of violent programs out of all programs in which element occurs
	All programs		Percent of programs which—				
			Contain no violence		Contain violence		
	N	Percent	N	Percent	N	Percent	Percent
1967:	(N 96)		(N 18)		(N 78)		
Due process of law (legal apprehension or trial) is indicated as a consequence of major act(s) of violence	18	18.7	0	0.0	18	23.1	100.0
Agent of law enforcement is American Negro	2	2.1	0	0.0	2	2.6	100.0
1968:	(N 87)		(N 16)		(N 71)		
Due process of law (legal apprehension or trial) is indicated as a consequence of major act(s) of violence	17	19.5	0	0.0	17	23.9	100.0
Agent of law enforcement is American Negro	4	4.6	0	0.0	4	5.6	100.0
1967 and 1968:	(N 183)		(N 34)		(N 149)		
Due process of law (legal apprehension or trial) is indicated as a consequence of major act(s) of violence	35	19.2	0	0.0	35	23.5	100.0
Agent of law enforcement is American Negro	6	3.3	0	0.0	6	4.0	100.0

Table 25.—Aspects of law enforcement in violent episodes

	1967	1968	Both years
Total number of violent episodes	478	394	872
Law enforcement agents or agencies play no role			
or no clearly identifiable role in connection	*Percent*	*Percent*	*Percent*
with violent episodes	87.4	87.8	87.6
When they do play a role—			
It is nonviolent................................	40.0	27.1	34.3
They commit violence in course of duty	53.3	64.6	58.3
When they are involved in violence—			
They initiate violence...........................	44.4	43.2	43.8
They respond to violence in violent manner	28.9	38.6	33.7
They respond in nonviolent manner	6.7	9.1	7.9
They become victims of violence	20.0	9.1	14.6
They employ only the level of violence			
necessary to accomplish their objectives........	79.5	83.8	81.6
They commit violence that appears to go			
beyond that necessary to accomplish			
objective	5.1	16.2	10.5
Both, uncertain	15.4	.0	7.9
Their actions are portrayed as—justified	81.6	56.8	69.3
Unjustified	5.3	29.7	17.3
Both, uncertain	13.2	13.5	13.3

Table 26.–Ethnicity in violent and nonviolent TV drama: 1967, 1968, and totals

Story element and year	Occurrence of story element in— All programs		percent of programs which— Contain no violence		Contain violence		Percent of violent programs out of all programs in which element occurs
	N	Percent	N	Percent	N	Percent	Percent
1967:	(N 96)		(N 18)		(N 78)		
Place of action partly or wholly outside United States	35	36.5	3	16.7	32	40.8	91.4
Minority groups, people, or foreign countries, people, play significant role	30	31.2	2	11.1	28	35.9	93.3
Agent of law enforcement is American Negro	2	2.1	0	0.0	2	2.6	100.0
1968:	(N 87)		(N 16)		(N 71)		
Place of action partly or wholly outside United States	17	19.5	1	6.3	16	22.5	94.1
Minority groups, people, or foreign countries, people, play significant role	39	44.8	5	31.3	34	47.9	87.2
Agent of law enforcement is American Negro	4	4.6	0	.0	4	5.6	100.0
1967-1968 totals:	(N 183)		(N 34)		(N 149)		
Place of action partly or wholly outside United States	52	28.4	4	11.8	48	32.2	92.3
Minority groups, people, or foreign countries, people, play significant role	69	37.7	7	20.6	62	41.6	89.9
Agent of law enforcement is American Negro	6	3.3	0	.0	6	4.0	100.0

Table 27.—Whites and non-whites among the "violents," "killers," and "killed"

	Totals		Whites		Nonwhites		Uncertain	
	N	Percent	N	Percent	N	Percent	N	Percent
All characters	455	100.0	351	100.0	30	100.0	74	100.0
Percent of total	(100.0)		(77.1)		(6.6)		(16.3)	
Those who commit violence:								
All "violents"	241	53.0	176	50.1	20	66.7	45	60.8
(Percent of total)	(100.0)		(73.0)		(8.3)		(18.7)	
"Killers" only	54	11.9	49	14.0	2	6.7	3	4.0
(Percent of total)	(100.0)		(90.7)		(3.7)		(5.6)	
(Percent of "violents")	(22.4)		(27.8)		(10.0)		(6.7)	
Those who die violent death	25	5.5	18	5.1	2	6.7	5	6.7
(Percent of total)	(100.0)		(72.0)		(8.0)		(20.0)	

Table 28.—Frequencies of violent acts in 112 plays in which violence
was significant to the plot

	1967	1968	Total
ABC	281	186	467
CBS	175	121	296
NBC	245	207	452
Total	701	514	1,215

Table 29.—Average number of violent acts per play

	1967	1968	Total
ABC	10.8	13.3	11.7
CBS	10.9	7.1	9.0
NBC	11.7	11.5	11.6
Total	11.1	10.5	10.8

Table 30.—Average number of violent acts recomputed per full program*

	1967	1968	Total
ABC	14.1	14.3	14.2
CBS	15.9	12.1	14.1
NBC	14.4	14.8	14.6
Total	14.6	13.9	14.3

*   "Full program" includes all plays on a multiplay program in a single
unit.

Table 31. – Reliability Coefficients and Frequency
Distributions of Violent Acts

Categories	Relia- bility*	Totals	ABC 1967	1968	CBS 1967	1968	NBC 1967	1968
Complexity of instruments	.68 I							
No instruments		494	122	87	47	44	105	89
Simple instruments		400	82	58	59	42	85	74
Complex instruments		321	77	41	69	35	55	44
Total		1,215	281	186	175	121	245	207
Seriousness	.83 N							
Humorous aspect present		249	42	74	22	38	43	30
Serious violence		966	239	112	153	83	202	177
Total		1,215	281	186	175	121	245	207
Distance source receiver	.73 N							
Close proximity		875	222	139	79	81	187	167
Far, but within sight		287	54	36	93	37	37	30
Without sight		53	5	11	3	3	21	10
Total		1,215	281	186	175	121	245	207
Beneficiary and source	.70 N							
Identical		712	168	91	113	72	154	114
Not identical		503	113	95	62	49	91	93
Total		1,215	281	186	175	121	245	207

(Continued)

Table 31.—Reliability Coefficients and Frequency Distribution of Violent Acts (Continued)

Categories	Relia-bility*	Totals	ABC 1967	ABC 1968	CBS 1967	CBS 1968	NBC 1967	NBC 1968
Immediate response	.75 N							
No resistance		711	174	97	93	84	150	113
Nonviolent resistance		72	18	17	7	5	15	10
Violent resistance		432	89	72	75	32	80	84
Total		1,215	281	186	175	121	245	207
Permanent consequences	.85 I							
Not evident		83	16	9	9	4	24	21
No consequences		935	219	146	130	97	192	151
Somewhat impaired or severely incapacitated		83	20	13	13	11	9	17
Dead or annihilated		114	26	18	23	9	20	18
Total		1,215	281	186	175	121	245	207
Amount of nonviolent interaction	.75 I							
None		595	155	66	112	62	93	107
Minor		311	65	70	31	26	83	36
Medium		144	22	35	13	15	35	24
Major		165	39	15	19	18	34	40
Total		1,215	281	186	175	121	245	207
Evaluative portrayal of Source	89I							
Good		515	129	80	75	49	94	88
Neutral, in between		183	39	30	16	15	49	34
Bad		517	113	76	84	57	102	85
Total		1,215	281	186	175	121	245	207

(Continued)

Table 31.–Reliability Coefficients and Frequency Distribution of Violent Acts (Continued)

Categories	Relia-bility*	Totals	ABC 1967	ABC 1968	CBS 1967	CBS 1968	NBC 1967	NBC 1968
Evaluative portrayal of receiver	.89 I							
Good		610	140	95	90	57	121	107
Neutral, in between		187	37	37	13	15	52	33
Bad		418	104	54	72	49	72	67
Total		1,215	281	186	175	121	245	207
Relation of source to law	.78 N							
Law enforcement officer		120	34	18	13	16	34	5
Semi-law-enforcement officer		94	13	29	14	10	13	15
Criminal		269	23	60	58	29	44	55
No special relation		732	211	79	90	66	154	132
Total		1,215	281	186	175	121	245	207
Relation of receiver to law	.78 N							
Law enforcement officer		92	24	19	13	12	18	6
Semi-law-enforcement officer		113	16	33	16	8	23	17
Criminal		209	21	47	51	28	27	35
No special relation		801	220	87	95	73	177	149
Total		1,215	281	186	175	121	245	207
Outcome for source	.79 I							
Winner		401	94	71	65	36	63	72
Winner but		122	29	10	15	15	30	23
Neither, irrelevant		199	56	29	16	11	57	30
Loser but		133	12	11	33	14	21	22
Loser		380	90	65	46	45	74	60
Total		1,215	281	186	175	121	245	207

(Continued)

Table 31.—Reliability Coefficients and Frequency Distribution of Violent Acts (Continued)

Categories	Relia-bility*	Totals	ABC 1967	ABC 1968	CBS 1967	CBS 1968	NBC 1967	NBC 1968
Outcome for receiver	.79 I							
Winner		423	97	83	71	32	65	75
Winner but		157	38	19	15	20	44	21
Neither, irrelevant		165	35	19	15	8	60	28
Loser, but		97	9	5	31	19	15	18
Loser		373	102	60	43	42	61	65
Total		1,215	281	186	175	121	245	207
Sexual aspect	1.00 N							
Not present		1,168	273	176	175	121	227	196
Present		47	8	10	0	0	18	11
Total		1,215	281	186	175	121	245	207
Sex of source	.92 N							
Indeterminate		118	22	15	51	17	8	5
Male(s)		983	241	148	117	92	208	177
Female(s)		86	15	18	3	7	23	20
Mixed group		28	3	5	4	5	6	5
Total		1,215	281	186	175	121	245	207
Sex of receiver	.92 N							
Indeterminate		81	16	9	43	8	5	0
Male(s)		993	238	149	115	97	209	185
Female(s)		72	21	20	5	6	15	5
Mixed group		69	6	8	12	10	16	17
Total		1,215	281	186	175	121	245	207
Serial classification of source	.88 N							
Program no serial		161	16	22	0	0	51	72
Regular part in serial		402	102	50	66	63	72	49
Other part in serial		652	163	114	109	58	122	86
Total		1,215	281	186	175	121	245	207

(Continued)

Table 31.—Reliability Coefficients and Frequency Distribution of Violent Acts (Continued)

Categories	Relia-bility*	Totals	ABC 1967	1968	CBS 1967	1968	NBC 1967	1968
Serial classification of receiver	.88 N							
Program no serial		161	16	22	0	0	51	72
Regular part in serial		476	115	68	84	70	82	57
Other part in serial		578	150	96	91	51	112	78
Total		1,215	281	186	175	121	245	207
Group belongingness of source	.84 N							
Isolated individual		242	72	39	32	17	45	37
Group leader		258	51	25	35	36	79	32
Group member		446	96	91	55	40	74	90
Group		269	62	31	53	28	47	48
Total		1,215	281	186	175	121	245	207
Group belongingness of receiver	.84 N							
Isolated individual		228	66	33	30	16	43	40
Group leader		219	40	26	32	28	75	18
Group member		487	112	90	70	44	74	97
Group		281	63	37	43	33	53	52
Total		1,215	281	186	175	121	245	207

*Coefficient, and whether nominal (N) or interval (I). See description of reliability tests in section on methodology.

Table 32.—Associations between evaluative portrayals and outcome for sources and receivers of violent acts

	Good	In-between	Bad	
Sources (total of 1,215 acts):				
Winner	363	35	3	
Winner, but ...	77	16	29	Kendall's tau$_c$=+.72
Neither	42	87	70	
Loser, but	24	9	80	
Loser	9	36	335	
Receivers (total of 1,215 acts):				
Winner	394	28	1	
Winner, but	117	19	21	Kendall's tau$_c$=+.70
Neither	48	74	43	
Loser, but ...	29	12	56	
Loser	22	54	297	

*Table 33:– Violence in Commercials**

	ALL			ABC			CBS			NBC		
	1967	1968	Both	1967	1968	Both	1967	1968	Both	1967	1968	Both
All commercials (N)	441	554	995	194	154	348	142	187	329	105	213	318
Violence in commercials (N)	45	31	76	18	2	20	18	13	31	9	16	25
Percent of total	10.2	5.6	7.6	9.3	1.3	5.7	12.7	7.0	9.4	8.6	7.5	7.9
Categories of commercials containing violence (in percents of all commercials containing violence):	Percent	Percent	Percent	Percent	Percent	Percent	Percent	Percent	Percent	Percent	Percent	Percent
Breakfast cereals, chewing gum, foods	24.4	48.4	34.2	16.7	.0	15.0	38.9	53.8	45.2	11.1	50.0	36.0
Automobiles	2.2	16.1	7.9	.0	100.0	10.0	.0	23.1	9.7	11.1	.0	4.0
Toys	4.4	9.7	6.6	5.6	.0	5.0	5.6	.0	3.2	.0	18.8	12.0
Tobacco	11.1	3.2	7.9	5.6	.0	5.0	16.7	7.7	12.9	11.1	.0	4.0
Promotional announcements	46.7	19.4	35.5	61.1	.0	55.0	33.3	15.4	25.8	24.4	25.0	32.0
Others	11.1	3.2	7.9	11.1	.0	10.0	5.6	.0	3.2	22.2	6.2	12.0

*These are the results of an informal tally of commercial and public service announcements observed on the programs. No reliability tests were performed. Furthermore, the 1967 commercials attached to tapes and films used were not necessarily those transmitted during the initial airing of these programs, and commercials for five 1968 programs were omitted because of mechanical recording difficulties.

Appendix III-K

THE VIEWS, STANDARDS, AND
PRACTICES OF THE TELEVISION INDUSTRY

By Robert K. Baker & The Media Task Force Staff

A. The Television Industry's View of the Research
on Effects of Violent Portrayals

Fifteen years ago (1954), industry spokesmen took the position that the research evidence on the effect of violent portrayals on children was inconclusive. However, they did acknowledge that there was a possible risk of adverse effects, and that for this reason the industry had adopted standards and regulations to govern the portrayal of violence. In addition, the President of the National Association of Broadcasters advised the Senate Subcommittee on Juvenile Delinquency (Senator Estes Kefauver, Chairman) that the industry could be relied upon to promote the needed research. This was to be a familiar pattern of response for fourteen years until the hearings of this Commission, in December 1968. At those hearings, the networks remained committed to the view that the evidence was inconclusive, but asserted that they had made an effort to promote research and had been unable to develop any sound research methodology; no one had provided a research procedure which, in their view, would produce an answer to the question. The following is a summary of the industry's position on research. It is regarded as relevant to the issue of whether the industry should be relied upon by this Commission to direct any additional research the Commission deems desirable.

In 1954, Harold E. Fellows, President and Chairman of the Board of the National Association of Broadcasters, while testifying before the Senate Subcommittee on Juvenile Delinquency, told the subcommittee that the NAB intended to undertake a survey of the impact of television programming on children. Such a survey was never done. Leroy Collins, Mr. Fellows' successor, while testifying before the same subcommittee on June 19, 1961 (Senator Dodd, Chairman), excused the NAB's failure to follow through:

Soon [after the representation made by Mr. Fellows], the television code review board undertook a pilot study of 'viewer attitudes' to determine the feasibility of a broader study, but about that time the Columbia Broadcasting System announced it was engaged in sponsoring a survey which, while broader, would cover essentially the same ground. In view of this overlapping inquiry, NAB deferred to CBS in order that the larger survey could go ahead in preference to the narrower inquiry which the NAB had initiated. It is anticipated the CBS' project will be completed by the end of this summer [1961] and that a final report will be published before the end of this year.

James T. Aubrey, then president of CBS, referred to the CBS study during his testimony before the subcommittee in 1961, "Among the areas covered in this study is the effect of television on children. We hope it will make a significant contribution to knowledge in this field."

The study referred to by Messrs. Collins and Aubrey was finally published in 1963.[1] On page 82 the author expressly states:

The present study provides no direct evidence on the effects of television on children. Our information refers entirely to *parents'* beliefs, attitudes, and behavior with respect to the television set vis-a-vis the child.

To the best of our knowledge, this is the only research resulting from the seven-year-old promise made by Mr. Fellows in 1954 and the representations of Mr. Aubrey in 1961.

In the 1961 hearings, the industry again asserted that the evidence of the effects of television's violent portrayals on children was inconclusive. Again the industry promised research.

The question of additional research arose in the context of a question to Mr. Leroy Collins:

Question: Dr. Wilbur L. Schramm, Director of the Stanford Institute of Communications Research, and a recognized expert in the field of behavioral research, stated in testimony before the subcommittee that the amount of extremely violent programs which we have on TV at the present time is just too dangerous to go on. In light of this situation, has the NAB sponsored or taken part in any research in this area? Does it plan any such activity in the future?

Mr. Collins: . . . . we are moving significantly in this area now. At a meeting of our joint radio and television board of directors last week approval was given to proceed with the initial planning of an NAB research and training center in association with one of the leading universities in the nation.

Mr. Collins told the committee of the need for,

"comprehensive and concentrated research project on a massive scale, conducted by the best professional resources in the social sciences and managed under impartial auspices."

He advised the Subcommittee that the NAB,

"will be glad to join with others in underwriting the cost of a comprehensive study . . . I have consulted with representatives of the networks, and feel confident that they would be willing to participate in the financing of a such continuing research project."[2]

Mr. Aubrey also told the Subcommittee that it was conceivable that the networks and possibly the advertisers might jointly underwrite the kind of research needed and that CBS intended to "continue to be interested in research to solve the problem with which we are faced as we have in the past." In a similar vein Dr. Frank Stanton, President of CBS, told the committee:

We have already told the NAB that we wanted to participate in an industry-wide research of this kind, but I believe that even the NAB's study should be a part of a much broader study that gets at all of the forces rather than just television because other influences affect juvenile delinquency.[3]

NBC and ABC also agreed to participate.

In 1962, the industry co-sponsored the Joint Committee for Research on Television and Children. Two years later, 1964, Senator Dodd held additional hearings on television violence and inquired about the state of the research. Walter D. Scott, then Executive Vice President and now Chairman of the Board of NBC, responded that he was not yet convinced that media portrayals of violence had a deleterious effect on children. He went on to refer to the work of the Joint Committee:

I think that all of us are looking forward to the work of the Joint Committee and counting heavily upon having some definitive work come out of that committee.

Senator Dodd pointed out that it had been two years since the formation of the Committee and then asked "What have they done, actually?" Mr. Scott replied:

I have asked the same question, Senator, because I have wondered why there has not been more in the way of results up to this point. I have been reminded by our people who are working very actively and closely with the Committee that it is appropriate to bear in mind that the work of scholars frequently sets its own pace and that time may be the price we must pay for meaningful results. As I understand it, they have had work done by a very large number of competent scholars in the field of social sciences. I understand that there have been something like one hundred separate projects that have been studied, that these have been narrowed down, that they are now at the stage of being ready to go ahead with, I believe, either five or six specific projects, out of which they hope to get some meaningful answers."[4]

So far as we have been able to determine, some six and one-half years after the Joint Committee's formation, only one report has been published—a paper by Dr. Ruth Hartley[5] which was the basis for Dr. Klapper's testimony before this Commission in October of 1968. The thrust of that testimony and the object of the paper was to analyze the inadequacies of the research performed by others—an approach which yielded a report which could be used to support the Network's thesis that the evidence was inconclusive.[6]

In addition to this one published paper, the Joint Committee has commissioned only two other papers relevant to the effects of media violence on children. One is a study by Dr. Seymour Feshbach. Prior to the commissioning of this paper, Dr. Feshbach was recognized as one of the leading proponents of the catharsis hypothesis—the theory that viewing violence reduces aggression. Dr. Feshbach's catharsis hypothesis had been effectively challenged. Although not a certainty, it could be reasonably expected that Dr. Feshbach's study would provide new support for his theory that viewing violence on television reduces aggression.

The third study was on the effect of repetition—only peripherally related to the effects of media violence—and was not completed because the contractor apparently abandoned the project.

NBC had these comments on the Joint Committee:

Any discussion of the effect on human behavior of the depiction of violence in television programs inevitably turns to research in the field. In several Congressional hearings on television and violence, NBC has urged objective research, keyed particularly to the influence of television on children. We have suggested that the research should be broad based, that it should be conducted under the direction of, or jointly with, foundations or other non-industry organizations to avoid any charge of biased results. We have offered to cooperate with other affected groups to support such projects including paying our fair share of the cost.

For a variety of reasons, it has not been possible to initiate a large scale research program of this type. A good start was made in 1963 with the organization of the Joint Committee for Research on Television and Children. The Joint Committee is made up of representatives of the three networks, the National Association of Broadcasters, the Foundation for Character Education and the Department of Health, Education and Welfare. Its chairman is a member of the faculty of Boston University.

In June, 1963 the Committee invited more than 4,000 social scientists to submit proposals for specific research projects in the area. Two dozen projects were proposed to the Committee in detail and evaluated by a special consulting panel. Four proposals that seemed most promising were selected to be underwritten. Only two materialized. One of these conducted by Dr. Seymour Feshbach, is a study of the actual television viewing of two groups of adolescent boys—including underprivileged and non-white youths. Their behavior was observed and measured before, during and after a six-week period. One group watched action programming, and the other saw more placid fare.

Our own research people feel it is the most valid research in this area to date, because it measures real-life television exposure and real-life aggressive behavior. I understand Dr. Feshbach has delivered a summary of the results to the Commission, although his final report will not be completed until early next year. The Joint Committee hopes to be able to repeat this type of research with other children in other areas to double check the validity of the present findings.[7]

Under the circumstances, it is difficult to believe that the promises to do research were regarded as seriously by the industry as they were by the Dodd Committee. Although all three networks stated that financing would be no problem, there has been no paid staff, no paid executive director, and each member of the Committee has been a volunteer whose principal occupation has been something other than the work of the Committee.[8]

Dr. Stanton best characterized the current state of the Joint Committee in the following passage:

> I am embarrassed and I referred to it this morning, about the fact that the industry committee, which is not industry purely broadcasting but involved representation from HEW and other outside organizations, fell apart. We financed our share. Others financed their share. Some of the money is still left. It has been a very dormant organization. We tried to stimulate it from Dr. Klapper. We have been unsuccessful in doing so.
>
> I have no doubt as a result of these hearings that this will be given more stimulation and in fact I promise you that it will be.[9]

It was reported in the trade press that the presidents of the three networks met shortly after the December hearings with the President of the National Association of Broadcasters to discuss possible research on the relationship between television and violence.[10]

Other than their participation in the Joint Committee, ABC and NBC have sponsored virtually no original research on the effects of television, and only recently has NBC begun to develop an inhouse capability for doing such research. In response to a request for all documents prepared by experts in the social sciences and funded in whole or in part by the network, NBC's and ABC's responses were insignificant. CBS funded both Dr. Hartley's paper and the study by Gary Steiner[11] (which was at best peripherally related to the subject). CBS does have in-house capability for evaluating the research of others in the person of Dr. Joseph Klapper.

At the present time, it is the view of ABC that for every one or two psychiatrists that may have presented themselves to the Commission, there are others who have conflicting points of view. The evidence is inconclusive.[12] Mr. Goldenson does believe that many of the research people who have provided reports to this Commission would agree that the normal child has not been affected by violence on television because of the countervailing effect of teachings by his parents of the difference between right and wrong. He does believe it has been indicated that a subnormal child may be affected.[13] Nevertheless, ABC believes that until the adverse effect has been *definitely* established, they are taking all of the necessary action which the possible risk of an adverse impact may require.[14]

Although ABC does not sponsor any research on the efficacy of its product, its research and standards and practices departments have attempted to keep abreast of current research and to interpret it for the benefit of relevant employees. ABC executives feel that it is pointless for them to sponsor research because any findings which this work might produce would be suspect:

Research should be done from an objective standpoint and one that the public would be satisfied with as being done objectively, rather than that which is directly financed by our particular company. [15]

They seem to assume that research sponsored by the industry would not present useful findings. When reminded of the fact that drug companies, as well as many other manufacturing and service organizations in this country, are held responsible for assuring the efficacy of their products before they are marketed, Mr. Goldenson responded that he thought ABC was "quite different in that respect from a drug company."[16]

Mr. Goldenson's grounds for declining to sponsor research has merit only if one assumes that the sole purpose of such research is to transmit the results to the public and have it accepted by the public. It has no merit if its purpose is to determine the efficacy of the product for purposes of its internal decision-making processes. If, for example, it were discovered that the portrayal of violence has no adverse effect upon viewers or that only certain kinds of violent portrayals had an adverse effect, then ABC would be in a much better position to meet its public interest obligations under the Communications Act of 1934. Moreover, in the case of a commission of this kind, such research could be submitted to consultants not connected with the industry for a determination of its validity.

Although the American Broadcasting Company is unwilling to undertake its own research projects, it *has* expressed a willingness to finance its share of jective research by an outside institution.[17]

Dr. Stanton strongly made the point that there was really no first-class research methodology available at the present time which would provide answers to the effects question:[18]

It isn't an unwillingness on the part of the industry to underwrite the research. It is that no one in the thirty-odd years I have been in the business has come up with a technique or methodology that would let you get a fix on this impact.[19]

In speaking of efforts to get research from the Joint Committee, Dr. Stanton said:

These people from the outside have been given every encouragement, every funding they have asked for to come up with methodology, and this is the field that is very illusive and it doesn't do any good to spend a lot of money and come up with facts somebody can punch his fingers through.[20]

According to Dr. Stanton, CBS had made "efforts to mount serious methodology studies long before the assassinations in 1968."

Mr. Goodman, President of NBC, also stated that there has been a great deal of difficulty in identifying worthwhile projects. He suggests that this Commission "by recommending a program under which sound and meaningful research projects could be identified and carried forward" would make a valuable contribution.[21]

It should be noted that CBS has funded more research than the other two networks and has made a more concentrated effort to keep abreast of the research developments on the question of effects. The CBS research budget during 1968 was almost $200,000. CBS also employs a full-time sociologist who reads most of the available literature and presents memoranda to CBS officials as an aid in making policy decisions.[22] NBC has allocated approximately $100,000 of its 1969 budget for effects research.[23]

The current position of the networks remains that the current evidence on the effects of portrayals of violence on viewers is inconclusive. At the same time, they do recognize that there is a risk in portraying violence on television, but believe that their present practices of reducing the amount of violence and limiting its treatment have been adopted with an adequate appreciation for the risks involved. In short, they believe that, in view of the possible risks, present standards and practices strike an appropriate balance between license and complete prohibition of violence in entertainment programming. In the words of Julian Goodman, President of NBC:

> We have the feeling that what we have done so far has reduced the scenes of conflict in our entertainment programming to a state where we feel we are, with the state of research as we now know it, . . . acting responsibility with what we have on the air now.[24]

Dr. Stanton took a similar position. He noted that the program schedule next fall will take cognizance of the evidence on the effect of violent programming on children and that we can expect the amount of violence to be substantially reduced.[25]

B. Industry Standards and Practices on the Portrayal of Violence

The television networks have persistently argued that their standards for the portrayal of violence and their machinery for enforcement of these standards—the National Association of Broadcasters (NAB) and the individual networks' Program Standards and Practices Departments (PSPDs)—are adequate to protect the public interest. We have examined this argument in light of current programming practices and found it wanting.

1. Enforcement of the NAB Code

The three networks and some two-thirds of the nation's commercial television stations subscribe to the NAB Code which sets overall industry standards for the portrayal of violence. The purpose of the code is:

> . . . cooperatively to maintain a level of television programming which given full consideration to the educational, informational, cultural, economic, moral and entertainment needs of the American public to the end that more and more people will be better served. (1968, NAB, The Television Code)

The Code Authority has a director and staff of 32 in Washington, New York and Hollywood. A Television Code Review Board, composed of nine subscribers to the Code, functions as a consultative and review body for the Code authority and can recommend the ultimate sanction—revocation of the authority to display the Code seal—for a violation of the NAB Code. The regulations provide that all hearings on the subject of code violations shall be closed and that all correspondence and transcripts concerning specific programming shall be confidential. No provision is made for publicizing a decision that the Code has been violated.

The responsibilities of the Code Authority are wide, and its powers are largely a matter or interpretation. These include the authority to hear complaints and inform subscribers; to advise subscribers of attitudes and desires of accountable organizations and institutions and the public in general; and to review and monitor, if necessary, "any certain series of programs, daily programming or any other program presentations of a subscriber as well as to request recorded material, or a script and copy . . . "

The various NAB standards calling for restraint in the portrayal of violence (whether in general programming or children's programming) are aimed primarily at screening material that might alarm or upset the audience. The only flat prohibition is that "The use of horror for its own sake will be eliminated . . . " Nevertheless, a distinctive characteristic of the Code is its insistence that television programming have a moral theme. Drug addiction, cruelty, greed, selfishness, criminality, murder, suicide, and illicit sex relations are to be portrayed in an unfavorable light. With respect to children's programming, the Code calls for avoidance of the "techniques of crime in such detail as to invite imitation" and recommends against the portrayal of violence and sex unless "required by plot development or character delineation."

As the distinction between standards for general programming and children's programming makes clear, broadcasters should exercise special care in the kinds of materials specifically aimed at children or shown during those times of the day when children are likely to constitute a substantial part of the audience. Superimposed on this requirement is Standard I-7 which encourages broadcasters to promote, "programs presenting genuinely artistic or literary material, valid moral and social issues, significant controversial and challenging concepts, and other subject matter involving adult themes."

Thus, in determining how necessary to the plot a particular portrayal of violence must be, how it may be emphasized, etc., the broadcaster should consider the time of day it is shown, the kind of audience it is likely to appeal to, and the artistic merit of the program. This leaves a wide margin for interpretation.

Despite vague protestations to the contrary, the NAB Code notably omits standards covering the larger issue of providing balanced program fare—i.e. rules relating to the number of programs which, because of their format, require the use of violence as the basic mode of conflict resolution. Similarly, nowhere in the Code is there any provision relating to the general question of the morality of using violence as a dramatic device.

The NAB's powers to enforce the Code are strictly limited by the consent of its subscribers. Prior to March of 1969, when ABC and NBC agreed to let the NAB pre-screen their programs, the NAB could, at best, make pre-screening requests, but had no assurance that such requests would be granted. Until now, the NAB's efforts to enforce the Code have been confined largely to the monitoring of on-the-air programs which represent a very small proportion of the total network entertainment schedule. "In-depth discussion" with network personnel is the strongest action the NAB has taken with regard to violations of its code. The only formal sanction which the NAB may impose upon a subscriber is denial of authorization to display the NAB seal of good practice—something which the NAB has not done in the past five years and which, in any case, would be of little consequence to the subscriber. Furthermore, the NAB's provisions for confidential proceedings on possible code violations and its failure to make any provision for publicizing violations keeps industry practices out of the public limelight, thus further weakening the Association's powers to effect changes and improvements.

2. Enforcement of Network Standards

Given the NAB's limited powers of enforcement, the primary responsibility for screening program content is placed upon the networks themselves. ABC, CBS, and NBC each has a Program Standards and Practices Department with independent authority to review scripts, roughcuts, and final films to assure adherence to NAB and network standards. The PSPDs have no responsibility for determining program mix in the network schedule; they are responsible only for the manner in which violent incidents are portrayed in particular programs.

Network standards are broadly similar and, on the whole, conform to the NAB Code. In practice, each of the networks professes to exercise particular care in the portrayal of violence in programs viewed by children, and NBC and CBS both have special admonitions with regard to thematic content in children's programs. This is particularly ironic in view of past network cartoon programming which, as an independent study funded by this Commission revealed, was almost completely violent.

In practice, the distinction between standards for children and adult programming seems largely irrelevant. Surveys on the population's media habits show that children watch a large number of programs aimed at adults, particularly during the early evening hours. Thus, stringent standards on violence should reasonably apply to *all* programs, not just to those aimed primarily at children.

As for the enforcement of existing standards, our review of PSPD documents reveals a common and over-riding preoccupation at all the networks: violence must not be portrayed in such a manner as to shock, upset, or otherwise have a negative effect on the audience. Given this preoccupation with viewers, the PSPDs focus primarily on reducing the quantum of violence (e.g. not showing the horrible consequences of violence, keeping fights short, not allowing wounds to bleed, reducing the number of arrows, blows, or shots necessary to accomplish the aggressor's purpose, not allowing bodies to be displayed in grotesque positions or with eyes open, not showing the impact of weapons on victims, not terrorizing children, etc.) and rarely on the elimination of violent acts altogether.

Our information on the implementation of codes, other than that generally available to the public comes basically from: interviews with personnel from the standards and practices departments of the three commercial networks; testimony of the heads of the standards and practices departments at NBC and ABC; a letter from Mr. Tanskersley, head of standards and practices at CBS; testimony of the presidents of the three commercial television networks; interviews with the persons involved in the production of TV programs; and examination of the standards and practices documents from 26 episodes of "Ironside," "High Chapparal," and "The Saint" (NBC); "The Avengers," "Felony Squad," and "Guns of Will Sonnett" (ABC); and "Cimaron Strip" and the "The Wild, Wild West" (CBS).

There are certain inherent limitations on this method of procedure. For example, there is no way to determine whether or not the instructions in the standards and practices documents were ever followed. There has been at least some evidence in the past to suggest that they are not uniformly followed. Ideally, the best course of action would have been to examine the standards and practices documents and compare them with the original scripts and the final product. Time, however, did not permit this more detailed approach. With these limitations in mind, we proceed to examine each of the three networks.

a. American Broadcasting Company

The general standards enunciated for controlling the portrayal of violence at ABC are: violence for the sake of violence or shock value is not permitted and the use of violence must be necessary to the development of the plot or character development. The relevance of violence to the plot or character development varies proportionately to the network estimate of number of children in the audience. One interesting characteristic is that each program is judged separately and on the basis of its time zone in the program slot. (Interview with Alfred R. Schneider of ABC.)

Among the more specific criteria which Mr. Schneider listed were:
(1) no sensationalism merely to attract audience.
(2) concern and awareness of the public's feelings.
(3) questions of public taste.
(4) desire not to generate a negative reaction in viewers.

With regard to the social science literature on the effects of violence on viewers, ABC does not deem it helpful in formulating specific policy recommendations on how violence should be portrayed in concrete cases—there are too many different points of view.

A review of the material we have examined shows that the most important criterion in determining what is acceptable is public taste. Examples of this concern may be found in the standards and practices documents for specific programs obtained by the Violence Commission from ABC. Consistent with their desire not to shock viewers, the following admonitions were found in the documents relating to the series "Guns of Will Sonnett:"

This beating of the sick boy is too sadistic and must be modified—to one blow—certainly not so vicious or so prolonged as described.
Caution on the appearance of dead bodies. Keep blood to a minimum and the eyes closed, please.
Caution. Do not overdo, re: display of blood here.

No close-ups of arrows piercing Milt's back or Dan's chest—and nothing too gruesome for audience in subsequent scenes, re: Dan's appearance.

In the program series "The Avengers," the following comments were typical:

In order not to repel too many viewers, the business with Grant and the boa constrictor will have to be handled with a minimum of close-ups of the snake and avoidance of shots showing it in contact with the man. When final struggle is on—his movements, moans, and facial expressions can only be approved after screening unless avoided for the most part.
Keep shots of snakes as distant and unrepulsive as possible.
Benstead's electrocution must not be too brutal for home viewing.
Gifford's screams should be kept to a minimum.

For reasons which are not entirely clear, "The Avengers" episodes contain far fewer admonitions and changes at the script and review stage than other programs. The reasoning behind this may be because the film was shot in England or because it is regarded as more comedy than serious dramatic programming. In any event, there are an unusually small number of cautions, deletions, etc.; generally, it seems less well supervised than the CBS program the "The Wild, Wild West" or NBC's "Ironside." It seems to be on a par with NBC's "The Saint," which is also filmed in England.

The following comments were found and are regarded as typical of those in the standards and practices documents for the ABC program "Felony Squad:"

Special caution that we do not demonstrate exactly how the fire is set; the chemicals being mixed not identified; in the scenes of the bug "working"—please suggest what he is doing rather than graphically detailing same.
Caution that, in script development, we do not reveal or give a demonstration of arson techniques, by action or dialogue, so as to invite imitation.
Just a caution that there is no sighting down the barrel of rifle with cross-hair effect.
Just a caution that wound-blood is not overdone.
Your usual care in seeing that bodies in death are not shocking or grotesque to view. Of course, eyes closed in death.
Please modify and keep action coverage so that we do not show how the "torch" is made and possibly invite imitation.
As described, these scenes seem too much. Please modify so that sequence is not overly-brutal. Also effects of beating not over-drawn. Special caution herein throughout (the handling of Julia, the fights); please more suggestion than graphic detailing; the struggles not unnecessarily prolonged. The acceptability of episodes depends on manner in which it is done and can only be approved on film.
It is not clear where the children are through most of this sequence. Be sure that they are not placed in jeopardy at any time. Also, they must not be witness to any act or intent of violence on their father's part or audience to any conversation to this effect.

Just a caution on choking sequence; please no close-uping of hand around the throat of victim's face. Of course, victim's features not grotesque (eyes bulging, etc.).

Please eliminate some of the killings, particularly in part one.

Substitute for "firing directly into Zachary's face."

Usual caution that fights are not overly brutal or prolonged and effects of beating not "overdrawn"—caution (scene 107) that we do not see Bradon's body hit the ground.

Special caution that the "young hoods" look to be at least in the 20 year age group. Of course, the "next scar" not too "over-drawn."

Page 12—should an officer, after he has disarmed the offender (even though he is personally outraged) then begin slapping him around? Kindly modify this action.

Do not close-up Declose's face as he is being choked. Please keep below camera frame or "covered." He can gasp, but caution that it is not a gagging or gurgling sound. Also caution that moment of contact with rock is off camera.

Delete shot of bloated face. Body may be floating up-side down but must not, in any way, be shocking to look at.

Again, the predominant concern appears to be with not shocking the viewers. Second to this is the desire to avoid illustrating graphically conduct which might be imitated. Finally, unlike the other two programs on ABC, a concern is expressed here for the proper portrayal of a police officer.

b. National Broadcasting Company

In addition to its adherences to the NAB Code, NBC has its own which provides:

> Whether in terms of human conflict or cruelty to animals, violence should never be presented for its own sake, for shock affect or as an audience stimulant and should never be carried to excess. Depictions of violence can be justified as an expression of conflict only to the extent essential to the advancement of plot or the depiction of characterization.

The NBC Code, unlike the NAB Code, provides that the use of violence must be justified as making an essential contribution to the plot or depiction of character—not simply, as in the case of the NAB Code, where the program is one which, because of subject matter or time slot, is likely to have a predominantly child audience. The NBC Code has a special precaution with regard to children's programming which provides in part:

> Programs for children and young people should be designed to convey the commonly accepted moral, social and ethical ideals characteristic of American life; to reflect respect for parent, good morals and honorable behavior; to foster healthy personality development; and to provide opportunities for cultural and intellectual growth as well as entertainment.

To determine how these standards and the NAB Code are applied in practical, we examined the standards and practices documents from three NBC Television programs: "High Chaparral," "Ironside," and "The Saint." The "High Chaparral" program is typical, and we will concentrate on it with such observations from the other two programs as seem appropriate.

Among the most frequently found cautions in the documents pertaining to "High Chaparral" were:

1. Avoid excessive bloodiness of wounds (there were a total of 21 cautions in 26 programs).
2. Delete the impact of the instrument of aggression, bullet, arrow, gun butt, etc. (a total of 32 instances where the impact was deleted or softened by showing it out of frame or moved off camera).
3. Fights are not to be unnecessarily long or brutal.
4. Victims of homicide are to be shown with their eyes closed and not positioned grotesquely.

In more detail, the PSPD urged the following cautions:

1) Eliminate any suggestion of sadism:

In the montage of warring Indians being hunted down and shot, take care that this is not overdone so that it becomes a brutal thing; nor should we see BUCK grinning fiercely just before the killing. This would give him the aspect of a sadist.

It is felt by this department that one blast from BUCK's shotgun is sufficient to stop CLEEG. Therefore, it is unnecessary for BUCK to fire both barrels which would lead our viewers into believing BUCK to be a sadistic killer.

2) Avoid brutality:

Please exercise caution on the "pier eight brawl." Avoid brutality such as kicks, low blows. Acceptability of this sequence will be determined at the rough-cut viewing.

Please exercise caution in presenting the fight between BUCK and BART. The fight must be brief and void of any brutality. Please avoid any low blows or kicking. Caution make-up of the combatants.

Please find another means for MANOLITO to knock the knife from CARLO's hand instead of MANOLITO kicking him somewhere below the belt line.

3) Eliminate excessive violence:

The killing of RICARDO is acceptable; however, the killing of the other RURALES, we feel, is excessive and unnecessary. Please find some other way of dispatching them without killing them.

CURRY slugging BLUE seems to be unnecessary as he has already clubbed him with his revolver. One or the other is acceptable, but not both.

The pistol slugging of BLUE appears to be utterly gratuitous and unjustifiable and should therefore be eliminated. It should be quite sufficient for BLUE to discover his father on the floor still severely stunned from the pistol slugging administered by BROOKES. BIG JOHN can then haltingly explain the circumstances and send BLUE in quick persuit of the fleeing BROOKES.

4) Avoid showing the misery, or consequences of violence:

Take care that the scene with an arrow jutting from ANNALEE's breast is not done in a shocking or objectionable manner.

Caution on MANOLITO's killing RINALDO with the scythe. As described in script, close-up on MANOLITO [the aggressor]. Caution that impact is out-of-frame.

A caution in the shooting of the battle scenes that you avoid any detailed misery, killing or blood. Please provide adequate cutaway shots so that this can be tempered at the time of rough cut viewing.

Please use off-camera technique in showing BLUE taking the thornes from underneath the nails of the tortured Indian.

Please avoid any close-up exposure of the dead body of BURNS pierced with arrows.

As the kid is shot and he starts to fall, please avoid sensationalizing his fall as he goes tumbling down the rocks. It will be unacceptable to see the kid bouncing from rock to rock in his fall.

Caution handling as John is depicted probing for the bullet and cauterizing the wound in these scenes. General caution on showing the cholla ball sticking into JOHN's leg and subsequent removal of the desert bush.

As MARIA cradles the dying RAMON in her arms, avoid showing the knife protruding from RAMON's chest.

5) Avoid scenes likely to terrorize children. This was a concern about which NBC seemed to be more concerned than the other two networks:

Please avoid prolonging or sensationalizing these scenes whereby ANGIE is trapped by the coiled rattlesnake. The child can be frightened but not terrorized by her dilema.

Please use care and restraint in presenting this scene as the mistreatment of children is a very sensitive area among our viewers.

6) Finally, an attempt to make sure that the overall moral tone of that story remains in accord with NAB standards:

On page 11 it is felt by this department that the pistol-whipping of the doctor's patient PEDRO is unnecessary. PEDRO can just be knocked cold to achieve the same effect. The ending as presently written is unacceptable to this department; there must be some retribution for DOC'S kidnappin и and extortion. He just can't ride off scot free.

The Standards and Practices documents relating to the first twenty-six programs of the fall 1967 season for the series "Ironside," have many of the same types of cautions and warnings found in the documents for the series "High Chaparral." These include:

1) caveats against showing victims of homocide with their eyes open and in grotesque postures.
2) no excessive bloodiness on wounds resulting from violence.
3) no knives or other weapons to be shown protruding from the bodies of victims.
4) a warning about making violent sequences unnecessarily shocking or alarming to viewers.
5) keep fights as short as possible.
6) not showing contact or impact of weapon on victim.
7) caution on make-up used on bruises.

There was also more emphasis in this series on the use of violence on women:

> Please use restraing when staging BILL's treatment of BARBARA since violent treatment of women is a very sensitive area.
>
> Violent treatment of women is a very sensitive area, and, rather than the action described as POGO hurls her viciously across the room, CONNIE should be pushed away as POGO reacts to the pain of the bite on the hand; this will eliminate what would be interpreted as unnecessary violence.

Apparently violence must be more necessary to the plot or the depiction of character when it is directed toward women than when directed toward men. There was also more need to caution the producers against the portrayal of scenes which were likely to be emulated:

> This outline is approved. It is necessarily violent but timely play which can make an effective statement against paramilitarism. However, in telling the story, it will be important to the network to avoid an over-emphasis of violence in the sense of not giving the less balanced members of the audience any extraordinary ideas. In my opinion, the heavies should be as odious and obviously contemptible as circumstances permit; they should in fact be shown as goons working stupidly under the direction of two deranged and basically weak subhumans (the "Admiral" and "Jeff").
>
> The fashioning of the weapon should not be in such detail as to invite imitation.

A similar caveat was applied to "The Saint", a program produced in Britain, in which the hero's unlawful exploits were not portrayed in detail:

> When Simon takes out lock picking tools and spends five seconds opening the door, please be sure that he is not using a celluloid strip and that we do not see any detailed use of the tool . . . the presentation of techniques of crime in such detail as to invite imitation shall be avoided.

c. Columbia Broadcasting System

While CBS has no formal written code in addition to the NAB Code, a memorandum by Mr. Tankersley, now head of CBS Standards and Practices, to his superior in 1960 was re-issued on March 25, 1968 and serves as the most complete statement of policy which we have found in the CBS documents. That memorandum provides in part:

> ... we make an affirmative effort to eliminate all violence that is not absolutely essential to plot development and further, to see that violence, whether considered necessary or not, is kept within the bounds of acceptable taste, with due regard for the composition of our audience at the time the show is broadcast in various time zones. Programs aired during children's hours are scrutinized with the most circumspect care to insure that they contain nothing which would be harmful in any manner, psychologically or morally,. . . Deletions and modifications are effected daily in the interest of our child audience . . .
>
> In evaluating an act of violence for editing purposes it is more equitable and logical to judge the individual script and its particular content. To regard a specfic act of violence in light of the total week's programming is hardly a sound basis for constructive editing and imposes an arbitrary standard.
>
> An act of violence is frequently the initial story point and the motivation for the story line, culminating in a final act of violence which punishes the antagonist or vindicates a protagonist. It is essential to evaluate which acts of violence are necessary to the story and which are used solely for visual interest and shock value. Requests for the deletion of violence are frequently necessary to eliminate the latter type of incident. In programs where violence is not an integral part of the theme, care is necessary to prevent violences being used as a means of holding interest in an essentially static dramatic situation.

Earlier in that memorandum Mr. Tankersley had enumerated the factors affecting the acceptability of an act of violence:

> The program, series and/or characters involved.
> The dramatic situation; considered separately and in script context.
> The degree of violence in the entire script.
> The specific act of violence.
> The weapon or means employed.
> The method and manner of the act: degree of realism or credence, make-up, sound effect, dialogue, actors reaction, wardrobe.
> Because acts of violence are subject to innumerable variations, degrees and interpretations, the final basis for acceptibility as the visual impact of the screen presentation.

In memorandum dated June 28, 1968 and addressed to Standards and Practices, Editors, he asked:

> In evaluating programs, please ask yourselves the following four questions:
>
> 1. Can the number of violent incidents within the program be reduced?

2. Can those which must remain be softened?

3. Does the program contain any scenes, which taken out of context, would defy explanation or justifications?

4. Does the program feature any cruel or unusual device which would have the effect of heightening the impression of violence?

Unlike the NAB Code, the CBS proscription against violence unessential to the plot applies comprehensively—it includes adult entertainment programming. In addition, CBS shows a special sensitivity for violence in children's programs, with particular emphasis on the time slot in which the program is scheduled rather than the subject matter of the program. The prohibition in children's programming states that they should contain nothing "which would be harmful in any manner, psychologically or morally." Whether this means that violence must be more essential to the plot for children's programs than for adult programs is not clear. There is, necessarily, a certain amount of subjectivity involved in this decision, as illustrated by some comments addressed to standards and practices editors by Thomas Downer:

Empirical evidence of children's reactions is provided nightly by my own two youngsters, ages 10 and 5, and while conceding that the emotional make-up of human beings is a variable factor, I do find that this is a help.

Those sections of NAB Code which are applicable specifically to children's programming are also probably given more force during the early viewing hours. These provisions prohibit the portrayal of frightened children. For example, the Brave New World episode of the "Lost in Space" series was found unacceptable because it portrayed a youngster in danger, very frightened, and ended with an unresolved horror situation in which a teenager was left at the mercy of a murderous robot. It was suggested by CBS that the script might be made acceptable by making the following changes:

We object to most of the dialogue on this page (9) where alien voice says, "Only a portion of it;" where SMITH says, "If you take out my brain, it will die;" the speech of the alien voice which follows in scene 30 is considered repugnant, as the audience will relate it to a later fate for WILL [teenager].

WILL should not have tears in his eyes or speak in an agonized whisper.

SMITH's attitude should not be "nakedly sinister" as shown in your stage directions, nor should WILL be overcome with fear.

For a youthful audience, the words "human specimen" in SMITH's line is considered unsavory and objectionable.

WILL's attitude should not be one of terror but rather bravado. If he is to enter the alien's space craft, he should do so willingly.

WILL's line, "You mean I have to stay with you forever and ever?" is, under the circumstances, too frightening for youthful audience.

WILL should not be fearful and hysterical, as described, at the end of the scene.

There are several additional considerations involved in the implementation of CBS's General Standards. Mr. Tankersley stated in an interview that the nearest thing the network has to an expressed standard is that the network shall present as little violence as possible without interfering with the creative process. In addition, the PSPD also considers the public attitude toward violence as well as what CBS believes is acceptable to the audience. This sometimes relates not only to the amount or mode of portrayal, but also to the subject matter. After the assassination of Dr. King and Senator Kennedy there was a general belief among the networks that the public's tolerance for violent content had been reduced and, accordingly, it was believed that there should be a reduction in the amount of violence shown on television. In addition, certain kinds of violence were considered to be in very bad taste. A scene showing an attempted assassination would probably have resurrected memories of the King and Kennedy assassinations—memories which would have had a negative impact on the audience. This, by network standards, is "bad taste." Finally, Mr. Tankersley suggested that CBS programming is probably a reflection of what they think the viewers want to see, rather than a reflection of society, but he emphasized that this was only a guess.

With regard to the portrayal of law enforcement officers and the possible effects of such portrayals on viewers' attitudes toward law enforcement officers, CBS follows the NAB Code and treats law enforcement officers with respect. They do not prohibit stories about a "bad cop"; however, when such a program is aired, CBS takes care to insure that it is not a general slur on the police profession.

Not only does CBS review each program with respect to the particular mode of portrayal of violence in each script and the amount of violence in each script, there is also an appraisal of theme. "[A] program which has special appeal for children or is broadcast at an early hour has thematic restrictions that another might not have." It is unclear whether this relates only to the morality of the overall theme or whether this includes an assessment of how much violence is necessary to make a quality dramatic program.

While CBS claims that it is responsive to its audience on questions of portrayals of violence, it should be pointed out that their sample of audience response is minimal. Between September 1967 and August 1968, 5744 letters were answered by the Program Practices department. Of these letters, only 76 related to violence, and only 50 of those mentioned specific CBS television porgrams; the remainder related to television violence in general. CBS's night-time action-adventure-crime programs during this period were estimated to have reached a cumulative audience of approximately 1,461,000,000 homes; [26] When this is taken into consideration, 76 letters is not much feed back.

Of the three networks, CBS has one of the most systematic procedures for providing information on the overall violent content of programming. In addition to the number of violent incidents in each program, standards and practices editors are required to report:

The kinds of animals portrayed and how they are treated.
Characterization of businessmen, craftsmen, foreigners, lawmen, professionals, public officials and other, and whether the portrayal is favorable or unfavorable.

Children in the story.

The types of crime and violence portrayed in the episode: Specifically listed are arson, attempted murder, extortion, fistfights, kidnapping, killing by lawman, knifing, lynching, murder, robbery, self-defense slaying, sex crime, shooting, strangling, torture, and other.

Liquor: whether it is shown in a cafe, restaurant, saloon, bar, nightclub, dwelling place, office or business place, other. Whether any liquor was drunk. The kind of liquor. Whether drunkenness was portrayed.

Whether narcotics was portrayed and, if so, how treated.

Whether profanity was portrayed, and if so, how treated.

Whether adultery, gambling, illicit sex or suicide was portrayed and if so how treated.

Whether smoking was portrayed and, if so, what was smoked and how treated.

The Violence Commission staff examined standards and practices documents from the first twenty-six episodes of the 1967 season—"The Wild, Wild West" and "Cimmaron Strip." [27] "The Wild, Wild West" was rated by the National Association for Better Broadcasting as one of the most violent programs on television, and our analysis of CBS standards in practice will focus upon this. Other programs will be mentioned to the extent that they offer additional insights. In "The Wild, Wild West" series, there were twenty-two episodes in which the number of violent incidents were determined by CBS S&P editors. In these twenty-two episodes, there were a total of 153 violent incidents—an average of 6.96 per program. By far the most common suggestion was aimed at reducing what was regarded as unnecessary or excessive violence. Other common cautions or deletions found in these documents related to:

(1) shortening the length and lessening the brutality of fist fights.
(2) cautions against the display of victims of homicide in grotesque positions.
(3) and softening of portrayals of the reactions of victims and others to the consequences of violence (e.g. bloody wounds, people screaming).

Typical examples of these and other cautions include:

1) Excessive violence:

The guard should shove, rather than kick the "prisoner."

Please exercise restraint in the gun battles and in the number of men killed.

It is understood that rather than a fusillade, only two arrows will strike the Digger, and this will be handled with appropriate caution.

It is understood that Slade will knock out the Indian rather than shoot him.

It is understood that the Gunsel will send Artemus staggering with a shove rather than hitting him.

In Scene 182, West should shove or knock Farnsworth into the group rather than hurl him bodily as indicated.

To avoid hitting the attendant, we suggest that West employ the pressure point gimmick.

We ask that West and Artemus sneak past the guard rather than have West knock him out.

Artemus should not shoot more than two of the deputies on camera.

It is understood that the Marshal will be wounded rather than killed, and the killing of the second passenger deleted.

Rather than blowing up the heavies' wagon, we request a method be devised to capture them.

2) Shortening the length or brutality of fights:

The fight between West and O'Reilly should not be excessively long or brutal.

Please exercise directoral caution in filming of the fights to prevent brutality or excessive length.

3) Eliminate traces of sadism:

To avoid any element of sadism, caution should be exercised in showing Enrique and the prisoner seen hanging in Sordo's camp.

4) Avoid grotesque positioning of dead bodies:

O'Reilly's . . . body should not be displayed in a grotesque manner [after he falls from the ledge.]

5) Soften or do not show the consequences of horror of violence:

It is our understanding the shot will be cut away as soon as Freemandle falls into the vat [of acid] .

To prevent an element of gruesomeness, the Heavy's being struck by the arrows should not be emphasized.

We should not see the mace embedded in his back as indicated.

We trust appropriate caution will be exercised in the make-up of the bloody Cassidy. Makeup caution should be exercised when showing the dead man. Obviously his being shown with "his skull neatly caved in" is unacceptable.

Caution should be exercised in showing Sordo's wounds.

The desk clerk should not be shown with his head twisted.

6) Restraint vis-a-vis women:

Please delete scenes of the restrained girl being slapped. Suggest only sound of slap before assumed shot of Dorcas, and in place of second slap she be shaken, or threatened with a second slap.

7) Drugs:

The use of the hypodermic needle should not be emphasized.
Artemus' use of the hypodermic syringe should not be emphasized.

8) Do not shock or frighten the audience:

We were assured that the masks seen here and throughout the film would not be of a grotesque or frightening nature.
To prevent morbidity, we ask that the coffin not be seen burning.
To prevent gruesomeness in this scene, caution should be exercised in the sound effects.
The cries coming from the man in the cave should not be "unnerving" ones of "horror" as indicated.
To prevent shock or horror, the business of Draja removing his iron hand should not be detailed or emphasized. The wounded Benje should not howl in pain as indicated.

In the "Cimmaron Strip" series, there were approximately 7.37 violent incidents per program as counted by CBS standards and practices editors. Some comments were made about the horrific nature of the opening teasers.

This portion of of the opening teaser could become unacceptably horrific for early evening home viewing. We hope undue emphasis on fear will not be an inherent part of the opening teaser.

There is also some evidence that several synopses were rejected completely or substantially as written because of the absence of proper moral values. For example: The episode "Before I Die" was rejected on August 8, 1963 with the following comment: "The moral problem left unresolved (perjury and murder) make this story unacceptable. It is felt that Mr. Hitchcock could not cover this properly by a disclaimer." (In another Alfred Hitchcock episode it was requested that the interrogation of LES by police should be in accord with acceptable standards of police procedure.") In the "Mannix" series, the episode "Man in the Shadow" was rejected because the network felt, "That it would be unwise to draw such a close parallel to the assassination of Dr. Martin Luther King. In view of the unsettled domestic climate and the sensitivity of the subject matter, we could not now accept this story."

C. *Conclusion*

In the final analysis, present network standards on portrayals of violence are weak because they appear to be based on little more than a fear of losing viewers. Little consideration is given to the issue of whether violence is indeed necessary to maintain dramatic tension in the resolution of conflict, and only cursory attention is paid to the larger question of reducing the number of violent programs in network entertainment scheuules.

REFERENCES

1. Gary Steiner, *The People Look at Television,* 1963.
2. U. S. Congress, Senate, *Effects on Young People of Violence and Crime Portrayes a Television,* Part 10, Hearings before the Subcommittee to Investigate Juvenile Delinquency, Committee on the Judiciary, 87th Cong., (Washington U. S. Government Proverty Office, 1963,) pp. 2244 and 2245.
3. *Ibid.,* p. 2559.
4. Juvenile Delinquency Subcommittee, *Hearings, op. cit.* note 2, Part 16, p. 3825.
5. Although we have been advised that this is the product of the Joint Committee there is some ambiguity. The internal correspondence of CBS indicates that they funded the operation, that her contract was with CBS, and that the product was used exclusively by CBS.
6. The suggestion that the paper was self-serving to the networks does not mean that it was not a scholarly, craftsman-like job. Nor is there any suggestion intended that the final product was biased because funded by a network. The sole point is that, the nature of the assigned paper made it self-serving for the networks.
7. *Testainment to Violence,* Hearings on the Mass Media before the National Commission on the Causes and Prevention of Violence, December 20, 1968.
8. *Ibid.*
9. *Ibid.*
10. *Broadcasting,* Jan. 13, 1969, p. 5.
11. Steiner, *op. cit.* note 1.
12. Testainment to Violence *op. cit.* note 7.
13. *Ibid.*
14. *Ibid.*
15. *Ibid.*
16. *Ibid.*
17. *Ibid.*
18. *Ibid.*
19. *Ibid.*
20. *Ibid.*
21. *Ibid.*
22. *Ibid.*
23. *Ibid.*
24. *Ibid.*
25. *Ibid.*
26. Tankersley speech before N. Y. Joint Legislative Committee, October 31 1968.
27. Although three series were examined from the other two metworks through an administrative error only two episodes were subpoenaed from CBS. After examining the documents submitted from all three networks it was decided that the CBS submission was sufficient for our purposes.